1995

MEDICAL AND HEALTH ANNUAL

Encyclopædia Britannica, Inc.

CHICAGO

AUCKLAND · LONDON · MADRID · MANILA · PARIS · ROME · SEOUL · SYDNEY · TOKYO · TORONTO

1995 Medical and Health Annual

Editor	Ellen Bernstein
Senior Editor	Linda Tomchuck
Contributing Editors	David Calhoun, Charles Cegielski, Robert F. Rauch
Art Director	Bob Ciano
Senior Picture Editor	Holly Harrington
Picture Editors	Kathy Nakamura, Karen Wollins
Art Production Supervisor	Stephanie Motz
Designers/Illustrators	John L. Draves (senior), Kathryn Diffley, Jon Hensley, Steven N. Kapusta
Art Staff	Diana M. Pitstick, Amy Segelbaum
Manager, Cartography	Barbra A. Vogel
Supervisor, Cartography	Brian L. Cantwell
Cartography Staff	David Herubin, Michael D. Nutter
Manager, Copy Department	Sylvia Wallace
Copy Supervisors	Lawrence D. Kowalski, Barbara Whitney
Copy Staff	Letricia Dixon, John Mathews, Jeffrey Wallenfeldt, Lee Anne Wiggins
Manager, Production Control	Mary C. Srodon
Production Control Staff	Marilyn L. Barton, Stephanie A. Green
Manager, Composition/Page Makeup	Melvin Stagner
Supervisor, Composition/Page Makeup	Michael Born, Jr.
Coordinator, Composition/Page Makeup	Danette Wetterer
Composition/Page Makeup Staff	Griselda Cháidez, Carol A. Gaines, Thomas J. Mulligan, Gwen E. Rosenberg, Tammy Yu-chu Wang
Vice President, Management Information Systems	Lawrence J. Merrick
Publishing Technology Group	Steven Bosco, Philip Rehmer, Vincent Star, Mary Voss
Manager, Index Department	Carmen-Maria Hetrea
Index Supervisor	Edward Paul Moragne
Index Staff	Katherine L. Boyd, Stephen S. Seddon
Librarian	Terry Passaro
Associate Librarian	Shantha Uddin
Curator/Geography	David W. Foster
Assistant Librarian	Robert M. Lewis
Yearbook Secretarial Staff	Dorothy Hagen, Catherine E. Johnson

Editorial Advisers

Stephen Lock, M.D.	Drummond Rennie, M.D.
Research Associate,	Professor of Medicine,
History of 20th Century Medicine,	Institute for Health Policy Studies,
Wellcome Institute for the History of Medicine, London;	University of California at San Francisco;
Editor Emeritus,	Deputy Editor (West),
British Medical Journal	*Journal of the American Medical Association*

Editorial Administration

Charles P. Trumbull, Director of Yearbooks
Elizabeth P. O'Connor, Vice President, Operations
Marsha Mackenzie, Director of Production

Encyclopædia Britannica, Inc.
Peter B. Norton, President and Chief Executive Officer
Joseph J. Esposito, President, Encyclopædia Britannica North America
Karen M. Barch, Executive Vice President, Operations

A Few Words
from the Editor . . .

ONE OF THE MOST DIFFICULT things about putting out a "yearbook" of medicine and health is to be "current." Hardly a day goes by without a new gene being identified, a new pathogen recognized, a new alarm raised about this or that drug, a new link established between mind and body, or a critical new finding published about the role of diet in causing (or preventing) disease. And reports of new and improved treatments and new or continuing environmental threats to health abound. While it would be impossible to include every late-breaking development in these pages, the *Medical and Health Annual* turns to experts to put recent medical news in perspective and to consider critical matters of current health concern. The more than 70 authorities who contributed to this volume are from countries around the world and are among the most knowledgeable in their diverse fields.

What will readers find in this 1995 edition of the *Annual*? Here are just a few highlights:

● **X-rays** were discovered 100 years ago. Where would the practice of medicine be today if the German scientist Wilhelm Röntgen had *not* come upon "a curious emanation" that made it possible to see inside things? What windows on the human body were opened by that amazing new power? "Röntgen's Remarkable Rays: Centennial Tribute" commemorates this important anniversary by looking back at the life of Röntgen the man and at the events that led to and followed his seminal discovery. (*See* page 172.)

● **Domestic violence** may touch as many as *one in four* American families. Many recent events have focused attention on this costly U.S. public health problem but perhaps none more than the murder in Los Angeles of Nicole Brown Simpson—allegedly by her ex-husband, the movie star and former football hero O.J. Simpson—and the execution of 11-year-old Robert Sandifer of Chicago, reportedly by members of his own gang, only a few days after he was accused of shooting and killing a 14-year-old girl. While those widely publicized acts of violence took on lives of their own in the press, they also "brought home" the message to a great many Americans that murder is often a "family affair." Moreover, children are not spared from this societal scourge. "Violence: America's Deadliest Epidemic" takes a probing look at what has become a U.S. public health *emergency* of the first order. (*See* page 70.)

● **The violence of war**—and particularly its impact on the lives and health of the civilian population of one region of former Yugoslavia—is the subject of "Trying to Help: Humanitarian Relief in Bosnia." In 1993 epidemiologist Michael J. Toole of the International Health Program Office of the Centers for Disease Control and Prevention served on a UN relief team that provided desperately needed food and aid to a besieged Muslim enclave in eastern Bosnia. He describes the enormous obstacles and constraints, the frustrations, and the frequent dangers that humanitarian aid workers throughout Bosnia and Herzegovina faced (and continue to face) in trying to help long-suffering citizens in the midst of a bloody ethnic conflict. (*See* page 150.)

● **The AIDS epidemic** has prompted an unprecedented response from the arts—unlike any other disease in history. From the red-ribbon symbol of "AIDS Awareness" on a U.S. postage stamp to the ghostly self-portraits of photographer Robert Mapplethorpe to John Corigliano's *Symphony No. 1* to the two-part Tony award- and Pulitzer Prize-winning Broadway play *Angels in America*, "Raising Spirits: The Arts Transfigure the AIDS Crisis" examines the vast outpouring of AIDS-inspired artworks. (*See* page 124.)

● **Citizens play a vital part in responding to medical emergencies.** An international consortium recently issued revised guidelines on when and how bystanders should use resuscitation techniques to provide basic life support for victims of respiratory or circulatory (cardiac) arrest—until emergency medical services arrive on the scene and can take over. These new recommendations are presented in "Saving Lives in the '90s"—an article that motivated *this* editor to enroll in a CPR (cardiopulmonary resuscitation) class and to learn the proper method of performing the Heimlich maneuver. (*See* page 193.)

● **U.S. health care reform** has arguably cornered more public and political attention in the past year than any other single topic. The '95 *Annual* not only covers the efforts to overhaul the world's most costly health care delivery system, which fails to cover as many as one-sixth of all Americans (*see* "News Makers," page 6, and "Health Policy," page 297), it also includes Special Reports on the health care crises and consequent reforms now under way in two other countries. (*See* "Health Care in France: Saving the System," page 303, and "Focus on Health in a Changing South Africa," page 309.)

● **The health and well-being of travelers** are considered in several articles in this volume. How can today's international tourists avoid malaria, cholera, and HIV? When is it safe to drink the water in a foreign country? Where can wayfarers turn for up-to-date information on infectious disease outbreaks and immunization requirements in their destination countries? And what are the mental and physical rewards of a health-and-fitness-oriented vacation? (*See* "Bon Voyage . . . but Beware," page 26, "Souvenirs Nobody Wants: Guidance for Globe-Trotters," page 48, and "Active Vacations: Exercise Your Options," page 424.)

● **The "Decade of the Brain"** reaches its halfway point in 1995, and the '95 *Annual* has not ignored the neurosciences. "Recent Developments from the World of Medicine" (pages 209–400) includes reports on Alzheimer's disease, amyotrophic lateral sclerosis (ALS, or Lou Gehrig's disease), epilepsy, schizophrenia, and chronic fatigue; looks at the phenomenon of "false memory syndrome"; and describes important recent advances in understanding, treating, or diagnosing multiple sclerosis, depression, and Huntington's disease.

● ***Your* health concerns** are addressed in "HealthWise." What does the testing of infants' vision involve? To what extent are computer users' wrists at risk? What drugs and other substances should pregnant women say "no" to? Is a vegetarian diet healthful? Experts provide the answers. (*See* pages 401–465.)

*   *   *

But there is a great deal more. To find out about the many other subjects covered in the 1995 *Medical and Health Annual,* turn the page. . . .

Contents

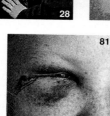

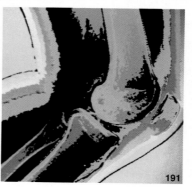

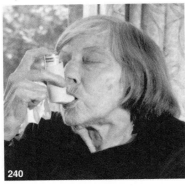

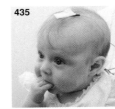

HealthWise

From the Pages of the 1994 Encyclopædia Britannica

4

5

6

7

8

9

10

11

News Makers

ALL HER "DOCTOR" **BARBIE,** IF YOU PLEASE. The favorite doll of girls in more than 140 countries celebrated her 35th birthday in 1994 with a midlife career change. The statuesque blond donned a white coat and became a pediatrician. Actually this was not Barbie's first venture into health care; in previous years she had been a candy striper, a nurse, a surgeon, and a veterinarian. While Barbie was not the most sensational news maker of the year, she was certainly among the most diverting in a world beset by an unabated AIDS pandemic and a host of other grave and difficult medical matters.

Hardly a day passed that the subject of overhauling the U.S. health care system was not in the news, and there was certainly no shortage of key players in that arena. **U.S. Pres. Bill Clinton**'s appointee **Hillary Rodham Clinton,** as head of the President's Task Force on

(Far left) Playwright Spalding Gray; (1) demonstrators demanding decent health care coverage; (2) AMA president Lonnie R. Bristow; (3) Lasker Award winner Nancy Sabin Wexler; (4) Syrian golden hamster, animal model for alcohol-abuse studies; (5) U.S. Surgeon General M. Joycelyn Elders; (6) Empress Michiko; (7) author Betty Friedan; (8) disaster survivor Tiffany; (9) Louise Brown, world's first test-tube baby, holding test-tube twins; (10) malaria survivor Mother Teresa; (11) "Doctor" Barbie.

National Health Care Reform, captivated the capital—and much of the rest of the nation—when she appeared before the House Ways and Means Committee on Sept. 28, 1993, and called upon Congress to "give the American people the health security they deserve." Even her critics were impressed by the first lady's mastery of the details of the complex Clinton administration health care proposal (the Health Security Act) as she responded to 12 hours of questions with poise and certainty—and without notes. The administration's official bill was formally delivered to Congress a month later.

A considerable boost for the Health Security Act came from former surgeon general **C. Everett Koop,** who urged physicians to support the plan even if they did not accept "every single point." Koop, one of the most outspoken and independent surgeons general in the history of that post, declared that President Clinton had accomplished more in health reform in four months than "all of his living predecessors put together." Two former first ladies, **Rosalynn Carter** and **Betty Ford,** and **Tipper Gore,** the vice president's wife, spoke out for insurance that would cover treatment of mental illness and drug and alcohol addiction, arguing that such provisions ultimately would save money.

The response from Congress to the president's Health Security Act was immediate and intense. Sen. **James M. Jeffords** (Rep., Vt.) distinguished himself as the only Republican to sign on in favor of the administration's proposal. Jeffords called for bipartisan support of the bill—support that was not to materialize. By the close of the first session of the 103rd Congress (November 1993), major figures who offered competing health care reform proposals included, among others, Rep. **Jim Cooper** (Dem., Tenn.), whose plan was dubbed "Clinton lite." Rep. **Jim McDermott** (Dem., Wash.), a former practicing psychiatrist, proposed the most polit-

ically liberal plan, a Canadian-style single-payer system. Sen. **John Chafee** (Rep., R.I.) favored a moderate approach to change and later led a bipartisan group of about 20 senators calling itself the "Mainstream Coalition," whose plan aimed to insure only about 92–93% of Americans by 2004 and would eliminate many provisions common to other proposals. Sen. **Phil Gramm** (Rep., Texas), on the other hand, contended that the U.S. health care delivery system needed only marginal repair.

Still other plans were put forward in early 1994 by Sen. **Daniel Patrick Moynihan** (Dem., N.Y.) and Sen. **Bob Dole** (Rep., Kan.). Then in late July **Richard A. Gephardt** (Dem., Mo.), the House majority leader, unveiled the "House plan," promising universal coverage by 1999. A few days later Senate Majority Leader **George Mitchell** (Dem., Maine) offered a more conservative bill than either Clinton's or Gephardt's, aiming for coverage of only 95% of Americans by 2000.

By mid-August (around the time this volume was "put to bed") long and heated debates on the floor of the Senate were under way. Many voices were heard, and there were daily compromises, shifts, setbacks, and a threatened filibuster on the part of Republicans. The House put off debates on health reform until after the Labor Day recess. Clinton seemed willing to compromise and support the so-called Mitchell plan. Mitchell pledged to keep the Senate in session until it acted on a health care bill but then relented, and senators took a vacation after all. At that point the prognosis for passage of any sweeping health legislation before the end of the year was not good. While the reform issue was not dead, it was clearly on the "critical list."

Although only fictional, **Harry and Louise,** the yuppie couple featured in an anti-Clinton-plan TV advertising campaign sponsored by the insurance industry, took on a life of their own. When first seen by TV viewers, they were sitting in their kitchen amid stacks of papers—presumably the Clinton administration's blueprint for health care reform. "It says here that under the president's plan we won't be able to choose our doctor," one of them observes. "There has got to be a better way," they conclude.

The couple was adopted by the Democratic National Committee and other parties to the debate in a series of spin-offs and parodies. Perhaps the funniest was that performed by none other than **Bill and Hillary,** in a video that was shown at the 1994 Gridiron Club dinner, at which the Washington press corps spoofs presidential politics. Hillary as Louise, with an enormous tome—

presumably the 240,000-word Health Security Act—on her lap, announces: "It says here on page 3,764 that under the Clinton health security plan we could get sick. . . . It says that eventually we are all going to die." (The actual document has only 1,342 pages.) Incredulously, her husband responds, "You mean after Bill and Hillary put all those new bureaucrats and taxes on us, we're still all going to die?" They, too, conclude in unison, "There's got to be a better way!" (*See* "Health Policy," p. 297, for more on U.S. health care reform.)

Arrivals and departures

Confirmed as U.S. surgeon general over the bitter objections of conservatives and fundamentalist religious groups was **M. Joycelyn Elders,** a sharecropper's daughter who became a pediatrician and later was appointed director of Arkansas's Department of Health by Gov. Bill Clinton. Outspoken and provocative, Elders was labeled the "condom queen" for her advocacy of condom distribution in schools to curb teenage pregnancy and the spread of AIDS. She made the point that U.S. teens get driver's education in school but not sex education: "We taught them what to do in the front seat of a car," she said. "Now it's time to teach them what to do in the back seat." A short time after her confirmation, she created a furor when she voiced her opinion that the legalization of drugs might help to reduce crime. In a further startling pronouncement, Elders criticized the U.S. Medicaid system, which, she said, must have been developed by a "white male slave owner." By failing to provide poor women with family-planning services to prevent unwanted pregnancies, Medicaid,

Elders opined, "contributes to poverty, ignorance, and enslavement." In August 1994 she helped launch a UNICEF campaign to promote breast-feeding worldwide. Appealing to U.S. mothers, nearly half of whom rely on formula rather than the breast, she said, "You can have a Ph.D. and not know how to feed a baby."

Another controversial official, **Bernadine Healy,** resigned under pressure as director of the National Institutes of Health (NIH) after politicians and scientists complained about her argumentative style and her awkward handling of investigations into misconduct in biomedical research. Not all of her efforts at the NIH drew opposition; she was widely lauded for instituting the Women's Health Initiative, a $625 million program to study health problems that affect women.

In contrast to the commotion over the appointment of Elders and the performance of Healy, the appointment of **Harold E. Varmus** as Healy's replacement was quickly confirmed in November 1993 by the Senate. Varmus, the first Nobel laureate to hold the office of NIH director, gained international renown for his research on cancer-causing genes. As head of the NIH, he will oversee a nearly $11 billion annual budget, which finances a major portion of the nation's biomedical research. His appointment was greeted with enthusiasm by dispirited researchers, who were elated that "one of their own" finally had been named to the office after a succession of clinicians. It was his own work at the NIH (from 1968 to 1970) that prompted Varmus to switch from clinical medicine to basic research.

The ranks of Washington, D.C., officials are minus one nurse. **Kristine M. Gebbie,** who served as the Clin-

Assembled in the House chambers (left to right), pediatrician T. Berry Brazelton, Hillary Rodham Clinton, C. Everett Koop, and Tipper Gore wait to hear an address on health care by the U.S. president. Other key players in U.S. health care reform (opposite page, left to right): Senators George Mitchell, Daniel Patrick Moynihan, Bob Dole, and Phil Gramm.

ton administration's AIDS policy chief for 11 months, submitted her resignation in July 1994. As Gebbie described it, the expectations about how she would perform the ill-defined job were "enormous and conflicting." She was often criticized by AIDS activists as ineffective, although none doubted her good intentions.

Also leaving the nation's capital in the summer of 1994 was **Joseph J. Jacobs,** director of the NIH's Office of Alternative Medicine (OAM). A pediatrician and a Native American familiar with traditional healing practices, Jacobs seemed the ideal choice to investigate the merits of unconventional therapies. His critics, however, found him slow to act and reluctant to offend the conservative elements of the medical establishment. For his part Jacobs was frustrated by a budget that was small by Washington standards and exasperated by the willingness of many people to accept less-than-scientific evidence of therapeutic benefits. Nevertheless, he maintained his wry sense of humor; at one point he reportedly suggested that the phone number of the OAM should be 1-800-Peyote.

David Satcher, the president of Meharry Medical College, Nashville, Tennessee, replaced **William Roper** as director of the Centers for Disease Control and Prevention (CDC) in Atlanta, Georgia, on Aug. 20, 1993. Satcher, an African-American, is an expert on minority and community health issues. **Donna E. Shalala,** secretary of health and human services (HHS), declared that Satcher brought "world-class professional stature, management skills, integrity, and preventive health care experience" to the CDC.

Another physician to reach high office was **Lonnie R. Bristow,** a California internist who in June 1994 became the first African-American president of the American Medical Association (AMA), which represents some 290,000 medical practitioners. Elected at a time when the U.S. seemed to be on the brink of enormous changes in health care delivery, Bristow said that his greatest concern was "to see that the doctor-patient relationship is protected in the health-care transition."

AIDS: no end in sight

As AIDS activists continued their angry protests, charging that the federal government has not paid adequate attention to the AIDS pandemic, Varmus made a widely heralded appointment of an official to spearhead U.S. research on the disease. He named **William E. Paul,** a highly respected immunologist and chief of the immunology laboratory at the NIH's National Institute of Allergy and Infectious Diseases since 1970, to direct the NIH's Office of AIDS Research. AIDS activist **Gregg Gonsalves,** a member of the Treatment Action Group, termed Paul's appointment "the biggest thing that the Clinton Administration has done in the fight against AIDS."

Other than sexual abstinence, the use of condoms during intercourse remains the only consistently effective barrier to the sexual transmission of HIV. Nevertheless, pressure from political conservatives and religious fundamentalists has impeded education about condoms, despite their acknowledged acceptance by the public health community. In 1994, however, in the face of vociferous criticism, the CDC introduced a series of radio and television public service messages to spread the word about the importance of condom use to prevent HIV transmission. The campaign targeted sexually active young adults—a high-risk group—with a series of ads that did not simply lecture but were designed to grab the audience's attention. One of the ads' stars was an **animated condom** that saved the day by making its way from the top drawer of a bedroom dresser, across the room, onto the bed, and under the covers of a young couple—just in time. But even after the reluctant acceptance of condom promotions by radio and television, the nation's newspapers remained largely resistant to accepting advertising for condoms.

On the other side of the globe, not nearly so reticent was **Mechai Viravaidya,** a Thai economist and restaurateur, whose Bangkok eatery, Cabbages & Condoms, offers departing diners condoms instead of after-dinner mints. "My philosophy," says Viravaidya, "is that contraceptives must be as easily accessible as vegetables."

One long-standing controversy in AIDS research largely faded on Nov. 11, 1993, when the U.S. government's Office of Research Integrity dropped all pending misconduct charges against AIDS researcher **Robert C. Gallo.** Those charges had centered on work carried out in the prominent virologist's laboratory at the National Cancer Institute over a period of many years. One of the accusations was that the AIDS virus Gallo claimed credit for discovering was one that had been appropriated from French scientists at the Pasteur Institute in Paris. A week before the Gallo charges were dismissed, a government appeals board had exonerated his former colleague and coresearcher **Mikulas Popovic,** concluding that "after all the sound and fury," there was no "residue of palpable wrongdoing."

In July 1994 NIH head Varmus announced that the U.S. had agreed to give the Pasteur Institute in Paris a larger share than it had been receiving of the royalties

(Above) Mechai Viravaidya, owner of the Bangkok, Thailand, restaurant Cabbages & Condoms, dishes out contraceptives as well as vegetables. (Left) Harold E. Varmus brings his research experience to the head office of the National Institutes of Health.

for the definitive blood test for HIV. This step was viewed as an acknowledgment that researchers in Gallo's lab had used a virus from the Pasteur Institute in developing the test. After his vindication in November, Gallo said that he was eager to get back to his research: "There is no doubt I lost significant time, and I feel obsessed to make up for it." In a written statement in July, he commented, "It is now time for this episode to be permanently closed. Pasteur scientists and I should focus all our energies on seeking a cure for AIDS."

While effective treatment for AIDS—or a vaccine that would prevent HIV infection—continued to elude researchers, the disease continued to take its relentless toll. Among AIDS deaths in the past year were those of two prominent journalists, **Randy Shilts** and **Jeffery Schmalz.** Shilts, who died on Feb. 17, 1994, at age 42, was the first openly gay reporter for a major metropolitan daily, the *San Francisco Chronicle,* and the first full-time reporter to cover the AIDS epidemic for a major paper. Schmalz, 39, a reporter for the *New York Times,* died of complications of AIDS on Nov. 6, 1993. He covered AIDS and gay issues for the *Times* and wrote openly of his own homosexuality and his life with AIDS. (*See* below for other AIDS activists who died of the disease. *See* also "AIDS," p. 215, and "Raising Spirits: The Arts Transfigure the AIDS Crisis," p. 124.)

Where there's smoke . . .

The flames of the antismoking movement were further fanned—confirming the adage "Where there's smoking, there's ire"—as tobacco companies came under increasing fire to curb their promotions and Americans were given yet further reasons to curb their smoking habits. Unsurprisingly, Surgeon General Elders, like her predecessors, accused cigarette manufacturers of using devious tactics to lure teenagers into a lifelong

Randy Shilts, journalist, died of AIDS on Feb. 17, 1994. Shilts was probably best known as the author of a groundbreaking history of AIDS in the U.S., And the Band Played On *(1987), which subsequently became a made-for-television movie.*

James D. Wilson—Gamma Liaison

addiction. She urged that all cigarette advertisements aimed at young people be banned and that the nation shift its antismoking efforts toward youth because most smokers "are hooked by the time they are 20." In the 1994 Surgeon General's Report, *Preventing Tobacco Use Among Young People,* Elders called upon the Federal Trade Commission to quash one of the most successful but irresponsible advertising campaigns, the **Joe Camel** cartoons, sponsored by R.J. Reynolds Tobacco Co., in which the debonair dromedary is depicted in trendy settings, puffing away on his Camel cigarettes. Capitalizing on the popularity of the suave Joe, the manufacturer recently launched an all-out ad campaign in widely read women's magazines featuring his female counterpart, the alluring **Josephine Camel.**

Meantime, a study by **John Pierce,** director of the Cancer Center at the University of California at San Diego, found that in the 1960s and '70s the tobacco industry had clearly succeeded in seducing teenage girls to smoke by promoting women's brands.

In one effort to counter the whimsical appeal of the smoking camels, FamilyCare Communications in Eden Prairie, Minnesota, developed its own crusader, **Rex A. Canine,** a pooch who, like other aspiring film stars, wears shades. Rex plays the lead in a 14-minute video, "Send Joe Camel Packing," designed for antismoking programs in schools. In a sequel, "Spitting Tobacco," **Rex II** will address the growing and equally dangerous use of smokeless tobacco by young people.

Rep. **Henry A. Waxman** (Dem., Calif.), chairman of the House Health and Environment Subcommittee, introduced the Smoke-Free Environment Act of 1993 to ban smoking in all restaurants and other buildings open to the public—legislation that in February 1994 received the endorsement of the Clinton administration and six former surgeons general as well as McDonald's Corp. and the National Council of Chain Restaurants. The act calls for an end to smoking in every public building regularly entered by 10 or more people at least one day a week. Companion legislation was introduced in the Senate by Sen. **Frank Lautenberg** (Dem., N.J.), who had previously succeeded in making domestic flights on all U.S. airlines smoke-free. At the same time, McDonald's announced that smoking would be banned in all of its 1,400 wholly owned restaurants and that it would encourage franchise owners to do the same. Waxman welcomed the corporation's support. "In the most elementary terms," he said, "members of Congress must now choose between Ronald McDonald and Joe Camel."

In February 1994 the tobacco industry came under fire for intentionally promoting and sustaining addiction by manipulating the levels of nicotine in cigarettes. During congressional hearings Food and Drug Administration (FDA) Commissioner **David A. Kessler** lambasted industry officials, saying there might be grounds for regulating the sale of cigarettes under drug laws, which could result in their removal from the over-the-counter market.

At the very time the tobacco industry was busy defending itself—calling for an "informed debate" in full-page newspaper ads—a hot new novel hit the stands, **Christopher Buckley**'s satirical farce, *Thank You for Smoking*. As *New York Times* reviewer Christopher Lehmann-Haupt observed, Buckley's book is "so timely that you have to wonder if [the author] has been orchestrating recent events in tobacco-land." Like the products his spoof is about, Buckley's book carries a warning: "This novel could be hilarious to your health." Buckley's protagonist is one Nick Naylor, who is chief spokesperson for the Academy of Tobacco Studies. He freely admits he works for an industry that kills "more than 400,000 a year! And approaching the half-million mark." Inevitably, a question Buckley was asked on the book-promotion circuit was whether *he* smokes. He does not—or at least he gave up cigarettes in 1988. He does, however, indulge in an occasional cigar, though he is quick to point out, "At the risk of sounding presidential, I don't inhale." (*See* "Smoking," p. 389, for more on tobacco-related developments.)

Diet delights and dilemmas

In an undiplomatic moment during a conference in Brussels, President Clinton, whose penchant for burgers, fries, and milk shakes is well-known, compared the rotund German chancellor **Helmut Kohl** to a sumo wrestler. Rather than taking umbrage, the jovial chancellor, whose avoirdupois does not grossly exceed that of the president, invited Clinton to dine with him a few weeks later when he visited the U.S.

The two leaders met at Filomena's, an Italian restaurant in Washington, D.C., where they engaged in some further caloric bonding. Chef **Vito Piazza** bragged, "There's no spa cuisine here. Our motto is *abbondanza*." And *abbondanza* ("abundance") the two world leaders consumed. They started with red wine, followed by hot and cold antipasti, fried calamari (squid), and ravioli stuffed with veal, cheese, and spinach and topped with marinara sauce. The president also had a Tuscan soup made with white beans, tomatoes, and spinach. The

SURGEON GENERAL'S WARNING: Smoking By Pregnant Women May Result in Fetal Injury, Premature Birth, And Low Birth Weight.

NEW FRIENDLY MARKET

Rex A. Canine (left) tells kids to send Joe Camel (above) packing.

(Above) David Weintraub—Stock, Boston; (left) © 1993 FamilyCare Communications and ITDA, Inc.

chancellor had a salad with Italian dressing. To top off the meal, both enjoyed a dessert of zabaglione with mixed berries. Amazingly, they were still able to walk out of the restaurant. The president's caloric consumption at the meal was estimated at 3,367, the chancellor's at 3,263; moreover, each ingested an amount of fat equal to more than a quarter pound of butter.

Such gourmandizing, however, apparently was a rare treat for President Clinton, who is attempting to eat more sensibly now that he is the nation's leader. He seems to have had some success. After a physical exam following an arduous first year in office, doctors at Bethesda Naval Hospital in Maryland pronounced Clinton to be "in excellent health." Though his cholesterol was borderline high (204 milligrams per deciliter), the president had "no indication of heart disease or other serious disorders," White House physician **Robert Ramsey** said.

Mrs. Clinton was making her own contribution to her husband's attempt to eat a prudent diet. She asked for and received the resignation of White House executive chef **Pierre Chambrin,** who had been hired as a sous-chef (assistant chef) by Barbara Bush. Chambrin prepared food in the French tradition, using liberal amounts of butter and cream. That the current first lady was opting for a dietary overhaul was apparent in her choice of **Walter S. Scheib III** as the new White House chef. The 39-year-old Scheib, a graduate of the Culinary Institute of America in Hyde Park, New York, previously held the post of executive chef at the venera-

ble Greenbrier Resort and Health Spa in White Sulphur Springs, West Virginia. With Scheib in the kitchen, the emphasis, both in first family meals and in state dinners, was to be on low-fat dishes using fresh ingredients and with a decidedly American flavor. A White House press aide confirmed that cardiologist **Dean Ornish** would be informally advising the new chef. On Ornish's recommendation Mrs. Clinton ordered numerous cases of fat-free, meatless "burgers" for White House consumption. (*See* below for more about Ornish's dietary approach.)

Thin may be in on the fashion scene, but researchers in Helsinki, Finland, reported that **Barbie**'s sylphlike figure is sending young girls the wrong message about what a healthy woman's body should look like. After giving the doll a complete physical, the Finnish doctors concluded that Barbie is anorexic. They calculated that she has far too little padding to give her the 17% to 22% body fat that experts say a woman needs to menstruate. Now that Mattel, the doll's manufacturer, has given Barbie an M.D., perhaps she may adopt a more nourishing diet and add some heft to her hips. Whatever her image, Barbie generates about $1 billion a year in sales for Mattel. The company announced in 1994 that it would contribute $1 million of the revenues from Dr. Barbie to support the immunization of U.S. children.

Sealed in

On Sept. 26, 1993, in Oracle, Arizona, **Abigail Alling, Linda Leigh, Taber MacCallum, Mark Nelson, Jane**

Poynter, Sally Silverstone, Mark Van Thillo, and Roy L. Walford emerged from two years of isolation inside a bubblelike structure known as Biosphere 2 (Earth is Biosphere 1). The volunteers ranged in age from their mid-20s to their mid-60s.

Biosphere 2 was widely criticized for being "more showbiz than science." Six months after the project began, the 11-member scientific advisory panel, headed by Thomas E. Lovejoy of the Smithsonian Institution, resigned en masse. Many scientists viewed the experiment as "a kook's dream" and "a rich man's whim." The kook they were referring to is Edward P. Bass, a Texas billionaire who put up most of the money for Biosphere Space Ventures, initially costing $150 million and scheduled to run for 100 years. Annual operating costs are subsidized by the $4 million a year collected from the more than 200,000 visitors who visit the Arizona-desert site to gawk at the Biosphereans inside and, of course, to purchase the inevitable T-shirts, mugs, bumper stickers, and other souvenirs so dear to tourists' hearts.

Biosphere 2 was designed to be a "closed" system that replicates Earth's environments. Air, water, and waste are recycled, and nothing is received from the outside except sunlight, electricity, and computer and telephone communications. The habitat is divided into seven distinct "biomes," or ecosystems: rain forest, savanna, marsh, ocean (complete with a wave machine that generates daily tides), desert, farm, and human living quarters. Living inside with the crew were 3,800 species of plants, animals, and insects. Fish, pigs, goats, and chickens were intended to provide food, but only limited amounts were available.

During the two-year stint of the Biosphereans, an unanticipated lack of sunshine produced a meager harvest, requiring the crew to rely on some stored grains and seeds as dietary supplements. At one point oxygen levels dropped to 15%—equivalent to an altitude of 4,200 meters (14,000 feet)—necessitating oxygen to be pumped in from the outside, and four crew members needed to take the drug acetazolamide to relieve symptoms of altitude sickness.

Despite the experiment's general lack of scientific rigor, some valuable information was gleaned, especially about the effects of the dietary regimen. Walford, a nutritionist and gerontologist at the University of California at Los Angeles, established the nutrient-rich, low-calorie, low-fat diet. The major items on the Biosphereans' menu were grains, legumes, fruits, and vegetables. The meal plan, which would strike many as spartan, consisted of about 1,750 calories a day and resulted in weight losses of 9–10% among the women and as high as 18% among the men; blood pressure and cholesterol levels declined—in some cases, dramatically. While certain home-grown staples such as sweet potatoes and beets were plentiful, some of the crew complained of being hungry a lot of the time, and others admitted to having fantasies about rich desserts. At least one crew member, Silverstone, liked the diet so much that she wrote a cookbook, *Eating In: From the Field to the Kitchen in Biosphere 2.*

After the Biosphere 2 experiment ended, Lisa Walford, Roy's daughter, collaborated with her father on another cookbook, *The Anti-Aging Plan.* New York Times food critic and nutrition writer Marian Burros attended a buffet where she had the chance to sample some of the recipes from the Walfords' book. "There was cold soggy 'pizza,' mushy, cold 'lasagna,' salad dressed with vinegar and 'chocolate' cake that stuck to the roof of your mouth," she reported. Not exactly four stars. (*See* below for more on recently published cookbooks.)

On March 6, 1994, taking with them the lessons learned by their pioneering predecessors, seven new Biosphereans entered the 1.3-hectare (3.15-acre), 10-story, glass-domed terrarium in the Arizona desert. The new recruits would not be subjected to quite the same test of endurance as were the first Biosphereans, who set a world record for living in isolation; rather, the new team would have staggered stays of four months to more than a year in the habitat. Also, visitors and

(Opposite page) U.S. Pres. Bill Clinton and German Chancellor Helmut Kohl face off at Filomena's. The score: Clinton 3,367 calories, Kohl 3,263. The first lady, who watches the presidential waistline, undoubtedly was not amused. In April 1994 she hired a health-spa chef, Walter S. Scheib III (left), to trim the fat from the White House menu.

(Opposite page) Dirck Halstead—Gamma Liaison; (left) Jeffrey Markowitz—Sygma outside scientists would be allowed to enter. According to the research director, **John Corliss,** the policy of allowing visiting scientists inside was intended to make the project into a true research laboratory.

Absent from the studies conducted during the occupancy of the first crew were efforts to assess psychological reactions to prolonged confinement. (There were, however, reports of frayed tempers.) Although the second crew would remain inside for shorter periods, psychologists intended to measure their stress levels and other psychological parameters.

Celebration and commemoration

Celebrating her 16th birthday in October 1993, **Louise Brown** of Bristol, England, was proclaimed by her parents to be much like any other teenager, with a fondness for "loud music and stupid clothes." The fact of her ordinariness only makes her birth—as the world's first "test-tube baby"—all the more miraculous. Today the procedure that made Louise's life possible, in vitro fertilization (IVF), is an established treatment for infertility that is responsible for as many as 16,000 births a year. The family now has another daughter, **Natalie,** also conceived by IVF.

The U.S. Postal Service announced in 1994 that it was honoring American physician **Virginia Apgar** with a commemorative stamp. Apgar, who died in 1974, was a delivery room anesthesiologist who became concerned that not enough medical attention was given to infants immediately after birth. She developed a simple method for assessing the physical health of newborns that is now used routinely all over the world. The "Apgar score" assesses five parameters—heart rate, breathing, muscle tone, reflexes, and the infant's color (a sign of adequate circulation)—at one minute and five minutes after birth. The method enables the delivery room staff to determine quickly which infants should be transferred to neonatal intensive care.

Until now France had never accorded to a woman the honor of burial in her own right in the Panthéon. **Marie Curie** (1867–1934), the Polish-born French physicist famous for her work with radioactivity, had been interred in the national shrine but shared the tomb of her husband and scientific collaborator, **Pierre Curie,** who died in 1906. In 1994 French Pres. **François Mitterrand** asked the family of Madame Curie for permission to move her remains to a separate vault, where she finally would be given the prestige she earned in life. Curie, the first woman to teach at the Sorbonne, shared the Nobel Prize for Physics with her husband in 1903 and

won the Nobel Prize for Chemistry in 1911. Much of her work was on the medical applications of radioactive substances. Her death from leukemia was the result of radiation exposure in the course of her scientific work.

Sickness and celebs

Illness strikes the famous and fortunate just as it does ordinary mortals. **Mother Teresa,** the Nobel peace laureate who has devoted her life to helping the "poorest of the poor" and the "sickest of the sick," fell ill with malarial fever in New Delhi in August 1993. But after a brief hospital stay, doctors allowed the indomitable sister to celebrate her 83rd birthday (on August 27) by returning to her work in Calcutta. Four years earlier she had had a pacemaker implanted following two major heart attacks, but illness had yet to keep her down.

Japan's **Empress Michiko** was struck mysteriously mute with an undiagnosed ailment but seven weeks later was able to speak again. The empress collapsed on her 59th birthday, Oct. 20, 1993; when she regained consciousness after a few hours, she could not speak. Doctors subsequently attributed the empress's sudden affliction to "strong feelings of distress" and "bitter grief," which palace officials ascribed to a series of recent articles in the Japanese press that accused her of

The eight Biospherreans emerge from two years' voluntary confinement in a $150 million habitat in the Arizona desert.

inordinate extravagances and of being a domineering figure at court.

Just before Christmas 1993, Gov. **Robert P. Casey** of Pennsylvania returned to work. Some 190 days earlier he had been on the brink of death. Casey, aged 61, suffers from a rare hereditary liver disease, familial amyloidosis. In May 1993 his health was rapidly failing; his disease had severely damaged his liver and heart and had affected his intestines. He began searching for his own cure, reading the medical literature and consulting specialists. Ultimately he turned to the pioneer transplant surgeon **Thomas E. Starzl** at the University of Pittsburgh, Pennsylvania. Starzl agreed to perform an experimental heart and liver transplant. The operation was a success. Though doctors were concerned about Casey's returning to such a demanding job, more than one year after his surgery the governor continued to do well. The cost of the 13-hour operation and related care was $353,772, paid for by the Pennsylvania state employees insurance plan. Some were critical of the fact that Casey received priority treatment for an experimental procedure—especially when there is such a scarcity of donor organs, and most patients are placed on waiting lists. (*See* "Transplantation," p. 395, for more on Starzl's recent work.)

Quite a few celebrities have channeled their energies into "causes" that benefit or bring attention to the sick and suffering. British actress **Jane Seymour,** star of the hit TV series "Dr. Quinn, Medicine Woman," in which she plays a pioneer doctor in the American West, was host of a three-part television special, "The Heart of Healing: Remarkable Stories of How We Heal Ourselves." The program profiled individuals who had found apparent cures for dire illnesses and explored the ways the mind can heal the body. Seymour shared a personal story: her mother recovered from what was thought to be inoperable cancer after she was given a bottle of holy water and told to pray.

In the fall of 1993, country music star **Reba McEntire** visited St. Jude's Children's Research Hospital in Memphis, Tennessee, and was so moved by the upbeat spirits of young cancer patients that she featured them in a music video. The courageous youngsters appear during McEntire's singing of "If I Had Only Known," a song she dedicated to the memory of her band members, who were killed in an airplane crash.

Actor **Gene Wilder,** husband of the late **Gilda Radner,** who died of ovarian cancer in 1989, helped establish "Gilda's Club" in New York City, intended as a special gathering place for cancer patients and their

Pennsylvania Gov. Robert P. Casey exercises on a treadmill five weeks after receiving a new heart and liver. A few months later he was back on the job.

Governor's Office, Commonwealth of Pennsylvania

families and friends. The center, which opened in the spring of 1994, got its name because Radner was often quoted as saying that having ovarian cancer gave her membership in an "elite club" to which she would rather not have belonged.

Illness on stage

New York City writer and actor **Spalding Gray** performed his autobiographical monologue *Gray's Anatomy* at Manhattan's Vivian Beaumont Theater at Lincoln Center. Gray suffers from the rare visual disorder known as macular pucker; the vitreous humor in his left eye has broken down and pulled away from the retina, leaving a small piece of skin on the macula. The macula, a structure at the center of the retina, enables the perception of detail. In essence, Gray's condition causes him to see differently out of each eye; as Gray puts it, "I'm a little cockeyed." The monologue recounted his idiosyncratic search for a cure. "I didn't want medicine," said the playwright. "I wanted magic." His quest took him on visits to an American Indian sweat lodge, a Filipino psychic surgeon, a nutritional ophthalmologist, a Brazilian healer, and a Christian Science practitioner—among others.

Another autobiographical effort was 32-year-old **Evan Handler**'s one-person show, *Time on Fire,* which played off-Broadway at the Second State Theater in Manhattan. Both comedy and tragedy, the play tells of Handler's successful struggle against acute myeloid leukemia, an often-fatal blood cancer. Over a period of four years, he was in and out of hospitals 10 times, enduring nightmarish chemotherapy, which cost him more than half a million dollars but failed to cure the disease. What finally saved him was a bone marrow transplant at Johns

Actor Nigel Hawthorne endures the tortures of the royal physicians in The Madness of George III.

Photograph, Donald Cooper—Photostage

Hopkins Hospital in Baltimore, Maryland. Handler was not gentle in his portrayal of the medical staff at Manhattan's Memorial Sloan-Kettering Cancer Center, where he was initially treated. Some doctors who saw *Time on Fire* thought it should be performed expressly for the hospital's staff, to enlighten them about their often-insensitive bedside manners.

The Madness of George III, by British playwright **Alan Bennett,** staged by the Royal National Theatre of Great Britain, has been a standing-room-only hit in London since 1992. The play examines the lunacy of the English monarch, who lost his mind after losing possession of the American colonies. *The Madness of George III* is based on the view of some contemporary physicians that the eccentric George, who reigned from 1760 to 1820, was afflicted not by mental illness but by a form of porphyria, a metabolic blood disorder. The play's villains are the doctors, who alternately inspect the king's bowel movements, check the color of his urine, gag him, give him emetics, blister him with hot glasses, put him in a straightjacket, and otherwise torture and humiliate him. The royal sufferer is played brilliantly by actor **Nigel Hawthorne.** After attending the performance, **Princess Margaret,** a direct descendant of George III, is reported to have gone backstage and asked, "Is it hereditary?" (It is.)

Two Harvard Medical School psychiatrists, **Samuel Shem** and **Janet Surrey,** coauthored the play *Bill W. and Dr. Bob.* The title refers to the cofounders of Alcoholics Anonymous, **Bob Smith,** a surgeon from Akron, Ohio, who abused alcohol for over 40 years, and **Bill Wilson,** a former alcohol-abusing New York stockbroker. The play was intended to enlighten medical students about addiction—a problem that traditional medical education often ignores. Performed by six professional actors of the Cambridge Theatre Company, the educational drama opened at Harvard's Hasty Pudding Theatre in October 1993 and then was to go on tour, being performed at medical schools, colleges, treatment centers, corporations, and prisons.

In the animal kingdom

Socks, the nation's "first cat," was not the only feline to enjoy celebrity in recent months. **Tiffany,** a part-Persian cat, was a miraculous survivor of the January 1994 California earthquake. Rescued after being trapped under rubble for 41 days, the pertinacious puss had her picture in newspapers around the world. "She's nothing but skin and bones," said veterinarian **Sandy Sanford.** "But she's alive and she's purring."

Krista, a seven-year-old Shih tzu, was one of several dogs making medical history as the first of the species to receive the widely publicized antidepressant Prozac. Its veterinary use thus far has been directed at compulsive behaviors—such as incessant licking or scratching—rather than at treatment of depression. Just as the drug has been reported to cause striking personality changes in some human patients, some dog owners have claimed that under its influence their canine companions became entirely new animals.

The **Syrian golden hamster,** a rodent with a unique proclivity for alcohol, came into the scientific limelight when it was discovered that the kudzu vine reduced the tiny tippler's alcohol consumption by half. Given the opportunity, the hamsters will consume 40 times as much as an average human alcohol abuser per ounce of body weight. Researchers from Harvard Medical School used an extract derived from the root of the plant to induce temperance in experimental animals. Their studies suggest kudzu holds promise as a treatment for human alcohol addiction. Kudzu has been used medicinally in China since 200 BC. (*See* "Armadillos to Zebra Fish," p. 100, for more on animal models of human disease.)

Our bodies, our best-sellers

Society's obsession with staying thin, remaining youthful, and defying death was reflected on the best-seller lists. Seemingly miraculous antidotes to illness, depression, and even personality flaws were also all-consuming interests of Americans, if the books they bought are an indication: *Food—Your Miracle Medicine* by **Jean Carper** and *Listening to Prozac* by **Peter Kramer** were consistently on the charts. (*See* "Mental Health and Illness," p. 325, for more on Kramer's book.)

Now in her 70s, **Betty Friedan,** the founding mother of the contemporary feminist movement, has published *The Fountain of Age.* Like many before her, Friedan has found that growing older is not all bad. Both men and women told her of their satisfactions in seniority. Among those she interviewed was senior citizen **Hugh Hefner,** creator of *Playboy* and father of the swinging lifestyle. Hefner confided to Friedan, "I'm savoring this autumn season of my life most of all." (*See* "Midlife: The Crisis Reconsidered," p. 60, for more about Friedan's philosophy of productive aging.)

Also savoring their autumn were the centenarian sisters **Sarah** ("Sadie") and **Annie Elizabeth** ("Bessie") **Delany,** daughters of a slave who became the first black bishop of the Episcopal Church in the United States.

Having Our Say: The Delany Sisters' First 100 Years is the memoir of their long and fulfilling lives, in which they overcame both racial and gender barriers. Bessie, a graduate of Columbia University, became New York state's second black female dentist; Sadie was the first black home economics teacher in New York City. The sisters attribute their longevity, at least partially, to yoga, cod liver oil, and a daily dose of finely chopped garlic.

One of the most critically acclaimed health-related books of 1994 was by a physician and academician who never intended to write a "popular" book. In *How We Die*, **Sherwin B. Nuland,** a surgeon and professor of surgery and medical history at Yale University, examines in detail what happens to human bodies dying of

At ages 104 and 102, respectively, sisters Sarah ("Sadie"; left) and Annie Elizabeth ("Bessie"; right) Delany have their say in a best-selling memoir.

Photograph, Jacques M. Chenet—Gamma Liaison

AIDS, cancer, heart attacks, old age, Alzheimer's disease, and trauma. He vividly describes cancer cells as "a gang of perpetually wilding adolescents . . . the juvenile delinquents of cellular society," and he writes movingly of the deaths of his mother and older brother. The book eloquently expresses Nuland's deeply held conviction that the role of the physician is *not* to extend life at any cost. Neurologist **Oliver Sacks** called Nuland's portraits "as powerful and sensitive, and unsparing and unsentimental" as anything he had read. (*See* below for more about the literary leanings of Sacks.)

One volume on death that may never make best-seller lists has yet to be written. **Jack Kevorkian,** the pathologist from Michigan who has been a controversial proponent of physician-assisted suicide, and his

outspoken attorney, **Geoffrey N. Fieger,** hired an agent to seek a publisher for the book they want to write, the stated intention of which is "to tell the truth about just who we are and how and why we decided to take on one of the greatest taboos of medicine and society itself: Death." Prospective publishers were leery of the idea, however, speculating that while the book would undoubtedly generate public interest, as Kevorkian himself certainly has, this interest might not translate into book sales. From 1990 to the time he submitted the proposal, Kevorkian had assisted 21 terminally ill individuals in taking their own lives. At the end of 1993, he redirected his efforts from assisting in death to changing Michigan's law against euthanasia.

Inevitably, diet books continued to be big sellers. **Susan Powter,** a motivational speaker and former diet-industry victim, rose to the top of the best-seller lists with *Stop the Insanity!*—the "insanity" being fad diets that promise instant weight loss. Readers also rushed to buy the latest book from **Dean Ornish,** *Eat More, Weigh Less.* Ornish's prescription is more stringent than most—calling for a diet in which no more than 10% of calories come from fat (compared with a limit of 30% in the current U.S. dietary recommendations)—but his record of success in treating people with coronary heart disease, using a combination of diet, exercise, and techniques for stress reduction, is indisputable.

Oprah Winfrey's chef, **Rosie Daley,** came out with her own prescription for staying slim: the best-selling cookbook *In the Kitchen with Rosie: Oprah's Favorite Recipes.* After years of yo-yo dieting, Winfrey attributes much of her success in maintaining her trim new silhouette to Daley's "fabulous" low-fat, low-sugar, low-salt cuisine. She also has adopted a daily exercise program and a new attitude toward food. "I once believed that eating healthy meant eating food that was missing something—TASTE," the TV personality wrote in the introduction to the book.

Apprized

The health and vigor of medical research are apparent in the numerous recent laurels awarded for outstanding contributions in the field. The following are some but by no means all of those who received honors. (*See* "Genetics," p. 292, for the 1993 Nobel laureates in medicine and chemistry.)

From the Charles A. Dana Foundation, **W. Maxwell Cowan,** chief scientific officer of the Howard Hughes Medical Institute, received the Dana Distinguished Achievement Award in Health "for a career marked by extraordinary contributions to neuroscience as research scientist, international lecturer, and leader of institutions." **Anders Björklund,** professor of histology at the University of Lund, Sweden, and **Fred H. Gage,** professor of neuroscience at the University of California at San Diego, received Dana Foundation Awards for Pioneering Achievements in Health for their collaborative work on "developing gene therapy and cell-replacement techniques to treat brain damage, long considered irreversible." **Larry R. Squire,** professor of psychiatry and neuroscience, also at the University of California at San Diego, received a Pioneering Achievement in Health Award for research that altered the "centuries-old understanding of human consciousness."

Medical awards in three categories were given by the Albert and Mary Lasker Foundation. **Günter Blobel,** of Rockefeller University, New York City, and the Howard Hughes Medical Institute, received the Basic Medical Research Award for his study of protein translocation across cellular membranes. **Donald Metcalf,** research professor of cancer biology at the Walter and Eliza Hall Institute of Medical Research, Melbourne, Australia, received the Clinical Medical Research Award for his discovery of four colony-stimulating factors (proteins that promote cell differentiation). Recipients of Lasker Public Service Awards were: **Nancy Sabin Wexler,** professor of clinical neuropsychology, Columbia University College of Physicians and Surgeons, and former U.S. representative **Paul G. Rogers** of Florida. Wexler was recognized for her ongoing investigations into Huntington's disease. Rogers, known in Congress as "Mr. Health," served eight years as chair of the House Subcommittee on Health and the Environment and played a significant role in getting health-related legislation passed.

The Pharmaceutical Manufacturers Association presented Discoverers Awards to three scientists at Eli Lilly and Co., **Ray W. Fuller, Bryan B. Molloy,** and **David T. Wong,** for their work in developing fluoxetine (Prozac), "the first of a revolutionary new class of antidepressants that has helped millions of people throughout the world."

No one was more surprised by the popular success of his book How We Die *than the author, surgeon and Yale University professor of surgery and medical history Sherwin B. Nuland.*

Photograph, James Keyser—Time Magazine

Ronald McDonald Children's Charities gave Awards of Excellence to two leaders in minority health care. **Margaret C. Heagarty,** director of pediatrics at Harlem Hospital Center, New York City, was honored for establishing a network of neighborhood satellite health clinics, a pediatric AIDS unit, and a group home for HIV-infected children. **Gerald C. Yost** was recognized for his work in the Indian Health Service, including establishing an immunization program that eradicated meningitis in Native American children.

Neurologist-writer Oliver Sacks won an award for his New Yorker *magazine profile of Temple Grandin, a respected animal scientist whose accomplishments represent a triumph over autism.*

Photograph, Steve Allen—Gamma Liaison

Both Spain and Scotland recognized the Colombian biochemist **Manuel Patarroyo** for his creation of a synthetic malaria vaccine, which could be the first inexpensive, safe means of preventing a scourge that infects an estimated 300 million to 500 million people a year and kills between 1.5 million and 3 million. Spain awarded Patarroyo the prestigious Prince of Asturia Prize, and Scotland honored him with the Edinburgh Prize. (*See* Sidebar: "Souvenirs Nobody Wants...," p. 48, for more about malaria and Patarroyo's vaccine.)

The 1994 George Polk Awards for excellence in journalism, given by Long Island (New York) University,

included three separate awards for health-related coverage. **Eileen Welsome** of the *Albuquerque* (New Mexico) *Tribune,* who spent seven years uncovering secret plutonium experiments on human subjects conducted by the United States government, won a Polk Award for her investigative reporting. (*See* Special Report: "Human Subjects: Used or Abused?" p. 229, for more on radiation tests on humans.) **Larry Keller** and **Fred Schulte** of the *Fort Lauderdale* (Florida) *Sun-Sentinel* received a Polk Award for their coauthored series on patient deaths and injuries caused by delayed or denied medical care at health maintenance organizations. **Oliver Sacks,** author and neurologist, received a Polk Award for his compassionate and insightful article published in the Dec. 27, 1993/Jan. 3, 1994, issue of *The New Yorker,* exploring the inner world of an exceptionally gifted animal scientist and university professor, Temple Grandin, who has autism.

Ruth Gilbert, a British pediatric epidemiologist, won a 1994 European Woman of Achievement Award "for her ceaseless work to promote equality and equal opportunity among doctors in Europe."

A Rolex Award for Enterprise went to **Aldo Lo Curto,** who describes himself as a "traveling volunteer doctor" and spends his holidays in remote parts of the world providing free medical care to people who have little or none.

The Sedgwick Memorial Medal, the oldest and highest honor of the American Public Health Association, went to **William H. Foege,** "the public health leader who is making the world realize that public health is social justice." Foege played a major role in the global campaign to eradicate smallpox. From 1977 to 1983 he was director of the CDC. In 1986 he became executive director of the Carter Center in Atlanta, which is currently engaged in the effort to eradicate the scourge of guinea worm disease, a parasitic disease transmitted by contaminated drinking water.

Gone but not forgotten

In the first seven months of 1994, death claimed the lives of many important figures in health and medicine. Among these luminaries were:

● **David Axelrod,** 59, New York's health commissioner from 1979 to 1991. Gov. Mario Cuomo, under whom Axelrod served, called him "the people's doctor."

● **Michael Callen,** 38, singer and activist, founder of the People with AIDS Coalition and the Community Research Initiative in New York City, and author of *Surviving AIDS* (1990).

- **Bernard D. Davis,** 78, microbiology professor at Harvard Medical School and New York University. A pioneer in bacterial genetics research, he led tuberculosis research at the U.S. Public Health Service.

- **Robert Malcolm Ellsworth,** 65, regarded as the world's leading authority on tumors of the eye, particularly retinoblastoma, a rare inherited eye cancer in children. Treatment advances he brought about increased the retinoblastoma cure rate from 10% to 90%.

- **Erik H. Erikson,** 91, who pioneered child psychoanalysis (with Anna Freud) in Vienna. Though he never studied medicine and had only a high school diploma from Germany, he was appointed to the faculty of Harvard Medical School in 1934 and later was on the faculties at the University of California at Berkeley and Yale University. Erikson was the originator of a classic theory of human identity formation. Among his widely read books were *Childhood and Society* (1950), *Young Man Luther* (1958), and *Gandhi's Truth* (1969), which won a Pulitzer Prize.

- **Wilbur J. Gould,** 74, a New York City otolaryngologist well known for his treatment of famous people's voice ailments. Among his patients were Frank Sinatra, Beverly Sills, Anna Moffo, Elizabeth Taylor, Al Pacino, Luciano Pavarotti, Linda Ronstadt, Dan Rather, Mike Wallace, Sen. Robert F. Kennedy, New York Gov. Nelson A. Rockefeller, Sen. John F. Kennedy (when he lost his voice during the 1960 presidential campaign), and Pres. Lyndon B. Johnson (from whose larynx he removed a benign polyp in 1966).

- **Dorothy Hodgkin,** 84, British scientist who won the Nobel Prize for Chemistry in 1964 for her work with X-ray crystallography, used to elucidate the structures of penicillin, vitamin B_{12}, and insulin. In 1965 Queen Elizabeth II honored Hodgkin by making her the first woman since Florence Nightingale to become a member of the Order of Merit.

- **Walter H. Judd,** 95, U.S. physician, medical missionary in Japan and China in the 1920s and '30s, and member of the House of Representatives from 1943 to 1960. In 1981 Pres. Ronald Reagan awarded Judd the Presidential Medal of Freedom.

- **Stephen Mark Kritsick,** 42, a veterinarian who appeared on "Good Morning America" and the children's show "Romper Room," a pet health columnist for newspapers and magazines, and the author of *Dr. Kritsick's Tender Loving Cat Care* (1987). In New York City he tended the pets of numerous celebrities. Most recently he was a staff vet and spokesman for the national Humane Society in Washington, D.C.

- **Mary Woodard Lasker,** 93, philanthropist and volunteer lobbyist who furthered medical research. She was president of the Albert and Mary Lasker Foundation, which she and her husband, an advertising executive, established in 1942. The foundation annually recognizes outstanding contributions to clinical and basic medical research. More than 50 Lasker Award winners have subsequently received the Nobel Prize for Physiology or Medicine. (*See* above for the 1993 Lasker Award recipients. *See* photograph and caption, p. 195, "Saving Lives in the '90s.")

- **Jérôme Lejeune,** 67, French geneticist who discovered the chromosomal defect responsible for Down syndrome, which affects about one in every 800–1,000 babies and causes mental retardation and various physical abnormalities.

- **J. Vernon Luck, Sr.,** 87, U.S. orthopedic surgeon who was among the first to successfully reattach a severed limb. He was also a renowned inventor—of the first motorized bone-cutting and drilling device (the Luck Bone Saw) and of a partial hip implant (the Luck Cup).

- **Charles G. Moertel,** 66, highly respected cancer researcher at the Mayo Clinic, Rochester, Minnesota. An outspoken advocate of scientific rigor in medical research, he was critical of fellow scientists who allowed premature findings to raise false hopes in patients. Among his major studies were those showing that laetrile and vitamin C are ineffective against cancer.

- **Lord Porritt,** 93, distinguished athlete and physician and the first native-born governor general of New Zealand. At the 1924 Olympic Games he won the bronze medal in the 100-meter run and later acted as an adviser during the filming of *Chariots of Fire*, the acclaimed 1981 movie about that race.

- **R.A. ("Russ") Radley,** 43, AIDS activist, founding executive director of the Design Industries Foundation for AIDS, an organization that funds AIDS service and prevention programs, and a founding board member of the Gay Men's Health Crisis.

- **Nicholas A. Rango,** 49, physician and director of New York state's AIDS Institute, the largest state AIDS program in the U.S.

- **Berton Roueché,** 83, medical writer for *The New Yorker,* who originated a series of scrupulously researched narratives of medical intrigue, many of which chronicled the difficult work of doctors and epidemiologists in tracking down the causes of mysterious illnesses and baffling epidemics. "Lay readers found [his stories] scary and exciting, while doctors, impressed by their learning and clarity, used them as medical texts," his *New Yorker* obituary noted. Though he had no formal medical training, Roueché received honors and awards from the AMA, the *New England Journal of Medicine,* and the Lasker Foundation, among others.

• **Petr Skrabanek,** 53, Czechoslovak-born Irish physician and humanist who was an authority on substance P, a critical brain chemical involved in the transmission of pain. A modern Renaissance man, he also taught seminars on the Irish novelist James Joyce and was a world authority on *Finnegans Wake.*

• **Howard Sochurek,** 69, one of the most widely published medical photographers, especially well known for his computer-enhanced X-ray and computed tomography images. His striking photographs have appeared in many volumes of the *Medical and Health Annual,* including this one (*see* pp. 190–191).

Lord Porritt, Olympic medalist and surgeon (below), died on Jan. 1, 1994. Mary Woodard Lasker, philanthropist and champion of medical research (bottom), died on Feb. 21, 1994. Both were 93.

Photographs, (below) Hulton Deutsch Collection Limited; (bottom) UPI/Bettmann

• **Paul E. Spangler,** 95, a retired U.S. Navy surgeon. At age 67 Spangler took up running and virtually never stopped. He claimed 85 firsts in national distance competitions, ran in more than 10 marathons, and just weeks before his death won several gold medals at a senior Olympics in his home state of California. Spangler was an active member of the Fifty-Plus Runners Association, a group that has participated widely in research on aging and exercise.

• **Roger W. Sperry,** 80, psychobiologist who shared the 1981 Nobel Prize for Physiology or Medicine. His research career was devoted to the study of the mechanics of the brain and the mysteries of the mind; he was best known for his work with "split brains."

• **Robert J. Stein,** 82, internationally recognized forensic pathologist and medical examiner for Chicago and Cook county, Illinois. Among the more than 20,000 deaths he investigated during his 17-year tenure were those of the 33 victims of serial killer John Wayne Gacy and the 279 passengers killed on a DC-10 jet that crashed in 1979 near O'Hare International Airport.

• **Howard M. Temin,** 59, cancer researcher on the faculty of the University of Wisconsin at Madison. In 1975 Temin won a Nobel Prize for Physiology or Medicine for his part in discovering reverse transcriptase, an enzyme that he demonstrated is relevant in the viral transmission of cancer. Temin's untimely death was from adenocarcinoma, a type of lung cancer unrelated to smoking. In fact, he was an ardent nonsmoker; when he accepted his Nobel Prize, he scolded members of the audience for smoking during the presentation of an award for cancer research.

• **Lewis Thomas,** 80, physician who held prestigious positions as president of New York City's Memorial Sloan-Kettering Cancer Center and dean of the medical schools at New York University and Yale but who is perhaps most remembered for his best-selling collections of philosophical essays about the mysteries and curiosities of biology and of life itself. These include: *The Lives of a Cell* (1974), *The Medusa and the Snail* (1979), *The Youngest Science* (1983), *Late Night Thoughts on Listening to Mahler's Ninth Symphony* (1983), and *The Fragile Species* (1992).

• **Dirk van Zyl,** 68, South African who lived longer than any other recipient of a heart transplant—23 years. Van Zyl was the sixth heart-transplant patient of the world pioneer of the operation, Christiaan N. Barnard.

• **Bruce Voeller,** 59, scientist and authority on human sexuality and sexually transmitted diseases, who was a leader in the fight against AIDS.

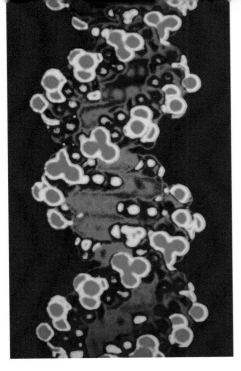

- **Janet G. Woititz,** 55, author, therapist, and lecturer who wrote more than a dozen best-selling self-help books, including *Adult Children of Alcoholics, Struggle for Intimacy,* and *Marriage on the Rocks.*
- **Sheldon M. Wolff,** 63, authority on infectious disease. In 1986 he served as cochairman of an Institute of Medicine review panel that urged the U.S. federal government to quadruple its support for AIDS research. Earlier he had been among the specialists who determined that high-absorbency tampons were associated with toxic shock syndrome, a potentially lethal staphylococcal infection.
- **Andrew S. Zysman,** 38, physician, AIDS activist, and member of the governing board of the American Association of Physicians for Human Rights.

—*prepared by Charles-Gene McDaniel, M.S.J., Professor and Chair, Department of Journalism, Roosevelt University, Chicago, and the* Medical and Health Annual *editors*

(Above) The computer-enhanced medical photographs of Howard Sochurek, who died at age 69, have been published in textbooks and magazines around the world. Nobel Prize-winning cancer researcher Howard M. Temin (below) died of a non-smoking-related form of lung cancer at age 59.

Bon Voyage... but Beware

by Richard Dawood, M.D., D.T.M.& H.

ILL HEALTH, INJURY, AND DEATH HAVE A historical link with travel that is every bit as ancient as the earliest human desire to seek new horizons. Each new environment—and every means of getting there—has always held risks for those brave enough to venture forth.

The woes of travel: ancient to modern

Humankind's ancient forebears knew that travel could spread disease. In biblical times strangers were feared for the contagion they might bring. Hippocrates, the "father of medicine," knew not only of the association between the movement of people and disease but of the most common affliction of travelers—travelers' diarrhea. In *On Airs, Waters, and Places* he wrote:

> I now wish to set out . . . what disadvantages and what advantages result from the waters we use, because they have a very great influence upon health. . . . The still and stagnant waters of marshes are the cause of diarrhea, dysentery, and intermittent fever. . . . Those cities which are favorably placed . . . are less touched by their disadvantages. But those where stagnant and marshy waters are used, and whose site is bad, suffer more from them.

He then went on to recommend boiling water before drinking it—advice that is still given to travelers who visit tropical and less developed countries.

Disease was not the only problem associated with travel. The harmful effects of exposure to environmental extremes were also recognized—even before Hippocrates. In 539 BC Cyrus the Great was so worried about how his conquering armies would be affected by intense heat that he ordered the troops to be taken into the desert every day and worked until they sweated. The dangers of cold-water immersion were studied during the naval wars between the Greeks and Persians, also in the 5th century BC.

Richard Dawood, M.D., D.T.M. & H.,
is Associate Specialist, Hospital for
Sick Children, London; Member of the
Executive Board, International Society of
Travel Medicine; Medical Editor, Condé
Nast Traveler; *and author and editor of*
books on travel medicine.

(Overleaf) Trekkers cross a suspension
bridge in Nepal. Nepal, in the Himalayan
foothills, attracts about 50,000 trekkers
from developed countries annually.
Photograph, Jock Montgomery

Quarantine was once virtually the only control measure possible against infectious diseases. The word itself derives from *quaranta giorni,* the 40 days that people traveling to Venice by sea in the 14th century would have to wait in isolation—because of the risk that they would spread bubonic plague.

In the 19th century French colonists called Africa "the white man's grave" because of the high risk of contracting blackwater fever (a complication of malaria), yellow fever, and other then inexplicable and untreatable diseases. One of the world's most distinguished centers for the study of tropical diseases, the School of Tropical Medicine of the University of Liverpool, England, was established at the turn of the century. Its location is no accident. Liverpool was the port to which ships from the British colonies would take their sick and dying—or at least those who survived the long voyage home. The pioneering work of Sir Ronald Ross, Sir Patrick Manson, and other parasitologists at the turn of the last century finally opened the door to the modern understanding of malaria and other scourges of the tropics.

During World War II it was not military might but malaria that determined the outcome of the struggle for control of Southeast Asia. Antimalarial drugs assumed strategic importance; neither before nor since has there been such intensive research into developing new drugs for tropical diseases.

Modern armies remain at risk. During Operation Desert Storm in Iraq in 1991, dozens of allied troops acquired leishmaniasis, an ancient parasitic disease that many military physicians had never heard of. Veterans of the Persian Gulf war still complain of mysterious symptoms, whose cause may yet prove to be an infectious or environmental agent to which the troops were exposed during their mission.

Travel in the 1990s

Travel has changed. The contemporary traveler is unlikely to be a colonist, a migrant, an explorer, a trader, or part of a conquering army. He or she

After their long journey by sea, c. 1905,
emigrants from Europe are examined for
communicable diseases on Ellis Island in
New York Harbor. Between 1890 and 1920
as many as 20 million immigrants were
screened for illness before being allowed
entry into the United States. Those found
to have infections were quarantined on the
island at the Marine Hospital.

is more likely to be traveling for pleasure or on business. Travel no longer necessitates weeks or months at sea, nor does it have to be an arduous feat of endurance (though some present-day travelers deliberately seek such adventure). For more and more people all over the world, travel has become easier than it ever was before. Likewise, once-remote places are now accessible.

Travel today takes place on a scale that could hardly have been imagined as little as 20 years ago. In 1990 there were over 1.2 billion air passengers; this figure included over 400 million international arrivals—representing more than an 18-fold increase since 1950. International and intercontinental tourism now accounts for 6% of world exports and 25% of world trade.

The Mediterranean coastline, with a resident population of 130 million, receives at least 150 million tourists every year. Nepal, in the Himalayan foothills, now draws some 50,000 trekkers from developed countries each year. Travel to tropical less developed countries is now commonplace for people from the developed world, and intercontinental travel is set for unprecedented growth throughout the '90s.

Travel medicine: a new specialty comes of age

Travel medicine is the modern study of the intricate relationship between travel and health. The myriad threats to the health and well-being of today's travelers are all within its scope. Travel medicine (also known as *empori-atrics,* from the Greek *empros,* meaning "to go abroad," and *iatros,* meaning "physician," "medicine," or "healing") is concerned with: tropical and

Intrepid mountain bikers are treated to a breathtaking view of the Colorado River from Dead Horse Point, Utah. "Adventure travelers" and those who journey to remote destinations face unique threats to their health. A whole new medical specialty, travel medicine, has evolved to study, treat, and find ways to prevent the myriad illnesses and injuries that today's globe-trotting tourists encounter.

29

infectious diseases; travelers' diarrhea; extremes of climate and altitude; adverse environmental conditions of every sort, as well as the effects that tourists have on the environment; jet lag; motion sickness; travel-related injuries; foodborne and waterborne ills; violence and terrorism; and even psychological reactions to travel—*e.g.,* fear of flying and culture shock.

Though the health hazards faced by travelers today are much less likely to be life-threatening than in the past, they are by no means inconsequential; roughly half of all travelers who go abroad suffer from health problems that, at the very least, interfere with the enjoyment of their trip. While ultimately much still depends on the resourcefulness of the individual traveler, there is now a much better understanding of what the risks are and of the many things that can be done to prevent and manage them.

Health problems: a changing pattern

Changes in the patterns of health problems that today's travelers face mirror trends in traveling itself and changes in people's travel habits over many decades. In general, the travelers of old who became sick were cared for while they were still abroad or, by ships' doctors, on the long sea voyage home. While physicians then had limited resources at their disposal and often could not cure their patients, they were at least familiar with their patients' diseases, especially those acquired in the tropics.

Today's jet aircraft have reduced journey times across the globe to a matter of hours, making short trips not only possible but the norm. This remarkable development means that symptoms of illnesses to which travelers are exposed while abroad are likely to appear *after* they return home. When today's travelers seek treatment at home, they often encounter physicians who do not recognize their illnesses and know little or nothing about how to treat them. Indeed, the long incubation period (*i.e.,* delay between exposure and onset of symptoms) of some infectious conditions often results in the link between the illness and the patient's having traveled being forgotten or ignored.

The impact of this change is particularly well-demonstrated in cases of malaria, perhaps the most notorious of all travel-related diseases. Malaria has an incubation period that ranges from five days to as long as a year; in the right setting the symptoms are easy to recognize: fever, headache, chills. Prompt treatment results in an almost certain cure, but a delay in diagnosis can be fatal. Once a traveler with malaria has returned home, the symptoms can easily be mistaken for those of the flu. It has been shown that the countries with the highest fatality rates for malaria are those in which physicians have the least familiarity with the disease. Thus, one of the worst places to be afflicted with malarial fever is Japan, as few Japanese travelers venture to malarial areas and very few Japanese doctors have ever seen cases of malaria. The malaria fatality rate in Japan is 10 times the rate in the United States and 20 times the rates in both Switzerland and Great Britain.

As another example, a disease with which most U.S. travelers and many U.S. physicians are unfamiliar is American cutaneous leishmaniasis (ACL), a protozoan infection that is endemic in the Americas in an area

Getting sick abroad*		
sickness or symptom	number	%
any	335	65
diarrhea	241	47
upper respiratory	142	28
skin rash or infection (including sunburn)	39	8
high-altitude effects	25	5
motion sickness	24	5
injury	24	5
medication side effect	20	4
fever not associated with other symptoms	12	2

*reported illness in 515 Americans traveling to less developed countries for three months or less (June 1989– June 1990); 38 (7%) sought medical care abroad for their illness

Adapted from David R. Hill, "Illness Associated with Travel to the Developing World," *Travel Medicine 2,* International Society of Travel Medicine, 1991

30

extending from northern Argentina to southern Texas. The disease causes skin lesions that typically evolve from papules to nodules to ulcers over a period of weeks to months. A recent study of U.S. travelers who had visited Mexico and Central America and acquired ACL found that 17% were home at least one month before they noticed lesions. Thirty-three percent consulted at least three physicians before leishmaniasis was diagnosed, and some consulted as many as seven doctors. Other diagnoses that were considered included skin cancer, syphilis, and fungal infections. One patient consulted six physicians, had two skin grafts, and paid $6,600 in medical bills before ACL was considered.

It is not just the way that people travel that has changed; what they do when they get where they are going is also important. For example, over the past 20 years, island destinations have become increasingly popular and affordable. Americans flock to Bermuda, The Bahamas, and the Caribbean; favorite holiday spots for Europeans are the Greek isles in the eastern Mediterranean and the Balearic Islands in the western Mediterranean, while Australians go to Bali to "get away from it all." These islands have many things in common—*e.g.,* the weather is hot and there is abundant sunshine. They also tend not to have well-developed public transportation systems. Many of those who visit these islands are young—or young at heart—and choose to explore them on motorbikes, often the most available and affordable means of getting around. Because they seldom wear crash helmets or protective clothing, their risk of injury is high. Another characteristic of these holiday islands is that their native populations are small and usually

Travel today takes place on a scale that could hardly have been imagined as little as 20 years ago. The World Tourism Organization estimated that in 1990 there were well over 400 million international travelers; by the year 2000 the annual number of international journeys is expected to increase by almost 50%.

31

Venturing beyond the tourist resorts, vacationers on the magical island of Bali explore the countryside on motorbikes. Because people on holiday commonly do not take adequate precautions, such as wearing helmets on rented motorbikes and driving slowly, they are at high risk for injury; indeed, more deaths among travelers occur on roads than are caused by infectious and tropical diseases combined. Furthermore, on Bali, as on most holiday islands, medical services are not likely to be up to Western standards. As Insights Guides: Bali *(Houghton Mifflin Co., 1993) cautions: "If you have a real emergency, get thee to Singapore. If your insurance policy covers SOS or medical evacuations, you're in luck. . . . If not, you need to put up $30,000 [in cash or on a credit card] for the special Lear Jet that will take you to Singapore." Tropical paradise seekers, take heed!*

too poor to support the kind of medical facilities necessary to take care of the large number of injuries that occur among tourist populations. On the Greek island of Crete, for example, the local population more than doubles with the annual influx of tourists. In the summer months the small local hospital in Iraklion has to cope with more than 10 injured vacationers every day, and not all of the injured survive the three-hour ambulance ride from the island's southwestern coast—a popular resort area and a haven for backpackers.

The changing pattern of disease in destination countries also has a clear impact on travelers. Some diseases have declined in importance. One of these, smallpox, was formerly a disease of travel par excellence; the availability of an effective vaccine, combined with a skillful strategy for deploying it, resulted in the global eradication of smallpox between 1967 and 1977. Smallpox, once prevalent throughout the world, is now a disease that travelers can consign to history books. Eradication of a small number of other diseases may follow. Dracunculiasis, or guinea worm disease, is a devastating but little-known parasitic affliction that is transmitted by unfiltered drinking water in parts of Africa and Asia. It, too, is likely to be eradicated before the end of the century. Poliomyelitis has also been targeted for global eradication by the year 2000, and much progress has already been made toward that goal—particularly in the Americas and Europe.

Many other tropical and infectious diseases, however, are on the increase: malaria, cholera, tuberculosis, diphtheria, yellow fever, dengue, HIV, and even the ancient scourge bubonic plague. At the same time, the

Ron Sanford—AllStock

places in the world where these diseases most often occur are increasingly accessible to everyone. Today's travelers need, as much as ever, to be fully informed about the risks.

"If it's Tuesday..."

While much of the recent progress in travel medicine has been motivated by the need to address the risk of life-threatening illness, today's travelers are also concerned about more subtle health issues than mere survival. The success or failure of a vacation that is intended to be pleasurable—or of a business trip involving delicate negotiations—can be dramatically influenced by such subtleties. One of the areas in which there has been much interest—and thus considerable research—is jet lag.

The syndrome of jet lag results from transmeridian (*i.e.,* east-west) travel between different time zones. (North-south travel does not cause jet lag.) The problem arises because modern air travel takes place at speeds that outstrip the body's ability to adapt to a new time zone. Almost all of the body's physiological processes have a rhythm, or pattern, that varies over the course of a day. The most obvious of these "circadian" rhythms are sleep and wakefulness, but the internal "body clock" also controls alertness, hunger, digestion, urine production, body temperature, and the secretion of hormones. Unfortunately, when these rhythms have been disrupted, they cannot all be brought back into synchrony at the same rates once the destination has been reached.

Jet lag thus is a state of physiological desynchronization; simply put, the clock says it is lunchtime, but one's body says it is the middle of the night. The severity and extent of the problem vary according to the number of time zones crossed as well as the direction of travel—most people find it more difficult to travel eastward (*i.e.,* to adapt to a shorter day as opposed to a longer one). The resulting symptoms are only too familiar to today's jet-setters: extreme fatigue, sleep disturbances, loss of concentration, disorientation, malaise, sluggishness, gastrointestinal upset, loss of appetite. Generally, adjustment to a new time zone takes one day for each hour of time difference.

In the past several years, researchers have discovered that the hormone melatonin plays an important role in controlling the body clock and that it can have powerful effects on jet-lag symptoms. These beneficial effects have been confirmed in numerous studies, including several double-blind, placebo-controlled trials in which some subjects were given melatonin and some were not and neither the investigators nor the travelers knew who was taking the hormone. Consequently, melatonin appears to be a promising remedy for world-weary long-haul travelers.

In the human body the pineal gland, a tiny cone-shaped structure in the brain, begins to secrete melatonin after the sun sets; melatonin secretion reaches a peak around midnight, then wanes through the rest of the night. In blind people there is no daily rhythm to melatonin secretion, and they often suffer from sleep disorders (which can be effectively treated with melatonin). Investigations have also shown that exposure to light—even in quite small amounts—depresses melatonin secretion and that judicious

Transmeridian travel that involves crossing time zones disrupts the body's normal physiological processes. The more time zones crossed and the less time spent crossing them, the more out of synch the internal body clock gets. In the illustration at right, in which New York City is the point of departure, each number corresponds to one time zone and roughly one day of jet lag. Flight A goes from New York to Los Angeles in 6 hours and crosses 3 time zones. Flight B is to London—7 hours, 5 time zones; flight C, to Sydney, takes a grueling 21 hours and crosses 9 time zones; flight D, to Delhi, is in the air for 17 hours, and 10 time zones are crossed. Even though flight E, from New York to Lima, takes 10½ hours, it crosses no time zones and therefore causes no jet lag—although it may cause stiff muscles, swollen ankles, and other unpleasant effects that are a consequence of sitting in a cramped airplane cabin for so long.

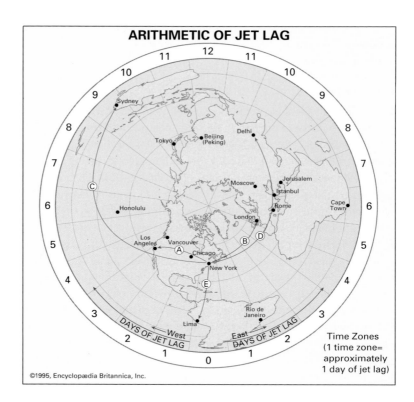

ARITHMETIC OF JET LAG

Time Zones
(1 time zone=
approximately
1 day of jet lag)

and carefully timed exposure to light can have a dramatic effect on jet lag. With this in view, various regimens of light exposure have been proposed as a way of alleviating jet-lag symptoms, but administration of melatonin seems to offer a much more direct and practicable way of actually speeding up the resynchronization of the body clock to a new time zone.

In studies the best results have been attained when a small dose of melatonin is given approximately two hours before bedtime on the first night in the new time zone and for several nights thereafter, depending on the distance that has been traveled. The number of doses is roughly the same as the number of time zones crossed. Thus, when traveling between New York and London, one would take melatonin for five nights upon arrival and upon return—to accommodate for the five-hour time difference.

Although melatonin has been widely studied and appears to be quite effective and safe, it has not been licensed for treatment of jet lag by the U.S. Food and Drug Administration (FDA) or by regulatory agencies elsewhere. This is partly for commercial reasons; no pharmaceutical company has yet considered it worthwhile to manufacture and market melatonin. In the U.S., however, a synthetic form of melatonin can be purchased at health-food stores, and some travelers are using it.

There is no doubt that with experience, frequent travelers almost subconsciously develop their own strategies for managing jet lag. That is one reason why formal evaluation of any one jet-lag remedy is so difficult—and why so many spurious "cures" and remedies abound. Whatever approach one takes, the following tips should help lessen the woes of long-distance travel.

- Flying westbound has the effect of lengthening the day. One should avoid taking naps during the flight, which may make it hard to fall asleep the night of arrival.
- One *should* sleep on eastbound overnight flights—such as the "red-eye" from California to New York or night flights from New York to London. It is a good idea to eat a light meal before taking off and then ask not to be disturbed by the cabin crew during the flight, so as to get the maximum amount of sleep possible.
- One should avoid alcohol and caffeine while flying; both can interfere with sleep.
- If one can, one should take daytime flights whenever possible; although they do not necessarily help in adjusting to the time difference, they cause the least loss of sleep and the least fatigue, allowing the traveler to arrive in the best possible shape.
- One should get adjusted to the new time zone as soon as possible— *e.g.,* by resetting one's watch upon arrival, eating meals and going to bed at appropriate times, and spending plenty of time during the day outdoors.
- Body temperature falls naturally during the night, and a common symptom of jet lag is to feel cold during the day. Some people find that hot baths help them feel better.
- The traveler should accept that there is bound to be some loss of performance when first arriving in a new time zone and should plan accordingly. For example, one should avoid important business meetings for the first 24 hours after arrival; if a first-day meeting is unavoidable, the traveler should choose a time of day when he or she would normally be most alert (on home time).

Cramped seats, dry air, and other discomforts

Many travelers confuse the adverse effects of the air journey itself with the symptoms of jet lag. While reduced cabin pressure and the dryness of the cabin air have shouldered much of the blame for in-flight discomforts, recent research has shown that these are much less important on long flights than was previously thought. Rather, many of the symptoms that long-haul passengers complain of are the direct consequence of cramped seating conditions.

In an interesting series of experiments conducted by Lufthansa German Airlines, researchers used a mock-up of a full-scale Boeing 747 interior in which 12 volunteers endured four simulated 12-hour flights (two daytime and two nighttime) sitting in "economy class." During the "flights" extensive physiological tests were performed. The experiments were then repeated at 10,600 meters (35,000 feet), in the cabin of a Lufthansa 747 during a 10-hour nonstop Seattle, Washington, to Frankfurt, Germany, flight. The tests demonstrated that restricted long-duration sitting resulted in significant movement of fluid into the tissues of the lower body—evident as the ankle swelling with which many travelers are all too familiar. In one of the subjects, as much as 2 kilograms (4.4 pounds) of fluid shifted into the lower extremities. Very little difference was found between the fluid measurements taken in the air and those taken on the simulated flights. There

The symptoms of jet lag—extreme fatigue, disorientation, general malaise—are only too familiar to anyone who has experienced a long-haul flight.

Jock Montgomery

35

Frequent fliers often complain of "sick plane syndrome"—malaise, headaches, nausea, sore throat, cough, and other symptoms that they attribute to the plane's poor air quality. As a fuel-saving measure, commercial airlines recirculate about 50% of the air on jets built after the mid-1980s. As the diagram at right shows, fresh air enters the aircraft through the jet engine; the air is then pressurized and chilled underneath the plane's cargo holds. The detail shows the pattern of air distribution within the cabin before the circulated air is removed through the exhaust system at the rear of the craft.

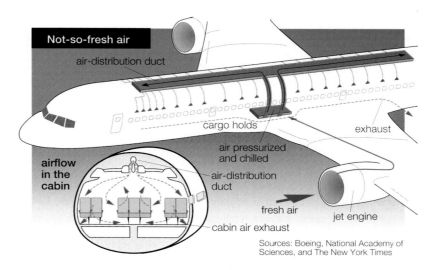

Sources: Boeing, National Academy of Sciences, and The New York Times

were, however, significant differences between passengers who stayed in their seats and those who walked about the cabin or made a conscientious effort to exercise during the flight.

These findings suggest that the dehydration, or fluid loss, usually associated with flying is actually a fluid shift. In fact, most of the symptoms that occur during long flights are almost entirely due to sitting cramped, motionless, and upright for hours at a stretch, which restricts normal blood circulation and thereby forces fluid out of the bloodstream and into the tissues of the lower body and legs. This effect can be prevented by frequent in-flight stretching and getting up and moving about the cabin. Another solution, though not always a very practical one, would be to fly in a reclining position—with the body as horizontal as possible.

Lufthansa has used the results of its research to produce a 12-minute exercise video, *Flyrobics,* which intercontinental passengers can follow during the course of their overseas flights to improve circulation and stretch cramped muscles. (Air New Zealand also has one, and Northwest Airlines offers a five-minute video exercise routine for passengers on its trips lasting longer than four hours.) The ideal solution, however, would be to provide air travelers with much more space and freedom of movement and with fully reclining (*i.e.,* flat, horizontal) sleeping facilities on long-haul flights.

Though many of the ill effects of flying per se are attributable to cramped seating, this does not mean that the cabin air is entirely blameless. In a pressurized cabin all fresh air is pumped in from the plane's engines, and as a fuel-saving measure, especially on newer aircraft, some of this air is constantly recirculated. Passengers and flight attendants have long complained of suffering from such symptoms as headaches and nausea—sometimes called "sick plane syndrome." The connection between cabin air and flyers' symptoms, however, has yet to be proved; as with so-called sick building syndrome, the jury is still out, and some of the effects in the case of planes may instead be due to chemical cleaning agents or aerosol insecticides that are used in the cabin. The practice of spraying aircraft cabins with insecticides while passengers and crew members are on board was discontinued on U.S. flights in the late 1970s. In March 1994, owing to concerns about long- and short-term health effects, the U.S. secretary of transportation called upon all foreign governments that still allowed or required spraying of planes before landing to halt the practice. Included were: Antigua, Argentina, Australia, Barbados, Belize, Bolivia, Brazil, Chile, Colombia, the Northern Marianas, Costa Rica, El Salvador, Guam, Guatemala, Jamaica, New Zealand, Nicaragua, Mexico, Panama, Peru, St. Lucia, St. Martin, and Venezuela.

Of much greater concern than chemical contaminants is the potential for transmission of infectious illnesses that are spread via airborne droplets from infected passengers. It is quite common for long-haul travelers to return from a trip with coughs, colds, or flu, which they may have been exposed to on the flight. Lately there have also been documented cases of the spread of tuberculosis among cabin crew members on commercial flights. On board an aircraft, in-flight humidity seldom rises above 2–10%. Virtually all the moisture in the cabin's air comes from the passengers. While recirculation of cabin air that is laden with infectious organisms may well result in exposure that is greater than would otherwise occur in a confined space, the dry air itself may also play a crucial part in transmission—irritating the nasal passages and damaging the body's natural barriers to infection.

Injuries: no accident!

The importance of injuries in relation to travel has already been alluded to. Fatal injuries in fact are the number one cause of death among intercontinental travelers and are responsible for approximately 25 times more deaths in travelers abroad than infectious and tropical diseases. Moreover, so-called accidents abroad tend to follow a depressingly repetitive pattern—the vast majority being readily preventable.

Most deaths occur on roads and involve motor vehicles. Often, motorists who normally wear seat belts, use child safety seats for their children, ob-

Robert Frerck—Tony Stone Images

Negotiating one's way through a typical midday traffic jam in Jaipur, the capital of Rajasthan state, India—with rickshaws, bicycles, cars, trucks, motorbikes, pedestrians, and animals all vying for a share of the road—is likely to be harrowing at best. Tourists who attempt to drive in an unfamiliar city may be taking their life in their hands.

Greg Huglin—Adventure Photo

Windsurfing is one of the thrills to be experienced along the Pacific coast of Baja California, in northwestern Mexico. Water sports draw millions of tourists annually to ocean beaches, rivers, lakes, and other waterways around the world but are also a leading cause of injury and death.

serve speed limits, and refrain from drinking and driving seem less inclined to do so abroad. One reason for this lack of caution is the absence of laws in many countries—or the fact that when rules exist they frequently are not enforced. Another, more important, reason is that people behave differently when they travel; they are more inclined to take unaccustomed risks. Some experts call this risk-taking proclivity the "escapist psychology of travel," which can extend to almost every activity—from choosing a sex partner to eating and drinking to carrying large amounts of cash.

Participation in water sports accounts for a great number of serious injuries that often result in disability or death among travelers. This includes swimming in dangerous areas, boating without wearing a life jacket, and diving into shallow water. Alcohol consumption is often a contributing factor.

Local safety standards can also be a problem. Unsafe hotel balconies, for example, are responsible for a large number of tourist casualties every year. Western travelers who visit less developed countries have come to expect that local safety standards will be the same as at home—especially when they stay at a hotel or resort that belongs to a large international chain. This is seldom a valid assumption, however. Fire safety rules, for example, differ radically among countries. While tour operators and others in the travel industry—as well as those who wield influence at a legislative level—need to do more to ensure safety, ultimately travelers must get used to the idea that their well-being depends on the safety standards that they set for themselves.

Medical care abroad: not to be counted on

Travelers should know that good medical care is not always available in foreign parts. This is especially true in some of the destinations that have the greatest tourist appeal: remote, isolated locations far from "civilization." Often such places are without roads or telephones, let alone intensive care units. It is simply an unfortunate fact of life that most less developed countries do not have medical facilities that are at all comparable to those in developed nations. The onus therefore is on the traveler to take every possible measure to *prevent* problems.

Travelers in less-than-perfect health should think carefully before visiting remote places with poor facilities. Similar considerations apply to dental care; one cannot count on dental facilities in most less developed countries—and even in some developed ones—to have sterile, disposable equipment. Having a dental checkup prior to travel is a much better idea—and certainly safer than any attempt at self-treatment using the do-it-yourself dentistry kits that have recently appeared on the market.

The growing prevalence of HIV in all parts of the world now raises important questions about travelers' risks of infection when they receive medical care. Of particular concern is the availability of safe blood for transfusion. In fact, most of the situations that might necessitate a blood transfusion abroad are preventable "accidents" of the kind referred to above, and it is far wiser for travelers to take preventive measures than to count on finding safe blood. Whether preventable or not, emergencies do occur. There are now sources of screened donor blood in almost every capital city in the

Doug Hulcher

A roadside dental practitioner offers his services on a busy street in Bangkok, Thailand. Before venturing to distant parts of the globe, anyone who might need dental work should have a checkup at home. In less developed countries and even in some developed ones, sophisticated dentistry is not likely to be available, and travelers cannot count on equipment's being sterile.

world, and embassies are often able to help in cases of urgent need. (The development of synthetic blood substitutes, on which there is currently intensive research, may ultimately solve this problem.)

Other types of medical care may place travelers at risk for bloodborne infections. There are numerous examples of people who developed hepatitis after undergoing immunization in poor countries where syringes are reused. In Turkey drivers who are involved in motor-vehicle collisions are required to provide a blood sample for measurement of blood alcohol level; the sterility of the needle that is used will depend on where the accident

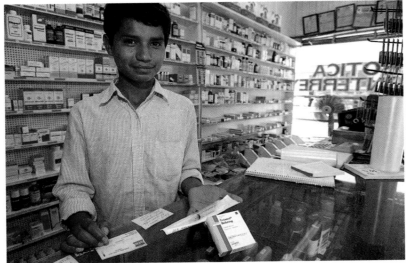

Lisa Quinones—Black Star

A young pharmacy employee sells do-it-yourself tetanus injections over the counter in Mexico. Drugs and vaccines that are available abroad may be quite different from those available at home. Some drugs may be imitations, some may be ineffective, and some may be quite dangerous. It is always wise for travelers to take along an ample supply of all medications they are likely to need on their trip.

takes place. In order to protect themselves, increasing numbers of travelers now also carry their own supplies of sterile disposable hypodermic needles and syringes—to be used by medical personnel in an emergency where sterile equipment is not available.

Travelers should also be aware that drugs and vaccines obtained abroad may be ineffective or dangerous. In some poor countries, where the likelihood of being bitten by a dog and the potential for contracting rabies are high, locally produced rabies vaccine may be almost as dangerous as the disease itself. Also, in many parts of the world, fake drugs are now a growth industry. Such drugs look like familiar medications but often contain chalk or talcum powder instead of active ingredients. They are usually ineffective but can be actively harmful. Either way, the underlying problem is not being treated, and in the case of a serious infection, the outcome could be fatal.

Although avoiding risks and preventing problems are always the wisest steps, emergency air-evacuation services are now increasingly sophisticated and are available to travelers through medical insurance schemes. Indeed, few parts of the world are out of their reach; nonetheless, travelers still need to have a means of summoning help. Furthermore, they need to be in a reasonably stable condition before medical evacuation can be attempted.

Shots for people going 'round the world

Unfortunately, only a small proportion of the diseases to which travelers are vulnerable are preventable by either vaccine or prophylaxis. This is in marked contrast to public perception; most travelers—and, indeed, many physicians—assume that once required travel vaccinations have been given, the traveler is safe. While the specific immunizations needed will vary widely, depending upon the destination, length of stay, nature of the trip, and personal habits of the traveler, there are some recent vaccine-related developments that are worthy of mention.

A vaccine against hepatitis A is now available. Hepatitis A is the most common serious infection that travelers are likely to encounter on trips to tropical countries. Hepatitis A is a viral infection that is most often spread by contaminated water or food; in many instances shellfish or other seafood is to blame. Infection produces fever, jaundice, malaise, and abdominal pain; in severe cases hepatitis A can lead to liver failure. Previously, the only method of protection was an injection of immune globulin containing hepatitis A antibody that was prepared from pooled plasma. While this was effective, protection lasted only about three months. The new vaccine contains a killed strain of hepatitis A virus, triggering active production of antibody by the immune system and giving reliable protection lasting at least 10 years.

Typhoid fever, a bacterial illness usually caused by *Salmonella typhi,* occurs worldwide. Travelers are most likely to be exposed when they eat contaminated foods in areas where hygiene practices are poor and a large proportion of food handlers are carriers of the infection. Typhoid fever symptoms include headache, confusion, cough, diarrhea, rash, and high fever. Although a typhoid vaccine was previously available, it had to

(Left) Western tourists sample northern Indian cuisine at a welcoming ceremony at their hotel in Jaisalmer, Rajasthan. (Below left) A traveler visiting Malaysia selects fresh vegetables at a street market in Kota Baharu. By far the most common illness in travelers is diarrhea that results from food or drink. To reduce the risk of travelers' diarrhea, the World Health Organization recommends avoiding all cooked food that is not hot when served or has not been cooked thoroughly and fruits and vegetables that have not been peeled or shelled or that have damaged skin. Depending on one's vacation spot, milk and ice cream, tap water, ice, and certain varieties of fish and shellfish should also be avoided. These safe-eating rules apply not only to food sold on the street by vendors but also to food that is served in restaurants and deluxe hotels.

be given in two separate doses at least four weeks before departure and caused unpleasant side effects, such as soreness at the injection site and fever. Travelers now have two new options: a single-dose injected vaccine or an oral vaccine taken in four individual doses. All three typhoid vaccines provide approximately 70% protection, but even those who are vaccinated need to be wary about what they eat and drink. The World Health Organization recommends that travelers:

• make sure that food has been thoroughly cooked and is still hot when served

• avoid uncooked food, except fruits and vegetables that can be peeled or shelled

• avoid fruits with damaged skin

• avoid ice cream from unreliable sources

• boil unpasteurized milk before consumption

41

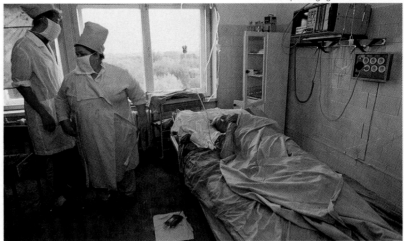

A patient with acute diphtheria is cared for in an isolation unit of a hospital in Moscow. An outbreak of diphtheria struck Russia, Ukraine, and other former Soviet states in 1993. In its first year the epidemic killed more than 150 persons. By mid-1994 tens of thousands of cases had been reported, and all travelers to the former Soviet Union were being advised to have a diphtheria booster if they had not been immunized against the highly contagious illness in the last 10 years.

A Japanese encephalitis vaccine is now available in many areas of the world and was recently licensed by the FDA. Japanese encephalitis is a sometimes fatal viral infection that causes inflammation of brain tissue. The disease is transmitted by *Culex* mosquitoes, and approximately 50,000 sporadic and epidemic cases are reported annually from China, South Korea, Japan, Southeast Asia, the Indian subcontinent, and parts of Oceania. It is most common in areas where the insects breed—*e.g.,* pig-farming and rice-growing regions. The risk of acquiring Japanese encephalitis is low for most travelers, but the risk for the individual will depend on the season, duration of the trip, and the traveler's personal habits and activities. Because the vaccine has resulted in some serious allergic reactions, it is generally not recommended for travelers unless they will be traveling in rural areas over a long period; most tourist destinations are safe. Mosquito avoidance measures in endemic areas, however, remain imperative.

A recent outbreak of diphtheria in Russia, Ukraine, and other former Soviet states has reached epidemic proportions. By mid-1994 well over 13,000 cases had been reported. This is the largest outbreak in the developed world in the past three decades. The highly contagious disease causes a toxin to spread throughout the body and a pseudomembrane lining to form in the respiratory passages; if untreated, it can affect the heart and central nervous system. Diphtheria is acquired from either contact with infected persons or environmental exposure. The risk of infection for travelers to the former Soviet Union is considered significant; therefore, it is recommended that all adult visitors have their diphtheria immunization status updated with a booster shot if they have not had one within the last 10 years.

The misery wrought by mosquitoes

In tropical countries a wide variety of diseases can be transmitted by insects, particularly by mosquitoes. The list includes viral infections such as dengue (an acute febrile illness transmitted by the *Aedes aegypti* mosquito and against which there is no vaccine), yellow fever (transmitted by *A. aegypti,* as well as other forest-canopy mosquitoes), and various types of encephalitis. It is the recent rise in drug-resistant malaria, however, that has aroused the greatest international concern. Moreover, in the absence of an effective vaccine, there has been renewed interest in protecting humans from bites of female *Anopheles* mosquitoes, which transmit malaria to humans, with nets and other anti-insect measures.

Modern mosquito netting is quite unlike anything used by the explorers of old; it is both lightweight and strong. The right mesh size is important; if the mesh is too small, the net is uncomfortable to use, while too large a mesh enables mosquitoes to get in. The standard mesh size for mosquito netting is 1.5 millimeters (0.006 inch; mesh sizes refer to the diameter of the hole plus its adjacent threads), or seven holes per centimeter. A coarser mesh (4 millimeters [0.16 inch]) can be used if the net is treated with an effective insecticide.

The synthetic fabrics used in today's netting, usually polyester, readily retain the insecticide permethrin, which dramatically increases the nets' effectiveness. Permethrin is a chemical compound that is related to

(Top) Peter Charlesworth—JB Pictures; (bottom) P. Carnevale—WHO

(Above left) A Thai village on the Cambodian border is fumigated for mosquitoes. Throughout Southeast Asia, drug-resistant strains of the mosquitoborne parasite that causes malaria have been rapidly gaining ground. (Left) In a village in Cameroon, in West Africa, bed nets are sprayed with the highly effective synthetic insecticide permethrin. In African villages where permethrin-treated nets have been widely used, malaria-causing mosquito populations have been markedly reduced.

pyrethrum, a natural insecticide extracted from chrysanthemum flowers. Pyrethrum is the active ingredient in "mosquito coils"—the slow-burning incenselike outdoor insecticide popular in many tropical countries. Similar compounds called pyrethrins are commonly used in insecticides that are sprayed, often indoors, and have a very low toxicity for humans, but permethrin is unique in that it binds so strongly to fabrics that it remains effective for months, killing mosquitoes on contact. Permethrin does not prevent bites when used on the skin, as the contact time would not be long enough; mosquitoes would bite first and possibly die later. Used on mosquito nets, however, it offers a near-ideal way of killing vast numbers of hungry mosquitoes; the sleeping traveler becomes the perfect bait and lures all nearby biting insects into direct contact with the treated netting. In African villages where treated nets have been introduced on a wide scale, mosquito populations have been drastically reduced.

The threat of malaria and other mosquitoborne infections is not limited to travelers in the tropics. "Hitchhiking" mosquitoes can travel overseas on planes and escape at destination airports. There are many well-documented cases of so-called airport malaria in Europe. Not only travelers at airports but residents of neighborhoods near airports have come down with mysterious fevers when bitten by imported insects. ("Airport malaria" is much less common in the U.S., probably because there are fewer direct flights arriving from Africa.) Although there are unresolved health questions about the spraying of pesticides in passenger cabins on planes, a strong argument in favor of the practice on intercontinental flights is that imported tropical diseases would be prevented.

The lure of high places

The world's highest places have been a source of wonder for travelers through the ages. Increasing numbers of travelers visit such places as Peru, Bolivia, and Tibet; for those who arrive by air, the sudden change in atmospheric pressure (atmospheric pressure decreases as altitude in-

Taking a breather from his ascent, a trekker in the Mt. Everest region of the Himalayas in Nepal has a view of some of the highest peaks in the world. The Great Himalaya Range, which extends through India, Bhutan, Nepal, and parts of Pakistan and China, has about 85 peaks rising to elevations of 6,000 meters (20,000 feet) or more above sea level. Among the earliest journeys through the Himalayas were those of Indian pilgrims who believed that the more arduous the journey, the closer they got to salvation. In modern times the Himalayas have attracted and challenged mountaineers from all over the world. As successively higher peaks have been scaled, climbers have sought more and more difficult tests of their skills and equipment. In the 1990s the number of Himalayan climbing and trekking excursions has grown to such a degree that tourists are now threatening the delicate environmental balance of the mountains.

Jock Montgomery

Climbers in the Annapurna region of the Himalayas inflate a Gamow bag, which can relieve the symptoms of altitude sickness. Approximately 20% of those who ascend above 2,000 meters (6,600 feet) suffer symptoms (including nausea, fatigue, and difficult respiration) as a result of reduced oxygen at high elevations. Rarer but more serious effects can lead to coma or death. Ascending slowly usually will prevent symptoms, and descending almost invariably relieves them. In cases where descent is not practical or possible, the pressurized Gamow bag can simulate actual descent. The altitude-sickness sufferer is sealed inside the device, which, when inflated, compresses air and thereby increases the number of oxygen molecules in a given volume of air so that with each breath the victim takes in more oxygen. This recent innovation has saved lives and brought expedition members from coma to consciousness in a matter of minutes.

creases) often leads to altitude sickness, and visitors must take great care to keep activity to a minimum over the first few days of acclimatization.

Climbing and hiking at high altitudes are ever increasing in popularity and, indeed, millions take to the world's peaks annually. As noted above, each year tens of thousands of adventure-bound Westerners trek in the Himalayan foothills. The best approach to avoiding altitude sickness is a slow ascent, but each year many overeager or unprepared trekkers and climbers suffer symptoms, and a few die. Because individuals vary in the rates at which they can ascend without symptoms, a climbing party should pace itself at the rate of the slowest and least experienced member.

The most obvious treatment for altitude sickness is to increase the atmospheric pressure; descending is usually the simplest and fastest way of doing this. Supplemental oxygen and the prescription medication acetazolamide (Diamox) are also used to prevent or relieve the symptoms of mountain sickness. An alternative is the use of a portable nylon compression chamber known as the Gamow bag (named for its developer, Igor Gamow, a chemical engineer at the University of Colorado). This new device looks like a sleeping bag with windows, weighs about 6.3 kilograms (14 pounds), and is inflated with a foot pump. To relieve symptoms it has to be pumped continuously to eliminate waste gases, which can be tiring at a high altitude; more elaborate models come with a carbon dioxide extractor. A larger model capable of accommodating two people is also available. Achievable compression with the Gamow bag is roughly equivalent to a 1,500-meter (5,000-foot) descent, depending on the altitude at which it is used, though for people who are seriously ill, there is no substitute for descent. The Gamow bag's use would certainly buy time in an emergency; it has already been used with great success on expeditions to remote places where rescue is difficult.

Embarking upon the future

Travel medicine has achieved an identity of its own. Around the world increasing numbers of physicians and other health care professionals are taking an interest in the subject—advising patients about preventing travel-associated health problems and improving their skill and expertise in diagnosing and treating the illnesses that travelers acquire. The International Society of Travel Medicine, founded in 1991, now has a membership of 1,300 and in March 1994 began publishing its own quarterly, peer-reviewed journal, the *Journal of Travel Medicine*. Its third international conference, held in Paris in April 1993, drew more than a thousand attendees from over 60 countries, and more than 450 scientific papers were presented. A fourth conference is scheduled for April 1995 in Acapulco, Mexico.

The number of travel clinics specializing in counseling international travelers has grown substantially. They can now be found in most major cities; the majority are affiliated with a medical school and staffed by physicians and nurses with training in tropical and infectious diseases. Before embarking on their foreign forays, prospective travelers not only can receive necessary vaccines and prophylactic medications but can get sound advice about everything from tropical diseases they might encounter (clinics generally have up-to-date reports on any recent outbreaks) to dietary prudence to preparing a medical kit. For returning travelers, clinics are usually better equipped than general practitioners to diagnose and treat any exotic illnesses they may have acquired.

The emergence of HIV as a new human pathogen, the recent outbreak of hantavirus infection in Native American communities of the southwestern United States, and the appearance of new, disease-causing strains of more familiar organisms have all focused attention on how the global community should prepare for the future. These infections are of considerable and growing concern to the specialty of travel medicine. Indeed, travel is a key factor in their dissemination. Clearly, avoidable delays in recognizing

The changing pattern of disease in destination countries has a clear impact on travelers. Whereas some diseases that once posed a serious threat to the health of the world's wayfarers have declined in prevalence or been eliminated entirely, new and potentially menacing infections have emerged, and others that had receded have reappeared, often with a vengeance. Moreover, since so many millions of people now travel widely, these infections are readily spread. The World Health Organization, the U.S. Centers for Disease Control and Prevention, and the International Society of Travel Medicine have recently joined forces to develop a global strategy for detecting and responding to pathogens that could endanger the lives of travelers. The map below shows selected emerging and resurgent infectious diseases in various parts of the world in 1993.

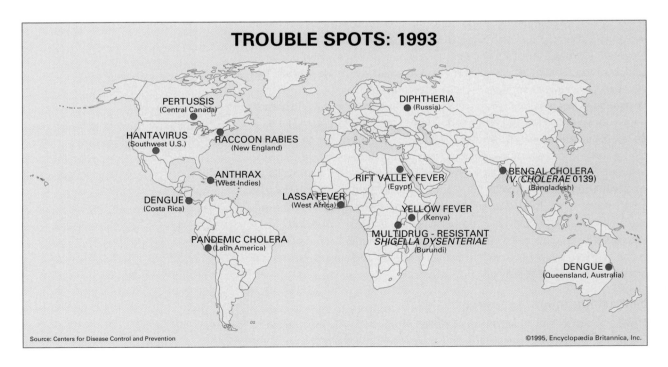

TROUBLE SPOTS: 1993

PERTUSSIS
(Central Canada)

DIPHTHERIA
(Russia)

HANTAVIRUS
(Southwest U.S.)

RACCOON RABIES
(New England)

BENGAL CHOLERA
(*V. CHOLERAE* 0139)
(Bangladesh)

ANTHRAX
(West Indies)

RIFT VALLEY FEVER
(Egypt)

DENGUE
(Costa Rica)

LASSA FEVER
(West Africa)

YELLOW FEVER
(Kenya)

PANDEMIC CHOLERA
(Latin America)

MULTIDRUG - RESISTANT
SHIGELLA DYSENTERIAE
(Burundi)

DENGUE
(Queensland, Australia)

Source: Centers for Disease Control and Prevention

emerging pathogens could have enormous costs in human suffering. The World Health Organization, the Centers for Disease Control and Prevention, and the International Society of Travel Medicine are now actively engaged in formulating a global strategy for detecting and responding to emerging pathogens that may threaten the health of future travelers and, indeed, of all humankind.

HEALTHY TRAVEL: SOURCES OF INFORMATION

Auerbach, Paul S. *Medicine for the Outdoors: A Guide to Emergency Medical Procedures and First Aid,* rev. ed. Boston: Little, Brown, 1991.

Dawood, Richard. *Travelers' Health: How to Stay Healthy All over the World.* New York: Random House, 1994.

Dawood, Richard, ed. *Travellers' Health: How to Stay Healthy Abroad.* Oxford: Oxford University Press, 1992.

Mooney, Blake. *Altitude-Related Places: A Medical Atlas. New Orleans, Louisiana: McNaughton & Gunn, 1933.*

Wilson, Mary E. *A World Guide to Infections: Diseases, Distribution, Diagnosis.* New York: Oxford University Press, 1991.

International travelers' hot line of the Centers for Disease Control and Prevention. Up-to-date health and disease information according to destination, available 24 hours a day: by phone (404-332-4559) and by fax (404-332-4565).

U.S. State Department Citizens Emergency Center. Information about political and other risks abroad (202-647-5225).

Immunization Alert. Computerized health briefings tailored to individual requirements and itineraries. 93 Timber Drive, Storrs CT 06268 (1-800-584-1999 or 203-487-0611).

International Association for Medical Assistance to Travellers (IAMAT). Free membership; provides a passport-sized directory of recommended physicians in about 120 countries, most of whom who have had some training in North America or the U.K., speak English or French, make hotel calls if necessary, and charge reasonable fees. The association also provides members with detailed pamphlets on immunization requirements worldwide and a personal medical record form that the traveler's regular doctor fills out, which gives foreign doctors a comprehensive medical history of the patient. 417 Center Street, Lewiston NY 14092 (716-754-4883), or 40 Regal Road, Guelph, Ont., Canada N1K 1B5 (519-836-0102).

International SOS Assistance. Thirty-two centers worldwide that provide referrals to physicians and hospitals. PO Box 11568, Philadelphia PA 19116 (1-800-523-8930).

International Society of Travel Medicine. Scientifically oriented organization that promotes free and rapid exchange of information on travel medicine issues; also publishes a newsletter and quarterly journal. Membership is open to the public. PO Box 15060, Atlanta GA 30333-0060 (fax: 404-488-4427).

SOUVENIRS
NOBODY WANTS: GUIDANCE FOR GLOBE-TROTTERS

Every year some 30 million to 35 million people from developed countries travel to less developed ones, many of which are in the tropics. At least 30% of those who venture forth succumb to illness; naïveté about risks greatly increases their chances of becoming sick. Pretravel information about potential health threats is therefore essential for any tourist about to embark for distant parts.

MALARIA

Today's international travelers may return home with more than their air mileage and a few tales to tell. Malaria parasites may have hitched a ride, too, threatening the health and even the lives of their unsuspecting hosts. Yet despite malaria's potential to kill, most travelers remain ignorant of the risks, and many would fail to recognize its symptoms.

Over the past decade, as tropical destinations in less developed parts of the world have become increasingly popular among Western tourists, the number of cases of "imported" malaria in industrialized countries has more than doubled. The World Health Organization (WHO) now receives reports of about 10,000 malaria cases a year in Europe alone; more than 1,000 cases a year are reported from the United States and Canada.

Tourists who travel to sub-Saharan Africa are at the greatest risk. As many as one in every 100 people from the industrialized countries who visit West African countries will get malaria; those who visit rural areas, away from the relative safety of air-conditioned urban hotels, are the most likely to become infected. African emigrants from the countryside who return to their villages to visit their families after their own immunity to malaria has waned are also particularly vulnerable. Even some major African metropolises are now experiencing malaria as a consequence of an ever increasing influx of people from rural areas seeking work.

Toll of a disease

Serious though the malaria problem is for travelers, their risk is dwarfed by the share of the burden borne by the less developed world. More than 40% of the world's population—or two billion people—are at risk of contracting the disease simply because they live in regions where the malaria parasites are endemic.

WHO estimates that between 300 million and 500 million people in less developed countries are stricken with malaria annually. No exact figures exist, but at least 1.5 million and perhaps as many as 3 million of these people die—the majority of deaths being among young African children. In the villages of The Gambia, for example, one in 20 children will die of malaria before his or her fifth birthday. This compares starkly with the mere handful of deaths that occur every year in each industrialized country, however tragic those deaths may be.

In less developed countries even the survivors and their families pay a heavy price for malaria. In highly endemic areas the disease is estimated to reduce the learning capacity of between 33% and 60% of schoolchildren. In sub-Saharan Africa the malaria burden, as measured by the World Bank (in "disability-adjusted life years"), outweighs that of all other diseases among women and ranks second only to respiratory diseases among men.

The economic impact of the disease varies from country to country. For Africa as a whole, the direct and indirect costs of malaria have more than doubled in the last decade, from $800 million in 1987 to an estimated $1.8 billion by 1992. A more meaningful estimate suggests that the average household's productivity may be reduced by almost one-third in the malaria season.

Presently the situation is actually worsening—a trend that directly affects international travelers. Drug-resistant strains of malaria parasites are spreading rapidly through Southeast Asia, in parts of Latin America, and, increasingly, in Africa. As more and more refugees flee war or seek work away from home, populations that lack immunity are suddenly exposed en masse to infection. In the economic "frontier" zones of Amazonia and Southeast Asia, where gold rushers and gem miners without immunity enter malarious areas, the incidence of malaria infection and death is extremely high. For example, in the Brazilian Amazon between 6,000 and 10,000 people die of the disease each year.

In 1992, at an international summit on malaria in Amsterdam, WHO's member states issued a declaration recognizing the worsening worldwide situation and the need to control the disease with better use of existing resources adapted to suit local communities. Whether the malaria parasites themselves will listen is another matter.

Malaria author: Phyllida Brown is a Senior Reporter for New Scientist *magazine, London.*

Complex creatures

Malaria is caused by four species of protozoan parasites of the genus *Plasmodium*. The most common is *P. vivax*. The one that kills and is spreading most rapidly is *P. falciparum*. The parasites are spread by the bite of infected female *Anopheles* mosquitoes, which feed on human blood, taking their meals between dusk and dawn.

More than almost any other organisms that cause disease in humans, the *Plasmodium* parasites are beguilingly adaptable, outsmarting their hosts at every turn. Their life cycle is complex. They infect red blood cells, entering the bloodstream from the gut of the mosquito in an immature form known as a sporozoite. The sporozoites migrate to the liver, where they mature into forms known as schizonts. Schizonts each contain as many as 30,000 organisms known as merozoites. Merozoites migrate from the liver to take up residence in the red blood cells, which they destroy in the process. The loss of red blood cells causes the anemia that so frequently accompanies malaria.

Most merozoites reproduce asexually—that is, by making identical copies of themselves rather than by mixing the genetic material of two parents. A few, however, develop into a sexual stage known as a gametocyte. These will mate only when they enter the gut of another mosquito that bites an infected person. Mating between gametocytes produces ookinetes, which

embed themselves in the mosquito's gut; ookinetes then ripen into oocysts, which release thousands of sporozoites, some of which will infect the next person the mosquito bites.

Detecting infection

Once infected by the malaria parasite, a person may or may not develop disease, and the symptoms can be variable. Partly for this reason, malaria may not always be easy to diagnose by symptoms alone. For more than a century the most reliable method of diagnosis has been a laboratory test in which a trained technician is able to see the parasites when a smear of blood from the infected person is examined under a microscope. The method, however, has obvious drawbacks. For example, the test is time-consuming, may fail to detect cases where there are very few parasites, and relies on a laboratory and skilled staff.

A more refined test, which makes it easier to detect low-level infections, uses acridine orange to stain the parasites, which are then visible under a special microscope. But this method is not perfect either. Consequently, scientists are working to develop alternatives, such as tests that would identify specific proteins from the parasites or tests that could detect tiny amounts of the parasites' genetic material, amplified thousands of times by a technique known as the polymerase chain reaction.

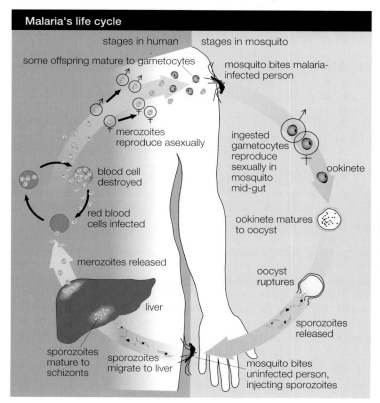

Malaria's life cycle

stages in human / stages in mosquito

some offspring mature to gametocytes

mosquito bites malaria-infected person

merozoites reproduce asexually

ingested gametocytes reproduce sexually in mosquito mid-gut

blood cell destroyed

ookinete

red blood cells infected

ookinete matures to oocyst

merozoites released

oocyst ruptures

sporozoites released

liver

sporozoites mature to schizonts

sporozoites migrate to liver

mosquito bites uninfected person, injecting sporozoites

The bite of the female Anopheles *mosquito (below) transmits the* Plasmodium *parasite that causes malaria. Both the mosquitoes and the parasites are remarkably hardy and adaptable—the insects growing resistant to pesticides, the parasites to antimalarial drugs. What has thwarted most efforts to develop a successful malaria vaccine is the complicated life cycle of the parasite—that is, its stages both in the mosquito and in the human (diagram).*

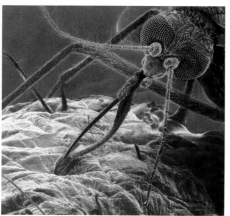

While better diagnostic tests are being sought, symptoms will continue to be an important clue in detecting malaria. This is true not only for people who live in rural areas that lack sophisticated laboratory facilities but also for international travelers. Most travelers will not develop symptoms until they return home to countries where malaria is not endemic and physicians are less likely to "think malaria." This makes it vital for travelers to recognize the possible early signs of infection themselves and then to visit their physician and tell her or him where they have been. Otherwise, the sickness may be dismissed as flu, with potentially fatal consequences. In some cases malaria can kill within hours.

Fever, aches, and pains

The period between infection and disease is usually between two and three weeks, but the disease can develop up to one year after a person leaves a malarious area. Malaria starts with vague, flulike symptoms, weakness, and lethargy; then a fever usually develops. The victim may also have severe headaches and aching limbs. He or she may vomit. Anemia may develop, with potentially severe consequences for pregnant women and young children.

Promptly treated, most cases of malaria can be cured, provided the parasites responsible are not resistant to the available drugs. But in cases caused by *P. falciparum,* malaria may progress rapidly to involve the brain, particularly in children; if it does, there is at least a 20% chance the patient will die. The person sinks slowly into a coma or, occasionally, has convulsions before losing consciousness.

Even after an apparent cure, however, symptoms may return. In the case of *falciparum* malaria, recurrence is common after just a few weeks. This is because treatment has failed to kill all the parasites. Two other species, *P. ovale* and *P. vivax,* can survive in dormant form in the human liver and months later cause symptoms.

A preventable disease

Many travelers believe that they are safe from malaria if they simply take prophylactic drugs such as chloroquine. They are wrong. Although the drugs provide some protection, none is completely effective against the parasites. The only way to be sure of avoiding malaria is to avoid being bitten by mosquitoes.

If one travels to a malarious region, essential equipment includes an insecticide such as diethyl toluamide, available from travel clinics in spray or roll-on form. This should be applied to any exposed skin (but kept off expensive sunglasses and watchbands). Long sleeves, trousers, socks, and shoes help to reduce the amount of exposed skin susceptible to biting. At night a bednet treated with insecticide, most notably permethrin, prevents the sleeping traveler from providing the mosquitoes with a meal. Burning a mosquito "coil," which contains the insecticide pyrethrum, will also deter the insects. Sonic buzzers, which are advertised as offering protection from mosquitoes, are useless.

In much of Africa and Southeast Asia, the treated bednet remains the mainstay of prevention. A study by researchers in The Gambia found that the use of treated nets cut the overall death rate sharply— by 70%. This is more than can be accounted for by malaria alone, so it is possible that malaria increases people's vulnerability to other potentially fatal diseases. Larger trials in other countries are attempting to confirm the Gambian results.

However important these physical measures may be, travelers should still take prophylactic drugs such as chloroquine, proguanil, or mefloquine. It is imperative that prospective travelers consult their physician or a specialized travel clinic for advice on the best current drug or combination of drugs for their particular destination. Parasites resistant to certain drugs are spreading rapidly, and the situation changes constantly. One should not be tempted to use leftover pills from a previous trip to the tropics without consulting a physician to check whether they are still effective. On returning home, it is vital that the traveler continue taking whatever drugs have been prescribed for at least four weeks; parasites may still be present in the body.

Treatment: few drugs, hardy parasites

The arsenal of drugs to treat malaria is remarkably small, and few new ones are in the pipeline. This is a serious problem because *Plasmodium* parasites evolve much more rapidly than new drugs. It appears that almost as soon as a drug reaches the market, parasites become resistant to it.

The original antimalarial, quinine, is based on an extract of the bark of the cinchona tree and was first recorded as a treatment for the disease in about 1630 in Peru. Despite a range of side effects such as tinnitus (ringing in the ears), blurred vision, and, less commonly, blood disorders and various allergic reactions, quinine is still used, especially for severe malaria and in cases in which the parasites are resistant to other, newer drugs.

Since the advent of modern pharmacology, new antimalarials have emerged slowly, and the few that do exist were developed largely in response to world wars or other events that have taken thousands of troops from Europe and North America into malarious regions. By the end of World War II, the drug chloroquine had been developed, and it is still the mainstay of antimalarial treatment worldwide. An alternative treatment of the same vintage is sulfadoxine-pyrimethamine. The Vietnam War stimulated the development of two more antimalarials, mefloquine and halofantrine.

A young girl ill with malaria is cared for in a Cambodian refugee camp. The burden of disease borne by people living in malaria-endemic areas in less developed countries is enormous. In most of Southeast Asia, the situation is presently worsening with the rapid spread of drug-resistant parasites.

The first chloroquine-resistant parasites emerged in the late 1950s and early 1960s in Asia and Latin America. Variant forms with slight genetic differences from their peers, these parasites happened to be unscathed by the drug. Naturally they prospered at the expense of the majority of drug-sensitive parasites. Under the so-called selection pressure of the drug, resistant variants gradually became the dominant population in certain regions. From these regions they spread—slowly but surely—and today almost no endemic country is without drug-resistant parasites.

Scientists in the United States have recently located a gene that governs chloroquine resistance; they hope that the knowledge will eventually enable them to design alternative drugs. But the pace of pharmacological research is glacial compared with the speed of the parasites' evolution. Within just five years of mefloquine's arrival in Thailand, for example, resistant parasites were emerging there. In parts of Thailand and Cambodia, there are now parasites that are resistant to *all* the conventional drugs. The shortage of drugs seems set to continue and even worsen. Moreover, because manufacturing such drugs tends to be unprofitable, fewer drug companies than ever before are now developing new antimalarials.

There is a glimmer of hope, however, on the pharmaceutical horizon. The Chinese have used extracts of the sweet wormwood plant, *Artemisia annua,* to treat malaria for more than 2,000 years; the first known record of its use was in 168 BC. In 1972 Chinese scientists identified the essential oil in the extracts, which is called *qinghaosu,* or artemisinin. The discovery remained unknown in the West until 1979, when scattered reports suggested that artemether, the drug derived from the oil, was highly effective. But Western scientists wanted rigorous clinical trials to prove its efficacy. Finally, in 1994, they got what they wanted. A two-year trial of artemether on the Thailand-Cambodia border among people with severe, multidrug-resistant malaria reduced the death rate threefold (compared with quinine). Eighteen of 50 patients treated with quinine died, while only 6 deaths occurred among the 47 treated with artemether. The drug has also been highly effective in reducing the death rate from malaria in Vietnam. The results of these recent studies were even more dramatic than what most scientists had been hoping for.

Elusive search for vaccines

Vaccines would be a cheap and effective way to prevent malaria parasites from infecting people, and they would gradually reduce the prevalence of disease. It is not surprising, therefore, that years have been devoted to the search for them. So far, progress has been painfully slow. The parasites are particularly difficult to immunize against. This is partly because the parasites appear to require a different response from the immune system at each of their different life-cycle stages (*e.g.,* at the sporozoite and merozoite stages). Moreover, the parasites' surface proteins change rapidly, forcing the immune system to follow a moving target. This means that a vaccine based on a particular "cocktail" of parasite proteins might not necessarily protect against all forms of the parasite that the immunized person might encounter.

Scientists, however, continue to work on a number of approaches to vaccines. One type of vaccine would aim to limit, or completely prevent, infection with parasites. This approach is being pursued by a number of research teams, whose vaccines are based on various proteins from the merozoite and sporozoite stages. The idea is to stimulate antibodies to the proteins that would block infection if the person subsequently encountered the real parasite. Another strategy is to develop an "antidisease" vaccine. This would not prevent infection, but it would block the body's harmful responses to infection, which are also thought to be responsible for many of the symptoms.

A third approach, known as an "altruistic" vaccine, would not stop either infection or symptoms in the individual but would prevent infection from spreading to others. Vaccinating people with a genetically engineered protein from the ookinete, which stimulates antibodies to the natural protein, would block the transmission of the parasite in mosquitoes because the antibodies interrupt the sexual stage of reproduction. Combined with drugs to treat the individual's disease, this approach could cut the rapid spread of malaria. Because it acts on a stage in the life cycle of the parasite to which humans are never directly exposed, this vaccine would also avoid the possibility of parasites' evading it through selection pressure.

All of these approaches are being tested, with results eagerly awaited. Only one vaccine, however, appears close to widespread use. Manuel Patarroyo, a Colombian biochemist at the Institute of Immunology in Bogotá, has developed a synthetic vaccine made from a string of peptides that mimic certain parasite proteins. Investigators claimed the vaccine was highly effective in trials involving more than 20,000 people in Latin America, but many scientists in other parts of the world were skeptical because some of the trials lacked proper controls. Recently, however, in rigorously controlled trials in Venezuela, the vaccine was shown to offer considerable protection, preventing infection in between 40% and 70% of people. WHO is now overseeing the trial and development of Patarroyo's vaccine, and trials in the much tougher environment of Tanzania are currently under way. In the foreseeable future, at least, it is unlikely that the vaccine will be given to travelers; rather, its use would be reserved for highly vulnerable populations living in endemic regions.

Manuel Patarroyo immunizes a Colombian child with the low-cost synthetic vaccine he developed against malaria. In extensive field trials in Latin America, the vaccine proved to be highly effective. Trials are currently under way in Tanzania, where the malaria challenge is much greater.

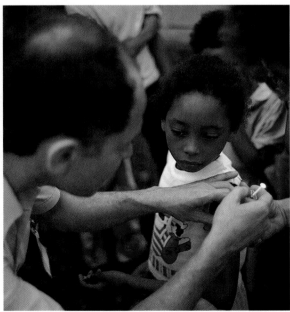

Timothy Ross—JB Pictures

Even if the Colombian vaccine is as successful in Africa as it has been in Latin America, it will not solve the world's malaria problem. Alternative vaccines will still be urgently needed, as will new drugs. Without major investment by the private sector or by the governments of industrialized nations, it is unlikely that these will emerge. For travelers, a journey free of the risk of malaria is not yet in sight.

HIV/AIDS

"Oh, yes, the truckers!" said Dr. O.E. Omolo, the provincial medical officer in Mombasa [Kenya]. . . ."They are true museums of disease! Chancroid, gonorrhea, syphilis, herpes, AIDS—well, the list goes on and on!"
—"Trucking Through the AIDS Belt,"
The New Yorker, Aug. 16, 1993

AIDS is the newest member of a group of diseases that are mainly transmitted from one person to another by sexual intercourse and so are collectively known as sexually transmitted diseases (STDs). The group includes illnesses caused by bacteria (syphilis, gonorrhea, chancroid, chlamydial infections), viruses (HIV infection, hepatitis B, herpes simplex infections, genital warts), protozoa, fungi, and ectoparasites. All STDs occur throughout the world, and some have been known since ancient times. Gonorrhea, for example, may have been described in early Chinese manuscripts and in the writings of the Greek physicians Galen and Hippocrates in the 2nd–5th centuries BC.

The association between STDs and travel has been recognized for almost as long; one popular explanation for the appearance of syphilis in 15th-century Europe is that it was introduced from the New World in 1493 by sailors who had accompanied Christopher Columbus' expedition. Nearly 500 years later, antibiotic-resistant strains of the organism that causes gonorrhea were first isolated from American and European patients who acquired the disease from sexual contacts in Southeast Asia and Africa.

Whereas the majority of international travelers were once soldiers and sailors, today's globe-trotters constitute a much more diverse population. They include tourists (now the largest group), foreign service personnel, business travelers, technical experts, students, amateur and professional athletes, expeditioneers, airline crews, refugees and immigrants, military personnel, missionaries, migrant workers, and volunteer aid workers. Certain groups of travelers—merchant seamen, long-distance truck drivers, flight attendants, prostitutes, and drug traffickers—have been instrumental

HIV/AIDS authors: At the Public Health Laboratory Service of the Communicable Disease Surveillance Centre, London, **Julia Heptonstall, M.Sc., M.B., D.T.M. & H.,** *is Consultant Microbiologist;* **O.N. Gill, M.Sc., M.B., B.Ch.,** *is Deputy Director and Consultant Epidemiologist; and* **Ahilya Noone, B.M., B.Ch., M.Sc.,** *is Consultant Epidemiologist.*

In Africa, where heterosexual transmission of HIV predominates, long-distance truckers have been instrumental in spreading the infection. In fact, the geographic pattern of the epidemic can be mapped along the continent's major highways. AIDS education teams are now working with truckers in peer-education programs; the sign on this driver's truck reads, "Condoms prevent AIDS."

in the international transmission of HIV infection. A homosexual flight attendant was identified as the central figure in a large cluster of U.S. AIDS cases in the early years of the American epidemic. The pattern of spread of HIV in Africa can be mapped along the major highways traveled by long-haul truckers, and the epidemiology of HIV infection in northeastern India, Myanmar (Burma), Thailand, and southern China is explained by cross-border movements of drug dealers and users and interactions of male visitors with female sex workers (prostitutes).

Ominous and inexorable

AIDS was first recognized in 1981 by experts from the U.S. Centers for Disease Control, in Atlanta, Ga. The earliest patients were homosexual men in New York City and California. Within a short period of time, however, as cases were recognized in intravenous drug users and in blood-transfusion and blood-product recipients, it became clear that the disease was not restricted to homosexuals. Cases also began to be reported in European countries. In 1983 the virus that causes AIDS, subsequently named the human immunodeficiency virus, or HIV, was isolated. Blood tests for the diagnosis of HIV infection were in widespread use by the end of 1985. During the mid-1980s the worldwide spread of AIDS became evident, and the rapidly increasing rate of HIV infection in Africa was revealed. By 1990 public health officials had become concerned about the growing numbers of HIV-positive individuals in Asia.

The initial stages of HIV infection may be completely asymptomatic, and those infected with the virus may remain perfectly well for many years. During this time, however, they are capable of transmitting the virus to others. Although treatment with antibiotics and antiviral drugs has improved the outlook for persons with HIV infection, overall the prospects remain grim.

Once AIDS has been diagnosed, average survival is between two and three years; more than 90% of AIDS patients will not survive five years. Survival time is even shorter in less developed countries. Current data suggest that the infection is progressing inexorably in at least 85% of HIV-infected adults and that all these persons will eventually die from their infection or a complication of the disease.

HIV infection is transmitted primarily through unprotected sexual intercourse (*e.g.,* sex without a condom), either homosexual or heterosexual. It is thought that the efficiency of transmission is generally low—that is, the virus is not readily transmitted—but may be enhanced in the presence of other STDs. Nonetheless, HIV is known to have been transmitted during single unprotected sexual acts. HIV is also transmitted by contact with infected blood and contaminated needles and syringes. Between 13% and 48% (the figures vary widely in different countries) of babies born to infected women acquire HIV before, during, or after birth. The virus is not transmitted by kissing, hugging, shaking hands, or sharing food or tableware. People cannot "catch" it from toilet seats or swimming pools or through everyday social or household contact with someone who is infected. There is no evidence that HIV infection is spread by insect bites.

Two types of HIV, with different patterns of geographic distribution, are known to exist. Type 1, called HIV-1, is the predominant virus, having spread rapidly worldwide from the mid- to late 1970s onward. WHO estimated that by mid-1993, 14 million people were infected with HIV-1, and this number was expected to rise to 30 million–40 million by the year 2000. The second type, HIV-2, appears to be both less infectious and less virulent than HIV-1. Although occasional cases of HIV-2 infection have been reported from outside Africa, at present this virus is largely confined to West Africa.

Passport, ticket, condoms . . .

The risk of HIV infection to an individual traveler depends on three factors: (1) knowledge of how the virus is transmitted, (2) chances of exposure to a situation where a risk of transmission exists, and (3) the pattern of HIV infection in the country or area to be visited. The duration and the social or cultural context of the visit are important to the extent that they affect the opportunities for exposure. For example, a man who attends a one-week business meeting accompanied by his wife is undoubtedly at lower risk of infection than an unmarried Peace Corps worker on a two-year tour of duty.

In recent years epidemiologists and infectious disease specialists have been actively investigating the risk of HIV infection to travelers. Much of the information comes from surveys of the knowledge, attitudes, and perceptions of people questioned at pretravel medical clinics. The results indicate that these individuals generally do know how HIV is transmitted and are aware of how to avoid infection, although a minority remain misinformed about the risks or unaware of them. Overall, however, even those with adequate knowledge about transmission of HIV underrate their own personal risks of infection during travel, fail to equip themselves to avoid sexual transmission (for example, by purchasing condoms), and are poorly informed about the existence of HIV infection in the area they intend to visit and about the risk of infection through blood transfusion or other medical care. The majority—but by no means all—of those who state that they plan to have sex with a new partner while abroad intend to use condoms. The data, however, also suggest that many people do not acknowledge that they might have unprotected sex while on holiday.

Sex away from home. Two different methods have been used to gather data on the risks to travelers of sexually acquired HIV. The first, mentioned above, involves questioning people prior to departure about their knowledge of HIV transmission and their intended sexual behavior. In one such study Australian researchers surveyed 213 patients seeking vaccinations and other medical advice preparatory to visiting Thailand. Only 34% reported that they definitely did *not* plan to have sex while traveling; 13% said they would not rule out having sex with a "bar girl." Of those who planned to be sexually active, 82% said they would use condoms 100% of the time.

Posttravel surveys are the second source of information regarding sexual behavior during travel. In such surveys conducted in England, varying proportions of vacationers, expatriate workers, and people attending STD clinics acknowledged having had unprotected sexual intercourse with a new partner while traveling. These partners included fellow travelers, residents of the locale visited, and local prostitutes. HIV infection has been reported among such returning travelers, and subsequent transmission to a regular partner at home has also been documented. Moreover, the occurrence of other STDs in British travelers returning home from areas where HIV infection is present confirms that they have engaged in high-risk behaviors even though they remain free of HIV. Travel abroad was a suspected risk factor in 101 of the 538 cases of hepatitis B reported to British communicable disease authorities in a single recent year.

A study of Peace Corps volunteers, published in 1993, revealed that only one-third of those who had been sexually active abroad had used condoms consistently, even though many had been stationed in countries where AIDS is a recognized public health problem. Eight had been infected with HIV. Having had too much to drink was cited by some as a predisposing factor for unsafe sexual behaviors.

Risks from "bad blood." Injuries are a common hazard for the international traveler. Such injury can

Teenage prostitutes await customers behind a display window in a Bangkok, Thailand, brothel. The thriving commercial sex industry has been a major factor in the spread of HIV in Asia. Public health authorities there are working hard to discourage the practice of "sex tourism."

sometimes be severe; motor vehicle collisions account for a large proportion of unexpected deaths among travelers, and in two studies of people who required emergency medical evacuation, nearly half were trauma cases. Emergency medical care may also be needed by pregnant travelers who suffer obstetric complications and by travelers who have preexisting medical conditions (*e.g.,* diabetes, chronic renal disease requiring dialysis). Still another category of people receiving medical care away from home consists of those who travel specifically to obtain treatment.

Since most industrialized countries had introduced effective techniques for screening donated blood for HIV infection by 1985–86, the risk of acquisition of HIV through blood transfusion in such countries is now minimal. In many parts of the world, however, blood transfusion may still carry an appreciable risk for the recipient.

HIV has been transmitted by the use of inadequately sterilized needles, syringes, and other medical equipment. Travelers should be aware that, in addition to injections or vaccinations, traditional healing practices, acupuncture, tattooing, and ear or body piercing may carry a risk of HIV infection. All travelers should be educated about the dangers inherent in unnecessary injections. Even such seemingly innocuous activities as getting a shave in a barber shop or a manicure or pedicure in a beauty salon could carry a risk of infection if razors and other implements are not scrupulously cleaned after each use. When traveling in areas where hygiene and sanitation are poor, travelers should probably forgo such services. Finally, since HIV is known to have been transmitted during dental procedures, it is probably best to avoid dental treatment in a place where sterilization may be less than thorough and the practitioner's infection-control practices are unknown. Those planning a trip would be wise to have incipient dental problems attended to at home prior to departure.

Interestingly, even travelers who are well equipped for potential health threats such as malaria and tetanus often do not know how to avoid or minimize the risk of HIV. At an occupational health conference for oil industry professionals held in Scotland in 1992, researchers questioned company doctors and nurses about the medical advice, vaccinations, and drug prophylaxis their corporations provided for employees traveling on business to such destinations as sub-Saharan Africa, Latin America, and Southeast Asia. Close to 80% reported that the company routinely provided vaccinations against tetanus, hepatitis B, typhoid, polio, and yellow fever, as well as drugs for malaria. Only 10% said that the company armed business travelers with protection against sexually transmitted diseases.

Clearly, all those who venture abroad—whether on business or on holiday—need to be better informed about the risks of HIV infection and how to protect themselves. Every traveler should bear in mind the following:

- Proper and consistent use of condoms and/or spermicides reduces the risk of exposure to HIV.
- Excess alcohol consumption increases the likelihood of unprotected sexual intercourse.
- Hepatitis B is the only vaccine-preventable STD; a vaccine against HIV is not available and is not likely to be in the foreseeable future.
- Travel can be hazardous, and serious injury may be unavoidable. Adequate medical insurance includes coverage for emergency medical evacuation.
- Unnecessary injections should be avoided.
- A blood test for HIV is widely available and is recommended for returning travelers who may have been exposed while away.

Informed, aware, prepared

The rapid increase in the volume of international travel in recent years and the speed with which movement now occurs between countries have been important factors in the developing HIV/AIDS pandemic. The pattern of infection varies from country to country, reflecting local social, cultural, and economic factors. Worldwide, three-quarters of HIV infections have resulted from sex between men and women.

The behaviors that place a person at risk of infection are the same in any geographic location, as are the preventive measures. These are being *informed* about, *aware* of, and *prepared* to avoid risk behaviors and minimizing exposure to situations where transmission is a possibility.

CHOLERA

The epidemic of cholera at Mecca worsens. A fortnight ago the deaths daily were counted in dozens. A week ago they numbered hundreds. Now they have reached the thousand mark. How much further the roll is to swell depends chiefly upon the number of pilgrims who remain in the stricken city. . . . An analysis of the well water shows it to be so contaminated by drainage from cesspools as to be rank poison, abounding with noxious impurities. . . . With thousands of pilgrims thronging about the well, with many sick and dying of cholera among them, the wells become as active and deadly a disseminator of disease as ingenuity could devise. . . . These pilgrims do not belong alone to Mohammedan countries. Many are from Great Britain, France and Italy. And not a few return home bearing thither the deadly infection.

—*Journal of the American Medical Association, 1893*

Cholera was formerly a disease of travel par excellence. Not so long ago travelers going to less developed countries used to dread the standard ritual of get-

Cholera authors: David A. Sack, M.D., is Associate Professor, Department of International Health, Johns Hopkins University, Baltimore, Maryland; Ronald Waldman, M.D., is Technical Director, Partnership for Child Health Care, Inc., BASICS Project, Arlington, Virginia.

ting painful cholera shots. Up until about 1973, along with yellow fever and smallpox vaccines, the cholera vaccine was legally required for travel to many parts of Asia and Africa. Now no country officially requires the cholera vaccine (though a few border crossings, especially in Africa, still require it "unofficially"). Why the shift in requirements? Has cholera, like smallpox, been eradicated from the face of the globe?

Unfortunately, cholera's impact around the world continues not only to be felt but to grow. Several million people are estimated to develop the disease each year, and over 100,000 are thought to die from it. Recently a new variety of *Vibrio cholerae,* the microbe responsible for the disease, has appeared, further increasing cholera's burden. In spite of these grim statistics, cholera today is a minimal risk for travelers, even in cholera-endemic areas; moreover, this small risk can be nearly eliminated with simple precautions.

The microbial enemy and the misery it causes

Cholera is a bacterial infection in which the organism *V. cholerae* colonizes the intestine; the bacterium secretes a toxin that causes the small intestine's mucosal lining to secrete copious volumes of fluid. The excessive secretion from the intestine far exceeds the ability of the mucosa to reabsorb the fluid, and the excess fluid is therefore expelled from the body. Hence, the major symptoms of cholera are severe watery diarrhea and vomiting. Usually these are associated with abdominal cramps, but there is no fever, nor is there blood in the stool. Patients with severe cases develop dehydration from the loss of so much fluid, and because the fluid losses are rich in salts and bicarbonate, patients develop electrolyte and acid-base-balance disturbances. Because all of the acute symptoms are related to the rapid fluid loss and attendant dehydration, treatment depends on rapid replacement of these losses.

Cholera is indeed a dangerous disease. Not only can it occur without warning, but it progresses rapidly. Cases have been described in which perfectly healthy young adults developed symptomatic cholera and within six hours were dead from dehydration and shock. If one does not have access to prompt and proper care, the risk of death can be great. In most of the fatal cases, death occurs within the first 24 hours.

Cholera is also dangerous because it spreads in epidemic fashion, striking one family after another. In severe epidemics many families within a region will be affected, and in the absence of treatment, many persons die. Not surprisingly, this is a disease that often incites panic among the public. In communities experiencing an epidemic, medical facilities are generally hard-pressed to cope with the large numbers of cases and are unable to prevent further spread.

Humans become infected by *V. cholerae* when they ingest water or food that has been contaminated; the bacteria are then excreted in the stools of patients who are ill with the disease and also in stools of persons who have no symptoms but are nonetheless infected. Even though cholera is a dangerous disease, about 80% of infected persons have either mild diarrhea or no symptoms at all. Only a small proportion have the severe form of the disease. Moreover, it is the asymptomatic individuals, who often are unaware they are infected, who are most likely to spread the infection from one region to another. Because these persons are healthy, they are mobile, facilitating *V. cholerae*'s rapid transmission to new regions. Thus, there is no benefit in quarantine of those who are ill, and although these means were commonly used in the past, all efforts to halt the spread of cholera through quarantine or by limitation of travel have failed.

In addition to the fecal-oral cycle of contamination, *V. cholerae* can survive in certain bodies of water free of human contamination. This has been the case in the Gulf of Mexico, where the bacteria have survived for many years even without renewed contamination by human feces. Environmental microbiologists also believe that the bacteria have been carried in coastal waters off Peru, the Chesapeake Bay, brackish waters near Bangladesh, and the Antarctic Ocean. The cholera-causing bacteria apparently live in aquatic microenvironments, where they attach to plankton and algae, breed on pollutants such as nitrogen and phosphorus, and eventually work their way into the human food chain. The seasonality and virulence of cholera may in this manner be coordinated with the seasonal cycles of these forms of minute aquatic plant and animal life.

Treatment: simple but spectacular

Even though cholera remains a dread disease capable of spreading rapidly and producing high case fatality rates, it is also a disease that is easily controlled and treated. Moreover, treatment is nearly universally successful. Whereas once about 40% of patients with cholera gravis (cholera with severe dehydration) died from the disease, now fewer than one-half of 1% will die if patients are given proper but simple treatment. Thus, the first rule for controlling cholera is that all patients should receive prompt treatment.

As early as the 1830s, scientists began investigating fluid replacement as treatment for cholera, but this did not gain favor until the 20th century, when suitable replacement fluids were developed and began to be used routinely. Beginning in the 1960s, scientists working in Calcutta and at the International Centre for Diarrhoeal Diseases Research in Dhaka, Bangladesh (then East Pakistan), carefully measured the volume and chemical composition of fluid losses in cholera patients. They postulated that if these fluids were replaced with sterile intravenous (IV) fluids as fast as they were lost, the patients might be saved. They also thought that the replacement fluids should have an electrolyte composition similar to that of the fluids being expelled. Studies dramatically demonstrated that these ideas were correct. In fact, patients so treated are not unlike the biblical Lazarus. Admitted to the hospital unconscious, with no detectable blood pressure or pulse, in as little as 15 minutes after the start of IV treatment, they awaken; within an hour or two, they may be sitting up eating a nourishing meal. Simply by replacement of the fluids, which restores the circulating blood volume, the shock is reversed and patients recover completely.

The next major advance in cholera treatment came when scientists learned how to replace these vital fluids by mouth rather than intravenously. In less developed countries, where cholera predominantly occurs, intravenous fluids are scarce and expensive, and trained health workers may not be available to treat the cases occurring during epidemics in rural or poor areas. But a simple solution of sugar, salt, and sodium bicarbonate in water, which was developed in Dhaka and Calcutta, now called oral rehydration salts (ORS) by the United Nations Children's fund (UNICEF) and WHO, can rehydrate all but the most severely dehydrated patients. ORS packets to make one liter of fluid cost about 10 cents to $1. Severely dehydrated patients would typically need a few liters for treatment. Thus, the cost for treating a case is less than $10. A similar solution can be made from four level tablespoons of sugar, one-half teaspoon of salt, and one-half teaspoon of bicarbonate of soda (baking soda) added to a liter of water. After rehydration, patients

Cholera patients in Cajamarca, Peru, are treated with oral rehydration solution. Widespread use of this simple and inexpensive form of therapy during the present Latin-American cholera epidemic has kept fatality rates to about 1%.

Gustavo Gilabert—JB Pictures

with cholera should eat a normal diet that includes fruits that are high in potassium, such as bananas, prunes, apricots, raisins, or oranges.

The availability of the ORS packets and the knowledge about how to make a similar fluid from home ingredients theoretically make simple and cheap treatment available to all cholera patients. Practically, however, ensuring that rehydration is available to all who need it is not so simple; nonetheless, programs around the world are working to disseminate this knowledge and to distribute ORS packets in countries where they are needed. Much still remains to be done, however, before this simple treatment becomes a consistent reality.

In addition to rehydration, patients with cholera and dehydration should also receive oral antibiotics to kill the bacteria and thereby shorten the duration of the illness. There is no advantage in receiving antibiotics by injection. Doxycycline, 300 milligrams, as a single dose is the recommended antibiotic, but tetracycline or trimethoprim/sulfamethoxazole for three days can also be used. Because some strains of *V. cholerae* have become resistant to these antibiotics, alternative antibiotics may have to be used. Fortunately, even without antibiotic therapy, patients will recover completely as long as their hydration is maintained.

Risk to today's travelers

The risk of cholera's occurring in contemporary travelers from the United States and other industrialized countries is very low—estimated to be in the range of one per 10,000 to 100,000 travelers who visit endemic areas. On the other hand, people who live in endemic areas typically will develop cholera at a rate of one per 1,000 per year. If municipal water supplies become contaminated, which often happens in poor countries during an epidemic, rates may be as high as 2 per 100 (2%). The explanation for the relatively low rate in travelers is that most travelers are careful about what they eat and drink; furthermore, they generally wash hands appropriately and are not likely to contaminate their food and drink. Travelers who assume the lifestyle of villagers will be at the same risk as the native population—and may even be at a higher risk because they lack the degree of immunity that those who are regularly exposed to *V. cholerae* develop.

Because cholera is a bacterial disease of the intestine, the *V. cholerae* organisms must be ingested with food or water if they are to make a person ill. Moreover, sufficient numbers of bacteria must be ingested in order to induce an illness; one or two will not cause cholera. (Those who are ill with cholera may excrete as many as 100 million organisms per milliliter of stool and may produce up to 10 liters or more of stool a day.)

Travelers can best prevent becoming infected by avoiding foods and drinks that might be fecally con-

The risk to travelers of contracting cholera is low, even in cholera-endemic areas of less developed countries—if they are careful about hygiene and what they eat and drink. Those who assume the native lifestyle may be at high risk.

taminated with large numbers of *V. cholerae* bacteria. Certain foods and drinks are more likely than others to be contaminated and thus should definitely be avoided in cholera-endemic areas. These include raw or undercooked fish or seafood dishes; food from street vendors, especially if eaten at room temperature; and drinks that are sold by street vendors or served in restaurants and that may be made with contaminated water or ice. The rare cases of cholera that have occurred in recent years in the United States have almost always been due to undercooked seafoods, especially crabs, from the Gulf Coast.

Though municipal water supplies are improving in many areas, travelers still should avoid drinking the local tap water; it is always safer to rely on boiled, bottled, or chemically treated water. The bacteria are easily killed by heating, so boiled water and cooked foods (if served hot) are safe. Carbonated soft drinks, too, are usually okay, and fruits that can be peeled are also safe. Because *V. cholerae* are killed by acidity, they are normally rendered harmless by the acidic conditions in the stomach. People taking antacids or other medications that decrease stomach acid must take extra precautions to avoid contaminated food and water. If not killed in the stomach, the bacteria can slip through to the more favorable conditions of the intestine.

A new epidemic strain

During the last two centuries, cholera has spread through the world in a series of seven pandemics—a pandemic being an epidemic involving many countries. Whether cholera occurred in Europe prior to the 1800s is still controversial, but it is clear that during the colonial period cholera spread from its "home base" in the Ganges delta in India to other parts of Asia, as well as to Europe and the Americas. The most recent (seventh) pandemic began in Indonesia in the early 1960s and over a period of several years spread to most Asian and African countries. Finally, in 1991, an explosive outbreak of cholera occurred in Peru and subsequently spread to nearly all South and Central American countries. For reasons that are still not understood, countries in the Caribbean have not been affected.

The bacterial strain responsible for this pandemic is El Tor *V. cholerae* 01. Though several hundreds of thousands of cases have occurred in Latin America since the epidemic struck in 1991, case fatality rates have generally been low (about 1%). Historically, this marks the first major epidemic in which treatment has kept up with the caseload, and it is thus a significant accomplishment for the health systems in the countries affected. Recently the numbers of cases reported to the Pan American Health Organization from most Latin-American countries have begun to decline,

Cholera in the Americas*			
	1991	1992	1993
Argentina	0	553	2,070
Belize	0	159	135
Bolivia	206	22,260	9,189
Brazil	2,101	30,054	49,956
Chile	41	73	28
Colombia	11,979	15,129	230
Ecuador	46,320	31,870	6,347
El Salvador	947	8,106	6,573
Guatemala	3,674	15,395	30,604
Guyana	0	556	66
Honduras	11	384	1,925
Mexico	2,690	8,162	10,712
Nicaragua	1	3,067	6,473
Panama	1,178	2,416	42
Peru	322,562	212,642	71,448
United States	26	103	18
Venezuela	13	2,842	409

* fewer than 20 cases reported in any single year from French Guiana, Paraguay, Suriname, and Costa Rica

Source: Pan American Health Organization

"Bengal cholera": epidemic in Bangladesh*			
clinical features	southern Bangladesh	Matlab Bazar	Dhaka
age of patients	all ages	all ages	adults
watery diarrhea	100%	99.6%	100%
mean duration of diarrhea before hospitalization	under 12 hours	19.2 hours	10.9 hours
severe dehydration	75%	55%	94%
vomiting	97%	86%	98%

*based on samples of patients admitted to hospitals in early 1993 with new strain of cholera

Adapted from Cholera Working Group, International Centre for Diarrhoeal Diseases Research, "Large Epidemic of Cholera-like Disease in Bangladesh Caused by *Vibrio cholera* 0139 Synonym Bengal," *The Lancet*, vol. 342 (Aug. 14, 1993), pp. 387–390

although Central America, Mexico, and Brazil are still having to deal with an increasing incidence.

In October 1992, as the seventh pandemic continued, an epidemic of cholera-like illness with pandemic potential broke out in Madras, India, and subsequently the responsible bacterium, designated *V. cholerae* 0139 ("Bengal cholera"), caused major outbreaks in other parts of India and in Bangladesh and spread to many neighboring countries, including Pakistan, Nepal, Thailand, Malaysia, and southern China. Additionally, imported cases have been seen in Hong Kong, Japan, the United States, and Europe, but they have not been associated with any spread within these countries. The symptoms produced by the Bengal strain are identical to those caused by earlier strains, and treatment is the same. The risk to travelers from *V. cholerae* 0139 is no different from that of other *V. cholerae*—i.e., minimal. However, the appearance of the new strain is important because those who reside in cholera-endemic areas had developed a degree of immunity to earlier strains of the bacterium but have no immunity against Bengal cholera.

New cholera vaccines

The formerly required cholera vaccine is not useful. It caused unacceptable side effects, required an injection, and induced only minimal protection (about 50%) for a short term (six months). Now, however, new vaccines are being developed for old strains as well as the new Bengal strain. These candidate vaccines fall into two general categories: killed, oral vaccines and live-attenuated vaccines. The former consist of killed *V. cholerae* bacteria mixed with a portion of the cholera toxin. The vaccines are given by mouth along with an antacid in a regimen involving two or three doses. In limited field trials thus far, there have been no evident side effects from the killed-bacteria vaccines. It is likely, however, that booster doses of these vaccines will be needed every few years by persons at risk for cholera.

A killed vaccine that was tested in Bangladesh in the 1980s was found to be completely safe and to decrease rates of cholera infection in adults by about 50% to 70% for about three years. Children under the age of five, however, were protected for only one year. Thus, if this vaccine is used, booster doses will be required more frequently for the younger age group. In 1994 two additional field trials of killed vaccines were under way in Peru to determine whether the vaccine performs as well in Latin America as it did in Bangladesh.

The live vaccines, which are also given orally, consist of *V. cholerae* bacteria that have been altered genetically to make them safe; the bacteria are still capable of minimal replication. The main advantage of the live vaccines is that they have the potential to protect against cholera after a single dose; booster doses thus will be needed less frequently. One live vaccine was found to be safe and effective in volunteers from nonendemic areas (Swiss and North American adults) and is currently being tested in a WHO-sponsored field trial in 66,000 people in North Jakarta, Indonesia. Additional studies will be needed to determine if and when these vaccines should be used routinely as public health measures in cholera-endemic countries. Both killed and live vaccines for the Bengal strain have been developed and can be added to existing new vaccines, but testing of these is still at an early stage. For travelers, even though their risk is slight, these vaccines will be available within the next few years.

Future outlook

Cholera continues to be a serious public health problem in less developed countries. Now that physicians have an understanding of how it is spread and how to treat it, the disease is no longer the threat that it once was. Still, treatment must be available and given promptly; there is no time to waste.

The main control measure that eliminated cholera as a risk in the United States and Europe was improved water and sanitation. Unfortunately, these are improvements that will take decades in most less developed countries. Hence, strategies to control death from cholera have focused mainly on ensuring that good treatment is available and on teaching inhabitants of cholera-endemic countries behaviors that decrease the risk of consuming contaminated food and water. Though cholera is a dread disease that will not soon be confined to history books, effective new vaccines are likely to be available soon that will be a substantial addition to the existing tools available to reduce its impact.

Midlife: The Crisis Reconsidered

by Robert Atkinson, Ph.D.

I T WAS ONCE THOUGHT THAT A PERSON HAD reached the limits of growth upon entering adulthood. According to prominent psychologists at the beginning of this century, life's major struggles and traumas were faced in childhood and adolescence; by the time people became adults, all was pretty much smooth sailing. Adulthood was seen by Sigmund Freud, the founder of psychoanalysis, and the American psychologist and educator G. Stanley Hall as a "mature" time.

Though that turn-of-the-century view of adulthood prevailed for a while, it was a narrow one that overlooked the views and experience of many earlier influential thinkers. As far back as the 14th century, for example, Dante described his own midlife situation quite differently in his monumental epic poem, *The Divine Comedy.* In the opening canto of *Inferno,* he writes: "I found myself in a dark wood, for the straight way was lost. Ah, how hard it is to tell what that wood was, wild, rugged, harsh; the very thought of it renews the fear! It is so bitter that death is hardly more so." It was not until the 1930s, however, with the pioneering work of the Swiss psychologist Carl Jung, that the various stages of adulthood were considered worthy of serious study.

By the 1970s the view that all of adulthood was a tranquil and uncomplicated time had been turned completely around. Dante's experience became the metaphor for the middle adult years. Popularized by Gail Sheehy's *Passages: Predictable Crises of Adult Life,* the phenomenon of the "midlife crisis" burst upon Western society's consciousness. Considering the extent to which the world had changed since the beginning of the century, it seemed quite reasonable that crisis might characterize midlife. Not only were people living longer, thus extending their middle years, but family life and society itself had altered appreciably and had become much more complex.

Robert Atkinson, Ph.D., is Associate Professor of Human Development and Director of the Center for the Study of Lives at the University of Southern Maine, Gorham.

Illustrations by Tim Jonke

Today a major *new* understanding of the middle adult years is emerging, providing a more hopeful picture—one that sees the life cycle as a whole and, most important, that puts "predictable crises" into their proper perspective. This new view recognizes that adults continue to grow and adapt to the various demands and roles of adult life, undergoing major physical and emotional changes in the process. Often they experience a transformation at midlife, becoming reinvigorated and recommitted to living the rest of life more fully.

An all-new scenario

The shift that can occur around midlife is now seen as a normal, healthy, and vital period of personal growth. No longer are the middle adult years viewed only, or primarily, as a time of crisis. Today's enlightened view appreciates middle age as the longest and perhaps *most* challenging developmental period of all. A considerable body of recent literature explains, among other things, why there are new and shifting commitments at midlife, why menopause is a crucial rite of passage, why there is so-called gender crossover, and why "caring for the soul" becomes important.

Books such as Mark Gerzon's *Coming into Our Own: Understanding the Adult Metamorphosis,* Cathleen Rountree's *Coming into Our Fullness: On Women Turning Forty* and *On Women Turning 50: Celebrating Mid-Life Discoveries,* Germaine Greer's *The Change: Women, Aging and the Menopause,* Faye Kitchener Cone's *Making Sense of Menopause,* and many others offer inspiring stories about real people who have found a "new lease on life" upon reaching middle age. While there may still be crises to face, it is now appreciated that a critical component of experiencing a crisis is being able to see it through to a resolution.

A multicultural perspective

In the context of a normal, socially prescribed rite of passage, a "crisis" is the halfway point through a natural process. If one focuses on only one part of a complete and purposeful process, one may miss the intent of the whole. People in traditional cultures accepted that the life cycle comprised stages and that getting through the times of transition was a natural process. They did not fear the middle (*i.e.,* the conflict or crisis) part of the process; they knew that it would lead to a resolution. Moreover, they had clearly defined, socially prescribed rituals that made it possible for them to see their way through each normal transition—without undue strife and in a reasonable period of time.

In fact, because of the central role that storytelling played in their lives, they were quite familiar with the process. Every traditional folktale or myth followed a similar pattern: a protagonist encounters adversity, which he or she must—and does—overcome. People therefore trusted that somehow the conflicts in their own lives would be resolved, that the ogre would be vanquished, or that an ally would be found in the wilderness who would help them see their way out.

It is notable that it was not a psychologist but a French ethnographer and folklorist who first laid the foundation for understanding the complexities of adult development. In *The Rites of Passage* (1909), Arnold van Gennep systematically described those ceremonies that celebrate an individual's transitions from one status to another within a given culture. "The life of an individual in any society is a series of passages from one age to another," Gennep wrote. He identified three very basic phases that constitute the scheme of all rites of passage. First, there is *separation* from the familiar and from the group. Next is a *transition,* in which the individual acquires new knowledge and new status. Finally, there is *incorporation,* or a return to the group, where the individual assumes his or her new role and carries out the functions associated with that position.

In the context of such traditional rites of passage, the contemporary midlife crisis can be viewed as an *incomplete* transition. When the process is allowed to complete itself, it will bring about a redefinition of roles, priorities, and values. Anthropologists have found that in many cultures, reaching middle age does not produce psychological stress and turmoil. The so-called midlife crisis, rather, is a culture-specific phenomenon, found primarily among people in today's technologically advanced Western societies. In fact, it may be Western society's *lack* of rituals designed to guide people through important transitions that makes midlife such a difficult time. Menopause, for example, tends to be much less problematic—both physically and emotionally—in societies where postmenopausal women become respected elders of their community, gaining power and status that they did not have during their childbearing years. As an example, Mayan women do not report having hot flashes, a menopausal symptom that women in many other cultures find extremely disturbing.

Of course, cultural differences within a pluralistic society can account for important variations in the way individuals experience the middle adult years. In the United States, for example, an adult member of a minority group who has to deal with destructive stereotypes that are perpetuated in everyday life—on television and in literature, movies, advertising, etc.—may have an especially difficult time getting through normal midlife changes. Members of certain ethnic groups that maintain close ties to their cultural heritage may experience struggles and challenges that are unique and that complicate the passage through midlife—especially when the values and traditions of that heritage are in conflict with mainstream values. On the other hand, it is also likely that a person from a strong traditional background, who is familiar with the natural pattern described above and whose culture provides rituals for getting through major life transitions, would be *better* able to cope with midlife difficulties than someone who lacks that familiarity and does not have prescribed rituals.

Over the hill at 40?

In contemporary industrial societies, where the average life span exceeds 75 years, age 40 has typically been considered the great divide between the first half of life and the last half. Even in earlier times, when life spans were much shorter, such a critical halfway-through-life juncture was recognized. Dante, who lived until the ripe "old" age of 56, identified such a midway marker. Jung broke new ground in psychology by comparing

63

midlife to noon in the daily course of the Sun; it is around the "noon" of life, which he saw as beginning between the 35th and 40th years, that a significant change in the human psyche is most likely to take place.

Today 40 no longer seems to hold the symbolic significance that it once had. People often do not feel the impact of having lived half their lives until the mid- or late 40s, or even age 50—if indeed at all. This may be due to what author Lydia Bronte calls the "longevity factor." Not only are people living longer—an average 25 years longer than at the beginning of the century and often into their eighth or ninth decades—but they are also maintaining more productive lives. Extended careers, better health, and increased opportunities have led to richer lives.

In *The Longevity Factor: The New Reality of Long Careers and How It Can Lead to Richer Lives,* Bronte describes a "second middle age," a time between 50 and 76, which is characterized by continued activity, greater vitality, and a more positive outlook. Bronte conducted interviews with 115 people aged 65 to 102 about their working lives. Over 60% reported that they never retired or planned to retire; nearly half said they reached a peak in their work after age 50; and many had made major achievements after the age of 60. Perhaps the most committed and personally involved student this author has ever had was a 70-year-old woman who had not been a student since she left medical school in her 20s to get married. Exactly 50 years after getting her undergraduate degree, she received her master's degree in adult education and gerontology. Then she decided to get her divinity degree—at age 72!

In many ways, age per se seems irrelevant in contemporary society. In fact, many scientists now maintain that the biological potential of the average healthy adult is about 120 years; midlife would then be closer to age 60. "Aging brings out the flavor of a personality," writes psychotherapist and best-selling author Thomas Moore in *Care of the Soul: A Guide for Cultivating Depth and Sacredness in Everyday Life.* Moore's point is that the "soul," which he describes as "a quality or a dimension of experiencing life and ourselves [that] has to do with depth, value, relatedness, heart, and personal substance," is not linked to the confines of physical life. Rather, the life of the soul goes on forever.

Biological changes: real but relative

Significant biological and physical changes occur for both women and men at or around midlife. Most people reach a peak in biological functioning at around 28 to 32, after which gradual shifts can begin to be noticed. By their 40s most people are aware that their bodies are slowing down; at the same time, the aging process begins to feel as if it is speeding up. This is often the time that people become aware of "middle-age spread"; they may start worrying about their cholesterol and blood pressure levels; they come to dislike the accumulating gray hairs; and they wonder whether they are remembering as well as they used to. There are, in fact, declines and losses. But the gains may be more important.

For men, though the changes are gradual, after age 40 it probably will take longer and require more breath to get around the bases in a softball game. In lovemaking, reaction time may also be somewhat slower, but staying power is often greater, allowing for a deeper, more intimate relationship. Though gradual drops in male hormone levels between the ages of 48 and 70 have been noted, there is no definitive indication that men undergo any precipitous changes in performance, strength, or inherent "maleness" in the second half of life. Moreover, many scientific questions would need to be resolved before middle-aged men were given testosterone supplements to maintain virility or ward off the aging process.

For women there is the dramatic change called menopause, which signals the cessation of the menstrual cycle and, as a rule, the ability to bear children. With menopause, ovarian estrogen production ceases, which may cause some disturbing physical symptoms. These include hot flashes, nighttime sweating, dryness of the vagina, and painful intercourse. Hormonal changes may also cause mood disturbances and a decline in sexual desire. Long-term effects include increased risk for heart disease and osteoporosis. Hormone replacement therapy can alleviate many of the short-term symptoms and minimize the long-term risks. However, estrogen supplements are not appropriate for all women.

Whereas in previous centuries women may not have lived long enough to go through menopause, today the average woman can expect to live a full 30 or more years beyond it. Unfortunately, menopause in present-day Western society is often perceived negatively. One of the major conclusions of a March 1993 workshop on menopause sponsored by the National Institutes of Health (NIH) was that menopause tends to be associated with illness and is often "treated" as a medical condition rather than as a normal life transition. This perception affects women's expectations about and probably the way they manage menopause.

Nevertheless, more and more women are discovering that the "change of life" is not something to be dreaded or feared and, furthermore, that the experience tends to be highly individualized. Although there may be discomforts, as there are with all life transitions, one can emerge from the experience feeling healthier, freer, and more confident—a phenomenon that anthropologist Margaret Mead aptly called "postmenopausal zest."

In *Drawing from the Women's Well: Reflections on the Life Passage of Menopause,* author Joan Borton invokes the traditional rite of passage to explain and honor menopause. She moves it from a passive state that is endured silently and alone to an active state shared with other women— where women consciously engage in changing and in "joining the community of our elders." This transformation is "life giving and thus sacred, connecting us with the Divine," says Borton. There is a great potential for spiritual learning when the choice is made to cooperate with "nature's amazing balancing process." The real *change* is not just a body event but a soul event, which Borton describes as becoming "one with the Mystery of life itself."

Embracing the experience of menopause rather than viewing it as an illness enables women to address important spiritual and emotional needs. A recent survey of over 500 U.S. women aged 41 to 55 found that the real issues that concerned them as they approached menopause were not physical ones such as hot flashes but matters such as relationships, the "empty-nest syndrome," and career assessment.

Indeed, there is more to the second half of life than holding back the tides of time. The acclaimed feminist author Betty Friedan suggests that the key to getting through midlife without crisis is not to look upon aging only as a decline from youth. If people hold that limited view, they "make age itself the problem," she writes in her book *The Fountain of Age*—published when she was 72. On the basis of her own extensive research, Friedan concludes that decline in various capacities with age is neither universal nor predictable. Those who view old age as yet another stage of potential development instead of as a terminal disease continue to have vitality and be productive and find many *new* possibilities for growth.

Elder tales: lessons for the second half of life

The 19th-century German philosopher Arthur Schopenhauer wrote: "The first forty years of life furnish the text, while the remaining thirty supply the commentary." Today, owing to the longevity factor, a few more years must be added to the commentary part, but Schopenhauer's premise—that people live the story of their lives in the first half and interpret or embellish those stories in the second half—is worth considering. The ability to see one's life as a comprehensible story may offer a key to prosperity and happiness. That, in fact, is what psychotherapy is all about—telling one's story to someone who can help interpret and make sense of it.

As noted earlier, in many traditional cultures stories have been told for centuries. Handed down and tested over many generations, myths and folktales are rich with human experience and wisdom; they are symbolic expressions of the human journey through life that provide insight and guidance. The French social anthropologist Claude Lévi-Strauss observed that stories are central to people's lives because they offer imaginary resolutions to real-life contradictions.

In most Western cultures storytelling plays an important part in the instruction and entertainment of children. "Fairy tales," however, are not only for children. "Real life does not end with youth or eternal happiness," points out psychiatrist Allan B. Chinen, who has compiled and interpreted "elder tales" from many cultures. His books *Once upon a Midlife: Classic Stories and Mythic Tales to Illuminate the Middle Years* and *In the Ever After: Fairy Tales and the Second Half of Life* offer traditional stories in which the protagonists are grown-ups and the lessons are "adult" ones. These elder tales are about the struggles, yearnings, and dilemmas of ordinary people in the second half of life. They warn of the difficulties that advancing years may bring but, more important, they preview the "promise and potential" still to come. Consider one example, "Fortune and the Woodcutter," an elder tale from Asia Minor, as Chinen retells it:

Once upon a time, there lived an old woodcutter with his wife. He labored each day in the forest, from dawn to dusk, cutting wood to sell in the village. But no matter how hard he struggled, he could not succeed in life, and what he earned in the day, he and his family ate up at night. . . .

After twenty years, the old man finally had enough. "I've worked for Fortune all my life," he exclaimed to his wife, "and she has given us little enough for it. From now on," the old man swore, "if Fortune wants to give us anything, she will have to come looking for me." And the woodcutter vowed to work no more.

. . . In fact, he decided to stay in bed.

Later that day, a stranger came knocking at the door and asked if he· could borrow the old man's mules. . . . The stranger explained that he had some work to do in the forest, and that he noticed the woodcutter was not using his mules. The old man agreed. . . .

The stranger then took the mules deep into the forest. He was no ordinary man, but a magician, and through his arts, he had learned where a great treasure lay. So he went to the spot and dug up heaps of gold and jewels, loading the booty on the two mules. But just as he prepared to leave, gloating over his new wealth, soldiers came marching down the road. The stranger became frightened. He . . . fled into the forest and was never seen or heard from again.

The soldiers went along their way, noticing nothing unusual, and so the two mules waited undisturbed in the forest. After many hours, they started for home on their own, following the trails they had used with the woodcutter for many years.

When they arrived at the woodcutter's home, his wife . . . ran to the mules and slashed the bags on their backs to lighten the load. Gold and jewels poured out, flashing in the sun.

"Gold! Jewels!" she exclaimed. In a flash, her husband was downstairs, and he stared in astonishment at the treasure spilling into their yard. Then he grabbed his wife and they danced deliriously. "Fortune did come to us after all!" he exulted.

And when the old man and his wife gave half their treasure to their sons and half the remainder to the poor, they were still as rich as rich could be!

What this elder tale is really about is the loss and the return of magic. For the woodcutter the hope and vigor of youth are gone, but when he least expects it, "magic" in the form of riches comes to him. Late in life he reaps his reward—the wealth gained for having worked long and hard in his younger years. The woodcutter's fortune is indeed a return on his investment. The elder's task, Chinen points out, is to be open to unexpected magic. "All too often adults dismiss the possibility of 'happy endings' in later life, and resign themselves to a slow decline."

Realizing the value of stories, middle-aged adults today are increasingly sharing their tales—in books, in formal workshops, and in informal support groups. Women, in particular, are joining together to dispel long-held myths and misconceptions about menopause; they are learning that life is not all downhill after age 40—that the "change of life" can signal a time of newfound freedom and blossoming.

Indeed, there is a power in the stories of others that helps people make sense of their own lives. Others' stories reveal the ways in which real people have endured deep change in their lives, drawing upon hidden inner resources. Such stories both inspire and invite introspection and help people realize their own inner strengths and potential to change and be renewed.

At the recent NIH workshop, women-to-women exchanges were cited as a key source of information about menopause. Women need to validate their own experiences, and other women are often seen as more credible sources than doctors because the issues of greatest concern to them are psychosocial rather than medical. Rountree, who has been leading workshops for women in their 40s and 50s for several years, has found that "women are comforted to hear the stories of other women and grateful to see how those women have changed their lives. Living examples remain the best source of inspiration."

Not a crisis after all

More and more people are discovering that midlife is not necessarily a time of crisis. Rather, it is a time of *quest.* Midlife can signal a quest for wholeness, a quest for integrity, a quest for love, a quest for independence as well as interdependence, or a quest for the "sacred." It can be a time for the healing of old "wounds" or for finding one's true calling.

Quest for wholeness. For many the midlife quest is for wholeness. Jung believed that in the second half of life people begin to discover and express qualities in themselves that were underdeveloped or neglected in the first half, and in doing so they achieve wholeness and balance. Gerzon compares the metamorphosis that occurs around midlife to that of a caterpillar becoming a butterfly. No one reaches the second half of life whole; everyone has been injured physically, psychologically, or spiritually, though some people may not be aware of those wounds. Those who do not resist or deny change will find that a new "self" is waiting to emerge.

Quest for love. Another common midlife quest is for love. There are often reevaluations of relationships and a search for deeper intimacy. Men and women may seek to free themselves from sex-role limitations and allow both the "masculine" and "feminine" in themselves to merge. In this quest for love, people search for "soul mates" who can be partners on a spiritual journey.

Finding one's calling. Today, with the average career spanning five or more decades, it is rare for most people to know what kind of work will satisfy them when they take their first job. Eventually, many begin looking for something that is more creative and fulfilling. Because people need to express themselves in their work, they begin to listen to their own inner voices to guide them to their "true calling." Success in the second half

does not always look the same as it did in the first. External achievements may no longer be primary. Many people become more attuned to internal feelings and recognize a desire to be of service to others. The midlife challenge becomes one of following their own dreams, and a midlife career change may provide the path to transformation.

A recent issue of *Fortune* magazine profiled middle-aged men and women in widely varied jobs who "beat" their midlife career crises and found new paths to job satisfaction and personal growth. A 38-year-old former banker took a huge cut in salary in order to join the staff of a major metropolitan newspaper as an editorial writer. What he lost in pay he gained in personal fulfillment. A 43-year-old executive at General Motors gave up her supervisory position to become a truck designer for the same company. An equal opportunity officer in Alabama was tired of paperwork, so he joined a construction crew for six months. He said he wanted to build "something tangible, like a bridge"—something he would be able to show his grandchildren.

Quest for the sacred. One of the most universal midlife needs is to overcome spiritual passivity—to begin "caring for the soul." Usually this means bringing some kind of regular discipline into one's daily life. "Taking an interest in one's own soul requires a certain amount of space for reflection and appreciation," says Moore in *Care of the Soul.* "A little distance" enables people to understand and cherish their own complexity. For some, discovering new meaning and purpose in life may come through achieving union with a "higher power"; for others, the quest involves cultivating what Moore calls "an appreciation for vernacular spirituality," which enables them "to see the sacred dimension of everyday life."

Indeed, midlife is much more than a time of crisis. It is in the second half of life that people discover what is personally sacred—what matters to them most in this life and beyond. Learning what that is may be the greatest midlife challenge of all.

Violence: America's Deadliest Epidemic

by George A. Gellert,
M.D., M.P.H., M.P.A.

THE UNITED STATES IS EASILY THE MOST violent of the peaceful industrialized countries (that is, those not engaged in civil war). Each year more than 1.5 million individuals are victims of assault. Every day more than 60 Americans are homicide victims. Among black men aged 15–24, homicide is the leading cause of death, and in the last 30 years homicide rates for children and adolescents have more than doubled. Violence between partners occurs at some time in 6 of every 10 marriages. A staggering two million to four million women are beaten by their male partners each year, more than 650,000 women are victims of rape, and 6–17% of women are physically assaulted during pregnancy. In 1991 two million to four million American children were abused or neglected by parents or guardians, and more than one million elderly people were mistreated by family members.

These statistics probably underestimate the true extent of the problem. More people are in U.S. prisons today than ever before, yet violence persists. In many quarters there is a growing sense that a "law-and-order" approach alone cannot substantially reduce levels of violence. Because violence is so prevalent and ubiquitous, and because U.S. society seems to accept violence, many have argued that violence in America is inevitable—a basic expression of American culture and values. Public health practitioners, however, argue that no civilized society should be so permeated by firearm assault, homicide, rape, and child abuse. They see violence in America as a social problem—indeed, as a public health emergency that demands immediate attention and corrective action.

For the purposes of this article, violence is defined as any abusive human action, usually intentional, directed against another person, which may result in injury. While violence is a worldwide problem and often involves international warfare and civil conflicts, the focus here is on the epidemic of violence now affecting the United States.

George A. Gellert, M.D., M.P.H., M.P.A., is Director of Medical Programs and Senior Consultant for Epidemiology/Public Health, Project Hope Health Sciences Education Center, Millwood, Virginia.

Friends come to view the body of 11-year-old Neil Maddox, the victim of a drive-by shooting in Chicago; photograph, Greg Mellis—Copley News Service

Starting in the home

Domestic violence is an extensive, pervading problem in the United States. It is an outrage to women and the entire American family.

—Office of the U.S. surgeon general, June 1992

Domestic violence may touch as many as one in four of all American families. Abusers perceive themselves as lacking power in their general environment and compensate for this by exerting power in relation to other members of the family. The perpetrators display their hostilities against a weaker target who cannot retaliate. David Finkelhor, a researcher in the field of domestic violence, has shown that abuse tends to involve relationships within the family where the greatest power differentials exist. Thus, the most common pattern of abuse is for the most powerful to abuse the least powerful family member; a father abuses the youngest child, for example.

Prior to the 1970s, violence in the family was thought to be infrequent and was not seen as a societywide problem. A recent survey of intact married couples found that nearly one of every eight husbands had carried out one or more acts of physical aggression against his female partner during the prior year; over one-third of these assaults involved severe aggression such as punching, kicking, choking, or using a knife or a gun. Even after marriages have been terminated through separation or divorce, women often continue to be victims of abuse by former spouses. Researchers generally believe that domestic violence involving women is underreported. There are frequently strong social and familial pressures not to report such violence. Fear of reprisal and emotional denial may contribute to underreporting.

Domestic violence between siblings is not uncommon, and research indicates that children learn about violence from witnessing abuse between parents. Corporal punishment may also be viewed as a form of domestic violence. In one study 40% of parents who used corporal punishment said that it occurred when they had had a bad day and that it bore no relation

Police in Minneapolis, Minnesota, arrest a man for attacking his wife. Domestic violence may occur in as many as one in four American families. Children who witness their father battering their mother are often profoundly traumatized by the event. Men who batter women frequently abuse children as well. The perpetrators of such violence generally perceive themselves as lacking power, and they take out their frustrations on weaker family members.

© 1991 Donna Ferrato—Domestic Abuse Awareness Project, New York City

to the child's behavior. Researchers have demonstrated that the later into adolescence a child was physically punished, the more likely it is that that person will subsequently abuse his or her own children. Five nations—Sweden, Norway, Finland, Switzerland, and Austria—now prohibit all forms of corporal punishment in homes as well as schools.

In the broad category of parent-child violence, adolescents are often overlooked. It is assumed that the majority of victims of child abuse are small children. Recent research, however, has revealed that adolescence is more abuse-ridden than early childhood. Adolescents experience not only disproportionately high levels of abuse but the most severe forms of abuse—those that result in serious injury or death. Youths aged 12–17 years constitute 38% of the child population, but 47% of the victims of all forms of child maltreatment are in this age group. Those in the 15–17 age group represent 19% of the child population, yet they experience 27% of the serious injuries and 23% of the fatalities that result from child abuse. As in the abuse of small children, the perpetrators of such violence are most frequently parents.

Violence against teens often extends beyond the home. A recent Justice Department report noted that U.S. teenagers are more likely than any other group to be victims of violent crime. In the 1980s surveys reported that 67 of every 1,000 teenagers were victims of rape, robbery, or assault annually, compared with 26 of every 1,000 adults. In 1990, 4,200 teens aged 15–19 years died from gunshot wounds. James Mason, a former assistant secretary of health and human services and head of the U.S. Public Health Service, noted that if the cause of these deaths were polio or untreated appendicitis, physicians would be taking action. He and many others now believe that physicians should be taking an active role in addressing the epidemic of violence.

Unsafe schools

The personal safety and security of young people are in jeopardy in schools across America. A 1991 national survey found that 26% of students in grades 9 through 12 reported carrying a weapon at least once during the prior 30 days. In New York City during the 1991–92 school year, 36% of all 9th- through 12th-grade public-school students reported being threatened by violence at school, and 25% were involved in a physical fight at school or outside school.

Physical fighting, a common form of interpersonal violence among adolescents, is a prominent cause of injuries and homicides. In one survey nearly 8% of all students in grades 9 through 12 reported that during the preceding 30 days they had been in at least one physical fight that resulted in injury requiring treatment by a doctor or nurse. Of these students, almost half had fought two or more times. The incidence of physical fighting was four times higher for male students than for female students and was highest for black male students, followed by Hispanic male students and then white male students.

Preventing physical fighting among young persons should be an important public health strategy for curtailing the overall incidence of violence-

Homicides in the home*	
detail	%
sex of victim	
female	36.9
male	63.1
race or ethnic group of victim	
white	33.3
black	61.9
Native American, Eskimo, Aleut	1.0
Asian or Pacific islander	1.7
other	2.1
age group of victim	
15–24	13.8
25–40	40.7
41–60	25.2
61 and over	20.2
circumstances	
altercation or quarrel	44.0
romantic triangle	6.9
murder or suicide	4.5
felony-related	21.9
drug dealing	7.6
homicide only	13.3
other	1.7
relationship of offender to victim	
spouse	16.7
intimate acquaintance	13.8
first-degree relative	9.5
other relative	2.9
roommate	2.9
friend or acquaintance	31.0
police officer	1.0
stranger	3.6
unknown (unidentified suspect)	17.4
other	1.4
method of homicide	
handgun	42.9
rifle	2.4
shotgun	3.6
unknown firearm	1.0
knife or sharp instrument	26.4
blunt instrument	11.7
strangulation or suffocation	6.4
burns, smoke, scalding	2.4
other	3.3
victim resisted assailant	
yes	43.8
no	33.3
not noted	22.9
evidence of forced entry	
yes	14.0
no	84.3
not noted	1.7

*based on data from 420 homicides in three U.S. metropolitan counties: Shelby county, Tennessee, King county, Washington, and Cuyahoga county, Ohio

Adapted from Arthur L. Kellermann, M.D., M.P.H., et al., "Gun Ownership as a Risk Factor for Homicide in the Home," New England Journal of Medicine, vol. 329, no.15 (Oct. 7, 1993), pp. 1084–91

Student attitudes about violence*		
	students involved in a physical fight (%)	students who carry a weapon to school (%)
effective way to avoid a fight		
threaten weapon use	36.2	43.9
carry a weapon	35.1	47.9
avoid/ walk away	35.5	43.8
apologize	19.0	24.5
family supports violent means of self-defense		
fighting	77.9	76.7
weapon use	54.8	67.5
feel safer with a weapon in a fight		
knife	48.9	64.2
handgun	50.7	60.5

*based on a survey of 1,339 9th–12th graders in New York City public schools

Source: "Violence-Related Attitudes and Behaviors of High School Students—New York City, 1992," *Morbidity and Mortality Weekly Report*, vol. 42, no. 40 (Oct. 15, 1993), pp. 773–777

related injuries and deaths. The demographic patterns of physical fighting are consistent with those that characterize homicide; the prevalence is greater among males and minorities than among females and nonminorities, and both occur most frequently among persons who know each other. Such similarities suggest that physical fighting is part of a spectrum of violent behavior that may ultimately culminate in homicide.

A 1992 survey of high-school students in Seattle, Washington, sought to determine the prevalence of handgun ownership. The findings were startling: 34% of students reported easy access to handguns, and 6.4% reported owning a handgun. Males were more likely to report both. A high rate of handgun use was reported, with 33% of student handgun owners stating that they had fired at someone. Gang membership, drug selling, suspension or expulsion from school, and assault and battery were associated with handgun ownership. The researchers concluded that the ready access to handguns of students in Seattle was probably representative of the availability of firearms to urban high-school students nationwide.

Gun-related victimization among inner-city youths in schools far exceeds that of students nationally. Whereas 2% of the nation's students report being victims of some sort of violence, 23% of inner-city students in one study had been victims of gun-related violence. Schools themselves do not generate this violence as much as they represent the location where violence stemming from forces outside the institution is played out. Gun-related violence in schools and on the way to and from schools often occurs because students come from social settings where carrying and using guns is commonplace.

It is uncertain whether increased security measures in and around schools will reduce levels of gun-related victimization. Many schools where children are carrying firearms already have tight security. Little difference has been found in the rates of violence between schools with and without conventional security measures such as patrolled hallways and visitor check-ins. Approximately one-fourth of large urban school districts in the

Students at an Indianapolis, Indiana, high school undergo a surprise weapons check. Weapon use among school-age children is a growing national problem. As many as one-quarter of high schools in large urban areas of the U.S. have installed metal detectors to curtail student violence. Tight security measures, however, may not be the solution. At least one study has shown that students who attend schools that have metal detectors still carry and use weapons; they simply do not take them into the school building.

Kelly Wilkinson—Indianapolis Star/Sipa

Volunteers for the "safe corridor" program patrol the streets of a high-crime neighborhood in North Philadelphia so that children can get to and from school safely. Before this program began, youngsters were frequently the victims of violent crimes.

U.S. have gone to the lengths of installing metal detectors in hopes of reducing weapon carrying. According to one survey, students who attended schools with metal detectors were as likely to carry and use weapons as those attending schools without detectors; they were just less likely to take the weapon inside the school building. Public health practitioners believe that a more direct form of intervention in the lives of youths at risk for school-related violence is needed. However, the ability to identify those at risk before they engage in or are victims of violence is seriously limited. It is clear that the problem of violence in inner-city schools cannot be isolated from the problem in greater society. Violent neighborhoods and communities will produce violent youths who attend schools where violence is played out, whatever measures schools themselves adopt. This larger problem will not yield to simple or single-dimensional solutions.

Women: battered and brutalized

As noted previously, estimates are that at least two million to four million American women each year are physically abused. One study found that violence was the second leading cause of injuries to women and the leading cause of injuries to women aged 15–44 years. As with other forms of violence, abuse of women often occurs at the hands of people the victims know well. According to the FBI, 30% of women killed by an act of violence in the U.S. in 1990 died at the hands of a husband or a boyfriend; more than 800 women were killed by their husbands, and another 400 were killed by their boyfriends. While women are also violent and frequently assault their male partners, they are generally neither as strong nor as large as men and thus inflict less harm. Furthermore, much violence committed by women against men is in self-defense against partners with a history of abusing women.

In the U.S. annually almost 100,000 rapes are reported to police. Actual incidence may be double that number. Officials consider rape to be greatly underreported. Some epidemiological studies have indicated that 20% of

75

adult women, 15% of college women, and 12% of adolescent girls have experienced sexual abuse and assault during their lifetime. Immediate medical concerns after rape include assessment and treatment of injuries and the need to obtain physical evidence for legal documentation. Pregnancy and sexually transmitted diseases are also major health concerns. The acute and long-term psychological effects of rape are often profound. Initial reactions to sexual assault include shock, numbness, withdrawal, and denial. Victims of attacks by strangers acutely fear that their assailant will return and further harm them. Long after the event, there may be self-blame, chronic anxiety, nightmares, sexual dysfunction, and feelings of vulnerability, loss of control, alienation, and isolation. An estimated 17–19% of rape victims make suicide attempts.

In the last 20 years a new national awareness of violence against women has emerged. As data on the prevalence of intimate violence have been gathered, various efforts have been directed at curtailing the problem. Responses have included increased prosecution of males who assault female partners and establishment of advocacy programs, counseling services, hot lines, and shelters for battered women. Nearly every state in the U.S. has now enacted laws addressing violence between adult partners, and rape laws nationwide have been amended to protect victims of assault by marital partners.

More than half of women assaulted by intimates are seriously injured, and at least 25% receive medical care. It has been estimated that 35% of women visiting hospital emergency rooms have symptoms of ongoing abuse. As in other areas of violence prevention, physicians are viewed as a front line for identifying female victims of abuse. However, physicians and other medical staff infrequently have the training necessary for intervention, and many are reluctant to get involved, especially in their patients' domestic affairs.

The American Medical Association believes that there are opportunities for physicians to intervene before intimate violence reaches life-threatening levels. It has recommended that medical professionals routinely screen female patients for victimization and develop treatment plans that address the cause of violent trauma as well as its manifestations. A protocol to assess current or past victimization should include asking nonjudgmental questions such as:

• Are you in a relationship in which you have been physically hurt or threatened by your partner?

• Has your partner ever threatened or abused your children?

• Has your partner ever forced you to have sex when you did not want to?

• Has your partner ever forced you to engage in sex that makes you feel uncomfortable?

• Do you ever feel afraid of your partner?

• Has your partner ever prevented you from leaving the house, seeking friends, getting a job, or continuing your education?

In addition, health care providers should develop links with a variety of resources in their communities to use when they detect victimization of women. These would include shelters for battered women, crisis interven-

Each year two million to four million women in the U.S. are physically abused. Among women aged 15–44, acts of violence are the number one cause of injury.

tion services, abuse hot lines, and counseling and treatment programs for currently abused women, adult survivors of child sexual abuse, and men who abuse women.

A public health emergency

Three consecutive U.S. surgeons general, C. Everett Koop, Antonia Novello, and, presently, M. Joycelyn Elders, have been outspoken about the violence "epidemic" in America, which they view as not only a public health problem but a public health emergency. Although violence is not a disease in the classic sense, its impact on personal and public health is more profound than that of many physiological diseases. Health professionals are firsthand witnesses to the consequences of violence. From the surgeon who removes the bullet from a patient who has been shot to the paramedic who responds to the call of a woman who has been battered by her husband to the pediatrician who sees an abused child in his or her office, doctors and other health professionals regularly diagnose and treat victims of violence and care for their families.

Despite the multiple causes of violence, health professionals have a clear duty to act as leaders in the movement against violence. Physicians not only can report acts of violence but can advocate for changes in economic conditions and insist on expanded access to health care. Health professionals can also inform and educate patients and the general public

Most U.S. states have enacted laws and established programs that address the huge public health problem of violence against women. Nationwide there are well over 1,000 shelters and safe houses for female victims of violence. The women pictured above have sought refuge from abusive male partners at Women's Advocates in St. Paul, Minnesota, which opened in 1974 and was the country's first shelter for battered women. In addition to providing bed, board, and a safe and supportive environment, Women's Advocates offers legal, financial, medical, and job assistance. Abused women can stay up to six weeks at no charge while they put their lives back together.

77

Family and friends grieve for Ramon Sanchez, Jr., a young boy killed by a stray bullet in the Watts area of Los Angeles in 1992. Ramon's funeral was paid for by singer Michael Jackson, who expressed his desire to help the Sanchez family after hearing about its terrible misfortune.

about the causes and effects of violence and support the establishment of violence-prevention programs in schools, clinics, churches, and other centers in the community.

The dramatic increase in societal violence since World War II is as difficult to understand as it is to control. Public health practitioners believe that while the criminal justice system has had and will continue to have an important role in societal efforts to combat violence, law-enforcement measures alone will not be adequate to curb the problem in a lasting way. The incidence of injuries and deaths from violence has continued to increase despite ever greater resources devoted to criminal justice. The criminal justice system relies on arrests and incarcerations to deter and punish offenders. Criminal justice professionals have themselves stated for years that violence is a broad social problem that extends far beyond their purview. Support for this assertion is found in the fact that more than half of all homicides stem from violence that occurs between family members or acquaintances. Furthermore, most injuries attributable to violence result not from criminal activities, such as robbery, but from violent arguments between people who know each other.

The Centers for Disease Control and Prevention (CDC) considers a public health approach essential to resolving the violence problem. A public health model looks at the root causes of violence and seeks to prevent violent acts before they occur. Prevention is far more desirable, humane, and cost-effective than either punishment or treatment after the event. Public health utilizes a systematic approach that depends on surveillance and epidemiological analysis to define risks and on community-based efforts to design and implement appropriate interventions. The same approach can be applied to violence that has been used to control infectious diseases and reduce the incidence of chronic diseases such as cancer and coronary heart disease. Public health campaigns often attempt to change public attitudes, promoting healthy behaviors while discouraging destructive ones. Such a strategy has proved successful in reducing cigarette smoking and

78

drunk driving and in increasing the number of people who engage in physical exercise and have adopted healthier dietary habits.

Despite the important role they can play, as noted previously, physicians on the whole have been reluctant to get involved. One survey of physicians showed that most viewed raising the matter of domestic violence with patients analogous to opening a Pandora's box. Their reasons included fear of offending patients, a sense that they lacked the ability to have an impact on the problem, fear that control of the therapeutic relationship may be lost, time constraints, and lack of training. For some physicians, identification with patients of a similar background also precluded their even considering the possibility of domestic violence as causing a patient's health problems. Many physicians felt that if they broached the subject of violence, patients would be likely to take offense at the implications of their questions. They also voiced concern that if they inquired about violence, it would be viewed by the patient as a betrayal of trust and could endanger the physician-patient relationship. Although they can intervene by referring patients to suitable community resources, physicians expressed fear that their attempts at intervention would not be meaningful—that ultimately the control of domestic violence is in the hands of patients, who may not be motivated to change.

In the aftermath of five days of civil unrest in Los Angeles in April–May 1992, which resulted in 58 deaths, 2,325 reported injuries, and more than 600 buildings completely destroyed by arson, the CDC sent a team of investigators to the city to assess the public health impact of the disturbance and to work with the community to develop ways to prevent future violence. Two strategies are currently being studied in pilot programs. The first is designed to teach young people not to be violent. For example, they are taught conflict-resolution techniques aimed at preventing the escalation of common disagreements to the point where an assault is likely to occur. The second involves intervening with victims of violence while they are still in the hospital emergency department. The thinking behind

Greg Mellis—Copley News Service

Teenagers suspected of drug dealing are frisked by police at an inner-city housing project in Chicago. Drug-related crime in large cities is rampant, and violence is an everyday reality that even the youngest children cannot escape. Many public health experts and, increasingly, government officials believe that national substance-abuse policies have failed. If substance abuse were treated as a public health problem rather than as a criminal justice problem, it is likely that the incidence of violent crime would be substantially reduced.

Relatives attending 11-year-old Neil Maddox's funeral are overcome by the sense of needless loss. Neil's mother believes that her son died because he was with the wrong people at the wrong time. On the night of Sept. 11, 1992, Neil was out with a group of older boys who presumably were trying to recruit him into a Chicago street gang. Five shots were fired into the group from a passing car. One of those bullets, which may have been intended for the gang's leader, struck Neil in the chest. Less than an hour later he was dead.

emergency department intervention is that those who sustain injuries from violent acts are frequently perpetrators of violence. They may go back out on the streets to seek revenge or else become involved in the same types of activities that resulted in their injuries. By reaching people in the hospital when they have been physically harmed by an act of violence, it may be possible to educate them about the risks that certain activities involve. At such a time the wisdom of avoiding violence and the many reasons for resolving conflicts without resorting to violence are likely to be obvious. Although this strategy has an immediacy that other approaches lack, emergency room physicians who encounter the victims of violence have expressed skepticism about its potential to have an impact.

Other violence-prevention approaches include innovative programs that target children at risk. Such programs go beyond the kinds of recreational activities that are traditionally offered to occupy young people. One ex-

Children in Los Angeles react to a rash of drug-related gang violence in their neighborhoods.

ample is mentoring by successful adults in the community who serve as role models. Programs that focus on building self-esteem are also likely to make a difference if they are offered in violence-ridden communities.

Public health scientists acknowledge that many of the factors contributing to acts of violence may not be amenable to traditional public health strategies. Unemployment, poverty, racism, lack of education and opportunity, inadequate health care, frustration and hopelessness, and exposure to violence all contribute to violent behavior. Unless these problems are addressed, the implementation of even the most innovative violence-prevention programs will have little, if any, impact.

Complexities of preventing violence: the case of child abuse

Public health and social welfare approaches to the problem of violence have clear advantages and can be both expedient and effective. They also have unique liabilities and limitations. A case in point is child abuse. Child abuse was formally identified as a medical condition in 1962 in an article that appeared in the *Journal of the American Medical Association*. Pediatrician C. Henry Kempe and colleagues brought international attention to the "battered child syndrome," in which chronic physical abuse of a child is manifested in a pattern of recurrent physical injuries. By 1967 all 50 U.S. states had enacted some form of legislation mandating that specified professionals report suspected cases of child abuse.

Such mandatory reporting has greatly facilitated recognition of the magnitude of the child-abuse problem. On the other hand, the laws are quite broad and in some cases vague, which means there is a dangerous potential for overreporting. Many state laws include a penalty for failure to report abuse or suspected abuse and provide immunity from both criminal and civil liability to persons making reports in good faith. Physicians, social workers, and other mandated reporters therefore tend to opt in favor of reporting. In some cases this has resulted in erroneous reports that have had damaging consequences for children and their families. In March 1994

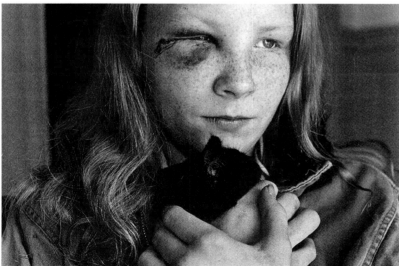

© Eugene Richards—Magnum Photos

The battered child syndrome was first brought to the attention of the medical community in 1962 when pediatricians described a pattern of recurrent physical injuries often seen in young children. Child abuse and neglect remain serious, widespread public health problems. Corporal punishment, though banned in many schools, is rarely regulated in homes. Studies have found that parents who physically punish their children often do so for reasons that bear no relation to the child's behavior; a more common reason is that the parent has had a bad day.

a federal appeals court in New York City ruled that the standard of evidence used by the state to place a suspect's name on its central child-abuse registry posed an "unacceptably high risk of error" and that many people who had been placed on the list did not belong there.

Despite the well-intentioned efforts of doctors, social workers, teachers, and others, there are enormous social and economic costs associated with an incorrect diagnosis of child abuse. Family privacy is violated, family relations are disturbed, and the child and his or her parents or caretakers are severely stigmatized. An allegation of child abuse subjects the child and family to investigation, medical and psychological examinations, possible court appearances, and often short- or long-term separation of the child from the family during the investigation.

At any one time nearly 500,000 U.S. children live apart from their biological parents. Over 50% of these children will be kept away from their homes for one year or longer; 60% will be placed in more than one setting, and some will have 15 or more "homes" during their childhood. Some will never again live with any permanent family. In the effort to prevent and reduce the level of domestic violence, it is important to be aware of the potential for excessive intervention and its consequences. It would be tragic and ironic if parents, and especially minority parents, hesitated to take their children for necessary medical care because they were afraid of being charged with abuse.

The case of child abuse clearly indicates that each strategy for controlling and preventing violence must include checks and balances aimed at reducing the frequency of misdiagnosis and error. Accuracy may be increased while efforts to detect all children at risk for abuse are maintained. Michael Durfee at the Los Angeles County Department of Health Services has implemented such a system. He has established and replicated throughout the nation a model interagency process for cases of alleged fatal child abuse. Child death review teams at the state and county levels bring together representatives of all the agencies in a jurisdiction that have interacted with fatally abused children. Through the exchange of information about specific cases, appropriate measures are taken to protect siblings and other children who are truly at risk of becoming victims of abusive parents or caretakers. Interagency interventions can also be extended to nonfatal cases of alleged child abuse. Strategies of this kind are required so that the "blind spot" that any single agency or profession brings to the effort to control violence can be eliminated.

A biological basis?

In their effort to identify the factors that contribute to violent behavior, scientists have long sought biological clues. In the 19th century, phrenology (measuring the size and shape of the skull) was advanced as a method for identifying innate personality traits, including criminal predisposition. The extent to which human behaviors are determined by nature (biology) versus nurture (the social and physical environment) continues to be a subject of considerable scientific interest. Recent advances in the medical sciences have stimulated much research aimed at identifying specific ge-

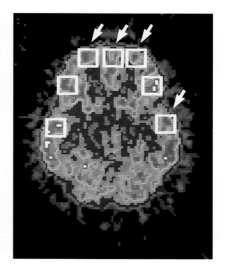

Scientists have long sought clues in the brain to explain violent behavior. Recently investigators have found a significant correlation between reduced cerebral glucose metabolism in specific regions of the frontal cortex and a tendency toward impulsive-aggressive behavior. In the positron emission tomography scan above, the four boxed areas indicated by arrows show distinct sites of low glucose metabolism in the cerebral cortex of a subject with a history of aggressive impulse difficulties. Even if such an abnormality in the brain is shown to predispose some individuals toward aggressive or destructive behavior, it is unlikely that any single biological or genetic factor will be any more important than the already well-established social and economic factors contributing to violence.

netic or physiological bases for violence. Underlying these investigations is the hope that a procedure to screen for and possibly methods of treating individuals at risk for violent behavior may result. In the 1970s efforts to identify locations in the brain that trigger violence were based on the hypothesis that chronic criminal behavior could be eliminated by selective ablation of certain brain regions. More recent research has focused on the roles of cerebral glucose metabolism and specific neurotransmitters (chemical signals in the brain), such as serotonin, in promoting aggressive behavior. Investigators in The Netherlands have recently identified a link between a gene and a rare hereditary predisposition for impulsive, violent acts among men in a Dutch family.

Unfortunately, many of the studies have been of poor quality and, consequently, the whole area of biological research on violence has become a controversial one. In the U.S. a disproportionate amount of violent crime is committed by members of minority groups, and representatives of those communities have decried genetic research on violence as racist. When socioeconomic status is factored into rates of violent crime, racial differences between groups disappear. While it is true that more violence is committed by members of minorities than by others, it is also true that there are more poor members of minorities in U.S. society. The most deprived people of any race or ethnic group commit the most violent crimes, and in a society that is economically stratified largely on the basis of race, the highest proportion of violent behavior will be seen among members of minorities that are at the lowest end of the scale.

83

In 1992 the National Institutes of Health canceled a highly controversial conference that was to be held on the genetics of criminal behavior. (Subsequently, there has been renewed support for such a meeting of scientists pursuing biological research into violent behavior, and the conference may proceed in 1995.) Certainly, the pursuit of biological causes of violence in isolation from other sociological contributors, such as poverty, is narrowly envisioned research at best. The appeal of such research is its simplicity and the hope that a readily identifiable marker will allow society to easily manage the violence epidemic. Even if such a biological basis for violence is established, however, it is unlikely that it will be one that can be shown to contribute to violence to a greater degree than, or independently of, the many known social and economic factors. Nor is it likely to be a universal biological trait. While such research should not be abandoned, its objectives and focus need to be more specifically stated, and its therapeutic potential as a response to America's violence epidemic needs to be responsibly—and conservatively—presented.

Impact of substance abuse

In 1992 Curt L. Schmoke, mayor of Baltimore, Maryland, examined the factors responsible for the epidemic of violence in his city. Handguns were an important part of the problem and were involved in more than 68% of all homicides. Firearms, however, were only one part of the problem. Schmoke argued that violence had become routine not only in his city but in urban American life primarily because of failed national substance-abuse policies. Baltimore's mayor and many other public officials believe those policies not only have failed to slow drug abuse, which rose 18% nationwide in 1991 alone, but have contributed to the epidemic of violence.

Mayor Schmoke has compared current substance-abuse policy with the U.S. experience during alcohol prohibition (1919–33), when efforts made to create an alcohol-free society resulted in large criminal enterprises, government corruption, and much violence. Prohibition was terminated as alcoholism began to be viewed as a disease.

The illicit-income potential of drugs is so great that traffickers and street dealers will go to any lengths, no matter how violent, to obtain those profits. At the same time, the lack of substance-abuse-treatment programs leads addicts to commit violent crimes to pay for illegal drugs. That pattern has not changed in the long history of the war on drugs, and many public health authorities now believe that it will not change until responsibility for fighting substance abuse is transferred from the attorney general to the surgeon general. The treatment of substance abuse as a public health problem, not a criminal justice problem, would represent a dramatic shift in social policy but may offer the best chance of substantially reducing the incidence of violent crimes in Baltimore and other American cities. The billions of dollars spent annually in attempts to arrest and incarcerate America's large addict population—a policy that leaves prisons overcrowded and violent offenders subject to early release and likely to commit more violent acts—could instead be transferred to the public health system and used for treatment, prevention, and education.

84

Recently both Pres. Bill Clinton and Surgeon General Elders have articulated the need to more effectively prevent and treat substance abuse as a fundamental component of a national violence-reduction effort. The Clinton administration has earmarked $13 billion for 1995 in support of a treatment-oriented national drug strategy.

A multibillion-dollar health problem

Approximately 200 million firearms are owned by private citizens in the United States, and estimates are that between one million and three million of these are assault weapons. According to the FBI, of the roughly 1.3 million crimes against individuals reported annually, almost one-fourth involve firearms. The average medical costs for treating a single case of penetrating trauma from a firearm range from $15,000 to $20,000; however, gunshot-wound victims often require intensive care, and costs for treatment and rehabilitation may be as high as $150,000 per incident. These patients need a great amount of care and place a serious burden on hospitals. A large percentage of gunshot victims have no private insurance; the costs for their care are reimbursed by government insurance programs or remain uncompensated. The public thus bears the major share of these costs. Annually the total direct cost for treating injuries attributable to firearms is probably in excess of $1 billion; indirect costs of firearm violence are at least $2 billion a year.

On a single day nearly 250 prisoners—70% of them repeat offenders—are processed at the Joliet (Illinois) Correctional Center Reception and Classification Unit. Prisons in the U.S. are filled beyond capacity, but the national epidemic of violence continues unabated. Criminal justice professionals increasingly agree that violence is a broad social problem that extends far beyond their purview. A public health approach to violence not only would be more humane but would also be more cost-effective than either punishment or treatment after the event.

85

Treating and rehabilitating victims of gun-related trauma in the U.S. cost well over $1 billion annually. Violence-related law-enforcement costs are also a huge drain on the national economy; however, while those costs continue to increase, so too does the incidence of violent crime.

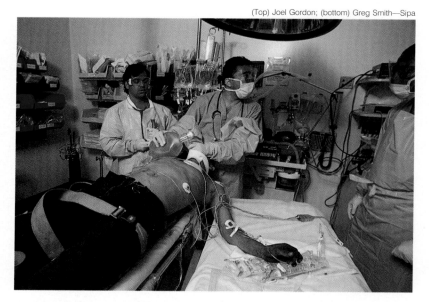

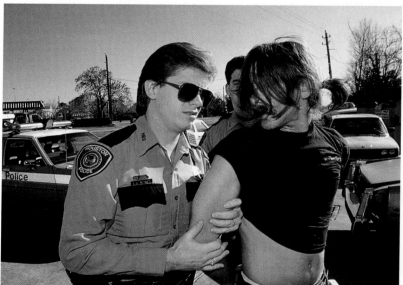

Consider the costs of violence against women. A 1993 national poll found that 34% of U.S. adults report having witnessed a man beating his wife or girlfriend and that 14% of women report that a husband or boyfriend has been violent with them. This level of domestic violence in a typical year may result in 21,000 hospitalizations, 100,000 patient hospitalization days, 29,000 emergency department visits, and 39,000 physician visits.

Recent estimates are that the annual incidence of family violence consumes $5 billion to $10 billion of resources, including not just health care costs but costs for other social services. In child-abuse cases, for example, investigative and protective services as well as foster home placements may consume up to $1.4 billion a year. Law-enforcement costs are also high. The nation's police forces spend approximately one-third of their time responding to domestic violence calls. Continuing use of medical services by victims of domestic violence, welfare and disability payments, and costs associated with shelters and other forms of care may consume an additional $5 billion to $10 billion annually. These direct and indirect costs of family violence alone confirm that this epidemic is one of America's most expensive health problems. Some public health authorities have even ventured that domestic violence may be the number one drain on the domestic economy.

America's love affair with firearms

Remarkably, every 14 seconds in the United States a new firearm is purchased. The U.S. is the only industrialized nation that does not effectively regulate private ownership of firearms. Consequently, the American civilian population is the most heavily armed of any civilian population in history; approximately one-half of U.S. homes have one or more firearms. Surprisingly, the U.S. has more than 20,000 laws that deal with the sale, distribution, and use of firearms; there is, however, little evidence that they are effective.

The prevalence of firearms in the U.S. is often attributed to the country's frontier heritage. Canada, however, has a frontier tradition similar to that of the U.S., but its homicide rate is only a fraction of the U.S. rate. In Australia, another frontier nation, private handgun ownership is one-seventh of that in the U.S., owing in part to an efficient system of gun regulation.

In recent years the sale of handguns and long guns in the U.S. has increased substantially; firearm manufacturers now sell more than 2.5 million handguns annually. Although only one-fourth of U.S. firearms are handguns, they are responsible for almost 75% of homicides involving firearms. Criminals use handguns as their primary weapons, and their ready availability makes it easy for a misguided individual to obtain a weapon that is nearly certain to kill. There is clear epidemiological evidence that the

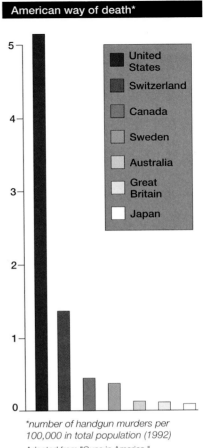

American way of death*

- United States
- Switzerland
- Canada
- Sweden
- Australia
- Great Britain
- Japan

number of handgun murders per 100,000 in total population (1992)

Adapted from "Guns in America," *The Economist*, vol. 330, no. 7856 (March 26, 1994), pp. 23–28; data from Handgun Control

Les Stone—Sygma

A father and son attend the Great Machine Gun Show in Bullitt county, Kentucky, at which attendees are able to try out a wide variety of weapons.

Les Stone—Sygma

Americans are the most heavily armed civilian population in the world; every 14 seconds in 1993, a new firearm was purchased in the U.S.

prevalence of firearms in a given society is directly associated with the level of firearm violence—the more guns owned, the more violent acts committed. Another part of the firearm problem is their longevity. When properly maintained, most guns have a life expectancy of decades, and many of the firearms used to commit crimes in the U.S. are several decades old. It has been pointed out that even if the U.S. were not to manufacture, import, or assemble any additional guns for the next three decades, enough firearms are already in the hands of owners to maintain, and indeed increase, current levels of violence!

The battle that has raged for decades between advocates of gun control and those who argue for unrestricted gun access has been dominated by rhetoric. The basic position held by those against any form of gun control is that decreasing the availability of guns will not eliminate homicides or nonfatal assaults. Gun-access advocates say that if guns are regulated, only criminals will have access to them through illegal means, such as theft or smuggling, leaving law-abiding citizens who constitute the majority unable to protect themselves.

In fact, the latter argument is not supported by the epidemiological data. The public has a misconception that most homicides are perpetrated by criminals killing to achieve profit. Rather, the majority of U.S. homicides are committed by previously law-abiding individuals who know the victim and who express their hostilities through the use of firearms.

The National Rifle Association (NRA) and gun manufacturers and merchants have articulated a broad range of constitutional and conservation arguments to defend their position. Gun-control opponents argue that any legislative action to control firearms is an abrogation of the constitutional right to keep and bear arms. The Second Amendment to the Constitution states: "A well regulated Militia, being necessary to the security of a free State, the right of the people to keep and bear Arms, shall not be infringed." When it was enacted in the 18th century, this amendment was important in

88

ensuring that a struggling young nation confronted by enemies would have the means to survive. Citizens then did not have modern protections such as mobile police forces and electronic communications, and they required a means to protect their homes and ensure their personal safety.

Advocates of gun control argue that the need addressed by the Second Amendment has long since disappeared and that a well-regulated militia as envisioned in the 18th century exists today in the National Guard. Furthermore, they maintain, another right entrenched in the Constitution is the assurance of domestic tranquillity, meaning that individuals are safe in their homes, at their workplaces, and on the streets of their communities. U.S. public health experts believe that the prevalence of firearms in contemporary U.S. society has made that right—the right not to be killed by another person who uses a gun with lethal intent—impossible to attain.

Steps in the right direction

Advocates of a legislative approach to firearms control do not believe that enacting a law will by itself provide a comprehensive solution to this complex problem. Even an effective gun-control law will not prevent gunshot incidents, but it may reduce their number. Gun-control laws, furthermore, do not have to prohibit gun ownership and access but may merely regu-

Chris Brown—Saba

During the first week in January 1994, $100 food coupons were offered to anyone who turned in a firearm in New York City—no questions asked. A highly successful "gun swap" two weeks earlier had given New Yorkers $100 gift certificates for toys and rounded up 317 weapons in 60 hours. Such amnesty programs are spreading nationally; everything from cash to mattresses to athletic footwear is being swapped for firearms—slowly putting a dent in the number of weapons in the hands of people who might otherwise use them in acts of violence.

late it. One recent nationwide survey of 1,500 adult Americans found that 84% favor the regulation of newly purchased handguns. Another survey indicated that most Americans favor a law requiring that privately owned guns be registered with federal authorities.

There is a growing scientific consensus among medical and public health practitioners that the wide availability of and immediate access to lethal weapons are key contributors to the high incidence of homicides. Just as public health efforts have reduced mortality from motor vehicle crashes without banning cars, many practitioners claim that injuries and deaths caused by firearms can be prevented without a total ban on guns. Reducing children's unsupervised access to loaded guns is just one example.

For many years the NRA has waged a strong—and apparently effective—lobbying effort. Members of the U.S. Congress have been influenced by and fearful of the NRA, which has threatened to ensure the defeat of any elected official who votes for a federal gun-control law. At the end of the 1993 legislative session, Congress showed modest political courage when it passed into law the Brady bill. The law mandates a waiting period of five working days for firearm purchases, during which a background check of the purchaser can be made. The law also raises licensing fees for gun dealers and requires that police be notified of multiple gun purchases by a single individual. However, this law is far from a comprehensive strategy to regulate firearms; it is widely acknowledged even by its originators that it represents only a first step in an evolving legislative process. Further legislation is required if the number of handguns used for malicious and criminal purposes is to be reduced (without limiting availability of guns for legitimate recreational uses). Without the support of U.S. voters, however, elected officials may not risk a conflict with the NRA.

Most public health practitioners recognize that effective legal regulation of firearms alone is too crude a vehicle to solve the problem of firearm injuries. There is evidence, however, that restricting access to guns has the

"How sweet it is; how long it took," commented James S. Brady on Nov. 30, 1993, as Pres. Bill Clinton signed the Brady bill into law. The new handgun legislation, first introduced in Congress in February 1987, mandates a five-day waiting period for purchasing firearms. Looking on at the White House signing ceremony were Brady (seated), who was wounded in a 1981 assassination attempt on then president Ronald Reagan, and (standing, left to right) Vice Pres. Al Gore, Attorney General Janet Reno, and Brady's wife, Sarah. Even Brady, who devoted seven years to getting his bill passed, acknowledges that it is only a preliminary legislative step.

Trippett—Sipa

potential to reduce the incidence of violent acts that result in death. In the District of Columbia it was found that the adoption of a gun-licensing law in 1976 coincided with an abrupt 25% decline in homicides resulting from firearm use and a 23% reduction in suicides in which a firearm was used. No similar declines were observed for homicides or suicides in which guns were not used, and no decline was seen in adjacent metropolitan areas of Maryland and Virginia, where restrictive licensing did not apply. These data suggested that restriction of access to handguns in the District of Columbia had prevented an average of 47 violent deaths each year since the law was implemented.

In a joint editorial, "Time to Bite the Bullet Back," published in the June 10, 1992, issue of the *Journal of the American Medical Association,* former surgeon general Koop and George Lundberg, the *Journal*'s editor, argued that the right to own and use a firearm involves certain responsibilities and that owners and users should have to meet criteria similar to those for motor-vehicle operators. Such criteria include: being of a certain age and in healthy physical and mental condition; demonstrating knowledge and skill in the proper use of firearms; being monitored in the use of firearms; and forfeiting the right to own or operate a firearm if the above conditions are not met. These public health leaders also felt that anything short of registration and licensing of all firearms owned or purchased in the U.S. would be too little action too late. In fact, a great deal of public sentiment supports their proposals.

No simple solutions

In early 1994, as debates over health care reform were getting under way in earnest on the floors of the U.S. Congress, Secretary of Health and Human Services Donna Shalala voiced support for President Clinton's reform plan, the Health Security Act, which is intended to provide all Americans with comprehensive health care and would also help reduce the levels of violence in U.S. society. Shalala made the point that because more children

91

*Residents of Chicago's West Side gather
to protest the senseless murders of young
people that occur with far too much
regularity in their neighborhoods.*

and families would have a regular health care provider, better surveillance
of and intervention in domestic violence would be possible and, in particular, child abuse could be curbed. Shalala also noted that young people
would have greater access to care in schools and therefore have more
opportunities to talk out and manage anger and conflicts nonviolently.

Health care reform will presumably ensure that more people will be able
to get help for mental health problems and substance abuse, which are
known contributors to violence. Hillary Rodham Clinton, Tipper Gore, wife
of U.S. Vice Pres. Al Gore, and former first ladies Betty Ford and Rosalynn
Carter have all been outspoken proponents of mental health coverage
under the new health policy.

The link between violence and lack of access to health and social services is indeed a strong one. It is a sign of progress in the mounting effort
against this epidemic that the issue of violence prevention has surfaced in
the national health care reform debate.

It is clear that many forces are responsible for violence in America.
Violence is not merely a matter of insufficient law enforcement but a public
health problem of major proportions. It cannot, however, be considered
exclusively as a public health issue, nor can it be approached in isolation
from its origins. Solutions will have to address root causes, including
social and gender inequities, failures of the educational system, unemploy-

92

ment, the lack of appropriate outlets for and means of resolving conflicts peacefully, and media that portray violence as an acceptable—and even a "glamorous"—way of life.

Like most human behaviors, violence is a complex phenomenon that resists one-dimensional solutions. There will be no one strategy that can more than modestly reduce the epidemic of violence that now tears at the very core of American life. As the country shapes itself for the 21st century, it is now clear that this public health emergency will challenge U.S. society's very concepts of a civil life. Such a revision is long overdue.

Where to turn for help and information

Most U.S. cities provide crisis intervention services for victims of violence. Listings of legal, economic, housing, and medical assistance services in one's own community can be found in the Yellow Pages of the telephone book under "Human services organizations" or "Social service organizations." There are also a number of national organizations that are sources of information on violence prevention. These include:

National Coalition Against Domestic Violence
1201 East Colfax Avenue
Denver CO 80218
(303) 839-1852

National Council on Child Abuse and Family Violence
1155 Connecticut Avenue NW, Suite 400
Washington DC 20036
(202) 429-6695

Domestic Abuse Intervention Project
206 West Fourth Street
Duluth MN 55806
(218) 722-4134

EMERGE (a men's counseling service on domestic violence)
18 Hurley Street, #23
Cambridge MA 02141
(617) 422-1550

National Victim Center
PO Box 17150
Fort Worth TX 76102
1-800-FYI-CALL

TV

THE MESSAGE IS MAYHEM by Brandon S. Centerwall, M.D., M.P.H.

In his 1962 novel *A Clockwork Orange,* the British writer Anthony Burgess creates a nightmarish futurescape: a world dominated by mayhem and fear, where street gangs run amok and the terrorized poor struggle to exist in vandalized housing projects while the anxious rich insulate themselves in oversized suburban homes. Burgess even invented an argot reflecting a culture dominated by television—in which *to viddy* means "to think, to feel, to see, to understand," all things superlative are "horrorshow," and the greatest high is to commit a bit of "the old ultra-violence."

The narrator is Alex, the leader of a street gang that patrols its turf armed with bats, chains, and switchblades. By and large, the gang is satisfied with giving its victims a mauling. By accident, however, Alex eventually kills someone and is arrested. At the climax of the book, as he is hauled off to prison, Alex reveals his age: 15.

Burgess intended his story to shock. There are limits, however; his artistic judgment undoubtedly told him that 15 was as young as he could make Alex and still maintain credibility with his readers. Today, 30 years later, a 15-year-old killer would hardly merit a raised eyebrow. Consider, for example, the widely reported 1992 murder of an English toddler by two Liverpool youths—aged 10.

TV and the public health

In Michigan a young teenager beat a transient to death with a baseball bat to see what it was like. Later, during the police interrogation, he recounted his surprise and dismay upon discovering that it was not as quick and clean as television had led him to think it would be.

Whether television increases levels of aggression and violence has been an issue ever since the medium became a part of cultural life. The first U.S. congressional hearings on the question took place in 1952, when fewer than a quarter of households in the United States had television sets. Over the ensuing decades the question has been explored in scores of research studies, as well as in several major government investigations and a RAND Corporation report— the broad consensus being that exposure to television violence *does* increase physical aggressiveness in young viewers.

Brandon S. Centerwall, M.D., M.P.H., is Assistant Professor of Epidemiology, School of Public Health, University of Washington, Seattle.

In 1975 the *Journal of the American Medical Association* published a "special communication" entitled "Effect of Television Violence on Children and Youth." The author, Michael Rothenberg, a pediatrician at the University of Washington, was the first to alert the medical community to the harmful effects of television violence on child development. In response to Rothenberg's report, which raised serious concerns among physicians, the House of Delegates of the American Medical Association (AMA) passed a resolution in 1976 declaring that TV violence threatens the health and welfare of young Americans. The AMA committed itself to taking remedial action, encouraging doctors to voice their opposition to TV programs that contain violence as well as to the sponsors of these programs. Many other professional organizations in the United States and elsewhere have since followed suit.

Imitation: a basic instinct

In Florida a six-year-old boy and his friend got into a scrap while playing at the boy's high-rise apartment. Finally, to settle the dispute, the boy maneuvered his friend onto the

Investigators who study the influence of television on behavior find that children are likely to imitate the actions of admired hero figures. Often these popular characters engage in destructive, antisocial acts.

Karen Wollins

balcony of the apartment and hoisted him over the railing, sending him 10 floors below to his death. Twenty minutes later the police came upstairs to ask some questions. The boy was watching cartoons on television. During the questioning he calmly continued to watch the TV and eat pizza.

The impact of television on children is best understood within the context of normal child development. As was shown in the 1980s in a series of studies by psychologist Andrew Meltzoff at the University of Washington, children are born with an instinctive capacity to imitate adult behavior. That infants can, and do, imitate an array of adult facial expressions has been demonstrated in newborns as young as a few hours old—well before they know that they themselves have facial features that correspond to those they are observing. The instinct to imitate is a useful one, as the developing child must master a vast repertoire of behavior in short order. It is, however, an instinct that operates indiscriminately. Infants are unable to judge whether a particular behavior ought to be copied and will imitate actions most adults would regard as destructive or antisocial.

It has been demonstrated, moreover, that children as young as 14 months old observe and repeat what they see on television. In an experiment conducted by Meltzoff, a series of infants viewing a video monitor looked on while an adult on the screen pulled apart a toy the youngsters had never seen before. Typically the infant would lean forward and watch the adult's actions with rapt attention. Next, the subjects were given the toy. Most immediately pulled it apart, exactly as they had seen done on the screen.

Television writers and producers are well aware of the medium's fascination for very small children. A glance at television industry trade journals reveals that programmers *advertise* their ability to attract and hold viewers as young as two years old. As might be expected, children are most likely to imitate those behaviors that most effectively capture and hold their attention—and there are few things more attention-getting than a rousing display of violence.

What is reality?

In Florida a woman who was being filmed for TV news was shot to death by her former husband while on camera. As the videotape rolled, he approached her, pulled out a gun, and shot her 12 times. The producer of the news program decided to broadcast the footage, and the tape was shown nationally on network TV and by many local stations. The producer explained that she was not troubled about showing the woman's murder because, she said, "It looks like a reenactment."

As of 1990, the average two-to-five-year-old American child was watching more than 27 hours of television per week, or almost 4 hours per day. This might not be harmful if young children understood what they were watching. However, the available evidence indicates that they do not. Up through ages three and four, even

Kids' TV: kinder, gentler programs?*		
	children's programs	prime time
violent acts per hour	32	4
violent characters	56%	34%
characters who are victims of violence	74%	34%
characters who kill or get killed	3.3%	5.7%
characters involved in violence as either perpetrators or victims	79%	47%

*based on 1991–92 television season

Source: George Gerbner, Ph.D., Annenberg School of Communications, University of Pennsylvania

with some coaching from adults, many youngsters are unable to distinguish fact from fantasy in television programs. In the minds of these young viewers, television is a source of entirely factual information about how the world works. There are no limits to their credulity. To cite one example, an Indiana school board had to issue an advisory telling young children that there is no such thing as a Teenage Mutant Ninja Turtle. Too many kids had been crawling down storm drains in search of the swashbuckling reptiles. Still, TV company executives continue to insist that "children don't *believe* this stuff!"

Naturally, as kids get older, they come to know better. Still, their earliest and deepest impressions are formed at a time when television is to them a source of factual information about the world. And this world is one in which violence is commonplace, and the commission of violence is generally portrayed as exciting, effective, and even glamorous. Children are most likely to imitate violent acts when they are committed by an admired hero figure and when violence is presented as fun, occurring without meaningful pain or injury and without lasting consequences. In real life, serious violence is most likely to erupt at moments of intense stress or frustration—and it is precisely at such moments that adolescents and adults are most likely to revert to their earliest, most visceral sense of the role of violence in society and in personal behavior. Much of this impression will have come from television.

A numbing effect

A California high school student told five incredulous classmates that he had murdered his girlfriend. He then took them to the site of the murder to show them her body.

Several days passed before one of them decided to notify the authorities.

A classic study by U.S. psychologists Ronald Drabman and Margaret Thomas demonstrated that children not only became more aggressive from watching television violence but also became more indifferent to the violence of others. The researchers randomly assigned fifth-graders to watch either 15 minutes of a television crime drama—including several shootings and other violent acts—or 15 minutes of a televised baseball game. Afterward the investigator left each child in charge of supervising two younger children by means of a television monitor, telling him or her, "I imagine they'll be OK, but sometimes little kids can get into trouble, and that's why an older person should be watching them. If anything does happen, come get me."

After the investigator left, the two youngsters on the TV monitor got into a quarrel, which escalated into threats and then physical blows; finally, the camera was knocked over and, amid shouts and crashing, the monitor went dead. (All of the older children witnessed exactly the same sequence because, unbeknownst to them, the fight was taped, not live.) As compared with the children who had watched the baseball game, those who had just viewed violent television were one-fifth as likely to summon the investigator. In all, 25% of the children who had watched the violent program failed to call the researcher to intercede.

Life before TV—and after

A number of long-term studies have focused on communities in which television was not introduced until relatively late. One such community, a remote rural town in British Columbia, dubbed "Notel" by the investigators, acquired television for the first time in 1973. The delay was due to problems with signal reception rather than to any rejection of TV by the residents. Psychologist Tannis Williams and her associates at the University of British Columbia seized on this opportunity to study a population of children before and after exposure to the medium. They compared the "Notel" youngsters to a control group of children in two similar towns that already had television. In this carefully designed study, before television was introduced into "Notel," 45 first- and second-graders in the three towns were watched while they played in a free, unstructured situation. The observers noted all instances of noxious physical aggression, such as hitting, shoving, and biting. The same 45 children were observed under similar circumstances two years later. To prevent bias the research assistants who collected the data were not told why they were watching the youngsters. Furthermore, an entirely new set of assistants was employed the second time around so that data gatherers would not be influenced by some recollection of a child's earlier behavior.

The sociopathic antics of MTV's Beavis and Butt-head have been copied by children, sometimes with tragic results. After Beavis urged, "Let's burn something," a five-year-old viewer set his family's home on fire; his younger sister died in the blaze.

As would be expected, the rates of aggression did not change over time in the two control communities. In contrast, two years after the introduction of television in "Notel," the level of physical aggression among the children had risen by 160%. The increase was observed in both boys and girls and in those who had been aggressive to begin with as well as those who had not.

In another Canadian study, anthropologist Gary Granzberg and his associates at the University of Winnipeg investigated the impact of television upon three Indian tribal communities in northern Manitoba that first acquired television in 1969, 1973, and 1977, respectively. In all three communities, rates of physical aggression increased among the children following the introduction of television.

Granzberg found, in addition, that specific TV episodes could be identified as triggers of specific violent incidents. A show about teenage gangs was followed by an outbreak of ganglike fighting at one school. The martial arts series "Kung Fu" prompted several incidences of stick and sword fighting in which some youngsters sustained injuries that resulted in the loss of an eye. Given that the traditional Indian cultures of these communities emphasized nonviolent approaches to conflict resolution, the effect of television upon the children's physical aggressiveness was all the more striking.

The child is father...

Psychologists Leonard Eron and L. Rowell Huesmann of the University of Illinois at Chicago followed the fates of 875 children living in a semirural U.S. county between 1960 and 1981. They found that for both boys and girls the amount of television the youngsters were watching at age 8 predicted the seriousness of criminal acts for which they were convicted by age 30. Among boys, even after the investigators took into account the youngsters' baseline aggressiveness, intelligence, and socioeconomic status at age 8, how much television violence they were viewing at that age was still a significant predictor of the seriousness of their criminal behavior in early adulthood.

In addition, Eron and Huesmann observed that the effects of TV viewing even extended to the next generation. Girls and boys who watched more television at age 8 were later, as mothers and fathers, punishing their own children more severely than those parents who had watched less television as children. Remarkably, how much television violence a 30-year-old man had been watching at age 8 predicted how physically aggressive his children would be even better than it predicted his own aggressiveness.

All in all, eight long-term studies conducted in Canada, the U.S., and England, including those described above, have demonstrated a relationship between early exposure to television and subsequent increases in physical aggression. The critical period of exposure is preadolescent childhood. Later exposure, in adolescence and adulthood, does not exert any additional effect. However, the aggression-enhancing effects of childhood exposure to television are chronic and extend into adulthood. This implies that children, rather than adults, should be the target of any interventions designed to mitigate the harmful effects of TV violence.

The "television hypothesis"

Nearly a decade and a half ago, the U.S. Centers for Disease Control (CDC) in Atlanta, Ga., initiated a violence research program. A central concern at the time was the doubling of the rates of violence in the United States since the 1950s. The question confronting researchers, this author among them, was why. Virtually every possibility was considered, including increased urbanization; changes in economic conditions; the effect of the post-World War II "baby boom"; trends in alcohol abuse, capital punishment, and civil unrest; changes in the availability of firearms; and the influence of television. Television was considered no more likely to provide an explanation than any of the other candidates. Over the course of seven years of research, first at the CDC and later at the University of Washington, this author tested and gradually eliminated the various possibilities. The "television hypothesis"—the theory that TV viewing is responsible for societal violence—stubbornly refused to be ruled out.

Intriguing as it was, this hypothesis remained to be proved. In order to put it to the test, it was necessary to devise a study that would compare the rates of violence in another, fairly similar country before and after the introduction of television. South Africa, which had no TV until the mid-1970s, provided an almost ideal subject for such a study, and Canada proved to be a useful "control group."

TV comes to South Africa: a natural experiment

Because the government of South Africa did not permit television broadcasting prior to 1975, the entire population—rich and poor, urban and rural, educated and uneducated—was excluded from exposure to television for a quarter century after the medium was introduced into the U.S. and Canada. In the mid-20th century the U.S., Canada, and South Africa were similar in many ways. Each was a multiparty, representative, federal democracy with strong Christian religious influences; in each, nonwhites were generally excluded from political power. Although South Africa had no television, the country boasted well-developed book, newspaper, radio, and cinema industries. Therefore, the effect of television on the populace could be isolated from that of other media.

To test the hypothesis that exposure to television is a cause of violence, the recorded homicide rates in South Africa, Canada, and the United States were compared before and after the introduction of TV. Because blacks in South Africa live under quite different conditions from those of blacks in the United States, it seemed logical to limit the comparison to white homicide rates in South Africa and the United States but to use the total homicide rate in Canada (which was 97% white in 1951). The data came from the respective government death certificate registries. Homicides were chosen as an index because they are subjected to intense investigation by law-enforcement agencies. Therefore, homicide statistics are exceptionally accurate and include more than 95% of all murders that occur. (In contrast, no more than half of assaults and rapes are reported to the police.)

The statistics showed that following the introduction of television into the U.S., the annual white homicide rate increased by 93% between 1945 and 1974. There was a parallel increase in homicides in Canada during this time. In South Africa during the same period, however, the white homicide rate *decreased* by 7%. In both Canada and the U.S., there was a lag of 10 to 15 years between the introduction of television and the subsequent doubling of the homicide rate. Given that homicide is largely an adult activity, if television exerts its behavior-modifying effects primarily upon children, the initial "television generation" would have to age 10 to 15 years before there would be a noticeable impact on the homicide rate. It would be expected that as the initial television generation grew up, rates of serious violence would begin to rise first among children, next among adolescents, still later among young adults, and so on. In fact, this is exactly what happened.

A comparison of South Africa with the United States alone at that time could easily have suggested that it was the U.S. involvement in the Vietnam War or the turbulence of the civil rights movement that was responsible for the doubling of the U.S. homicide rate. The inclusion of Canada in the analysis precluded those possibilities, however, since the Canadians also experienced a doubling of their homicide rate without any significant civil unrest or social upheaval.

Still, it remained to be proved that there was not some other factor, overlooked in the research, that could account for the doubling of U.S. and Canadian homicide rates. Therefore, it was necessary to devise further tests for the theory that exposure to television causes violence. The test of any theory's validity is whether its predictions prove true. For example, if the introduction of television in the 1950s did indeed cause a subsequent doubling of the U.S. homicide rate, it could be predicted that those populations that acquired television earlier would have had an earlier increase in their homicide rates, while those that acquired television later would be seen to have a later increase in homicide rates.

Because of socioeconomic factors—TV sets being a fairly expensive luxury item in the 1950s and blacks being generally less affluent than whites— black households in the U.S. acquired their first sets approximately five years later than white households. If the introduction of television was responsible for the doubling of the homicide rate, then the white homicide rate should have begun to increase approximately five years before the black homicide rate. The statistics show that white homicide rates began to increase in 1958. At the time, black homicide rates were declining; they continued to decline and did not begin to rise until 1962—four years later. Moreover, in the U.S. as a whole, where different regions of the country acquired television at different times, a strong relationship was observed between the arrival of TV in a particular region and a subsequent increase in the region's homicide rate.

From 1975 to 1987 the white South African homicide rate increased 130%. (As of 1991, the South African death certificate registry no longer categorized death certificates by race.) In contrast, the Canadian and white U.S. homicide rates did not rise during that period. Since Canada and the United States had become saturated with television by the early 1960s, it was expected that the effect of TV on rates of violence would likewise reach a saturation point 10 to 15 years later—*i.e.*, by about 1974 or '75.

On the basis of the above data, this author concluded that the introduction of television into the United States in the 1950s was responsible for a subsequent doubling of the homicide rate. This suggests that childhood exposure to television is likely to have contributed to roughly half of the U.S. homicides—or

approximately 10,000 deaths—per year. Although the association is not as clear for other forms of violence, the data indicate that exposure to television is also a factor in perhaps half of all rapes, assaults, and other forms of interpersonal violence. On the other hand, when the same analytic approach was taken to investigate the relationship between TV viewing and suicide, it was determined that the introduction of television had no significant impact upon suicide rates.

To say that childhood exposure to violence on TV contributes to a large proportion of violent acts is not to discount the importance of other factors—poverty, lack of education, unemployment, drug and alcohol abuse, low self-esteem, access to firearms, and others. Nevertheless, if television technology had never been developed, there would likely be 10,000 fewer murders in the U.S. each year and possibly as many as 70,000 fewer rapes and 700,000 fewer injurious assaults.

Voluntary standards: a solution?

In December 1993, in response to growing criticism, the major U.S. TV networks announced that they were adopting voluntary guidelines regarding violent programming. Parents, educators, and concerned health professionals were understandably skeptical. Network producers, when questioned by reporters, indicated that the new standards would require no changes in their programming. Moreover, when U.S. Sen. Paul Simon (Dem., Ill.) held a press conference to announce the internetwork agreement, industry executives were

Views on violence*		
	public	entertainment industry leaders
How serious a problem is violence on television and in the movies?		
very serious	50%	24%
serious	29	35
not very serious	14	35
not at all serious	5	5
To what extent does violence in the entertainment media affect the level of violence in the U.S.?		
no effect	7	13
major contributing factor	54	30
minor factor	37	57
Can the government play a constructive role in regard to TV violence?		
yes	59	40
no	33	60

*based on a poll of 1,001 registered voters and 867 entertainment industry executives, directors, writers, and actors

Source: Jeffrey Cole, Director, UCLA Center for Communication Policy, and *U.S. News and World Report*

not even present. None of this came as a surprise to long-standing advocates of nonviolent children's TV.

While the United States equivocates, Canada takes action. In October 1993 the Canadian Radio-television and Telecommunications Commission (CRTC) announced a new television violence code. Developed in consultation with all sectors of Canadian broadcasting, the code secured concrete commitments from private broadcasters, scheduled to be implemented in 1994. These stipulate that no broadcast may contain gratuitous violence (based on a clear definition of what constitutes "gratuitous violence"); programs containing scenes of violence suitable "for adults only" may not be aired before 9 PM; a national program classification system will be established within a year; children's animated programming must not have violence as a central theme or invite dangerous imitation; children's programming must not show violence as a preferred way of solving problems; and children's shows that include acts of violence must also portray the consequences of that violence.

The Canadian code makes for interesting reading. Most striking is the clear and shared sense of social responsibility on the parts of the television industry and the government, responsibility that has been pitifully absent from all efforts thus far in the U.S. (One can obtain the full text of Canada's television violence code [Public Notice CRTC 93-149] by writing to the CRTC, Ottawa, Ontario K1A 0N2, Canada, or by phoning 819-997-0313.)

Mastering the medium

Television violence is everybody's problem. Parents may feel assured that *their* child will never commit heinous violence despite a steady diet of television mayhem, but they cannot be assured that their child will not be murdered or maimed by somebody else's child raised on a similar diet. The issue of children's exposure to television violence must become part of the public health agenda, along with such universally recognized measures as child safety seats in cars, bicycle helmets, regular immunizations, and good nutrition. Part of the public health approach should be to promote affordable child care alternatives to the "electronic baby-sitter."

Parents should guide what their children watch on television and how much. The American Academy of Pediatrics recommends that parents limit children's television viewing to one to two hours per day. One newly available means of limiting viewing is the time-channel lock, an electronic device that permits parents to choose the programs, channels, and times that the TV set can be turned on; if a particular program or time of day is locked, the set cannot be tuned to that channel or turned on at that time. Time-channel locks are becoming increasingly available as an optional feature on new TV sets, and legislation under con-

For parents who do not want kids to see such "adult" TV shows as "NYPD Blue," with its raw language and frank portrayal of urban violence, one solution may be a device that enables them to lock out certain channels at certain times.

gressional consideration in 1994 would require that all new sets have them.

Restricting TV viewing is only one approach, however. Another is to teach children to master television. Mastery is control. When the child masters television, the medium no longer controls the child. In practice, this means teaching children how television technology works, why it works, who is determining program content, and to what ends. So-called media literacy education is a burgeoning new field. It includes giving children hands-on experience in using a television camera to create their own programs, which in turn enables them to rely upon their own creativity and teaches them how to distinguish fact from fantasy. Such media literacy education is already part of the mandated core curriculum of schools in the Canadian province of Ontario.

Interestingly, those who teach the hands-on use of television technology have noted that it is those young people most alienated from the educational process in general who become most engaged in the mastery of television. Whereas *watching* television seems to encourage youngsters' passivity and apathy, *making* television instills them with purpose. As one student operating a TV camera commented, "I feel in control."

*   *   *

Recent books on media literacy include *Visual Messages: Integrating Imagery into Instruction* (1992) and *Parenting in a TV Age* (1991). The latter is endorsed by the American Academy of Pediatrics.

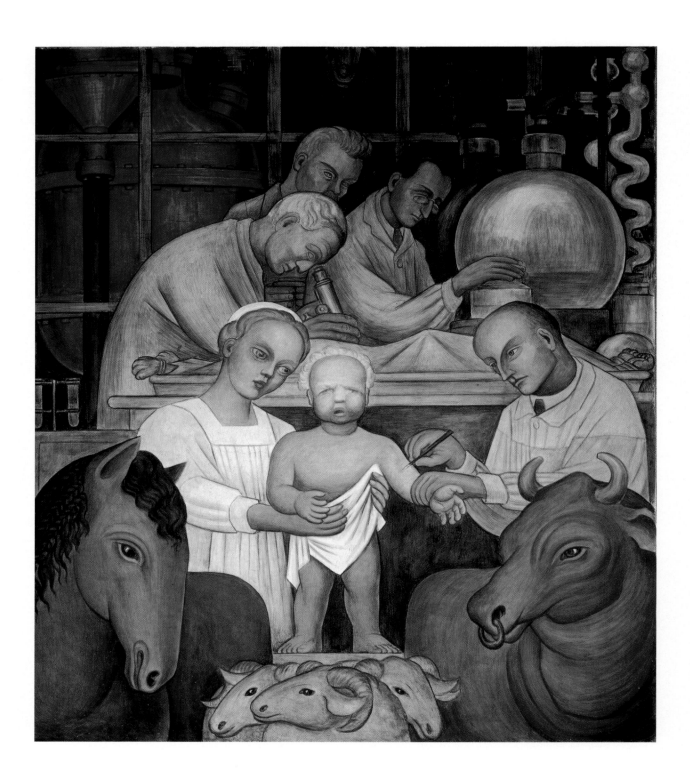

Armadillos to Zebra Fish

Animals in the Service of Medicine

by Fred Quimby,
V.M.D., Ph.D.

IN 1921 PHYSICIAN FREDERICK BANTING, working with Charles Best in the laboratory of J.J.R. Macleod at the University of Toronto, was attempting to isolate the substance that regulates blood sugar in the human body. Aware of the plight of thousands of children with diabetes who rarely lived to become adults, Banting had discovered that removing the pancreases of dogs created a similar condition in the animals, characterized by prolonged elevation of blood sugar—in other words, he had succeeded in creating an animal model of humans with diabetes. From this discovery Banting reasoned that the sugar-regulating substance must be made by the pancreas, and he thus began isolating the various constituents from that organ. An alcohol extract of whole pancreas was then tested in dogs. As Banting recounted later, "[I found that] diabetic dogs seldom live more than 12 to 14 days. But with the daily administration of this whole gland extract we were able to keep a depancreatized dog alive and healthy for ten weeks."

Banting and Best were the first to isolate insulin. A year later diabetic patients were being treated with the hormone—the first of the millions who would have the opportunity to live long, productive lives, thanks to the availability of insulin. In 1923 Banting and Macleod were awarded the Nobel Prize for Physiology or Medicine for this discovery.

Banting would not have found his treatment for diabetes had he not been able to study an animal model of the disease, for he could not ethically or legally experiment on humans. The same can be said of thousands of other biomedical achievements of the past few centuries, which came about only because there were animal models to serve as human surrogates. The tremendous contributions of animal models to biological and medical knowledge have been recognized by medical societies and health agencies around the world. As further testimony to their importance, more than two-thirds of all the Nobel Prizes for Physiology or Medicine since 1901 have been awarded for discoveries that required the use of animals.

Frederick Banting (right) and Charles Best pose with a diabetic dog that they succeeded in keeping alive and healthy with daily doses of extract of whole pancreas. To create an animal model of humans with diabetes, the two researchers surgically removed pancreases from dogs. They then used their model to discover the pancreatic hormone insulin and employ it successfully as a treatment for diabetes.

Fred Quimby, V.M.D., Ph.D., *is Professor of Pathology, New York State College of Veterinary Medicine, Cornell University, Ithaca, New York, on the Graduate Faculties in Veterinary Medicine, Immunology, and Toxicology. He is also Director of the Cornell Center for Research Animal Resources.*

(Page 100) "Vaccination" by Diego Rivera; collection, Detroit Institute of Arts, Founders Society Purchase, Edsel B. Ford Fund and a gift of Edsel B. Ford

A long tradition of animals in medicine

Humans have a history of close interaction with animals that extends back thousands of years to the domestication of dogs and, later, of buffalo, cattle, horses, sheep, poultry, and cats. The earliest written records involving animals in medicine date to 2000 BC, when Babylonians and Assyrians documented surgery on humans and animals.

True scientific inquiry began in the intellectually liberal climate of ancient Greece, where reasons were sought for natural phenomena without resort to mysticism or demonology. The first documented animal experiments were conducted by the anatomist Erasistratus, who in the 3rd century BC demonstrated the correlation between food intake and weight gain in birds. In the 2nd century AD, the physician Galen used a variety of animals to show that arteries contain blood and not air, as had been previously believed. During that period physicians carried out careful anatomic dissections and, on the basis of the comparative anatomy of animals and humans, accumulated a remarkable list of achievements, including a description of embryonic development, the establishment of the importance of the umbilical cord for fetal survival, and the recognition of the relationship between the optic nerves, which arise from the eyes, and the brain. The Greeks and later the Romans developed schools of higher learning, which included medical schools, and documented their findings in libraries. This brief flowering of scientific inquiry ended in Europe with the Middle Ages, during which the writings of ancient Greece and Rome were the final word on science and medicine until the Renaissance.

Medical education was revived in 10th-century Salerno, Italy, but because of a prohibition on human dissection, which lasted into the 13th century, animals substituted for humans in the instruction of anatomy. Because no investigations took place, virtually no new discoveries in medicine were made. How handicapped must have been those medieval physicians, who still did not know, for example, that filling of the lungs with air is necessary for life, that the body is composed of many cells organized into tissues, that blood circulates and that the heart serves as its pump, and that blood traverses from arteries to veins in tissue via capillaries. These basic facts were revealed only in the 1600s, and in each case the discoverer used animals to demonstrate the basic principle.

The pace of biomedical research increased during the 1700s. Pioneering scientists showed that the life-promoting constituent of air is oxygen, described the relationship between nerve impulses and muscle contraction, observed tissue repair and cellular division, discovered that food is digested by secretions of the stomach, and measured the heat generated by body metabolism. Again, in each case the discovery was made by means of observation in animals. The first measurement of blood pressure, made in horses in the early 1700s, paved the way for the development a century later of the mercury manometer, the instrument used to measure blood pressure in humans. The stethoscope was perfected in 1816 on the basis of animal experimentation.

In the 1860s the French scientist Louis Pasteur discovered that microscopic particles, which he called vibrions (*i.e.,* bacteria), were a cause of

a fatal disease in silkworms. When he eliminated the vibrions, silkworms grew free of disease—the first demonstration of the germ theory of disease. In 1877 Pasteur turned his attention to two diseases that infect animals, anthrax in sheep and cholera in chickens. He isolated the bacterium for each disease, reduced its virulence with high-temperature treatment, and showed that upon injection the attenuated organism in question did not cause disease but rather imparted protection against future exposure. Pasteur referred to this process as vaccination (from Latin *vacca,* "cow") in homage to the English surgeon Edward Jenner, who discovered that injection of matter from cowpox lesions into humans protected them against smallpox. Pasteur went on to develop the first vaccine against rabies, again using animals as surrogates for humans.

The second half of the 19th century began a new era in biology and medicine. In addition to such medical developments as vaccination, anesthesia, and blood transfusion, each of which depended on animal experimentation, two other events changed the direction of biological science forever. In 1859 the English naturalist Charles Darwin published *On the Origin of Species,* in which he hypothesized that all life evolves by selection for traits that give one species an advantage over others. In the 1850s and '60s the Austrian botanist Gregor Mendel used peas to demonstrate that specific traits are inherited in a predictable fashion. Nearly a half century later, about the time that Mendel's work was becoming recognized, the English biologist William Bateson reached the same conclusion by using

A 19th-century illustration shows the ancient Greek physician Galen employing animal skeletons during an anatomy lecture in Rome. In the 2nd century AD, Galen used animals to demonstrate that the arteries carry blood and not air, as had been taught for hundreds of years.

103

A variety of animals, including silkworms, sheep, chickens, and rabbits, served Louis Pasteur (above) in his research into microbial diseases and vaccine therapy. To study rabies and isolate its causative agent, Pasteur devised a reliable system based on rabbits for transmitting and maintaining the disease. (Below) Edward Jenner's technique for protecting humans against smallpox by vaccinating them with matter from cowpox lesions is practiced on a busy street in 19th-century Paris, with a cow as the source of the vaccine.

chickens. During the 20th century scientists systematically investigated the biochemical nature of inheritance, an endeavor culminating in the 1980s and '90s with the artificial synthesis of genes and their therapeutic application to correct inherited disorders in animals and humans.

For much of his vaccine research, Pasteur depended on a steady, fresh supply of the infectious agent under study, which he maintained in living animals by inoculation. In 1876 the German microbiologist Robert Koch demonstrated a technique for growing bacteria outside an animal in pure culture; *i.e.,* in vitro. This technique reduced the number of animals required for conducting research on infectious agents and is still widely used today. Koch developed postulates upon which the entire field of microbiology came to be based. According to his postulates, a microorganism could be related to a specific disease only if (1) it was demonstrated in every case of the disease, (2) it could be cultivated in pure culture, (3) upon inoculation into susceptible animals it reproduced the disease, and (4) it could be recovered from the diseased animals in pure culture. Using these postulates, scientists in the late 1800s and early 1900s went on to isolate and identify most of the important bacterial diseases of animals and humans.

At the start of the 20th century, the U.S. pathologist Leo Loeb and the French surgeon Alexis Carrel devised methods for growing cells and tissues in artificial media. These techniques revolutionized science not only because they allowed the isolation and propagation of viruses, which cannot thrive outside living cells, in systems less complex than whole animals but also because they permitted important studies in such fundamental areas as cell growth and differentiation, cellular interactions, the transformation of normal cells to cancerous cells, cellular aging, and molecular genetics.

Much of what is taken for granted in biology and medicine today is based on animal studies conducted during the past century—from the discovery of chromosomes and DNA to the elucidation of the dietary constituents critical to growth and survival (*e.g.,* essential fatty acids, amino acids, vitamins, and minerals) to the procedures, materials, and equipment used in modern surgery. The dramatic overall gains in life expectancy seen in most parts of the world since 1900 are due in large part to advances in nutrition, vaccines, antibiotics, and other areas in which animal experimentation played a major role. Some important examples of achievements made possible by animal research are listed in Table 1 on pages 106–107.

What is an animal model?

Like physicists, climatologists, and other investigators, biomedical scientists use model systems when it is difficult or impossible to use the system of interest. In biomedicine that system of interest is often in a human being, the intended beneficiary of the research. Although medical researchers sometimes do test their hypotheses directly on human subjects, when that is impossible (for instance, when the disease being studied is so rare as to preclude there being enough subjects for testing, or when evaluating the effect of a treatment requires the subject to undergo unacceptable invasive surgery), they seek a biological model system that is as similar to the human system as can be found. Types of model systems for biomedical research include whole living animals, tissues from humans and animals, nonliving physical systems, and mathematical models.

Occasionally biological phenomena can be investigated with nonliving model systems. For example, fluid collected from horseshoe crabs can be used to test samples for extremely low levels of bacterial toxins. The procedure, which causes no harm to the crabs, replaces one in which samples are administered to rabbits, which develop a fever if a toxin is present. Likewise, the synthesis of proteins and DNA can be studied through the use of cell-free chemical systems allowed to react on the laboratory bench.

Many kinds of studies, however, require some form of life. When the object of the research is to investigate a process found in single cells, such as the factors that control cell growth, cultured cells may be the most appropriate system. When the interaction of similar cells constituting a tissue is the object of investigation, such as the effect of a new drug on heart-muscle contraction, entire organs maintained in culture may be the most appropriate choice. And when the object is to observe the integrated activity of several organ systems, such as the protective effect of an antiviral vaccine, whole living animals—*i.e.,* animal models—are the appropriate choice. In some instances scientists' ability to use a system less complicated than a whole animal is limited only by the technology available.

(continued on page 108)

ENSURING THE BEST CARE FOR RESEARCH ANIMALS

Animal models have given scientists insights impossible to imagine coming from any other source. On the other hand, scientists over the years have become increasingly mindful of the imposition they place on their research subjects. Consequently, various regulations have been developed to protect research animals and assure the public that every consideration is given to animals before they are allowed to be used in experiments.

In the U.S., federal laws enforced by the Department of Agriculture and the Public Health Service dictate the manner in which animals are bred, housed, transported, and employed in biomedical research. Each institution receiving federal research funds, as well as funds from most private agencies, is required to establish a committee that reviews the proposed use of vertebrate animals. Consideration is given for the necessity to use animals, the need to alleviate their pain, and the opportunity for their socialization and exercise as appropriate. Education programs must also be offered so that all individuals who handle animals are properly trained in the specific needs of each species. Special attention is given to the qualifications of researchers performing surgery on or administering anesthesia to animals. Housing for research animals is constructed according to strict codes that minimize changes in environmental temperature and humidity, reduce the spread of infection, and promote biologically and behaviorally sound animals. Most animals used in research are specifically bred for the purpose and are free of known infectious diseases. Sanitation practices must conform to high standards to ensure the health of the animals, and veterinary care must be available 365 days of the year.

In addition to federal monitoring of research animal use, grant-funding agencies and manuscript reviewers for many scientific journals include humane animal care as part of their review. Finally, some individual states have passed laws and created monitoring agencies that provide further oversight of research animal use.

Legislation protecting research animals in the U.S. has paralleled the enactment of legislation in countries throughout Western Europe. As a result, the cost of conducting research on living animals has increased dramatically. Perhaps more important, however, the sensitivity of all individuals responsible for animal care and use has been raised.

Table 1: Examples of major advances that depended on animals

	advance	animals used
early 1900s	treatment of pellegra (niacin deficiency)	monkeys, dogs
	treatment of rickets (vitamin D deficiency)	dogs
	cardiac catheterization techniques	dogs, rabbits
	identification of the components of blood and plasma	dogs, rodents, monkeys, rabbits
	cardiovascular surgical techniques	dogs
	diphtheria vaccine	guinea pigs
	elucidation of the malaria-parasite life cycle	pigeons
	tuberculosis research	cattle, sheep
	elucidation of mechanisms of immunity	guinea pigs, rabbits
	characterization of the central nervous system	horses, dogs
	procaine (Novocain) and other local anesthetics	many species
	treatment of beriberi (vitamin B_1 deficiency)	chickens
1920s	intravenous feeding	dogs, rabbits, rodents
	open-chest ventilation (necessary for thoracic surgery)	dogs
	discovery of thyroxine (thyroid hormone)	dogs, others
	discovery of insulin and the treatment of diabetes	dogs
	typhus research	rodents, pigs, monkeys
1930s	transfusion, blood groups, blood typing	many species
	modern anesthesia and neuromuscular blocking agents	rodents, rabbits, dogs, monkeys
	anticoagulants	cats
	pump oxygenator (heart-lung machine)	cats, dogs
	monitoring electroencephalogram (EEG)	many species
	tetanus (lockjaw) vaccine	horses, others
	sulfa drugs	mice, rabbits
	penicillin	many species
	discovery of vitamin K	rats, mice, dogs, chickens
1940s	treatment of rheumatoid arthritis	rabbits, monkeys
	whooping cough (pertussis) vaccine	guinea pigs, rabbits
	chlortetracycline (Aureomycin)	many species
	streptomycin	chickens, guinea pigs
	discovery of Rh factor in blood typing	rhesus monkeys
	antimalarial drugs	many species
	diphtheria vaccine	horses
	electrical stimulation of paralyzed limbs	cats
	yellow fever vaccine	mice, monkeys
	antiarthritic effects of adrenal hormones	cows, others
	antihistamines	several species
1950s	blood preservation	many species
	measurement of oxygen, carbon dioxide, and pH (acidity or alkalinity level) in blood	many species
	cardiac pacemakers	dogs
	open-heart surgery	dogs
	treatment of hypertension with oral diuretics (thiazides)	dogs, others
	poliomyelitis vaccine	rodents, rabbits, primates
	tranquilizers for treatment of hyperactivity and anxiety	rats, rabbits, primates
	discovery of DNA	rats, mice
	cancer chemotherapy	rodents, rabbits, monkeys, dogs

	advance	animals used
1960s	selective coronary angiography (imaging of the heart's blood vessels), ventriculography (imaging of the brain's ventricles)	dogs
	hypothermia (body-temperature-lowering) techniques	dogs
	defibrillation of the heart	dogs
	coronary bypass surgery	dogs
	modern cardiopulmonary resuscitation (CPR)	dogs
	rubella (German measles) vaccine	monkeys
	lithium for treating manic-depressive illness	rats, guinea pigs
	antipsychotic and antidepressant drugs for treating various mental illnesses	rats, mice
	discovery of tumor-inducing viruses	chickens
	hormonal treatment of cancer	rats, rabbits
	role of genetic code in protein synthesis	rats
	corneal transplantation	rabbits, monkeys
	cortisone therapy	rabbits, monkeys
	kidney and liver transplantation	dogs
	prevention of hemolytic disease of the newborn	rabbits, others
1970s	vascular anastomosis (surgical connection of blood vessels)	dogs
	principles of intensive care	dogs
	heart transplantation	dogs
	bone marrow transplantation (to treat leukemia and sickle-cell disease)	many species
	measles vaccine	many species
	computed tomography (CT scan)	pigs
	treatment of leprosy	monkeys, armadillos
	therapies for treating eating disorders (*e.g.,* anorexia nervosa, bulimia)	rats, monkeys
	cimetidine (Tagamet) for treating gastric ulcers	rats, rabbits, others
	cerebral revascularization procedures (rerouting of blood to brain tissue)	monkeys
	treatment of scoliosis by electrical stimulation	sheep
	nonaddictive painkillers	rats, monkeys
	total hip replacement	sheep
	discovery of the infectious agent of Creutzfeldt-Jakob disease	primates
	discovery of natural endogenous-opiate pain-control systems	many species
1980s	cyclosporine and other immunosuppressant drugs	monkeys
	artificial heart	dogs, cows
	surgical repair of congenital heart defects	rodents, dogs, monkeys, sheep
	discovery of causative agent of AIDS	primates
	elucidation of visual-information processing by brain	cats, monkeys
	in vitro fertilization techniques	mice, primates
	intraneural electrical stimulation of paralyzed muscles	rabbits
	communication research leading to techniques for teaching language to children with mental retardation	primates
	gene replacement therapy	mice, rats
	hepatitis B vaccine	primates
	hepatitis A vaccine	marmosets
	elucidation of mechanisms involved in atherosclerosis	rabbits, monkeys, pigeons
	development of amantadine antiviral therapy	many species

(continued from page 105)

Before researchers can investigate disease conditions, they must first understand how the healthy body works. A living animal may thus serve as a model for normal body functions. Animals—particularly mammals—breathe, consume food, grow, reproduce, see, hear, and move by using processes similar to those of humans. In general, animals that are more closely related to human beings have more similarities than those that are distant. Dogs have served as excellent models for studies of cardiovascular function, respiration, transplantation biology, endocrinology, gastrointestinal function, and blood. Nonhuman primates, particularly the great apes, are

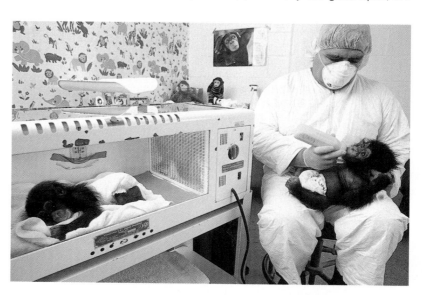

Healthy chimpanzee infants bred for AIDS and hepatitis research are cared for in a sterile room at the Southwest Foundation for Biomedical Research on the outskirts of San Antonio, Texas (top). When the studies in which they will take part are finished, the animals will go into lifelong retirement.

Chimpanzee playgrounds (below) form part of the extensive living areas designed for the animals at the foundation. Even the facility's quarantine areas, which house the animals in which AIDS and hepatitis vaccines are tested, are equipped with a variety of enrichment devices, including radios and color TV sets, and are overseen by a full-time animal behaviorist.

(Top) Michael Nichols—Magnum; (bottom) Southwest Foundation for Biomedical Research, San Antonio

108

extraordinarily similar to humans and are often the only nonhuman animals susceptible to human diseases. Because these animals are often rare in the wild, they are usually used only when no other system will suffice. Among the great apes, chimpanzees are used today only for limited studies, primarily vaccine trials for hepatitis B virus and human immunodeficiency virus (HIV), the cause of AIDS. Not wild chimpanzees but captive-bred ones are used in the U.S.; when the study is complete, the animals go into lifelong retirement as breeders. (Hepatitis B virus and HIV cause only transient illness in chimpanzees, with close to 100% recovery.) Fewer than half of 1% of the animals used in research in the U.S. are nonhuman primates.

Some animals not closely related to humans still may be similar enough in a given respect to allow meaningful investigations. For instance, since the 1930s the squid, a marine invertebrate, has been used to investigate the function of nerves. The squid has very large nerves and a much simpler nervous system than that of humans. These nerves allowed early investigators to measure electrical changes between the outside and inside of the nerve cell, studies that led to a modern scientific understanding of how impulses travel through the nervous system.

More recently human developmental biology has benefited from studies involving the zebra fish, a small, fast-maturing freshwater fish popular in home aquariums. The zebra fish has two primary advantages over other models: its embryo is transparent, allowing investigators to observe clearly how development unfolds, and the individual traits of color, shape, and function can be easily mutated in the laboratory and perpetuated in the offspring. In addition, zebra fish eggs can be induced to develop into embryos without fertilization. The resulting animals carry two sets of identical maternal chromosomes; since a mutation on one chromosome is duplicated on the other, the effect of the mutated gene can be observed quickly. Some mutations seen in zebra fish share striking similarities to developmental anomalies seen in children.

Although not closely related to humans, squids (below left) possess large nerves and a comparatively simple nervous system that make them valuable for neurological investigations. The squid's giant nerve axon (below), the long fiber along which a nerve projects its signals, is as much as 100 times as thick as its human counterpart, making it easy to see and manipulate in studies of the way nerve cells work.

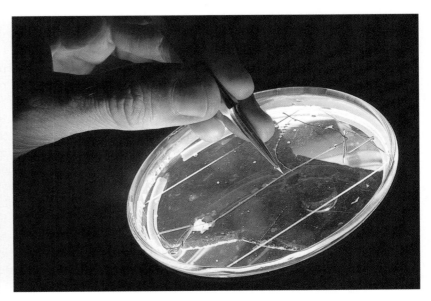

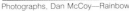
Photographs, Dan McCoy—Rainbow

109

Photographs, Zebrafish Laboratory, Institute of Neuroscience, University of Oregon

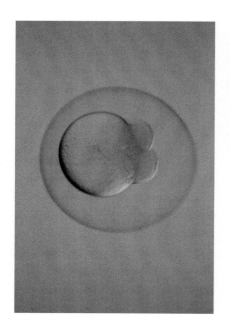

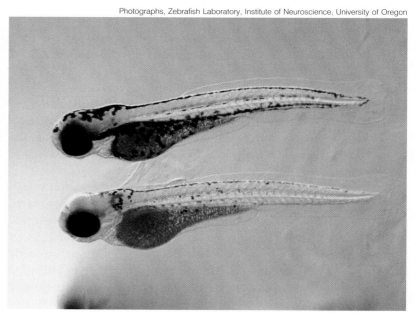

The zebra fish, a small freshwater species often found in home aquariums, is benefiting research into human developmental biology because of its transparent embryo and the ease with which it can be mutated in the laboratory. A two-cell zebra fish embryo, still in its egg, is shown in a photomicrograph (above). At this stage the embryo is less than a millimeter (0.04 inch) across. Two zebra fish siblings, just hatched following three days of development (above right), are compared. The bottom fish carries a genetic mutation, called "sparse," that affects its pigmentation.

Another category of animal model comprises those animals that have a disease in common with human beings. Humans and animals share hundreds of common illnesses, among them allergies, glaucoma, lupus erythematosus, muscular dystrophy, scoliosis, various forms of cancer, and such infectious diseases as hepatitis, Lyme disease, malaria, and tuberculosis (see Table 2). As a result, animals are often used as surrogates for humans in investigations concerning the cause and treatment of disease. In addition to sharing a disease with humans, an animal may possess certain attributes that make it more or less useful as a model. The ideal animal model accurately reproduces the disorder being studied; it is available for use by more than one investigator (to confirm scientific findings and extend the investigations); it is easy to handle and house; it is large enough to provide a number of samples over time; it produces large numbers of offspring (important if the disease is inherited); and it lives long enough to be usable.

Animal models may have either spontaneous or induced diseases. Cats, for example, naturally acquire the parasitic disease toxoplasmosis in the outdoor environment, develop viral infections that lead to leukemia, and can inherit the genetic defect responsible for muscular dystrophy. Although scientists do take advantage of such spontaneous diseases, often a particular study makes it necessary to induce a disease or disorder in an animal under carefully controlled conditions. Animals may be susceptible to human infectious diseases by injection even though they do not contract them naturally. Diseases and disorders also can be induced surgically; such was Banting's strategy when he created his dog model of diabetes. Occasionally chemical compounds are used to induce a disease, although to produce a useful model the compound must exert its effect very selectively. X-rays and radioactive isotopes likewise have been employed to induce diseases and disorders.

110

Using genetic engineering techniques, scientists can now add, delete, or disrupt given genes in animals and thus produce animal models with any of a broad array of desired characteristics or induced abnormalities. This type of genetic manipulation has been particularly successful with mice. For example, in 1994 researchers transferred into mice human-derived genes that caused the animals to express either normal or mutant forms of an enzyme called superoxide dismutase (SOD). Such mice, whose genetic material is taken partially from other organisms, are termed transgenic mice. Whereas the transgenic mice that received the nonmutated SOD gene developed normally, those that received the mutant gene developed motor neuron disease. Thus, for the first time, researchers succeeded in creating a model of familial amyotrophic lateral sclerosis (ALS, or Lou Gehrig's disease), which can be used to evaluate drugs for treating the disorder in humans.

Another kind of genetically altered mouse, called a knockout mouse, is produced when a normal gene in the mouse embryo is specifically disabled, or "knocked out." As a result, the mouse develops without the influence of the protein product of this gene. One type of knockout mouse, created with a defective gene for a protein that regulates the passage of chloride ions across the cell membrane, mimics the genetic mutation in humans that is responsible for cystic fibrosis. Although the induced disease is not identical to the human disorder, the mouse model has led to a better understanding of how the mutated gene in humans actually causes cystic fibrosis and to the development of experimental gene therapy for cystic fibrosis patients. It also has been used to develop a new drug to treat the excessive mucus produced in the illness.

Finding the "right" animal

Although good science requires careful planning, astute observation, and skillful practice, sometimes luck also plays a role. Many inherited models of disease in nonrodent species were recognized first by veterinarians who communicated their observations to researchers by word of mouth or in the professional literature. Dogs that were discovered to have hemophilia or Duchenne muscular dystrophy are typical examples. Because many of these inherited disorders are not treatable and are invariably fatal, pet owners and breeders often opt for euthanasia. Fortunately, some owners have offered their pets for adoption to research institutions, where breeding has preserved the genetic defect for study. The chance that a specific type of inherited disease of humans will be serendipitously discovered in an animal is low. Nevertheless, in dogs alone more than 100 models of human inherited disease are known, and many of these dogs are bred and available to investigators. Unfortunately, maintaining large animals with genetic defects is time-consuming and expensive, and thus most investigators prefer a small animal model.

For more than six decades, the U.S. has been the home for research institutions having a primary interest in the breeding and characterization of rodents. The Wistar Institute, Philadelphia; the Institute for Cancer Research, Fox Chase, Pennsylvania; the Roswell Park Cancer Institute,

Table 2: Some diseases shared by nonhuman animals and humans	
allergies	muscular dystrophy
anemia	narcolepsy
asthma	nerve damage
atherosclerosis	osteoarthritis
botulism	periodontal disease
bronchitis	
cancer	poliomyelitis
cardiovascular disease	rabies
cataracts	retinal atrophy
cholera	retinitis pigmentosa
congenital heart defects	rheumatoid arthritis
deafness	ringworm
diabetes	roundworm
diphtheria	rubella
emphysema	schistosomiasis
epilepsy	scoliosis
glaucoma	Sjögren's syndrome
hemophilia	skin diseases
hepatitis	spina bifida
herpesvirus infection	tetanus
hypertension	thyroiditis
infertility	toxoplasmosis
influenza	trypanosomiasis
kidney disease	tuberculosis
leprosy	typhus
lupus erythematosus	ulcers
Lyme disease	vitamin deficiencies
malaria	yellow fever
measles	

111

The dog above, a model of hemophilia B from a mixed beagle strain maintained at the University of North Carolina at Chapel Hill, has been partially cured by means of a gene therapy technique being developed for humans with the disease. Many inherited models of disease in species other than rodents, such as hemophilia or Duchenne muscular dystrophy in dogs, were first recognized by veterinarians while treating the animals of pet owners and breeders.

Buffalo, New York; the National Center for Research Resources, Bethesda, Maryland; and the Jackson Laboratory, Bar Harbor, Maine, are typical examples. Initially such centers maintained comparatively small numbers of different stocks, but after inbred strains of mice and rats were developed and their usefulness for investigating the influence of heredity on disease was recognized, the numbers of different stocks, lines, and strains of mice and rats expanded in response to worldwide demand.

As these collections of inbred mice grew, animal attendants occasionally would recognize individual animals that did not appear normal. In some instances the abnormality was due to a spontaneous mutation that, once studied, was found to be analogous to a human condition. Preservation of these chance mutations arising in breeding colonies has been the greatest single source of models of inherited diseases since the 1970s. Exciting new mouse models for disorders involving skin, muscle, the nervous system, and blood have been identified. One institution, the Jackson Laboratory, identifies about 20 new inherited conditions in mice annually. In recent years the technology for creating knockout mice has grown especially fast, and such mice, whose genetic mutations are known precisely, are replacing mice with spontaneous mutations as a source of animal models.

When an appropriate animal is needed for a disease that must be induced, the search can be difficult. In some instances the best approach involves a careful review of the information known about a species, with an eye to selecting an animal whose biological system of interest is analogous to that of humans. If, for instance, the animal is to serve as a model for heart transplantation, then the most appropriate species would have a heart similar in size and structure to that of humans, blood vessels of about the same size and configuration, blood that can be oxygenated and that responds to anticoagulants, and an immune system with a similar mechanism of transplant rejection. Also of possible importance are the structure of blood vessel walls, their ability to hold sutures, and the healing

The two mice are representatives of the first animal model of cystic fibrosis, created with a recently developed technology that allows researchers to disable, or "knock out," a specific gene in the embryo. The mouse on the left possesses only one copy of the defective gene in its cells and is thus a symptomless carrier of cystic fibrosis. The mouse on the right, which has inherited two copies of the gene, manifests the symptoms of the disease.

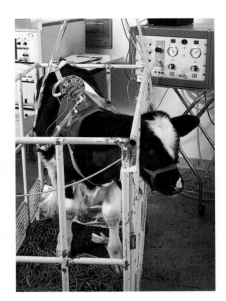

response of the animal. Given these considerations, when investigators have sought an animal model for heart transplantation research, they often have chosen the calf.

In other instances, finding a good model is hampered by lack of knowledge of the disease. For example, for years researchers had no animal model for leprosy, a bacterial infection characterized by skin lesions and nerve destruction, which in turn may result in erosion of the tissues of the face, ears, fingers, and toes. The causative organism, *Mycobacterium leprae,* proved very hard to grow in artificial media, and lack of a susceptible animal hindered work to develop vaccines. Finally, in the early 1970s it was reported that the nine-banded armadillo is susceptible to the disease, and at last scientists had a model that could contribute to future studies. The key factor in the susceptibility of the armadillo is its low body temperature, which is consistent with the predilection of the disease in humans for the extremities, where body temperature is lowest.

The range of useful models

Traditional animal models include mice, rats, guinea pigs, hamsters, rabbits, and dogs but, depending on the process being studied, any animal has the potential to serve as a model. For instance, various insects have been useful in clarifying physiological processes because they provide a less complex system for study. Crickets and katydids make sounds that the intended insect recipient immediately recognizes as mating signals. This fact has been used by scientists seeking to understand how the auditory system processes signals and translates them into meaningful acts. Whereas humans have 10,000–30,000 auditory receptors, crickets have only 70. Despite the disparity in numbers of receptors, such cellular phenomena as cell-to-cell communication are very similar between vertebrates and crickets, and the information gleaned from the study of crickets can aid in understanding of the more complex systems of vertebrates.

Lack of knowledge about leprosy hindered the search for a good model of the disease until the nine-banded armadillo (above left) was found to be susceptible to infection with the causative bacterium. The key factor in the success with the armadillo turned out to be the animal's low body temperature, a finding consistent with the preference of the leprosy bacterium for the human body's cooler extremities, such as the face, ears, and toes. A calf with a surgically implanted artificial heart (above) is used to evaluate the device for its suitability in humans. Because the heart, blood, blood vessels, and immune system of calves and humans are analogous in many respects, the calf is often used as a model for human heart transplants or artificial heart replacements.

113

Because all animals are evolutionarily related, certain basic physiological mechanisms remain virtually the same among species that otherwise can be quite different. Such is the case in the genetic control of prenatal development. Invertebrates were useful in discovering a set of genes, called homeobox genes, that are repeated on different chromosomes in the cell. Homeobox genes were found to control development directly by turning on and off the activity of other genes in the chromosome in a precise order, thereby triggering an orchestrated cascade of developmental changes in the embryo. Homeobox genes have been found in insects, earthworms, frogs, and humans, and in all species they appear to act in precisely the same way. Mutations in homeobox genes lead to developmental defects. Understanding their action is essential for understanding developmental abnormalities in higher animals, including human beings.

Whereas the types of animals used as models vary from alligators to tree shrews, the species is not as important as the biological system being explored. In instances in which the genetic composition of the animal must be held constant, only a single inbred strain of animal will suffice. In instances in which the biological phenomena are very basic, such as nerve impulse transmission, any of a large number of animals may suffice. To avoid choosing an inappropriate model, scientists must carefully define the problem to be studied and select the model only after reviewing the information known about the system under study. The animal's genetic makeup, its nutritional and housing requirements, and the microorganisms that it normally harbors may also enter into the selection process. Whenever possible, nonliving models must be considered either to reduce the need for living animals or to provide additional information that will better characterize the biological system.

When the cause of a disease in humans is multifactorial—having many potential contributors—it is often best explored with a number of models, from which comparisons can be drawn. One such disease is atherosclerosis, the accumulation of fatty deposits in the heart's coronary arteries, the known factors for which include hypercholesterolemia (elevated levels of cholesterol in the blood), stress, sex hormones, and diet, to name a few. Researchers studying the disease have employed a variety of models: pigeons, rabbits, and swine for investigating cholesterol metabolism and monkeys for elucidating the role of stress and sex hormones as factors.

In Japan in the late 1970s, a mutant stock of rabbit, called the Watanabe, was found to have persistent hypercholesterolemia. This rabbit has an inherited defect in which its liver cells lack the ability to capture low-density lipoprotein (LDL) that is circulating in the blood. Without the ability to remove LDL, which is rich in cholesterol, from the blood and metabolize it in the liver, the animal suffers from extremely high blood cholesterol levels and develops atherosclerosis. The Watanabe rabbit has helped clarify some of the most basic factors involved in the cause of hypercholesterolemia and atherosclerosis. Significantly, some human families have the same genetic defect, and affected individuals often die from a heart attack at a young age. In 1991 a line of pigs was identified with hypercholesterolemia and atherosclerosis. The animals have a genetic defect resembling another hu-

114

The Watanabe rabbit derives from a chance genetic mutation, discovered in the 1970s, that causes the animal to have elevated levels of cholesterol in the blood (hypercholesterolemia) and to develop atherosclerosis. The animal's condition mimics a genetic disease of humans in which afflicted individuals suffer from extremely high blood cholesterol and usually die from a heart attack at a young age. The Watanabe rabbit model has helped clarify some of the most basic factors involved in hypercholesterolemia and atherosclerosis and is aiding in the development of effective treatments, including gene therapy and cholesterol-lowering drugs.

man disease; in this instance a change in the LDL itself prevents its capture and removal from the blood. Such examples demonstrate the advantage of involving more than one animal model in pursuing answers to complex human diseases.

Animals in current research: three ongoing challenges

Although animal studies were responsible for many discoveries leading to improvements in human and animal health, the use of microbes, cell culture, and biochemical models has brought about a monumental expansion of knowledge in human molecular genetics. The achievements in molecular genetics in turn are now being applied in the treatment of such diverse diseases as cancer, AIDS, and a variety of inherited disorders. In most instances animal models are aiding molecular geneticists and physicians in defining the usefulness and limitations of these emerging treatments.

Cancer. Cancer is not a single disease; rather, the term describes a large group of diseases characterized by the loss of genetic control over cell growth and normal function. The consequence is an uncontrolled proliferation of cells, which may spread from their site of origin to other parts of the body (metastasize). A number of agents are known to promote cancer, among them certain viruses, ionizing radiation, asbestos, components of tobacco smoke, and various environmental pollutants. Although the precise manner in which these agents induce normal cells to become abnormal is not fully understood, it is now known that all cells that become cancerous undergo genetic alteration.

The genetic alterations caused by viruses and other agents have been the object of many investigations. In 1910 the U.S. pathologist Peyton Rous discovered that chickens infected with a transmissible agent, later shown to be a virus, developed malignant tumors called sarcomas. The Rous sarcoma virus (RSV) subsequently became the subject of many studies in both animals and cell culture. As a result, researchers found that RSV and

115

similar viruses that produce cancer in mice and cats carry specific, cancer-inducing genes, which were termed viral oncogenes, and that the viruses cause cancer by inserting their oncogenes into the genetic material of the cells that the viruses infect. Next, scientists found that normal cells contain remarkably similar genes that are intimately involved in cellular growth and proliferation. In normal cells these genes turn on and off under appropriate circumstances—for example, during wound healing. When cancerous cells were examined, investigators found that some of these cellular genes were abnormally expressed and were not turned off. The genes, named cellular oncogenes, continue to be expressed in cancerous cells because they have mutated or have relocated to a new position in the chromosome and away from genetic elements that normally control them.

Independently, investigators studying chemicals involved in cancer causation found that animals exposed to one chemical would develop many more malignancies if they were then exposed to a second chemical. These studies led to the concept of tumor initiators (chemicals resulting in cancer) and promoters (chemicals that augment the effect of initiators). Only recently have researchers learned that cellular oncogenes are involved in initiation and in some instances promotion.

As of 1994, scientists had identified more than 60 cellular oncogenes, many of which are specifically associated with human and animal tumors. The oncogenes are highly conserved in evolution, and counterparts may be found in all mammals. In fact, it is thought that the presence of viral oncogenes in RSV and related tumor viruses occurred as a result of the viruses' inadvertently picking up cellular oncogenes during infection of mammalian cells. The oncogene-equipped virus is able to insert the gene into the chromosome of another cell. When the oncogene is inserted at the right location, its gene product is continuously expressed, leading to cancer.

The original cancer-producing virus discovered by Rous is now known to be one of a family of tumor viruses called retroviruses, some of which cause cancer in various species of birds and mammals. Additional cancer-producing viruses that were first discovered in animals—for example, papillomaviruses, herpesviruses, and hepadnaviruses—each turned out to have a counterpart virus that produces cancer in humans. The first successful anticancer vaccine to be developed is one that prevents lymphoma in chickens caused by the Marek disease virus, a herpesvirus. Today, vaccines designed to prevent human liver cancer caused by hepatitis B virus, a hepadnavirus, are being tested in humans as well as woodchucks, which develop a similar illness. The recent success of a vaccine preventing virally caused leukemia in cats (FeLV vaccine) brings hope that a similar vaccine may prevent certain forms of leukemia in humans.

The cells of the body's immune system normally are well equipped to recognize altered cells, including cancerous cells, and kill them. The decrease in immune function seen as the body ages helps explain why most cancers arise in the elderly. The incidence of cancer is also higher in immunosuppressed patients, such as those receiving drugs to prevent transplant rejection. To overcome such problems, scientists have discovered ways to boost immunity in cancer victims by stimulating certain cells

Mice serving as models of humans with cancer are pictured with researcher Steven A. Rosenberg of the National Cancer Institute, Bethesda, Maryland. In the mid-1980s, working with mice, Rosenberg showed that a natural immune mediator, interleukin-2, could stimulate certain cells of the immune system to attack tumor cells. Subsequent experimental immunotherapies based on interleukin-2 have shown promise for combating specific types of cancer in humans.

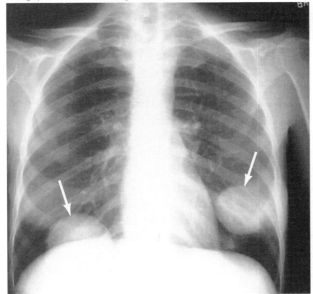 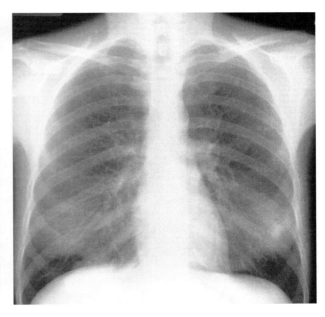

with a natural immune mediator, interleukin-2. The technique, originally developed in mice, has shown promise for specific types of cancer in humans. Other, related immune mediators such as interleukin-4 and alpha interferon have been shown to decrease tumor mass in animals, and alpha interferon has been shown to be effective against hairy-cell leukemia in humans.

Another approach to cancer therapy involves chemically attaching a powerful bacterial or plant toxin to a biological substance that naturally seeks out or is attracted by cancer cells—for example, an antibody that binds selectively to cancer cells or a growth factor needed by the cells. When tested in animals, both approaches have succeeded in killing tumor cells while causing fewer side effects than traditional chemotherapy and without inducing cross-resistance to chemotherapeutic drugs. Clinical trials are being conducted in humans in which these approaches are being used in conjunction with standard therapy to decrease the mass of the primary tumor and to kill spreading cancer cells.

AIDS. HIV is a retrovirus that shares many of the characteristics of the tumor-causing retroviruses. It does not directly cause cancer, however, but rather causes severe depression of the immune system and brain lesions. Certain species of nonhuman primates are afflicted with similar viruses and in some instances are susceptible to infection with HIV. Because it is now obvious that the great majority of HIV-infected humans will go on to develop AIDS, the safety of any experimental vaccine must be thoroughly verified in animals before it can be tested in humans.

Several approaches to AIDS vaccine development have taken place simultaneously. First, the simian immunodeficiency virus (SIV) has been used in an inactive or a genetically altered form to vaccinate monkeys, and several trials have demonstrated protection in monkeys against the simian form of AIDS. A second approach has involved inoculating chimpanzees with inactivated HIV or some of its molecular components and then chal-

The X-ray images above are of a human patient with spreading melanoma who was treated with an experimental interleukin-2-based immunotherapy developed in mouse models. The image at left, taken before treatment, shows tumors in the patient's lungs (arrows). The image at right, taken two months later, reveals that most of the tumors have disappeared as a result of the therapy.

117

Adrienne T. Gibson—Animals, Animals

The pigtail macaque was recently found to be susceptible to infection with HIV, the virus that causes AIDS, and to show symptoms of acute disease. Heretofore, the only nonhuman primate model for HIV infection had been the chimpanzee, which not only is scarce and expensive to breed and maintain but also shows no symptoms of AIDS after infection. The achievement offers researchers the prospect of a good animal model for monitoring the course of HIV infection and expediting animal-based vaccine and drug trials.

lenging the animals with the human virus. Until recently the only nonhuman primate susceptible to HIV was the chimpanzee, an endangered species. For this reason researchers have been eager to test vaccine strategies in other monkeys first. In 1992 a new nonhuman primate, the pigtail macaque, was shown to be susceptible to HIV, a finding that promises to expedite animal vaccine trials using HIV-based vaccines.

Since the late 1980s the U.S. National Institutes of Health (NIH) has sponsored a number of AIDS vaccine trials in uninfected humans to evaluate the safety (not efficacy) of the vaccines. From this work two candidate vaccines have been shown to elicit strong and lasting immune responses to the viral materials used in the vaccines. Nonetheless, the question of whether humans can be protected by vaccines against "field strains" of HIV (strains encountered in the real world) remains unanswered, and the rapid rate of mutation seen in HIV has left some scientists skeptical that a single vaccine can stimulate the immune system against HIV's many variants. Studies with chimpanzees reported in 1994 suggest that the two candidate vaccines do protect the animals against challenge by field strains of HIV. If animal experiments continue to show reason for optimism, the NIH may begin trials of the vaccines in people at risk of developing HIV infection.

In addition to vaccine developments, new anti-HIV therapeutics are being developed. A number of them are drugs that interrupt HIV replication at specific locations in its infection cycle. Trials of anti-HIV drugs are advancing through nonhuman primate models quickly, and several are now in human clinical trials.

Genetic defects. There are more than 3,500 known inherited diseases resulting from abnormalities in the genetic constitution. Taken together they afflict one in 200 people worldwide. Genetic mutations have been shown to cause, or have been implicated in, some forms of atherosclerosis and Alzheimer's disease, muscular dystrophy, cystic fibrosis, hemophilia, sickle-cell disease, thalassemia, and various immune system disorders, as well as a host of defects that affect important enzyme-mediated chemical reactions in the cell (inborn errors of metabolism).

With the discovery of retroviruses and their ability to insert genes in cells, investigators have developed retroviral vectors for the purpose of carrying normal, nondefective genes into the cells of persons with defective genes. A retroviral vector is a retrovirus that has been rendered incapable of multiplying and engineered to contain the appropriate nondefective gene. When allowed to infect cells of a patient with a genetic defect, the virus can integrate its therapeutic cargo into the chromosomes of those cells and thus correct the defect. The general technique is called somatic-cell gene therapy, so named because only the somatic cells (nongerm, or body, cells) are treated, not the sperm or egg cells. Therefore, the transferred gene is not heritable itself. It will ameliorate the condition in the patient only as long as the treated cells remain alive and functional; it will not prevent the disease in offspring.

The first attempts at somatic-cell gene therapy, which were successfully conducted in the early 1980s, involved mice. In 1990 and 1991 humans received gene therapy for the first time. Researchers transferred

118

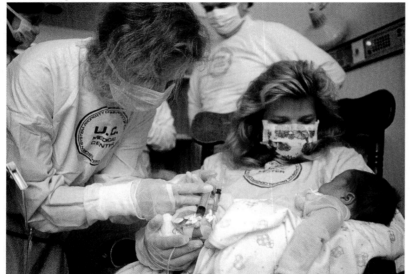

An infant boy is injected with his own gene-corrected stem cells to treat a severely impaired immune system resulting from a deficiency of the enzyme adenosine deaminase (ADA). The strategy behind this type of gene therapy is that the stem cells, which have been engineered with copies of functioning genes for ADA, will take up permanent residence in the infant's bone marrow and produce the enzyme in sufficient amounts for the rest of his life. The technique is a direct outgrowth of pioneering gene therapy experiments conducted successfully on mouse models in the early 1980s.

a nondefective gene into cells of two children to correct a biochemical abnormality, adenosine deaminase (ADA) deficiency, which results in severe immune deficiency. Other diseases now being addressed with gene therapy include hemophilia B, familial hypercholesterolemia, several forms of cancer, cystic fibrosis, Gaucher disease, and AIDS.

Progress to date in gene therapy owes much to a number of animal models of inherited diseases. In most instances the disease-causing gene mutations in the animals appeared spontaneously, like their counterparts in humans. One recent and promising gene therapy study involved endowing liver cells of the Watanabe rabbit, a model for familial hypercholesterolemia, with the gene that allows the cells to remove LDL from the blood. The treated rabbits showed a rapid drop in LDL levels for the 122-day duration of the experiment. Encouraged by this success, medical researchers carried out the same treatment in 1992 on liver cells of a woman with familial hypercholesterolemia. In 1994 the researchers reported on the results, describing a moderate lowering of the patient's blood cholesterol levels that lasted for the nearly two years of the reporting period.

As the genetic causes of more diseases are uncovered, new animal models wait to be treated. Among those available are mice with Sly syndrome, Gaucher disease, ornithine transcarbamylase deficiency, and Lesch-Nyhan syndrome (all four are metabolic disorders); dogs with Duchenne muscular dystrophy, hemophilia A, and hemophilia B; and rats with Crigler-Najjar syndrome (a metabolic disorder).

Humans and animals: mutual beneficiaries

Precisely because human life and animal life are interrelated, advances sought for humans through the use of animal models can travel a two-way street. Thus, the knowledge gained through animal research is used to repay these surrogates of humans by enhancing their well-being and treating, curing, or preventing animal disease.

119

Humans and other vertebrate animals are each susceptible to a large number of infectious diseases, and more than 200 of them afflict both. Some in the latter category, called zoonotic diseases, or zoonoses, are frequently transmitted from pets and domestic animals to people—for example, rabies, anthrax, and psittacosis (parrot fever). Certain vaccines that were developed to guard people against zoonotic diseases—*e.g.,* rabies, anthrax, tetanus, and Lyme disease—are now also used to protect animals. Monkeys were, and continue to be, instrumental in the development and testing of polio vaccines for human use. However, when the British animal behaviorist Jane Goodall reported an epidemic of polio among a colony of East African chimpanzees, human polio vaccine was used to immunize the chimpanzees and save the colony. In other cases vaccine technology originally developed for human needs has been turned to making vaccines that immunize species of animals against their own more serious infectious diseases.

Antibiotics, tranquilizers, steroids, insulin, sulfa drugs, anesthetics, analgesics, chemotherapeutic agents, anticoagulants, antiparasitics, antiepileptics, and antihistamines are all in common use in veterinary practice owing to the similarity of their effects in animals and humans. Surgical techniques developed for human use in blood transfusions, cancer treatment, spinal-cord trauma, hip replacement, fracture repair, congenital heart defects, and burns also benefit animals. Veterinarians, like medical doctors, take advantage of X-ray machines, computed tomography, ultrasonography, fiber-optic endoscopy, electrocardiography, electromyography, and renal dialysis equipment.

In yet another kind of turnabout, some drugs developed specifically for animals later have been found useful in humans. Ivermectin, developed to prevent heartworm infection in dogs, is now being used against onchocerciasis (river blindness), a parasitic disease that afflicts millions of people in tropical countries. Levamisole, developed as a cattle wormer, recently has been shown to greatly increase the survival of humans undergoing treatment with the chemotherapeutic agent 5-fluorouracil for colon cancer.

Finally, the results of animal research have been applied in efforts to save species from extinction. Knowledge of artificial insemination, semen storage, egg incubation, and behavioral adaptation was employed, for example, in the successful captive breeding of the peregrine falcon and restoration to its native habitats in the eastern U.S. Assisted reproduction has also helped to increase populations of wild cats and ungulates (hooved mammals) bordering on extinction. Likewise, knowledge of the detrimental effects on animals of human-made chemicals can prevent catastrophic environmental pollution, which may jeopardize the lives of animals throughout the food chain.

Future directions for animal research

Despite the incredible technical achievements in molecular biology and biotechnology of the past two decades, many questions remain that can be addressed only with the use of animals. Such afflictions as Parkinson's disease, Alzheimer's disease, AIDS, Lyme disease, chronic pain, spinal

At the National Zoo in Washington, D.C., the reproductive system of a female lion is observed with a laparoscope to monitor response to hormone treatments. The examination is part of a captive-breeding effort to increase genetic diversity in lions by impregnating receptive females with semen taken from wild lions in Africa. Much of the medical knowledge, techniques, and equipment now being applied to save species from extinction was first developed for human use through animal research.

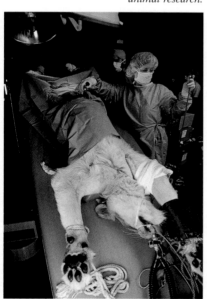

Michael Nichols—Magnum

A conspicuous success story for conservationists has been the successful captive breeding of the peregrine falcon and restoration to its former habitats in the eastern U.S. The effort has depended critically on knowledge of artificial insemination, semen storage, egg incubation, and behavioral adaptation to new environmental conditions—knowledge originally achieved with the help of animal studies.

trauma, drug addiction, atherosclerosis, and cancer will not be solved by in vitro methods alone, and animal studies will almost surely be involved with the development and testing of future therapies and vaccines.

These disorders represent only the known, familiar ones. The unexpected emergence of drug-resistant microorganisms, which presently include agents known to cause respiratory, urinary, and intestinal disorders as well as tuberculosis, malaria, and venereal diseases, presents an ongoing challenge. Drug resistance has also been demonstrated in HIV and herpesviruses. Although many in vitro systems for the culture and propagation of bacteria and viruses have been developed, newly emerging microorganisms do not always cooperate with scientists, and living animals may be needed to isolate them. New drugs, including an increasing number designed by computer and based on the molecular structure of the target site, will be synthesized and tested for efficacy. The concept of computer-designed drugs that are fully tested in other model systems before being tried in animals arose during the last decade and has helped ensure that only the best candidate drugs are submitted to animal testing.

Research in neurobiology has been, and will continue to be, greatly advanced through knowledge gained by animal experimentation. Correlating anatomy and function for various brain and spinal-cord structures and components in animals has aided in investigations of human disease. For instance, animal studies first identified the neurotransmitter acetylcholine in the brain and later showed that it is important in cognition. Alzheimer's disease, a chronic progressive degenerative disorder that affects memory and concentration, is the result of nerve-cell loss in the cerebral cortex and progressive loss of acetylcholine. Some aged monkeys show many of the characteristics of Alzheimer's disease. Employed as animal models in future studies, they may provide useful insights into the cause and treatment of the disorder.

121

Research using rodent models of diabetes is pioneering new potential treatments for the cause of the disease itself. Patients with insulin-dependent, or type I, diabetes have insulin deficiency due to loss of the cells in the pancreas that make insulin. Animal studies into the nature of insulin-dependent diabetes have demonstrated that it is an immune-mediated illness that is genetically induced. New therapies designed to block the genetic triggering of autoimmunity, an abnormal immune response to the body's own components (to pancreatic tissue in the case of insulin-dependent diabetes), are being evaluated in rodent models of diabetes.

No single biomedical research project appears to carry more potential for human health than the international Human Genome Project to identify, map, and sequence every human gene. In the late 1970s only 15 genes had been identified from the 100,000 contained in human chromosomes. By 1994 between 3,000 and 4,000 were known, with new genes being elucidated at a rate of one per day. In the end, scientists and physicians will know the precise location of each human gene and each gene's sequence of building-block molecules, the nucleotides, which carry the genetic code. With this information they will be able to pinpoint specific mutations responsible for the 3,500-plus known inherited diseases and possibly to correct many of them.

In support of the human genome effort, investigators are working to identify as many genes as possible in such animals as fruit flies, nematode worms, dogs, and mice. The order of certain genes on chromosomes and their functions are remarkably similar among species; therefore, knowledge gained about one species contributes to knowledge about all the others. To illustrate, two recent findings in mice may prove to have important implications for human genetics. In one, researchers identified the genes in mice for epilepsy; their precise chromosomal location in the mouse should greatly assist others in identifying one or more genes for epilepsy in humans. The second finding began with the discovery of a spontaneous genetic mutation in mice that leads to an illness characterized by multiple intestinal polyps. An inherited human illness, familial adenomatous polyposis, has the same pathology, and individuals with the condition go on to develop intestinal tract cancer. Upon investigating the mouse model, researchers found that the genetic defect involved a tumor suppressor gene, again similar to findings about the human illness. Significantly, however, the researchers also discovered and mapped a new gene that decreased tumor production in the mice. If this new cancer-inhibiting gene exists in humans, its discovery could have profound implications.

The achievements in biology and medicine of the past century have greatly depended on animal models. From the development of such procedures as kidney dialysis, organ transplantation, and coronary bypass surgery to cancer chemotherapy and the elimination or control of many contagious diseases, animal models have played a major—indeed a critical—role. Much of modern research conducted on animals involves rodents; in fact, 92% of all animals used for research and testing in the U.S. are rats and mice. Scientists are quite aware of the burden they place

122

(Top) Leonard Lessin—Peter Arnold; (bottom) Peter Menzel

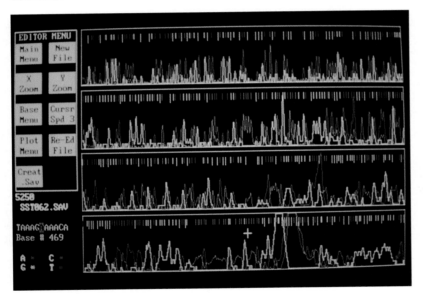

The diminutive nematode Caenorhabditis elegans *(above), measuring about a millimeter in length and possessing a three-day life cycle, has already served researchers well as a model system for the genetics of development. It now promises to aid the human genome effort by means of a project to decipher the worm's complete genetic instructions. Because the order of certain genes on chromosomes and their functions are similar among species, knowledge gained about even such simple animals as nematodes will contribute to the research under way to identify, map, and sequence every human gene (left).*

on these human surrogates and make every attempt to avoid the need for vertebrates or to reduce the number used. Furthermore, in the past three decades, biomedical advances have rapidly changed the nature of—and occasionally the requirement for—animal use. For such reasons total numbers of animals employed in biomedical research have fallen since the 1970s, despite ongoing research programs. Nevertheless, although strides in computer modeling, cell culture, molecular genetics, and bioassay techniques will surely yield ever more useful and suitable experimental models, animals will remain a vital part of research into health and disease for the foreseeable future.

123

Raising Spirits:
The Arts Transfigure the AIDS Crisis

THE DREAM OF FLOWERS

N O EPIDEMIC IN THE HISTORY OF HUMAN SUFFERING HAS prompted a more urgent, sustained, and tumultuous outpouring of responses from the arts than the global trauma of AIDS. Where other dreaded diseases are merely fatal, AIDS seems peculiarly fateful. It impresses some as a grim metaphor for the human condition, others as a dire symptom of the decline of modern civilization, and still others as a terrifying omen of the last judgment. Despite the media's demoralizing efforts to represent AIDS as an inevitably "deadly disease," AIDS patients themselves are struggling to live with the clinical and cultural consequences of their diagnosis. Many have defiantly cast themselves in the role of People Living with AIDS (PLWAs)—thus resisting a tragic destiny imposed on them by the rueful guardians of public health.

Viewing AIDS as a tragedy (as many people do quite reflexively) can be

by James Miller, Ph.D.

D.

S.

a constructive way of knowing it. So too is viewing it as a morality play, an existential farce, a soap opera, or a disaster film. In the decade of the '90s, the persistent effort to "capture" AIDS not just on stage and screen but in virtually every artistic medium has become a subject for artistic meditation in its own right.

Why AIDS should be so bound up with the arts and the arts with AIDS is a medical mystery wrapped in a cultural enigma. Hansen's disease may have had a longer history of maledictions and martyrdoms behind it than AIDS, but Broadway does not routinely stage new plays celebrating the dauntless spirit of People Living with Leprosy. Gonorrhea and syphilis may rival AIDS in souring "love's old sweet song," but rarely are new show tunes belted out to heighten "clap" awareness or to raise money for "pox" research.

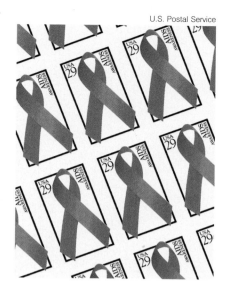

Positively negative: celebrating World AIDS Day

The urgently optimistic theme chosen by the World Health Organization (WHO) for the sixth annual World AIDS Day, Dec. 1, 1993, was "Time to Act!" and the arts responded, as usual, with plenty of timely action. However, with the cumulative total of adult human immunodeficiency virus (HIV) infections (including AIDS cases and deaths) reaching about 14 million worldwide, the arts had difficulty suppressing the sense that the time to act had been many years ago, when governments were routinely ignoring the gravity of the crisis.

Commemorations of the dead rather than confrontations with the living dominated the year's "celebrations" of this grimly ironic day. The red AIDS ribbon, now the epidemic's commemorative symbol par excellence, appeared with the vague message "AIDS Awareness" on a stylish new 29-cent stamp issued by the United States Postal Service. Ubiquitous but tiny, this image perfectly captured the widely diffused fear that the little that can be done here or there or anywhere to raise awareness is too late to save the millions already stamped with the mark of AIDS.

On World AIDS Day 1993, art galleries became envelopes of awareness stamped by the signs of the time. Paintings about AIDS by Joseph Bertiers, a self-taught artist from Kenya, were displayed at the Fowler Museum of Cultural History in Los Angeles to remind visitors that the epidemic affects artists all over the world. An empty "chair of mourning" surrounded by discarded dance slippers, abandoned art supplies, and unfinished works of literature materialized in the rotunda of the Chicago Cultural Center. Musicians played beside this allegorical installation for 15-minute intervals throughout the day; however, most of the time a dismal pall of silence fell over the scene. In Kansas the sheer size of the loss was commemorated at the Wichita Art Museum's special exhibition of works by American artists who had died of AIDS.

In New York City a less-is-more ethos seems to have reigned in the larger institutions. The Metropolitan Museum of Art discreetly took selected works, including a Rembrandt self-portrait, off the wall to mark the incalculable

James Miller, Ph.D., is Faculty of Arts Professor, University of Western Ontario, London. In 1988 he organized Canada's first interdisciplinary seminar on AIDS and the arts and curated "Visual AIDS," a traveling exhibition of AIDS posters from around the world. He is Editor of the anthology Fluid Exchanges: Artists and Critics in the AIDS Crisis *(University of Toronto Press, 1992) and currently teaches an undergraduate course on post-Stonewall gay history and culture.*

(Overleaf) "A Dream of Flowers" by Duane Michals, 1986. Courtesy of the artist and Sidney Janis Gallery, New York

Painting (oil on wood) by Joseph Bertiers from "AIDS in Africa: Through the Eyes of Joseph Bertiers," exhibition in UCLA's Fowler Museum of Cultural History, 1993. Courtesy of Ernie Wolfe Gallery, Los Angeles; photograph, Denis Nervig

loss of masterpieces now never to be painted because AIDS has taken such a huge toll on artists. The Museum of Modern Art covered a single wall in the Garden Hall with cards signed by gallery staff and visitors to commemorate lost artists, friends, lovers, and relatives.

Smaller institutions paid their respects in more overtly religious or pedagogical ways. The Museum for African Art, for instance, darkened the galleries of its exhibition "Face of the Gods: Art and Altars of Africa and the African Americas" to draw attention to a spotlighted Omolu altar dedicated to those who had died of "slim disease" (as AIDS is often called in Africa). The role of the graphic arts in promoting safer sex messages was highlighted in the Cooper-Hewitt National Museum of Design's "Living with AIDS: Education Through Design" display. Meanwhile, in the lobby of the Whitney Museum of American Art, busy volunteers from the Gay Men's Health Crisis were handing out brochures on the proper use of condoms to all who would take them. A neon sign flashing the word *Silence,* part of an installation by Barbara Steinman, provided visitors to New York's Jewish Museum with a red-alert reminder of the politically charged analogy between the epidemic and the Holocaust. This sign also alluded to the famous "Silence = Death" neon that first appeared in the AIDS art exhibit "Let the Record Show . . . " at Manhattan's New Museum of Contemporary Art in 1987, an exhibit that helped launch the AIDS activism movement. Did Steinman's sign commemorate the deaths of millions silenced by the epidemic or the censoring of controversial art and the demise of AIDS activism as a vital force on the New York cultural scene? It was hard to tell.

Elsewhere in the city and the world, however, silences around AIDS were being aesthetically broken. At United Nations headquarters, Liza Minnelli premiered a new AIDS anthem (originally an inspirational number from the

World AIDS Day 1993: (opposite page, top) the U.S. Postal Service issued a 29-cent "AIDS Awareness" stamp. Museums and galleries became envelopes of awareness, commemorating the vast numbers of artists lost to the global AIDS crisis: some shrouded works in black; others removed selected works for the day; still others mounted special exhibits. (Opposite bottom) Paintings by Kenyan artist Joseph Bertiers at the Fowler Museum in Los Angeles presented a bewildering array of images and messages about a bewildering illness and the terrible toll it has taken in Africa. Barbara Steinman's installation at Manhattan's Jewish Museum (above) recalled the trenchant motto of ACT UP New York and other AIDS activist groups, "Silence = Death" (above left).

gay-but-not-AIDS-related musical *Kiss of the Spider Woman*), accompanied by a youthful and very starry-eyed choir. "Someday we'll be free," she reassured the international community in her showstopping way: "I promise you we'll be FREE/ If not to-mor-row/ Then the day after that!" Even showbiz must have its kitschy moment of glory in the spotlight on World AIDS Day (if not on "the day after that").

Not to be outdone in charisma by anyone on the AIDS celebrity circuit, a sequined Princess Diana joined 11,000 music fans for a rock concert at London's Wembley Stadium to benefit AIDS research in England. The now-elusive Princess of Wales shared the stage with performers such as David Bowie, bad-boy rocker George ("Monogamy") Michael, and Canadian country music star k.d. lang. Absurd juxtapositions of high and low culture continued all day to bespeak the world's high-energy confusion over AIDS as a "cultural event." In the Philippines a group of nurses paraded through the streets of Manila chanting, "Condom, condom the best . . . safe sex, safe sex!" and pulling a float carrying votive candles twined with red ribbons. No comment was heard from the normally censorious leaders of the country's powerful Catholic Church.

In China, which has typically regarded AIDS as a foreign problem, it was finally time to act; medical scientists were called to a meeting in Beijing (Peking) to discuss strategies for coping with the ever rising numbers of adults infected with HIV in East Asia and the Pacific. Japan, too, shook off its xenophobic attitude toward the crisis. Celebrities took to the streets and handed out AIDS information to commuters in busy train stations. A major newspaper in India dared to publish an explicit guide to safer sex practices. On a more playful though no less serious note, the Gospel of Safer Sex was preached to Christmas shoppers in Berlin by latex missionaries from the Deutsche AIDS-Hilfe (German Aid for AIDS). Dressed in head-to-toe body-condoms, they easily stood out in the crowd on the Kurfürstendamm as they handed out free *Pariser* (condoms).

Filipino nurses artistically observe World AIDS Day with posters, floats, balloons, and the chanting of "safer sex" messages during a parade through the streets of Manila.

In an early-morning World AIDS Day ceremony, Place de la Concorde in Paris briefly becomes Place de la Condom.

Standing even taller was the 23-meter (75-foot) hot pink condom unfurled down the Obelisk on the Place de la Concorde in a predawn "zap" (attention-getting action) organized by volunteers from the Italian clothing company Benetton and activists from ACT UP Paris, a chapter of the AIDS Coalition to Unleash Power. The Obelisk under wraps was certainly a sight to behold. The joyous absurdity of the 35-kilogram (77-pound) *préservatif* covering the 3,300-year-old pink granite monument temporarily transformed the august square into the waggish Place de la Condom. Cheers went up as the unlubricated "Mega-Safe" unrolled in the right direction. Had the lowly condom at last attained the status of a high art object? Like its functional counterparts, it had a short life. Riot policemen ripped the offending sheath down an hour later.

The aestheticizing of AIDS: four theories

Explanations for the unprecedented engagement of the arts in what might at first look like a purely medical concern (as if the world of medicine was ever distinct from the encompassing spheres of culture) range from the journalistically simple to the academically arcane. At the simplistic extreme is a stereotyping syllogism that boils down to this: (a) lots of artists are gay; (b) lots of gays are "AIDS victims"; (c) therefore, lots of AIDS art is created to make the gay community feel better. This argument might be called the "theory of aesthetic compensation." It presupposes a fairy-tale transformation of the decadent "beautiful people" into the "living dead" under the baleful influence of HIV.

In the February 1989 issue of *Vanity Fair*, the photographer Robert Mapplethorpe lamented, "This disease is hideous." He died a month later. Where one might expect the aesthete's eye to be blinded with tears of self-pity, Mapplethorpe's ever cruising lens was pitilessly focused on his own wasted appearance; it seemed to fascinate him as much as it repelled him. In an exultant 1988 self-portrait, for instance, he cast himself in the role of

129

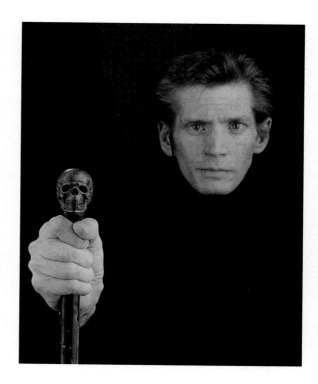

Mesmerized by the effects of AIDS on his own appearance, photographer Robert Mapplethorpe took this and other self-portraits before he died of the disease in March 1989 at age 42.

"Self Portrait," 1988; © 1988 The Estate of Robert Mapplethorpe

the "King of Death," his haggard face emerging out of the shadows of the underworld and glowing palely beside a carved skull forming the knob of a scepterlike cane. Eerily, the skull's blank eyes parallel the hypnotic glower of the ghostly Mapplethorpe.

Closely related to the aesthetic compensation theory is what can be called the "theory of aesthetic distance." According to this popular explanation of the epidemic of AIDS art, works like Mapplethorpe's last self-portraits set "us," the warily sympathetic general public, at a safe, contemplative distance from "them." Such a theory not only is naive in its moralistic impulse to disidentify the sick from the well but also is absurdly narrow in its gender bias and social focus. For one thing, it fails to explain why so many artists who are neither gay nor male have responded to AIDS in complex and challenging ways across the broad range of representational media. For another, it cannot account for the production of heterogeneous folk works such as the NAMES Project AIDS Memorial Quilt, which has been sewn, patched, painted, and assembled by thousands of hands around the world since 1987. Nor can it explain the organization of safer-sex "happenings" such as the 1990 benefit concert, held in a suburb of Mexico City, at which rock bands celebrated the saving graces of *el preservativo* ("the condom") while crowds of jiving teenagers and university students celebrated *vida contra Sida* ("life against AIDS").

A third explanation for the engagement of the arts with AIDS might be called the "theory of aesthetic crisis" since it is based on the observation that the epidemic happened to strike at a turning point in contemporary art and cultural history. In the late 1970s a generation of artists with academic training in semiotics (the language-based science of reading

130

cultural signs) was emerging from the ruins of modernism. A collective identity crisis in the wake of '60s liberalism and the slowdown of the gay and women's liberation movements was sapping their creative energies. They were "postmodernists without a cause"—until they discovered the "Big One" in the seismic repercussions of the AIDS epidemic. Subjects for radical artistic attack were swiftly found in the stigmatizing classification of people according to risk groups, in the immigration policies designed to stop the virally unclean at the border, in the conservative advertising campaigns promoting "family values" as the key to health, and in the media's representation of the so-called AIDS virus as a secret weapon or a terrorist agent.

Inevitably, some explorers of this forbidding terrain have come to regard AIDS as the perfect metaphor for the "postmodern condition." Insofar as these critical observers tend to read culture in terms of AIDS, instead of AIDS in terms of culture, their explanation for the artistic obsession with the epidemic might be labeled the "theory of aesthetic displacement." As an inversion of the periodizing "theory of aesthetic crisis," theory number four goes well beyond the notion that AIDS amounts to a deep-seated crisis of representation. In fact, if AIDS did not actually exist, postmodern theorists would surely have invented it as a projection of their all-consuming anxiety over existence and nonexistence on the howling brink of meaninglessness. Perhaps artists have been drawn to AIDS like martyrs to the arena simply because the syndrome serves as an imaginary stage upon which the major taboo-flagged subjects of traditional cultural interest—sex, death, life, birth, body, soul, blood, and so on—spectacularly converge and conflict before the distanced eyes of the well. According to the displacement theory, there can be no distance (aesthetic or critical) between the sick and the well these days, for dying is an inseparable complement to living.

One might wonder, however, how the women photographed by Ann Meredith in an AIDS ward in Kenya, far from the asylums of academic theory, would feel about being viewed as defenseless "carriers" of the postmodern condition. Would they rejoice to learn that their T cells, ruined by postmodern panic, were a hot topic in philosophy of contemporary culture lecture halls?

Art is not enough: activism versus aestheticism

World AIDS Day has become a "Day Without Art." Since 1989, when it was first celebrated in this positively negative way by a handful of galleries (mostly in New York City) with the encouragement of an ad hoc committee of activist-curators calling themselves "Visual AIDS," the event has grown to include some 5,300 art groups and cultural institutions throughout North America and Europe. As an aesthetic protest, these annual gestures of self-censorship affirm what they ironically seem to deny: take away the pleasures of art for a day, and society at large will then realize how much it depends on art for consolation in the midst of this tragic crisis. Perhaps as an ascetic exercise, enduring a Day Without Art is meant to sustain the frail hope that eventually the world will rejoice in a "Day Without AIDS"—or even a "Day Without Death."

131

As the parody of a famous soft-drink logo grimly suggests, no one with AIDS could possibly "enjoy" zidovudine (AZT; Retrovir), the costly mainstay of anti-HIV therapy that offers no hope of a cure. Nor, for that matter, do "things go better" with AZT; often they get worse.

But will the days of draped canvases and years of gala benefit concerts ever compensate for the brutally unaesthetic toll the epidemic has taken on this person's flesh or that person's spirit? "With 42,000 dead ART is not enough" was the sobering message that appeared on a poster produced by the graphic arts collective "Gran Fury" in 1988. If art is not enough, then what is? The same poster goes on to urge people to "take collective direct action to end the AIDS crisis." Such activist actions have taken various forms—among them satirizing dominant cultural practices, exposing the elitist policies of Manhattan galleries, shaming rich art consumers into an awareness of the infected homeless, and literally throwing the latest AIDS statistics back in the faces of the medical officers at the U.S. Centers for Disease Control and Prevention (CDC), Atlanta, Georgia, who had collected them for the *Morbidity and Mortality Weekly Report*.

The satiric impetus of activist art perhaps reached the limits of cynical bleakness in 1990 with Vincent Gagliostro and Avram Finkelstein's pop-arty parody of the internationally familiar red and white "Enjoy Coke" sign. The slogan had been grimly changed to "Enjoy AZT." Fine print at the bottom of the sign claimed:

The U.S. government has spent one billion dollars over the past 10 years to research new AIDS drugs. The result, 1 drug—AZT. It makes half the people who try it sick and for the other half it stops working after a year. Is AZT the last, best hope for people with AIDS, or is it a short-cut to the killing Burroughs Wellcome is making in the AIDS marketplace? Scores of drugs languish in government pipelines, while fortunes are made on this monopoly.

Clearly the debate, begun in the late '80s, over the efficacy of activist versus aesthetic strategies for reaching the promised "end" of the AIDS crisis has been a bitter and dispiriting one. Today, as artists and authors reckon with the increasingly gloomy possibility that such an end will not come in their lifetimes, they are struggling through days without art and attempting to move beyond the spiritually draining impasse of that debate. They are also creating an unprecedented number of powerful AIDS-inspired works—which may or may not be "enough."

Envisioning a new disease

Words and images, in fact, were busy representing the new syndrome—giving its vague presence definition and visibility—long before it was officially recognized as a threat to public health. Consider how and why AIDS received its name. In 1981, when American doctors began to perceive clusters of opportunistic infections, unusual cancers, and lingering malaises as symptoms of a hitherto unrecognized immunologic disorder that seemed to be striking mainly gay male patients, a variety of discriminatory-cum-diagnostic names cropped up in the medical press and in gay community newspapers for want of a single standard term. These included GRID for "gay-related immune deficiency," CAID for "community-acquired immune deficiency," "gay plague," "gay cancer," and even WOG for "Wrath of God."

Representatives of the arts were not present at the fateful meeting of epidemiologists and blood-industry officials in Washington, D.C., on July 27, 1982, when the syndrome first received its now all-too-familiar official medical designation. However, the highly inventive act of naming—ritually christening this new child of science—can be regarded as more than a mere bureaucratic labeling decision. It was also an inherently literary effort: the coolly impersonal components of the name, "acquired immune deficiency syndrome," especially "acquired," were carefully chosen to capture and fix the officially sanctioned character of AIDS as a strictly medical problem of apparently universal concern. That effort amounted to a clear renunciation of earlier prejudicial labels.

Images, no less than words, played a critical role in shaping early perceptions of the epidemic. Before it was realized how or even that AIDS could be "acquired" by anyone, the mysteries of its infectious transmission and pathogenic impact were being probed by the arts of medical imaging. Among the images surfacing in autopsy reports, clinical reports published in medical journals, and epidemiological bulletins in 1981–82 were blood cells enlarged by electron microscopy, close-ups of purplish lesions identified as Kaposi's sarcoma (KS), X-rays of pulmonary passages clogged by *Pneumocystis carinii* pneumonia, and clinical photographs of ulcerated feet, cadaverous torsos, swollen eyes, and tongues blanched with candidiasis. These prophetic pictures were certainly not artistic representations of disease and death in any traditional sense but, like any painting in the Louvre, they portrayed (rather than merely mirroring) what their observers wished to capture within a clarifying frame of reference. Patients all but vanished under the microscopic lens and fiercely focused beam of medical scrutiny. Since the earliest visual icons of the epidemic appeared, the "vision of AIDS" has been radically abstracted from its human sufferers.

As early as December 1981, San Francisco nurse Bobbi Campbell (the 16th diagnosed case of "gay cancer" in the Bay Area) styled himself as the "KS Poster Boy" and hung xeroxed photographs of his own KS lesions as warning signs in the windows of a Castro Street drugstore in the heart

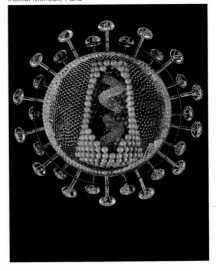

A drug company's computer graphic envisions the virus responsible for AIDS.

(Below left) In 1982 residents of San Francisco's Castro Street neighborhood learn about the "gay plague" from a poster in a drugstore window. News of the devastating new disease first reached the gay community largely because San Francisco nurse Bobbi Campbell went public with his diagnosis—making himself the KS (Kaposi's sarcoma) Poster Boy. (Below) As medical scientists were witnessing the evolution of a previously unknown syndrome, they, too, were viewing images of KS lesions published in the medical literature.

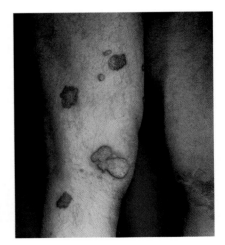

of the city's gay community. "Look at the lesions on my feet," Campbell warned. "What is happening to me could happen to you."

Was this the humble beginning of what *Newsweek* magazine was to hail over a decade later on its Jan. 18, 1993, cover as the glamorous connection between "AIDS and the Arts" forged by "A Lost Generation"? Pictured on that cover in an otherworldly ecstatic pose was the ballet star Rudolf Nureyev, who had died a week and a half earlier. While the shot may have done him justice as a *danseur noble,* it misleadingly represented him as the prototypical artist cruelly cut down yet ennobled by disease. Unlike Campbell, Nureyev kept his diagnosis a closely guarded secret to the bitter end. Campbell (who died in 1984) had neither aesthetic principles nor spiritual losses in mind when he turned his own image into an icon of the mysterious disorder he was fighting—a disorder as yet unblazoned with tragic grandeur. Rather, he was earnestly intent on warning fellow mortals about the frailty of the flesh while grimly laughing at his own plight. Needless to say, the KS Poster Boy did not make *Newsweek*'s two-page roster of creative worthies—"foot soldiers of the arts" mourned in Nureyev's shadow.

Following the unlikely and largely unacknowledged lead of pioneers like Campbell, artists in every field of representation have taken up the enormous challenge of humanizing the imagery and rhetoric of the Age of AIDS. Composers have filled with song the cavities of silence around AIDS; sculptors have fleshed out the cadaverous torsos in the clinical records with resurgent dignity; painters have scraped off the glossy sur-

In ceremonies at the Opéra-Garnier in Paris on Oct. 8, 1992, a gaunt and ailing Rudolf Nureyev received France's highest cultural honor, Les Insignes de Commandeur des Arts et des Lettres. The world-renowned ballet star died three months later, never having revealed publicly that he had AIDS.

J. Moatti—Sipa Press

faces of glamorized "loss" to find the agonized faces of the forgotten, the dispossessed, the excluded, the desperate. Filmmakers have panned across the social landscape of the sick and the well and zeroed in on specific community contexts in which the public spectacle of the "war on AIDS" is being waged. Novelists have conveyed the day-to-day struggles and anguish of protagonists living with AIDS, and autobiographers have magnified their own complex psychosexual experiences. Poets and play-wrights have given voices to the tongues depressed (but not silenced) by the Medical Establishment. The arts have also amplified the voices and feelings of doctors, nurses, buddies, and other caregivers, who play such crucial parts in the lives of PLWAs.

Fantasies of a cure

In 1990 one of Campbell's many anonymous successors plastered the Castro Street neighborhood with posters bearing the provocative slogan "Imagine a cure." How could anyone imagine a cure for a disease so fatalistically equated with death itself? Yet that sign did not go unheeded, for many artists have striven to defy the gloomy equation by imagining a cure for both AIDS and death.

"Art *does* have the power to save lives," insisted the American cultural critic Douglas Crimp in 1987, "and it is this very power that must be recognized, fostered, and supported in every way possible." Despite its obviously secular context, this proclamation is not so far removed in spirit from Dante's insistence that art has the power to save souls. Poet and novelist Paul Monette, for one, has proposed that the grieving process itself might be construed as "a cure that isn't in the books." In his elegy "The Worrying" (from *Love Alone,* 1988), Monette reflects on his own frantic state of hypochondria and survivor guilt mixed with intense poetic creativity following the death of his lover, Rog, in 1986.

A simple way to imagine a cure for AIDS is to rename it so that the fear-ful implications of the acronym magically, if temporarily, vanish. Canadian director John Greyson, for example, changed AIDS to ADS (for "acquired dread of sex") in his 1987 mock-rock video, "The ADS Epidemic," which, among other things, hailed latex condoms as "the very latest thing to wear."

In her 1992 dream play, *The Baltimore Waltz,* Paula Vogel dealt with the loss of her brother Carl to AIDS by renaming the syndrome. The protago-nist, Anna, who takes on Carl's identity, is diagnosed with ATD ("acquired toilet disease"). As a primary-school teacher, Anna is in a high-risk group—confronted by legions of ATD viruses breeding on the surfaces touched by children who do not heed their mothers' warnings about spreading "germs." The maternally instilled nightmare of catching a fatal illness from a toilet seat comes comically true in Anna's phobic journey through the conflicting memories and desires stirred up by her brother's death.

Rather than renaming it, some artists imagine AIDS cures by re-diagnosing it. Keith Haring's punchy poster called "Art Attack on AIDS" shows two simple white figures outlined in black confronting each other against a yellow background. Each throws two punches: one through a hole in the head and the other through a hole in the chest of the opposing

James Miller

In 1990 a poster challenges San Francisco's gay community to do what medical science had not succeeded in doing: end the AIDS crisis. While the tide of the epidemic has not yet been stemmed nor a cure for AIDS found, artists in virtually every discipline have responded in force—creating unprecedented numbers of imaginative works that console, offer hope, or otherwise make some religious or political sense out of the confused and conflicted "spectacle" of AIDS so often presented in the media.

Through writing her play The Baltimore Waltz, *Paula Vogel was able to come to terms with her brother Carl's AIDS death. The character Anna—played by Jenny Bacon (right) in a highly acclaimed Goodman Studio Theatre production in Chicago in April–May 1993—is the playwright's alter ego. Actor Jerry Saslow (sitting) plays Carl. In this empathic dream play it is Anna (rather than her brother) who is afflicted with a dire terminal disease; as a schoolteacher who shares bathroom facilities with her unhygienic pupils, she contracts ATD ("acquired toilet disease"). She and Carl then set off, in a daydream, in search of a miracle cure. In Europe they visit the clinic of a mad urologist named Todesröcheln ("Deathrattle"), who prescribes some highly unconventional medicine.*

figure. The words *art attack,* of course, suggest heart attack, as do the chest blows the two boxing figures deliver. Is the artist likening AIDS to a cardiological crisis—treatable through open-heart surgery—or open-heart boxing? Perhaps the message is that AIDS is a heartbreaking, or heart-opening, struggle. The head blows might be viewed as an attack on the apathy of those who refuse to act up against AIDS.

Scientific hopes for discovering a "magic bullet" have all but died as medical researchers confront the complexities of HIV and AIDS. Nevertheless, in the art world the old dream of a chemical cure has been kept alive. The Canadian artists Jorge Zontal, A.A. Bronson, and Felix Partz, the witty anatomists of consumer culture better known collectively as General Idea, exhibited "One Year of AZT and One Day of AZT" in their last touring show in 1993. (Zontal and Partz died of AIDS—in February and June 1994, respectively.)

"One Year . . . One Day . . ." consisted of a bas-relief of 1,825 styrene capsules stacked horizontally from floor to ceiling along two closely adjacent walls. On the floor rested five giant three-dimensional capsules that replicated zidovudine (AZT; Retrovir) in design—white with a blue band. The smaller ones, each about one-third meter (about one foot) long, represented an average annual supply of the drug. The larger ones, representing a daily dose, were each two meters (seven feet) long. At first glance the installation looked like an ironic pop-art joke. However, to those who have to pop zidovudine every five hours, day and night, for the rest of their lives, the message is no laughing matter.

A poster in much the same vein by Visual AIDS (1994) not only lashes out at the manufacturers of AZT, whose bitter pills are no panacea, but comments on the failure of all concerned to come up with an effective therapy. The poster shows a large bowl filled to the brim with pills and declares, "This is one week's medication for a person with AIDS. This is not a cure. Hard to swallow, isn't it?"

136

Prescriptions for bewilderment

From the late British director Derek Jarman's 1993 film *Blue,* an intensely subjective "vision" of life from the perspective of one who is blind as a result of AIDS (a not-infrequent complication), to the safer-sex Punch and Judy shows performed on the streets of Cape Town (Gary Friedman's "Puppets Against AIDS" project) to the "Love Messages" recorded in Amsterdam by rock stars and fashion models for MTV Europe (Jim Cook's contribution to World AIDS Day 1993), works on AIDS are everywhere, combining words and images with sounds and movements in increasingly complex expressions of rage, remembrance, and religious yearning. The artists behind these works stand apart from the aesthetes and activists in that they simply do not know what to think about the crisis anymore. Fantasies of a cure do not work for them, at least not for long. Cynicism of the "Enjoy AZT" kind leaves them cold—or more confused than ever before. Blinded by grief or burnt out by anger, they seek something firmer than what Monette called "the thin white cane of outrage" to see them through the dark. They seek something more positive than a negative diagnosis. And those with a positive diagnosis seek something more than drugs and hugs.

For those who find this profusion of AIDS representations perplexing—as perplexing perhaps as the epidemic itself with its mutating viruses and multitudinous losses—the works themselves provide an outlet, or at least support, for their confusion. "It's hard to be clear about a decision for

A "magic bullet" for AIDS has yet to be developed, though many have been imagined. A mocking rendering of the hard-to-swallow AIDS drug AZT ("One Year of AZT and One Day of AZT") by Canadian artists Jorge Zontal, A.A. Bronson, and Felix Partz (known collectively as General Idea) was exhibited at Toronto's Power Plant Gallery as part of the group's last touring show, "Fin de siècle," in 1993. Shortly before Zontal died of AIDS in February 1994, the artistic collective received a lifetime achievement award from the city of Toronto.

"One Year of AZT" (1991, 1,825 units of vacuum-formed styrene, 5 x 12 x 2½ inches each) and "One Day of AZT" (1991, 5 units of fiberglass, 33½ x 84 x 33½ inches), installation by General Idea from "Fin se siècle" exhibition in the Power Plant Gallery, Toronto, 1993. Courtesy of General Idea; photograph, Cheryl O'Brien

my own treatment," confessed architect George Gannett, one of the 15 PLWAs whose perplexed eyes stare out hypnotically from the black-and-white photographs taken by Boston-based photographer Nicholas Nixon. As Gannett reflected in a 1988 journal entry (quoted in Nicholas and Bebe Nixon's book *People with AIDS*): "It's terrible when you see people chasing every imaginable cure, any treatment, any therapy. Some people are so obsessed with 'doing something' that they can't see what's happening. Which is, that they're dying."

Anxious curiosity about the meaning of safer sex turns to agonizing confusion over the paradoxical death wish at the heart of erotic desire in the nervous opening lines of Thom Gunn's poem "In Time of Plague": "My thoughts are crowded with death/ and it draws so oddly on the sexual/ that I am confused/ confused to be attracted/ by, in effect, my own annihilation."

No character has clearer moments of prophetic fury, or thinks he has a more clarifying impact on the morally muddled world of the epidemically challenged, than AIDS-stricken Ned Weeks, the Jeremiah-like alter ego of playwright Larry Kramer. In his first dramatic incarnation, *The Normal Heart* (1985), as the impassioned but impatient organizer of a New York activist group modeled on the Gay Men's Health Crisis, Ned has all the answers to the political and medical problems plaguing his community. "I hear you have a big mouth," his doctor Emma Brookner remarks as she examines her patient. "Is big mouth a symptom?" he rejoins. "No," snaps the doctor, "a cure." With his big mouth thus opened by hallowed medical authority, Ned proceeds to say more than "aaah." He finds his vocation as a prophet and fulfills Brookner's moral commandment: "Tell gay men to stop having sex."

And a hard sell it is as he attempts to bring "the word" to his sexually liberated but morally limp friends. Even the prophet of prophylactic abstinence has moments of doubt when his message seems to be falling on deaf ears despite its apocalyptic urgency. At a low point he cries out, "We're all going to go crazy, living this epidemic every minute, while the rest of the world goes on out there, all around us, as if nothing is hap-

Boston-based photographer Nicholas Nixon and writer Bebe Nixon say in the foreword to their book People with AIDS *(David R. Godine, Publisher, 1989): "Our purpose from the outset of this project was to record with honesty and compassion what it can be to have AIDS." In words and pictures they capture the impact AIDS has on the lives of 15 individuals "as precious time slips away." George Gannett, a full-time architecture student at the Rhode Island School of Design, was photographed in 1987 (below), the year he was diagnosed with Kaposi's sarcoma and full-blown AIDS. (Below right) One of the last photographs Nixon took of Gannett was shortly before the architect died, in February 1989, at his home.*

 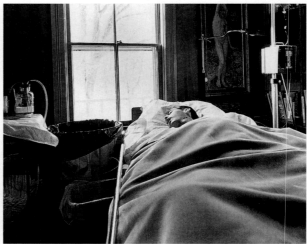

Photographs, (left) "George Gannett, Providence, Rhode Island, October 1987" and (right) "George Gannett, Barrington, Rhode Island, February 1989" by Nicholas Nixon. From *People with AIDS* © 1989 David R. Godine, Boston

William Gibson—Martha Swope Associates

In Larry Kramer's play The Destiny of Me, *the sequel to his fiery polemic,* The Normal Heart, *the protagonist, Ned Weeks, previously an impassioned AIDS activist battling at the front lines, is now a more introspective AIDS patient undergoing experimental treatment. His activist anger has not diminished so much as deepened by his moody reflections on his former life, growing up in a dysfunctional family in suburban "Eden Heights." In this scene in his hospital room (from the play's opening run in New York's Greenwich Village), Ned the patient (foreground, played by Jonathan Hadary) is visited by his younger self (actor John Cameron Mitchell).*

pening, going on with their lives and not knowing what it's like, what we're going through."

Weeks's thunderous railings continue in Kramer's second AIDS play, *The Destiny of Me* (1993), but furious perplexity is now Ned's unwavering response to the mysterious workings of the illness within his own body, which he has checked into a hospital to undergo "top-secret" trials of an experimental treatment. Will the Big Mouth be able to keep the promise of this new therapy a secret from the activists clamoring for any sign of hope from the Medical Establishment? While his dauntless spirit still remains on the activist front lines, the unexpected peace of his 11th-floor hospital room on the infectious diseases unit gives his daunted heart room to grieve for his tormented youth, his wasted energies, and his lost friends. Ned then allows himself an 11th-hour indulgence in bewilderment. "When I started yelling," he cries out in an impassioned soliloquy, "there were 41 cases of a mysterious disease. Now a doctor at Harvard is predicting a million by the turn of the century. And it's still mysterious. And the mystery isn't why they don't know anything, it's why they don't *want* to know anything."

But the doctors themselves (represented by the *life*-affirming character appropriately named Tony Della *Vida*) are bewildered by the antagonism of activists. "All your anger has kept us on our toes," says Della Vida. "So why is my hospital surrounded by your army of activists? Am I going to be burned at the stake if I can't restore your immune system?"

Warding off the plague

Artists have traditionally raised spirits above (and against) the torments of this world in three ceremonious ways. In the most ancient and most basic of these, art has an *apotropaic* function; it ritualistically wards off demons, monsters, evil spirits, or anything else perceived as harmful to the health or harmony of society—often by magical or mystical means.

No realm of the arts has seen more purely apotropaic action since the epidemic began than the dance world (both classical ballet and contem-

In less than a decade, Keith Haring (above right, painting a section of the Berlin Wall in 1986) rose from obscure subway graffitist to one of the best-known and best-loved pop artists in the world. When Haring was struck with AIDS, he battled against the disease with the same kind of determination and vigor that he devoted to all his projects. Almost until the day he died, Feb. 16, 1990, at age 31, he worked indefatigably—creating sculptures for children's playgrounds, painting murals on inner-city walls and in hospital wards, and speaking to groups of children about AIDS. One of his punchier posters attacking AIDS apathy is shown above.

porary dance theater). On the surface it may seem ironic that the majority of choreographers have been reluctant to create dance works openly addressing AIDS, particularly when it has taken such a terrible toll on the ranks of most of the world's major dance companies. Mark Morris, for instance, has strategically avoided creating "AIDS works" for his American dance company (even though he is open about his seropositive status). Dance, he believes, is primarily a fantasy medium that is best suited to the exploration of universal themes such as desire, despair, and death. Nureyev entertained a similarly romantic view.

Perhaps the reluctance of Morris and Nureyev and many other gay choreographers to address AIDS springs from an unwillingness to collapse their identities as free-spirited artists into the activist role of the PLWA. Their aesthetic detachment from the crisis might be construed as a strategy of self-defense; the body-wasting horror of AIDS is simply "too close to home." When AIDS strikes painters, it does not affect the materials of their art, but when it strikes dancers, it wastes the basic medium through which their art has life and visibility.

A few choreographers have boldly broken the creative bloc around AIDS. Douglas Wright of New Zealand dedicated his solo work *Elegy* to three of his friends who had recently died of AIDS, and the BBC broadcast it on Nov. 27, 1993, as a preview to its coverage of World AIDS Day. African-American dancer Bill T. Jones's *Last Supper at Uncle Tom's Cabin/ Promised Land* (1990) grew out of his grieving meditations on the enslaved body following the loss of his lover and dance partner, Arnie Zane, to AIDS in 1988. In 1994 Jones, whose creative energy had not been slowed by his own struggle with AIDS, was choreographing another AIDS work that he defiantly called *Still/Here*.

Where the dance world has chosen to pour most of its physical and spiritual energies against AIDS has been into many gala fund-raising events. The 1994 benefit performance of "Dancers for Life," staged annually in Toronto, had the subtitle "A Leap of Faith." Most of the selections on the

140

program were from ballets or modern dance works that were not created in response to AIDS. The sole exception was a work by choreographer and dancer William Douglas—his dramatic solo *Anima*—a dance that represents the passionate struggle of the soul to find release from the torments of a dying but still erotically driven body.

Clad in green briefs and a loose green overshirt resembling a hospital gown, Douglas (who does not hide his seropositive status) twisted and stretched his long body in a sequence of agonized poses. His costume became the encumbering body, which he desperately sought to escape. Accompanying his jerky movements was a mix of fluid sound effects suggestive of blood pumping, IV tubes dripping, bodily fluids ebbing. Near the end a buzzer sounded for several tense minutes. Had a medical monitoring device gone off, signaling the cessation of breathing or the flattening of a pulse? Slowly, as if in a dream, the dancer removed his sweaty shirt and dropped his briefs to the floor. Naked in the spotlight, but upright at last after so many painful bends and extensions, he stood for a few seconds and then strode ceremoniously forward toward the audience into an electrifying blackout.

Raising the dead

Spirit raising through the arts can also have an *animistic* function. In this case the spirits raised are usually those of the dead. Ned Weeks spends much of his time in the hospital communing with the raised spirits of his spooky family, who suddenly appear to him onstage just as he knew them decades ago when he was growing up innocent of AIDS in suburban "Eden Heights." He is also visited by himself as a boy. From his lost and all-but-forgotten younger self, the fountain of his pre-AIDS creativity, Ned finds a way to affirm life in the depths: "You are not going to die!" his younger self proclaims.

An animistic vision plays an important part in the 1993 Home Box Office television adaptation of *And the Band Played On,* Randy Shilts's 1987 chronicle of the first five years of the AIDS epidemic. A large crowd of AIDS ghosts perform a prophetic dance of death for actor Richard Gere, cast in the closeted cameo role of a legendary Broadway choreographer (à la Michael Bennett, who died of AIDS in 1987). Gere pays a secretive visit to a CDC epidemiologist in San Francisco to report his ominous symptoms. Gloomily stationing himself at a window, he assumes his new role as a doomed but repentant representative of the "beautiful people" as he watches a parade of gay revelers celebrating Halloween on the street below. Suddenly Gere has a glimpse of his future; the parade is transformed into a *danse macabre* with cadavers and skeletons led by the ghoulish figure of Death.

This apocalyptic vision of the epidemic is effectively satirized by Greyson in his film *Zero Patience* (1993), a musical about AIDS mythologies and activist resistance to them. Shilts's character "Patient Zero" (a Canadian airline steward blamed for "carrying" AIDS to the United States) returns from the dead as a blithely homoerotic spirit eager to subvert the homophobic myth of his villainous promiscuity.

Though AIDS has severely diminished the ranks of professional dancers, few choreographers have chosen to create specific works about the disease. Dancer and choreographer William Douglas is an exception. In a performance of Anima *(below), Douglas writhes out of his hospital-gown-like costume, seeking release for his soul from his AIDS-stricken body.*

Anima, dancing and choreography by William Douglas. Courtesy of William Douglas Dance; photograph, Cylla Von Tiedemann

141

Art has the "anagogic" potential to raise human spirits beyond the sphere of fate to everlasting bliss, which John Copoulos achieved in his memorial to his friend Mark Sorrell, an uplifting panel for the NAMES Project Quilt.

Dancing in paradise

When the arts raise human spirits above the storms of history or beyond the spheres of fate into a state of everlasting life, blissful peace, or abundant health, they perform their third and most complex function. The *anagogic* function takes its name from the ancient Greek *anagōgē,* a "leading up" of the soul into mystical heights. A striking example of an anagogic vision in AIDS art may be found on a panel of the NAMES Project Quilt—John Copoulos' tribute to Mark Sorrell.

Sorrell is shown reaching the heavenly end of his search for transcendence, with his head and shoulders rising up through the dancing stars, the tip of his head crossing the frontier of eternity, above which beckons a blue sky with his name inscribed in a rainbow of colors. Whereas Sorrell and Copoulos—and other worldly dancers—sought momentary ecstasy in their orgiastic dancing rites at the New York City club the Paradise Garage, the post-AIDS reveler, in Copoulos' anagogic vision, will find everlasting bliss in the "Paradise" beyond.

Eternity in sound waves

The second decade of the epidemic has seen the emergence of a new group of challenging works that cannot easily be labeled "activist" or "aesthetic" responses to AIDS because they are neither—or both at once. Music is no less capable of expressing the transcendental aspirations of the Age of AIDS than are the visual and literary arts. After seeing the NAMES Project Quilt, American composer John Corigliano was inspired "to memorialize in music those I have lost, and reflect on those I am losing." The creative result of his meditations was his *Symphony No. 1,* a "quilt-like interweaving" of melodic motifs in four movements, which was first performed in March 1990 by the Chicago Symphony Orchestra under the baton of conductor Daniel Barenboim.

The ghosts of the AIDS dead are not quiet in Corigliano's symphony. They literally haunt the score with the nostalgic echoes of their favorite dance tunes, their own chamber works, even their fleeting improvisations recovered from old tape recordings. In the first and fourth movements, for instance, sweetly remote phrases from an Isaac Albéniz tango (composed in 1921) float over the raging brass and percussion to evoke the erotic

142

lightheartedness of a lost friend whose piano renditions of the tune used to delight the composer. The second movement is a tarantella, a lively dance form in $\frac{6}{8}$ time. (This apotropaic dance has its origins in 15th-century Italy, where frenzied dancing was thought to cure the hysteria associated with a venomous spider's [tarantula's] bite.) The animistic design of the symphony as a whole is most elaborately worked out in the third movement, "Giulio's Song." Giulio was an amateur cellist whose friendship the composer had enjoyed since his college days, when they used to improvise and record duets for cello and piano. Giulio died of AIDS several years before the composition of the symphony; his musical spirit rises again in all its improvisatory immediacy for an extended cello solo near the start of the third movement's chaconne.

Though "Giulio's Song" ends explosively with a trumpet sounding a violent A, the final movement, "Epilogue," drifts quietly beyond the storms of time and memory without the anticipated furious fanfare of doom. Corigliano's final melodic recapitulation of themes from the previous movements gathers the spirits of his friends together into a slow meditative current flowing into an oceanic soundscape; the formerly desperate A is transfigured into a quiet note of hope in an immortalizing diminuendo.

The streets of *Purgatorio*

When the filming of *Philadelphia,* the first mainstream, high-budget motion picture about AIDS, began in October 1992, the working title was *Probable Cause*. But this is much more than another glitzy Hollywood

When the NAMES Project Quilt was displayed in October 1987 on the Mall in front of the U.S. Capitol in Washington, D.C., it covered a space larger than two American football fields. It has been growing ever since. For society at large it serves as a reminder of the vast numbers of men, women, and children who have been lost to a cruel epidemic. For the bereaved who have lost individual loved ones, it provides a therapeutic community of sorrow.

Photograph, Trippett—Sipa

melodrama about Law and Justice. By renaming the film after the City of Brotherly Love, writer-director Jonathan Demme (who is straight) and his writing partner Ron Nyswaner (who is gay) evidently wished to signal their "brotherly" intention to work together on a redemptive labor of love. Their "unusual" collaboration, according to their own much-hyped account, was a soul-searching mission that took them back and forth across the heavily guarded "homo-hetero" boundary through the taboo zones of the epidemic. Demme's "risky" undertaking has clearly been projected into the conflictual dynamics of the film's two main characters: Joe Miller (played by Denzel Washington), a straight lawyer with homophobic attitudes, and his client Andrew Beckett (Tom Hanks), a gay lawyer who loses his high-ranking job at a prestigious Philadelphia law firm when an AIDS-phobic colleague notices a KS lesion on his face.

The opening shots, accompanied by Bruce Springsteen's Oscar-winning dirge, "Streets of Philadelphia," zoom from steely downtown office towers full of malevolent heterosexual lawyers to the spray-painted backstreets of South Philadelphia with its slumming derelicts, deadbeats, and other alienated souls. One might hardly expect anything beautiful or brotherly to come from all this. Yet the streets of Philadelphia are truly closer to heaven than they at first appear—at least for those who have eyes to see them through the magic lens of Hollywood. Demme as director is closer to Dante than he lets on. His Philadelphia might be seen as an American version of *Purgatorio,* where the upwardly mobile soul of the gay lawyer patiently endures the combined torments of AIDS and AIDS discrimination before being mystically released into a "home movie" of his paradisiacal childhood. En route, he miraculously converts his straight black lawyer from "homophobe of the year" into an honorary member of the congregation of the aesthetically redeemed (through the divine intervention of Maria Callas, singing a paean to love, the aria "La mamma morta" from Giordano's verismo opera *Andrea Chénier*).

In the box-office smash Philadelphia, *Andrew Beckett (Tom Hanks, left), an AIDS-stricken gay lawyer who has been fired by his prestigious Philadelphia law firm, is defended in court by Joe Miller (Denzel Washington, right), a decidedly straight lawyer. As they endure the grueling trial, Miller rather miraculously overcomes his deep-seated homophobia. Ironically, however, shortly after their legal victory, Beckett loses his battle against his disease.*

This Philadelphia is, like its poor struggling namesake in the book of Revelation (3:8–10), a point of spiritual illumination in a darkening world, where otherworldly messages are sent through prophetic channels to a congregation of aspiring converts. "Because you have kept my word of patient endurance," the risen Christ assures the Philadelphians in a letter sent through his prophet John, "I will keep you from the hour of trial which is coming on the whole world, to try those who dwell on the earth." Throughout his earthly trial, which functions as a symbolic prelude to the Last Judgment, Andrew Beckett remains true to his martyrological name by facing his powerful opponents (led by a glowering Jason Robards as the head of his former law firm) with unrelentingly patient endurance.

A confusing vastness: angels on Broadway

In 1993 the Tony award for best new play went to playwright Tony Kushner for Part One of his "Gay Fantasia on National Themes," *Angels in America*. In this complex and remarkable work, Kushner treats AIDS primarily as a spiritual crisis that literally requires an angel to resolve. That audiences are stunned and confused by the sudden appearance of an angel on Broadway is not surprising. Her manifestation in the theater is so spectacular, so visually embodied, that one might think she is merely a stage trick or a hallucination caused by some kind of collective AIDS dementia. "God almighty," gasps the play's gay fantasist at these heavenly special effects, "*Very* Steven Spielberg." Her entrance, in fact, poses a difficult theological question: Is she the angel of death or the messenger of divine love?

The character who must wrestle with this question and eventually with the angel herself is an ex-drag queen named Prior Walter, whose physical frailty is offset by a spiritual toughness. Prior must fight the viral legions of death whose angel has left her "wine-dark kiss" (a KS lesion) on his skin as an erotic as well as an epidermal omen of what he will suffer as a gay PLWA abandoned by his lover.

Significantly, most of the play's fictional history takes place in the mid-1980s, when Ronald Reagan's America was reeling from the first shock waves of AIDS phobia in the wake of Rock Hudson's death. Reagan himself was scandalously unshaken by the sudden springing of the epidemic to public attention. Though Kushner pulls no punches in his satiric allusions to "Reagan's children," for the most part he leaves the contentious social arena alone. His characters are not stirred by the war drums of activism. Indeed, his version of the "AIDS apocalypse" proceeds on its relentlessly aesthetic course as if no tempers had ever flared at the Gay Men's Health Crisis and no crowds had ever blocked traffic on the Brooklyn Bridge to protest the tardiness of AIDS drug trials.

As the tutelary spirit of America, the angel is also the celestial source of the political and personal freedoms (including erotic liberty) that have been eroded by the collective experience of AIDS as an unending series of dark injustices. The angel's climactic breakthrough "in a shower of unearthly white light" in Part One, *Millennium Approaches,* is the coup de théâtre that fractures Kushner's marathon play into its two complementary parts, each a three-and-a-half-hour drama in its own right.

The Angel of America (Ellen McLaughlin) makes her spectacular appearance before Prior Walter (Stephen Spinella), the ex-drag queen with AIDS, in Millennium Approaches, *Part One of Tony Kushner's award-winning play,* Angels in America.

Photograph, Joan Marcus

The angel's infernal counterpart in the play is a figure dredged up from the very darkest undercurrents of the American dream. "I wish I was an octopus. Eight loving arms and all those suckers," this diabolical character proclaims in his demonic opening speech. In contrast to the play's other leading characters, who are largely fictional, this villain is based on the New York lawyer and Washington, D.C., wheeler-dealer Roy Cohn. As Sen. Joseph McCarthy's legal adviser and fellow witch-hunter for the Senate Committee on Government Operations in the early 1950s, Cohn played a Machiavellian role in the exposure of the supposed "commie-homo" plot to corrupt the moral purity of America. Kushner's Cohn is a pernicious "closet case" whose self-loathing has fueled a lifetime of aggression against homosexuals. Though diagnosed with AIDS at the end of *Millennium Approaches,* he refuses to be exposed as a gay man by the dreaded disease. Moreover, his denial of his "diseased" sexual identity will persist to the end of his life—in fact, even beyond that, as will be revealed in *Angels in America* Part Two.

Kushner began to write Part Two in 1989, and the drama that emerged bravely reflects the new world order suggested by its grandiose title, *Perestroika.* A first version, which opened in Los Angeles in November 1992, was rewritten before it opened in November 1993 in London and a few days later in New York. The rewritten drama was certainly worth the wait, for the two great wings of the play work brilliantly together. Part One is chiefly concerned with justice (or, rather, its absence). Part Two (which

146

in June 1994 earned Kushner his second Tony award for best new play) struggles to transcend the vanity-of-vanities world of the law by fusing the cosmic power of love with the social power of forgiveness. As Kushner constantly suggests in the biblical allusions that vibrate through *Angels,* its two parts are bound together in contentious concord like the Old and New Testaments.

While the five acts of *Perestroika* cover only two months of calendar time—January and February 1986—they are set against a limitless expanse of theorized future evoked by "The World's Oldest Living Bolshevik," a blind prophet of Marxist utopianism identified as Aleksii Antedilluvianovich Prelapsarianov. As his mock-theological name suggests, his archaic views predate the fall of Soviet-style communism and are therefore innocent of the momentous political implications of Mikhail Gorbachev's reconstructive rise to power. These ironies aside, Prelapsarianov wisely deplores the obsessive nostalgia and shrinking prospects of the Americans caught up in the disillusioning Age of AIDS. They are too concerned with the practical task of day-to-day survival. They either lack vision in a prophetic sense or so distrust the imagination as a source of healing power that their fantasies of a cure fail to raise their spirits above the bewilderments of the diseased present. "You who live in this Sour Little Age," this prophet harangues the audience, "cannot imagine the grandeur of the prospect we gazed upon: like standing atop the highest peak in the mighty Caucasus, and viewing in one all-knowing glance the mountainous, granite order of creation."

If the Sour Little Age of AIDS is not sweetened much in Part Two, it is at least broadened and deepened for all the characters. Though *Perestroika* is full of up-in-the-air visionary moments, its main action is at ground level, where all divine revelations are ultimately rejected. Part Two clears up an important question about the angel's theological role, which was literally left hanging at the ambiguous end of Part One. From Prior's revisionist perspective, the angel looks less and less like a messenger from the

Joan Marcus

The pernicious Roy Cohn (played by Ron Leibman), a McCarthyite lawyer during the witch-hunting 1950s, is the angel's infernal counterpart in Kushner's two-part drama. A deeply closeted homosexual, he deals with his intense self-loathing first by directing his destructive energies against the gay community (which he regards as utterly "without clout") and then by refusing to "come out" as a gay man with AIDS after his diagnosis.

God of the Judeo-Christian tradition the more he interacts with her as the embodiment of a desire-driven universe. She swiftly sheds her chastening image, revealing to Prior that there's more beneath her flowing robes than God cared to reveal in the Bible.

After a knock-down-drag-out fight between the now-hospitalized Prior and the angel, the patient wins the right to ascend into heaven to see for himself whether he should throw the prophetic book *Anti-Migration* (which the angel had previously delivered to him, literally hot off the heavenly press) back at the overseers of the universe. When a shaft of pure white light shoots a ladder of even purer whiter light into his hospital room, he hoists himself, with some difficulty—his lungs not being what they once were—but still with heroic resolve, into the beyond.

In the end, Prior returns their tome without a qualm and beats a hasty retreat back to postlapsarian New York. Kushner's post-Hollywood heaven might be viewed as an Oz without a wizard. If AIDS is the tornado stirred up by the Wicked Witch of Republicanism, Prior is a gay version of Dorothy, whose flight over the rainbow is ironically destined to reinforce the simple heartfelt desire to return home. His waking-up scene is a bittersweet parody of Judy Garland's teary homecoming to Auntie Em's Kansas. "I've had a remarkable dream," he cries, "And some of it was terrible, and some of it was wonderful, but all the same I kept saying I want to go home."

In the epilogue of Angels *Part Two,* Perestroika, *Prior Walter (standing) meets friends at the Bethesda fountain in Central Park. By this time he has had a knock-down-drag-out fight with the angel and won, been to heaven and confronted the overseers of the universe, and returned (without qualms) to postlapsarian New York. Still living with AIDS after nearly half a decade, he confesses that he prefers stone angels atop fountains to the celestial ones.*

Joan Marcus

The annual tides of the AIDS epidemic in Canada are measured on the concrete columns of the Cawthra Park AIDS Memorial (designed by architect Patrick Fahn) in downtown Toronto. Unveiled in June 1993, the monument is devoted to the memory of a community's and a country's AIDS dead; the pillars bearing their names are arranged along an open-ended pathway, articulating a space for contemplating the epidemic's expansion.

The play's epilogue, which is dated February 1990, takes place in New York City's Central Park. Four years have passed since Prior's heavenly ascent, but he is still proudly—if perversely—clinging to life with AIDS. Gathered with friends around the Bethesda fountain, with the angel Bethesda represented in stone at the top, Prior concludes: "I like them best when they're statuary. They commemorate death but they suggest a world without dying."

Open endings

Postactivist works such as Kushner's *Angels in America,* Demme and Nyswaner's *Philadelphia,* and Corigliano's *Symphony No. 1* favor open endings. Their plots expand outward, upward, and onward, tacitly acknowledging that there are no aesthetically satisfying resolutions to the "AIDS crisis," just as there are no easy political ways to tie up the loose ends of the "AIDS story." Although they are intended to change the popular image of the epidemic as an exclusively gay plague, the inclusive design of these recent AIDS-inspired creations is more than just socially transformative; it is also spiritually transfigurative.

AIDS art in the '90s looks beyond the tentative short-term prognosis that medicine has to offer and cannot easily be associated with any one art of raising spirits—for sometimes it raises hell, sometimes ghosts, and sometimes angels. That these works should be full of miraculous breakthroughs, magical empowerments, supernatural solicitations, clairvoyant dreams, apocalyptic illuminations, and "special effects" in a holy (as well as a Hollywood) sense is not surprising in light of their spiritual function as antidotes to all the gloom and doom on the medical front. Turning to the arts for hope, the bereaved and the bewildered are finding a new set of prophets who are reinventing Heaven in boldly transfigurative visions of the harrowing—and hallowing—of AIDS.

At age 42, choreographer and dancer Bill T. Jones has lost none of his creative energy or commanding stage presence. Much of his recent work reflects his personal struggle to defy the common misperception of People Living with AIDS as passive victims. In June 1994 he received a prestigious MacArthur Foundation fellowship—$265,000 over five years—to pursue his work. The award came at the time he was choreographing a dance about AIDS to be called Still/Here.

149

Trying to Help: Humanitarian Relief in Bosnia

by Michael J. Toole, M.D., D.T.M. & H.

Michael J. Toole, M.D., D.T.M. & H., is a medical epidemiologist with the International Health Program Office, U.S. Centers for Disease Control and Prevention (CDC), Atlanta, Georgia. This article was prepared in his private capacity; no official CDC support or endorsement is intended.

(Opposite) Sarajevo, 1993; photograph, Christopher Morris—Black Star

AS 1994 BEGAN, THE PEOPLE OF FORMER YUGOSLAVIA WERE struggling to survive their third year of war. Since Slovenia and Croatia declared their independence in June 1991, the six republics that made up the old Socialist Federal Republic of Yugoslavia—Serbia, Montenegro, Slovenia, Croatia, Macedonia, and Bosnia and Herzegovina—have turned backward to rediscover their past and attempt to build a future. The consequences have been violent warfare, ethnic persecution, economic collapse, death, and destruction—to a degree not seen in Europe since World War II. Although each republic has been affected to an extent, the bloodshed and suffering have been the greatest among the populations that inhabit the remnants of Bosnia and Herzegovina.

In the absence of peace, the international community mounted a massive relief program aimed at keeping the civilian population alive. This report looks at that operation, which has been marked since its start by awesome constraints, limited achievements, and constant dangers; included are selected extracts (not necessarily in chronological order) from the journal kept by this author while serving as a relief worker accompanying a United Nations relief convoy as it struggled to reach a besieged Muslim enclave in eastern Bosnia in the winter of 1993.

A war against civilians

It has been snowing steadily for three days, and Zepa village shimmers in the late afternoon light. From this distance it is difficult to see that almost every house has been damaged by the artillery shells that have bombarded it almost daily for the past year. I am one of a team from the U.S. Centers for Disease Control and Prevention (CDC), sent to carry out an assessment of the public health needs in Bosnia and Herzegovina. We are accompanying a convoy of food provided by the international community for the besieged inhabitants of the Zepa valley. Only one week earlier there had been four such enclaves in central and eastern Bosnia; however, on the 2nd of March, Serbian forces captured Cerska, 60 kilometers [one kilometer = 0.62 mile] to the north. Another enclave, Srebrenica, 30 kilometers northeast of Zepa, was under siege by Serbian military forces; no food convoy had reached the 60,000 inhabitants since December 1992. Srebrenica was soon to become famous around the world when the French commander of the United Nations Protection Force (UNPROFOR) in Bosnia and Herzegovina, Gen. Philippe Morillon, refused to budge from the post office until the Bosnian Serb military permitted a food convoy to enter the town. The fourth enclave, Gorazde, is a city of 50,000–60,000 people and lies approximately 50 kilometers to the south of Zepa.

—March 6 (the day we reach our destination)

In January 1994 the inhabitants of Bosnia and Herzegovina were trying to survive a second winter of war—their physical and psychological reserves vastly depleted. Particularly threatened were the long-suffering citizens of the capital, Sarajevo, and of the remaining Bosnian government-controlled enclaves of Tuzla, Zenica, Srebrenica, Zepa, and Gorazde.

The conflict in Bosnia and Herzegovina and in the devastated Serb-dominated areas of Croatia, known locally as the Krajina and by the international community as the UN Protected Areas (UNPAs), has been a war against civilians. The goal has been to kill, injure, disable, intimidate, and remove civilians of opposing ethnic groups, creating "ethnically cleansed" zones. The exact death toll from this violence may never be known; estimates in early 1994 ranged between 115,000 and 200,000 deaths. Violence is the single most important public health risk factor in these war-ravaged areas, and the primary public health consequences of the war have been deaths and injuries directly caused by that violence. In Sarajevo alone, for example, there were 4,600 violence-related deaths and 16,000 injuries during the first year of the war. In the central Bosnian province of Zenica, hospital admissions due to war-related trauma rose from 22% in April 1992 to 78% in December of the same year.

Signs of anguish on the faces of long-suffering Sarajevans reflect the horrors they are daily forced to endure as a war that has been directed expressly against civilians rages on.

Luc Delahaye—Sipa

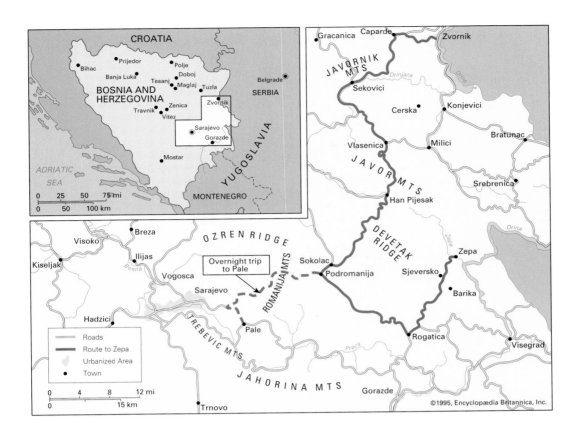

The secondary effects of the war on public health have been mediated through severe food shortages, mass population displacement, destruction of health facilities, medical supply shortages, and disruption to water, electricity, fuel, and gas supplies. In previous and ongoing wars in less developed countries, such secondary effects of war often cause more deaths than the violence itself—a consequence of high rates of malnutrition and epidemics of infectious diseases. In Bosnia and Herzegovina, however, neither widespread famine nor large epidemics of communicable diseases had occurred by early 1994. Nevertheless, the potential for such calamities remained high unless the international community could successfully gain access to the affected population and provide sufficient aid.

In March 1993 the author was part of an international humanitarian aid team that brought desperately needed food and medical supplies to residents of the Zepa valley, a besieged Muslim enclave in eastern Bosnia and Herzegovina. The map traces his route through Bosnia and Herzegovina.

Food relief: urgent and obstructed

Shortly before dawn three days ago, our convoy left Belgrade, the capital of the Republic of Serbia and what remains of the Federal Republic of Yugoslavia (Serbia and Montenegro). About 50 metric tons of food and medical supplies had been loaded onto 10 Belgian army trucks, their white canopies marked with the letters UNHCR (standing for United Nations High Commissioner for Refugees), the international organization charged with providing humanitarian assistance to former Yugoslavia. Several small four-wheel-drive vehicles and a military ambulance complete the convoy. The trucks are being driven by young Belgian soldiers, members of one of the many national military contingents that constitute UNPROFOR. Other convoys are managed by Swedes, British, Canadians, Danes, and Russians. The convoy starts its journey on the modern international superhighway that was once a busy route for commercial trucks traveling from Greece and Turkey to the rich markets of Western

153

Gen. Philippe Morillon (above), the French commander of the United Nations Protection Force (UNPROFOR) in Bosnia, is pictured alongside a food convoy at the UN base in Vitez. In March 1993 Morillon accompanied a convoy to Srebrenica, one of the remaining Muslim holdouts in eastern Bosnia; after the town was shelled by Serb tanks and rockets, he sought to ensure the security of the town's 60,000 inhabitants, many of whom were on the brink of starvation. The commander refused to leave until food and essential supplies could be delivered and Serbian forces allowed the safe passage of refugees seeking to leave the devastated enclave. (Above right) Winter snow and cold prevail in April 1993 as white-canopied UN trucks attempt to reach eastern Bosnia, where hundreds of thousands of residents were dependent on food aid for survival. By early 1994 well over four million people in former Yugoslavia were in need of relief assistance.

Europe. On this day, however, the road is empty, its tollbooths almost deserted. International economic sanctions against Serbia and Montenegro and occasional shelling along the portion of the road between Belgrade and Zagreb have effectively rendered it traffic-free.

—*March 4*

Food is the most pressing need in Bosnia and Herzegovina. UNHCR estimated in early 1994 that a total of 4.5 million people throughout former Yugoslavia were in need of relief assistance. Of these, 2.7 million were in Bosnia and Herzegovina; most of the others were refugees and displaced persons scattered throughout Croatia, Serbia, and Montenegro. UNHCR appealed for $522 million to finance the relief operation during the first six months of 1994. Since 1991 the relief effort in former Yugoslavia had cost almost $2 billion, of which the United States government had provided approximately $436 million.

The UNHCR daily ration for persons dependent on food aid in former Yugoslavia consists of 450 grams (one gram = 0.035 ounce) of wheat flour; 60 grams of beans and other pulses; 40 grams of fish, meat, or cheese; 30 grams of vegetable oil; 25 grams of sugar; and 4 grams of yeast. This provides an average of approximately 2,400 kilocalories per person per day, an adequate amount for persons performing light work, even during the cold winter months. Dried orange juice powder was also distributed in areas where the people were likely to suffer from vitamin C deficiency (this included Sarajevo and the other Bosnian enclaves). The estimated total requirement of food aid in the first six months of 1994 was 450,000 metric tons, of which 61,000 had already been committed by the U.S. In addition to family food rations, the United Nations Children's Fund (UNICEF) and nongovernmental aid organizations were providing supplemental feedings to individuals at high risk—mainly young children. In late 1993 UNICEF was providing supplemental meals to approximately 200,000 of the estimated 500,000 children living in war-affected areas.

Despite the apparently adequate food ration and generous donations by Western nations, the actual delivery of this food to the beneficiaries is inordinately difficult and dangerous. Most food convoys are organized by either UNHCR or the International Committee of the Red Cross (ICRC). Armed forces of the various factions, especially Serbian soldiers in eastern and northern Bosnia and around Sarajevo and Croatian militia in southern and central Bosnia and western Herzegovina, have obstructed food convoys for weeks at a time and, in many cases, confiscated their contents. For example, food convoys destined for the central Bosnian towns of Maglaj and Tesanj were held up for over 100 days, finally reaching them on Oct. 20 and 22, 1993, respectively. Overall, during the first week of November 1993, only 35% of the required food aid was successfully delivered to Bosnia and Herzegovina and the UNPAs.

During the fall of 1993, it was clear that there would be severe food shortages during the impending winter. Fighting between Bosnian government and Croatian forces escalated steadily, making food aid deliveries increasingly difficult and sometimes impossible. Commercial food traffic into central Bosnia had almost totally ceased owing to disruption by Bosnian Croat forces. The southern Bosnian city of Mostar was under siege, and approximately 50,000 Muslims were trapped in the eastern side of the city. Even in Sarajevo, where international efforts to furnish and maintain food supplies had previously been successful in most instances, the airport was often closed toward the end of 1993; this was due to repeated, heavy shellings. During the month of October, for example, a total of 6,323 metric tons of aid was delivered to the capital city—an amount that was 1,098 short of UNHCR's minimum requirements.

The scene at the Zvornik border crossing is the first of many surreal sights on this journey. On both sides of the road leading up to the bridge over the Drina River, rows of white-canopied relief trucks are parked, waiting for permission to cross into Bosnia and proceed to various destinations: Sarajevo, Tuzla, and the enclaves in eastern

James Mason—Black Star

UN protection forces wait at a Serb-controlled checkpoint on the road to Vitez. The will of peacekeepers serving as armed escorts for relief convoys is repeatedly tested as the delivery of humanitarian aid is impeded, often for weeks at a time, or prevented altogether. In some instances the contents of convoys have been confiscated, and many relief workers have lost their lives in the line of duty.

Bosnia. However, the officials who grant (or, more often, do not grant) permission to cross the bridge are not working for the internationally recognized government of Bosnia and Herzegovina. The border guards represent the Bosnian "Serb Republic," since Serbs now control 70% of the land area of the country. Before the war Bosnia and Herzegovina had a population of 4.4 million, of whom 44% were Muslims, 33% Serbs, 18% Croats, and the remainder of mixed or other ethnicity. The Muslim-dominated government, based in Sarajevo, now controls less than one-fifth of the country, although this territory includes most of the major urban areas.

After a delay the convoy moves across the bridge into Zvornik, where, on a small hill, one is immediately confronted with a large cemetery containing dozens of new, crudely erected wooden crosses marking recent burials. Only 10 kilometers from Zvornik, on the road to Tuzla, the village of Caparde appears to have been totally destroyed, almost every house having been shelled or burned and the only sign of life an elderly couple pulling a handcart loaded with their belongings. In the stark black and white of a late winter snowstorm, these refugees appear to have emerged from a World War II newsreel.

After a five-hour delay, we proceed to the next town on the route. We arrive at Rogatica around 3 in the afternoon and park at the police checkpoint. It is immediately evident that the police here are far more hostile than those we had earlier encountered at Podromanija. There will be no sharing the warmth of woodstoves at this checkpoint. A group of workers representing the European Community and charged with monitoring aid delivery are told that they will not be allowed past the checkpoint and are given five minutes to leave town. We are informed that it is too late to start checking the contents of the convoy and that we must spend the night in Rogatica. The Belgian soldiers driving the food trucks and the French security escorts who joined us in Podromanija set up camp in an abandoned brick works on the edge of town; the UNHCR relief workers and I spend the night in a private home.

—March 5

During the first several months in 1994, the food-supply situation began to improve significantly. In January a total of 30,000 metric tons of food aid was moved into Bosnia and Herzegovina; this compared with an average of 23,000 metric tons per month during 1993. By March there was still further improvement following threats of air strikes by NATO against Bosnian Serb positions and a cease-fire between Croatian and Bosnian government forces. During the week of March 5–12, trucks carried 9,146 metric tons of food into Bosnia and Herzegovina, which amounted to 94% of the estimated minimum requirements. Exceptions to this improving trend in food delivery were seen in Maglaj, Doboj, Tesanj, and Gorazde. For example, only one food convoy had managed to enter Maglaj during the 10 months between May 1993 and March 1994; the 103,000 mostly Muslim residents of Maglaj district were surviving mainly on airlifted food. The situation for the 750,000 desperate residents of the besieged Muslim-dominated stronghold of Tuzla improved greatly in late March when the UN finally reopened the city's airport and began to organize an airlift of food and other much-needed humanitarian supplies.

The presence of UNPROFOR in Bosnia and Herzegovina has been essential for the safe delivery of food to the besieged enclaves of central and eastern Bosnia. Although the protection forces' numbers have never exceeded 13,000 (mostly Western European and Canadian soldiers), food convoys have relied on these armed escorts to help negotiate passage past hostile militia checkpoints. In March 1994 the UN Security Council requested an additional 8,250 peacekeepers to reduce tensions in Sara-

(Left) Food is unloaded from UN trucks in Mostar. From the start of the conflict in Bosnia and Herzegovina, food has been the most pressing civilian need. As early as January 1993, data collected by the World Health Organization (WHO) indicated that residents of war-affected zones were suffering progressive deterioration in nutritional status. In Srebrenica and Zepa there was clear evidence of increased mortality due to malnutrition. (Below left) Bosnian women retrieve Meals, Ready-to-Eat, air-dropped by U.S. military planes. Many reports indicated that a significant proportion of relief supplies, airdropped over a period of several weeks in the early spring of 1993, failed to reach the civilians for whom they were intended.

jevo and to enforce the new agreement between Muslims and Croats in central Bosnia.

In addition, Western military aircraft have played a critical role in transporting food supplies into the region. For example, between July 1992 and November 1993, U.S. aircraft flew 2,220 sorties delivering 24,600 metric tons of relief supplies into Sarajevo. During the first year of the Sarajevo airlift, a total of 46,000 metric tons of supplies were delivered by aircraft of some 20 nations in more than 4,150 sorties. Also, U.S., French, and German aircraft have air-dropped food and medical supplies directly into the besieged enclaves of eastern and central Bosnia. Between Feb. 28, 1993, when the airdrops began, and March 19, 1994, more than 2,500 such missions were flown, and a total of 16,500 metric tons of food, clothing, and medicines were dropped into Gorazde, Zepa, Srebrenica, Tuzla, Cerska, Konjevici, Tarcin, Polje, Zenica, Maglaj, Tesanj, and eastern Mostar.

157

On this morning the convoy assembles at the checkpoint, where each truck is systematically unloaded and every box and sack counted and its contents checked by the Serbian police. The unloading is done by a group of 15 male Muslim prisoners-of-war; most of them are quite old, a few are adolescents, and none appears to be of combat age. If the number of boxes in a truck does not correspond with the convoy manifest, the excess is retained by the police. Sacks of flour are removed and loaded onto police pickup trucks. The police commander demands that half of the 89 cartons of medical supplies we are carrying be given to the Rogatica Hospital. We had visited the small town hospital and observed serious shortages of a range of basic medical supplies. However, the hospital had received a donation of drugs the week before, and it was obvious that no surgery was performed there. Back at the checkpoint the negotiations continue in a threatening environment until a compromise is reached. Fifteen of the 89 cartons are left behind.

Wrangling continues for hours in the intense cold—the temperature hovering at about −15° C [5° F]. All guns and ammunition belonging to the UNPROFOR soldiers are checked, counted, and registered. All jerricans of fuel are unloaded and left behind at the checkpoint, to be retrieved on the return journey. The Serb police chief gives us a long speech about Zepa and its people, who he claims converted to Islam relatively recently (during the late 17th century), several hundred years after the arrival of the Turks. Although they continue to observe many local Serbian customs, such as the baking of traditional Serbian Orthodox Christmas cakes, he tells us, the people of Zepa are extremists and are particularly dangerous during this holy month of Ramadan. This harangue seems part warning and part lament for a perceived historical betrayal by people who were once his "Serb brothers."

—March 6

Most of the food that was air-dropped in 1993 consisted of Meals, Ready-to-Eat (MREs), precooked 3,600-kilocalorie food rations designed to feed U.S. troops in the field. During the summer of 1993, in response to criticism that these MREs were inappropriate for certain cultural groups (many meals contained pork) and even dangerous for children (their salt content was high), the U.S. Department of Defense (DOD) developed a new variety of prepared meals for airdrops. Called a Humanitarian Daily Ration (HDR), each meal package supplies between 1,900 and 2,200 kilocalories, or close to the recommended daily minimum human caloric requirement.

(Below) A Bosnian senior citizen enjoys a nourishing hot meal at one of the feeding stations established by the International Committee of the Red Cross. (Below right) Residents of Sarajevo, dependent on generous food donations from the international community, are served at a local soup kitchen.

(Left) Masao Endo—Saba; (right) Jean-Claude Coutausse—Contact Press Images

A hungry youngster in Gorazde eagerly eats supper; his mother and grandmother appear relieved that he is able to have this hard-to-come-by meal. Those at highest risk of malnutrition in war-ravaged Bosnia and Herzegovina are the children. By late 1993 UNICEF was providing supplemental meals to approximately 200,000 of an estimated 500,000 children in the war zones.

The HDR contains legumes, grains, and vegetables but no meat, making it acceptable to most of the world's ethnic groups. In late 1993 the DOD donated 1,940,000 of these meals, worth $7.6 million, to the relief effort in Bosnia and Herzegovina.

Nutritional status

Despite the difficulties in delivering food aid, surveys by the World Health Organization (WHO) in various parts of Bosnia and Herzegovina during the summer of 1993 found that acute malnutrition rates among children under five years of age had remained below 5%. However, the surveys found that adults had lost an average of 12 to 15 kilograms (26.5 to 33 pounds) in body weight since the beginning of the war, and 10% of women in Zenica and Sarajevo were found to have nutritional levels just above the critical cutoff point for acute malnutrition. Most people appeared to have been able to find enough food to maintain adequate caloric intake; however, in many regions their consumption of food containing essential micronutrients such as iron, folic acid, and vitamin C had been inadequate. The same WHO surveys found that 18% of persons had below-normal hemoglobin levels, indicating that they were anemic. During the war the Sarajevo Hospital transfusion department was regularly turning away 30–35% of potential blood donors because of anemia.

Malnutrition levels may have remained low because of continuing commercial deliveries of food into the central and western regions of Bosnia and Herzegovina well into 1993. In addition, aid agencies distributed large amounts of agricultural seeds during the spring of that year, a program that was notably successful—to the extent that farmers planted seeds on two to three times the acreage normally sown. Even in Sarajevo most apartment-building balconies could be seen to have pots of tomatoes and other vegetables growing during the summer months.

During the summer of 1993, it was feared that the lack of refrigeration in Bosnian cities might cause food to spoil or become contaminated. How-

159

Having endured a long winter of food shortages, a Sarajevan tends a vegetable garden in the early summer of 1993.

ever, because of the general unavailability of foods such as meat and dairy products that require cold storage, this did not occur.

Less than 10 minutes after we leave the last Serb village, Sjeversko, a motley group of men armed with hunting rifles and World War II-vintage guns wave us to a halt. This is the Muslim frontline. After passing through a further three or four kilometers of forest, we slowly descend the narrow dirt road that winds its way into the valley, cross a narrow wooden bridge, and move into the main village of Zepa. In the faint evening light, we can see a large crowd of perhaps 1,000 villagers who have turned out to welcome the convoy—only the third to make it since May 1992. We park next to the cemetery, and even in the dim light, freshly erected wooden plaques are clearly visible. There is a frenzy of activity; medical supplies are unloaded at the small hospital, and the food trucks are taken down to the school, where the contents are stacked in a storeroom in the basement. Here we see cartons containing food packages that were retrieved from the previous night's airdrop by American planes. There have been two such airdrops, yielding a total of 17,000 packages of the U.S. military rations. Unfortunately, each of the drops had been followed by fierce Serbian shelling; that morning's bombardment by Serbs had killed five Zepan villagers.

—March 6

Sarajevans cross a bombed-out bridge and expose themselves to sniper fire to secure desperately needed water (below), while other residents of the capital city (below right) line up in the rain to collect water, glad for whatever scarce supply they are able to obtain. Disruption of public water and sanitation systems during war poses a major threat to the public health. By late summer 1993, water supplies in Sarajevo had been reduced to an average 5 liters (5.3 quarts) per person per day; WHO recommends 20 liters (21.1 quarts) daily for maintenance of health.

Desperate for water

Another major threat to public health in Bosnia and Herzegovina is the destruction and breakdown of municipal water supplies. Breakdowns in sewerage systems and cross-contamination of piped water supplies had led to widespread contamination of drinking water. These problems were compounded by a lack of electricity and diesel fuel needed to run generators. In the summer of 1993, Sarajevans had on average only 5 liters (5.3 quarts) of water per person per day, compared with the minimum of 20 liters (21.1 quarts) recommended by WHO. Although widespread epidemics of diarrheal disease had been avoided, local health department data showed that the incidence of communicable diseases had increased significantly since the beginning of the war. For example, the incidence of hepatitis A (spread by contaminated water) had increased 6-fold in Sarajevo, 12-fold in Zenica, and 4-fold in Tuzla since 1991. The incidence of dysentery caused by the bacterium *Shigella* increased 12-fold and 17-fold in Sarajevo and Zenica, respectively, during the same period.

Larger epidemics of diarrheal disease may have been prevented by the remnants of relatively high-quality medical services still functioning in the country—despite the fact that health workers had not been paid since mid-1992—and the high level of personal hygiene among the generally well-educated population. In addition, WHO and UNICEF distributed large numbers of iodine and chlorine tablets in Sarajevo during the summer of 1993 for use in home disinfection of drinking water. In late 1993 the International Rescue Committee, an American aid agency, brought in and assembled a new $2.5 million public water system for Sarajevo that would provide up to 450,000 liters (475,510 quarts) of clean water per hour at full capacity. This project was funded by the New York-based Soros Foundation, which had also provided $2.7 million to connect 20,000 Sarajevan families to a natural gas line so that they could heat their homes and cook. Other central Bosnian cities such as Zenica and Tuzla had also suffered severe water shortages.

Health services deteriorate

Many essential disease-prevention programs collapsed in Bosnia and Herzegovina because most health services were diverted toward treating the war injured. In addition, the violence prevented much of the population from reaching health facilities, many of which had been destroyed or heavily damaged. There were numerous reports of heavily damaged and intentionally destroyed medical facilities, including Kosevo Hospital, the main hospital in Sarajevo, serving the largest number of patients; hospitals in Breza, Bihac, and Mostar were also systematically attacked.

Consequently, antenatal care and child-immunization programs were severely curtailed. In 1993 only between 22% and 34% of children in Sarajevo, Zenica, Bihac, and Tuzla had been immunized against measles, an average of only 49% against polio, and 55% against diphtheria and whooping cough. Outbreaks of these diseases were not reported; however, their occurrence would be inevitable if vaccination rates remained low. On the other hand, the incidence of new cases of tuberculosis (TB) report-

A woman in Sarajevo gathers wood for fuel. The public health impact of war is exacerbated by destruction of power supplies. Shortly after Serbian forces began all-out shelling of Sarajevo in May 1992, electricity losses and fuel shortages were common.

161

edly was rising; this was attributed to a shortage of appropriate drugs for treating the infection and to the lack of access many TB patients had to treatment facilities.

Sokolac military hospital is the largest medical facility in Serb-controlled eastern Bosnia. It was completed in 1992 to replace an adjacent mental hospital; however, it was quickly transformed into a surgical facility as soon as the war began. The hospital is modern but has a somewhat unfinished feel about it. Patients—men in military uniforms and a few civilians—huddle on benches in bitterly cold waiting areas. There has been no electricity for the past six months, and a small generator provides power during surgical procedures. There is no running water; once a day a military truck delivers water, which is stored in a rubber bladder tank on the ground floor. Staff members carry the water by bucket to the wards and operating rooms. These scenes would be commonplace in the Third World; it is difficult to comprehend that we are in late 20th-century Europe.

The hospital director, Tausan Tomislav, pours us a glass of brandy in his office and talks about his makeshift facility. A colonel in the former Yugoslav National Army, Tomislav describes his hospital as being overwhelmed by the demands of war casu-

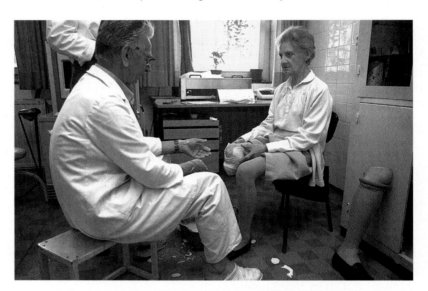

The paramount public health problem in the war-torn former Yugoslavia is violence. Widespread trauma is a direct consequence. Medical facilities, many of which have been specific targets of attack, have not been able to handle the vast number of injuries. Limb wounds requiring amputation are among the most common injuries. A woman who lost her lower right leg in a cross fire is fitted for a prosthesis (above right); a wounded Muslim child waits in a Sarajevo hospital to be evacuated for treatment (right).

(Top) Filip Horvat—Saba; (bottom) Wesley Bocxe—JB Pictures

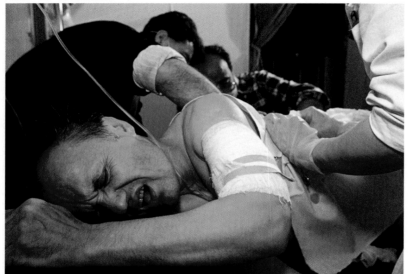

Operating in a makeshift facility, doctors remove a bullet from the back of a trauma victim without the aid of anesthesia.

alties. Almost 40% of his patients are civilians; two-thirds of them are admitted with war-related injuries. Although his staff of 18 doctors and 60 nurses includes many trained surgeons, their work is hampered by severe shortages of all kinds of basic medical and surgical supplies. When he shows us the intensive care unit, Tomislav is careful to point out a Muslim patient, one of three being treated at the hospital. He implies that Muslim patients who are often harassed by Serbian soldiers are protected by the medical staff, which treats all patients, regardless of their ethnicity.

—March 4

Although the worst impact of the war has been felt by the population of Bosnia and Herzegovina, the quality of medical care and public health deteriorated in all the republics of former Yugoslavia, with the possible exception of Slovenia. By early 1994 Croatia had received more than 570,000 refugees, straining the capacity of its health facilities. The international economic sanctions against Serbia and Montenegro (the only remaining republics in Yugoslavia) devastated the economy, costing $25 billion in lost revenue and producing unprecedented rates of inflation that reached *six trillion percent* in March 1994! Although medical supplies were exempted from the sanctions, these two republics lacked the foreign currency to purchase imported drugs and other needed provisions. Widespread shortages of drugs such as insulin, laboratory supplies such as the reagent to test blood for the AIDS virus, and filters for kidney dialysis severely affected the adequacy of medical care. In addition, the influx of 520,000 refugees placed an added burden on health facilities.

Reports have documented extensive sexual violence perpetrated by all the warring ethnic factions in Bosnia and Herzegovina.

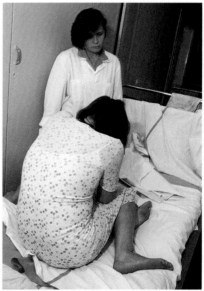

The suffering of women and children

When we ask the director of Sokolac Hospital whether he has seen evidence of sexual abuse among his female patients, Tomislav answers that he has seen very little. However, he does relate several stories of wartime rape. He tells of a Christian Serb nurse at the Sarajevo military hospital who was abducted and repeatedly raped, presumably by Muslim men, and who later attempted to commit suicide. He also tells the story of a Muslim woman who was raped, presumably by Serbs, and fractured her

163

Many babies born to Bosnian women as a result of rape are unwanted and abandoned.

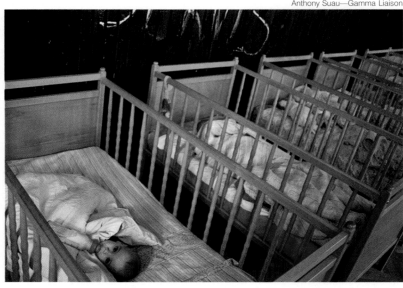

spine while trying to escape her tormentors. She was admitted to Sokolac Hospital and then transferred to Belgrade for further treatment.

—March 4

Perhaps the most terrible weapon employed in the ethnic war in former Yugoslavia was rape. The number of women raped by men on various sides of the conflict may never be known; however, independent investigations by Amnesty International and the European Commission concluded that possibly tens of thousands of Muslim girls and women had been raped as part of a systematic campaign of terror.

The public health impact of the war on women and children has been severe. The terrible effect on children is illustrated by UNICEF's estimate that as of early 1994, 15,000 children had been killed and 35,000 injured by the war. In Sarajevo alone, UNICEF estimated, 30% of children lost a family member, 40% were shot at by snipers, 19% witnessed a massacre, and 72% saw their homes shelled or attacked. UNICEF established an emergency program of counseling and psychological support for traumatized children that by mid-1994 had reached 150,000 children through a network of teachers and psychologists in all parts of former Yugoslavia.

We spend the night at Pale—the headquarters of the Bosnian Serb authorities—a modern mountain-resort town situated behind the Serbian artillery emplacements that constantly pound Sarajevo 16 kilometers away. At the entrance to the town, rows of rusting flagpoles and a faded "Welcome" billboard are reminders of the 1984 winter Olympic Games that were held there in an era when Yugoslavia was still a member of the civilized world community. We sleep in a makeshift guest house run by a family from Sarajevo; the family had owned a prosperous transport business before the war; this was their vacation home.

Next morning, I watch our hosts' 16-year-old son set out for school. Walking jauntily along the snowy street with his friends, wearing jeans and a brightly colored parka, he looks like any typical European or American teenager. But this is no average European town; it is the capital of a renegade republic founded on the basis of ethnic hatred and intolerance. I can't help but wonder what kind of place in Europe,

164

The book I Dream of Peace: Images of War by Children of Former Yugoslavia *was published in December 1993—a joint project of UNICEF and HarperCollins Publishers. In the introduction James P. Grant, executive director of UNICEF, says that in "dozens of schools and refugee camps . . . children have been encouraged to draw and write as a way to unlock the doors to their inner emotions. Assisted by parents, teachers, psychologists, and art therapists, the children recall not only traumatic events but also happy memories from the past. They also create promising dreams of the future." One young Bosnian artist (far left) displays her drawing of everyday life amid war. (Left) No one can know what the future holds for a generation of Bosnian children who have grown up with bloodshed, ethnic hatred, and intolerance all around them. UNICEF, working on all sides of the conflict, has responded by training professionals to identify the childhood victims of posttraumatic stress disorder and to offer group and individual psychotherapy. The agency is also helping educate parents about ways to prevent long-term psychological damage.*

in the world, his generation will find when his country emerges from this hateful war. Will he ever again share his life with the Muslim kids with whom he once shared a Sarajevo classroom?

—*March 5*

Although the war's full psychological toll on children may not be known for years, by early 1994 serious declines in child health status had already become apparent. For example, in Sarajevo perinatal mortality increased from 16 deaths per 1,000 live births in 1991 to 27 per 1,000 during the first four months of 1993. During the same period, the rate of premature births increased from 5.3% to 12.9%, the stillbirth rate increased from 7.5 per 1,000 to 12.3, and the average birth weight decreased from 3,700 to 3,000 grams (8.2 to 6.6 pounds). There was also a dramatic increase in spontaneous and therapeutic abortions; at Kosevo Hospital in mid-1993,

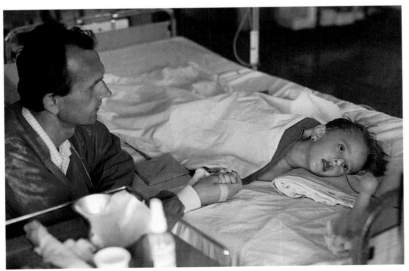

Five-year-old Irma Hadzimuratovic and her father wait in an old military hospital in Sarajevo until she can be airlifted out of the country for treatment. The mortar fire that killed Irma's mother severely damaged the girl's spine and ruptured her intestines. Her only hope for survival was specialized treatment that Bosnian doctors were unable to provide. Bureaucratic entanglements delayed her evacuation for 10 days until British Prime Minister John Major sent a Royal Air Force plane to take her to London's Hospital for Sick Children, where doctors saved her life.

the abortion rate was twice the rate of births. All of these problems were directly linked to the deterioration in quality of antenatal and perinatal care in the capital city.

In August 1993 the world was alerted to the plight of a five-year-old Bosnian girl, Irma Hadzimuratovic, who had been severely wounded by a mortar shell that killed her mother. A fragment of ammunition had entered her back, compressing her spine and rupturing her intestines. Her doctors tried in vain for 10 days to have Irma evacuated on a United Nations military plane so that she could receive specialized treatment abroad. Bosnia and Herzegovina had neither the facilities nor the medical expertise to provide the care she needed. Her situation highlighted the time-consuming bureaucratic procedures that were necessary to allow such medical evacuations. Worldwide publicity finally led to intervention by British Prime Minister John Major, who personally ensured Irma's prompt departure to London. Her arrival at the Hospital for Sick Children in Great Ormond Street on August 9 was witnessed by television viewers around the world.

In response to Irma's case, UNHCR and the International Organization on Migration joined efforts to facilitate and expedite subsequent evacuation of patients requiring medical care that was not available in Bosnia and Herzegovina. Patients are transported to Sarajevo, Belgrade, or Zagreb, where they are then referred to hospitals in more than 30 countries. By Feb. 17, 1994, the medevac program had benefited 510 patients, of whom more than 200 were treated in the United States. Following the marketplace massacre in Sarajevo on Feb. 5, 1994, which killed 68 civilians and wounded more than 200, a rapid evacuation was organized on U.S. and ICRC aircraft. By the end of the day on Sunday, February 6, 177 injured patients had been flown to Ramstein Airbase in Germany. Three days later 37 patients had been moved to hospitals in Italy.

No place to call home

Rogatica shows ample evidence of war-induced destruction. One corner of the town has been heavily shelled; however, most of the damage is of a different kind. Burned-out shells of houses are scattered throughout the town in a seemingly random fashion. These are the homes of Muslims who had once lived peacefully in this medium-sized town; Rogatica's prewar population was about 12,000. When we ask our hosts why the adjacent house was burned down, we are told that their former neighbors became "Muslim extremists." Before the war these neighbors worked together, their children studied at the same school, and their sons played soccer on the local team. We do not ask where the residents of this silent, ruined house are now; we have already been told of a detention camp somewhere in town.

—March 5

The elders of the Zepa enclave produce an extensive list of destroyed property and livestock in the valley. Seven of the valley's 33 villages have been destroyed completely. More than 800 buildings—including six schools, three mosques, and nine restaurants—have been shelled or burned. More than 1,000 head of cattle, 3,500 sheep, and 95 horses have been killed or stolen. As for the human cost, the statistics are even grimmer. The prewar population of approximately 7,200 has swollen by more than 25,000 with refugees from the surrounding towns of Han Pijesak, Vlasenica, and Rogatica. Among this population of 33,600 persons, there have been 1,190 deaths since April 1992; 675 deaths have been hunger-related and 445 due to war injuries.

Muslim refugees from the "ethnically cleansed" Banja Luka region in northern Bosnia and Herzegovina are sheltered in a gymnasium in the town of Travnik in the central part of the republic. By 1994 more than 700,000 persons inside the republic had been displaced, which severely exacerbated the problem of providing adequate shelter and protection against the winter cold. International relief agencies mounted massive humanitarian aid operations to provide what basic necessities they could, but continued fighting virtually ensured that much human suffering would occur.

There is no way to verify these figures; however, if they are accurate, the death rate in Zepa valley during the past 12 months would be four times the prewar death rate in all of former Yugoslavia.

—March 6

The war has wrought widespread damage and destruction of housing throughout Bosnia and Herzegovina. By 1994 the displacement of more than 700,000 persons inside the republic had exacerbated the problem of providing adequate shelter, especially during the bitterly cold winter months. International relief agencies mounted massive operations to provide building materials to repair damaged houses, as well as sleeping bags, blankets, clothing, and various kinds of fuel to help the population protect itself from the weather. Whereas the airlift of winter-protection materials into Sarajevo in December 1992 was highly successful, in late 1993 Bosnian Serbs denied passage to land convoys carrying winter supplies into eastern and central Bosnia, claiming that these materials were not strictly "humanitarian aid."

The war has resulted in extensive property damage. The remains of shelled houses are commonplace in Sarajevo and many of the besieged towns and enclaves; families usually are displaced as a result of the damage.

At dawn we have our first look at Zepa by daylight. We visit several houses and speak with many of the refugees who streamed into the valley last summer. Most are cramped into the remaining rooms of shelled houses. In one basement room four women, a teenage girl, and an old man lie under blankets on the floor. The old man has vacant eyes and does not speak; he seems to have removed himself from the reality of this room and of the events outside. None of the women know the whereabouts of their husbands, sons, or brothers. Six months earlier these six Muslims from Rogatica had been exchanged for the bodies of dead Serb soldiers. Prior to the exchange they had endured the most awful torments in a detention center in the town. The young girl had been raped, we are told later by Zepa's mayor, who is also a physician; he is careful not to speak of these events in her presence. The girl's mother becomes hysterical when we start to leave; she pleads with us to help them leave the valley. She cries that they have nothing, only these blankets and the clothes they are wearing. She wants to escape to the relative security of Tuzla, or even Gorazde.

—March 7

Signs of hope

I take a quick look at the cemetery as we prepare to leave the Zepa valley after finally accomplishing our mission, but I soon lose count of the wooden plaques marking the recent burials—perhaps more than 1,000 are dispersed through the graveyards of Zepa's remaining 26 villages. As we move across the bridge and begin the corkscrew climb up the mountain, I feel an overwhelming sense of helplessness. Having delivered the food and observed the conditions of these people's trapped lives, we were now leaving them with little hope of permanent relief. There are no cheering crowds to see us off; the people of Zepa are getting on with what is left of their lives. At the top of the ridge, I try to catch a last glimpse of Zepa, but a curtain of snow removes it from sight.

—March 7

During the three months that followed the UN convoy's March 1993 aid delivery to Zepa, only one more food convoy made it safely into the valley. In May 1993, during a brief flurry of diplomatic activity to try to end the war, Zepa was under intense siege by Bosnian Serb forces. The United Nations

In Sarajevo, a city where parks and recreation areas have become vast graveyards, a Muslim funeral is held in what was once a soccer field. No one knows exactly how many deaths there have been in this war. Government-released estimates indicated that 4,600 were killed in the capital city alone in the first year of fighting, and by the end of 1993, 21 months into the conflict, there had been 9,700 Sarajevan deaths.

Antoine Gyori—Sygma

Flowers serve as a memorial to the 68 people killed on a single day in February 1994 when a mortar shell exploded in a crowded Sarajevo market. The marketplace massacre triggered a sharp response from the international community. NATO issued an ultimatum to Serb forces to withdraw heavy artillery from areas surrounding the city or face air strikes. Intense negotiations followed, and a period of relative calm ensued—the first true lull in fighting in 23 months.

Security Council passed a resolution declaring Zepa to be a "safe haven" that would be protected by UNPROFOR on the ground and by the explicit threat of NATO air power. With the ongoing presence of humanitarian aid workers and UNPROFOR soldiers, by July the situation in the valley had improved. However, other so-called safe havens protected by the same UN resolution—Srebrenica, Gorazde, Sarajevo, Tuzla, and Bihac—had not fared so well. Serb forces had persistently denied international aid workers free access to Gorazde and Srebrenica; Sarajevo was still being shelled daily during the winter of 1993–94; and in Tuzla and Bihac, which were swollen with tens of thousands of refugees, access routes for aid delivery had been almost totally cut off.

A profound change in the attitude of the international community occurred with the marketplace massacre in Sarajevo on Feb. 5, 1994. Within days, NATO issued an ultimatum to Bosnian Serb forces, threatening air strikes if heavy weapons were not withdrawn from the area surrounding Sarajevo. Following intense diplomatic efforts carried out by the Russian government, the Serbs complied with NATO's demand. A period of relative calm ensued in Sarajevo, allowing its residents to move around the city without fear for the first time since the beginning of the war; even the long-immobile streetcars began a limited service in early April. This lull in the shelling also allowed the international community to move relief supplies into Sarajevo almost unhindered, and plans were being developed in April to commence reconstruction and rehabilitation of public buildings and utilities that had been badly damaged or destroyed.

Other promising developments in March 1994 included the signing of a cease-fire between Croatian and Bosnian government forces and an agreement to form a federation of Croat- and government-controlled areas of Bosnia. Relief convoys were able to enter the devastated city of Mostar in late March, and a South African-donated field hospital was established to provide medical care. Nevertheless, the war raged on in northwestern Bosnia, with reports of numerous murders and severe human rights abuses against Muslims and Croats in Prijedor, Banja Luka, and Bihac. The situation in Prijedor became so serious that UNHCR and ICRC began to evacuate thousands of civilians from the area. Neither agency had engaged in such mass evacuations previously for fear of being parties to the Serb campaign of ethnic cleansing. In addition, Serb forces continued to shell the eastern Bosnian city of Gorazde, where its estimated 65,000 residents had been trapped since the middle of 1992. In April 1994 NATO planes employed air strikes for the first time since the beginning of the war in an attempt to prevent the Serbs from entering the city. By April 25 the Serb onslaught had caused 715 deaths and injuries to 1,970 among residents of the city.

Yet the war rages on

"Resentment has grown beyond easy soothing, remorse beyond the point of repentance, and grief beyond sensible forgiveness," observed Milos Vasic, reporter for the Belgrade opposition weekly newspaper *Vreme,* as the fall and winter months of 1993 approached. The war, he predicted, would "burn out" only when its fuels had been depleted. The international relief operation in former Yugoslavia has been one of the most difficult, dangerous, and costly ever mounted in world history. By the summer of 1993, a total of 51 soldiers of UNPROFOR and 8 UNHCR relief workers had been killed. In addition, ICRC lost one senior foreign delegate, and both local and foreign staff of several other nongovernmental organizations were killed— all in the course of providing or attempting to provide humanitarian aid. On June 1, 1993, a convoy was ambushed outside the central Bosnian town of Maglaj, and three of its drivers, including two Danes, were killed. In early 1994 the killing of foreigners continued, with a British aid worker killed in a convoy near Zenica in January; soon after, three Italian journalists were killed by shrapnel in Mostar.

The cost of this operation has been high in both human lives lost and dollars spent. Still, in April 1994 the war continued unabated in certain areas of northwestern and eastern Bosnia, and an overall peace agreement appeared to be a distant prospect. Moreover, the Bosnian government controlled less than 20% of the territory of the republic.

Benjamin Kulovac, Zepa's physician-mayor—a fit-looking, bearded man in his early 30s—takes us through the hospital, which is really a small dispensary with two rooms converted into wards. In the dim yellow lamplight we can barely make out the eight inpatients, six of whom are recovering from war injuries. Every window is broken and has been replaced with crude plastic sheeting. A huge hole beneath one of the windows has been covered with wooden planks; a shell entered there, passed through the small ward and across the corridor, and exited through the only bathroom situated on the other side of the building. Kulovac is assisted by his wife, who is a dentist, and two other doctors. All four worked in Rogatica before the war and fled to Zepa last May. None of the three doctors has had any specialized surgical training, but all are forced to perform extensive surgical procedures on injured villagers in Zepa. Before the first medical supplies arrived, amputations and other operations had been performed without anesthesia. Some patients were given alcohol to numb the terrible pain; others could only pray for relief.

—March 6

Violence remains the leading threat to the health and well-being of the people of Bosnia and Herzegovina. The international relief effort has not stopped the fighting. Representatives from the International Health Program Office of the U.S. Centers for Disease Control and Prevention who carried out an assessment of the public health situation concluded that traditional tools of public health had not been effective in lessening the impact of the war on the population and that the international public health community needed to actively explore methods for promoting a sustainable *peace that encourages* unity *rather than division.*

The paramount public health issue in Bosnia and Herzegovina and other war-torn areas of former Yugoslavia remained the violence and its direct consequences: trauma-related deaths, injuries, and disabilities; sexual violence; and the immeasurable psychological effects of the war. However, as the war dragged on without clear hope of resolution, the potential for major epidemics, widespread malnutrition, and elevated child and maternal mortality steadily mounted. The displacement of more than two million people would normally create the environment for such public health problems; fortunately, most of the refugees and displaced persons in former Yugoslavia avoided the crowded and unsanitary camps associated with high mortality rates in less developed countries. More than 80% were housed with local people; however, the generosity of these hosts might eventually run out, and more and more refugees would be exposed to the health risks of collective centers.

While the massive international relief effort probably averted many thousands of deaths from hunger and disease, it did not stop the fighting and was unable to prevent the violent deaths of hundreds of thousands of mostly innocent civilians. The draft report of the assessment of humanitarian needs carried out in March 1993 concluded that "the best humanitarian assistance program will be of limited utility as long as more direct and forceful means are not applied to end the conflict itself or, at least, to shift its focus away from the civilian population." It is perhaps a measure of the lack of willpower on the part of one of the world's most powerful nations that this phrase was omitted from the final summary of the report that was released to the U.S. Congress and the media.

On the last day of 1993, *New York Times* columnist Anthony Lewis summed up the situation in former Yugoslavia particularly well: "The people of Sarajevo and the other Bosnian enclaves are holding out somehow, trying to keep alive their dream of a country without hate." He then went on to speculate that perhaps "someday a world that now cynically disregards their fate will honor them."

171

Röntgen's Remarkable Rays: Centennial Tribute

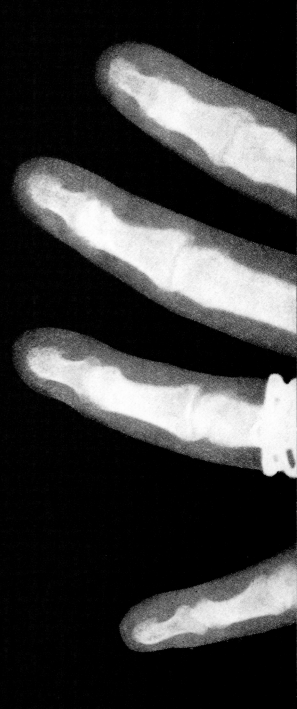

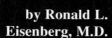

by Ronald L. Eisenberg, M.D.

I T WAS LATE AFTERNOON ON NOV. 8, 1895. Wilhelm Conrad Röntgen was working alone in his laboratory. He had recently repeated the experiments of the German physicist Philipp Lenard, in which invisible cathode rays escaping from the thin aluminum window of a glass vacuum tube produced luminescent effects on certain fluoroscopic salts and darkened a photographic plate. It had occurred to Röntgen that if similar experiments were made with heavier-walled Hittorf-Crookes vacuum tubes without aluminum windows, the cathode rays might penetrate the glass directly and excite a cardboard screen painted with fluorescent barium platinocyanide. However, this effect might be obscured by the strong luminescence of the tube itself. Taking a pear-shaped tube, Röntgen carefully shielded it with pieces of black cardboard and then hooked the tube onto the electrodes of a Ruhmkorff coil (an apparatus that produces intermittent high voltage). After darkening the room to test the opacity of the shield, Röntgen passed a high-tension discharge through the tube. No light penetrated the cardboard.

As he was preparing to interrupt the current, he noted a flickering glow on a small bench located nearby. It was as though a faint spark from the coil had been reflected by a mirror. Not believing this possible, Röntgen passed another series of charges through the tube, and again the same fluorescence appeared. Excitedly, Röntgen lit a match and, to his

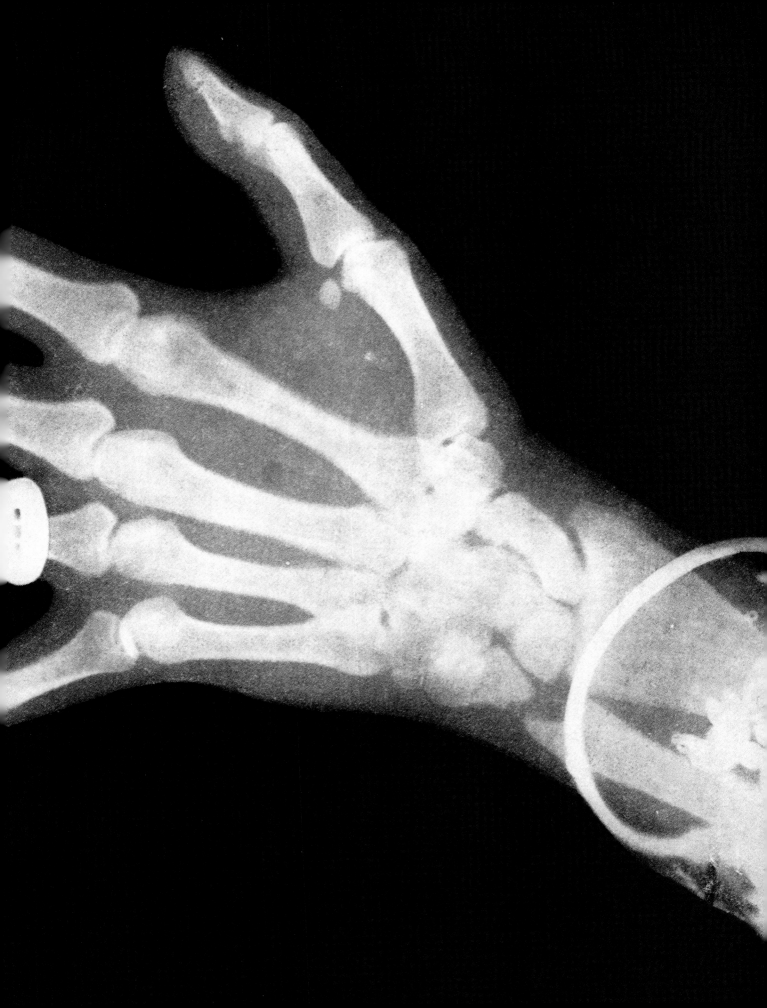

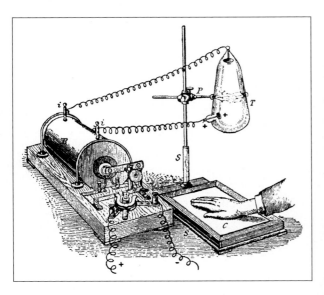

Wilhelm Röntgen was an obscure physics professor conducting experiments with cathode rays when he accidentally stumbled upon a new form of light whose invisible rays were capable of penetrating solid objects. The discovery earned him instant renown and a preeminent place in the history of science. The diagram depicts the simple apparatus he employed to take his first radiographs, including an X-ray of his wife's hand.

Ronald L. Eisenberg, M.D., is Chairman of Radiology, Highland General Hospital, Oakland, California, and Clinical Professor of Radiology, University of California at San Francisco and Davis. His book Radiology: An Illustrated History, *published by Mosby-Year Book, Inc., St. Louis, Missouri (1992), was written "to give radiologists an understanding of the rich tradition of their specialty and to offer other physicians and the lay public an insight into the historic developments that have propelled radiology from the obscure province of engineers and photographers to one of the most rapidly growing fields in medicine." This article is adapted from that book, with kind permission from the author and publisher.*

(Overleaf) Photograph, Historical Pictures/ Stock Montage, Inc.

great surprise, discovered that the source of the mysterious light was the barium platinocyanide screen lying on the bench a few meters away. He repeated the experiment again and again, continually moving the screen farther from the tube. But the glow persisted even when the painted surface of the fluorescent screen was turned in the opposite direction. There seemed to be only one explanation: something was emanating from the tube that produced an effect on the fluorescent screen at a much greater distance than he had ever observed in his cathode-ray experiments.

If this curious emanation could escape the cardboard shield, perhaps it could penetrate other substances. To test this conjecture, Röntgen held a variety of objects between the tube and the screen and closed the switch to the inductor. Most objects caused little or no reduction in the intensity of the glowing screen. Only lead and platinum seemed to obstruct the rays completely. As he held the various materials between the tube and the screen, Röntgen was amazed to see the ghostly shadow of the bones and soft tissues of his own fingers. The flesh was transparent, the bones fairly opaque.

How could he document these evanescent images? Fortunately, Röntgen remembered that cathode rays darkened a photographic emulsion. He replaced the fluorescent screen with a photographic plate and succeeded in producing an image by using the vacuum tube as a light source. When he placed a piece of platinum on the plate before the exposure, a light area appeared on the developed plate where the platinum had absorbed the rays. It became clear to Röntgen that this was a new form of light, which was invisible to the eye and had never been observed or recorded. Thus, X-rays were discovered, and radiology was born.

"I have discovered something interesting..."

For the next seven weeks, Röntgen remained secluded in his laboratory, concentrating entirely on a large number of carefully planned experiments. He was determined to continue his work in secret until he was certain of the validity of his observations and was confident enough to hand the results over to other scientists for confirmation or refutation. As his wife, Bertha, reported, Röntgen had his meals served in the laboratory and even had his bed moved there so that he could remain undisturbed and ready day or night to try out any new ideas that might come to him. Only once did he mention to one of his few good friends, the German zoologist Theodor Boveri, "I have discovered something interesting, but I do not know whether or not my observations are correct."

Röntgen constructed a sheet metal cabinet about 2.1 meters (7 feet) high and 1.2 meters (4 feet) square at the base to have a permanent darkroom instead of draping his laboratory with ineffective blinds and curtains. Into one side of the zinc-walled chamber he inserted a circular aluminum sheet one millimeter (about 0.04 inch) thick and about 46 centimeters (18 inches) in diameter, through which the new rays would pass. A zinc door on the side of the booth opposite the aluminum disk permitted his entry and exit. The vacuum tube was placed outside and focused on the disk's center. A lead plate was added to the zinc wall between the tube and himself. In this way Röntgen effectively protected himself from the yet-unknown harmful effects of radiation.

One evening Röntgen persuaded his wife to be the subject for an experiment. He placed her hand on a cassette loaded with a photographic plate and made an exposure of 15 minutes. On the developed plate the bones of her hand appeared light within the darker shadow of the surrounding flesh. Two rings on her finger had almost completely stopped the rays and were clearly visible. When he showed the picture to her, she could hardly believe that this bony hand was her own and shuddered at the thought that she was seeing her skeleton. To Bertha Röntgen, as to many others later, this experience gave a vague premonition of death.

Epochal announcement

After extensive experimentation Röntgen was convinced that he was dealing with an entirely new kind of ray different from all others. Knowing that the announcement of such a discovery could not be long delayed, Röntgen prepared a short manuscript entitled "On a New Kind of Rays: A Preliminary Communication," which he handed to the secretary of the Würzburg (Germany) Physical Medical Society on Dec. 28, 1895. Since no meetings or lectures were to be given during the long Christmas vacation, Röntgen made the unusual request that the paper be published in the annals of the society even before it had been presented at one of the meetings.

In this epochal announcement, which appeared in the last 10 pages of the 1895 volume, Röntgen reviewed his wealth of experimentation estab-

Bertha Röntgen was taken aback by this ghostly image of the skeleton beneath her transparent flesh.

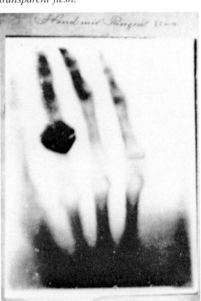

175

lishing the existence of these new "X-rays" (a name he coined to distinguish them from other rays already known), as well as a perceptive description of their properties. He first described the generation of X-rays and stressed that the black envelope around the tube, which was opaque to visible light or to ultraviolet rays from the Sun or from an electric arc, did not filter or reduce the effect of the rays on a fluorescent screen. Röntgen demonstrated that almost all materials were transparent to the X-ray, although in widely differing degrees. As he wrote, "Paper is very transparent: I observed that the fluorescent screen still glowed brightly behind a bound book of about 1,000 pages; the printer's ink had no noticeable effect. Likewise, fluorescence appeared behind a double pack of whist cards; the eye can hardly detect a single card held between the apparatus and the screen." Similarly, a single sheet of tinfoil was hardly observable, and only the addition of several layers began to show a distinct shadow on the screen. Pine boards 3 centimeters (1.2 inches) thick remained partially transparent to the rays. The behavior of glass remained a special phenomenon because, although generally transparent to visible light, the amount of lead contained in the glass showed up markedly on the screen. Most dramatically, Röntgen described the stark image produced by the shadow of a hand with its relatively transparent fleshy parts and darker shadows of the bones.

Various substances—gases, liquids, and solids—were shown to be as transparent as air. Sheets of copper, silver, lead, gold, and platinum showed transparency of different degrees. Röntgen concluded that "the transparency of various substances assumed to be of equal thickness depends primarily upon their density" (that is, inversely as the molecular weight of the substance). Platinum and lead were the most opaque substances. Noting that 1.5-millimeter-thick lead was practically opaque, Röntgen used this substance in his experimental work to show its contrast effect on photographic plates. For example, a stick of wood having a 20-millimeter-square cross section that had one side painted white with lead paint acted differently depending on how it was held between the glass tube and the screen. Although it had practically no effect when the direction of the X-rays was parallel to the surface, the stick showed as a dark streak on the plate when the painted face was turned across the beam.

Röntgen showed that barium platinocyanide was not the only substance that fluoresced when exposed to X-rays. He also listed calcium compounds, uranium glass, ordinary glass, calcite, and rock salt. He considered it fortunate that photographic dry plates were sensitive to X-rays since "one is able to make a permanent record of many phenomena whereby deceptions are more easily avoided." Simply wrapping the photographic plate in heavy black paper or a routine holder enabled Röntgen to perform his experiments in daylight. However, it was no longer possible to leave wrapped photographic plates lying around the laboratory lest they be exposed to incidental X-rays that would spoil them.

To differentiate the new rays

Röntgen showed that the new rays were propagated in straight lines and that they were neither reflected nor refracted. He proved that the X-ray intensities followed the inverse square law relative to the distances between the screen and discharge apparatus.

A critical issue was to differentiate the new rays from the cathode rays described by Lenard. Röntgen showed that air (and most other substances) absorbed a much smaller portion of transmitted X-rays than cathode rays. The fluorescent glow from X-rays could be produced as far as 1.8 meters (6 feet) from the discharge tube, compared with only several centimeters for cathode rays. Unlike cathode rays, X-rays could not be deflected by a magnet, even in strong magnetic fields. Röntgen showed that the area on the wall of the discharge apparatus that showed the strongest fluorescence had to be considered the main point of emission of X-rays, which radiated in all directions. Thus, the X-rays were arising from the area where previous investigators had determined the cathode rays impinged on the glass wall. If he deflected the cathode rays within the discharge apparatus by means of a magnet, he observed that the X-rays were now emitted from another area, namely from the new terminating point of the cathode rays. Therefore, Röntgen concluded that "X-rays are not identical with cathode rays, but they are produced by the cathode rays in the glass wall of the discharge apparatus."

Röntgen also showed that the new rays were not ultraviolet rays since they were not refracted in passing from air into various substances nor were they polarized. Because they formed shadows, fluoresced, and exerted chemical effects, Röntgen postulated that the new rays might be related to light and speculated that they might represent "longitudinal vibrations in the ether."

Röntgen then reviewed the various photographs taken with his apparatus to demonstrate the true "ray" character of the emanations. The most dramatic were photographs of the hand showing the bony structures and one made through his laboratory door that showed not only the varying thickness of stiles and panels but also several streaks representing areas

Early on, Röntgen demonstrated that nearly all materials are to some degree transparent to X-rays. Among the first experiments he undertook to demonstrate the true "ray" character of the new light form were a radiograph of a wooden box containing a set of metal weights and another of a compass—the magnetic needle and degree markings of which are clearly visible despite being shielded by a metal case.

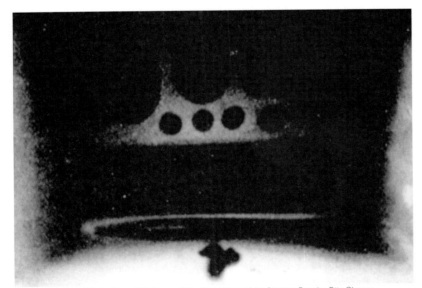

Photographs, from *Wilhelm Conrad Röntgen and the Early History of the Röntgen Rays* by Otto Glasser;
© 1934 Charles C. Thomas, Springfield, Illinois

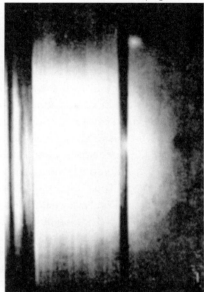

The door of Röntgen's laboratory (right) was the subject of one of his early experiments demonstrating the X-ray's ability to pass through various substances. Visible in the radiograph (far right) is the door's internal framework. The circular white area indicates a part of the door that had been brushed with lead-based paint.

on which lead-based paint had been brushed. Other radiographs showed a set of weights in a covered wooden box, the shadow of a wire wrapped around a wooden spool, and the needle and degree markings of a compass enclosed in its metal case.

To speed critical reading and evaluation of his work, on Jan. 1, 1896, even before news of the discovery was published, Röntgen sent copies of the article and examples of prints of the X-ray pictures he had taken to a number of well-known physicists, many of whom he knew as friends. Probably sensing that his days of peaceful relative obscurity were coming to an end, he exclaimed to his wife after dropping the reprints in the mail, "Now the devil will be to pay!"

News of the sensational discovery spreads

Franz Serafin Exner of Vienna, a friend of Röntgen's since their college days in Zürich, Switzerland, received one of the New Year's packets and showed the pictures to a small gathering of fellow scientists. One of them, Ernst Lecher of Prague, asked Exner to lend him the prints until the next morning. Lecher, in turn, showed them at once to his father, Z.K. Lecher, then the editor of the *Vienna Presse*. Realizing the enormous news value in the story of the new rays, the editor immediately prepared an elaborate article on the revolutionary discovery by the "Würzburg professor" for the next morning edition. Rushing to meet his deadline, Lecher misspelled Röntgen's name, and the discovery of "Routgen" echoed throughout the world. Nonetheless, Lecher perceptively appreciated that "biologists and physicians, especially surgeons, will become interested in the Ray as it might open new trails for diagnostic purposes."

The news was quickly copied by other European papers, and on the evening of January 6, it was cabled from London to countries around the world in the following words:

The noise of war's alarm should not distract attention from the marvelous triumph of science which is reported from Vienna. It is announced that Prof. Routgen of the Würzburg University has discovered a light which for the purpose of photography will penetrate wood, flesh, cloth, and most other organic substances. The Professor has succeeded in photographing metal weights which were in a closed wooden case, also a man's hand which showed only the bones, the flesh being invisible.

Ironically, Röntgen's hometown paper did not report the news of the sensational discovery until January 9. Compounding delay with inaccuracy, the Würzburg newspaper assumed that scientific societies met during the Christmas holidays and stated that Röntgen had first presented his discovery in a lecture.

The most astounding confusion concerning Röntgen's discovery was created by Thomas Smith Middleton, an American student at the University of Würzburg. Upon returning home to Chicago, he came up with this widely circulated fable:

On the afternoon of April 29, 1895, Roentgen was suddenly called to the telephone while observing the fluorescence of a tube connected with a Ruhmkorff coil. Without disconnecting anything, he placed the loaded tube on a book which contained a key as page marker. A photographic cassette happened to lie underneath the book. On his return from the telephone, Roentgen disconnected the tube and spent the rest of the afternoon outdoors, photographing flowers. The following morning, while developing the plate, he noticed the radiograph of the key.

Thus, in Chicago and elsewhere where the imaginative public believed in the myth of the book and the key, April 30, 1895, was marked as the anniversary of the great discovery.

An appreciation of the potential medical use of the new rays could be found in the morning edition of the *Frankfurter Zeitung* on January 7:

At the present time, we wish only to call attention to the importance this discovery would have in the diagnosis of diseases and injuries of bones, provided that the process can be developed technically so that not only the human hand can be photographed but that details of other bones may be shown without the flesh. The surgeon then could determine the extent of a complicated bone fracture without the manual examination which is so painful to the patient; he could find the position of a foreign body, such as a bullet or piece of shell, much more easily than has been possible heretofore and without any painful examinations with a probe. Such photographs also would be extremely valuable in diagnosing bone diseases which do not originate from an injury and would help to guide the way in therapy.

Domestic peace is gone

Almost overnight, Röntgen was no longer an unknown middle-aged professor of physics at the Physical Institute of the University of Würzburg but the focus of international praise, condemnation, and curiosity. From all over the world came letters of congratulation and incredulity as well as reports of duplication of the original experiments and a few of failures. To the Würzburg institute were sent tubes of various construction and other equipment for the production of the rays. Through its modest doors passed scientists, reporters, the sympathetic, and the curious. The location of the Röntgen's private residence on the second floor of the institute left no escape from the heterogeneous horde that descended upon it. "Our domestic peace is gone," complained Bertha Röntgen to a friend, and Röntgen was forced to adjust from the satisfying freedoms of a quiet private life to a tacit acceptance of public demands. Some visitors went so far as to filch X-ray photographs from the laboratory, and postcards with Röntgen's signature failed to reach their destination.

The response of scientists and laymen seemed completely out of proportion to the simple, unpretentious, rather dry style of the published communication. Unquestionably, if not for the many pictures of hands made quickly after the communication was published, which demonstrated the importance of the new rays in the study of anatomic structures and pathological changes, the discovery might have been consigned for some time to the relative oblivion of the physical laboratory.

Röntgen received 1,000 pieces of mail during the first week alone. Among these were several suggesting that there might be monetary gains in the proper exploitation of the new rays. Sometime later Max Levy, an engineer in the German electric firm AEG, who had done some excellent work with X-rays, approached Röntgen regarding the firm's interest in the development of the rays. Röntgen answered him without hesitation: "According to the good tradition of the German university professors, I am of the opinion that their discoveries and inventions belong to humanity and that they should not in any way be hampered by patents, licenses, contracts, nor should they be controlled by any one group."

The opposite point of view was taken by the American inventor Thomas A. Edison, who freely admitted to the commercial exploitation of science

The mysterious new rays immediately captured the popular imagination, inspiring an outpouring of stories, poems, caricatures, and jokes. Many of these were based on the lay public's erroneous impression that radiography was exactly like ordinary photography except that it was able to penetrate paper, cloth, flesh, and other opaque substances. The cartoon (right) appeared in Life *magazine in February 1896. The caption read: "The new Roentgen photography. 'Look pleasant, please.'"*

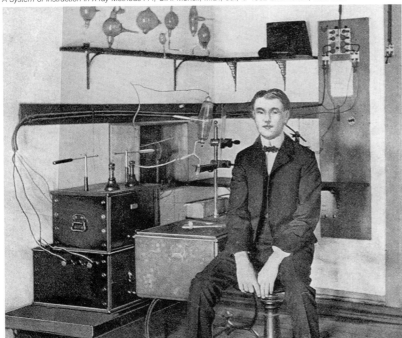

The dental profession was quick to develop clinical applications for the X-ray. Just two weeks after Röntgen's announcement of his discovery, a German dentist made an intraoral radiograph of his own teeth; the image required an exposure time of 25 minutes! The first dental radiography laboratory in the U.S. was established in July 1896 by a New Orleans, Louisiana, dentist, C. Edmund Kells. A patient about to have his teeth X-rayed by Kells is shown at left.

for personal gain. He was quoted by an American newspaper as saying, "Professor Roentgen probably does not draw one dollar profit from his discovery. He belongs to those pure scientists who study for pleasure and love to delve into the secrets of nature. After they have discovered something wonderful, someone else must come to look at it from the commercial point of view. This will also be the case with Roentgen's discovery. One must see how to use it and how to profit by it financially."

Röntgen's communication was immediately translated into several languages. The newspaper speculations on the medical use of X-ray photographs, although seemingly unwarranted at first, led to innumerable experiments that offered unequivocal proof of the value of the new rays. Within two months virtually all the major medical and nonmedical scientific journals had printed X-ray illustrations and articles on the value of X-rays in medicine. In all of 1896 more than 1,000 papers relating to X-rays were published.

Röntgen detested the excessive publicity and complained that "on January 1st I sent out the offprints and then all hell broke loose!" He declared that "they blew the trumpet out of proportion." Röntgen especially disliked the sensationalism of radiography, which he considered only as a means to document his astounding fluoroscopic observations.

First public demonstration

The first public demonstration of X-rays before a scientific body occurred on the evening of Jan. 23, 1896, when Röntgen addressed the Würzburg Physical Medical Society before a large and crowded audience. Every seat in the auditorium was filled long before the meeting began, and

Röntgen's appearance was greeted with a veritable storm of applause that was repeated several times during the presentation. With genuine modesty Röntgen first gave credit to his predecessors in the investigation of cathode rays, mentioning the German physicist Heinrich Rudolf Hertz, Lenard, and the English physicist Sir William Crookes in particular. After a discussion of his experimental protocol and results and a demonstration of several radiographs, Röntgen invited a university colleague, the famed anatomist Albert von Kölliker, to have his hand photographed by the new rays. Kölliker eagerly complied, and a little later an excellent X-ray picture of his hand was shown to the audience amid tremendous applause. The anatomist then noted that in his 48 years as a member of the society, he had never attended a meeting with a presentation of greater significance, either in the field of natural science or in medicine. After leading the audience in three cheers for the discoverer, Kölliker proposed that the new rays henceforth be designated "Röntgen's rays," and this proposal was approved by unanimous and enthusiastic applause. Although Röntgen lived 27 years longer, this was the only formal lecture he gave on the subject of the discovery of X-rays.

Two more "communications"

Ten weeks after his initial paper, Röntgen issued his second "communication" (March 9, 1896). Röntgen observed that positively or negatively electrified bodies in air were discharged by X-rays. Replacing air with hydrogen or reducing the air pressure caused a corresponding reduction in the rate of discharge. He reported a scale for measuring the intensity of the rays by observing the degree of fluorescence on a screen or the intensity of blackening of a photographic plate. He recommended the insertion of a Tesla apparatus (condenser and transformer) between the vacuum tube and the induction coil. This arrangement generated less heat and maintained the vacuum for a longer period, produced a more intense penetrating beam, and could compensate for vacuum tubes that had been too much or too little exhausted.

The third and final communication by Röntgen, "Further Observations on the Property of the X Ray," appeared in May 1897. It was submitted to the Prussian Academy of Sciences in Berlin rather than the Würzburg Physical Medical Society, to which the first two communications had been sent. In this work Röntgen discussed X-ray diffraction and proceeded to an analysis of the variables that produced differing intensities of X-ray brightness on a fluorescent screen. As the eminent British physicist Silvanus P. Thompson complained in a book written that year, "Roentgen had so thoroughly explored the new properties of the new rays by the time his discovery was announced, that there remained little for others to do beyond elaborating his work."

Röntgen: the man and his life

After the news of Röntgen's discovery was published, the general public wanted to know more about the man himself. The first newspaper accounts were meager and inaccurate. Because news of the discovery had come from Vienna, it was erroneously reported that Röntgen was an Austrian professor. Soon, however, enterprising reporters were able to find out more about his personal affairs and were able to present their readers with good biographies of the great scientist.

Early years and schooling. Wilhelm Conrad Röntgen was born on March 27, 1845, in Lennep, a small town on the lower Rhine in the heart of the industrial Ruhr Valley of Germany. He was the only child of Friederich Conrad Röntgen, a manufacturer and textile merchant, and Charlotte Constance Frowein, who came from a Dutch family well-known in industrial and shipping circles. When Wilhelm was three years old, the Röntgens moved to Apeldoorn, The Netherlands, about 160 kilometers (100 miles) to the northwest, where Charlotte's parents made their home. As the only child of a conservative and well-to-do merchant, Wilhelm had a pleasant childhood and was certainly indulged if not spoiled. His initial schooling was erratic, and at age 17 he began his studies at the Utrecht Technical School. This institution prepared its students in two years for entrance into a technical high school but did not fill the prerequisites for matriculation to a university. Although only an average student, Röntgen was progressing satisfactorily until a harmless student prank got him into trouble. Unwilling to divulge the name of a fellow student who drew a caricature of an unpopular teacher, Wilhelm took the blame and was expelled from the school.

When this unfortunate incident promised to be serious enough to interrupt Wilhelm's education, his father obtained permission for a private examination that would give his son credentials to enter a college. Wilhelm prepared for the examination for almost a year. Unfortunately, on the day before the examination the examiner, who was sympathetic toward Wilhelm, became ill and was replaced by a teacher who had taken part in the former suspension proceedings. With this handicap Wilhelm failed the examination. Again his path to a university had been blocked.

Posing for a formal portrait photo, the young Röntgen (below left) adopted a serious demeanor. A later, more informal photo shows Röntgen (standing, center) with his parents and other relatives and gives a sense of his comfortable, bourgeois upbringing.

Photographs, from *Wilhelm Conrad Röntgen and the Early History of the Röntgen Rays* by Otto Glasser; © 1934 Charles C. Thomas, Springfield, Illinois

Wilhelm and his parents had almost become resigned to his seeming inability to adjust to the requirements of the Dutch educational system and to obtain the credentials necessary to become a regular university student. Luckily, a Swiss friend living in Utrecht informed them that the Polytechnical School in Zürich would accept students lacking the usual credentials if they could pass a stiff entrance examination. Thus, Wilhelm began classes in Zürich in November 1865 and received his diploma as a mechanical engineer two and a half years later. Ironically, Röntgen had only a single course in physics, given by the German mathematical physicist Rudolf Clausius, the father of thermodynamics.

Of all the professors who helped shape Röntgen's mind during these formative years, the one who proved to be of greatest influence was August Kundt, a brilliant experimental physicist who succeeded Clausius in the chair of physics at the Polytechnical School. Röntgen remained in Kundt's laboratory after graduation and began physical experiments on various properties of gases. After one year he submitted his thesis to the University of Zürich, housed in the same building as the Polytechnical School, and on June 22, 1869, Röntgen obtained his doctorate in philosophy from that university.

While living in Zürich, Röntgen often visited a popular student café run by Johann Gottfried Ludwig, a former student at the University of Jena who had fled from Germany in the 1830s during a revolutionary uprising. He fell in love with Ludwig's daughter, Anna Bertha, who was six years older than Röntgen and "a tall slender girl of extraordinary charm." Although his parents, who were anxious to see him married to the daughter of some prominent and wealthy family, expressed some disappointment, Wilhelm and Bertha married on July 7, 1872.

Ascending the academic ladder. When Kundt moved to the University of Würzburg, he invited Röntgen to become his assistant. However, once again Röntgen was held back by his inadequate formal education. Before he could be appointed to a salaried position on the faculty, it was necessary that he climb the first step of the academic ladder and be appointed a privatdocent, or unpaid lecturer recognized by the university. Lacking the high school matriculation degree, as well as satisfactory training in the classical languages, Röntgen was prevented by the strict traditions of the old institution from getting this initial academic title. Fortunately, this disappointment was short-lived, for two years later both Kundt and Röntgen accepted appointments to the faculty of the newly established University of Strasbourg. After two years of hard work, Röntgen was appointed a privatdocent, and the stage was now set for an unimpeded academic career.

During the seven years that he spent at Strasbourg, Röntgen investigated a wide variety of problems in physics. These included the determination of specific heats, electrical discharges, the Sun's radiation, telephonic improvements, electromagnetic rotation, and the properties of crystals.

Röntgen's work began to appear in publications and to attract interest in the rapidly expanding field of physics. In 1879 he was invited to become professor of physics at the University of Giessen in Hesse, an important post that he accepted when only 34 years old. While at Giessen,

Röntgen intensified his research on electromagnetic and gas phenomena, on pyroelectric and piezoelectric properties of crystals, and on surface phenomena of liquids. He also undertook an extensive investigation of the "Rowland effect," named for the American physicist Henry Rowland, who had shown that a charged body in motion produced a magnetic field similar to that generated by an electric current in a conductor.

Würzburg years. On Oct. 1, 1888, Röntgen was offered the prestigious post of professor of physics and director of the new Physical Institute of the University of Würzburg. Unlike his old, meagerly equipped laboratory at the university where he had begun work 16 years before as a newlywed, the new Physical Institute on the broad, tree-lined Pleicher Ring had two spacious floors, a basement, and a lecture room. The second floor comprised the private residential quarters of the director of the institute and had ample room for a conservatory, much to Bertha Röntgen's delight. One can only imagine Röntgen's feeling of triumph on assuming the chair of physics at the same university that had previously refused to give him an academic title.

At Würzburg, Röntgen obtained important results in studies on the influence of pressure on various physical properties of solids and liquids. He investigated the compressibility of many liquids, notably ether and alcohol, and continued studies of the effect of pressure on the dielectric constants of water and ethyl alcohol. He examined the refractive indexes of these liquids and the conductivity of various electrolytes.

In 1894 Röntgen became rector of the University of Würzburg. In his inaugural address he repeated the words of Athanasius Kircher, one of his predecessors in the chair of physics and philosophy, who had stated more than two centuries before, "Nature often reveals the most astonishing phenomena by the simplest means, but these phenomena can only be recognized by persons who have sharp judgment and the investigative spirit, and who have learned to obtain information from experience, the teacher of all things." Little did Röntgen realize that in less than a year these words would apply to him.

By October 1895 Röntgen had found his entire attention captivated by the work of Crookes, Hertz, Lenard, and the German physicist Johann Wilhelm Hittorf on cathode rays. As noted above, he had already repeated some of Lenard's original experiments, notably his observations on the effects produced by cathode rays in free air and hydrogen. Although at first he used Lenard's aluminum-window tube, Röntgen found that he could obtain the same results with ordinary (glass) tubes, which he preferred since flaws in the thin aluminum window tended to weaken the vacuum in the Lenard tube. By now totally absorbed by this field that challenged the most competent experimental talent, Röntgen decided to devote himself exclusively to research on cathode rays.

Reluctant luminary. Following Röntgen's discovery of X-rays, numerous decorations and special honors poured in from all over the world. Among the most outstanding ones were the gold Rumford Medal from the Royal Society in London, the Elliot-Cresson Medal of the Franklin Institute in Philadelphia, and the Barnard Medal awarded by Columbia University, New

York City, at the recommendation of the American Academy of Sciences. In 1901 Röntgen became the first recipient of the Nobel Prize for Physics. Contrary to his usual rule of not personally attending the awarding of an honor, Röntgen traveled to Stockholm to receive the diploma, gold medal, and prize from the hands of the Swedish crown prince in a ceremony at the Music Academy. He declined to give an official Nobel lecture, but at the impressive supper after the ceremony, he spoke a few words of appreciation for the honor and said that this recognition would stimulate him to continue scientific research that might prove of benefit to humanity. Röntgen gave the prize money to support scientific research at the University of Würzburg, the site of his immortal discovery.

Röntgen was summoned to Potsdam by German Emperor William II to demonstrate the new ray at the imperial palace. Prince Regent Luitpold of Bavaria awarded him the Royal Order of Merit of the Bavarian Crown, which carried with it not only the honor and decoration but also personal nobility. Röntgen accepted the decoration but declined the status of nobility. Although now entitled to call himself Wilhelm von Röntgen, he also declined to adopt the coveted "von," a symbol of status in a most status-conscious nation. Busts and monuments were erected in Röntgen's honor, and even a statue on the Potsdam Bridge in Berlin. Röntgen's portrait could be found on special stamps in various lands and on German currency.

Later life. In 1900, at the special request of the Bavarian government, Röntgen agreed to become professor of physics at the University of Munich and director of the new Physics Institute. He resumed his research on the physical properties of crystals, their electrical conductivity, and radiation influences on them. The outbreak of World War I and the ultimate defeat of Germany affected Röntgen deeply. Strong national feelings persuaded him to turn in his gold decorations when the call for gold was made to continue the war effort. He even was persuaded by some patriotic colleagues to

Röntgen receives the first Nobel Prize for Physics from the Swedish crown prince in Stockholm on Dec. 10, 1901. Röntgen himself had been one of the distinguished scientists asked to submit names of candidates for the signal honor. With characteristic modesty, he suggested the eminent British physicist Lord Kelvin.

The Nobel Foundation

An early 20th-century illustration depicts European physicians in consultation over a youthful patient's chest X-ray. Radiography of the chest became possible only with improvements in methods and equipment that decreased the exposure time of radiographic plates to one second or less. This instantaneous process allowed rapidly moving anatomic structures to be captured in clear, unblurred images.

Photograph, Mary Evans Picture Library

sign a proclamation of 93 intellectuals in an "appeal to the civilized world" not to believe the reports of German excesses during the war. Later, in his older and calmer years, he regretted both of these actions.

In October 1919 Röntgen's beloved wife, Bertha, died after a prolonged illness. The memory of their wonderful companionship for almost 50 years intensified Röntgen's loss, and in his loneliness he would read important news items to her picture and pretend that she still shared his thoughts.

Röntgen retired from his post as professor of physics early in 1920, but two laboratory rooms were set aside for his continued use. Three years later, at age 78, Röntgen was still able to walk to the laboratory to eagerly complete some experimental investigations that he had begun some months earlier. However, he complained that walking was becoming more difficult and that his sight and hearing were proving inadequate for the observations required. On Feb. 10, 1923, the discoverer of X-rays died in Munich.

The funeral cortege assembled prominent scientists from all parts of Germany and neighboring countries, who came to pay their respects to a great fellow researcher and benefactor of humankind. Then, in accordance with his will, his body was cremated and his papers and personal correspondence also given to the flames.

Among the many eulogies was one by Rudolph Grashey, a pioneer radiologist, who stated:

An angel from heaven presented the wonderful new ray to the scientists. Medicine has received the lion's share of his discovery. Nature manifests itself in such a way only to those who, through restless exploring, have developed an instinct for its

187

The humorous potential of X-rays seems to have been virtually irresistible. The caption on this 1897 cartoon read: "Whether stout or thin, the x-ray makes the whole world kin."

intricacies and laws. . . . Nobody could have been more dignified, predestined to receive this present from nature. Life has given him much, but more than he has received he has given us. A spark of his mind has kindled a light which illuminated dark trails of science. Immortal is his work, immortal his name.

Right to priority

Was Röntgen the first to produce X-rays? As with all major discoveries, a number of often vociferous scientists came forward to claim priority in having observed the penetrating rays.

The first X-ray picture was actually produced almost six years before Röntgen's discovery. After an experimental session testing electrical sparks and brush discharges as photographic light sources, Arthur W. Goodspeed at the University of Pennsylvania began demonstrating the properties of a Crookes cathode-ray tube to William Jennings, a photographer. Next to the tube Jennings had stacked several unexposed photographic plates, on top of which were two coins, reportedly his trolley fare. When Jennings later developed the plates, some were mysteriously fogged, and one contained two dark round disks, as well as the usual tracing of the electrical sparks on the negative. This curious shadowgraph could not be explained, and so the plates were filed away and forgotten. Only after Röntgen's discovery did the men re-create the setting of their earlier experiment and grasp the magnitude of the observation that they had failed to make. Although he claimed "no credit for the interesting accident," Goodspeed maintained that "without doubt, the first Röntgen picture was produced on February 22, 1890 . . . [at] the University of Pennsylvania."

In 1890 Ludwig Zehnder, Röntgen's assistant at Würzburg, was using black cloth to cover a vacuum tube and thus eliminate the disturbing light emanating from the cathode. In this way he hoped to detect fluorescence

188

of the screen not only nearby but also at some distance from the tube. When Zehnder turned the current on, he noticed a momentary flash where the remote screen was lying, but the tube was immediately punctured. Zehnder felt terribly upset and was willing to replace the tube at his own expense. Röntgen, however, consoled his friend with the prophetic remark that "many more tubes will have to be punctured before all their mysteries are solved." After the discovery of X-rays, Zehnder recalled the incident and that he had noticed the instantaneous glow from the nearby fluorescent screen. However, Zehnder never made a priority claim and remained a loyal friend of Röntgen for the rest of his life.

A number of scientists working with electrical discharges through evacuated glass tubes had in all likelihood produced X-rays. Crookes, Hittorf, and Lenard, among others, had observed the fluorescent glow in materials located near their tubes. However, none had properly recognized or identified the nature or source of the fluorescence, let alone reproduced the phenomenon with full awareness and command. As one of the earliest investigators of X-rays, Max Levy of Berlin, reminisced later, "I have no doubt that X-rays were seen in laboratories even before Röntgen's time, but they were not recognized as such by the investigators. The credit due Röntgen is not decreased but is considerably increased by this fact because his genius discovered the significance of a thing which others had seen but did not recognize."

The Nobel Prize: untold story

The most bitter contender for the credit given Röntgen was Lenard. Lenard initially respected and admired Röntgen and sent him a letter congratulating him on "your great discovery." In turn, Röntgen acknowledged the work of Lenard and his teacher Hertz in his Würzburg lecture. Röntgen and Lenard even shared two prestigious prizes, in Vienna in 1896 and in Paris a year later.

Lenard's unquenchable animosity began when Röntgen alone was awarded the first Nobel Prize for Physics in 1901. Lenard felt not only disappointed but actually betrayed, for he had been certain that he would share the prize. Consequently, Lenard proclaimed himself the true discoverer of the X-ray.

The real story of the Nobel decision was kept secret for almost 70 years, until the transcripts of the many meetings were made available to the public. A board of members of the Swedish Academy of Sciences was empowered to make the selection. A special advisory committee of five leading Swedish physicists (headed by Svante Arrhenius and Anders Ångström) was also appointed. Physicists in different parts of the world were invited to submit names for the prize. Among these physicists was Röntgen himself, who suggested Lord Kelvin.

When the time for nominations had expired, 29 proposals had been submitted. Of these, 12 suggested Röntgen, 1 suggested Lenard, and 5 recommended a division of the prize between these two scientists. The advisory committee recommended that the prize be divided equally

(continued on page 192)

189

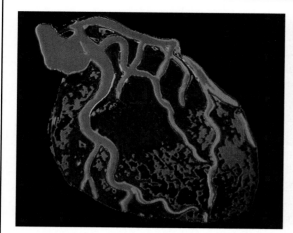
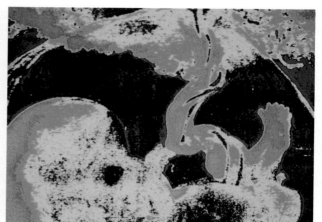
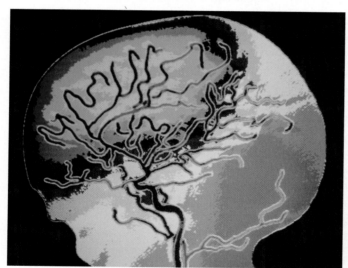
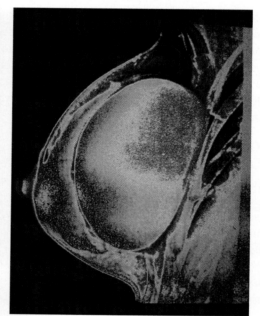
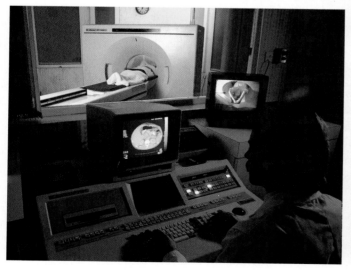
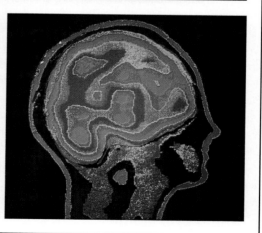

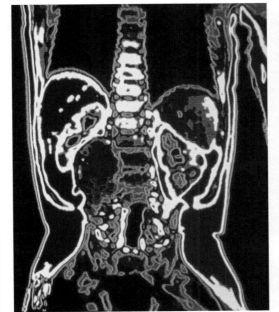

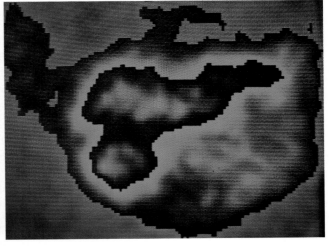

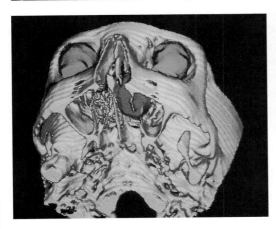

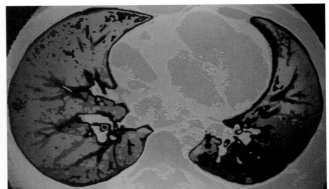

Today's sophisticated imaging technologies are direct descendants of Röntgen's radiographs, although both the images and the equipment that produces them are vastly more complex than anything radiology's originator could have imagined. With such techniques as computed tomography (CT) scanning, magnetic resonance imaging (MRI), positron emission tomography (PET) scanning, and emerging applications of spectroscopy, virtually every structure in the body and many physiological processes can be captured visually. On the opposite page (clockwise from top left): digital subtraction angiography showing blockage of coronary arteries; ultrasound image of fetus in first trimester; mammogram of silicone breast implant; PET scan of brain; CT scan in progress; CT scan of brain, showing arteries. On this page (clockwise from top left): MRI of lower trunk, revealing tumor between kidney and spine; PET scan of heart; CT scan of lungs, showing pulmonary function; CT scan of knee; three-dimensional CT scan of skull.

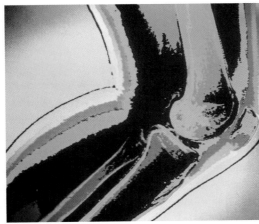

(continued from page 189)

between Röntgen and Lenard. Nevertheless, the academy in full session disregarded the recommendation of the advisory committee. They decided against sharing the prize since the late Swedish inventor and philanthropist Alfred Nobel, who established the award, had specified that it be given only to the most distinguished scientist of the year. The decision was unanimous in favor of Röntgen.

Even after being awarded his own Nobel Prize in 1905, Lenard continued unabated in his animosity. Among his statements downgrading Röntgen's efforts while glorifying his own are the following:

A comparison can best make clear to the neutral observer Roentgen's role in the discovery. I shall make this striking comparison here because it may throw a light on the even now widespread historical confusion and untruth! Roentgen was the midwife at the birth of the discovery. This helper had the good fortune to be able to present the child first. She can only be confused with the mother by the uninformed who knows as little about the procedure of the discovery and the preceding facts as children of the stork.

I am the mother of the x-rays. Just as a midwife is not responsible for the mechanism of birth, so is Roentgen not responsible for the discovery of x-rays, which merely fell into his lap. All Roentgen had to do was push a button, since all the groundwork had been prepared by me.

In effect, Lenard claimed that anybody could have discovered X-rays after his (Lenard's) work on cathode rays. However, Lenard never gave a satisfactory explanation as to why he himself had not accomplished this task. Also, he never mentioned that the so-called Lenard tube was actually based on Hertz's work.

Röntgen took all these insinuations philosophically and contended it was beneath his dignity to react publicly. To his friend Zehnder he wrote, "Well, dear heaven, the envious are never lacking when something occurs as with me. That is always the case."

History's judgment

Lenard's unbridled hatred of Röntgen climaxed during the time of his lofty position in the Nazi hierarchy of scientists. In his four-volume work on German physics, there is no mention of Röntgen (or Einstein) in the text, but the foreword is a lengthy diatribe against the Jews. The implication, drawn by many in Germany, was that Röntgen was a Jew. In answer to a direct query from the American radiologist Lewis E. Etter, "Was Röntgen a Jew?" Lenard replied, "No, but he was friend of Jews and acted like one."

It is interesting to note that at the time of the 50th anniversary of Röntgen's discovery, the Physical Medical Society of Würzburg applied to the Nazi minister of post and telegraph to have a memorial stamp made for Röntgen similar to the ones issued for Robert Koch and other scientists. It so happened, however, that the minister had been a physicist and a student of Lenard's at Heidelberg. He rejected the request, saying the proposal was not in order since such an honor was reserved "only for the illustrious." One hundred years after Röntgen's seminal discovery, on which an entire science is now based, neither his preeminence nor his place in history can be denied.

192

SAVING LIVES
IN THE '90s

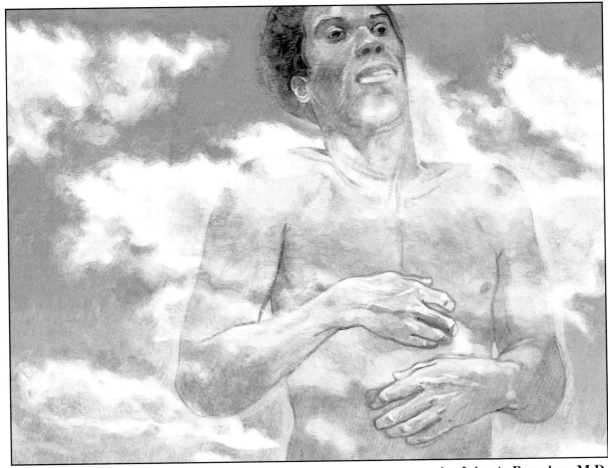

by John A. Paraskos, M.D.

Cardiopulmonary resuscitation (CPR) is the attempt to provide artificial breathing and circulation of blood to a person in whom spontaneous breathing has ceased (respiratory arrest) or in whom the heart has stopped beating (circulatory, or cardiac, arrest). Since the introduction of modern techniques of CPR, dramatic advances have been made in the emergency care of victims of respiratory and cardiac arrest. Under the right circumstances, virtually anyone can reverse "sudden death" by using his or her hands, lungs, and brain.

Attempts to revive victims of cardiac or respiratory arrest are not new. Sporadic reports of successful resuscitations were recorded in antiquity. These included biblical accounts of the resuscitations of young boys by Elijah (1 Kings 17:18–22) and Elisha (2 Kings 4:32–35). Nevertheless, until about 40 years ago, successful resuscitation was largely limited to rare instances of artificial ventilation for victims of respiratory arrest (*e.g.,* near drowning, smoke inhalation, and obstruction of the airways).

Evolution of CPR

In 1958 Hugh E. Stephenson, professor of surgery at the University of Missouri School of Medicine, reported on the use of "open-heart massage"—opening the chest and squeezing the heart. He advised its use in the operating room when the normal heart rhythm had stopped from an anesthesia accident and an ineffective and disorganized rhythm called ventricular fibrillation had supervened. This open-heart massage was occasionally successful if the heart rhythm could be rapidly restored by an electric shock applied directly to the heart surface. This was achieved with electrode paddles (*i.e.,* an "internal defibrillator"). Two years earlier, in 1956, Paul Zoll, at Beth Israel Hospital in Boston, had described the use of externally applied electrodes in reversing ventricular fibrillation. This "external defibrillator" allowed the reversal of this type of fatal heart rhythm without opening the chest. This newly acquired ability—to shock the heart back to life—challenged medical investigators to develop a method of providing artificial breathing and artificial circulation of blood that would keep the patient alive long enough to bring the defibrillator to his or her aid.

Shortly thereafter Peter Safar and James Elam, anesthesiologists at Johns Hopkins Hospital in Baltimore, Maryland, described a "mouth-to-mouth" breathing technique that was an excellent method of lung ventilation that provided oxygen to the blood but did not produce any circulation. Then, in 1960, William B. Kouwenhoven along with colleagues, also at Johns Hopkins, described "closed-chest cardiac massage," performed by pushing down rhythmically on the sternum (breastbone), which introduced the modern era of cardiopulmonary resuscitation. The simplicity of this technique led to its widespread use; as Kouwenhoven stated, "All that is needed are two hands." The combination of this technique with mouth-to-mouth ventilation evolved as the basic method of CPR.

In 1966 interested scientists gathered at a conference sponsored by the National Research Council of the U.S. National Academy of Sciences. This conference recommended that the American Heart Association (AHA) develop training programs and set up guidelines for the optimal performance

John A. Paraskos, M.D., is Professor of Medicine and Director of Diagnostic Cardiology, University of Massachusetts Medical School, Worcester, and served as Chair of the 1992 National Conference on Cardiopulmonary Resuscitation (CPR) and Emergency Cardiac Care (ECC).

(Overleaf and page 208) Illustrations by Jody Williams

of the CPR technique. The second national conference on CPR in 1973 was cosponsored by the AHA and the National Academy of Sciences and recommended that instruction in CPR be extended to the general public. Instruction in CPR for both health care professionals and laypersons soon followed as community programs were established in basic life support (BLS). The American Red Cross has played a key role in the instruction of the public through its wide-reaching programs in CPR.

In addition to its BLS programs for laypersons, the AHA developed professional teaching programs in advanced cardiac life support (ACLS). The 1973 conference set guidelines for both BLS and ACLS and also mandated the development of programs in neonatal and pediatric life support. Guidelines for all these procedures were updated in 1979, 1985, and again in late 1992. The most recent national conference on CPR and emergency cardiac care (ECC) was cosponsored by the AHA, the American Red Cross, the American Academy of Pediatrics, the American College of Cardiology, the European Resuscitation Council, the Heart and Stroke Foundation of Canada, and the U.S. National Heart, Lung, and Blood Institute. Many other groups cooperated, thus guaranteeing a broad-based consensus on emergency rescue programs and methods.

Matters of life and death

For individuals with adequately preserved cardiopulmonary and neurological systems, respiratory and circulatory arrest can be reversed if CPR and definitive ACLS care, such as defibrillation, are quickly available. CPR buys time by supplying life-sustaining oxygen to the brain and other vital organs until emergency medical personnel arrive on the scene and can shock the heart back to life. For many of these victims, prolonged and vigorous life ensues if such restoration of ventilation and circulation occurs before vital structures have been irreversibly damaged.

The short period during which loss of breath and pulse can be reversed is referred to as "clinical death." This is distinguished from "biological

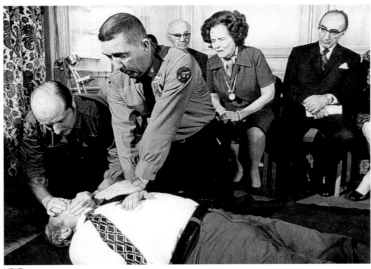

UPI/Bettmann

In 1973 emergency medical services personnel of the New York City Police Department demonstrate the technique of closed-chest cardiac massage, which was first described in 1960 by William B. Kouwenhoven of Johns Hopkins Hospital, Baltimore, Maryland. Combined with mouth-to-mouth ventilation, this easy-to-perform technique became the basic approach to cardiopulmonary resuscitation recommended for use by any trained bystander. In the background observing are (left to right) Kouwenhoven; Mary Lasker, president of the Albert and Mary Lasker Foundation; and Michael E. DeBakey, world-renowned heart specialist and president of Baylor College of Medicine, Houston, Texas. On that occasion Kouwenhoven was a recipient of the 1973 Albert Lasker Clinical Medical Research Award for lifesaving advances against acute heart attacks; Lasker presented the award, and DeBakey was the chairman of the awards committee.

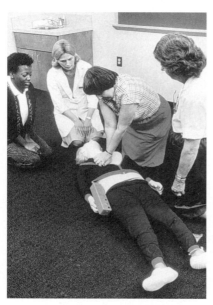

(Top) Using a doll to demonstrate, an instructor shows two members of an American Red Cross class the correct method of removing a foreign object from the obstructed airway of an infant. (Bottom) A student in a CPR class practices delivering chest compressions on a dummy.

death," the state of *irreversible* death. The best single criterion (medical or legal) for establishing the *ultimate* death of an individual is "brain death." For the brain-dead individual, it is generally inappropriate to continue life-sustaining measures to keep the rest of the body alive. The one exception is the continuation of circulation to maintain viability of vital organs in the potential organ donor.

Cardiac emergencies: magnitude of the problem

Cardiovascular disease accounts for nearly one million deaths in the United States annually. This represents almost half of deaths from all causes. Approximately 500,000 deaths, most of which are "sudden," are due to coronary heart disease. More than 160,000 of these deaths occur in people under the age of 65, and more than half of all cardiovascular deaths occur in women. Safar, now professor of anesthesiology at the University of Pittsburgh (Pennsylvania) School of Medicine, has estimated that for the 750,000 victims of sudden death in the U.S. every year, there are fewer than 200,000 attempts made at resuscitation. Of these attempts approximately 70,000 are initially successful, but only about 7,000 of the victims are returned to their former life. Thus, a mere 1% of all cardiac arrests are successfully reversed.

In marked contrast to these dismal statistics stand the data from Seattle (King county), Washington, which has the nation's best record for survival after cardiac arrest. Seattle is a community with a large percentage of the population (two-thirds of adult residents) trained in CPR and a well-organized emergency medical system (EMS) capable of rapid response and the provision of early defibrillation. A study carried out in King county indicated that approximately one-third of patients with documented ventricular fibrillation (an uncoordinated quivering of the heart muscle) or ventricular tachycardia (a life-threatening sustained rapid heartbeat) without a pulse were successfully resuscitated if CPR was provided promptly (within four minutes) and defibrillation delivered rapidly (within eight minutes). In the absence of prompt CPR followed rapidly by defibrillation, the likelihood of success was negligible. From these and more recent statistics, it is estimated that if CPR training were instituted for a large segment of the U.S. public and emergency medical systems capable of providing early defibrillation were established nationwide, as many as 100,000 to 200,000 lives could be saved annually.

The concept of a four-linked "chain of survival" has been used by the AHA to underscore the importance of (1) early access to emergency care (rapid notification of EMS, phoning 911), (2) early institution of CPR, (3) early defibrillation, and (4) early advanced care (ACLS). A delay in any of these constitutes a "broken link," which compromises the chance of a successful outcome.

Early attempts at reproducing the Seattle experience have met with widely divergent results. While in some suburban and semirural areas the results have been encouraging, in large metropolitan locations such as New York City and Chicago, the results have been disappointing. The poor results in urban areas appear to be the result of multiple breaks in the "chain of survival." In New York and Chicago, as compared with Seattle, the arrival of the emergency team is delayed significantly by city traffic, bystander CPR is much less likely to be provided (at least in part because smaller proportions of the respective populations have been trained), and the time from cardiac arrest to defibrillation is much longer. For the outcome in large cities to be improved, access to early CPR must be improved and the automated defibrillator needs to be made more widely available. Theoretically, local police and fire department personnel and security personnel for large buildings and apartment houses could not only be trained in CPR but be given access to ventilating masks and automated defibrillators and trained in their use.

Reluctance to perform CPR: the public's fears

At the 1992 national conference on CPR and ECC, it was emphasized that because the majority of cardiac arrest victims die suddenly—before they arrive at a hospital—the community must be recognized as "the ultimate coronary care unit." The layperson, therefore, is the most important link in the CPR-ECC system. However, a relatively small proportion of the lay public is trained in basic life-support techniques, and many who have had training are reluctant to perform CPR.

Complications of BLS procedures. Proper application of CPR should help minimize serious complications. Nonetheless, there are risks inherent in BLS procedures. Gastric distension and regurgitation are common complications of mouth-to-mouth ventilation. Complications of sternal compression include rib and sternal fractures. While rib fractures are common during CPR, especially in the elderly, no serious effects are likely. Though rare, other potential complications of BLS procedures are injury to part of a lung, bleeding into the chest cavity, and lacerations of the liver or spleen.

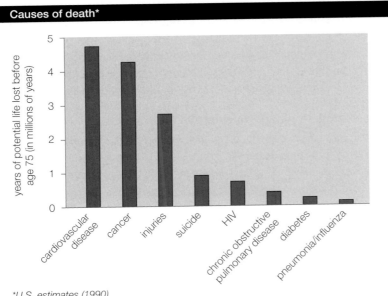

Causes of death*

U.S. estimates (1990)
Sources: Centers for Disease Control and Prevention and the American Heart Association

The rescuer's awareness of these potential complications is important, but the successful resuscitation of the cardiac arrest victim—*i.e.,* saving a life that would otherwise be lost—is even more important. Laypersons should be reassured by the fact that Good Samaritan laws in most jurisdictions protect individuals who do not have a duty to respond and who are acting "in good faith" and are not guilty of "gross negligence." Such laws are intended to minimize the public's fears about possible legal ramifications of performing CPR; moreover, *not* providing BLS hinders or precludes subsequent emergency medical intervention.

Fear of infection. The widespread public fear provoked by the spread of HIV is understandable, given the seriousness of the infection. Unfortunately, this anxiety may lead to excessive caution when dealing with strangers; it has certainly decreased the willingness of the lay public as well as health professionals to learn and perform CPR. The effect of this fear on CPR is serious and must be addressed.

While mouth-to-mouth ventilation results in the exchange of saliva between the victim and the rescuer, saliva has not been implicated in the transmission of HIV. This is true even after contamination of open wounds with saliva from known HIV-positive individuals. It has also been shown that hepatitis B-positive saliva is not infectious when applied to oral membranes. Other diseases, such as tuberculosis, herpes, and respiratory viral infections, however, are potentially spread during mouth-to-mouth resuscitation.

Health professionals often use protective equipment to prevent such transmission. *All* health care providers who are called upon to provide CPR as part of their duties should have special equipment available to allow artificial ventilation without direct contact with the victim (*e.g.,* masks with one-way valves).

While there is no legal obligation for a trained layperson to provide CPR, the informed layperson should be motivated by the knowledge that a delay in initiating ventilation could result in death or disablement for a victim who could otherwise be saved. The potential rescuer should also recognize that the risk of infection, even with a known HIV-positive victim, is extremely low. More laypersons may be motivated to learn lifesaving techniques if they realize that if they are ever called upon to provide CPR, it will most likely be for members of their own family or close acquaintances.

Responding to cardiopulmonary emergencies

Citizens play an important part in responding to cardiopulmonary emergencies by providing basic life support for victims of respiratory and/or cardiac arrest. Training in BLS is widely available and usually involves a three-hour course.

The recommendations given here are intended as guides for the proper performance of CPR by laypersons who have taken a course. They are based on the guidelines issued following the 1992 national conference on CPR and ECC and represent the consensus of experts from many disciplines.

The bystander must react promptly to assess the responsiveness of a seemingly unconscious victim by attempting to wake and communicate with the victim; he or she should tap or gently shake the victim and shout, "Are you okay?" After determining unresponsiveness, the rescuer should call for help, summoning anyone within earshot. If no other person is immediately available, the rescuer should call for emergency medical services immediately (dialing 911 in most localities) and identify the location and nature of the emergency. This dictum of "phone first" assumes that telephone services are reasonably close by and that EMS is available. After summoning help and activating the EMS system, the rescuer should begin BLS. The situations calling for BLS are:

● Respiratory arrest. The victim of respiratory arrest may have an obstructed airway or may be a victim of drowning, stroke, smoke inhalation, drug overdose, electrocution, or physical trauma. In such cases the heart usually continues to circulate blood for several minutes, and the residual oxygen in lungs and blood may keep the brain viable. An attempt at CPR is the proper first step. Opening the airway and providing ventilation may be all that is required for restoration of spontaneous breathing. Often such early intervention will result in the prevention of cardiac arrest.

● Cardiac arrest. The cardiac arrest victim experiences rapid depletion of oxygen to vital organs. After six minutes without oxygen, brain damage is likely, except in hypothermic conditions (*e.g.,* near drowning in cold water). Therefore, early bystander CPR (within four minutes) and rapid ACLS with attempted defibrillation (within eight minutes) are essential for survival and neurological recovery.

The ABCs of CPR

The sequence of steps in CPR may be summarized as the ABCs of CPR— *A* referring to airway, *B* to breathing, and *C* to circulation. After unresponsiveness has been established, the victim must be supine and on a firm flat surface for effective CPR to be administered. If the victim is lying face down, the rescuer must roll the victim over so that the head, shoulders, and torso move together without twisting of the neck (Fig. 1). In this way the torso, head, and neck are moved as a unit, and the potential for neck injury is lessened. The rescuer then must open the airway (Fig. 2) and check for spontaneous breathing (Fig. 3). The most common way to open the airway

Figure 1

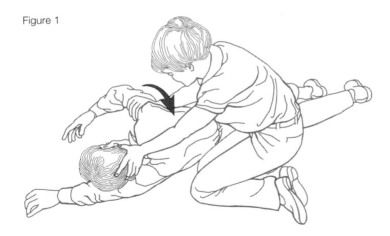

Fig. 1: Rescuer positions victim for CPR after establishing his or her unresponsiveness and summoning emergency medical services.

Illustrations (Figures 1–15), adapted from Emergency Cardiac Care Committee and Subcommittees, American Heart Association, "Guidelines for Cardiopulmonary Resuscitation and Emergency Cardiac Care," Part II: "Adult Basic Life Support" and Part V: "Pediatric Basic Life Support," *JAMA,* vol. 268, no. 16 (Oct. 28, 1992), pp. 2184–98 and pp. 2251–61. Copyright 1992, American Medical Association

Fig. 2: (A) Victim's airway obstructed by tongue and epiglottis (arrows); (B) airway opened by means of head tilt-chin lift maneuver. Fig. 3: Rescuer determines breathlessness by placing ear over victim's mouth and nose. Fig. 4: While maintaining open airway, rescuer gently pinches victim's nose closed, establishes an airtight mouth-to-mouth seal, then delivers two slow breaths followed by 10–12 breaths per minute as long as needed. Fig. 5: To determine pulselessness, rescuer locates larynx in victim's neck (A), then slides fingers to left to find pulse at carotid artery (B).

Figure 2

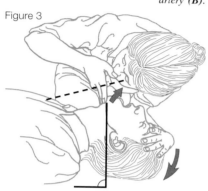

A B

Figure 3

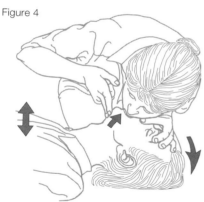

Figure 4

(Fig. 2B) is to place one hand on the victim's forehead and tilt the head back with pressure from the palm. The fingers of the rescuer's other hand are placed under the bony part of the jaw near the chin and lifted to bring the chin forward. This is known as the "head tilt-chin lift maneuver." If the victim has a serious neck injury, tilting the head may cause spinal damage. Therefore, if neck injury is suspected, it is best to open the airway without extending the neck or tilting the head. If the victim is breathing, it is best not to attempt moving the victim until the emergency team has arrived to stabilize the neck with proper equipment.

If spontaneous breathing is absent, rescue breathing must be initiated. The rescuer pinches the victim's nostrils with the thumb and forefinger and begins mouth-to-mouth ventilation (Fig. 4). First, the rescuer takes a deep breath and positions his or her mouth over the victim's mouth, making a tight seal. Next, the rescuer breathes into the victim's mouth twice, completely refilling his or her lungs after each breath. Each of the first two breaths should be delivered over 1½ to 2 seconds, allowing the victim's lungs to deflate between breaths. The reason for delivering the breaths at this relatively slow rate is to prevent the air from going into the victim's stomach instead of the lungs. Thereafter, the rate of 10 to 12 breaths per minute is maintained for as long as is necessary. If attempts at ventilation are unsuccessful, the victim should be considered to have an obstructed airway, and attempts should be made to dislodge a potential foreign-body obstruction (*see* below).

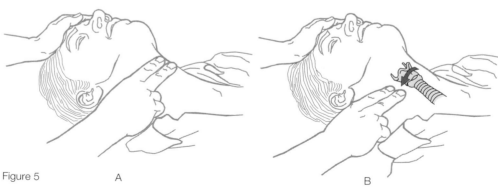

Figure 5 A B

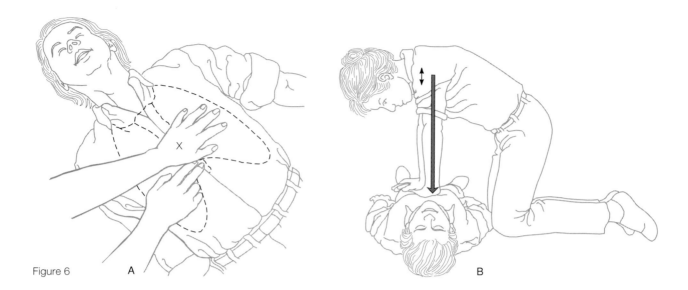

Figure 6   A   B

If the victim lacks a pulse, chest compressions should be initiated. In the adult one can best determine the absence of a pulse by feeling the carotid artery, the large artery in the neck (Fig. 5). If a pulse is not felt after 10 seconds of careful searching, the rescuer should proceed to deliver chest compressions.

Artificial circulation depends on adequate chest compression, which one achieves by depressing the victim's sternum. The rescuer places the heels of his or her hands on the lower half of the victim's sternum, with the fingers kept off the rib cage (Fig. 6A). If hands are placed either too high or too low, or if the fingers are allowed to lie flat against the rib cage, broken ribs and laceration of internal organs can result. The rescuer's elbows should be kept locked, and the arms should be straight, with the shoulders directly over the victim (Fig. 6B). This position allows the rescuer's upper body to provide a perpendicularly directed force.

The sternum is depressed approximately one and one-half to two inches at a rate of 80 to 100 compressions per minute. At the end of each compression, pressure is released and the sternum is allowed to rebound, but the rescuer's hands are not removed. Equal time should be allotted to the compressions and release of pressure; the movements should be smooth—*i.e.,* done without jerking or bouncing on the sternum. After 15 compressions the rescuer gives two full breaths and then delivers another 15 compressions.

Pediatric resuscitation

The majority of infants and children who require resuscitation have a respiratory problem that causes cessation of breathing. Cardiac arrest, when it occurs, results from the ensuing lack of oxygen; therefore, the focus of pediatric resuscitation is on opening the airway and providing ventilation. In a child the cessation of cardiac activity is usually the sign of a prolonged lack of oxygen. The outcome of CPR in these children is therefore

Fig. 6: (A) Correct hand position for delivering chest compressions; *(B)* proper body position of rescuer for providing artificial circulation to a pulseless victim: rescuer's shoulders directly above victim's sternum, arms straight, and elbows locked to provide a perpendicularly directed force.

Fig. 7: Child's airway opened with head tilt-chin lift maneuver; rescuer should begin CPR for a nonbreathing unconscious infant or child before *calling for help.*
Fig. 8: Rescue breathing for an infant or small child, with rescuer's mouth covering victim's mouth and nose. Fig. 9: Mouth-to-mouth ventilation for a larger child, with one hand lifting chin and the other hand maintaining head tilt while thumb and forefinger gently pinch the victim's nose closed. Fig. 10: Pulselessness of an infant determined by palpation of brachial artery in upper arm.

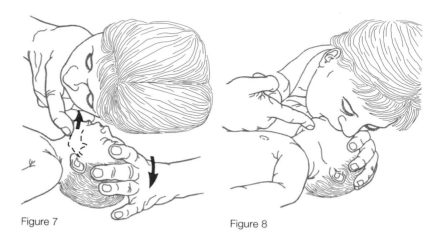

Figure 7   Figure 8

Figure 9

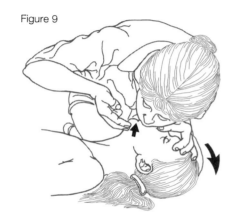

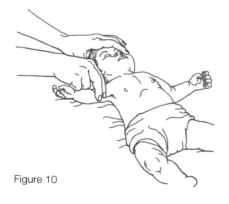

Figure 10

poor, and brain damage is all too common. On the other hand, if a child suffering from respiratory arrest is promptly treated—before cessation of cardiac activity—the outcome is often favorable. It is for this reason that it is recommended that the rescuer initiate CPR *before* taking time to telephone for emergency assistance. The first minute of CPR will allow opening of the airway and the beginning of artificial ventilation. If an obstructed airway is found, attempts at dislodging a foreign body should not be delayed.

Effective techniques for ventilation and chest compression vary with the size of the child. "Infant" procedures are applicable for victims who appear to be under one year of age. "Child" techniques are applicable for those who appear to be between ages one and eight. "Adult" techniques are appropriate for a victim who appears older than eight years.

If the child is not breathing, the head tilt-chin lift maneuver is used to open the airway (Fig. 7) after he or she is placed in a supine position. Usually providing rescue breathing for infants and small children requires the rescuer's mouth to cover both the victim's mouth and nose to make an effective seal (Fig. 8). If the child's face is too large to allow a tight seal to be made over both nose and mouth, the mouth alone is covered while the nose is pinched closed, as in the case of an adult (Fig. 9).

The ventilation rate for infants and children is 20 breaths per minute (one every three seconds). Artificial ventilation for an adolescent is done at the adult rate of 10 to 12 breaths per minute (one every five seconds). The time that should be taken to fill the lungs of the infant or child is 1 to 1½ seconds (this is faster than in the adult or adolescent, as a lesser volume of air is needed).

Artificial circulation is instituted in the absence of a palpable pulse. The pulse of the larger child or adolescent can easily be detected at the carotid artery; the presence of an infant's pulse is best determined by palpation of the brachial artery in the upper arm between the elbow and the shoulder (Fig. 10).

To deliver chest compressions to an infant, the rescuer's index finger is placed on the sternum just below the nipples. The proper area for compression is the lower third of the sternum but avoiding the lowermost portion

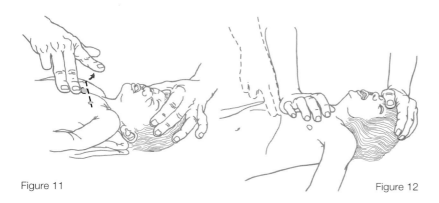

Figure 11

Figure 12

Fig. 11: Proper placement of fingers on sternum of an infant for delivering chest compressions (one finger's width below the imaginary line running between nipples); other hand maintains head position to facilitate ventilation. Fig. 12: To give CPR to a child between one and eight years old, the rescuer first traces the lower margin of child's rib cage (using the middle and index fingers) to the notch where ribs and sternum meet; middle finger is placed on notch and index finger next to it; heel of same hand is then placed next to spot marked by index finger. Compressions should be delivered smoothly at a rate of about 100 per minute, with pauses at the end of every fifth compression to provide rescue breathing; the hand that is not compressing the chest maintains the head position to facilitate ventilation. Fig. 13: Correct position for performing Heimlich maneuver on a conscious victim who is standing; same position is used for an adult or child.

(Fig. 11). Using two or three fingers, the rescuer compresses the sternum one-half to one inch. For delivering chest compressions to a child, the heel of one hand is positioned on the lower third of the sternum (Fig. 12), which is compressed about one to one and one-half inches. The frequency of sternal compressions for infants and children is 100 per minute. The ratio of compressions to ventilations is 5:1 for most small children and 15:2 for larger children.

Obstructed airways: the Heimlich maneuver

Airways can become obstructed in a variety of ways. An unconscious person can develop airway obstruction when the tongue falls backward into the throat. In persons who are sedated, inebriated, or ill, regurgitation of stomach contents into the back of the throat obstructs the airway and is a frequent cause of cessation of breathing and subsequent death. Even otherwise healthy individuals may develop a life-threatening foreign-body obstruction of the airway from poorly chewed or improperly swallowed food or from a large wad of gum that has been inadvertently inhaled. (Meat is the most common cause of "café coronaries"—so called because such emergencies, which often occur in restaurants, may be mistaken for heart attacks.) It is not uncommon for children's smaller airways to become obstructed by small nuts, candies, toys, or other objects accidentally inhaled.

Victims of complete airway obstruction may still be conscious, but they will be unable to cough or speak. They can be saved if the foreign body is expelled from the airway. Often a properly timed and executed abdominal thrust (Heimlich maneuver) will force air from the lungs in sufficient quantity to do this.

To perform the Heimlich maneuver on one who is still conscious and standing, the rescuer stands behind the victim and wraps his or her arms around the victim's waist (Fig. 13). The fist of one hand is placed with the thumb side against the victim's abdomen, slightly above the navel. The fist is grasped with the other hand and a quick inward and upward thrust is delivered. It may be necessary to repeat the thrust 6 to 10 times to clear the airway. Each thrust should be a separate and distinct movement.

Victims who are unconscious or lying down should be placed in the supine position with the face up. The rescuer kneels astride the victim's

Figure 13

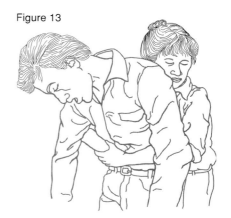

Figure 14

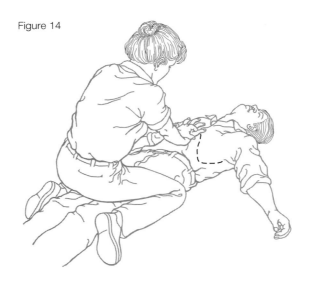

Figure 14

Fig. 14: Proper position for performing Heimlich maneuver on an adult or child who is unconscious or lying down. Fig. 15: Positions for administering back blows (A) and chest thrusts (B) to dislodge a foreign body that obstructs the airway of an infant; infant is supported on rescuer's forearm; up to five back blows are delivered alternately with up to five chest thrusts until the object has been removed.

Figure 15

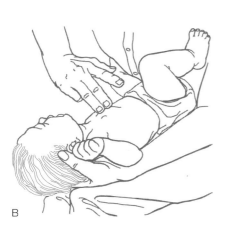

A

B

thighs and places the heel of one hand against the victim's abdomen, slightly above the navel. The other hand is placed directly on top of the first and pressed inward and upward with separate quick, forceful thrusts (Fig. 14). If no object is expelled or the maneuver is not successful, the mouth should be opened and the back of the throat inspected. If an object can be seen and grasped, it can often be removed. Care should be taken, however, not to thrust it deeper.

The Heimlich maneuver is not appropriate for infants because abdominal thrusts could easily result in organ damage. Back blows and chest thrusts are therefore recommended (Fig. 15). These are delivered with the heel of the rescuer's hand while the infant is supported in the prone position straddling the rescuer's forearm, with head lower than trunk—face down for back blows and face up for chest thrusts. The rescuer delivers up to five forceful back blows between the infant's shoulders, then turns the infant and gives up to five quick downward chest thrusts. If the airway remains obstructed, back blows, chest thrusts, and rescue breathing are repeated until the foreign object has been removed and the infant is breathing on his or her own.

Advanced lifesaving

Once a victim has been successfully resuscitated and EMS personnel have arrived promptly on the scene—within 8 to 10 minutes—ACLS can begin. ACLS is delivered by paramedics and trained emergency medical personnel and directed by a physician (at the scene or by direct telemetric communication). The aim of advanced life-support methods is to defibrillate the heart if necessary—shocking it back to a more normal rhythm—and to further stabilize the patient before transport to a hospital. Stabilization includes the use of special equipment to support ventilation and circulation, cardiac monitoring, establishment of intravenous access, and administration of drug therapy (*e.g,* morphine for pain, drugs to control abnormal heart rhythms, and drugs to improve cardiac output and rate).

Defibrillation is the definitive treatment for the vast majority of cardiac arrests. It should be delivered as early as possible and repeated frequently until an effective rhythm has been reestablished.

The drug most frequently used in ACLS is epinephrine, which constricts blood vessels, thereby raising blood pressure and improving blood flow into the heart and brain. If defibrillation has failed (or is not an option), an adult in cardiac arrest should be given a one-milligram dose of epinephrine, which is repeated every five minutes as needed. Animal studies have suggested that doses as high as 10 milligrams are advantageous. However, two human trials have failed to demonstrate a better outcome with a higher dose, although no detriment was shown; therefore, higher doses are now considered optional as therapy.

Drugs that stabilize the heart rhythm (antiarrhythmics) play an important role in many resuscitation situations. Lidocaine has proved the most useful in counteracting potentially life-threatening ventricular arrhythmias. Other drugs with similar action that may be used are bretylium, procainamide, and various beta-blockers.

Changes in CPR and ECC guidelines

While most of the guidelines for CPR and ECC remained unaltered, the 1992 national conference reached a strong consensus for several major changes. Among them were the following:

● "Phone first"—i.e., call 911 promptly after an adult victim has been found to be unresponsive—before initiating CPR—unless another person is available to make the call.

● One minute of immediate CPR is still recommended in the case of infants and children—before summoning emergency services (assuming another person cannot make the call).

Surviving cardiac arrest			
location	number of victims receiving defibrillation by emergency medical personnel*	number surviving	% surviving
large urban			
New York City	415	22	5.3
Chicago	371	15	4.0
midsize urban/suburban			
King county, Washington†	2,074	705	34.0
Tucson, Arizona	118	18	15.3
suburban/rural			
Pennsylvania	382	47	12.3
Minnesota	107	11	10.3
Iowa	51	10	19.6

*may or may not have received bystander CPR
†includes Seattle

Adapted from Gary Lombardi, M.D., et al., "Outcome of Out-of-Hospital Cardiac Arrest in New York City," JAMA, vol. 271, no. 9 (March 2, 1994), pp. 678–683. Copyright 1994, American Medical Association

Physio-Control Corporation

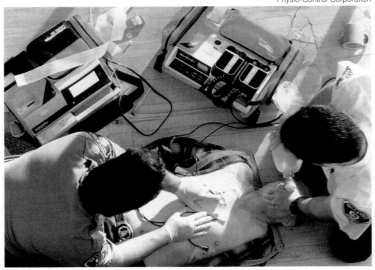

Paramedics demonstrate the use of an automatic external defibrillator on a dummy. Defibrillation is the definitive treatment for the majority of cardiac arrest victims. It should be delivered as early as possible (within eight minutes of the victim's collapse) and repeated until an effective heart rhythm has been reestablished. Today's automatic defibrillators can read the victim's heart rhythms, determine whether shocks are needed, and, if so, administer the appropriate shocks.

● The time taken to fill the lungs during artificial ventilation has been increased from 1 to 1½ seconds to 1½ to 2 seconds per breath to decrease the likelihood of filling the stomach with air.

● The initial dose of epinephrine (one milligram) for the pulseless victim remains unchanged; higher repeat doses are now considered optional.

● New detailed protocols have been outlined for treatment of arrhythmias, pulseless cardiac electrical activity, shock and hypotension, acute pulmonary edema, refractory ventricular fibrillation, and hypothermia.

● Various new drugs have been introduced for treating a variety of heart rhythm disturbances.

● Placement of a needle directly into the marrow cavity of an infant or child (intraosseous route) is now considered safe for delivering drugs if a vein cannot be easily found.

● Because ethical considerations are important in resuscitation and advanced life support of cardiac arrest victims, recommendations were made for assisting EMS personnel in responding to advance directives (living wills) and do-not-resuscitate orders.

Future refinements

It is likely that basic life-support techniques could be further refined to provide better blood flow during cardiac arrest and thus improve success rates. Although many case reports describe complete recovery in humans even after prolonged administration of CPR, investigators have measured blood flow during CPR in cardiac arrest victims at no better than 25% of normal.

As researchers continue to evaluate new CPR approaches and techniques, they are seeking a better understanding of the mechanism by which blood flows during resuscitation efforts. In 1960, when Kouwenhoven reported on the efficacy of the closed-chest cardiac-massage technique, most experts accepted that "squeezing," or compressing, the heart that is "trapped between the breastbone and the backbone" propels the blood. This was known as the "cardiac-compression theory." In 1976 J. Michael Criley, at Johns Hopkins Hospital, brought the theory of cardiac compression into question when he reported that during cardiac arrest, repeated forceful coughing was capable of generating arterial blood pressures comparable to those of normal cardiac activity. This finding strongly suggested that high pressures in the chest, or "thoracic cavity," were capable of sustaining blood flow without sternal compression. Subsequently, it was proposed that the propulsion of blood even with sternal compression was due to the mechanism of increased intrathoracic pressure—the "thoracic pump theory." Researchers have attempted to increase this pressure further by a number of maneuvers. In 1982 Sandra H. Ralston and colleagues at the Biomedical Engineering Center at Purdue University, West Lafayette, Indiana, reported on the effects of compressing the abdomen when the sternum is not being compressed, known as "interposed abdominal compression." This technique promises to improve blood flow by increasing the amount of blood in the chest cavity when the sternum is being compressed. While early reports suggested an improved outcome in humans, the technique unfortunately requires more than one rescuer. Furthermore, the method cannot be readily taught to the lay public. Other experimental CPR techniques are under investigation. These include the use of a plungerlike device ("compression-decompression CPR") and the use of a pneumatic chest vest analogous to a large blood-pressure cuff, which increases chest pressure uniformly and automatically.

Preventing needless deaths

Sudden death related to coronary artery disease is the most prominent medical emergency in the United States. A large number of these deaths could be prevented by prompt action in alerting the EMS (calling 911), prompt delivery of bystander CPR, and early delivery of electrical defibrillation. Many victims of near drowning, electrocution, suffocation, and drug intoxication could also be saved by the early initiation of CPR and advanced life-support measures.

Programs aimed at modifying risk factors for cardiovascular disease have already reduced mortality from heart attacks. More efforts need to be directed toward prevention, which would further reduce the number of victims requiring CPR and ECC.

Not only does the prompt application of lifesaving techniques in newborns, infants, and children promise to save lives but, by preventing brain damage, it will avoid lifetimes of unnecessary suffering and expense. Trauma is the major cause of death and debility in the pediatric and young adult population. Here, too, emphasis on trauma prevention could reduce the need for pediatric resuscitation.

Training programs by the AHA and the American Red Cross reach millions of persons, both lay and professional. Because of this enormous penetration, strong messages about risk factors for coronary disease and injury prevention delivered at the time of CPR training will undoubtedly have an impact on cardiovascular mortality and trauma statistics.

207

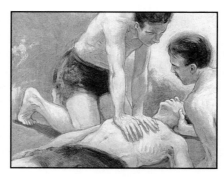

Many organizations, such as the American Red Cross, hospitals, and YMCAs, offer adult courses in basic life-support methods for laypersons. In addition, many large companies conduct CPR training sessions for employees. Local affiliates of the American Heart Association maintain lists of courses in their regions. To find a nearby course one can call 1-800-AHA-USA1 (1-800-242-8721).

RECENT DEVELOPMENTS FROM THE
WORLD OF
MEDICINE

Aerospace Medicine

Humankind lives in a complex and ever changing world and is continuously subjected to myriad environmental factors that shape all life processes. The effects of many of these factors are transient in nature. Some, however, significantly contribute to the maintenance of human health and sometimes even induce adaptive changes that can affect the very evolution of the species.

Humans, as living organisms, interact with the environment through a series of complex sensory and motor interfaces. When the body senses changes in the environment, it responds with an outpouring of enzymes and hormones that regulate its response to the stimulus. Day and night cycles, temperature and humidity, atmospheric pressure and gas composition, ionizing and nonionizing radiation, and gravity are among the important physical factors that act as stimuli and thereby affect the quality and time course of human life.

Gravity is a universal force that has influenced the evolution of life on Earth in important ways. It is also one of the least understood factors of biological evolution. Like most physical elements of the environment, the effects of increased gravitational forces can be experimentally manipulated in a laboratory setting. However, removal of gravity for any significant period of time is impossible in ground-based settings.

Greater understanding of physiological processes and how they are influenced by gravity has been made possible by research conducted in spaceborne laboratories. During spaceflight the influence of gravity can be effectively removed and the body's response to its absence measured. Analysis of these measurements has revealed that significant changes occur in several body systems. These changes reflect the body's attempt to adapt to this unique environment and the situation of weightlessness it produces. The emphasis of biomedical research in space has been on documenting these changes and understanding the mechanisms responsible for them. This focused area of research contributes to ensuring the health, safety, and productivity of humans in space; in addition, this knowledge contributes significantly to the promotion of health and the prevention and treatment of disease in people on Earth.

In order to ensure success of space missions involving humans, the National Aeronautics and Space Administration (NASA) supports a comprehensive life sciences research program that utilizes the space shuttle carrying the Spacelab. The Spacelab is a European-built, 10,000-kg (22,000-lb) pressurized module carried in the shuttle orbiter payload bay. It provides a "shirtsleeve" environment in which to conduct scientific experiments in microgravity, the condition of weightlessness in space in which only minuscule forces are experienced—*i.e.*, in the virtual absence of gravity. NASA's life sciences flight experiments program uses the Spacelab to carry out extensive biomedical research on the body's adaptation to spaceflight, some of which is designed to study physiological problems associated with extended spaceflight durations in the future. The first Spacelab mission dedicated entirely to biomedical research was the Spacelab Life Sciences-1 (SLS-1) mission in June 1991. The highly successful flight lasted nine days, carried seven astronauts, who had spent approximately seven years preparing for the mission, and 29 rodents and 2,478 jellyfish. It included 18 specially designed animal and astronaut biomedical studies.

Spacelab Life Sciences-2

SLS-2 was the second in this series of dedicated life sciences missions. These missions, in addition to biomedical studies carried out on other shuttle flights and in ongoing ground-based studies conducted in NASA laboratories, have provided scientists with much new understanding of human physiological responses. On Oct. 18, 1993, the space shuttle *Columbia,* carrying the Spacelab module, was launched from the John F. Kennedy Space Center in Florida; the flight landed at Edwards Air Force Base in California on Nov. 1, 1993. This 14-day mission was the longest shuttle mission flown since the NASA space shuttle program began in 1981. The mission-specific objectives addressed the acute (*i.e.,* short-term) physiological responses to microgravity, longer-term adaptation problems, and the readaptation to Earth's gravity. An additional goal was to demonstrate the utility of rodents as a suitable experimental model for physiological changes that occur in humans.

The seven-member crew, selected from NASA's astronaut corps and the scientific community at large, possessed a variety of complementary backgrounds that enabled them to achieve the mission's goals. The three orbiter crew members were: the mission's commander, Col. John E. Blaha of the air force; air force Lieut. Col. Richard A. Searfoss, pilot; and mission specialist Lieut. Col. William S. McArthur, Jr., of the army. Together they maintained and operated the shuttle systems and voluntarily participated as subjects and operators in several experiments. The four payload crew members were: M. Rhea Seddon, who was payload commander; David A. Wolf and Shannon W. Lucid, mission specialists; and payload specialist Martin J. Fettman.

The payload crew members were selected for this mission because their combined biomedical expertise was particularly suited for the SLS-2 investigations. Seddon, who also flew on the SLS-1 mission, is a medical doctor who continues to work as an emergency physician. Her firsthand experience with investigations on SLS-1 was fundamental to SLS-2's success. Wolf is a surgeon who helped develop the American Flight Echocardiograph, an instrument used to monitor the cardiovascular system during spaceflight. In 1992 Wolf was named NASA Inventor of the Year for developing a bioreactor, a device that promotes the growth of cell cultures in space. Lucid, a biochemist with extensive laboratory research experience who had previously flown on four shuttle missions, set the record for the longest time spent in space by a woman: 838 hours 27 minutes. Fettman, selected from a list of highly qualified candidates, is a practicing veterinarian who used his skills to perform the first rodent dissections in space.

Fourteen experiments were selected from proposals submitted by the scientific community to be carried out on SLS-2. These experiments focused on changes in the cardiovascular, pulmonary, musculoskeletal, vestibular, and regulatory physiology systems. Eight of these investigations used humans as subjects, and six used rodents. Several similar investigations were conducted on the SLS-1 mission; the SLS-2 data added to the statistical analysis of the previously collected data and also extended the data collection by utilizing more advanced techniques. In addition, several entirely new experiments were conducted.

As noted above, rodent dissections were performed in flight for the first time; their purpose was to provide tissue samples for postflight analysis. Because previous dissections had been done only postflight, it had been difficult to distinguish between those changes that occurred as a result of adaptation to microgravity and those that were a response to the stress of reentering Earth's gravity. To determine the physiological adaptation to microgravity and the subsequent readaptation to Earth's gravity, data collected during and after the mission were compared with preflight baseline data.

Physiology in space

Each physiological system varies in its speed of response to the stresses of spaceflight. The most rapid effects are observed in the vestibular system and in the systems that respond to fluid volume change—notably the fluid-and-electrolyte-regulation and cardiovascular (circulatory) systems.

Vestibular system adaptation is usually accomplished in three to five days, during which space motion sickness may be experienced and subtle changes in balance, orientation, and proprioception (the body's response to internal stimuli) may occur. The initial entry into weightlessness causes body fluids to redistribute into the upper body—a direct response to the lack of gravity, which on Earth pulls fluids toward the feet. The body, in turn, perceives this upward fluid shift as a fluid overload, and the kidneys respond by excreting the "excess"—a process that causes a reduction in plasma blood volume, which in turn signals a more gradual decrease in red blood cell mass, commonly known as "space anemia."

Slower, more gradual changes are observed in the cardiovascular/cardiopulmonary and musculoskeletal systems. The fluid redistribution due to the lack of gravity is thought to affect the function and structure of the heart and lungs as well as the blood pressure within the arteries and veins. On Earth the heart is forced to work hard every time a person stands up, walks, runs, or performs any activity that opposes gravity. In contrast, in microgravity the heart is no longer being stressed, and like any muscle that is not properly exercised, it will lose some of its strength. This phenomenon, called "cardiovascular deconditioning," is also observed in patients who are bedridden for long periods of time. On Earth gravity also causes a relatively greater amount of blood to flow to the lower portion of the lungs and a relatively greater volume

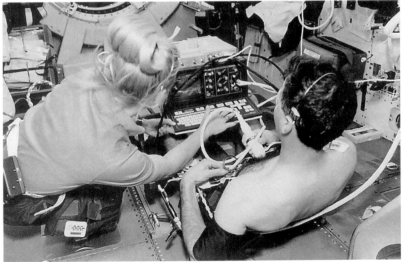

M. Rhea Seddon, payload commander on the October 1993 Spacelab Life Sciences-2 mission, assists payload specialist Martin J. Fettman in a self-administered echocardiography study. The noninvasive test uses high-frequency sound waves that are beamed at the heart and then reflected, or "echoed," back. The echoes produce images of cardiovascular structures and provide information about the functioning of the cardiovascular system. The resulting data are displayed on a television-like screen.

of air to fill the upper lungs. Experiments conducted in microgravity indicate that lung structure changes in flight such that perfusion of blood and ventilation in the lungs are evenly distributed.

Structural change also plays a part in musculoskeletal adaptation in space. In the weightless environment the muscles and bones are no longer required to support the body's weight. The leg muscles of astronauts weaken, losing mass as well as protein, the major component of muscle. Minerals such as calcium and phosphorus are lost from the bones, which induces a condition similar to the bone-weakening disorder osteoporosis.

SLS-2 findings

As already noted, the results of studies conducted on the SLS-2 mission contributed to the understanding of how humans and various species of animals respond to spaceflight. Some experiments confirmed previous observations and hypotheses; others shed important new light on specific responses.

Regulatory physiology. Carolyn S. Leach of the NASA Johnson Space Center in Houston, Texas, designed a study to investigate the mechanisms that contribute to decreased fluid volume and the resultant adaptive responses caused by the upward fluid shift that occurs upon entering microgravity. Blood, urine, and saliva samples were collected from the astronauts to monitor the time course of changes in body fluid volumes, kidney function, electrolytes, and hormones. Prior to the sample collections, crew members injected and ingested chemical tracers that would show up in body fluid samples; this enabled the monitoring of plasma volume and levels of extracellular fluid and total body water as well as renal (kidney) function (specifically, glomerular filtration rate and effective renal plasma flow).

Results indicated that the glomerular filtration rate, a key measure of kidney function, increased, with a corresponding decrease in total body water. Plasma volume, extracellular fluid volume, and total body water decreased within 21 hours of the onset of weightlessness. Decreased activity of plasma renin (a kidney enzyme) and decreased levels of the hormone aldosterone, which functions in the regulation of the body's balance of salt and water, were found to occur a few hours after the beginning of spaceflight; these findings are consistent with the operation of mechanisms for reducing plasma volume. Increased glomerular filtration rate is also consistent with the operation of these plasma-reducing mechanisms.

Clarence P. Alfrey, a hematologist at Baylor College of Medicine, Houston, designed an experiment that examined the regulation of total blood volume and red blood cell (RBC) mass. Plasma volume, RBCs, the hormone erythropoietin (which stimulates RBC production in the bone marrow), and iron levels were measured from the collected blood and urine samples to evaluate erythropoiesis (*i.e.,* RBC production). The results showed that in space bone marrow maintains the same rate of RBC production as on Earth; however, the release of new RBCs into the blood is decreased, as some of these blood cells are retained in the bone marrow. This adapted RBC level is an appropriate physiological response to decreased plasma volume.

Alfrey also designed and analyzed the results of an experiment investigating the physiology of RBCs and blood volume in rodents. This investigation used chemical tracers to study the rate of production and destruction of the RBCs and showed that RBC mass decreased. Decreases were also seen in the white blood cells and the peripheral blood lymphocytes. A decrease in white cells and lymphocytes could indicate a compromised immune system.

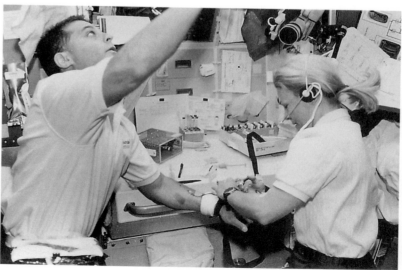

Seddon obtains a blood specimen from mission specialist David A. Wolf. At various points during the SLS-2 mission, blood, urine, and saliva were collected from crew members. The samples made it possible to assess regulatory physiology and monitor the time course of changes in body fluid volumes, kidney function, electrolytes, and hormones. One of the notable physiological responses to microgravity is a reduction in plasma blood volume, which in turn causes a gradual decrease in red blood cell mass and the condition known as "space anemia."

NASA

Hematologist Albert T. Ichiki of the University of Tennessee at Memphis investigated the physiology of the immature red blood cell precursors in rodents' bone marrow. By using a novel technique, that of stimulating precursor RBCs with the hormone erythropoietin prior to the bone marrow collection, Ichiki's experiments provided more comprehensive data in this area than had previously been collected in space. Postflight analysis showed that the number of precursor RBCs was decreased, which implies that microgravity depresses erythropoiesis by suppressing the response of the RBC precursor cells in the bone marrow to erythropoietin. The injection of erythropoietin, however, did not appear to stimulate an expected release of additional blood cells.

Cardiovascular/cardiopulmonary physiology. Cardiologists C. Gunnar Blomqvist of the University of Texas Southwestern Medical School and Leon E. Farhi of the State University of New York at Buffalo assessed the adaptation of the cardiovascular/cardiopulmonary system. Data on cardiac blood volume, the distribution of blood and blood gases in the lungs, and cardiac output were collected from the astronauts during resting periods and while they exercised at graded levels on a bicycle ergometer. The data indicated that resting cardiac output seemed to be elevated throughout the period of microgravity exposure, with blood pressure normal and heart rate low. Astronauts (who were all well-conditioned before the space mission) were able to maintain a maximal level of exercise in space. However, postflight there was a significant decrease in their exercise capacity, and immediately postflight there was a reduced ability to maintain a normal cardiovascular state while standing.

Blomqvist also investigated the central venous pressure (blood pressure near the heart) of two subjects—Fettman and Lucid—who each had a venous catheter inserted near the heart's right atrium prior to launch. The SLS-1 finding of a decrease in central venous pressure was confirmed during SLS-2, which has led scientists to reevaluate the previously held concept of early cardiovascular adaptation. Because central venous pressure is an indicator of the filling capacity of the heart, and early measurements of heart size and stroke volume in space suggested increased filling of the heart, it had been hypothesized that the central venous pressure would increase.

John B. West, an expert in pulmonary physiology at the University of California at San Diego, analyzed various gas mixtures that were inhaled by the crew members so as to determine how well the lungs function in weightlessness. West found that lung diffusing capacity and blood flow increased significantly in flight, and the normal inhomogeneity of ventilation and blood flow decreased; these preliminary results indicate that pulmonary function is not significantly altered by a two-week absence of gravity.

The cardiovascular/cardiopulmonary status of SLS-2 crew members was monitored at rest and during exercise at various levels of intensity. Here mission specialist Wolf prepares for an exam on the Spacelab's bicycle ergometer.

Musculoskeletal physiology. Physiologist T. Peter Stein of the University of Medicine and Dentistry of New Jersey in Camden designed tests to study protein metabolism in humans in order to identify the cause of in-flight decreased muscle mass. Blood, urine, and saliva samples were analyzed postflight for the presence of ingested tracers and certain metabolic byproducts. Results suggested that the body perceives spaceflight as a stress situation, with responses similar to those seen with infection or injury. In the first four to five days of spaceflight, the body loses protein in response to microgravity, but it achieves an adapted steady state after that. Stein's analyses also suggest that muscle damage occurs postflight, owing to the sudden imposition of gravity on muscles that had become weakened or atrophied in space in response to stress factors and disuse.

Muscle tissue was obtained in flight from six rodents and preserved for postflight analysis. The outstanding condition of the returned samples from these first-ever in-flight dissections demonstrated that tissue samples can be attained successfully in space. Danny A. Riley,

213

A pulmonary function test allows the analysis of gases that mission specialist Lieut. Col. William S. McArthur, Jr., inhaled moments earlier. Data obtained on the 14-day SLS-2 mission indicated that the astronauts' lungs were not significantly affected by a two-week absence of gravity.

an anatomist at the Medical College of Wisconsin in Milwaukee, performed the postflight analysis on muscle tissues and measured a significant decrease in size of the antigravity muscle fibers. On Earth muscles must counteract the forces of gravity; muscle tone is the constant state of readiness of muscles, which prevents the body from falling. In space muscles adapt to the state of weightlessness by losing tone. Also, the muscle fiber samples showed no evidence of tearing, a phenomenon previously observed in tissue samples collected postflight rather than in flight. It is now believed that tearing may be a consequence of damage caused when atrophied muscle fibers bear weight upon landing. These findings are important because they can be applied to the development of countermeasures that will enable astronauts to readapt to gravitational forces without experiencing muscle injury following long-term spaceflight.

Kenneth M. Baldwin, a physiologist at the University of California at Irvine, compared the structural, chemical, and metabolic properties of rodent muscle fibers exposed to microgravity with muscle fibers from control rodents that remained earthbound. It was noted that microgravity induced a change in the fiber type (from slow- to fast-twitch) in antigravity muscles. Slow-twitch fibers contract and fatigue slowly, whereas fast-twitch fibers contract and fatigue quickly. Thus, in space the skeletal muscle fibers contract faster, affecting the ability of the antigravity postural muscles to support weight-bearing activity upon return to Earth. It was also found in postflight analyses that the ability of skeletal muscle to use fatty acids as an energy source was reduced, which implies that microgravity impairs the capacity of muscles to sustain prolonged exercise.

Claude D. Arnaud, professor of medicine at the University of California at San Francisco, studied the mechanisms causing the changes in the human body's calcium balance. Analysis of the collected blood and urine samples from astronauts showed increased urinary calcium excretion, elevated plasma calcium, and bone mineral loss. In addition to confirming SLS-1 findings of hormonal studies, the SLS-2 experiment measured biochemical markers of bone resorption and formation and intestinal dietary calcium absorption. Data analysis suggested that abnormal losses of calcium from bone in microgravity are caused by increased bone resorption that is not compensated for by an equivalent increase in bone formation. Arnaud is in the process of developing a working conceptual model of bone and calcium regulation in space, which, importantly, may lead to methods for treating osteoporosis on Earth.

Physiologist Emily M. Holton from NASA Ames Research Center, Moffett Field, California, studied the effects of weightlessness on bone growth and changes in calcium metabolism in rodents. Postflight analysis of bone structure labeled by ingested calcium markers confirmed that the rate of bone development in rodents is slower in space than on Earth, which is analogous to the findings in humans.

Neurophysiology. Lawrence R. Young, a human factors engineer at the Massachusetts Institute of Technology, tested the sensitivity of the otolith organs in the inner ear to see how these organs interpret sensory signals that contribute to posture, equilibrium, and perception. SLS-2 results confirmed the previous finding that gravity plays an important role in maintaining positional sense (*i.e.,* an individual's mental awareness of his or her bodily position).

Neurophysiologist Muriel D. Ross of the NASA Ames Research Center investigated spaceflight's effects on the vestibular maculae (sensory cells in the inner ear that contribute to the sense of equilibrium) of rodents. These cells were removed and preserved late in the shuttle's flight. Postflight analysis showed that the neural synapses of gravity sensors changed in microgravity. These in-flight synaptic changes are an example of the process known as neural plasticity, by which the nervous system adapts to, remembers, and learns from a new sensory condition.

Continuation of life sciences research

Together, the SLS-1 and SLS-2 missions laid the groundwork for life sciences research of physiological adaptation to microgravity during short-term missions. The next SLS mission will focus on in-depth investigations of the neurophysiological responses to spaceflight. This "Neurolab" mission is being planned as a cooperative effort between NASA, the National Institutes of Health, and other U.S. and international agencies. Cellular, molecular, and developmental neurobiology as well as sensory-motor and nervous system adaptation to microgravity are likely to be studied.

Biomedical and fundamental biological research is also conducted to a lesser extent on other shuttle and Spacelab missions. The shuttle/Spacelab mission launched on July 8, 1994, included studies on human and aquatic animal adaptation—the results of which will be published in 1995.

The Russian Space Agency and NASA have planned to fly a series of missions utilizing the Russian space station *Mir* and the U.S. space shuttle, which will conduct ongoing biomedical research and research on long-duration human adaptation in space (*i.e.*, on missions exceeding 90 days). Russian cosmonauts have already spent one year aboard *Mir*. The first joint mission is scheduled for 1995. Subsequent *Mir*/shuttle missions will test various means of counteracting adverse physiological changes that otherwise might interfere with long-duration stays in space.

Earthbound health: space science pays off

NASA's study of the adaptation of living systems to space began with the early Mercury missions, where the primary concern was astronaut survival, and consisted of preflight and postflight measurements of basic physiological parameters. During the Gemini and Apollo missions, the emphasis shifted to the routine but limited in-flight monitoring of health parameters (heart rate, body temperature, and respiration). During Skylab a broad range of life science studies were performed, mainly to study in a general way how different body systems responded to exposure to microgravity. With the advent of the Spacelab missions, detailed investigations began to be conducted to discern the underlying causes of these changes and, where appropriate, how to counteract them.

As the number of flights, the length of stays, and the size of the population exposed to spaceflight increase, so will the list of life sciences issues that will need to be addressed. The results from the SLS-1

and SLS-2 missions and future Neurolab findings will provide a knowledge base from which definitive and unique solutions to space-induced changes in the human organism can be developed.

Importantly, these results may also be used to address life sciences concerns on Earth. This occurs either through technology transfer (some examples being biotelemetry systems and "telemedicine," sophisticated diagnostic imaging machines, and innovative tissue-regeneration devices) or by a knowledge transfer—*i.e.*, using what spaceflight reveals about physiological adaptation to better appreciate the fundamental functioning of the human body.

—*Arnauld E. Nicogossian, M.D.,
and Howard J. Schneider, Ph.D.*

AIDS

Despite the fact that scientists have made enormous strides in unraveling the molecular secrets of the human immunodeficiency virus (HIV), the benefits of current therapies are limited, and a vaccine to prevent infection is not yet on the horizon. The AIDS epidemic therefore continues to have a devastating impact.

In 1994 a reevaluation of the research effort resulted in an increased emphasis on the complex interactions between HIV and the immune system that eventually lead to the development of AIDS. Many authorities now believe that more imaginative approaches to treatment and prevention will come only through a better understanding of the pathogenesis of AIDS—the process by which the virus actually causes disease.

Patterns in populations

The World Health Organization estimated in 1994 that nearly 14 million people worldwide were infected with HIV: 9 million in sub-Saharan Africa, 2 million in Southeast Asia and the Indian subcontinent, 1.5 million in South America, and 1 million in North America. During the past couple of years, the growth of the epidemic has been particularly explosive in India and Thailand. A study conducted in northern Thailand estimated that about 12% of military recruits were HIV-infected. Of that group, 96.5% had a history of sexual contact with female prostitutes. A combination of poverty, trade in illicit drugs, and commercial sex fuels the spread of the virus in Asia; if unchecked, the Asian toll from HIV infection is expected to exceed that in sub-Saharan Africa by the year 2000.

Whereas about 47,000 new cases of AIDS were reported to the U.S. Centers for Disease Control and Prevention (CDC) during 1992, the total for 1993 was over 100,000. This dramatic increase did not represent an actual doubling of new infections but rather resulted from the expanded case definition adopted by the CDC in January 1993. The new definition includes as a criterion for AIDS severe depletion of T helper

215

lymphocytes (also known as CD4+ T lymphocytes, or simply CD4+ cells), even in the absence of so-called AIDS-defining illnesses, those opportunistic infections considered characteristic of the disease. One consequence of the new case definition was a significant increase in the number of infected persons eligible for AIDS-related benefits and services. Some argued that adoption of the new definition was driven by political and social pressures. However, CD4+ cells are the principal target of HIV in the body, and progressive depletion of these cells is the primary consequence of HIV infection. Opportunistic infections, by contrast, are secondary events that occur as a result of impaired CD4+ cell function. The new case definition, therefore, reflects more accurately than the old one the current understanding of AIDS pathogenesis.

Although the number of new cases of AIDS in the U.S. is no longer increasing as rapidly as it was a decade ago, public health officials estimate that approximately 50,000 new HIV infections occur in that country each year. One-quarter of these involve people younger than 22 years of age. The growing proportion of infected individuals who acquire HIV as adolescents or young adults suggests that AIDS-prevention programs have had only limited success in modifying risk behaviors, such as unprotected intercourse or needle sharing, in this group.

As of 1992, AIDS had become the leading cause of death for U.S. men aged 25–44 years and the fourth leading cause of death among women in this age group. The impact of HIV infection continues to be disproportionately large among African Americans; the death rate from AIDS for black men was three times as high as for white men, and for black women 12 times as high as for white women. As the HIV epidemic matures, patterns of transmission in the U.S. have come to resemble more closely those observed in the less developed world, where heterosexual transmission is the predominant way the virus is spread. Although the largest proportions of U.S. AIDS cases in 1993 consisted of men who have sex with men (47%) and individuals who use intravenous drugs (28%), heterosexual transmission of HIV continued to account for an increasing share of cases (9% in 1993, compared with 8.5% in 1992). Moreover, in 1993 for the first time, homosexual males accounted for fewer than half of the new U.S. cases. One consequence of the growing incidence of heterosexual HIV transmission is the rise of AIDS among women, who now constitute 16% of cases.

The incidence of AIDS in children younger than 13 years of age has risen in parallel with the increase in HIV infection among women of reproductive age. Although estimates vary, it is generally accepted that the risk of HIV transmission during pregnancy from an infected woman to her child is 15–25%. Three mechanisms are responsible for mother–infant transmission of HIV: infection of the fetus as a result of virus crossing the placenta, transmission to the newborn at the time of birth, and transmission to nursing infants through breast milk. Specific interventions aimed at interrupting maternal transmission of HIV by each of these mechanisms are the subject of intensive study, and one strategy appears extremely promising (see below).

While epidemiologists were continuing to investigate the means by which a Florida dentist could have transmitted HIV to several patients—even considering the possibility that he may have infected them on purpose—another instance of transmission of the virus in a health care setting was reported. Australian health officials announced in December 1993 that four people who had undergone minor operations in a surgeon's office on the same day in 1989 became infected with HIV, presumably as a result of inadequate infection-control measures. The source of the infection was not the physician but another patient (since deceased), who also underwent a surgical procedure that day. A CDC official commented that this was the first known case in which HIV was transmitted from patient to patient in a health care setting. Moreover, no additional cases of HIV transmission from health professionals to patients in the U.S. had been discovered by the CDC after investigation of nearly 16,000 individuals cared for by HIV-infected health care workers.

Several other reports of unusual transmission concerned the spread of the virus between household members. In two instances uninfected boys living in the same house with youngsters with HIV apparently acquired the virus via contact of open skin lesions with infected blood. A shared razor was presumed to be the instrument of viral spread in one of these cases. Another case involved an elderly woman who had cared for her adult son while he was dying of AIDS. While noting the rarity of such occurrences, public health officials also emphasized the importance of infection-control precautions in the home setting.

Clues to the disease process

The factors that determine the progression of HIV disease in an individual are complex and remain poorly understood. Although the median time between HIV infection and development of full-blown AIDS in adults is about a decade, the disease progresses more slowly in some and more precipitously in others. Many theories have been put forward to account for this difference. The results of recent studies strongly suggest that the principal factor in determining disease progression is the virus itself.

HIV is a member of the lentivirus (slow virus) family of retroviruses. Retroviruses are viruses whose genetic material is composed of RNA, which must be converted into DNA during infection of a host cell. Each virus particle, or virion, contains two copies of the viral genetic material, single strands of RNA, packaged inside a protein core. The core is surrounded by a lipid membrane in which are embedded two so-called envelope proteins. HIV binds to lymphocytes and monocytes, types of white blood cells, through specific interactions with the CD4 receptor molecule on the surface of these cells. Following this initial step, called adsorption, the virus envelope fuses with the cell membrane, allowing the virus core to enter the cell. Once inside, single-stranded viral RNA is converted into double-stranded DNA, the same substance that makes up the host cell's genetic material, through a process known as reverse transcription. This process is mediated by a special enzyme, reverse transcriptase, which is packaged with viral RNA in the core particle. The completed DNA copy of HIV RNA then integrates itself into the host cell's chromosome, where it remains for the life of the cell.

Primary infection. During initial, or primary, HIV infection, large numbers of infected cells can be found in the individual's peripheral blood circulation, and high concentrations of infectious virus are present in the plasma. These concentrations fall dramatically as the individual's immune system responds and produces effective virus-specific immunity. At this stage infectious virus often becomes undetectable in the plasma, and the number of infected cells in the circulation may drop to fewer than one in a million peripheral blood mononuclear cells. Despite the apparent disappearance of infectious virus from the infected person's blood circulation, the virus continues to replicate unabated in lymphoid tissues. Studies by investigators at the National Institutes of Health (NIH), Bethesda, Md., and the University of Minnesota provide evidence of active virus replication in the lymph nodes even during the clinically "latent" stage of infection—*i.e.,* the asymptomatic phase of the disease. These re-

sults indicate that HIV is never truly latent but instead causes a chronic active infection with continuous virus production at all stages of disease. With advancing disease, HIV-specific immunity declines, and infectious virus is once again detectable in the plasma. The concentration of virus generally correlates with the disease stage; thus, patients with AIDS have 100 to 1,000 times more infectious virus detectable in their blood than asymptomatic individuals.

Rapid viral mutation. One of the many remarkable features of HIV is its high mutation rate. As a consequence, no two virus particles are exactly alike. Related strains that share genetic similarities can be grouped into clades (lineages descended from a common ancestor). At the 1994 Keystone AIDS Symposium, held at Hilton Head, S.C., scientists from the Los Alamos (N.M.) National Laboratory and the Henry M. Jackson Research Laboratory, Rockville, Md., presented data that provide evidence for the existence of at least eight distinct clades of HIV. The genetic diversity of HIV in a particular human population reflects the length of time the virus has been present in that population. It is likely, therefore, that new clades will emerge over time in populations in which only one or two clades currently are found.

A similar sequence of events is recapitulated in microcosm in infected individuals. During primary infection there is relatively little genetic heterogeneity among viral DNA sequences cloned from an individual patient. With time, however, the genetic diversity of the HIV population that can be recovered from the patient increases. This increasing heterogeneity may be responsible for the emergence of mutants that "escape" the control of the patient's immune system and may lead to the emergence of more virulent isolates.

Virulence. Recent reports from several research groups suggest that the growth properties of HIV may

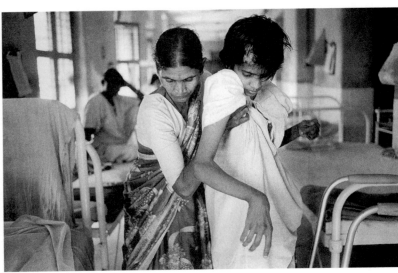

Forced into prostitution at age 12, a 15-year-old Indian girl, terminally ill with AIDS, is cared for in a hospital in Bombay. The explosion of the AIDS epidemic in Asia is attributed in large measure to a thriving commercial sex industry.

Dayanita Singh—JB Pictures

also play a role in disease progression. In most patients early after infection the virus grows relatively slowly and grows equally well in monocytes and in T lymphocytes. Virus isolated at this time usually does not induce cell fusion, a property correlated with the ability of HIV to kill infected cells. Later a more virulent, or cytopathic, variant capable of inducing cell fusion can be isolated from many patients. These cytopathic viruses differ from their predecessors in that they grow more rapidly in the laboratory and are characterized by their preference for growth in T cells (T-cell tropism). Specific molecular changes in the virus envelope protein are responsible for this transformation. A number of recent studies suggest that the emergence of T-cell tropic HIV variants correlates with an accelerated decline in the number of CD4+ cells and more rapid progression to AIDS. However, AIDS also develops among individuals with less cytopathic forms of the virus. Although the switch to T-cell tropism appears to be a predictor of disease progression, it apparently is not a necessary step in the complex process of AIDS pathogenesis.

Treatment: no real breakthroughs

The past year was marked by continued controversy over results of the Concorde study, a collaborative effort by British and French investigators that examined the benefits of initiating treatment with zidovudine (AZT; Retrovir) in HIV-infected persons while they were still asymptomatic as compared with deferring therapy until symptoms appeared. At the end of three years, the Concorde researchers concluded that no differences in disease progression or survival could be found between the two groups. These results were at odds with the findings of several earlier studies conducted at 32 collaborating centers of the AIDS

Clinical Trials Group (ACTG; an NIH-sponsored multicenter research group), which observed a significant reduction in disease progression among patients receiving zidovudine. Moreover, a study by European and Australian investigators concluded that early initiation of zidovudine therapy reduced by nearly one-half the risk of disease progression over a three-year period, reinforcing the results of the ACTG studies.

A closer look at Concorde results. A number of important distinctions have been lost in the debate over these seemingly conflicting reports. First, all of the patients in the Concorde study who showed evidence of disease progression subsequently were treated with zidovudine. Therefore, this study did not challenge the benefits of zidovudine in those with more advanced, symptomatic HIV infection. Second, once results of the U.S. studies became known, Concorde participants were given an opportunity to receive zidovudine regardless of whether they had been assigned to the immediate or deferred therapy group. These mid-trial changes in protocol design may have limited the ability of the study to discern differences between the two treatment groups.

Concorde also highlights the difficulties of translating into medical practice the results of large-scale clinical trials conducted over many years in a field of research that is rapidly evolving. During the course of the study, two additional anti-HIV drugs, didanosine (Videx; formerly called dideoxyinosine, or ddI) and zalcitabine (Hivid; formerly called dideoxycytidine, or ddC), were licensed for use in the U.S., and several other investigational agents became available. Introduction of these drugs shifted the debate away from questions of when antiretroviral therapy should be initiated to the question of how combinations of anti-HIV drugs could be used to greatest effect.

A physician discusses the option of taking the drug zidovudine (AZT; Retrovir) with an HIV-positive patient. Questions about the drug's benefits were raised by the Concorde study, conducted in England, France, and Ireland, which found that zidovudine therapy begun early in the course of HIV infection did not prolong survival. In the meantime, more anti-HIV drugs are being approved, and many doctors now consider regimens combining several drugs to hold the greatest promise.

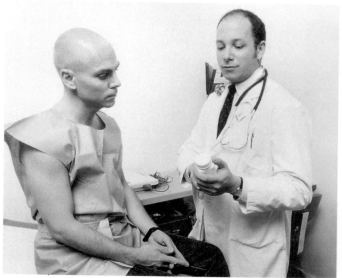

Hank Morgan—Science Source/Photo Researchers

The Concorde study nevertheless had a profound impact on AIDS therapy in the U.S., where zidovudine use fell sharply after results of the trial were made public. Since many U.S. AIDS experts still recommend early initiation of anti-HIV therapy, it is uncertain to what extent this drop in zidovudine use reflects growing disenchantment among HIV-infected individuals who have elected not to undergo therapy, as opposed to changing medical practice.

Combination therapy: two drugs better than one? The results of the first large-scale clinical trial of combination anti-HIV therapy were presented at the Ninth International Conference on AIDS in Berlin in the summer of 1993. That study, conducted by the ACTG, evaluated the effectiveness of zidovudine plus zalcitabine as compared with either drug alone in patients who had received at least six months of prior therapy with zidovudine only. No additional benefit of the combination was found in the study group as a whole, but there was a clear trend toward greater efficacy of the combination in patients with higher CD4+ cell counts (*i.e.,* those in earlier stages of disease progression). Although there are differences of opinion among AIDS investigators about how to interpret those results, the ACTG study lends further weight to the argument that more thorough virus suppression earlier in the disease may produce greater clinical benefit than has been observed with zidovudine alone.

"Convergent chemotherapy": research flaws revealed. The growth of HIV in the presence of a variety of anti-HIV drugs leads to the emergence of drug-resistant mutants. Investigators at Harvard Medical School reasoned that simultaneous treatment with several drugs in combination—so-called convergent chemotherapy—might lead to HIV mutants that would have an impaired ability to replicate. Laboratory experiments appeared to support this hypothesis.

Unfortunately, media accounts of these findings inflated their significance and unreasonably raised the hopes of thousands of patients. In response to public pressure for access to an experimental multidrug treatment regimen based on the Harvard data, the NIH doubled the size of a clinical trial of the regimen being conducted by the ACTG. Four hundred patients rushed to enroll in this study over an eight-week period. When other research groups were unable to repeat results of the original experiments, the Harvard team reviewed their data and found a previously overlooked error that negated their hypothesis. An important lesson from this experience is that preliminary results based on laboratory models should be evaluated critically before being accepted at face value. In the emotionally charged arena of AIDS research, the adage from the Reagan-Gorbachev era, "Trust, but verify," is particularly apt.

Even though the concept of convergent chemotherapy was disproved, it remains possible that three-drug combinations might inhibit HIV more effectively than one- or two-drug regimens. Pilot studies in patients at the University of Alabama at Birmingham have shown that a combination of zidovudine, didanosine, and the experimental drug nevirapine does in fact substantially decrease the amount of HIV circulating in the bloodstream.

New anti-HIV drugs. In June 1994, in keeping with its practice of accelerated approval of promising drugs for AIDS, the U.S. Food and Drug Administration (FDA) approved stavudine (Zerit; formerly known as d4T) for individuals in whom zidovudine fails or cannot be tolerated. The preliminary results of a clinical trial indicated that patients who switched to stavudine after more than six months of zidovudine treatment had significant increases in CD4+ cell counts and significant decreases in the amount of circulating HIV as compared with those who continued on zidovudine. The final results of the trial, which should be available by the end of 1994, were expected to provide additional information on the clinical outcomes of patients treated with these two drugs.

Among the clinical trials that got under way during the past year were those of lamivudine (3TC), a new nucleoside analog (the category that also includes zidovudine, didanosine, and zalcitabine), and delavirdine (like nevirapine, a nonnucleoside analog). Expanded studies of the proteinase inhibitor saquinavir (formerly known as Ro 31–8959) were also initiated. A great deal of attention has been focused on the proteinase inhibitors, a class of drugs that act at a completely different stage in the viral life cycle than other currently available antiretroviral agents. Although chemically dissimilar to each other, both the nucleoside analogs and the nonnucleoside analogs act by inhibiting the activity of reverse transcriptase, the enzyme required for transformation of viral RNA into DNA. The proteinase inhibitors, on the other hand, block the action of another enzyme, HIV proteinase, which is required for viral particle maturation. When HIV proteinase is blocked, the resulting virus lacks the capacity to cause infection. Preliminary studies indicated that Ro 31–8959 has antiviral activity in patients but is poorly absorbed; the results of larger trials using the drug in combination with zidovudine or zalcitabine were expected by the end of 1994. Several other proteinase inhibitors are in earlier stages of development and should enter clinical trials soon.

Prevention of maternal–fetal transmission

Perhaps the most significant advance of the past year was the finding that zidovudine reduces the risk of HIV transmission from pregnant women to their babies. In a study conducted by the ACTG, 477 HIV-infected women in their 14th to 34th week of pregnancy were randomly assigned to receive zidovudine or a placebo during pregnancy and labor. For the first six weeks

In a year not otherwise distinguished by optimistic AIDS news, one hopeful note in 1994 was the finding that zidovudine therapy during pregnancy can significantly reduce an infant's risk of acquiring HIV from an infected mother. With the increasing incidence of HIV infection among U.S. women of childbearing age, strategies to prevent mother-to-infant transmission of the virus are likely to assume growing importance.

of life, the infants received the same treatment as their mothers, either the drug or a placebo. Therapy with zidovudine reduced the rate of HIV transmission by two-thirds, from 25% to 8%. Zidovudine treatment was not associated with any serious side effects in either the women or their infants. This finding could have a dramatic effect on the rate of HIV infection in U.S. children since nearly all cases—an estimated 1,800 per year, according to the CDC—are the result of maternal transmission. At the same time, the study raises troubling questions about access to drugs in the Third World, where maternal transmission accounts for a significant proportion of total AIDS cases. In parts of central Africa, for example, more than 20% of pregnant women are HIV-positive. Zidovudine use has been limited in this region owing to the high cost of the drug and the meager health care budgets of less developed countries.

A clinical trial of another potential strategy for preventing maternal HIV transmission began in late 1993. The substance being tested is HIV immune globulin (HIVIG), a blood product that contains antibodies to HIV. Originally, trials of HIVIG in pregnant women had been scheduled to begin in 1992, but they were delayed when the company that was to manufacture the product withdrew because of liability concerns. After a new manufacturer was found, recruiting of subjects had to begin again because the women enrolled in the 1992 trial had already given birth. Still another approach to preventing the passage of HIV from infected women to their babies involves the use of vaccines to stimulate maternal immune responses. Several such vaccines are also being tested in clinical trials.

Project Immune Restoration

Even if an antiretroviral drug were available that completely arrested HIV infection, patients in advanced stages of the disease would still be at risk of developing opportunistic infections because of their compromised immune status. In the United States a coalition of leading AIDS researchers and activists, known as Project Immune Restoration, has been assembled to develop innovative strategies for AIDS treatment that would combine anti-HIV drugs with immune-based therapies. The goal of such an approach is to reconstitute the immune function of those who are infected with HIV.

Much of this work has focused on the use of cytokines to stimulate the failing immune systems of infected individuals. Cytokines are proteins that are released by cells of the immune system to regulate, or modulate, immune responses. Individual cytokines may have positive or negative effects on cell proliferation and on immune function. Unlike hormones, which are secreted in relatively large amounts into the blood and act on cells throughout the body, cytokines are released in minute quantities and act locally, usually on neighboring cells in the lymphoid tissues. Systemic administration of cytokines may therefore have unwanted side effects. For example, a report presented by investigators from the NIH at the First National Conference on Human Retroviruses, held in Washington, D.C., in December 1993, described a study in which intermittent high-dose interleukin-2 (IL-2) was used to stimulate T helper cells in patients at different stages of HIV infection. Although this treatment resulted in dramatic increases in the number of CD4+ cells in patients with less advanced disease, significant toxicity occurred in a large number of patients. In addition, IL-2 administration was associated with an increase in the concentration of HIV in the blood, perhaps as a result of direct stimulation of virus production by IL-2. Clinical trials of other cytokines are therefore proceeding cautiously.

Vaccine research

Little progress toward the development of an effective AIDS vaccine was reported at the sixth annual meeting of the National Cooperative Vaccine Development Groups for AIDS, held in Alexandria, Va., in November 1993. Although infected individuals' immune responses to HIV have been characterized in detail, scientists have been unable to determine whether any of these responses have the potential to protect against infection. Particularly discouraging was a December 1993 report by several groups of researchers who had been testing potential HIV vaccines. The experimental vaccines had been shown to induce antibody production in human volunteers. Even more promising, in the laboratory, antibodies recovered from the volunteers had effectively blocked white blood cells from becoming infected with laboratory-grown strains of HIV. Much to the surprise of the investigators, however, the same antibodies failed to prevent infection of white blood cells by samples of virus that were isolated from human patients. The reason for the difference between laboratory-grown HIV and so-called field isolates was unclear, and a debate ensued over whether field trials of the vaccines should proceed as scheduled.

Another setback to the vaccine effort came in May 1994 when NIH officials announced that five subjects participating in preliminary studies of two different AIDS vaccines had become infected with HIV. The vaccines in question, which were produced by recombinant DNA technology, consisted only of the virus envelope protein and did not contain any infectious HIV particles. In each case the volunteers who became infected acquired HIV through sexual contact with an infected partner, not from the vaccine. These particular studies were being conducted to test the safety of the vaccines and to determine their ability to produce an immune response against HIV. Because the studies were not designed to test the effectiveness of the vaccines in preventing HIV infection, no conclusion can be drawn from the fact that five volunteers became infected.

Advocates of a preventive vaccine continue to argue that even a partially effective vaccine might lead to a substantial reduction in the numbers of AIDS cases in parts of the world where HIV transmission is rampant. Skeptics insist that field trials are premature and that the enormous costs of such trials would divert resources from basic research that might lead ultimately to a clearly effective vaccine.

No less controversial was the special appropriation by Congress of $20 million for the Department of Defense (DOD) to study an HIV envelope protein-based vaccine produced by the Connecticut biotechnology firm MicroGeneSys as a potential therapeutic—rather than a preventive—agent. The goal of therapeutic vaccination is to boost virus-specific immune responses in infected individuals in the hopes of maintaining immune-mediated virus suppression. Lobbying efforts on behalf of MicroGeneSys had secured the appropriation over the objections of experts who felt that the available data did not justify proceeding with a large-scale trial of the MicroGeneSys product. Particularly irksome to many AIDS researchers was the provision that MicroGeneSys would be paid for providing the vaccine to the DOD. In other AIDS trials sponsored by the NIH, pharmaceutical companies have provided their products at no cost to the government. After a year of delays, the project was finally shelved when the secretary of defense, along with the director of the NIH and the head of the FDA, signed a memorandum in which they stipulated that the study should not be performed. It is unclear how the $20 million will now be spent.

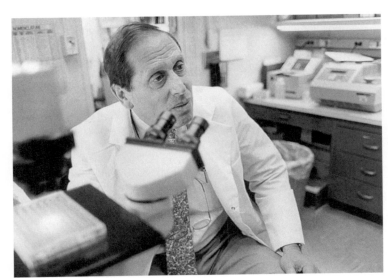

David Scull—The New York Times

Named in February 1994 to head the Office of AIDS Research of the National Institutes of Health, William E. Paul, a highly respected immunologist, assumed his new post at a critical juncture in the AIDS research effort. In August, at the Tenth International Conference on AIDS in Yokohama, Japan, Paul announced that the U.S. would cut spending on clinical trials of new therapies and increase funding for much-needed basic research.

Toward a new U.S. research agenda

In February 1994 William E. Paul was named director of the Office of AIDS Research (OAR) at the NIH. Although new to AIDS research, Paul is a widely respected immunologist who served as chief of the laboratory of immunology at the NIH before taking the OAR post. The NIH Revitalization Act of 1993 provided expanded authority to the OAR in response to pressures from community activist groups for better coordination of NIH-sponsored AIDS research.

A key element in crafting an AIDS research agenda is control of the NIH's $1.3 billion AIDS research budget, which funds the majority of basic and clinical AIDS research in the U.S. The OAR director has been granted unprecedented control over this budget, including a $10 million discretionary fund that can be allocated to speed progress in promising new areas of research. In addition, the OAR will henceforth submit its annual budget requests directly to the U.S. president, bypassing the usual NIH channels.

Paul moved quickly to assemble a group of outside experts to reevaluate NIH programs in HIV pathogenesis, epidemiology, drug and vaccine development, and behavioral research. He will also need to examine how research dollars are distributed between intramural research programs (conducted by scientists at the NIH) and extramural programs (conducted by university-based investigators through NIH grants and contracts). If successful, this process should lead to a clearer set of goals and priorities for U.S. AIDS research in the coming years.

—*Daniel R. Kuritzkes, M.D.*

Alzheimer's Disease

Alzheimer's disease (AD), a degenerative disorder that attacks the brain and leads to dementia, is one of the most common dementing disorders of old age, affecting nearly four million individuals in the U.S. alone. If a cure is not found and current demographic trends continue, it is estimated that the number of persons affected by AD will double every 20 years.

Dementia is a group of symptoms characterized by an insidious decline in intellectual functioning of sufficient severity to interfere with a person's normal daily activities and social relationships. The most serious aspect of the loss in intellectual functioning is in the domain of cognitive ability. The dementia of Alzheimer's disease is distinguished from that seen in such conditions as age-associated memory impairment and benign senescent forgetfulness in that it is inevitably marked by progressive, irreversible declines in memory, performance of routine tasks, time and space orientation, language and communication skills, abstract thinking, and the abilities to learn, carry out mathematical calculations, and construct an object with blocks. In addition, AD is distinguished by

personality changes and impairment of judgment. The rate of deterioration varies, but invariably the disease eventually renders patients unable to care for themselves. The time from the onset of symptoms to the end of life can vary from 2 to 20 years.

The increasing visibility of Alzheimer's disease, evidenced by the amount of attention it receives in both the scientific community and the lay community, may create the impression that AD is a newly discovered illness or that it is now being more widely or perhaps inappropriately diagnosed. There is, however, no evidence to indicate that the incidence of the disease—that is, the rate of occurrence of new cases—has increased over the years. (Incidence is distinguished from prevalence—the percentage of a population that is affected with a particular disease at a given time.) In fact, ancient Greek and Roman writers as well as Elizabethan chroniclers accurately described the symptoms of AD, thus suggesting that it or very similar dementing disorders have long been part of the human condition.

Because dementia typically makes its appearance in the later years of life, the signs and symptoms of dementia have been mistakenly assumed to be indicators of old age. In fact, the term *senile* was once used almost interchangeably to describe the conditions of being demented or being aged. In recent years, however, as scientists have learned more about the processes of aging and the neurobiology and diseases of the aging brain, it has become apparent that the aging process does not, by itself, lead to dementia or neurodegenerative disease. AD and other dementing disorders of old age are caused by specific pathological conditions. In the absence of disease, the human brain can and does continue to function unimpaired—often well into the 10th decade of life.

Who is at risk?

Although aging per se causes neither dementia nor Alzheimer's disease, it is the most strongly associated risk factor for AD. Family history, or genetic predisposition, is another important risk factor; a history of AD in a first-degree relative (parent or sibling) increases the odds of developing AD threefold to fourfold. A history of severe head injury that leads to brief loss of consciousness doubles the risk of developing AD. These three risk factors—age, genetic predisposition, and head trauma—meet the accepted epidemiological criteria for causal factors: (1) they provide a plausible biological explanation, and (2) their effects are strong and consistent. Other risk factors that have been investigated—such as maternal age, hypothyroidism, and exposure to environmental toxins such as aluminum or to chemicals such as benzene and toluene—have not been shown to meet the above criteria.

Factors that apparently *decrease* a person's risk for AD have also been identified. Among these, the

Studies in several different countries have shown that people who have high levels of educational attainment are less likely than their less well-educated peers to develop Alzheimer's disease later in life.

most important appears to be educational and occupational attainment. People who achieve only a low level of education have double the risk of developing AD compared with those who have had six to eight or more years of schooling. Education presumably increases the brain's reserve capacity such that the clinical manifestations of AD are delayed or become more difficult to detect. Other factors that have been implicated as having a protective effect—but need to be confirmed by further and more careful studies—include postmenopausal estrogen replacement therapy, long-term use of anti-inflammatory drugs, and cigarette smoking.

As an increasing proportion of the population survives beyond the age of 85 years, increasing numbers of individuals will be at risk for developing a dementing disorder. Recent well-designed epidemiological studies have assessed the prevalence of all dementias (including Alzheimer's disease) in diverse communities around the world. These surveys indicate that 25–35% of those 85 and over are affected by some form of dementia. In one such study, conducted in East Boston, the prevalence of AD alone in the 85-and-over age group was found to be 47%. The variations in prevalence rates are due primarily to differences in the criteria used by investigators to identify individuals with dementia and, more specifically, with AD. One of the major problems in all such community surveys of dementia is that 15–30% of the sample population may be unwilling, unable, or unavailable to participate. Because it is possible that dementia might be more frequent among those who do not participate, the reported prevalence rates may actually underestimate the true prevalence.

Regardless of these problems in methodology and the differences in the estimates, two important facts have emerged from the epidemiological studies conducted during the past several decades:

• The prevalence of dementia increases in an exponential fashion with increasing old age; that is, the percentage of the population affected doubles for every decade people live beyond the age of 65. Thus, if 10% of all people 65 and older have AD, 20% of the over-75 population will be affected and 40% of all those over age 85.

• Since the Industrial Revolution, but particularly starting at the turn of the last century, life expectancy has been increasing. And during the past three decades, improvements in public health measures, diet, and health behavior have brought about dramatic demographic changes, including a lower birthrate. Thus, today in most industrialized countries, the 85-and-older age group is the fastest-growing segment of population.

These two facts, the increasing number of older people and the increasing incidence of dementia with age, point to an ever larger group of those at risk for Alzheimer's disease.

Neurobiological basis of AD

Although AD is a distinct disease defined by its characteristic clinical course and pathology, it is a heterogeneous condition with varied manifestations. The rate of cognitive impairment, for example, differs markedly among individuals. The characteristic features of AD brain pathology also differ sharply among people. Though the onset, course, and sequence of events may vary widely, it seems likely nonetheless

223

that the destructive forces involved ultimately converge to cause nerve cell (neuron) dysfunction, loss of connections between nerve cells, and death of some nerve cells. The quest for the mechanisms by which neurons lose their ability to communicate with each other and the reasons for selective neuronal death are at the heart of the worldwide scientific effort to discover the cause—or causes—of AD.

It has been known for some time that the survival of nerve cells in the brain depends on the proper functioning of many interrelated systems. These systems can be characterized by the three aspects of neuronal activity they modulate: communication, metabolism, and repair.

The communication system used by most neurons relies on a vast array of chemicals to carry information between and within nerve cells, as well as to cells outside the nervous system. Through this complex chemical signal transduction system, the brain functions as a master control center for the whole body. Depletion or absence of any of these chemicals disrupts cell-to-cell communication and interferes with normal brain function.

The metabolic activity of neurons depends on the blood circulation provided by a complex system of both large and extremely small blood vessels in the brain. The supply of oxygen, glucose, and other nutrients to nerve cells is critical to the health, survival, and normal functioning of the brain. A sustained reduction in the supply of oxygen or glucose can lead to cell death.

The third system involves the repair and cleanup functions of the neuron. Unlike other types of cells in the body, nerve cells do not replicate after birth. Instead, they constantly degrade or digest old, worn-out parts of themselves and synthesize new proteins for replacement parts. This system of continuous protein synthesis and degradation is finely regulated, and any disruption could have disastrous consequences for nerve cell function.

These three interrelated systems normally work in synchrony. Sometimes, however, internal (endogenous) factors, such as changes in an individual's nutritional, immune, or neuroendocrine status, interfere with the normal functioning of one of these systems, thus disrupting the delicate balance. Alternatively, external (exogenous) factors such as toxins, trauma, or infectious agents might disrupt the equilibrium. There is evidence that the pathology seen in AD is associated with changes in all three systems. The following will examine what is known with respect to each of these systems in AD.

Cell-to-cell communication

Changes in the brain's communication systems ultimately affect the individual's behavior. The behavioral effects of alcohol consumption, for example, are me-

diated through changes in the signal transduction pathways of large numbers of nerve cells. In the case of the specific behaviors seen in AD patients—namely, cognitive impairment and performance decline—the most immediate precipitating events in the brain are alterations in the chemical communication pathways within and among neurons.

A vast repertoire of chemicals—including neurotransmitters, neuroendocrine peptides, growth-promoting factors, metal ions, and many others—is used by each neuron for different kinds of communication, much as multilingual individuals in a cosmopolitan community may use different languages for different conversations. In the mid-1970s, AD researchers found that an enzyme necessary for the synthesis of one such chemical, the neurotransmitter acetylcholine, was deficient in the brains of AD patients. This was an important discovery in that it provided the first link between AD and a specific biochemical defect in the brain.

The scientific community was particularly ready to accept the challenge of AD at this time because, in the preceding few years, research in neurotransmitter chemistry had revealed that acetylcholine-containing neurons (i.e., cholinergic neurons) play an important role in memory. Since the initial discovery of a cholinergic deficit in AD, it has been shown that the disease also involves abnormalities in other neurotransmitters, as well as in other chemical signals that modulate neuronal activity. However, over the years animal studies and analysis of human brain tissue obtained at autopsy have consistently confirmed the relationship between cholinergic deficits and memory impairments.

In the early 1980s the "cholinergic hypothesis" of AD engendered great optimism that the cholinergic deficits could be corrected—and the disease cured—through pharmacological manipulations. The confidence that many scientists placed in this approach was based on the apparent similarity between AD and another neurodegenerative disorder, Parkinson's disease, in which neurotransmitter deficits can be ameliorated by an increase in the supply of the deficient chemical. In subsequent years a number of strategies were tried for correcting the cholinergic deficits in AD, all designed to maintain or improve the availability of acetylcholine by increasing its synthesis, facilitating its release at the synapse (the contact point between nerve cells), or slowing the rate of its breakdown. Generally, these approaches have not fulfilled their initial promise, in spite of modest successes in small groups of patients for short periods.

Promise and problems of tacrine. One of these experimental efforts involved a multicenter clinical trial of tetrahydroaminoacridine (THA). This substance was approved as a treatment for AD by the U.S. Food and Drug Administration in September 1993 under the name tacrine (Cognex), despite controversy about its effectiveness. Tacrine is a cholinesterase inhibitor, one of a class of compounds that slow the degradation, or breakdown, of acetylcholine, thus allowing the small amounts of neurotransmitter that are released to remain at the synapse a bit longer than usual. The rationale was that prolonging acetylcholine availability at the synapse would effectively facilitate the transmission of information from one cell to the other. A number of studies with various cholinesterase inhibitors have shown that in some AD patients these compounds do slightly slow the rate of decline in performance on some neuropsychological tests. Tacrine is not without drawbacks, however. It can cause liver toxicity, and it does not appear to help all patients. Therefore, studies are being conducted to find an optimal dosage of tacrine and to identify subgroups of patients who stand to benefit most from the drug. More important, however, the search continues for more effective treatments with fewer side effects that would help more AD patients for longer periods.

There are several possible reasons why treatment strategies directed at correcting cholinergic deficits have not been as successful as expected. One is that the most effective compound for correcting the chemical deficiency or the appropriate molecular target has not yet been found. Another potential reason is that the cholinergic neurons are selectively vulnerable in AD and are dying; therefore, therapy to increase available acetylcholine is too little and too late. Still another distinct possibility is that some other biochemical abnormalities may occur first, placing the cholinergic system at risk; this antecedent event, therefore, should be the target of treatment. Finally, it is highly likely that an effective treatment for AD would need to select multiple targets since it is known that the disease affects many biochemical systems, all of which influence the neuronal signal transduction pathway.

Multiple therapeutic targets. Many groups of researchers at major universities and at biotechnology and pharmaceutical companies around the world have become interested in the problems of AD and committed to developing active agents to intervene at various stages of the signal transduction process. Neuroscientists have made significant advances in discovering the details of molecular mechanisms in cell-to-cell communication and the intricate signal transduction pathways within a neuron. This knowledge now provides a vast array of molecular targets for intervention. To promote and facilitate drug-discovery efforts at academic institutions and to accelerate the testing of promising compounds, the Alzheimer's Disease Cooperative Study Unit (ADCSU), a 33-site U.S. consortium, has been established. It represents a major national resource for developing improved technologies for clinical trials, for conducting clinical trials, and for testing new diagnostic procedures.

At present, many potential treatments aimed at enhancing neuronal communications are in various stages of planning for testing. The following are representative:

● There is some evidence that nerve cell death in AD results from increased production of free radicals, unstable molecules that can wreak havoc in the body. An accumulation of oxygen free radicals, in particular, leading to breakdown of neuronal cell membranes, has been postulated as a mechanism of cell death in AD. The ADCSU has been assessing the efficacy of the Parkinson's disease drug deprenyl (selegiline; Eldepryl) and the antioxidant vitamin E, separately or in combination, in delaying the progression of AD.

● In some preliminary epidemiological studies, women on estrogen replacement therapy have been found to be at somewhat reduced risk of developing AD. A short-term pilot study is being planned to evaluate the efficacy of this treatment approach.

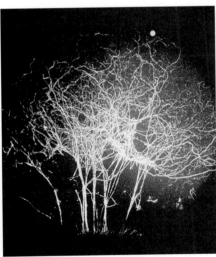 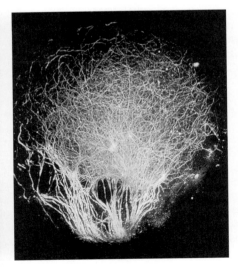

A comparison of normal rodent brain tissue (far left) and tissue that has been exposed to high levels of estrogen (left) shows a proliferation of neuronal connections in the estrogen-treated tissue. Epidemiological studies have found that postmenopausal estrogen replacement therapy reduces a woman's risk of developing Alzheimer's disease, adding to the evidence that the hormone could have a role in maintaining the critical connections between nerve cells.

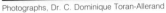
Photographs, Dr. C. Dominique Toran-Allerand

• Studies of arthritis patients who regularly used anti-inflammatory drugs such as indomethacin and naproxen showed them to be at reduced risk of developing AD. Anti-inflammatory compounds also have been reported to delay the progression of symptoms of AD. A pilot study testing the effects of the anti-inflammatory agent prednisone is scheduled to begin in 1994.

• Acetyl-L-carnitine, a naturally occurring substance, can act on the neuron by providing important constituents for the synthesis of acetylcholine and also can assist the cell in its metabolic activity by reducing the production of free radicals. A similar compound is being tested in a large clinical trial.

• In a normal healthy nerve cell, the level of calcium is extremely low compared with that outside the neuron. Many complex systems work to maintain low intracellular calcium levels; failure in any of them can cause levels to rise, with fatal results. Clinical studies are under way to determine whether the regulation of calcium within a cell may have beneficial effects.

• Another drug trial scheduled to start in 1994 involves a combination of pharmacological and behavioral approaches—psychoactive drugs (haloperidol, trazodone) and behavior-management techniques—to reduce disruptive, agitated behavior in AD patients. It is expected that as scientists learn more about behavioral methods for improving the care and management of AD patients, clinical trials will be initiated specifically to test the efficacy of such techniques.

• Some loss of neurons is a central feature of AD pathology, and therapy based on naturally occurring nerve growth promoters has been the subject of intense interest and study by many groups. On the basis of the successes observed in animal studies, one such substance, nerve growth factor (NGF), has been proposed as a means of treating loss of cholinergic neurons in AD. NGF administration has been shown to prevent cholinergic degeneration associated with normal aging in animals. Many scientists believe that NGF or other growth-promoting factors could delay or stop the behavioral impairments associated with loss of cholinergic neurons in humans. A clinical trial is being planned to determine the efficacy of NGF as a treatment for AD.

Metabolic stress: causes and effects

The second system that is important for neuronal survival consists of the structural and functional elements that regulate nerve cell metabolism. Scientists have known for some time that without an adequate supply of oxygen and glucose, neurons will die. Moreover, these cells are extremely demanding and fussy about the metabolic fuel they consume; they need an abundant supply of pure glucose, and any sustained deprivation, as occurs in asphyxiation or stroke, has disastrous consequences.

A number of studies have demonstrated that vascular changes in the brain are intrinsic to the pathology of AD. Profound structural and biochemical alterations in tiny blood vessels in the brain can lead to chronic deprivation of blood flow, resulting in a progressive decline in neuronal function in selected brain areas. Pathological changes in the capillaries of the brain imply that the functioning of the blood-brain barrier (BBB) is altered in AD. The BBB allows oxygen, glucose, and other essential nutrients and chemicals to pass from the capillary circulation into brain tissue while at the same time preventing the passage of undesirable compounds such as environmental toxins, pathogens, and drugs. The association of severe head trauma with an increased risk for AD is probably related to damage to the brain microvessel system and possible failure of the BBB.

In recent years the application of sophisticated medical imaging techniques to the study of the brains of AD patients has yielded insight into metabolic abnormalities. One such technique, positron emission tomography (PET), has shown that in AD patients certain parts of the brain involved in cognitive functioning are unable to utilize glucose properly. Scientists are not certain whether these deficits are due to microvessel pathology or dysfunction in other parts of the metabolic cascade, such as a defect in the protein that transports glucose. The end result, however, is that in AD certain parts of the brain are under a condition of chronic metabolic stress. Continuous malnutrition of neurons, for whatever reason, could have several important implications for understanding of the pathologies associated with AD. The synthesis of acetylcholine, the key neurotransmitter for memory, is highly dependent on glucose metabolism in the brain. Thus, the selective vulnerability of cholinergic neurons might actually be a consequence of inadequate blood circulation to those parts of the brain, resulting in a gradual starvation of these cells. The cholinergic deficits and associated cognitive decline could be the result of metabolic abnormalities that may have proceeded unnoticed for a long period before the onset of obvious, disabling cognitive changes.

Another consequence of chronic glucose insufficiency in the brain is the conversion of a harmless and essential neurotransmitter, glutamate, into a potent killer of neurons. Glutamate is an excitatory amino acid; in appropriate amounts it is essential for development and normal functioning of neurons but, as with other excitatory amino acids, in excessive amounts it can become toxic to the very neurons it normally stimulates. Glutamate becomes neurotoxic when too much of it is present at a synapse or when, in normal amounts, it stimulates a glucose-deprived neuron. Glutamate toxicity is mediated by the influx of calcium into the cell, and it is the excessive internal concentration of calcium that eventually kills the cell.

Although the rate of deterioration varies from person to person, in time Alzheimer's disease inevitably renders patients unable to care for themselves, placing an enormous physical and emotional burden on families and other caregivers.

In recent years scientists have become especially interested in the biochemical mechanisms of neurotoxicity for two reasons. First, it has been shown that a wide variety of toxic compounds, some present in the environment (exogenous toxins), such as aluminum, and others naturally present in the body (endogenous toxins), such as glutamate, can lead to selective neuronal dysfunction and death. Second, neurotoxins have become an important analytical tool, allowing neuroscientists to study different characteristics of nerve cells as reflected by their selective vulnerability.

Among the many potentially neurotoxic compounds in the environment, aluminum has captured the most attention. Aluminum is a ubiquitous element. While autopsy analyses of the brains of AD patients have produced conflicting results depending on methods used, there appears to be a modest accumulation of aluminum in the brain lesions—the neuritic plaques and neurofibrillary tangles—that are characteristic of the disease. Nonetheless, the possible role of the element in AD remains controversial. It still is not clear whether aluminum buildup contributes to, causes, or results from the cellular pathology associated with AD. Many scientists believe that aluminum is unlikely to be a primary causative factor but may have a secondary role in the pathogenesis of AD.

Synthesis and degradation: a delicate balance

The third essential system for maintaining the health of a neuron is its ability to control and balance two opposing biochemical events, one involving the mechanisms of protein and membrane synthesis, the other involving the processes that degrade or digest proteins. It is through this complex balancing act that neurons repair and renew themselves and derive their unique ability for self-modification in response to stimuli, experiences, or injuries.

Most nerve cells, once fully developed, are designed to provide a lifetime of service. A neuron, to function properly, must renew between 50,000 and 100,000 different types of proteins. A mistake in the synthesis of any one of these proteins could interfere with an essential cellular function and lead to a failure in a neuron's ability to communicate vital information. Such errors could result in too much or too little of a protein or one with the wrong sequence of amino acids (the building blocks of protein), something like a string of words with spelling and grammatical errors. Errors in amino acid sequence, in turn, could influence the three-dimensional structure of the protein, thus affecting how well it does its job. What might appear to be a minor change in the position of one or two amino acids could become the cause of a disease such as AD. Errors in protein degradation can have equally disastrous consequences. Proteins that are not properly digested or broken down could accumulate, forming new, harmful aggregates.

As mentioned above, the neuropathological hallmarks of AD are two kinds of microscopic lesions, called neuritic (or senile) plaques and neurofibrillary tangles, which are found in the brains of AD patients at autopsy. Both are the consequences of abnormalities in the processing of different types of proteins. The major constituent of the tangles is a protein called *tau,* which is present in normal brain tissue. Tangles apparently form as a result of abnormal phosphorylation (the addition of phosphate molecules) of tau, a process that interferes with the protein's role in the construction of vital intracellular transport structures known as microtubules.

The other major lesion associated with AD, the neuritic plaque, has as its principal constituent beta-amyloid protein. Amyloid is derived from a larger protein, called the amyloid precursor protein (APP), which is normally found partially embedded in the membrane of the neuron. The function of APP is not known, but it is believed that it may play an important role in stabilizing synaptic contact points. It is very likely that APP is critical to the plasticity of the nervous system, thus being of great importance for understanding the neurobiology of cognitive functioning. It must also play other, undiscovered roles in the normal functioning of neurons because there are many different forms of APP, each with a sightly different amino acid sequence; they have been found in all kinds of animals, from fruit flies to humans.

Amyloid protein has the unusual characteristics of being highly insoluble and resistant to degradation, thus readily accumulating within the nervous system. How it interferes with cell functioning is not totally clear, but there are some suggestions that aggregations of beta-amyloid become highly toxic to neurons in a way similar to glutamate. In fact, both of these substances may inflict their damage by disrupting the internal homeostasis of calcium ions. Recent discoveries concerning the nature of amyloid protein, how it is formed and processed, what it does to a cell, and the genes that determine its structure have created tremendous excitement among neuroscientists. Many believe that pursuit of this clue will lead to discovery of the specific cause or causes of AD.

Genetic keys?

The scientific enthusiasm about the possible role of amyloid protein in the pathology of AD has been further fueled by the results of molecular genetics studies that have identified genes associated with familial (inherited) Alzheimer's disease on chromosomes 21, 14, and 19. The first specific gene linked with familial AD was the APP gene on chromosome 21, which is responsible for producing amyloid protein. After the initial report, several other mutations were found in the region of the APP gene in members of families that had a history of AD onset at a relatively young age. How these mutations alter the behavior of APP and their significance to normal cell functioning are not known. Subsequently, a region on chromosome 14 was also linked to an early-onset form of the disease. The exact gene has not yet been pinpointed, and its function is still unknown.

The third and most recently discovered gene linked to AD is the apolipoprotein E (ApoE) gene on chromosome 19, which has been associated with many late-onset familial cases of AD as well as sporadic cases in the over-60 age group. (Sporadic cases are those occurring in individuals who have no strong family history of the disease.) The ApoE gene directs the synthesis of a cholesterol-transporting blood protein. The gene occurs in three different forms: apoE2, apoE3, and apoE4. One of these, apoE4, is found in 14% of control populations but is present in 30–40% of the late-onset sporadic cases of AD and 80% of the late-onset familial cases. In certain families the chance of developing AD before age 85 rises to 90% for individuals who are homozygous for apoE4, which means they have inherited this form of the gene from both parents. These people have 5:1 odds of developing AD, compared with 15:1 odds in individuals who have a single ApoE4 gene. It has been estimated that between 25% and 40% of AD cases can be attributed to the presence of this form of the gene.

Not only does the ApoE gene have a strong and consistent relationship with the disease, but within a few months after it was identified, researchers postulated a plausible biological explanation for its role in the pathological processes of AD. It has been shown that the protein encoded by the ApoE gene has a high affinity for and binds with beta-amyloid in the plaques. Among Alzheimer's patients, those who have the gene for apoE4 have larger plaques than those who lack the gene. It appears that apoE4 acts as a chaperone to APP and, in some unknown way, promotes the formation of neuritic plaques. It has also been postulated that it plays an important role in the formation of neurofibrillary tangles. In the brain ApoE proteins are taken up by neurons in large quantities after neuronal injury and appear to play an important role in various recuperative processes and in neuronal plasticity.

The excitement and optimism generated by the discovery of a relationship between Alzheimer's disease and ApoE is well-warranted; epidemiological studies of AD will now have a biological marker for sorting patients into homogenous groups and studying them with the hope of finding other contributing factors. At the same time, this research has provided new opportunities for developing alternative treatment strategies.

The campaign against AD

The crisis in U.S. health care costs, the rapidly growing number of older people in the population, and the devastating toll of AD have led to the formulation of a public-private working proposal for a major campaign against the disease. This national initiative is called the "Five-Five, Ten-Ten Plan for Alzheimer's Disease." The goal is to slow the rate of deterioration in AD patients by 5 years during the next 5 years and by 10 years within 10 years. The overriding aim of this initiative is to discover treatments that will allow patients to continue to function independently. Importantly, this approach will target not only the cognitive dysfunction associated with AD but also the behavioral disturbances that often leave some families with no choice but to institutionalize their loved ones.

The progress made to date is, in large measure, due to the successful partnership between family-support groups such as the Alzheimer's Association and government-sponsored researchers. Now the partnership is being expanded to include private foundations such as the newly established Zachary and Elizabeth M. Fisher Medical Foundation in New York City. This collective effort is certain to yield results.

—Zaven S. Khachaturian, Ph.D.,
and Teresa S. Radebaugh, Sc.D.

Human Subjects: Used or Abused?

by George J. Annas, J.D., M.P.H.

Important ethical issues in biomedicine have been widely publicized during the past year. These included revelations about secret radiation experiments conducted by the U.S. government during the Cold War, continuing controversies about medical research on patients dying of AIDS and cancer, and questions regarding human embryo and fertility research. These issues have a common theme: the inadequacy of the standards for protecting the rights and welfare of human subjects of medical experimentation.

Radiation experiments: shocking disclosures

In 1986 Rep. Edward J. Markey released a report from the House Subcommittee on Energy Conservation and Power entitled "American Nuclear Guinea Pigs: Three Decades of Radiation Experiments on U.S. Citizens." The report detailed 31 experiments conducted on more than 700 Americans by the federal government from the 1940s to the 1970s, most designed to test the effect on the human body of exposure to radiation. The experiments included injection of plutonium or uranium into terminally ill patients; irradiation of the testicles of prisoners to study the impact of radiation on fertility; exposure of nursing home residents to radium or thorium, either injected or ingested, to measure the passage of these radioactive substances through the body; and feeding of radioactive fallout to human subjects to see how the body would excrete it. Although the 1986 report was carefully documented and cited specific published reports on the studies, it went virtually unrecognized and unheralded, primarily because the administration of Pres. Ronald Reagan dismissed it as overblown.

Under the administration of Pres. Bill Clinton, the reaction to similar disclosures, involving thousands of Americans, has been dramatically different. In October 1993 reporter Eileen Welsome of the *Albuquerque* (N.M.) *Tribune* wrote a series of articles about five individuals who, without their knowledge or consent, had been injected with plutonium in 1945–47 as part of an Atomic Energy Commission (AEC) study of the impact of plutonium on human beings. The information was sought to help determine how to treat workers and scientists exposed to plutonium at weapons development and production plants.

It was believed at the time that the subjects had terminal illnesses and were not likely to live long, al-

though this turned out not always to be the case. For example, plutonium was injected into the leg of a 36-year-old man who was thought to have bone cancer. The leg was then amputated for study. As a result of the amputation, the man could no longer work and was dependent upon his wife to support him. He died 45 years later, in 1991. Another subject was misdiagnosed as having stomach cancer and was injected with plutonium in 1945. He lived to age 79, dying in 1966. The subjects were not told the purpose of the experiments, either at the time or later when follow-up studies were conducted.

When these stories came to light, Hazel O'Leary, secretary of the U.S. Department of Energy (DOE; successor to the AEC), said that she was "appalled, shocked, and saddened" by the plutonium experiments. She took steps to begin an investigation of other radiation experiments conducted by the AEC and suggested that a way should be found to compensate the victims. This reaction was shared by President Clinton, and a task force was created to conduct a similar review of all federal agencies that might have been involved in radiation experiments during the Cold War.

The ongoing investigations may last for years since there are 32 million pages of DOE documents alone to review, all classified as top secret. Nonetheless, it is already possible to conclude that there were at least two different kinds of experiments sponsored or cooperated in, each conducted with varying degrees of consent on the part of the subjects. The first involved the use of relatively harmless radioactive isotopes as tracers to measure the route, absorption, and elimination of substances introduced into the human body; in the second, toxic doses of radioactive materials were used to study the effect of radiation on the body. The first type of experiment, which might be called the "peaceful" use of radiation, would be ethically acceptable today if performed on subjects who could and did give informed consent. The second type, referred to as "Cold War" experimentation, usually put the subjects at such a high risk of harm that it could not be ethically justified, then or today, even with informed consent. An example of each type of experiment illustrates the differences.

"Peaceful" atomic studies. Perhaps the most widely publicized radiation tracer studies were performed on

mentally disabled children living at the Fernald School in Waltham, Mass., in the mid-1950s. Three of these studies, all published in the medical literature at the time, involved the placement of radioactive isotopes of calcium (Ca^{45}) in milk to measure the differences in absorption of calcium when ingested with different kinds of breakfast cereals. The amounts of radiation were presumed to be harmless. Nonetheless, the consent form signed by the parents did not mention the use of radiation at all. The major ethical and legal objections to the study do not stem from the risk to the subjects, however; rather they stem from the selection of the subjects in the first place—a captive population of so-called expendable individuals—and the lack of informed consent.

There is general agreement that vulnerable populations should be used as subjects only if the experiment cannot be done on less vulnerable populations, the experiment is important and cannot be performed without human subjects, and the results of the experiment can help other members of the vulnerable population itself. These ethical guidelines were not followed in this experiment. It seems that the mentally disabled residents of Fernald were chosen only because they were convenient and their parents were not likely to object. If young people were needed for the study, healthy youngsters living at home or students from the Massachusetts Institute of Technology, the university that employed the scientists, should have been recruited. The Fernald residents were used as objects or guinea pigs instead of human beings with rights, an affront to both their human rights and their human dignity. Such treatment is not countenanced by law or ethics, either by today's standards or by those of the 1950s.

"Cold War" studies. Perhaps the clearest illustration of the Cold War radiation experiments funded by the AEC is one that took place at Boston's Massachusetts General Hospital in the mid-1950s, at the same time the radioisotope studies were being done at Fernald. The Massachusetts General experiment was designed to find the dose of uranium that could be tolerated by humans. Six patients terminally ill with brain tumors were injected with uranium (U^{235}). Five of the six were semicomatose or in a coma at the time; most died within 2 months, but one lived for 17 months. There is no evidence of consent by anyone, although permission to perform an autopsy was refused by the family of the only woman in the study. The published report of the experiment, which indicated that the subjects had been exposed to a range of 10% to 30% of a lethal dose of uranium, concluded, "Of the common laboratory animals, man appears to correspond most closely to the rat in regard to intravenous tolerance to uranium." Human subjects were used in this case because they were captive and available. No consent was sought or obtained, apparently because the re-

searchers believed that terminally ill individuals could not be harmed.

The Nuremberg Code
The Nuremberg Code, the primary document setting forth the legal and ethical requirements of experimentation with humans, was enunciated by U.S. judges at the trial of the infamous Nazi doctors at Nuremberg (Nürnberg), Germany, in 1946–47. The doctors were accused and convicted of performing brutal experiments on concentration camp inmates during World War II. Most of these investigations, such as those involving exposure to freezing temperatures and high altitudes, had as their end point the death of the "subjects." The Nazis justified these cruel practices on the basis that it was wartime and sacrifices were expected of everyone. The court, in finding most of the defendants guilty of war crimes and crimes against humanity, set forth the Nuremberg Code not as a revolutionary pronouncement but rather as an authoritative restatement of basic human principles that "must be observed . . . to satisfy moral, ethical, and legal concepts."

The 10 points of the Nuremberg Code make it clear that researchers are obligated to respect and protect both the rights and the welfare of subjects of human experimentation. The subject's rights are protected by the first provision of the code, which requires voluntary, competent, and informed consent, and by the ninth provision, which gives the subject the right to end the experiment at any time. The requirement of the code for consent is uncompromising; those who cannot consent must not be used for human experimentation that is not for their own benefit. The welfare of subjects is protected by the code's remaining eight provisions, requiring a reasonable experiment and research design, prior animal studies, avoidance of unnecessary suffering and injury, a ban on experiments that are likely to result in death or disabling injury, proper facilities, and a qualified researcher who is willing to halt the study to protect the welfare of the subjects.

U.S. government researchers were well aware of both the trial of the Nazi doctors and the authority of the Nuremberg Code. In a 1950 memorandum, for example, the AEC's chief health officer, Joseph Hamilton, commented that radiation exposure studies on soldiers—who were ordered to stand in the desert while an atomic bomb was being exploded—conjured up the activities of the Nazi doctors: "If this is to be done in humans, I feel that those concerned in the Atomic Energy Commission would be subject to considerable criticism, as admittedly, that would have a little of the Buchenwald touch." (Buchenwald was the site of a Nazi concentration camp.) In 1953, shortly after the election of Pres. Dwight Eisenhower, the secretary of defense formally adopted the Nuremberg

U.S. Army soldiers observe the subsurface detonation of an atomic bomb on Yucca Flat, Nevada, in March 1955. In the 1950s military personnel were used regularly as guinea pigs in radiation-exposure studies, although some of the scientists involved in the research questioned the ethics of the practice.

Code as the official policy of all branches of the U.S. armed services.

Nonetheless, little progress was made in applying the precepts of the code until 1966, when an influential article by physician Henry Beecher was published in the *New England Journal of Medicine.* Beecher described some particularly unethical experiments that had been conducted in the U.S. during the 1950s and '60s. All had been carried out and their findings published without comment on their ethics. Beecher's article prompted the federal government to seek ways to monitor research and to recommend that institutions establish committees to review research protocols and consent forms for studies involving humans. In 1974 Congress passed the National Research Act, which established a commission to draft regulations applicable to all federally funded research. The commission, which disbanded in 1978, drafted regulations on several different categories of research, including that involving fetuses, adults, children, prisoners, and the institutionalized mentally disabled.

All of the commission's recommendations, except those related to the institutionalized mentally disabled (such as the residents of Fernald), were adopted by the U.S. Department of Health, Education, and Welfare (predecessor to the Department of Health and Human Services). The regulations regarding adults (but none

of the others) were eventually adopted by all federal agencies. Under these regulations local panels, which consist primarily of researchers and are called institutional review boards (IRBs), are required to review and approve all research protocols and consent forms before research on human subjects begins.

These procedures have had a major impact in that virtually no research on prisoners is currently done in the United States and most routine research on drugs and medical devices (both regulated by the U.S. Food and Drug Administration) is well reviewed. On the other hand, as the type of experimentation on human subjects has changed, it has become apparent that IRB review of protocols and consent forms does not protect those who have always been the most vulnerable and who now are often the most valuable research subjects—terminally ill patients. A brief look at research involving AIDS and cancer helps explain why.

"Nothing to lose"?

Perhaps the primary reason that existing guidelines have little practical relevance for the terminally ill is that their prognosis alone determines both what researchers and physicians deem "reasonable" and what patients themselves find acceptable, or even desirable. Like the AEC investigators during the Cold War,

231

many of today's researchers believe that terminally ill individuals cannot be hurt—they are "going to die anyway"—and therefore have "nothing to lose." Prior peer review of protocols and consent forms thus becomes pro forma and provides no meaningful protection for subjects. Likewise, patients who are told that accepted therapies offer them no hope have come to view experimental protocols as treatment. In fact, instead of being suspicious of experimentation, such patients may demand access to experimental interventions as their right. One such intervention is the experimental use of autologous bone marrow transplantation, in which the patient's own marrow is removed, treated, and reinfused. Informed consent provides no meaningful protection in such circumstances.

The Nazi doctors' chief defense at Nuremberg was that experimentation was necessary to support the war effort. Today combating disease is often conceived in military terms—the "war on cancer" or the "war on AIDS." In such "battles" patients, especially terminally ill patients, become conscripts. As a former editor of the *New England Journal of Medicine,* Franz Ingelfinger, put it, "The thumb screws of coercion are most relentlessly applied to the most used and useful of all experimental subjects, the patient with disease." Or as writer Susan Sontag has eloquently argued in *AIDS and Its Metaphors* (1989), war metaphors (including Cold War rationales) are dangerous to patients because they encourage authoritarianism, overmobilization, and stigmatization. Sontag writes:

No, it is not desirable for medicine, any more than for war, to be "total." Neither is the crisis created by AIDS a "total" anything. We are not being invaded. The body is not a battlefield. The ill are neither unavoidable casualties nor the enemy.

We—medicine, society—are not authorized to fight back by any means whatever.

Cancer specialists (and their patients) have an increasingly difficult time distinguishing not only between experimentation and therapy but also between the role of the researcher-scientist testing a hypothesis (the ideology of science) and the role of the physician treating a patient to the best of his or her ability (the ideology of medicine). It is also worth emphasizing that most studies on the terminally ill, including cancer and AIDS clinical trials, are funded by drug companies with a tremendous financial stake in the enterprise. Clinical investigators may also have financial interests in the pharmaceutical companies, which calls their own objectivity into question.

Medical ethics is thus being eroded by a new commercialism in medicine and is in danger of being eclipsed by business ethics. This fact has led most leading medical journals in the United States to require financial disclosure by the investigators prior to publication of research results. Neither IRBs nor individual subjects are routinely informed of the financial aspects of proposed clinical trials, however, even though the financing may create potential conflicts of interest among the sponsor, the researcher, and the patient-subject.

Because there is no cure for AIDS, it has been perceived as the disease in which there is no distinction between treatment and experimentation. The disease primarily strikes those in the prime of life, leading to a death that is premature by virtually any standard, and even treatments that may prolong life are far from satisfactory. In addition, many people with the disease do not have health insurance to cover the costs of medical care; the only way such uninsured individuals can obtain treatment is to enroll in an experimental drug trial. In fact, an espoused slogan of the group ACT UP (the AIDS Coalition to Unleash Power), "A Drug Trial Is Health Care Too," is factually correct in many U.S. settings. Nonetheless, the slogan wrongly conflates experimentation with therapy, encourages people with AIDS to seek out experimentation as treatment, and validates the physician-researcher's view

New York City AIDS activists demonstrate outside City Hall on the first day of Rudolph Giuliani's term as mayor. AIDS patients have been among the most vocal in demanding access to unproven therapies. Because of the grim prognosis of the disease, patients and researchers alike often fail to make a distinction between experimentation and treatment.

Mark Peterson—Saba

of AIDS patients as experimental subjects who have "nothing to lose."

The goal of research is to produce generalizable knowledge—"to yield fruitful results for the good of society," in the words of the Nuremberg Code—*not* to treat a particular person. Because consent is not an ethical excuse or a justification for inhumane treatment or poorly designed research, the experiment must be valid and the potential harm minimized *before* consent is even sought. To protect subjects it seems reasonable that researchers who believe their subjects cannot be harmed by experimental interventions be disqualified from doing research on humans on the basis that such researchers would not protect their subjects' welfare appropriately.

Likewise, patients who believe that they have nothing to lose and are desperate to "try anything" should be disqualified as research subjects because they would be unlikely or unable to protect themselves adequately by giving voluntary and competent consent and thus would be vulnerable to exploitation. If both researcher and subject share the view that there is nothing to lose, there is virtually no limit to the harm that can be visited on the research subject. Clearly, additional regulations regarding terminally ill patients need to be adopted to supplement existing federal research guidelines.

Reproductive research: how far is too far?

Like human beings facing the end of life, human embryos and fetuses also present unique issues in the research context. Experiments involving the beginning of life, like those involving the terminally ill, must be held to high ethical standards and subjected to rigorous scrutiny. One of the more controversial news stories of recent months led to allegations that medical scientists had gone too far in intervening with natural reproductive processes.

The discussion began at a conference on fertility research when two investigators from George Wash-

ington University, Washington, D.C., announced that they had "cloned" human embryos and that a number of the "clones" had continued to develop in the laboratory. All of the embryos were eventually destroyed.

Cloning, the creation of a genetically identical offspring from a somatic (*i.e.,* nonreproductive) cell of a parent organism, has been the subject of science fiction and speculative ethical debate for decades. It has never actually been done in humans or any other mammals. Strictly speaking, the technique used by the George Washington researchers was *not* cloning but rather *blastomere separation.* In nature, after the joining of sperm and egg, the fertilized egg divides, forming two genetically identical cells called blastomeres. Each of these then divides again, resulting in 4, 8, 16, and 32 blastomeres. Each blastomere has the potential to develop into a separate individual. Over the past 20 years or so, scientists have isolated and separated blastomeres from the embryos of experimental animals. The technique, which has been referred to by various names, including "twig cloning" and "embryo twinning," has been used to produce twins in rodents, lambs, and cattle. It had not previously been applied to human reproduction.

Arguments in favor of extending the procedure to humans center around the shortage of eggs for in vitro fertilization (IVF) and the difficulty of surgically removing eggs from the ovaries. Using blastomere separation, a single fertilized egg could potentially produce multiple embryos. Opponents regard the process as unnatural—a Vatican spokesperson called it "perverse"—and some fear that it could lead to commercialization of human embryos and, ultimately, to selective breeding of humans. In one futuristic scenario one of several identical embryos might be permitted to grow and be born, while the others would be frozen. The child could then be subjected to various medical and intelligence tests. This information, along with a photograph, could appear in a "catalog," so that prospective adoptive parents could "shop" for a child with known characteristics. An explicit "market price" might then be set, based on the child's physical and mental traits. This practice, in turn, could be used to put a specific price on human characteristics in general. The point is not that such a practice would necessarily lead to baby buying but that a market in human embryos might directly affect how people feel about (and value) children with specific desirable or undesirable characteristics. Primarily in response to the debate triggered by this experiment, the director of the National Institutes of Health established an ethical advisory board to make recommendations for the conduct of embryo experimentation in the U.S. The board was scheduled to make its recommendations in the fall of 1994.

Two other controversial procedures recently in the news related to the practice of IVF itself. The first involved the implantation of an embryo (using a donor egg) into women past the age of menopause—in one case a 62-year-old Italian woman who gave birth to a son in July 1994. The fact that men can become fathers at virtually any age while women are limited by the cessation of the menstrual cycle has led some to feel that age restrictions on motherhood are arbitrary and sexist. Others note that the women in these cases receive a donor egg fertilized with their male partners' sperm and so are giving birth not to their own genetic children but rather to their partners'. Others simply find it surprising that women in their 50s and 60s would want to become pregnant, given that they would be in their 70s or 80s before the child reached adulthood.

Even more controversial was the suggestion by a British researcher that eggs—and perhaps ovaries— from aborted fetuses be recovered and used in IVF. The arguments in favor of such a procedure cite the growing acceptability of the medical use of fetal tissues and the shortage of available eggs for IVF. The arguments against focus on the issue of consent, specifically that it is difficult to understand why a woman who decides not to have a child—and therefore terminates her pregnancy—would, at the same time, agree to allow her genetic "grandchildren" to be borne by someone else. Because the donation of gametes (sperm and eggs), unlike that of other fetal tissue, involves a decision to procreate, the consent of the biological "father" of the fetus (who would be the genetic "grandfather" of any resulting children) would also be required. Both the use of fetal eggs and the use of IVF in older women are considered so ethically problematic that the ethics committee of the American Fertility Society has been asked to make recommendations concerning these procedures.

Getting serious about subjects' rights
Revelation of past radiation experiments and analysis of contemporary research on the terminally ill raise two additional issues: how can victims of experimentation be compensated for past harm, and how can future harm be prevented? Compensation would require a legislative act similar to the legislation the U.S. Congress enacted to compensate Japanese Americans wrongly detained in camps during World War II. Another precedent is the 1990 radiation exposure compensation statute, which was designed to compensate those exposed to radioactive fallout from nuclear testing in Utah, Nevada, and Arizona. The victims of Cold War radiation experiments are owed both a formal apology and monetary compensation from the government. The country should also get a full accounting of all the experiments done in the name of its citizens and financed by them.

As seemingly inadequate as it is to make up monetarily for lives damaged as a result of medical experimentation, compensation for past harm may be easier than prevention of future harm. When governments feel that their security is threatened by an enemy, they seem to be able to justify virtually any "defensive" action, including unlawful human experimentation. What is needed is more effective public oversight of all human experimentation that carries a risk of death or threatens deeply held values.

The U.S. has had three national advisory commissions on human experimentation. Nonetheless, current research regulations are inadequate to prevent abuses, and the IRB mechanism, relying as it does on peer review by other researchers, cannot adequately protect the human rights and welfare of research subjects. Accordingly, it would be timely and appropriate for the federal government to establish a national human experimentation agency. Such an agency would be similar to the Securities and Exchange Commission or the Federal Trade Commission in being independent and having both regulatory and adjudicatory authority. It would promulgate and enforce rules governing research with terminally ill patients and oversee the conduct of all research on human beings, including that on embryos and fetuses. In addition, such an agency would review all unusual research protocols proposed, such as those involving genetic engineering, artificial organs, and xenografts (animal-to-human transplants).

Biomedical research involves values and indicates what kind of life a society wants for itself and its children. Therefore, a national human experimentation agency should be composed exclusively of nonscientists. Moreover, it would also be sensible to change the composition of local IRBs so that a majority of the members were laypersons. These measures might not solve all the problems in human experimentation, but they undoubtedly would solve some. Perhaps most important, such actions would indicate that the U.S. is serious about protecting *both* the rights and the welfare of research subjects.

Asthma

In many Western countries the prevalence of asthma is about 4–5%. The incidence of asthma worldwide has doubled in the past two decades, as has the incidence of allergic disease. In the United States there are approximately 15 million people who suffer from asthma, and the disease is the country's sixth most common cause of hospitalization. Asthma is the most frequent hospital admitting diagnosis for children and teenagers. There are now more than 5,000 recorded asthma deaths per year in the U.S.—more than twice as many as there were in 1977—and African-Americans are about three times more likely to die from asthma than are whites.

In 1990 the cost of asthma was estimated to be more than $6 billion, and it is certain to be much higher now. Asthma-associated emergency room visits alone cost at least $200 million annually, and treatment of asthma accounts for about 10% of the medical costs of most health maintenance organizations. Asthma is the major chronic disease responsible for school absenteeism, and it is a rare teacher who has not had to respond to a wheezing child in class.

A problem of trapped air

Asthma is a lung disorder marked by attacks of breathing difficulty, wheezing, and coughing and by the presence of thick mucus in the lungs. The word *asthma* derives from the Greek and means "to blow, or breathe hard"; the attacks occur because air is unable to escape the "blown-up," or overinflated, chest once inspired. Ordinarily, air flows smoothly into the chest during inspiration and empties from the chest passively during exhalation. With normal breathing, the chest empties owing to the elastic recoil of the lungs after they are inflated. Thus, the actual "work" of breathing is exclusively devoted to breathing in; one ordinarily exhales without exerting energy.

In asthma the airways (bronchi) become thickened owing to a combination of processes: the bronchial muscle that surrounds the airway constricts, which narrows the bronchial cavity (lumen); the lining of the airway swells owing to fluid buildup (edema) and infiltration by immune system cells; and the airway secretes increased amounts of thick mucus. As a result of these processes, airflow in the small, narrow airways (bronchioles) is obstructed.

During the normal process of inspiration, the chest wall moves outward and the diaphragm downward, increasing the actual volume inside the chest cavity. Owing to the outward pressure created by the movement of the rib cage, the airway actually widens as air flows from the bronchi through the bronchioles to the alveoli (small air pockets in the lungs where carbon dioxide and oxygen are exchanged). Once inhalation has stopped, the diaphragm collapses, the ribs relax, and the chest cavity gets smaller. At this stage the thickened asthmatic airways collapse and act as one-way valves; air is able to get through the airways during inhalation but then gets trapped and partially fills the lungs. Amazingly, an asthmatic can trap as much as two liters (about four pints) of air—enough to fill a basketball. Indeed, much of the discomfort of asthma is due to this air trapping.

Air exhaled through narrowed airways becomes turbulent, causing a wheezing sound. Listening to the chest of an asthmatic, one hears high-pitched wheezes that often sound as if many piccolos are being played inside the patient's chest. The presence of increased mucus complicates the asthmatic's breathing, causing raspy, gravely sounds, called rhonchi. If the patient gets very short of breath, the rush of air during inhalation also causes wheezing. But the major problem is

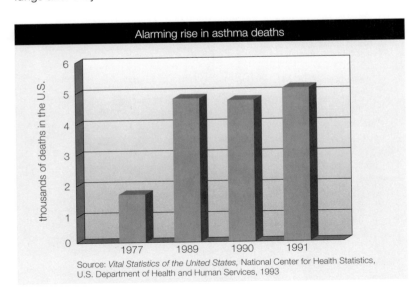

Source: *Vital Statistics of the United States*, National Center for Health Statistics, U.S. Department of Health and Human Services, 1993

The incidence of asthma worldwide has doubled in the past two decades. Even more alarming is the rising asthma death toll, despite better treatments. In the United States there were more than 5,000 recorded asthma deaths in 1991—a rate that has more than doubled since 1977. The sharpest increases are among the elderly and African-Americans.

in emptying the chest, and it is only when the air trapping is relieved and the wheezing and shortness of breath disappear that the patient feels well.

Asthma's symptoms

Patients with asthma complain of tightness of the chest, often felt beneath the sternum (breastbone); they cough and feel short of breath. Shortness of breath may occur during asthma attacks or exercise. Exercise-induced asthma is a very common way for the disease to first manifest itself. Patients get short of breath after a few minutes of exercising and experience wheezing, coughing, and mucous production, which may resolve itself spontaneously in 30 to 60 minutes, even if exercise is continued. Exercise-induced asthma is seen in most children with asthma if they exercise vigorously. Running is the most likely form of exercise to provoke asthma; biking and swimming are less likely to do so. The underlying event in exercise-induced asthma is cooling of the airways due to hyperventilation. Air passing quickly over the airway removes some of the water that coats the airway. This evaporative process leads to airway cooling. Breathing dry air facilitates the cooling process and, therefore, running is more likely to cause exercise-induced asthma than swimming because the air the swimmer breathes is highly saturated with water. Likewise, wearing a face mask or respirator while exercising reduces wheezing by providing humidified air.

In 1991 the National Heart, Lung, and Blood Institute (NHLBI) of the National Institutes of Health issued new guidelines on the diagnosis and management of asthma. In this advisory, sent to all U.S. physicians, patients are classified on the basis of their symptoms as having mild, moderate, or severe asthma. Patients with wheezing or breathing difficulty less often than two days per week are considered to have mild asthma; when wheezing occurs two to five days per week and is associated with some degree of dimin-

ished lung function, asthma is considered moderate; severe asthma is that in which patients have continuous symptoms, frequent worsening of symptoms, and impaired lung function. These classifications were formulated to serve as guides for treatment that is aimed at controlling asthma and preventing acute attacks. Unfortunately, these guidelines have not been widely followed. Some doctors may still treat symptoms rather than the underlying disease. As a result, some of the asthma deaths and emergencies that occur could have been prevented.

Complications: explaining the high death toll

Uncomplicated asthma (mild asthma or moderate asthma that is controlled) does not lead to bronchitis, a disease of inflamed bronchi most often triggered by cigarette smoking or airway infections and manifested as a regular cough with significant mucous production. Uncomplicated asthma does not lead to emphysema, a disease in which the alveoli are destroyed and the ability to exchange oxygen for carbon dioxide is impaired. Uncomplicated asthma may, however, increase the loss of normal lung volume and may lead to complications if not properly treated. Severe asthma may lead to asthma attacks that are difficult to treat.

In the past decade, not only has the incidence of asthma increased but so has the death rate. As noted above, in the U.S. more than 5,000 asthmatics now die each year. There are a number of potential reasons for this increased death rate, among which are increased exposure to indoor air pollution—some of the major culprits being house dust mites, molds, animal emanations, and insect parts; an overreliance on bronchodilators as a means of treating asthma, which may mask the progression of the underlying disease; and the inability of people in lower socioeconomic groups—especially inner-city asthmatics—to obtain good medical care. A sizable portion of asthma deaths occur in major metropolitan areas.

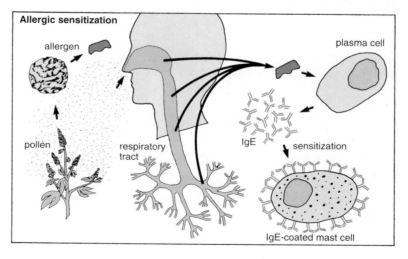

An individual becomes sensitized to an allergenic airborne substance—in this case, plant pollen—after prolonged exposure to it. The allergen, a protein on the surface of the pollen source (e.g., a ragweed plant), is inhaled into the respiratory tract, where it is taken up and presented to plasma cells. The plasma cells make immunoglobulin E (IgE) antibodies capable of recognizing the specific allergen that stimulated their production. The IgE goes on to sensitize nearby mast cells, binding to "high-affinity" receptors on each cell's surface. Once an IgE antibody has fixed to a mast cell, it stays there—usually for prolonged periods—capable of initiating an allergic response.

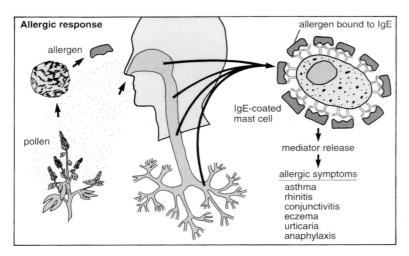

Allergic response

allergen

pollen

allergen bound to IgE

IgE-coated mast cell

mediator release

allergic symptoms
asthma
rhinitis
conjunctivitis
eczema
urticaria
anaphylaxis

Once an individual has become sensitized to an allergen, reexposure to the same substance (e.g., ragweed pollen) can set off an allergic response. On entering the respiratory tract, the allergen binds to IgE-coated mast cells, activating them and stimulating the release of chemical mediators (e.g., histamine, leukotrienes, prostaglandins, cytokines). The mediators then interact with surrounding tissues to produce allergic symptoms.

King's county, N.Y., and Cook county, Ill., are two urban centers with very large populations of poor people who often use emergency rooms for crisis care but do not receive ongoing care. They also have very high asthma death rates. Many experts believe that a part of the problem of increasing asthma mortality reflects inadequate treatment of inner-city asthmatics. In an effort to reduce the number of asthmatic episodes and deaths, particularly among minority children, the National Institute of Allergy and Infectious Diseases is currently funding the National Cooperative Inner-City Asthma Study to design and evaluate comprehensive interventions in eight U.S. urban areas.

A chronic inflammatory condition

One of the fundamental abnormalities in asthma is hyperresponsiveness, or irritability, of the airway. All asthmatics experience airflow obstruction when they breathe irritating fumes or are exposed to nonspecific irritants. Over the past 15 years, respiratory specialists have come to appreciate that airway irritability is in large part due to chronic inflammation of the airways; the airway walls are infiltrated with inflammatory cells from the immune system that readily respond to irritation. The mechanism leading to such airway inflammation that is now best understood is the late-phase allergic reaction, which helps explain the relationship between allergy and asthma.

Allergy and asthma: intimate connection

Allergies are the most common cause of asthma. Among children under age 16, 90% of those with asthma are also allergic; about 70% of asthmatics aged 16 to 30 are allergic; and half of asthmatics aged 30 and over are allergic.

The allergic reaction is dependent on three components: an allergen, immunoglobulin E (IgE) antibody, and a tissue cell called the mast cell (*see* diagrams). In a nutshell, the allergic reaction involves the pro-

duction of IgE antibodies directed against ordinarily harmless allergens—water-soluble proteins that are derived largely from airborne particles.

Atopy—the capacity to become allergic—is determined largely by genetic factors. If one partner of a couple is allergic, there is about a 33% chance that the offspring will become allergic. If both partners are allergic, it is possible that all of their offspring will be allergic. However, the genetic predisposition is only one determinant. The genetic control influences the synthesis of IgE antibodies, but these IgE molecules are produced only when there is exposure to appropriate allergens.

Allergens. Inhalant allergens, or antigens, which act directly on the mucous membranes of the respiratory tract, are usually derived from natural organic sources such as house dust, pollens, mold spores, and insect and animal emanations. Such allergens are responsible for most allergic rhinitis, conjunctivitis (inflammation of the eye), and asthma; less often, they cause dermatologic reactions such as urticaria (hives) and eczema (dry or crusty inflammation of the outer layer of skin) or systemic anaphylaxis (shock).

Inhalant allergic diseases may be episodic, seasonal (such as seasonal allergic asthma), or perennial. The most important seasonal allergens are pollens. Despite popular belief, the heavy, sticky pollens of brightly colored flowers seldom cause allergy symptoms, as these pollens are spread by insects and not by wind currents. Most tree pollens are released during the early spring. In most parts of the U.S., the height of the grass pollen season is late spring to midsummer. Although some species of weed pollen are airborne in spring and early summer, the greatest problems are caused by weeds in the late summer and early fall. In the eastern and midwestern U.S., ragweed is by far the worst offender.

Exposure to allergens in the home environment accounts for year-round allergies. Among the inhalants dust mites, molds, animal emanations, and cockroaches are responsible for most perennial allergic rhinitis and asthma. In the past several years, there has been increasingly clear evidence that exposure to cigarette smoke in the home is associated with exacerbated asthma in children.

House dust itself is a mixture of lint, mites, mite feces, animal danders, insect parts, fibers, and other particulate materials. Overwhelming evidence indicates that the mites *Dermatophagoides farinae* and *D. pteronyssinus* are the principal sources of antigen in house dust. These arachnids cohabit with humans in all temperate climates, subsisting on shed human skin. Their fecal materials are encased in a rich coating of intestinal enzymes; an enzyme within this coating known as a protease is the primary allergen. Mite feces are relatively large and heavy compared with other allergens and thus are airborne only briefly. Mites living in bedding, mattresses, and carpets require a warm, relatively humid environment for proliferation—18°–21° C (65°–70° F) and 50% relative humidity. Both live and dead mites are thought to contribute to allergic reactions.

Cat dander is a very potent allergen that derives from both salivary and skin sources, is much smaller and lighter than dust allergens, and is found ubiquitously and continuously in the air in households with

The dust mite, which subsists mainly on shed human skin, thrives wherever dust accumulates. It is these microscopic creatures and their feces that are the principle source of antigen (allergenic substance) in common house dust.

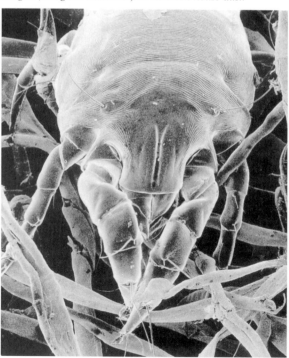

David Scharf

cats. Recent data suggest that weekly washing of the cat, when combined with other avoidance measures, greatly reduces the allergen load in the house. Dog allergens are found in saliva, serum, epidermal scales, and urine but not in hair. Thus, contrary to widespread belief, both short-haired and long-haired breeds may be equally allergenic.

In urban environments cockroaches are now known to be a major allergen. Commercial spraying is the only measure that has been shown to reduce cockroach infestation.

Among the inhalant antigens, molds, which are multicellular fungi, occupy a unique position because they are found in both outdoor and indoor environments. *Alternaria* and *Cladosporium* are major outdoor allergens. *Penicillium* and *Aspergillus* are the most prevalent molds found in basements, bedding, and damp interior areas. While pollen allergens typically become windborne during dry weather and are removed from the air during rain, high mold-spore counts are found in clouds and mist. Many upper respiratory tract allergy symptoms during periods of high humidity are therefore attributable to molds. Indoor mold exposures are reduced but not eliminated by the use of home dehumidifiers; often the use of bleach or other disinfectants to remove mold from damp areas and other places in the house where molds tend to grow works well.

IgE production. The IgE antibody is a member of a group of proteins called immunoglobulins that contribute to the functioning of the immune system. IgE has the capacity to bind avidly to particular molecular receptors on mast cells and related white blood cells.

Exposure to allergens in susceptible individuals leads to the production of IgE antibodies. It usually takes two to five seasons of exposure before sufficient IgE has been produced to sensitize the patient toward a particular allergen. The sensitization process requires that enough IgE become fixed to the surface of mast cells to initiate the release of histamine and other chemicals from mast cells upon subsequent exposure to that allergen. Current data suggest that there must be between 10 and 100 IgE molecules directed against a specific allergen on the surface of a mast cell before that cell can respond to an allergen.

IgE itself is a so-called trace molecule; *i.e.,* one that is found in concentrations so small that they cannot be easily detected. However, the action of IgE is amplified by the presence of "high-affinity" receptors on individual mast cells, to which up to one million IgE molecules are able to bind. A single mast cell is thus armed to respond to any of hundreds of common allergens. Moreover, once an IgE antibody has fixed to the surface of the mast cell, it stays there for extended periods (usually years).

Mast cells are found in the lining of the nose, the airways, the gastrointestinal tract, and the skin and,

Allergies are the most common cause of asthma; among children under age 16 who suffer from asthma, 90% have allergies. Contrary to widespread belief, dog allergens are derived not from the pet's hair but from its saliva, its urine, and scales shed from its skin. Youngsters therefore are just as likely to be allergic to short-haired dogs as to long-haired ones. The same is true for allergic adults.

not surprisingly, these are the major sites of allergic reactions. Once a mast cell has been sensitized, another exposure to the inciting allergen can trigger the allergic response. This response involves the secretion of inflammatory chemical mediators, including histamine, leukotrienes, prostaglandins, and cytokines, among others.

Late-phase allergic reactions. It is easy to appreciate that an allergic person who visits the home of a friend with a cat would develop itchy eyes, sneezing, or wheezing within a few minutes. It is harder to appreciate that an allergic person with asthma would be exposed to a provocative allergen and then experience difficulty breathing 8 to 12 hours later. Until about a decade ago, allergic processes had been thought to be short-term responses. It is now known that mast cells exposed to allergens not only cause an acute allergic reaction but also initiate a prolonged inflammatory response known as the late-phase allergic response. This response involves the prolonged elaboration of cytokines (powerful chemical substances secreted by mast cells). Nearby lymphocytes (small white blood cells that are paramount in immune defenses) become activated to synthesize and release additional inflammatory cytokines, and other lymphocytes are attracted to the site of the reaction. An abundant type of white blood cell known as the neutrophil also migrates from the blood to participate. However, the type of blood cell that plays the most important role in asthma—and in all allergic reactions—is the eosinophil. Eosinophils are thought to be the cause of many of the inflammatory changes seen in asthma, and many investigators now think they may actually cause asthma.

The presence of eosinophils and other inflammatory cells and the chemical products they release into the tissue result in increased airway hyperresponsiveness. Thus, when an allergic reaction occurs, it leads

not only to an immediate response but to a prolonged increase in airway irritability.

Enlightened treatment

A dramatic shift in asthma treatment has taken place over the past several years. Airway reactivity and the other underlying causes of asthma have become the primary therapeutic targets; in the past, treatments were mainly symptomatic, relying on bronchodilators.

Allergen avoidance. Prevention, which addresses asthma's underlying causes, is now considered a basic part of the therapeutic approach. Thus, allergic asthmatics who avoid exposure to allergens reduce the likelihood of experiencing asthma symptoms and decrease airway reactivity.

Immunotherapy. Although there is little controversy regarding the role of immunotherapy (allergy shots) in the treatment of allergic rhinitis, immunotherapy specifically for asthma remains controversial. Many studies have addressed this approach, and one can find both positive and negative results in the medical literature. However, when allergic asthmatics sensitive to single allergens, such as cat or dog dander, are treated with purified allergen by immunotherapy, improvement is generally noted in both asthma and airway responsiveness. This finding and other recent evidence indicate that immunotherapy can be used to specifically treat allergic asthma. Moreover, immunotherapy is the only treatment that has a long-lasting effect; it is often more feasible than avoidance and, when effective, reduces the need for most medications.

Anti-inflammatory agents. Cromolyn sodium and nedocromil (a new product that became available in 1993) are agents that have the ability to reduce or prevent the release of chemical mediators from mast cells and minimize allergic inflammation. Given prophylactically, cromolyn or nedocromil can prevent allergen-induced early asthmatic responses, late asthmatic responses, and the increased airway reactivity that ordinarily results from these changes. Both drugs are highly effective agents with few side effects.

Corticosteroids (*e.g.,* beclomethasone dipropionate, flunisolide, triamcinolone acetonide) have many actions that make them useful in treating asthma—the most relevant being the ability to reduce inflammation and airway reactivity. Worldwide, inhaled corticosteroids are becoming increasingly more popular as long-term therapy for asthma, although certain questions regarding potential minimal effects on growth in children and subtle adrenal suppression are still of concern. The recently issued guidelines on asthma treatment developed by the National Asthma Education Program of the NHLBI advocate the regular use of cromolyn (or nedocromil) early in asthma treatment for virtually all asthmatics; daily use of inhaled corticosteroids is recommended as very useful in the treatment of moderate to severe asthma.

One or more than one of these agents are continuous therapies meant to reduce the need for symptomatic treatments. However, most patients with moderate to severe asthma also require symptomatic therapies in order to keep airflow under control.

Symptomatic therapies. Although beta agonists have been available for the treatment of asthma for more than three decades, it was only with the development of safer, specific beta$_2$ agonists that these compounds came into widespread use. These bronchodilator agents are selective for beta$_2$ receptors in the airway, the stimulation of which produces smooth muscle relaxation and reduced vascular permeability and thus inhibits airflow obstruction. When it was still thought that the root cause of asthma was tightening of the muscles around the airways, these drugs were widely prescribed as the sole medicine to relieve asthma attacks. Although beta agonists are still the primary symptomatic treatment for asthma, it is now recognized that the bronchodilator effects of these agents may potentially mask airway inflammation and disease progression. Studies from New Zealand have suggested that the use of beta agonists only in response to symptoms may have advantages over regular use. Recent Canadian reports suggest an increased risk of death or near death among asthmatic patients who regularly used more than two canisters of beta agonist medication per month.

It has been speculated that increases in bronchial responsiveness may have contributed to mortality in these cases. While an inhaled beta$_2$ agonist can inhibit allergen-induced early asthmatic responses, unlike cromolyn, nedocromil, and inhaled corticosteroids, it does not protect against chronic increases in nonspecific bronchial responsiveness—*i.e.,* the late-phase asthmatic response.

It is currently recommended that beta$_2$ agonists be used at the lowest possible dosage and only for as

In the past, asthma therapy was primarily aimed at alleviating acute symptoms. Today's more enlightened approach targets asthma's underlying causes. Medications used prophylactically generally reduce the need for symptomatic treatment.

long as necessary to control symptoms. However, given that these drugs are the most effective agents available for relieving bronchospasm, patients who are constantly symptomatic may need to use them regularly.

A new, long-acting beta$_2$ agonist was introduced in the U.S. in 1994. Salmeterol is a beta$_2$ agonist capable of keeping the airways open for at least 12 hours. In clinical trials salmeterol was more effective than short-acting beta$_2$ agonists (used four times a day) in decreasing symptoms. Salmeterol may be especially useful for nocturnal asthma, asthma causing the frequent need for bronchodilators, and exercise-induced asthma. Although the clinical experience with long-acting bronchodilator therapy is limited, this product should prove useful in the treatment of difficult-to-control asthma.

American physicians have gained extensive experience with the drug theophylline as a bronchodilator in the treatment of asthma in children and adults as both emergency and routine therapy. This agent works by opening up the smaller passageways in the lungs, allowing sufficient air to enter in order to normalize breathing. Theophylline is not without drawbacks, however. The drug has a very narrow therapeutic index; therefore, blood levels need to be monitored. Theophylline's clearance from the body may be modified by a variety of clinical situations, including concomitant use of such drugs as cimetidine, erythromycin, and allopurinol. Side effects, which tend to increase with increasing blood levels, include gastrointestinal discomfort, headache, nausea, vomiting, nervousness, insomnia, and seizures. It is for all these reasons that the use of theophylline has declined over the past decade.

Theophylline is nevertheless a time-tested drug that is safe and effective when prescribed and monitored appropriately by an experienced physician. Moreover, it is useful for providing prolonged bronchodilation, particularly at night. Thus, theophylline remains an important agent in the symptomatic treatment of moderate to severe asthma.

Ipratropium and atropine are the anticholinergic drugs that are available for the treatment of asthma. Anticholinergics act on the nervous system, which is believed to play a role in causing the airways to constrict during an attack. Atropine is now infrequently prescribed owing to its unacceptable side effects (e.g., dry mouth, blurred vision, central nervous system stimulation). Inhaled ipratropium has proved effective in the treatment of excessive mucous secretion (bronchorrhea). As a mild bronchodilator, ipratropium is useful in children with asthma and for chronic obstructive pulmonary disease.

Future directions in asthma treatment

Research scientists continue to look for new treatments for asthma. Several new, potent inhaled corticosteroids are near release for clinical use. Various anti-inflammatory agents that have been found to be useful in treating rheumatoid arthritis or psoriasis are currently being examined in the treatment of severe asthma. Other classes of drugs such as leukotriene antagonists, platelet-activating-factor blockers, 5-lipoxygenase inhibitors, and mucolytics are also being studied for asthma therapy, and several products are nearing the stage where they may be approved by the U.S. Food and Drug Administration. Recent reports from several groups of researchers suggest that a genetic basis for atopy may have been discovered. As allergy plays such a vital role in asthma, these discoveries may have important implications for the future diagnosis, prevention, and treatment of asthma.

With these advances the pharmaceutical approach to asthma is certain to change during the next several years. The greatest advance, however, has been the change in the aim of therapy. Until very recently, therapy was directed toward controlling patients' symptoms. Now, for the majority of asthmatics, the aim is to reduce or virtually eliminate the disease itself. This very basic conceptual change is already having profound effects on asthma therapy, and it is hoped that it will ultimately have an impact on the unacceptably high morbidity and mortality associated with the disease.

—*Michael A. Kaliner, M.D.*

Cardiovascular Disease

Cardiovascular disease, including coronary artery disease and related atherosclerotic disease of other blood vessels, continues as the primary cause of death in industrialized regions of the world. In the United States alone, it is estimated that there are 1.5 million heart attacks annually, resulting in some 500,000 deaths.

Despite a reduced incidence of myocardial infarction (heart attack) over the past two decades, as well as a significant improvement in survival after myocardial infarction attributable to advanced medical techniques, the social and economic burden of heart disease remains enormous. More and more heart attack survivors have impaired function of the heart muscle and progressive atherosclerosis of the coronary arteries. Many survivors of myocardial infarction later develop congestive heart failure, life-threatening arrhythmias, or angina pectoris (chest pains), for which they require additional medical attention and procedures. Similarly, there are hundreds of thousands of patients each year who fully avoid a myocardial infarction by coronary bypass surgery or angioplasty (catheter treatment of narrowed arteries). Their conditions are palliated but not cured. They remain at risk for occlusive disease (artery obstruction) in coronary bypass grafts, restenosis (renarrowing) of arteries that have been treated with angioplasty, and development of new narrowings in untreated vessels.

Technological advances to treat cardiovascular disease account for clear successes, but the underlying disease process seems to continue in contemporary society at a pace that has been only slightly slowed. Medical science has refocused its efforts on understanding biochemical and cellular mechanisms of atherosclerosis; it is hoped this research will lead to new methods of prevention as well as better treatments. Advances are also accruing from the improved quality of clinical research trials. Large multicenter studies are yielding statistically meaningful results to guide therapy with old and new procedures and drugs. Adequate numbers of women are for the first time being included in many of these research projects, and some new studies are focusing specifically on questions about women's cardiovascular health.

Pathogenesis of atherosclerosis

For several years the hypothesis of endothelial injury has served as a conceptual framework and a guide for laboratory studies of atherosclerosis. The endothelium is the single-cell layer that lines the inside of a blood vessel wall. Endothelial cells normally produce nitric oxide, which prevents the adhesion of blood cells and the formation of clots. Nitric oxide also promotes vasodilation, a relaxation of the arterial wall, which increases vessel diameter. In response to various adverse stimuli, including abnormal levels

241

of serum lipids, hypertension, diabetes, and cigarette smoking, the endothelium supersedes its normal function of protecting the artery and initiates the process of atherogenesis. Ultimately, a dense buildup of atherosclerotic plaque obstructs blood flow in the vessel. The molecular and cellular interactions leading up to such obstructive atherosclerosis continue to be clarified by basic research.

The current understanding of the atherosclerotic process is as follows: the injured and dysfunctional endothelium traps increased amounts of lipoprotein, a molecular complex laden with cholesterol. Oxidized low-density lipoprotein (LDL) is formed in the endothelium and contributes further to endothelial injury. Adhesive substances appear on the endothelial cell surface, and circulating monocytes (a type of white blood cell) and T lymphocytes (another type of white blood cell) from the bloodstream adhere to this surface and migrate into the arterial wall. The monocytes change their form to become macrophages. These macrophages and the T lymphocytes accumulate, and smooth muscle cells in the arterial wall migrate into the incipient plaque and begin to proliferate. The smooth muscle cells manufacture a matrix of complex proteins and protein-carbohydrate molecules. Cholesterol builds up in the cells and in the surrounding matrix. The early lesion is a lipid-rich "fatty streak," which transforms to a fibrous plaque as smooth muscle cells and matrix accumulate.

Messenger molecules known as growth factors and cytokines attract the macrophages, T lymphocytes, and smooth muscle cells into the growing atherosclerotic plaque. Numerous molecules with such "chemoattractant" properties are being discovered. Notable among them is platelet-derived growth factor, which is released by adherent blood platelet cells, the endothelium, and macrophages and attracts smooth muscle cells.

Cell proliferation is also stimulated by chemical messages. Tumor necrosis factor alpha and transforming growth factor beta are examples of the several chemical agents that stimulate proliferation of smooth muscle cells. Some substances are secreted by multiple cell types, and some serve multiple functions. Moreover, some substances can both attract cells and stimulate their proliferation; platelet-derived growth factor plays this role in the case of smooth muscle cells. Thus there is a complex interplay of chemical messages between cells as the atherosclerotic lesion progresses.

Despite this complexity, certain steps in the pathway are already being targeted for clinical intervention. The pivotal role of oxidized LDL has led to an increasing interest in antioxidant therapies to help prevent atherogenesis; e.g., the administration of specific vitamins that inhibit oxidation in the cells. Specifically targeted antibodies produced by genetic engineering techniques that block the action of platelet-derived growth factor and other growth factors might be used to modify the arterial response to injury.

Genetic insights

Although the importance of elevated serum cholesterol has been recognized for decades, the genetic basis of cholesterol elevations and other forms of abnormal lipid metabolism is still in the process of being elucidated. Genetic factors and lifestyle, particularly diet, contribute to elevations of serum cholesterol in the form of LDL cholesterol. However, not all individuals with high serum cholesterol develop heart disease, and as many as half of those with documented coronary disease do not have high serum cholesterol.

These apparent discrepancies are beginning to be understood as medical scientists learn more about a special type of lipid-carrying particle known as lipoprotein(a). Lipoprotein(a) is a genetic variant of LDL, the common cholesterol carrier in the blood. The former is a much less plentiful particle than LDL, but its serum level appears to correlate closely with the risk of heart disease. In laboratory studies lipoprotein(a) displays a strong affinity for entering into the atherosclerotic plaque and initiating blood clots.

The genetic determinants of lipoprotein(a) levels may soon be understood. A gene known as the ATHS gene has been located on human chromosome 19, and the presence of this gene correlates closely with an accentuated risk of heart attack. The risk is nearly three times higher in those who have the gene than in those without the gene. Moreover, individuals with the ATHS gene have atypically high amounts of lipoprotein(a). Screening tests may soon be available to identify families and individuals with this genetic and metabolic defect; dietary counseling and other interventions that would reduce the high risk of coronary heart disease could then be offered.

Recent findings from Framingham

The epidemiology of cardiovascular disease has been greatly clarified by the ongoing Framingham Heart Study. Over 5,000 residents of Framingham, Mass., have been studied since 1949. Their habits and health parameters (e.g., cigarette use, physical activity, body weight, blood pressure, and cholesterol levels) have been followed and correlated with clinical events for four and one-half decades.

The children of the original participants have also been studied; these offspring are now middle-aged. To some extent they show improvements in health over that of their parents, but there have also been important health declines in this second generation of subjects. Fewer smoke cigarettes, and blood pressure and cholesterol levels are lower than they were among their parents' generation. The underlying prevalence of hypertension, however, is unchanged, although

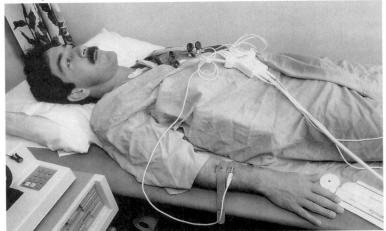

A second-generation subject in the Framingham Heart Study undergoes an electrocardiogram. Since 1949 the health, lifestyles, and cardiovascular-disease risk factors of over 5,000 residents of Framingham, Mass., have been carefully studied. The middle-aged offspring of the first-generation subjects generally smoke less and have lower blood pressure and cholesterol levels than did their parents. However, the prevalence of hypertension, obesity, and non-insulin-dependent diabetes in the offspring suggests that they may be overly complacent about their risk of heart disease.

high blood pressure is detected earlier and better controlled in the younger generation. More alarming is the fact that the second generation of men have become heavier, and they get less exercise. Moreover, both men and women show increasing rates of adult-onset diabetes, with its attendant serious complications.

Sedentary occupations and increased consumption of fattening restaurant food may account for these distressing trends. This younger generation has witnessed a falling cardiovascular death rate in the U.S. and may have become too complacent about its own cardiovascular risk.

Continuing prevention efforts

Lifestyle changes to modify risk factors continue as the basic premise behind public health efforts to prevent atherosclerosis. A diet low in cholesterol and saturated fat, weight loss, regular exercise, control of hypertension and diabetes, and cessation of cigarette smoking are all important features of preventive programs. Meanwhile, new interventions to further reduce heart disease risk are still being sought.

Antioxidants. Since oxidation of LDL appears important in atherogenesis, blocking this chemical step with so-called antioxidants could theoretically reduce the risk of cardiovascular disease. Two major studies, one in men and one in women, have shown impressive reductions in heart attack risk in those who take regular doses of vitamin E, which has antioxidant characteristics. Supplemental vitamin E in a dose of at least 100 international units per day reduced the risk of heart disease by 46% in women and by 37% in men. An earlier study found that supplemental beta-carotene reduced heart disease risk by 22%. Although these vitamin supplements are generally safe and relatively inexpensive, a public health recommendation for their use will likely await the results of carefully controlled therapeutic trials that compare the effects of antioxidants with those of placebos.

Alcohol consumption. In recent years, the potential of moderate consumption of alcohol (usually defined as two drinks a day) to reduce the risk of heart attack has garnered considerable scientific interest. Studies have compared drinking habits and heart disease rates within populations and among people residing in various countries. Red wine first received specific credit for the beneficial effects that were seen, but more recent studies have found that the favorable cardiovascular effect seems to be attributable to ethanol itself. The mechanism may be an ability of alcohol to raise levels of high-density lipoprotein (HDL) cholesterol, the "good cholesterol," which has a mitigating effect on atherogenesis. At present, however, without clear-cut findings from intervention trials, a public health recommendation for alcohol consumption is certainly unlikely, particularly considering the abuse potential and the need to weigh benefits against the burden of alcohol-related disease and of motor vehicle deaths and disabilities attributable to alcohol consumption.

Estrogen therapy. Women are largely protected from coronary disease until menopause. Then, over the course of the decade between the ages of 50 and 60, their heart attack rate gradually increases to approach that of men. Postmenopausal women have lipid profiles similar to those of men; their levels of atherogenic LDL increase, and their levels of protective HDL decrease. The abrupt decline in estrogen level after menopause probably accounts for these changes. Estrogen replacement therapy, which has been clearly shown to lower the risk of osteoporosis (bone thinning), is currently being examined for its potential to prevent heart disease in postmenopausal women. Some early studies had shown that estrogen reduces the risk of coronary heart disease and cardiovascular death in women by as much as 50%. Larger studies, with many thousands of women enrolled, are now under way. Several clinical parameters will be tracked in addition to cardiovascular events. These

243

include the effects of estrogen and progestin (which is often given in conjunction with estrogen to reduce the risk of uterine cancer) on lipid and bone metabolism as well as possible beneficial or detrimental effects on rates of various cancers. The estrogen-blocking agent tamoxifen, which is currently being studied to see if it prevents breast cancer in women at high risk for the disease, is also being evaluated for its effects on heart disease risk.

Many women in industrialized countries are already treated with supplemental estrogen after menopause, usually to reduce short-term effects such as hot flashes or to prevent osteoporosis. If, indeed, their heart disease rates are reduced as well, the public health implications would be enormous—resulting in huge reductions in both financial and human costs.

Drugs for congestive heart failure

Congestive heart failure is a condition in which the heart is unable (or fails) to pump an adequate amount of blood through the circulatory system. When the heart is not doing its job effectively, the system gets backed up, causing the lungs and peripheral tissues as well as the heart itself to become congested with fluid. Symptoms include fatigue, shortness of breath, and swelling (edema) of the feet and legs.

Angiotensin-converting enzyme (ACE) inhibitors are a class of drugs that has been used for several years to treat active congestive heart failure and to prevent recurrences. Captopril, enalopril, lisinopril, and other drugs in this group reverse many of the neurohormonal disturbances of congestive heart failure. With treatment, there is less resistance to blood flow in the peripheral arteries. This improves the pump performance of the heart and helps to reverse the build-up of salt and water in the lungs and other tissues. In conjunction with these clinical effects, ACE inhibitors

have been shown to improve the survival of heart failure patients. More recently, ACE-inhibiting agents have been shown to be effective in preserving left ventricular (cardiac muscle) function and preventing heart failure in patients with asymptomatic left ventricular dysfunction. A number of injurious processes can cause the heart to fail. In the majority of cases, congestive heart failure involves an impaired ability of the heart's left ventricle to contract and eject blood, known as systolic dysfunction. Many people with a slightly or moderately weakened heart can now completely avoid developing symptoms if treatment with ACE inhibitor therapy is begun early, when their disease is still in a subclinical stage.

The class of medications used to treat congestive heart failure known as inotropic drugs augments the force of contraction of the diseased ventricle. Vesnarinone is a new inotrope (booster of cardiac contraction). Initial studies suggest that vesnarinone not only improves the clinical condition of patients but also increases survival.

It is essential to evaluate the long-term effects of a new therapy on patient survival, even when the therapy is clearly effective for acute treatment. Phosphodiesterase inhibitors—a subcategory of inotropic drugs—inhibit activity of the enzyme phosphodiesterase. This raises the level of cyclic adenosine monophosphate in heart muscle cells and thereby stimulates contractility of the heart muscle. One of these drugs, milrinone, appeared promising for congestive heart failure, being effective as a short-term intravenous therapy for severely ill patients, but chronic use of an oral form of this drug was found to increase the rate of death when compared with a placebo.

Vasodilators relax the smooth muscle cells in the walls of veins and arterioles. Vasodilator treatment of congestive heart failure increases venous capacity,

Normal blood flow is obstructed in a plaque-laden coronary artery (right); in the open, healthy artery (far right), circulation is unimpeded. The molecular and cellular mechanisms of the complex atherosclerotic process are continuing to be clarified by cardiovascular research.

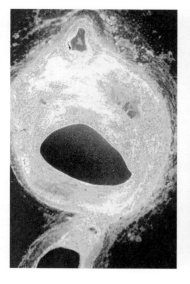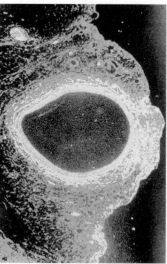

which shifts the blood volume away from the overfilled heart chambers. Arterial resistance also decreases, enabling the left ventricle to pump the blood forward more efficiently. The most effective oral agents with vasodilator action are ACE inhibitors. Flosequinan is a new vasodilator that can reduce symptoms and improve exercise capacity in the short term. It was approved by the Food and Drug Administration (FDA) in 1993 for treatment of congestive heart failure but later withdrawn from the market because it, like milrinone, appeared to be associated with increased mortality.

Aspirin: wider use

Whereas aspirin has been recommended for many years for preventing heart attacks in asymptomatic middle-aged men and in men who have already experienced an initial heart attack, doubts have remained regarding the safety and efficacy of prophylactic aspirin in women, diabetics, hypertensives, and the elderly. Results of 300 studies of aspirin therapy were recently pooled to reevaluate these subgroups. The findings from this meta-analysis showed a clear benefit for all patients at risk for heart attack and thus support the use of aspirin irrespective of sex, age, blood pressure, or presence of diabetes in patients who have already experienced a heart attack. Prophylactic aspirin use has also been shown to be beneficial in preventing stroke in patients who have had a previous stroke.

There are not adequate data to indicate whether the use of aspirin by all people who have not had a heart attack or stroke would be beneficial (although there has been such evidence for middle-aged men). Further information regarding that question, and specifically on the effects of aspirin use in women, is expected from an ongoing study of 40,000 nurses.

Anticoagulants

During the type of arrhythmia, or irregular heart rhythm, known as atrial fibrillation, blood clots may form on the walls of the inactive atrial chambers and dislodge into the bloodstream. A resulting stroke is the most frequent serious complication of atrial fibrillation. Warfarin is an anticoagulant that can prevent blood-clot formation and stroke in patients with this condition. Its use was mostly confined to the highest-risk patients, such as those who also had severe heart valve disease, until large controlled clinical trials were completed. The efficacy and safety of warfarin to prevent stroke now have been shown for a wider group of patients with atrial fibrillation, including the elderly.

Anticoagulation therapy with warfarin has become safer and more effective owing to a laboratory innovation known as the International Normalized Ratio (INR). The warfarin dose must be adjusted so that the blood coagulability is in a therapeutic range. Too little anticoagulation is ineffective, and too much anticoagulation poses a risk of hemorrhage. Blood coagulation

is measured with a test called the prothrombin time, but results can vary considerably among different laboratories owing to different potencies of the main reagent used for the test. To overcome this confusion, laboratories around the world have agreed upon a way to standardize the reporting of prothrombin times. This method, the INR, permits easy comparison of prothrombin time results between different laboratories and between different reagents used by the same laboratory. With more reliable prothrombin time measurements, patients who take anticoagulants can now be more easily maintained within a therapeutic range. For those with atrial fibrillation, this international effort means better protection against stroke and fewer bleeding complications. The advantages of the INR also apply to patients who have mechanical heart valves and receive anticoagulation therapy and to those who receive warfarin for venous disease (e.g., phlebitis).

For many years the agent that cardiologists relied upon for acute anticoagulation was heparin, which is essential during certain angiographic procedures, during heart and vascular operations, and for initial treatment of various conditions in which clots tend to form. Heparin is a rapidly acting drug that is administered intravenously or subcutaneously. It acts in conjunction with the circulating cofactor antithrombin III to inactivate thrombin, the critical enzyme in blood-clot formation. However, heparin has important limitations. It does not inhibit the thrombin that has already become bound to a growing blood clot. Furthermore, heparin does not stop thrombin from stimulating platelets (circulating blood-clotting cells) that adhere to the vessel wall and further the clotting process.

Among several new thrombin inhibitors that are under evaluation, the hirudins show particular promise. Hirudins are specific thrombin inhibitors that bind directly to thrombin. Originally purified many years ago from the medicinal leech (*Hirudo medicinalis*), hirudin is now available as the recombinant product r-hirudin and as the synthetic peptide hirulog. Unlike heparin, these hirudin derivatives directly inactivate thrombin without requiring a cofactor molecule. Hirudins neutralize thrombin even when it is already bound to a propagating clot, and they also block the ability of thrombin to stimulate platelets.

These potential advantages over heparin have prompted a growing number of clinical studies of the efficacy and safety of hirudins. In patients undergoing coronary angioplasty, r-hirudin appears to be better than heparin in preventing thrombotic occlusion of the treated artery. Hirulog is also effective in coronary angioplasty. Both hirudins have also been shown to prevent venous thrombosis after hip-replacement surgery. Although there is much potential for hirudins, as with use of other anticoagulants a risk of bleeding complications exists. Quick reversibility is therefore a necessary feature of anticoagulation therapy. An effective antidote for heparin is available, but further work is needed to develop such a reversal agent for the hirudins.

Renarrowing of arteries after angioplasty

Balloon angioplasty, also known as percutaneous transluminal coronary angioplasty, is still the mainstay of catheter therapy for coronary disease. In 1990 more than 300,000 of these procedures were performed in the U.S. alone. A tiny balloon, usually 2 to 3.5 mm (0.08 to 0.14 in) in inflated diameter, compresses the artery wall and opens a channel through the segment of atherosclerosis. Unfortunately, the technique remains limited in two major ways. First, an acceptable opening of the artery cannot be accomplished in 5% to 10% of cases. This lack of initial success varies with the expertise of the clinician who inserts the catheter and with patient selection. Although the initial success rates have improved considerably since the advent of balloon angioplasty in 1977, a significant number of patients still do not benefit. Second, the rate of restenosis (gradual renarrowing) of treated arteries remains high, at 30% to 40%.

The concept of having tools that readily open narrowed coronary arteries is attractive, and new devices that appear to do this capture the limelight in cardiology. Directional atherectomy is a method that utilizes a device that slices off strips of atheromatous material from the artery wall. Despite the theoretical advantage of actually removing artery-clogging tissue, two recent studies comparing directional atherectomy with balloon angioplasty did not show a significant difference in rates of restenosis. Moreover, one of the studies suggested a higher complication rate with the newer device. It is hoped that directional atherectomy can be refined further to achieve better results.

Rotational angioplasty utilizes a rapidly spinning device to shave off the obstructing atheromatous material, which then flows downstream in the artery and is flushed through the microcirculation. The material is ground into such tiny particles that it passes through the vascular bed of the cardiac muscle without major problems. This device is superb for treating long and complex narrowings that are not optimal for the balloon method. Though rotational angioplasty offers the advantage of higher initial success rates on difficult arteries, the restenosis rates are, unfortunately, at least as high as those for balloon treatment.

Coronary stenting has been developed to improve initial results of conventional angioplasty and prevent restenosis. A tiny cylindrical metal wire tube is placed over an angioplasty balloon, delivered to the site of coronary narrowing, and deployed by inflation of the balloon. Inflation expands the stent, which then provides mechanical support for the dilated artery. Stents improve initial results by preventing the occasional

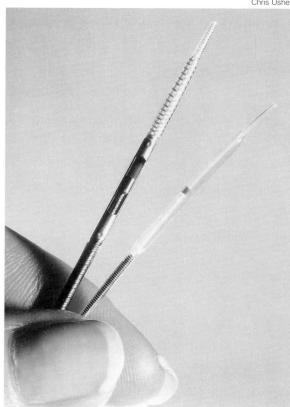

Chris Usher

An atherectomy device (left) cuts away plaque from an occluded artery. Thus far, this new tool does not appear to offer a more effective means of treating clogged coronary arteries than the angioplasty balloon (right).

acute closure of a treated artery. Long-term restenosis rates are probably improved as well. A greater initial vessel diameter is achieved with stenting, and this may account for the smaller number of patients returning with severe restenosis.

Stents are currently used for larger coronary arteries and diseased saphenous-vein bypass grafts but not for small to medium-sized coronary arteries. This is because stents have a tendency to promote clotting at the angioplasty site, and this tendency is greater in vessels with a smaller diameter and limited flow. Attempts are under way to develop more versatile stents with surface properties resistant to thrombosis.

Restenosis remains a major limitation of conventional coronary angioplasty. The artery does not become renarrowed because of a recurrence of cholesterol-laden plaque but because there is cellular proliferation that generally narrows the artery by about four months after the angioplasty procedure. In response to the inevitable mechanical injury of the arterial wall during angioplasty, a multifactorial process ensues with thrombus formation and growth factor stimulation of smooth muscle cells. Since newer methods to open an artery, including atherectomy, rotational angioplasty, and even excimer lasers (which use ultraviolet light to break the chemical bonds between arterial plaque molecules), do not appear to reduce the rate of restenosis, researchers have tried to prevent the process with pharmacological measures. To date, there has been a frustrating lack of success with various drugs, including arterial-dilating, antiplatelet, antithrombotic, and lipid-lowering agents. Efforts are now focusing on the role of growth factors, such as platelet-derived growth factor and transforming growth factor beta. If a critical growth factor can be suppressed with a drug or antibody, perhaps the restenosis process would then be interrupted.

Lifesaving implants

Ventricular tachycardia and ventricular fibrillation are the life-threatening arrhythmias most often associated with sudden cardiac death. In ventricular tachycardia the heart beats rapidly and steadily (usually between 140 and 250 beats per minute). Symptoms range from palpitations and weakness to full collapse and unconsciousness. In ventricular fibrillation, impulse conduction within the ventricle is chaotic and mechanically ineffective. Fatal cardiac arrest occurs unless resuscitative measures are immediately undertaken. Ventricular fibrillation may be preceded by ventricular tachycardia, or it may occur suddenly and without warning.

As the population ages, growing numbers of patients have either survived a heart attack or have dysfunction of the heart muscle from other causes; it is these patients who are at highest risk for sudden cardiac death. There are antiarrhythmic drugs that in some cases suppress ventricular arrhythmias, but often the available drug therapies are ineffective or not well tolerated. Additionally, it remains difficult to predict in individual patients whether a particular drug can provide long-term protection from a potentially fatal event.

Since the first use of an implanted cardioverter-defibrillator (ICD) to treat ventricular arrhythmias nearly 15 years ago, the device has continued to gain applicability and acceptance. Recent technical advances have substantially improved the performance and tolerability of the ICD. The sensing system of the most recent generation of implantable defibrillators can better distinguish between different types of arrhythmias. This permits delivery of individualized and specific treatment. With the ICD, ventricular tachycardia is initially treated by antitachycardia pacing. This low-energy pacing can terminate ventricular tachycardia without the need for a high-energy shock. A patient who has such a device implanted may not even know that this lifesaving function has occurred. If repeated antitachycardia pacing is not successful or if ventricular fibrillation is detected, the ICD delivers a shock (usually 5 to 10 joules). If it is still unsuccessful, a

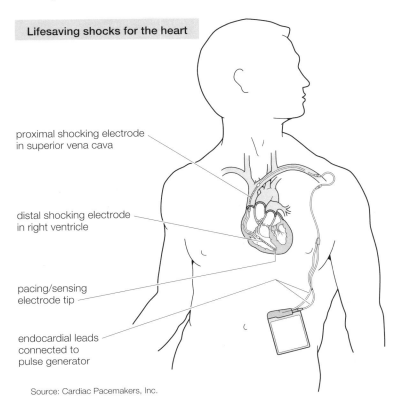

Lifesaving shocks for the heart

proximal shocking electrode
in superior vena cava

distal shocking electrode
in right ventricle

pacing/sensing
electrode tip

endocardial leads
connected to
pulse generator

Source: Cardiac Pacemakers, Inc.

Recent technical improvements in the pacing and shock-delivery capacities of the implanted cardioverter-defibrillator (ICD), as well as simplification of the surgical procedure for its implantation, are making it increasingly practical to offer this lifesaving device to a growing number of patients at high risk for sudden cardiac death. (Left) An ICD lead extending from a pulse generator, situated in a subcutaneous pocket below the rib cage, terminates in the right heart chambers, where sensitive electrodes monitor the heart rhythm. Rapid low-energy pacing can terminate an episode of ventricular tachycardia. If this is not successful or if ventricular fibrillation intervenes, higher-energy shocks are delivered at progressively greater voltages until a stable rhythm has been established.

backup or rescue shock of 30 joules is delivered. When the shock is delivered, the patient feels a strong jolt in the chest. This tiered approach is made possible by an improved computer program that can be tailored and adjusted to the needs of the individual patient by means of a radio transmitter.

With successful termination of ventricular tachycardia or fibrillation, either by pacing or shock, an abnormally slow heartbeat (bradycardia) ensues in about 30% of episodes. The improved ICD now has the capacity to act as a conventional antibradycardia pacemaker, supporting the heart rhythm until the patient's own heartbeat returns to normal. The ICD also records and later transmits the details of the arrhythmia and treatment sequence so that the cardiologist is able to closely monitor the condition of the patient.

A very conservative approach to patient selection for these lifesaving devices has generally been followed thus far. Most ICDs have been implanted in patients with spontaneous ventricular tachycardia or those with ventricular fibrillation in whom drug therapy is ineffective or not tolerated owing to side effects. Some ICDs have also been implanted in patients with syncope (blackout spells) who are shown in the laboratory to have ventricular tachycardia or ventricular fibrillation inducible by electrical stimulation. The criteria for use of the ICD will become more liberal as the surgical implantation technique becomes less invasive. Indeed, with the advent of a transvenous lead system, this trend has already begun. The original ICDs required a surgical opening into the chest cavity (open thoracotomy) for placement of the patchlike leads on the cardiac surface. In contrast, the new transvenous leads are positioned into the heart via the subclavian vein (the vein under the clavicle, or collar bone) under fluoroscopic guidance (X-ray images viewed on a fluorescent screen). The procedure is now much like the implantation of a conventional pacemaker, a relatively minor surgical procedure.

The implications of these developments are that a minor-risk ICD implant could be offered to increasing numbers of patients who are at high risk for sudden death. There may even be a prophylactic use of the device in heart patients who have not yet demonstrated ventricular arrhythmias or syncope. It should be emphasized, however, that this high-tech medical procedure is at present very costly and requires extensive follow-up care. Also, the implantation is still not completely free of risk, and even the newest devices do not always function perfectly.

Several multicenter randomized trials are now under way. These trials should clarify which patients would truly benefit from implantation of a cardioverter-defibrillator and which patients would not. Some patients with life-threatening ventricular arrhythmias have severe underlying left ventricular dysfunction and may be destined to succumb to congestive heart failure or

a new heart attack in the near future; the implantation of an ICD in patients such as these would give minimal benefit.

Implanted devices that malfunction

When medical devices that are implanted, such as an artificial heart valve or a battery-powered pacemaker, save lives, which they often do, patients are generally grateful and relieved. If the device malfunctions or is judged prone to malfunction, the sense of security otherwise afforded by the device may be replaced by fear and anxiety.

Prosthetic heart valves. Worldwide, over 80,000 patients have had their diseased heart valves surgically replaced with Björk-Shiley convexo-concave valves, which were first introduced in 1976. (All models of the convexo-concave Björk-Shiley valve were withdrawn from the market in 1986.) These prosthetic valves have a tilting disk mechanism, supported by metal struts, that controls blood flow. The valves fail when the struts crack or fracture—a situation that often leads to fatal cardiovascular collapse of the patient. Usually patients who have Björk-Shiley valves do not experience warning symptoms before such an event.

The incidence of fractured struts varies among models of this type of valve, depending on the valve opening angle and position (aortic or mitral). The highest-risk implants are the larger valves (greater than 29-mm [1.14-in] diameter), which have a disk that tilts 70°; failure rates are 1.3% to 1.4% annually. These larger (mitral) valves have been implanted in Europe but not in the U.S. Prophylactic replacement of artificial mitral valves is generally recommended because it increases life expectancy in this subset of patients. Valves that are smaller in size (less than 29 mm) with a 60° tilt or those in the aortic position pose such a low risk of fracture that prophylactic replacement is

Swedish surgeon Viking O. Björk displays the replacement heart valve he invented. Björk-Shiley convexo-concave heart valves were taken off the market in 1986 when it was discovered that a key component in some models can fracture.

not warranted. For valves with an intermediate annual fracture risk (0.3% to 0.6%)—under 29 mm, 70° valves and equal to or greater than 29 mm, 60° valves—recommendations for prophylactic reoperation depend on a patient's age and individual surgical risk. The best candidates for reoperation in the intermediate risk group are those younger than 50 years of age.

Because of the alarm caused by malfunctioning Björk-Shiley valves, attempts have been made to detect strut fractures noninvasively before a valve fails. Computer-enhanced X-rays have revealed minute defects in the struts of some asymptomatic patients. This new diagnostic procedure enables early detection of potential malfunction and selective reoperation.

Pacemaker leads. The implantation of artificial pacemakers is now quite common. These electrical devices, too, occasionally malfunction. Although the pacemaker's pulse generator, the power source that contains the battery and circuitry, is electronically more complex than the wire lead that conducts the electrical stimulus from the generator to the cardiac muscle, it is the lead that fails more often. A lead must be constructed of flexible material; once implanted, the leads are subject to physical wear. Some pacemaker leads have been found to fail at unexpectedly high rates. Those that have failed most often have been coaxial bipolar leads (containing two sets of wires), which fail owing to disruption of insulation between or around the wire components. Initially, lead failure may be manifested as abnormal sensing; thus, the device may read a spontaneous heartbeat when there is actually none. Later, as electrical energy is lost at the site of the broken insulation, the pacing system may fail to deliver adequate stimulus to maintain a heartbeat.

The consequences of pacemaker lead failure vary among patients. Many patients with pacemakers today are not fully dependent upon the device for every heartbeat. They may still have some underlying heart rhythm of their own but receive a pacemaker as a backup to prevent an occasional pause. Other patients are much more pacemaker-dependent and would collapse if their unit failed to pace. These latter patients should be considered candidates for prophylactic replacement of the lead if they have a device that is particularly prone to failure or if there are signs that leads are not functioning properly. Fortunately, the sophisticated pacemaker generator connected to the lead can assist the physician in monitoring for a break in insulation. The newer generators are capable of measuring electrical impedance along a lead and transmitting this measurement by radio signal. A very low impedance warns the physician that the lead is not functioning normally and should be replaced.

Economic influences on cardiovascular services

Health care expenditure in the United States amounts to 14% of the gross national product, which is higher than that in most other countries. Accordingly, there is a strong trend toward packaging medical care into large conglomerates of hospitals and doctors in an effort to contract for services and contain costs. It is hoped, but not yet proved, that these conglomerates can deliver high-quality services at low cost, two attributes that heretofore have seemed more divergent than compatible.

Cardiovascular services constitute an important segment of the health care budget. Heart and peripheral vascular diseases are common, and the concomitant diagnostic and therapeutic procedures are some of the most technically advanced and costly in health care. The numbers of diagnostic cardiac catheterizations and coronary angioplasties have climbed as an aggressive approach to coronary disease has become the norm. Such procedures are currently made available on a nearly unrestricted basis, including to elderly patients if their medical conditions do not otherwise pose a contraindication.

When complications arise during angioplasty or cardiac surgery, the cost of care increases considerably. Such complications usually lead to more procedures and a longer hospital stay. An example is that of acute vessel closure during coronary angioplasty, which occurs in 2% to 8% of patients undergoing the procedure. A costly emergency coronary bypass surgery is then performed as a salvage procedure, extending the hospital stay by at least a week.

There are approximately 468,000 coronary bypass operations performed annually in the U.S. Death rates after bypass vary widely; a recent study of New England hospitals found that death rates varied by as much as 400%. Rates of nonfatal complications also vary considerably. The reasons for such wide differences thus far have been somewhat elusive. Patient selection, skill of the surgical team, and postoperative nursing care all contribute to the outcome. Hospitals with large caseloads of coronary bypass operations generally achieve better results than smaller programs, presumably because of the expertise and experience of surgeons and the availability of skilled support services.

For these reasons, the federal government and private insurers now seek to identify regional centers that can handle a high volume of cardiovascular procedures with low complication rates and containable costs. Consequently, hospital administrators and doctors are scrambling to gather their performance data in the hope that they can be presented in the most favorable possible light to potential payers. It will be to the public's great advantage if health care delivery systems with the best medical outcomes are selected by this process. Unfortunately, however, there are reasons to be skeptical when the primary forces driving these policies are economic.

—*Marc K. Effron, M.D.*

Perspective on Pesticides

by Philip J. Landrigan, M.D., M.Sc.

The release in mid-1993 of the report "Pesticides in the Diets of Infants and Children," written by a panel of experts convened by the National Research Council of the U.S. National Academy of Sciences (NAS), prompted renewed scrutiny of the effects of these chemicals on human health. Although this particular document focused on the special vulnerabilities of the young—because of their smaller, developing bodies and the unique characteristics of their diets—it also questioned some of the general procedures used to determine the safety of pesticides. The report, bolstered by new findings on a possible link between DDT and breast cancer and by further conclusions about the health effects of the herbicide Agent Orange, helped spur a reevaluation of U.S. policies and regulations regarding all such chemicals.

Many chemicals, many uses

Pesticides are used widely in nations around the world. More than 600 different products—insecticides, herbicides, and fungicides—are currently registered with the U.S. Environmental Protection Agency (EPA). In 1992 in the U.S. alone, approximately 400 million kg (800 million lb) of pesticides were used in agriculture, and additional quantities were applied in other settings, both indoors (homes, schools, hospitals) and out (lawns and gardens, forests, public lands).

When they are applied effectively, pesticides can control insects, fungi, bacteria, weeds, rodents, and other pests. Pesticides have reduced infestations, limited the spread of disease, and contributed to dramatic increases in yields for many food crops, thus increasing the amount of food available and variety of the diet. Many pesticides, however, are harmful to the environment, and their use has caused severe damage to ecosystems. Many are also known to be toxic to humans, and others are suspected of being toxic. They can produce a wide range of harmful effects on human health, including acute and chronic injury to the nervous system, lung damage, injury to the reproductive organs, dysfunction of the immune and endocrine systems, birth defects, and cancer.

Most pesticides in commercial use today are synthetic chemical products, the majority derived from petroleum. (There are also naturally occurring pesticides produced by plants and other organisms.) The era of modern pesticides began in the 19th century when sulfur compounds were developed as fungicides. In the late 19th century, arsenic compounds were introduced to control the insects that attack fruit and vegetable crops; for example, lead arsenate was used widely on apples and grapes. All of these substances were highly toxic. In the 1940s the chlorinated hydrocarbon pesticides, most notably DDT (dichlorodiphenyltrichloroethane), were introduced. For a time DDT and similar chemicals were used extensively in agriculture and in the control of malaria and other insectborne diseases. Because they had little or no immediate apparent toxicity, they were widely hailed and initially were believed to be safe.

With the publication of Rachel Carson's prophetic book *Silent Spring* in 1962, the potential of the chlorinated hydrocarbon pesticides for long-term toxicity and for accumulation in the food chain became recognized. It was shown, for example, that DDT caused reproductive failure in eagles and ospreys, species that had accumulated large doses of DDT because of their position high in the food chain. In 1972 DDT was banned in the U.S. by the newly created EPA. Heavy application has continued, however, in many nations, and especially in less developed countries.

In most industrialized countries today, the principal classes of insecticides in use are organophosphates, carbamates, and pyrethroids. Unlike the chlorinated hydrocarbons, these compounds are short-lived in the environment and do not "bioaccumulate"; *i.e.*, build up in body tissues and in the food chain. Some of them, however, can affect the nervous system, causing serious acute and chronic toxicity.

Insecticide use has declined in recent years, reflecting the adoption of integrated pest-management systems. Such programs emphasize the use of nonchemical means of pest control as partial or complete replacements for pesticides. In agriculture, for example, integrated pest management may involve crop rotation and the use of resistant plant strains. In homes and buildings such programs incorporate the regular cleanup of food residues, the sealing of foundation cracks, and good maintenance. Unlike insecticides, fungicides have continued in steady use, and herbicide use has increased dramatically. Further, there are considerable discrepancies among countries in the patterns of pesticide use, despite the increasing globalization of food markets and efforts to standardize regulations across borders.

Balancing risks and benefits

The response to the dual nature of pesticides—to their combination of benefits and toxicity—has been to develop an extensive regulatory system. In the U.S. the principal law governing these substances is the Federal Insecticide, Fungicide, and Rodenticide Act (FIFRA), enacted in 1947 and amended several times since then. (Pesticide-control provisions are also contained in the Federal Food, Drug, and Cosmetic Act of 1958.) Intended by Congress to be a "balancing," or risk-benefit, statute, FIFRA declares that a pesticide must not cause "unreasonable adverse effect" on the environment or on human health. According to the law, the balancing process must take into account "the economic, social and environmental costs as well as the potential benefits of the use of any pesticide."

The key to pesticide control under FIFRA is a registration process; each potential use of every pesticide must be registered with the EPA. For a pesticide to be registered, its manufacturers must submit data on intended uses and potential risks. Pesticides intended for use on food crops must also be assigned a "tolerance" by the EPA, defined as the maximum amount of residue of the pesticide permitted to be present on or in a particular foodstuff. Tolerances, established by weighing economic and agricultural considerations against concerns for human health, are the single most important mechanism by which the U.S. government controls levels of pesticide residues in food.

The Alar controversy

The possibility that chronic exposure to pesticide residues in food might have long-term effects on human health burst upon the public consciousness in the U.S. in 1989 with revelations about Alar (daminozide). A synthetic chemical once widely used on fruit crops, especially apples, Alar acts as a growth retardant, delaying crop ripening and thus prolonging shelf life. The compound was not adequately tested for toxicity before it was introduced in the U.S. in 1963. Subsequently, toxicity studies were begun by the manufacturer, but they were poorly designed and produced inadequate data on the health effects of the chemical. Meanwhile, the product remained on the market.

In February 1989 scientists with the Natural Resources Defense Council (NRDC), a nongovernmental U.S. environmental organization, reported that the principal metabolic by-product of Alar, a compound called unsymmetrical dimethylhydrazine (UDMH), was a potent carcinogen (cancer-causing agent). The finding received intense publicity because of widespread concern that children, in particular, were at high risk of exposure to Alar in their diets. The NRDC report noted that children eat six or seven times more fruit than adults and drink 18 times more apple juice.

A vigorous counterattack was launched by the pesticide-manufacturing industry, which claimed that the

(Below) A swarm of locusts darkens the sky over the arid Ethiopian plains. After years of battling these destructive pests with chemicals, scientists are now working to develop alternative means of control. One strategy relies on using natural insect enemies, such as toxic fungi. The dead grasshopper at left is a victim of one such fungus; its remains contain fungal spores that will infect and kill other grasshoppers.

(Left) United States Department of Agriculture; (right) Gianni Tortoli—
Photo Researchers

An expert panel concluded in 1993 that the standards used to assess the risks of pesticide residues in food fail to take into account the dietary patterns of children and the special vulnerability of their developing bodies.

NRDC findings were inaccurate. Further assessment of Alar and UDMH was, however, undertaken by the National Toxicology Program of the U.S. Public Health Service. In this scrupulous and thorough evaluation, the carcinogenicity of Alar was fully confirmed, supporting the NRDC findings. It indicated that American children had indeed been extensively exposed to this carcinogenic pesticide in their diets. Shortly thereafter, Alar was withdrawn from the market.

Risks to children

In 1988 the U.S. Congress directed the NAS to undertake a systematic study of pesticides and children's health. A committee of experts was assembled to address the issue. Its long-awaited report, published in June 1993, reached the following conclusions:

• The pesticide-regulatory system in the U.S. is seriously flawed. The basic problem lies in the approach to the setting of tolerances. The committee found that too often the legally mandated balancing of economic interests against health concerns unduly favors agricultural interests. Consequently, the legally permitted levels of pesticide residues in many foods substantially exceed safe levels, in some cases by a factor of several hundred. The committee thus recommended that the process for setting tolerances be revised.

• The committee also found that the tolerance-setting process pays little heed to the special susceptibilities and unique dietary exposures of infants and children. Indeed, the experts observed that the current system of assessing the health risks of pesticides is based almost entirely on the diets and susceptibilities of adults. They therefore recommended that the system

of risk assessment be revamped to provide specific protection for the health of infants and children.

• The committee expressed its concern about the inadequate testing of many pesticides before they are marketed. Especially lacking were data on long-term hazards affecting young people. The panel thus recommended that such gaps be closed and that more accurate laboratory testing methods be developed. It also recommended that testing look beyond cancer to assess other potential adverse effects of pesticides, such as effects on the neurological, endocrine, and immune systems.

Legislative reform

In September 1993 the administration of Pres. Bill Clinton announced proposals for revising the laws that govern U.S. policies on pesticides. Among the suggested changes were a provision for quicker review of pesticides already on the market and a ban on the export of chemical products that are prohibited in the U.S. The administration would continue use of the concept of "negligible risk" (defined as the level of exposure that could be expected to cause one case of cancer in one million people over a lifetime) as the basic standard of safety but would also reduce the levels of proof required. No proposal caused as much controversy, however, as the administration's suggestion for modification of the so-called Delaney clause, which in its strictest interpretation can prohibit all harmful pesticide residues in processed foods.

The Delaney clause, passed into law in 1958 as an amendment to the Federal Food, Drug, and Cosmetic Act, bans from processed foods any pesticide that has been shown to cause cancer in humans or animals. The clause has from the beginning been highly controversial, with representatives of the pesticide and food industries arguing that it is too inflexible since it totally prohibits in processed food even the smaller amounts of chemicals that may be allowed in raw foodstuffs. Environmentalists, however, have long considered the Delaney clause a bulwark of public health and environmental protection. For many years the EPA did not strictly enforce the Delaney clause and allowed very low, or "de minimis," levels of pesticides in processed foods—levels that in the agency's opinion posed no more than a "minimal risk" to health. In 1992, however, a U.S. appeals court ruled that this approach directly contravened the intent of the Delaney clause and thus was not legal.

There are two ways in which the U.S. Congress might decide to deal with the Delaney issue. One would be simply to reaffirm the clause. The alternative would be to replace the clause with a regulatory process based on quantitative risk assessment, an approach by which cancer risk to humans is computed on the basis of results from animal studies. Such an approach would mandate that quantitative consideration be given to dietary exposures and to the hazards of pesticides as a formal component of the regulatory process for processed foods. It would take into account carcinogenic potential but would also consider toxic effects other than cancer.

The pesticide and food industries favor the latter process, which they claim would be more realistic than the approach embodied in the Delaney clause. Environmentalists, however, are concerned that adoption of a regulatory program based on risk assessment would perpetuate the unsatisfactory balancing approach that now operates in the setting of tolerances. Quantitative risk assessment would be more acceptable to environmentalists if it insisted that tolerances be based on health, rather than economics, and that they be designed specifically to protect children, as was recommended by the NAS.

Public health advocates also argue that any new legislation should include so-called sunset provisions, which would require that registration be removed from the most toxic pesticides within a few years. At the heart of this proposal are data indicating that a preponderance of pesticide-related health risks can be attributed to a relatively small number of substances, largely older compounds introduced before the current requirements for premarket testing were in place.

Further findings

Concern about the safety of pesticides was also heightened during recent months by two other reports. One of these involved the release of data suggesting a correlation between DDT and breast cancer. The other, concerning the much-studied Agent Orange, reached conclusions about the relation of the herbicide to a number of diseases suffered by those exposed to it.

DDT and breast cancer. The finding of a possible association between exposure to DDT and breast can-

cer in women was made public in April 1993. Studies undertaken in the New York City metropolitan area found that breast cancer was four times more likely to occur in women with the highest body concentrations of DDT as compared with those with the lowest. This striking finding represented the first instance in which a specific environmental factor had been correlated with human breast cancer. A subsequent study conducted in California found evidence for an association between DDT and breast cancer in white and African-American women but not in Asian women.

This and other recent research suggest that some chemicals, DDT among them, might affect the human body by mimicking the action of natural hormones such as estrogen. Indeed, Rachel Carson's observation of a link between DDT and impaired reproduction in eagles and ospreys may in fact have reflected the estrogenic activity of DDT in those species. The recent data on DDT and breast cancer suggest that the estrogenic risks of certain pesticides might extend to humans.

Agent Orange and cancer. The herbicide Agent Orange was used widely by U.S. forces in the Vietnam War to defoliate the jungle and destroy food crops. It is a fifty-fifty mixture of two herbicides—2,4-dichlorophenoxyacetic acid (2,4-D) and 2,4,5-trichlorophenoxyacetic acid (2,4,5-T). The latter was contaminated during its manufacture by 2,3,7,-8-tetrachlorodibenzo-p-dioxin (dioxin), a highly toxic chemical and a potent carcinogen. Dioxin contamination was especially heavy in 2,4,5-T produced in the early years of the war.

After the war U.S. veterans began to express concerns that health problems experienced by them and their children—particularly birth defects—might have been caused by exposure to Agent Orange and dioxin. In addition, studies were published suggesting

In West Islip, N.Y., women study a map showing the distribution of breast cancer cases, seeking a pattern that might provide clues to the unusual prevalence of the disease on Long Island, which has a higher rate of breast cancer than other parts of New York state. The possible contribution of environmental factors— including exposure to the insecticide DDT—is coming under increased scrutiny.

Vic DeLucia—The New York Times

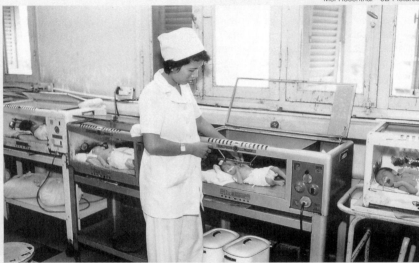

A pediatric hospital in Ho Chi Minh City, Vietnam, treats an unusual number of cases of birth defects and childhood cancers—conditions attributed to exposure to the herbicide Agent Orange, used as a defoliant during the Vietnam War. U.S. veterans of that war have long complained of similarly attributed health problems. A panel of experts convened by the National Academy of Sciences in 1991 concluded that there were sufficient data to support a link between Agent Orange and certain cancers—but not enough to support an association with birth defects.

that birth defects in Vietnamese children might be related to such exposures. A study of chemical industry workers involved in 2,4,5-T production, conducted by the U.S. National Institute for Occupational Safety and Health, found excess deaths (*i.e.,* more than could be due to chance) from two kinds of cancer—soft-tissue sarcoma and non-Hodgkin's lymphoma.

To further assess the hazards of Agent Orange, the NAS convened a panel of experts in 1991. After evaluating the epidemiological and toxicological data, this committee concluded that there was strong evidence for a positive association between herbicide exposure in Vietnam and soft-tissue sarcoma, non-Hodgkin's

lymphoma, and Hodgkin's disease. The committee also concluded that there was strong evidence for a link between Agent Orange and the skin condition chloracne (characterized by eruptions produced by exposure to chlorine) and for a link between exposure to 2,4,5-T and the metabolic disease porphyria cutanea tarda (a liver ailment that also produces skin lesions). In addition, the committee found weaker evidence of association between exposure to herbicides and cancer of the lungs, larynx, and trachea, as well as prostate cancer and multiple myeloma. The data did not permit conclusions on an association between Agent Orange and some diseases—*e.g.,* immune disorders, leukemia, and birth defects—and suggested no association with others—*e.g.,* cancers of the skin, bladder, and gastrointestinal system.

The committee based its findings on research carried out on industrial and agricultural workers exposed to Agent Orange at high levels over long periods of time and not on Vietnam veterans, whose actual exposure to the substance was more difficult to determine. Nonetheless, the U.S. Department of Veterans Affairs accepted its conclusions for purposes of determining disability benefits.

An ongoing story

Pesticides will continue to be a two-edged sword, permitting more food to be produced for the world's growing population but also posing substantial risks to ecosystems and to human health. With continuing scientific advances, new toxic effects will undoubtedly be recognized. However, improvements in testing methods should also enable more accurate assessments of the health hazards of environmental chemicals. In the future, therefore, regulations regarding pesticide use may be based on more precise data than are currently available.

"Well, I'm not sure. . . . I guess it's been washed."

Dentistry

The art and science of dentistry are evolving rapidly to meet the challenges of the 1990s. The needs and desires of dental patients are being served by innovative materials, improved techniques, and emerging technologies. One result of the tremendous amount of new information and knowledge is that many dentists are narrowing the focus of their areas of expertise. While this increased specialization may require a patient to see more than one dentist in order to complete a comprehensive treatment process, the increased quality of care is well worth it.

Current trends in dentistry are governed by several guiding principles. By far the most important is that maximum effort should be made to conserve healthy tooth structures. As preparation techniques improve, there is less need to remove healthy enamel and dentin, the materials composing the principal mass of a tooth, along with the decayed portions; dentists are therefore able to preserve more of the natural tooth than was possible in the past. Likewise, innovative methods of restoration involve *adding* ceramic materials to the existing dental structures rather than *removing* large portions of the teeth prior to treatment. Other guiding principles in dentistry today are an emphasis on achieving the most natural-looking results possible and increasing the involvement of patients in planning their own treatment.

Doing away with the drill

Dread of the dental drill causes many people to avoid seeking care until their problems become too painful to endure. In fact, until relatively recent times, much of dental treatment was essentially driven by disease and pain; one went to the dentist only when the agony of a decayed tooth was too intense to bear or the swelling of the face too unsightly to tolerate. The course of treatment was decided upon by the dentist with little patient involvement. Procedures were designed for rapid relief of the problem, even if this entailed some discomfort for the patient.

Today's dentistry, on the other hand, is constantly seeking ways to make a visit to the dentist's office more comfortable. Toward this end, technology to replace the drill has always been considered desirable. One such technology involves microabrasion, the use of a fine stream of tiny aluminum oxide particles, to remove decayed tooth material. Not only is it virtually painless—in most cases, no anesthetic is needed—it is also faster than conventional drilling.

Microabrasion is based upon the principle that a moving particle has an energy equal to half of its mass times the square of its velocity. While the aluminum oxide particles used in this procedure have a negligible mass, their velocity upon exiting the nozzle of the instrument is tremendous. The kinetic energy stored in the velocity of the particles is directed at the tooth surface. As the particles strike this surface, only very tiny portions of the decay are abraded, one layer at a time. The fine focus of the stream of particles permits precise targeting of only those areas affected by cavities. Since the decay is removed layer by layer, under dry conditions, the dentist can see exactly how much of the tooth structure is being removed and is able to determine the minimum depth required for adequate preparation of the tooth. The purity of the aluminum oxide that is used ensures minimal toxicity.

As noted above, microabrasive preparation is faster than preparation with the conventional drill—and far more comfortable for the patient. The air that propels the particles is warmed to body temperature and causes no thermal sensitivity when it touches the tooth. The particles themselves are too large to enter the dentinal canals and thus do not enter into the tooth itself. Because decay is much softer than healthy tooth structure, it is air-abraded preferentially. In most situations there is no need for a local anesthetic, thus freeing the patient from the unpleasant after-effects—the droopy or swollen feeling of the cheeks or tongue—that often follow a dental appointment.

Microabrasion leaves the enamel and dentin with a somewhat rough surface texture. This surface is ideal for the bonding procedures that are commonly used in filling teeth. Furthermore, tooth structure removal is kept to a minimum, a conservative approach that offers the best prognosis for long-lasting, natural-looking restorations. Microabrasive preparation, however, is indicated only for small and moderate cavities and for the replacement of composite resin fillings. It is not applicable to preparing teeth for crowns or removing old amalgam fillings.

Spare the tooth

Ultraconservative treatment—achieving maximum results with minimum removal of healthy tooth structure—would seem to be the natural goal of all dentistry, but it is only in recent years that materials and techniques have advanced to a point where it is a realistic objective. Traditional amalgam fillings required a certain bulk if they were to be effective. Thus, the preparation of the teeth often included the removal of small areas of otherwise healthy enamel in order to create space for the necessary bulk of the filling. Composite resin fillings, on the other hand, require no minimum size of preparation; they can be successfully placed in the tiniest of pits and grooves and, once bonded, will exhibit a tremendous tenacity regardless of bulk.

In the past the preparation of a tooth for a crown (cap) required that the outer portion of the tooth be removed to make space for the restoration. With conventional crowns, which were made of porcelain fused to metal, a 1.5–2-mm (0.06–0.08-in)-thick layer of tooth structure had to be removed. The dental tissue being removed often was weak or decayed, but in some cases healthy enamel had to be sacrificed as well.

Recently introduced leucite-reinforced porcelains reduce the required thickness of removal to one millimeter (0.04 in) or less. (Leucite is a white or gray mineral consisting of a silicate of potassium and aluminum.) Crowns made of these materials need no metal substructure. Because the crown itself can be made far thinner (porcelain-fused-to-metal crowns require a relatively thick layer of opaque porcelain for masking the dark color of the metal), less of the natural tooth needs to be removed. And while traditional crowns are cemented to the remaining tooth with a relatively insoluble, nonreactive agent, the leucite porcelains are bonded to the tooth with a resin material that interacts chemically with both the porcelain crown and the tooth. In addition to their tooth-sparing properties, leucite-reinforced porcelains also provide an advantage in terms of appearance. The color of the porcelain is selected to match the natural shade of the teeth. Since leucite porcelains are partially translucent, they transmit the color of the underlying tooth.

Leucite-reinforced porcelain is also being used to create veneers for teeth that are discolored, too small, or unevenly shaped or spaced. Previously, the preparation of teeth for veneers required removal of $\frac{1}{2}$ mm or more of a tooth's surface to accommodate the thickness of the porcelain. With leucite-reinforced porcelain, however, the veneer need be only $\frac{1}{2}$ mm thick at most. In many cases the amount of tooth structure that must be removed is so small that patients require no anesthetic.

This innovative material is even strong enough to be used on the molars, which must withstand tremendous pressures during biting and chewing. A variety of processes (chewing extremely coarse foods, habitual grinding or clenching of the teeth) can cause the back teeth to become unduly worn down. When these posterior teeth no longer support the bite, the front teeth also begin to wear down in an abnormal fashion. To correct this problem, the biting surface of the posterior teeth must be built up by means of onlays. Not only is leucite-reinforced porcelain durable enough to be used in restoring the vertical dimension of molars, but once it is bonded to the tooth surface, it becomes an integral part of the dental structure and is unlikely to break off. Except where it is necessary to replace old or faulty fillings, the dentist can cover healthy molars without any prior preparation, thus preserving as much healthy tooth structure as possible.

Say "cheese"

Their faces and smiles play important roles in the way that people are perceived and also contribute much to their self-images. The accepted picture of youth and health would not be complete without sparkling white teeth. Thus, it is no surprise that whitening of the teeth should be one of the most popular dental procedures performed. Most dentists offer tooth whitening, and millions of patients have undergone this procedure.

Discoloration of the teeth is dependent on several factors. Certain habits, such as smoking or chewing tobacco, tend to yellow the teeth rapidly and deeply. Coffee, tea, colas, and certain foods, such as beets and pomegranates, as well as food products that contain artificial colorings, also tend to stain the teeth. Obviously, the more that the teeth are subjected to staining influences, the faster they will discolor. Generally, yellow and brown stains are fairly readily removed through whitening procedures, while gray stains tend to be more resistant to treatment.

A number of safe and effective whitening systems have been developed during the past few years. Most involve bathing the teeth in a whitening gel for several hours, usually overnight. Important factors that govern the safety of the procedure include the type of whitening agent that is used and the acidity of the gel. The active ingredient should not be capable of destroying tissue and should react relatively slowly with the stains, which are located in between the enamel crystals of the tooth. Rapidly acting chemicals will dry the tooth surface excessively, making it more brittle.

The most commonly used whitening agent is 10% carbamide peroxide, which will react completely over several hours. Because of the difficulty of keeping such a liquid in contact with the teeth for an extended period, the agent is delivered via a thick gel. The more viscous (sticky and glutinous) the gel, the greater the intimate contact between the whitening agent and the tooth and the more rapid the whitening process. In terms of acidity or alkalinity, the gel should be neutral; any deviation of pH will cause irritation of the gums and will make the teeth overly sensitive.

Before beginning the procedure the dentist will check the teeth and gums to make sure that whitening is appropriate and that it will be effective. Then a custom-fitted thin acrylic tray is fabricated on a model of the patient's teeth. At bedtime, after brushing and flossing, the patient fills the tray with whitening material; the tray is then fitted over the teeth and worn overnight.

The effects of the whitening are often clearly visible after the first night, but the entire treatment takes from two to four weeks for most patients. The effects last several years, after which a shorter course of treatment (usually two to three nights) will restore the desired color. In addition, a maintenance program can prolong the effects of the treatment. Special whitening toothpastes contain decolorants (*e.g.*, Calprox) that help to eliminate stains from teeth that have already been whitened.

In the past the best remedy for stained teeth was to cover them with lighter-colored crowns. This process involved removing large portions of the enamel and dentin. With chemical whitening, only the stain molecules are eliminated; the tooth structures and surfaces remain intact. This is an important consideration because most patients seeking whitening have relatively strong and healthy teeth. The immense popularity of these lightening procedures is providing dentists with an opportunity to determine the long-term benefits and to fine tune the treatment in order to make the application time shorter and the duration of the effect longer.

A few years ago a number of commercial tooth-bleaching products were removed from the market. These had been sold directly to consumers in supermarkets and drug stores, and some contained materials that were potentially caustic to the teeth or the oral tissues. Because these products did not require the supervision of a dentist, harmful effects could not be quickly detected.

Picture this

Some of the least pleasant moments in the course of the dental exam occur as the dentist, through a series of grunts, sighs, and often unintelligible comments, describes the condition of the patient's teeth to an assistant. These mysterious utterances are all the more disconcerting to the patient because he or she cannot observe what is being described. In recent years, however, the introduction of intraoral cameras has helped both patients and dentists to readily view the condition of the teeth and gums. The newest and most sophisticated instruments consist of a very small television camera (in a sterilizable casing), a monitor to display a video image, and a light source to illuminate the darker reaches of the mouth. The image is a greatly magnified full-color view of any structure at

which the camera is directed. For the dentist this is an invaluable aid to diagnosis; teeth and gums can be examined in far greater detail than was ever possible before. Even the smallest problems can be seen, usually at an early stage when treatment can prevent extensive damage from occurring.

The intraoral video camera also serves as an educational tool. The dentist or hygienist can conduct a real-time visual tour of the mouth, showing the patient an image of his or her own teeth on the TV monitor. This allows patients to understand more fully the impact of regular brushing and flossing (or lack thereof) and the processes involved in tooth decay and gum disease. As patients become more involved in the evaluation of their oral status, they are likely to take better and more regular care of their own teeth.

The intraoral camera also helps patients understand why certain treatments are required. While it may take many minutes to explain the particular problems of a tooth, often these TV pictures are worth the proverbial thousand words; even to the untrained eye, the damaged condition of the tooth or the gums is readily visible. By eliminating the mystery and the fear of the unknown, intraoral cameras also help make patients more comfortable.

The images may be printed on thermal paper and stored in an album as part of the patient's dental record, stored on a floppy or hard disk, or kept on a WORM (write once, read many times) optical disk and available to view at the touch of a button. These pictures are especially useful for monitoring a changing clinical situation over a period of time and evaluating the rate of the change. Long-term documentation of the state of the teeth enables analysis both of the individual patient's condition and of disease processes in general.

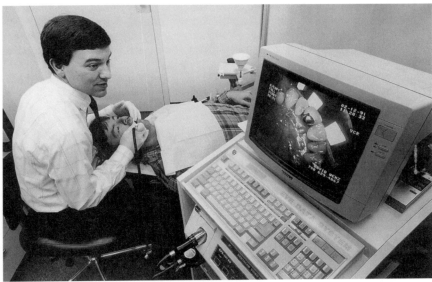

A dentist uses an intraoral camera to produce a video image of a filling on the lingual (tongue) side of a patient's tooth. An invaluable aid to diagnosis, the tiny camera enables dental practitioners to examine teeth and gums in far greater detail than was previously possible. The video display is also useful for explaining problems and procedures to patients.

Rich Chapman—Chicago Sun-Times

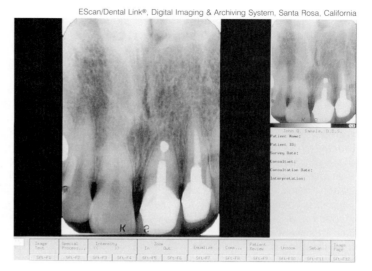

EScan/Dental Link®, Digital Imaging & Archiving System, Santa Rosa, California

An intraoral radiograph is displayed on a computer screen. By means of a system that includes a computer, a digital sensor, and a special software program, a dentist not only can review X-rays on-screen but also can store them efficiently on an optical disk that holds up to 30,000 images. The same technology makes it possible to transmit dental X-rays across town or across a continent. The application of computer technology and telemetric communications has revolutionized the practice of dentistry.

Telediagnosis

Dentistry has not been left out of the technological revolution that has been sweeping the health sciences. The increasing use of computerized instruments and electrodiagnostic tools during regular checkups is changing dental treatment from a catch-up process to an interceptive one; many dental problems now can be detected and treated relatively easily even before they have been noticed by the patient. Also, as noted above, there has been a tendency toward increasing specialization among dental practitioners. A number of recognized specialties now exist, along with an even greater number of specific interest areas within which individual professionals have expertise.

In order to provide the best possible diagnosis or treatment, a dentist may wish to consult an expert in a specific field. The consultant may practice hundreds of kilometers away, however, making it impractical, if not impossible, for the specialist to examine the patient in person. Fortunately, in dentistry most clinical situations can be well described by means of pictures or radiographs, and a consultation can be undertaken without the patient's being physically present. The major problem in the past has been the quick, efficient transportation of these images from the treating dentist to the consultant and back again.

Intraoral cameras and radiovisiography (low-radiation X-ray) devices provide digitized images highly suitable for electronic transfer via the information superhighway. Recently a group of dental practitioners formed an electronic interchange called the Dental Link Network to facilitate the exchange of information and opinions. Using a computer, a modem, and the "Link" software program, the dentist seeking an expert opinion sends the relevant images to a consultant. The consultant examines the pictures and radiographs, enters treatment or diagnostic suggestions into the computer, and retransmits the package to the requesting dentist. At all times the identities of the patient and the requesting dentist are kept confidential. The exchange of information is rapid so that treatment need not be delayed. The system provides clear advantages for both the patient and the treating dentist; expert opinions can be solicited prior to commencement of treatment, and all available clinical options can be considered and, if necessary, modified to suit the situation. Distance from a major urban center or a particular specialist is not a deterrent to consultation.

The future

The pace of dental research and development has never been greater; more new materials and techniques have been introduced in the last 10 years than in the previous 100. Some new developments on the horizon include home electric toothbrushes that floss as well as brush, argon lasers to make fillings harder and produce them faster, and porcelain materials that are strong enough to use in place of metals. Even with all the advances that have taken place in recent years, the practice of dentistry continues to evolve at a rapid rate.

—*George A. Freedman, D.D.S.*

Diabetes

Diabetes mellitus is a medical condition characterized by an abnormally high concentration (level) of glucose (sugar) in the blood. For diagnosis a blood specimen is obtained in the morning with the subject having eaten nothing since bedtime (a fasting blood glucose specimen). In healthy individuals the concentration of glucose in such a blood specimen should not exceed 140 mg/dl (milligrams of glucose per deciliter of blood). When it does and when the abnormal value is verified by another abnormal value on a second occasion, the diagnosis of diabetes mellitus is justified. The type of test that is performed and the interpretation of the test result can be changed so as to identify other individuals with lesser degrees of glucose intolerance (sometimes called borderline diabetes). Except in the case of pregnancy, modified tests (including the so-called glucose tolerance test) are not recommended as a component of standard medical care.

When the blood glucose elevations are extreme (200–300 mg/dl or more), the person with diabetes usually has the characteristic symptoms of excessive urinary volume (polyuria), excessive thirst (polydipsia), and excessive eating (polyphagia) associated with hyperglycemia (high blood glucose concentration). Diabetes mellitus is not a single disease with a single cause but has many different causes, both genetic and environmental, all of which result in an elevated blood glucose concentration. This makes it unlikely that a single treatment will be appropriate for all persons with diabetes or that a single cure or preventive strategy will be discovered.

Two types

So that the diagnosis and treatment can be simplified, most people with diabetes are grouped into one of two categories: (1) those with insulin-dependent diabetes mellitus, abbreviated IDDM and sometimes called type I diabetes, and (2) those with non-insulin-dependent diabetes mellitus (NIDDM), also called type II diabetes. Although there are undoubtedly subgroups within these categories, subgrouping is generally unnecessary for routine medical purposes. There are between 12 million and 14 million Americans today with diabetes. Of these, about 5% (700,000 individuals) have IDDM, while the vast majority (approximately 95%) have NIDDM. About half of the 11 million to 13 million Americans with NIDDM are not aware that they have the condition because the symptoms are often subtle and not specific for diabetes. The prevalence of diabetes is not uniform throughout the world or across different cultures and ethnic groups. In general, IDDM is more prevalent in the Scandinavian countries and less prevalent in the tropics. NIDDM is more prevalent in urbanized, overnourished Western cultures. Diabetes is unusually widespread among Native Americans; notably, the incidence of NIDDM among the Pima Indians of Arizona is the highest in the world, with nearly half of the adult population being affected.

Insulin-dependent. Persons with IDDM are usually young (under 35 years of age) at the time of diagnosis and often have the characteristic symptoms noted above that are associated with extreme hyperglycemia. The diagnosis is straightforward since the fasting blood glucose is often 300 mg/dl or above. When the disease is fully developed, most patients have a complete absence of the hormone insulin. Since insulin is produced exclusively by the beta cells (ß cells) of the islets of Langerhans in the pancreas, the absence of insulin in the blood implies that the insulin-producing ß cells are nonfunctioning or have been destroyed. In most instances this destruction results from the body's antibodies' being directed against its own ß cells or their contents, as if they were foreign invaders. Thus, IDDM is generally considered to be one of the group of so-called autoimmune diseases.

The cause of the autoimmune destruction of the ß cells is unknown. There is a definite hereditary component, but heredity alone is not the total answer. Most people with IDDM do not have a history of diabetes in their immediate family, and diabetes is not invariably transmitted from parent to offspring. Although a predisposition for IDDM is associated with genes in the HLA-D region of the short arm of chromosome 6, no specific diabetes genes have been identified.

Since the hormone insulin is essential for life, all persons with IDDM require insulin treatment. Insulin treatment, combined with the other elements of good diabetes management, will generally prevent death from diabetic coma (diabetic ketoacidosis) and permit normal growth and development in children with IDDM. Nevertheless, the management of IDDM with insulin is difficult, time-consuming, costly, and associated with the risk of both mild and severe hypoglycemia (low blood sugar). Furthermore, persons with IDDM have a greatly increased risk of developing long-term complications some 15 to 40 years after diagnosis of the primary disease.

Non-insulin-dependent. Persons with NIDDM are usually older (beyond age 35 at the time of diagnosis) and are often obese. The diagnosis may be missed easily since the symptoms may be few or nonspecific and the blood glucose level not greatly elevated (*i.e.,* it is in the range of 140–240 mg/dl). Compared with IDDM, the causes of NIDDM are more obscure. In most persons with NIDDM, insulin is not absent from the blood and the insulin-producing ß cells have not been destroyed by an autoimmune process. Although there is a striking tendency for NIDDM to run in families, it does not have the strong association with HLA-D region genes that has been noted with IDDM. Although it can still be said that no diabetes genes per se have been identified, there has been recent progress in identifying specific genetic abnormalities in certain subtypes of NIDDM. Specifically, mutations in the gene that codes for glucokinase, a key enzyme regulating the metabolism of glucose by ß cells, have been discovered in families with the subtype of NIDDM known as maturity onset diabetes of the young, or MODY. MODY has an onset early in life and is inherited in an autosomal dominant manner.

The common feature found in persons with NIDDM is that they have two abnormalities: insulin resistance and relative insulin deficiency. Insulin resistance means that a larger than normal amount of insulin is required for producing a biological effect (*i.e.,* for lowering the blood sugar). Relative insulin deficiency means that although individuals with NIDDM have insulin, the quantity is insufficient to overcome the insulin resistance and thereby maintain the blood glucose level within the normal range. It is probable that both abnormalities are inherited.

Obesity is the most common lifestyle-related cause of insulin resistance. Most obese persons with NIDDM do not require insulin treatment since they have sufficient insulin to maintain their blood glucose at an acceptable level if they restrict their caloric intake and lose weight. However, since this is seldom achieved, many people with NIDDM are treated with drugs that stimulate the secretion of insulin from the person's own ß cells (sulfonylurea drugs). Later in the course of NIDDM, the insulin deficiency may worsen, and insulin replacement may be required.

Although the symptoms of NIDDM may be nonspecific and persons with NIDDM are not at great risk from death due to diabetic coma, it is a mistake to consider NIDDM a mild disease. Persons with NIDDM develop the same long-term complications of diabetes as persons with IDDM and, in addition, have an even greater risk of accelerated atherosclerosis with myocardial infarction, stroke, and vascular disease of the legs.

Complications: common and costly

The major long-term complications of diabetes involve the eye (diabetic retinopathy), the kidney (diabetic nephropathy), the nervous system (diabetic neuropathy), and the vascular system (myocardial infarction, stroke, and inadequate blood circulation, leading to gangrene). Most persons with diabetes will develop some degree of diabetic retinopathy, a leading cause of severe visual impairment, during their lifetime. In retinopathy, lesions and hemorrhages form in the retinal vessels. About 8,000 new cases of blindness a year in the U.S. alone are caused by this significant

complication of diabetes. Among persons with diabetes, nephropathy is the leading cause of kidney disease requiring dialysis or transplantation. It is also the specific diabetes complication associated with the highest mortality. About 35–45% of persons with IDDM and 20% with NIDDM develop diabetic nephropathy. Diabetic neuropathy affects the conduction of sensory and motor nerve signals, especially in the feet and legs. Reduced sensation in the feet can lead to foot ulcers and infection. Diabetic neuropathy with insufficient blood flow to the legs is the leading cause (excluding trauma) of foot or leg amputations in the U.S. Cardiovascular disease is a common complication, and persons with diabetes have a threefold-to-fourfold excess risk of death due to myocardial infarction.

The American Diabetes Association has estimated the economic cost of diabetes in the U.S. to be $92 billion annually. Thus, the progress made in understanding the causes of diabetes and in developing treatments to prevent the early complications of diabetes have not eliminated the long-term complications of diabetes as a major cause of human suffering.

Most important discovery since insulin

In 1980 the National Institute of Diabetes and Digestive and Kidney Diseases, one of the 13 institutes of the U.S. National Institutes of Health, initiated a research program to investigate the relationship between the type of treatment given to patients with IDDM and the rate at which they develop long-term complications. This study was called the Diabetes Control and Complications Trial (DCCT). It was carried out in 29 clinical centers in North America—26 in the United States and 3 in Canada. The research question that the investigators were attempting to answer was whether a form of diabetes management called intensive treatment (sometimes called "tight glycemic control") was more effective than standard or conventional treat-

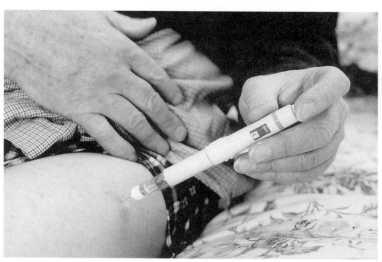

Because persons with insulin-dependent diabetes lack the hormone insulin, which regulates the body's metabolism of sugar (glucose), they require insulin treatment. It has now been established beyond a doubt that intensive treatment aimed at maintaining blood glucose levels as close to normal as possible will delay the onset of the many serious complications of diabetes. Intensive treatment, or "tight glycemic control," involves multiple injections of insulin on a daily basis or continuous insulin delivery via a pump.

ment in delaying the onset or slowing the progression of diabetic complications. Despite extensive studies of diabetes treatments in both experimental animals and humans, this fundamental question had remained unanswered.

The first volunteer in the DCCT was enrolled in August 1983. The study ended in June 1993, which was about one year ahead of schedule. Ultimately 1,441 persons with IDDM were randomly assigned to receive either intensive or conventional treatment. Random assignment means that the treatment group was not chosen by the participant or the doctor but was decided by a procedure similar to the toss of a coin. This type of study, called a randomized clinical trial, is the only way to determine whether an observed difference in the development of complications is caused by the treatment itself rather than by various other potential factors. For example, if persons with less severe diabetes chose to receive intensive treatment, then an apparent beneficial effect of intensive treatment might be, in reality, an effect of a difference in disease severity.

Patients in the conventional treatment group received one or two insulin injections daily—treatment that was standard in American and Canadian medical centers in 1983 and remained the accepted form of therapy until the results of the DCCT were published in September 1993. Patients in the intensive treatment group followed a form of treatment that was designed to maintain the blood glucose levels as close to normal as possible; they used a finger-stick procedure to measure their own blood sugar four or more times daily and took insulin either by multiple injections (three or more per day) or by the use of an external insulin pump that provided a continuous injection of insulin into the tissue beneath the skin.

The results were surprising and important. First, 99% of the volunteers (1,422 of 1,441) completed

the study despite its length (almost 10 years for the first patients enrolled) and complexity (multiple finger sticks and multiple injections or the use of insulin pumps for the intensive treatment group, multiple tests to assess the outcomes, multiple visits to the clinic, etc.). Second, the beneficial effects of intensive treatment were greater than expected. The average risk for the development or progression of diabetic retinopathy was reduced by more than 50% (probably by about 80%). The average risk reduction for diabetic nephropathy (kidney disease) was approximately 54% and for clinical neuropathy (mainly peripheral nerve disease) about 60%. What these results mean is that a 27-year-old with IDDM who switches to a program of intensive treatment can expect, on average, to live a life without symptoms from the complications of diabetes until age 65 or beyond, a 20-year gain in symptom-free life!

Two major risks were associated with intensive treatment. Hypoglycemia (low blood sugar) occurred three times more often in persons on intensive treatment than in those on conventional treatment, and some of these episodes were severe enough to cause unconsciousness or a seizure. There was no permanent neuropsychological impairment, however. The second adverse effect was that about 30% of the people on intensive treatment had substantial weight gain. Despite these adverse effects, there was no reduction in the subjects' self-perception of their quality of life; this was true even before the beneficial effects of intensive treatment were known. Once the beneficial effects of intensive treatment had been demonstrated and made known to the DCCT volunteers of both treatment groups, most opted to remain on or to change to an intensive treatment program.

The DCCT, together with all other medical evidence to date, has established beyond reasonable doubt that intensive diabetes treatment will delay the onset and

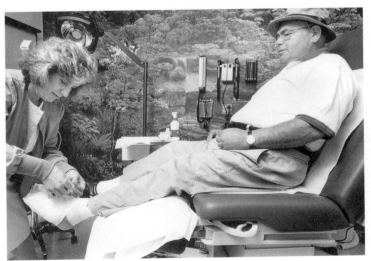

A steel worker who has diabetes receives daily foot care in his company's clinic. In both insulin-dependent and non-insulin-dependent diabetes, many organs and systems of the body—including eyes, kidneys, nervous system, and vascular system—are affected. Diabetic neuropathy, in which the conduction of sensory and motor nerve signals, especially in the feet and legs, is diminished, can lead to foot ulcers, infection, and sometimes gangrene. Excluding trauma, diabetic neuropathy is the leading cause of foot and leg amputations in the United States.

Kevin Monko—Kelsh Wilson

slow the progression of the major microvascular (eye and kidney disease) and neurological complications of IDDM. Thus, the question that has plagued physicians and persons with diabetes since the discovery of insulin in 1921 has finally been answered.

At the same time, the DCCT findings raised new and important questions. Thus, there remain major challenges.

Implications and challenges

It is now reasonable for most persons with IDDM to be offered a program of diabetes management that will lead to close-to-normal blood glucose levels. For perhaps 430,000 persons in the U.S. alone, this means a form of treatment that approaches the intensive regimen used in the DCCT. Currently, the U.S. health care system would be unable to meet that challenge because of the regimen's complexity and the fact that it requires an interdisciplinary health care team (endocrinologists and other physician-specialists, nurses, dietitians, and behavioral scientists) trained and skilled in intensive management of diabetes. Most medical settings presently do not have the necessary personnel with the requisite training. Furthermore, intensive treatment is two to three times more costly than conventional care, and the cost savings that would be derived from the avoidance of complications would not be realized for 20 years! Finally, the common adverse effect of hypoglycemia is always unpleasant and sometimes dangerous. For all these reasons, simpler and better methods for achieving near-normal blood glucose levels are urgently needed.

Another important question raised by the DCCT is whether the conclusions, which were derived exclusively from a study carried out on persons with IDDM, should be extended to the vast majority of people with diabetes who have NIDDM. Unfortunately, there have been no reliable clinical trials that answer the question directly. The rationale for extending the conclusions is that because elevated blood glucose levels are the proximate cause for development of complications, the type of diabetes (whether IDDM or NIDDM) is not relevant. The public health implications of extending intensive treatment to persons with NIDDM would be enormous. In the U.S. alone this would include 11 million to 12 million more people.

At present it seems prudent for most persons with NIDDM to strive for improved blood glucose control through weight loss, improved nutrition, and elimination of cardiovascular risk factors—especially cigarette smoking, high blood pressure, and high cholesterol. Recent nutritional guidelines from the American Diabetic Association are less restrictive than the traditional "diabetic diet." Thus, ice cream, frozen yogurt, and other sweets that were once forbidden are now allowed in moderation. One recent study suggests that a diet high in monounsaturated fats (*e.g.,* olive oil) may be preferable to a high-carbohydrate diet for many people with diabetes. These new recommendations may make it easier for people with NIDDM to adhere to a long-term program of improved eating habits.

Even with these lifestyle changes, some persons with NIDDM will require treatment with sulfonylurea drugs or insulin. The use of insulin should probably be limited to those persons with NIDDM who are truly insulin deficient and then used in sufficient doses to maintain the blood glucose levels as close to normal and as safely as possible.

In various stages of development are several approaches to the problem of how to maintain the blood glucose in the normal range without the risk of hypoglycemia. Transplantation of the pancreas has received the most attention and is currently considered a therapeutic option. All transplant recipients, however, require the use of immunosuppressive drugs,

A patient participating in the Diabetes Control and Complications Trial receives instruction on the use of an insulin pump. The large-scale study, involving 1,441 subjects with insulin-dependent diabetes, lasted nearly 10 years. Once the benefits of intensive treatment were made known to the subjects in the two treatment groups (intensive versus conventional), most chose to follow a regimen of intensive blood sugar control.

Courtesy of William Tamborlane, M.D., Yale University; photograph, Kathleen Apicelli

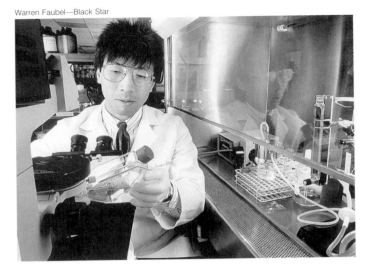

Patrick Soon-Shiong and colleagues at the Veterans Administration Wadsworth Medical Center in Los Angeles have successfully transplanted insulin-producing islets of Langerhans in diabetic dogs; in 1993 they received approval from the U.S. Food and Drug Administration to begin preliminary trials of islet-cell transplants in humans. A major problem that must be overcome before the procedure can have widespread application for patients is the immunogenicity of transplanted islet cells— i.e., the capacity of the cells to elicit an immune response in the recipient, resulting in graft rejection. Scientists are seeking methods of reducing the risk of rejection. Soon-Shiong and his team have protected islet cells by encapsulating them in a semipermeable gel membrane or in pea-sized bubbles made from seaweed extract.

probably for a lifetime. Most patients who receive pancreas transplants are in kidney failure and receive a combined kidney-pancreas transplant. This allows the treatment of pancreatic rejection at an early stage by using signs of kidney rejection as a early warning signal. Approximately 500 persons receive such transplants in the U.S. annually.

Transplantation of the islets of Langerhans (which, as previously noted, contain the insulin-producing ß cells) instead of transplantation of the whole pancreas is another approach. Thus far, this procedure is still experimental and not widely used in humans. Various procedures are being tested to reduce the immunogenicity of the islets and thereby lower the risk of rejection. These include removal of the most immunogenic cells from the whole islet and methods of isolating the islet from destructive forces by encasing it in a semipermeable membrane. Still farther down the developmental chain are genetic engineering methods for inserting the genes that regulate the production and secretion of insulin into the nonfunctioning islets of patients ("gene therapy").

Other scientists are using a mechanical rather than a biological approach to blood glucose control. The success of this approach will hinge on the development of an implantable device that senses the level of glucose in the blood and feeds the information to a microcomputer chip that governs the amount of insulin injected by a microinfusion pump and flowing directly to the liver.

The ultimate aim of the biomedical research teams working on the problem of diabetes is to prevent the onset of diabetes altogether. This is indeed a formidable challenge. Since IDDM is an autoimmune disease, there is great promise for methods to interrupt the immune destruction of the insulin-producing ß cells before all the cells are destroyed. Some of these methods are currently undergoing testing in

randomized clinical trials. For example, the Diabetes Prevention Trial of Type I Diabetes, sponsored by the National Institutes of Health, is now testing whether intervention with insulin injections (using small doses) during the prodromal period (early phase) will delay or prevent the onset of clinical disease. Other methods, such as the induction of so-called immune tolerance, are in earlier stages of development but show considerable promise. The heterogeneous nature of NIDDM will likely mean that prevention approaches will need to target various stages of the disease and that different methods of prevention will be found for the different causes of the condition.

—Oscar B. Crofford, M.D.

Diet and Nutrition

Over the past year or so, the U.S. public has been bombarded by magazine and newspaper articles about studies of the efficacy of vitamins in preventing disease. People have read, for example, that nurses who had high intakes of vitamin E had a reduced risk of heart disease and that people in rural China who took a dietary supplement of beta-carotene, vitamin E, and selenium had a reduced risk of cancer. They learned of findings suggesting that people can lower the risk of cataracts by taking vitamins C and E. Americans also read of an investigation in Finland involving lifelong cigarette smokers that concluded, contrary to previous reports, that vitamin supplements do not protect against lung cancer; moreover, the Finnish study indicated that beta-carotene supplements may actually increase the risk for both lung and heart disease. As with other nutrition news in recent years, consumers, instead of feeling enlightened, are growing increasingly confused and exasperated. The following is intended to provide a reasonable perspective on the nutrition-vitamin controversy.

You are what you eat

It has long been known that the vitamins, minerals, calories, and protein supplied by food are necessary for the body to grow, develop, and regenerate. Increasingly, however, scientists have come to recognize that the so-called macronutrients (sources of calories) and micronutrients (noncaloric sources of essential substances) present in food have the ability to prevent—or promote—chronic disease. The scientific evidence supporting the relationship of diet to chronic illness is nutrient- and disease-specific. For example, it is now widely accepted that the ingestion of excessive amounts of one macronutrient, saturated fat, promotes the development of coronary heart disease. This finding has led to a drop in Americans' consumption of saturated fat from 17% of total calories in the 1960s to 12% of calories in the 1990s. It has also resulted in the burgeoning of a market for fat-free and reduced-fat food products.

Preliminary evidence suggests that the ingestion of vitamin-rich foods or vitamin supplements (or both) might prevent the development of cancer and coronary heart disease. This revelation, although premature and nonspecific, has resulted in increased sales of vitamin supplements—now a $2.9 billion-a-year industry—and has fueled an enormous debate about the optimal intake of specific vitamins and the value of vitamin supplementation.

Nutrition science: a brief history

Many societies have believed that ingestion of specific foods could either enhance the enjoyment of life or hasten its end. For example, chocolate has been considered an aphrodisiac; the vegetables in the nightshade family—eggplant, peppers, tomatoes, and potatoes—were once believed to be toxic. Some plant-derived substances have been consumed for their medicinal properties.

Many of these practices and beliefs—grounded in tradition, myth, and superstition—turned out to be based on biologically plausible principles. Many non-nutritive extracts of plants were eventually found to contain biologically active substances that are now, in a purified form, classified as drugs. Digoxin, for example, a drug for the treatment of heart failure, is derived from the leaves of the foxglove plant, and vinblastine, an anticancer agent, is made from the periwinkle plant. However, the efficacy of plant-derived compounds was not proved beyond doubt until their biologically active constituents were isolated and purified. Once a reputedly active compound was identified, rigorous testing and retesting were required before a cause-effect relationship could be established. To ensure that the beneficial effect attributed to a particular substance was not due to chance, these tests also included comparisons between the compound in question and a compound that had no suspected effects (placebo).

Once they had developed techniques to chemically separate foods into their constituent nutrients, micronutrients, and indigestible components, scientists were able to use the methods described above to isolate and test how a specific food could provide health benefits. They found that three major classes of macronutrients in the diet—fat, protein, and carbohydrate—provided the body with energy. Following this discovery, biochemists were able to elucidate the process by which the body, using oxygen, metabolizes these macronutrients. They demonstrated that there is an obligatory balance between the energy extracted from the diet, on one hand, and the energy expended by the body or stored as fat, on the other. As a result of this research, minimum caloric and protein requirements for a healthy diet were established.

The role of dietary micronutrients—vitamins, minerals, and the like—became apparent when individuals consuming deficient diets developed symptoms that could be reliably reproduced—that is, the symptoms developed after a short time in people who were fed a deficient diet and abated when the micronutrient was restored. For example, in the 18th century it was common for sailors on long ocean voyages to develop the condition called scurvy, characterized by gum disease and spontaneous bleeding into the skin and mucous membranes. The disease could be prevented if citrus fruits were included in the sailors' diet. Vitamin C was not identified as the active substance in citrus fruits until the first half of the 20th century, a time when many vitamins were isolated and characterized. Following this accomplishment, the U.S. National Academy of Sciences established recommended dietary allowances (RDAs) for protein, 10 vitamins, and 6 minerals. The RDA corresponded to a level of intake twofold to sixfold greater than the minimum level needed to avoid a state of deficiency.

In the past 50 years, macronutrients have been further subdivided: fat into saturated, monounsaturated, and polyunsaturated fatty acids; protein into essential and nonessential amino acids; and carbohydrate into simple, complex, digestible, and indigestible. Using the chemical composition of foods as a standard, nutrition scientists have been able to compare the nutrient content of diverse diets. Finally, epidemiologists, observing population differences in nutrient intakes and disease rates, have formulated hypotheses relating specific dietary constituents to specific illnesses.

Diet and disease: establishing links

The first diet-disease relationships to be uncovered involved diseases that had short periods of incubation—*i.e.,* dietary changes rapidly resulted in the appearance or disappearance of symptoms. Only a few significant associations between diet and disease were observed this way, however, and most of these involved vitamin deficiencies.

Ailing sailors aboard an 18th-century ship are given citrus fruits to eat by order of Scottish naval surgeon James Lind. In 1753 Lind, who is credited with establishing the concept of dietary deficiency as a cause of illness, demonstrated that the disease known as scurvy—later identified as vitamin C deficiency—could be prevented or cured by ingestion of the juice of oranges, lemons, or limes. Scurvy was once a major cause of sickness and death among sailors on long sea voyages, during which fresh fruits and vegetables were scarce.

The more recent diet-disease links to be elucidated involve common ailments that have longer incubation periods. Because these disorders take years to develop, medical scientists seeking to confirm such relationships needed to identify an intermediate step in the disease process, a risk factor that could predict the development of the disease. The risk factor could then be considered as a surrogate for the disease itself. Some risk factors can be altered by diet, and this short-term relationship between food intake and a particular risk for disease could allow for extensive testing of any hypothesis linking diet to the development of a predisposing condition—*i.e.* a risk factor—and, ultimately, to a specific ailment.

The diet-heart disease hypothesis provides an example of how this stepwise approach can prove a diet-chronic disease link. Excess dietary intake of saturated fat and cholesterol will in the short term raise serum cholesterol levels; elevation of serum cholesterol over the long term will increase the risk for coronary heart disease. Evidence supporting this hypothesis has come from multiple complementary lines of scientific investigation (observational studies in humans, animal experiments, human intervention trials), and it now has widespread support and acceptance.

Establishment of relationships between macronutrients and chronic disease suggested that similar links might be found for micronutrients and disease. Like macronutrients, vitamins and minerals could play a role in disorders that are more chronic and multifactorial in nature than the acute and self-limited conditions associated with vitamin deficiencies. Moreover, the same population databases used for seeking correlations between macronutrient intake and disease could be employed to look for similar correlations involving micronutrients.

As noted above, a *relationship* between reported intake and disease does not prove *causality*. If there is sufficient evidence of a relationship, however, animal experiments can be employed to test biologically plausible roles for the micronutrient in question. As a next step, human intervention trials—in which subjects are randomly assigned to receive supplements of the biologically active substance or a placebo—could be conducted.

To date, only two large-scale population studies of Americans have amassed sufficient data to evaluate vitamin intake and correlate it with disease rates. One of these investigations involved women (the Nurses' Health Study), while the other enrolled only male health care professionals (the Health Professionals Follow-up Study). Both collected information on food intake by asking participants to fill out questionnaires concerning their typical intake of 61 to 131 common foods. Both studies also queried participants about their use of vitamin supplements. After estimating the combined intake of vitamins from foods and supplements, the investigators then evaluated correlations between vitamin intake and incidence of disease. Several vitamins appeared to show a graded protective effect against the subsequent development of disease (*see* table, page 266). It must be emphasized that these findings are merely observations; a cause-effect relationship can be established only through an intervention trial.

Many more observational studies focusing solely on cancer rates have shown an inverse association between fruit and vegetable intake and the development of disease. Whether this protective effect is due to fruit and vegetable consumption per se or to behavioral factors associated with eating these foods is unknown—for example, people with better diets are likely to be more affluent, obtain better health care, have healthier lifestyles, and so forth.

Further, it is not known whether vitamins or other substances contained in fruits and vegetables are re-

Protective effect of vitamins: observational studies			
vitamin	disease	population studied	observed effect
E	coronary heart disease	87,245 women*	women who consumed 21.6 IU–1,000 IU daily had one-third lower rates than those whose daily intake averaged 1.2–3.5 IU
E	coronary heart disease	39,910 men†	men who consumed average of 419 IU daily had one-third lower rates than those who consumed average of 6.4 IU per day
C			no benefit
beta-carotene			no benefit in nonsmokers; some benefit in smokers
folate	colon cancer	15,984 women* and 9,490 men†	subjects who consumed average of 750 µg per day had one-third lower rates of polyp formation than those who consumed 200 µg per day
C	breast cancer	89,494 women*	no benefit
E			no benefit
A			low intake (less than 6,630 IU per day) may increase risk; no benefit seen with high intakes

*participants in Nurses' Health Study
†participants in Health Professionals Follow-up Study

sponsible for this "protective" effect. If micronutrients in the diet do indeed offer protection against disease, a logical next step is to elucidate the mechanism by which they do so. One potential explanation currently receiving a great deal of acceptance is the antioxidant theory.

The antioxidant theory

Every organism has evolved strategies for preventing premature death. Whereas single-cell organisms can employ only limited defenses, multicellular organisms (such as humans) have mechanisms for decreasing the chances of death that involve the whole body, specific organs, and individual cells. At the whole-organism level, behavior strategies (e.g., food-preservation techniques, proper hygiene) and manipulation of the environment (e.g., sanitation systems) lead to a reduced likelihood of death. At the organ level, mechanisms such as the blood circulation—providing oxygen, energy, and infection-fighting cells and removing toxic wastes—can prevent organ failure and consequent death. At the cellular level, enzymes are produced to defuse cellular toxins.

Since every organism and every organ are made of cells, defenses against death must be initiated at the cellular level. Damage to a cell's DNA (the basic genetic material) will impair most cell functions and can result in cell death. A common mechanism leading to DNA damage occurs when free radicals—unstable molecules—discharge energy into the cell in an attempt to achieve a stable state. The most common free radical is oxygen in an unstable form (O^{3-}) that must give up an electron in order to achieve a stable state (O^2). The donation of an electron to a nearby molecule transfers the unstable state to the

acceptor molecule; as a consequence, the acceptor molecule is damaged and can no longer perform its normal function.

Since free-radical formation is a common biological occurrence, an organism must be able to defend itself against this form of cellular damage. Vitamins recently have been shown to play a vital role in these defenses. For example, vitamin C, which is present in circulating blood, is part of the first line of defense against free radicals. Vitamins A and E have also been shown to absorb free radicals. Moreover, an interrelationship between these defense processes exists—vitamin C has been shown to regenerate the electron-absorbing capacity of vitamin E. Because of their capacity to defend the body against the ravages of oxygen free radicals, vitamins A, E, and C have been termed *antioxidants*.

Antioxidants and cancer. After cancerous tumors were discovered to have abnormal cellular DNA, speculation arose that antioxidant vitamins might play a role in treatment. Megadose vitamin C therapy was tried in patients with terminal cancer but did not affect symptoms, tumor size, or survival. An important question remained unanswered by such trials: Could vitamin C, by preventing DNA damage, prevent the cancer from forming in the first place? The concept is attractive and has some support from clinical observations. For example, smoking is associated with low blood levels of vitamin C. Does this reduction in circulating vitamin C then increase smokers' risk for lung cancer? Or is this finding merely an association that plays no causal role in the development of lung cancer?

Intervention trials in humans are under way to test whether smokers who receive antioxidant vitamin supplements will have a lower incidence of lung cancer than smokers who receive a placebo. (The findings of one such study are described below.) A number of similar, specific vitamin-cancer theories have been proposed; to test them, the National Cancer Institute is funding several "chemoprevention" trials in people who are at high risk for cancer.

The results of the first cancer chemoprevention trial were published in the *Journal of the National Cancer Institute* in 1993. This landmark five-year study was conducted among approximately 30,000 people in Linxian (Lin Xian) county, China, where the world's highest rate of esophageal and stomach cancers has been observed. Because of the limited variety of food-stuffs available in this rural community, the diet is extremely low in both macronutrients and micronutrients. Four different vitamin supplements were tested either alone or in combination: (1) vitamin A (5,000 IU) plus zinc (22.5 mg); (2) riboflavin (3.2 mg) plus niacin (40 mg); (3) vitamin C (120 mg) plus molybdenum (30 μg [micrograms]); and (4) beta-carotene (15 mg), selenium (50 μg), and vitamin E (30 mg). The trial found that the fourth regimen—a combination of beta-carotene, selenium, and vitamin E—was associated with a lower rate of all cancers and, more specifically, esophageal and stomach cancers. This study provided the first scientific evidence that vitamins may play a role in the prevention of cancer.

Although the proponents of vitamin supplements heralded this trial as definitive proof of the benefits of vitamins, several facts must be noted. First, the experiment was performed in a population whose diet is deficient in micronutrients. Second, this population has a very high risk of developing relatively unusual forms of cancer. Third, the dose of vitamins used in the trial was comparable to the vitamin intake provided by the average American's diet and was less than the megadoses used by many supplement takers. These three considerations limit the generalizability of this

study to the U.S. population—among whom the overall diet is micronutrient sufficient, the rates of esophageal and stomach cancer are low, and megavitamin supplementation is common. Whether megadose vitamin supplements will prevent cancer in Americans remains to be seen.

Another cancer chemoprevention trial was recently completed in Finland. Nearly 30,000 male smokers received one of four daily supplements: vitamin E (50 IU), beta-carotene (20 mg), vitamin E (50 IU) plus beta-carotene (20 mg), and a placebo pill containing no vitamins. After more than five years, lung cancer incidence in the four groups of subjects was compared. Not only was there no benefit observed in the three vitamin-supplemented groups, but both groups that received beta-carotene had *higher* rates of lung cancer than those receiving vitamin E alone or the placebo.

Those who are skeptical about vitamin supplements were quick to cite the Finnish trial as strong evidence that supplementation not only lacks benefits but may be harmful. This conclusion may be too facile, however. Several points must be taken into consideration. First, participation in the trial was limited to smokers, and vitamins may not be capable of counteracting the harmful effects of smoking. Second, the selection of vitamins tested was small, and the dose of vitamin E was far lower than the 400 IU (440 mg) taken by most who use supplements. Finally, the findings suggesting a deleterious effect for beta-carotene could be due to chance. The specific role of vitamin supplements in cancer prevention awaits the results of more clinical trials. Moreover, each trial, while important in itself, must be evaluated with respect to the consistency of the findings with data from other scientific investigations.

Heart disease and antioxidants. The theory behind the probable role of antioxidant vitamins in the preven-

Residents of Linxian (Lin Xian) county, China, wait to be screened as part of a five-year cancer chemoprevention trial conducted by the U.S. National Cancer Institute. The results, published in 1993, showed that a combination of beta-carotene, selenium, and vitamin E significantly reduced the risk of all types of cancer in this population.

Phillip Taylor, M.D., National Cancer Institute; photograph, The New York Times

*"What do you have that's
rich in antioxidants?"*

tion of coronary heart disease is perhaps less straight-forward than the theory that accounts for vitamins' efficacy against cancer. In coronary heart disease, heart muscle cells die as a result of reduced blood flow through the coronary arteries, which supply blood to the heart. The arteries become narrowed by deposits of cholesterol-laden plaque. If a blood clot forms in a narrowed part of the vessel (coronary thrombosis), blood flow may be completely obstructed. Without the oxygen and nutrients carried by the blood, heart muscle cells are damaged; *i.e.,* a heart attack occurs.

The arterial plaques in coronary heart disease contain intracellular and extracellular cholesterol, and initial interest in the risks of coronary disease focused on factors that could explain how these plaques developed. For example, an elevated blood cholesterol level could increase the risk for plaque development by increasing the availability of cholesterol. Elevated blood pressure might injure the blood vessel wall, and plaques are more likely to develop at sites of injury.

Recently, attention has focused on the early stages of plaque development, during which cholesterol is deposited only in specific cells called macrophages. Studies on the life cycle of macrophages show that these cells do not readily take up the common form of cholesterol found in the bloodstream, low-density lipoprotein (LDL). However, macrophages avidly ingest LDL cholesterol particles that have been oxidized by free radicals. If vitamins could prevent the oxidation of LDL cholesterol particles, could they prevent the uptake of cholesterol particles by macrophages, thereby preventing the development of coronary disease? This theory has so far been supported by observational associations—people with higher vitamin intakes have lower rates of coronary disease than people who have lower vitamin intakes—and by in vivo experiments—LDL particles obtained from subjects taking vitamin supplements are less easily oxidized

than LDL particles from subjects taking placebos. It is not clear, however, whether it is vitamin intake itself or the healthier lifestyle of vitamin-supplement takers that accounts for this protective effect. Nor is it clear where in the human body LDL particles undergo oxidation. Several controlled trials are under way to assess the effects of vitamin supplementation on the risk of coronary disease.

Evaluating vitamin intake: no simple task

Whether dietary supplements alone or behaviors associated with taking vitamin supplements are responsible for the apparent healthiness of vitamin takers is unknown. To even begin to answer this question, one needs to know how much of a specific micronutrient is being consumed by the general public and how much is being consumed by supplement takers. There are two ways to arrive at estimates of these data. First, the vitamin intake of the population as a whole can be estimated by use of what the food industry calls "food disappearance data," which in turn can be used to calculate per capita consumption of a given foodstuff. A more precise assessment of individual intakes can be arrived at through techniques such as a 24-hour dietary recall, food records kept by subjects, and responses to questions about the frequency of consumption of specific foods; these individual estimates can then be averaged for an overall estimate of population intake. Regardless of the method used, food consumption must be translated into nutrient and micronutrient consumption through the use of a database of the nutrient content of foods.

Among nutrition authorities around the world, the U.S. Department of Agriculture (USDA) *Handbook 8* has long been considered the most reliable such database. It is used as a basis for public nutrition policy and nutrition-related medical research. In November 1993, however, a report by the General Accounting Of-

268

fice revealed that the handbook contains inaccuracies and inconsistencies. One problem is that the value reported for a given food may be based on an average of too few measurements; as more reliable assay techniques become available, the currently used values may be found to be erroneous and will need to be revised. Another potential source of error is that the micronutrient content of an edible plant can vary depending upon its genetic variety, where it is grown, the nature of the growing season (e.g., wet, dry, hot, cold, long, short), and the processing and cooking procedures used to prepare it for consumption. Thus, the recorded vitamin content of a given fruit, grain, or vegetable may not accurately represent the actual vitamin content of the food item as consumed. Last, the micronutrient content of some foods has not been determined, making the database incomplete. Despite these drawbacks, the USDA Handbook 8 remains the best available source for the nutrient content of common foods.

Putting the brakes on health claims

On Feb. 14, 1994, the FDA formally adopted long-awaited new food-labeling regulations. The new rules spell out how the nutrient content of foods must be listed on package labels and specify the nature of the health claims that can be made for a food. They also require manufacturers to express the essential vitamin and mineral content of their products as a percentage of the current RDAs, established in 1989 by the National Academy of Sciences and recently renamed "recommended daily intakes," or RDIs.

Whereas food manufacturers can make only very limited, FDA-approved health claims for their products under the new law, dietary-supplement manufacturers would have been able to continue the long-established practice of making unsubstantiated and exaggerated claims. In 1993, therefore, the FDA also proposed rules for the labeling of dietary supplements; these were finalized in January 1994 and scheduled to take effect in July 1995. In effect, the agency redressed the disparity in requirements of the two industries, extending to supplements the same regulations that govern labeling and health claims of foods. The new regulations will benefit consumers by standardizing supplement labels and limiting product claims to prevent misleading labeling.

Initially, the health claims permitted for vitamin and mineral supplements were to have been limited to the same areas as are allowed for foods. The FDA had considered 10 potential diet-disease relationships; however, only seven of these (calcium/osteoporosis; sodium/hypertension; fat/cancer; saturated fat-cholesterol/coronary heart disease; fiber-containing grain products, fruits, and vegetables/cancer; fruits and vegetables/cancer; and fiber-containing grain products/coronary heart disease) were felt to have sufficient

scientific consensus to be allowed as the basis for a health claim for foods.

Before ruling that the health claims for dietary supplements would be identical to those allowed for foods, the agency reevaluated the scientific data supporting the role of folic acid in preventing the birth defects known collectively as neural tube defects (NTDs). In December 1992 the Public Health Service had issued a recommendation that all U.S. women of childbearing age who are capable of becoming pregnant consume 0.4 mg per day of folic acid to reduce the risk of these defects. In support of this recommendation, the FDA decided to allow dietary supplements that contain folic acid—but not folic acid-containing foods and food products—to make the claim that they help prevent NTDs.

The FDA will continue to monitor the safety of dietary supplements. In 1989 one product—L-tryptophan—was responsible for an outbreak of a mysterious disease that affected some 1,500 people and caused more than 35 deaths. Appropriately, the agency immediately removed L-tryptophan from the market. How it will handle such products in the future is unclear. Historically, the agency has intervened only when adverse effects were associated with a supplement. Whether it will adopt a proactive role—requiring safety data prior to the marketing of a new product—remains to be seen.

Supplements: to take or not to take?

Vitamins are touted as a "natural" way to increase the likelihood of achieving many desirable attributes: youthfulness, energy, resistance to colds, and increased endurance, to name a few. The new labeling regulations will put a stop to these unsubstantiated claims. With or without advertisements, however, consumers must still decide whether to take vitamin supplements.

No definite link has been established between vitamin intake and chronic disease prevention. The antioxidant theory appears biologically plausible, and many people would like to be assured that antioxidants can protect them against cancer and heart disease. However, even if the theory is proved to be true, it still remains to be shown that vitamin supplementation—as opposed to eating foods that are rich in antioxidants—will decrease the likelihood of disease. Moreover, exactly how much of a particular vitamin would be protective and whether other substances in the food supply are also needed to maintain optimal health are unknown. Whereas taking a vitamin supplement is quick and easy, there may be an equally effective strategy available, namely, eating a wider variety of fruits, vegetables, and grains and controlling other modifiable risk factors, such as cigarette smoking, physical inactivity, and obesity.

—Margo A. Denke, M.D.

Ancient Ways for Modern Ills: Hawaiians Go on a Diet

by **Terry T. Shintani, M.D., J.D., M.P.H.**

After just five days of following a program based on traditional Hawaiian principles of eating and living, a 38-year-old Hawaiian woman with diabetes no longer needed the 80 units of insulin she had been taking for years. After four months on the program, she had lost more than 23 kg (50 lb), despite eating *more* than she did before; three years later she still requires no medication for diabetes. A 44-year-old man who was diagnosed as dying of heart failure and expected to live less than a year is alive and well over two years after that dire diagnosis. Startling results like these are occurring on a regular basis under a program that uses ancient principles to treat a population plagued by modern chronic diseases.

A Hawaiian paradox

Hawaii is considered by many as the quintessential tropical paradise. Its very name conjures up images of pristine beaches, pounding surf, and palm trees swaying in the trade winds. A popular vacation destination, it is thought of as a place where body, mind, and spirit can be rejuvenated in the gentle hands of nature.

Hawaii is also nicknamed the "health state," and for good reason: it is the healthiest state in the U.S. from the standpoint of longevity. Americans of European ancestry live longer in Hawaii than their counterparts in Europe, and Americans of Asian ancestry in Hawaii reach greater ages than their counterparts in Asia. It is therefore a tragic irony that in the healthiest U.S. state, the native Hawaiian people have the worst health statistics in the nation. This is the "Hawaiian paradox."

The native people, then and now

The natives are in general above the middle stature, well formed with fine muscular limbs; their gait graceful and sometimes stately.
—description by a European missionary visiting Hawaii, 1832

In ancient times the Hawaiian population flourished, nurtured by the environment of pure water, warm temperatures, and abundant vegetation. Early photographs show that as a people the native Hawaiians were tall, graceful, and slim. Their athletic ability and robust health were legendary. Historical accounts such as the one above suggest that there was little

heart disease, cancer, diabetes, or obesity among Hawaiians of the past. Cultural values and practices that emphasized a spiritual tie with nature helped to protect their health, as well as to conserve their food supply and natural resources.

Since the arrival of Westerners, however, the native Hawaiian population has declined precipitously. First it was ravaged by infectious diseases. More recently, in the past 100 years, the destruction of Hawaiian culture and the abandonment of traditional ways have resulted in another wave of diseases—those primarily related to diet and lifestyle.

Of all the cultural changes that have come with modernization, perhaps the most detrimental has been the adoption by the Hawaiians of the high-fat Western diet. It is this change in eating habits that appears to be responsible for most of the chronic disease and excess mortality of the islands' native people today. Indeed, most Americans die of diet-related diseases, according to current statistics. In 1987, 35.7% of all U.S. deaths were caused by heart disease, 22.4% by cancer, 7% by stroke, and 1.8% by diabetes. In the same year, a survey of causes of death among people of pure Hawaiian descent indicated stunning rates of mortality from chronic disease, including deaths from heart disease (178% higher than the U.S. average), cancer (126% higher), stroke (145% higher), and diabetes (588% higher). The percentage of native Hawaiians who are obese (*i.e.,* more than 20% over normal body weight for height) is among the highest in the country—approximately 66%.

The phenomenon of dramatic increases in chronic disease with the adoption of the typical Western diet is not unique to Hawaii, however. Hawaii may be simply the best—or worst—example of what happens when people stray from their traditional eating habits and way of life. A similar trend occurs in just about all peoples around the world who begin to adopt a "modernized" diet and lifestyle. While industrialization tends to increase life span—primarily because of reductions in infant mortality, childhood illness, and infectious diseases—it also tends to result in a precipitous rise in the incidence of chronic conditions such as those besetting native Hawaiians today.

Moreover, among many indigenous peoples these fairly sudden and drastic changes in diet and lifestyle seem to have had an exaggerated health impact. Among the Pima Indians in the southwestern U.S., for example, the death rate from diabetes is much higher than average, as is the prevalence of obesity. A similar phenomenon has occurred among the natives of Nauru, an independent Pacific island nation that has become wealthy as a result of its phosphate-mining industry. Their diet has been largely Westernized, and the prevalence of diabetes is 44%—among the highest in the world. In the 1970s researchers who studied the native population of another Pacific island, Palau, found that cholesterol levels averaged 160 mg/dl (milligrams per deciliter). The people ate a diet similar to that of their ancestors. By comparison, the average cholesterol level of Micronesians living in California was 210 mg/dl. In Western Samoa, where some of the traditional eating patterns have been preserved, the prevalence of obesity is approximately 45%. While this may seem high, nearly 80% of Samoans in the U.S. eating a typical "American" diet are obese.

Thrifty genes

One of the hypotheses that has been proposed as an explanation for the high rates of obesity among the native peoples mentioned above is that of "thrifty genes." This hypothesis suggests that the genetic makeup of such native populations allows them to utilize calories in a very economical manner, burning them slowly and storing any excess in the form of body fat. Such a process would explain why obesity rates among certain populations are higher than among others who eat similar high-fat diets.

The hypothesis goes on to suggest that the presence in some populations of thrifty genes was a result of generations of adaptation to periods of calorie deprivation. Among the Polynesians, for example, those with such genes could have survived long ocean voyages more easily than others and would be better adapted to a situation in which food was alternately abundant and scarce. Similarly, the ancestors of today's Pima Indians had to endure prolonged periods of drought and starvation, and those who were able to store calories most efficiently survived—and thus contributed to the gene pool of the present-day Pima—while others who did not have this adaptive advantage would have perished, many before they had a chance to pass their genes on to another generation.

So-called thrifty genes, however, are clearly not the sole reason for obesity in these or any people. As mentioned above, early accounts of native Hawaiians indicate that they were a tall, slim, and athletic population in the 1700s and 1800s. One early 19th-century visitor to Hawaii noted that "the common people are of a thin rather than full habit." Thus, while thrifty genes may foster obesity, their effect has become manifest only with the adoption of Western eating habits.

Nutrition profiles, ancient and modern

In sharp contrast to today's practices, the diet of Hawaii in ancient times was low in fat, high in fiber, and primarily starch-based. The staples were taro (a tuber) and poi (fermented taro starch), along with sweet potatoes, yams, and breadfruit. Large amounts of greens and other vegetables were consumed, as were seaweed, fruits such as mountain apple and banana, and, in smaller amounts, fish. Chicken was eaten occasionally, but pork—although legendary as the centerpiece of the feast, or luau—was actually not eaten by the common people. Such food, if available, would have been reserved for the *ali'i* (royalty), who were also the only members of society who were obese. Dairy products were unknown in this culinary tradition. Cooking methods included baking, steaming, and roasting over an open fire. Foods were never

Douglas Peebles

The very same foods that sustained Polynesian peoples in ancient times may prove to be the answer to the persistent health problems—obesity, diabetes, high blood pressure, heart disease—that plague native Hawaiians today. The staples of the traditional Hawaiian diet, shown at left, include tubers such as sweet potatoes and taro, the starchy breadfruit, bananas, seaweed, and the dish known as poi—fermented taro starch. Though not an everyday feature of the traditional diet, which derived most of its calories from complex carbohydrates, steamed fish wrapped in taro leaves (center of plate) is a tasty addition to the menu.

fried, as there were no metal pans for frying, and oil was not consumed as such. The nutrition profile of such a diet is about 7–12% fat, 78–80% carbohydrate, almost all of it complex carbohydrate, and 12–15% protein. The fiber content is high (about 50 g per day).

This traditional eating pattern is radically different from the diet of most Hawaiians today. Of course, eating habits in Hawaii are quite similar to those in the rest of the United States, with a few notable variations. Fast-food chains are every bit as evident as they are on the mainland, and burgers, fries, pizza, tacos, and the like are popular. What differs in Hawaii is the large quantity of Asian foods that are consumed, including teriyaki beef and chicken, Chinese dishes, Korean-style barbecue beef, and various other ethnic specialties. Also unique to Hawaii is the high consumption of white rice by the islands' fairly large Asian-American population. In terms of its nutrition profile, however, the current diet of Hawaii generally reflects that of the United States at large: about 37–40% of calories come from fat, 29% from starch (*i.e.,* complex carbohydrates), 10–15% from sugar, and about 12% from protein. The fiber content is relatively low (approximately 10 g per day).

The Waianae plan: a diet and more

On the semirural west side of the island of Oahu, 56.3 km (35 mi) from Honolulu, is an area that has the poorest health profile, the lowest socioeconomic status, and the largest native Hawaiian population of any community in Hawaii. The area is served by the Waianae Coast Comprehensive Health Center (WCCHC), where the unique Waianae Diet Program was developed. The program was conceived in 1987 by this author and developed along with Claire Hughes, a native Hawaiian nutritionist, Helen Kanawaliwali, a community health worker, and the WCCHC staff.

The first group of participants was recruited in 1989. In this initial study, 20 people of native Hawaiian ancestry were placed on a strict diet of traditional Hawaiian food for a period of 21 days and then provided with a maintenance diet of traditional foods from a variety of cultures. During the three weeks, participants were permitted to eat as much as they wanted of the Hawaiian staple foods; fish and chicken were allowed but were limited to a maximum of 113 to 170 g (4 to 6 oz) per day. At regular intervals participants were weighed and had their cholesterol and triglyceride levels, blood pressure, and other indicators measured. For those who had diabetes, blood sugar levels were checked on a daily basis.

The program extended far beyond dietary measures, however. In keeping with the ancient Hawaiian concept of *Lokahi,* or "oneness," it emphasized a holistic approach to health, taking care of all aspects of the person. Each evening during the three weeks of the plan, after a dinner eaten communally, participants attended either a health education session or a cultural activity. These events were designed to reinforce the spiritual, mental, and emotional aspects of well-being, as well as to promote physical health. Traditional Hawaiian practitioners were included among the speakers, along with Western-trained health professionals.

As mentioned above, in keeping with Hawaii's custom of embracing other cultures, traditional foods of other peoples were introduced at the end of the three-week period. These foods included whole grains, whole grain breads, potatoes, and pastas; vegetables of all kinds, including leafy greens, squashes, and turnips; fruits such as oranges and pineapples; and protein primarily from vegetable sources, such as beans, lentils, and tofu (soybean curd). Like the traditional Hawaiian foods, all of these are high in complex

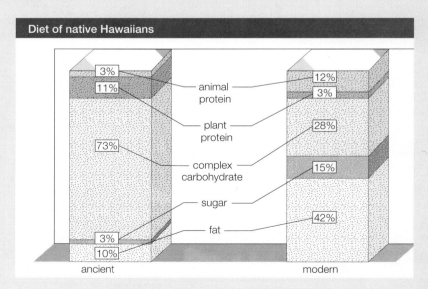

Diet of native Hawaiians

ancient
3%
11%
73%
3%
10%

animal protein
plant protein
complex carbohydrate
sugar
fat

modern
12%
3%
28%
15%
42%

carbohydrates and low in fat. Expanding the diet to include a broad range of foods that are nutritionally equivalent to the traditional diet had several benefits. It made adherence to the diet easier, more convenient, and often less expensive.

Astonishing outcome

The clinical results of the program were startling. In the initial group cholesterol levels fell 14.1%, and triglycerides, also a risk factor for heart disease, decreased 22.3%. In those with diabetes overall average blood sugar levels fell from an initial 161.9 mg/dl to 123.4. In those who had high blood pressure, systolic pressure decreased by about 11% and diastolic pressure by about 10%. The weight loss achieved by the participants was remarkable, and it demonstrated another paradox: people ate more food than usual during the program but weighed less at the end of the three weeks. In the first group an average weight loss of 8 kg (17.1 lb) was recorded in 21 days.

Perhaps most astonishing, however, was that many in the program were able to achieve control of a number of hitherto intractable health problems. Several people with diabetes no longer needed insulin or oral antidiabetes medication. One individual who had been taking 100 units of insulin per day no longer needed insulin after two weeks; others with various insulin requirements decreased or eliminated their need for medication. The need for insulin returned, however, in those who did not maintain the diet. Another participant, who previously had been treated for asthma in the emergency department four or five times per year, no longer had acute attacks and was able to reduce the need for asthma medication. Still another, who was housebound at the beginning of the program because of arthritis, astonished the group by dancing the hula at the end of the three weeks.

Limitless applications

By early 1994 some 160 people had completed the formal three-week Waianae Diet Program. While it is not a weight-loss regimen per se, the program has done well when compared with others that focus on weight reduction as their main goal. Over 20% of the Waianae Diet Program participants had maintained significant weight loss over an average follow-up period of 24 months. This is considerably better than most commercial diet programs, which have a long-term success rate of about 10% or less.

The formal diet is only one component of the project, however. A growing number of people—thousands per year—are reached by educational activities conducted by WCCHC staff members and through books and articles distributed by the WCCHC. Several communities on neighboring islands have been assisted in creating similar programs.

Beyond its clinical implications, the Waianae Diet

Douglas Peebles

Terry T. Shintani, a physician at the Waianae Coast Comprehensive Health Center, near Honolulu, is one of the originators of the regimen that has helped many native Hawaiians to overcome chronic diseases.

Program provides a structure for promoting healthy lifestyles, preserving traditional culture, and, by encouraging traditional agricultural practices, protecting the environment. It also demonstrates how cultural values can motivate people to adopt healthy habits. Rather than repeatedly exhorting participants to count calories or cut down on fat, the WCCHC staff makes a concerted effort to put the plan into a cultural context, emphasizing, for example, that returning to a traditional diet is one way for people to show respect for their ancestors. The inclusion of foods from many ethnic traditions makes the program adaptable for use anywhere in the world. In Hawaii it has proved successful not just with native Hawaiians but with individuals from a variety of ethnic groups.

A further advantage of the program as a public health strategy is its relatively low cost. Studies suggest that a nutrition-centered approach such as this one would, in most cases, be more effective for the treatment of heart disease than coronary bypass surgery, which can cost from $25,000 to $100,000. Considering that bypass surgery is performed more than 400,000 times a year in the U.S., at a total cost of nearly $90 billion—and in most cases requires repeat surgery in an average of four years—it becomes clear that a regimen such as the Waianae Diet Program would be a cost-effective primary intervention for heart disease.

Hawaii is a classic example of what happens to people's health when they lose touch with their cultural origins and abandon their traditional diet. It is also a microcosm of what is happening elsewhere in the world. Now it may also provide one possible solution to the virtual epidemic of obesity and chronic disease in affluent nations around the world.

Epilepsy

One of every 200 people has epilepsy—*i.e.*, is susceptible to recurrent seizures. Although in many cases seizures can be completely prevented by the use of antiepileptic drugs, a sizable minority of people continue to have seizures despite drug treatment. The frequency of attacks may vary from fewer than one per year to many seizures per day.

Even when medication completely controls seizures, however, the side effects of antiepileptic drugs may range from the annoying to the disabling, making therapy less than successful. The therapeutic index—the difference between the amount of drug necessary to produce the desired effect and the amount that produces dose-dependent side effects—is very small in this class of drug. Thus, many patients who depend on drugs in doses that provide seizure control do so at the expense of quickness of thought, memory skills, or physical agility.

The lack of a perfect treatment for epilepsy has led to a recent surge of interest in new therapies. The most exciting of these are surgical treatment, new antiepileptic drugs, and an innovative procedure called vagal nerve stimulation.

Surgery: drastic but often successful

Although brain surgery for medically intractable serious seizure disorders has been practiced since the 1940s, the treatment has become widespread only within the last 10–15 years. Prompted by the failure of drugs to provide completely successful, symptom-free eradication of seizures in everyone with epilepsy, neurologists and neurosurgeons at large medical centers that specialize in the treatment of epilepsy joined forces to develop a drastic but often successful alternative to drug therapy.

Surgery is an option mainly for those with focal epilepsy—that is, seizures that begin in a single, localized brain area that is the site of irritation from benign tumors, scars, or trauma. Surgery is a reasonable treatment for epilepsy if seizures can be shown to arise from this kind of lesion and if the location of the seizure focus is an area that can be removed or severed from adjacent brain tissue without disabling the patient. Satisfying these criteria is not an easy task; it requires the efforts of a clinical team consisting of epileptologists (neurologists who specialize in epilepsy), neurosurgeons, neuropsychologists, neuroradiologists, and clinical neurophysiologists. Because of the dramatic impact on the patient of both the disease and the treatment, clinical nurse specialists, social workers, and clinical psychologists are usually part of the treatment team as well.

Evaluation of a patient who is a possible candidate for surgery begins with a review of his or her medical history; the purpose is threefold: to confirm the

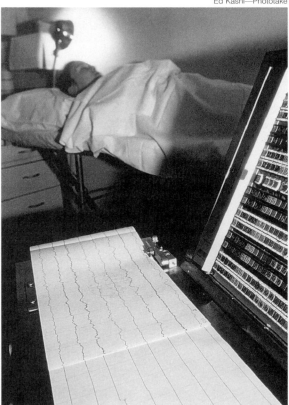

An electroencephalogram, or EEG, can help confirm that a specific brain area is responsible for a patient's epileptic seizures. If a discrete seizure focus can be pinpointed, surgical removal of the abnormal tissue may be an option.

diagnosis of epilepsy, to ensure that all reasonable and appropriate drug treatments have been tried, and to assess the patient's ability to withstand the stress of the diagnostic process and the surgery itself. The subsequent clinical investigations are aimed at determining the site of onset of seizures within the brain and the risks to the patient's normal functioning if that site is removed.

First, because different brain areas are involved in various motor, sensory, and emotional processes, a meticulous description of the individual's attacks often suggests which brain area produces them. Seizures that begin with twitching of the left hand, for example, usually originate on the right side of the brain in a region that controls the movement of the fingers. An electroencephalogram (EEG) may demonstrate an area of irritation, and magnetic resonance imaging (MRI) of the brain often shows a brain lesion such as an area of atrophy or scarring. Some research centers use positron emission tomography (PET), an imaging technique that can picture brain *function* (as distinct from *structure*) in the form of metabolic activity and blood flow. A battery of neuropsychological tests is used to assess specific cognitive skills such as language or memory; such tests often reveal selective or relative impairments mediated by a specific region of the brain. Specialized tests of language and memory, during which each of the two cerebral hemispheres (the two halves of the brain) is temporarily anesthetized, help to confirm the ability of the healthier hemisphere to function adequately if the abnormal focus is removed from the other hemisphere.

Finally, the surgical candidate is hospitalized in order for the surgical team to observe the seizures firsthand. Antiepileptic drugs are reduced in order to hasten the appearance or frequency of the attacks, which are captured on videotape and recorded on EEG. The seizures can then be reviewed to ensure that only one seizure type, and therefore one abnormal cerebral site, is involved, and the location of the abnormal EEG activity at the onset of the seizures can be pinpointed. Some seizure foci prove so elusive that more elaborate diagnostic studies may be necessary, such as seizure monitoring with the EEG recording electrodes surgically positioned under the skull or even implanted into brain tissue.

If all of these clinical investigations point to the same cerebral site as the likely seizure focus, and if the focus lies in an area that can be safely approached and removed, surgery may be recommended. Although most tissue removals are small, entire cerebral hemispheres have been surgically removed in cases where brain damage was already extensive and normal function much impaired.

Most surgical procedures involve excision of abnormal segments of brain. The most common is temporal lobectomy, or removal of the temporal lobe. However, other techniques are sometimes used. Some patients have more than one seizure-producing area or seizures that begin in a widespread, nonlocalized network of brain cells. Severing the connections between the hemispheres, a procedure known as a corpus callosotomy, sometimes succeeds in reducing or stopping the most severe types of seizures. Another procedure, called multiple subpial transection, involves making a series of tiny cuts on the surface of the brain; this sometimes allows seizure foci in nonremovable brain areas to be rendered free of epileptic potential while preserving the function of the area.

Temporal lobectomy results in complete cessation of seizures in a majority of patients. After a recovery period, many are able to stop antiepileptic drugs permanently. Corpus callosotomy tends to be less successful and is often undertaken simply in an attempt to reduce the number of a person's severe seizures. Because brain surgery poses significant risks, it is an option suitable only for those epilepsy patients who cannot be successfully treated with medication. The expense of such surgery and of the necessary preliminary testing is prodigious, and careful cost-benefit analyses have not yet been done; these would weigh improvements in patients' social and psychological well-being against the financial costs of the procedure.

New—and better—drugs

Until 1993 it had been more than 15 years since the last major new antiepileptic drug was approved for use in the United States. Within the last several years, however, at least two significant new antiepileptic drugs have appeared in Europe and Japan, and these appear to be the harbingers of a series of innovative medications for the treatment of epilepsy.

Vigabatrin and lamotrigine were released in Great Britain and other European countries several years ago and have joined the ranks of major antiepileptic drugs there. Similarly, zonisamide, developed and approved for use in Japan in 1988, has proved to be a safe and effective drug. The U.S. Food and Drug Administration (FDA) approved felbamate (Felbatol) and gabapentin (Neurontin) in 1993. FDA approval of lamotrigine is expected to follow.

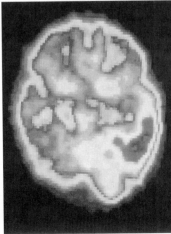
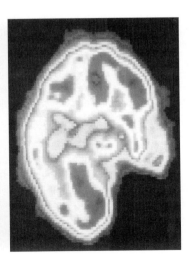

To cure an intractable form of epilepsy in a three-month-old, surgeons removed about one-fifth of his brain. Positron emission tomography (PET) scans of the brain before the operation (far left) and after (left) reveal dramatically how much tissue was excised. Within weeks of the surgery, the remaining part of the brain assumed the functions of the missing areas. Such treatment relies on the fact that the infant's developing brain is extremely adaptable.

Photographs, Alan D. Levenson

While none of these drugs is a panacea, all have distinct advantages over older medications or may offer alternative therapy for patients in whom the older medications have not been satisfactory.

Vigabatrin and zonisamide, for example, are effective in the treatment of seizure types previously treated with the drugs phenytoin and carbamazepine. But neither of the new agents causes the overgrowth of gum tissue associated with phenytoin, and both may succeed when carbamazepine fails to control seizures. Both, of course, have occasional side effects of their own, such as weight gain or altered cognition.

Felbamate was approved in August 1993 for use alone or in combination with other antiepileptic drugs. One year later, however, in response to reports of 10 cases of a serious blood disorder in people taking felbamate along with other medications, the FDA recommended that the drug be discontinued in all patients not receiving significant benefit from it. Meanwhile, the safety of the drug was under careful scrutiny.

Lamotrigine has been shown to be effective in some with intractable types of epilepsies, but it may be associated with side effects when used with carbamazepine and so must be introduced with care. Gabapentin is remarkably free from interactions with other antiepileptic drugs, and the way it is metabolized makes it exceptionally simple to use. However, because it is rapidly eliminated from the body, gabapentin must be taken several times a day to be effective.

Thus, although several new drugs have arrived, and newer ones are on the way, the ideal antiepileptic drug has not yet been discovered. The search continues.

Stimulating method for control of seizures

An entirely new approach to the treatment of epilepsy began with the observation that seizures in rats could be blocked by electrical stimulation of the vagus nerve, using a surgically implanted device similar to a cardiac pacemaker. The two vagus nerves (left and right) normally carry electrical impulses to and from the brain as part of the control mechanism for autonomic (involuntary) functions such as gastrointestinal activity, heart rate, respiration, and blood pressure control. Artificial stimulation of these nerves directly and indirectly affects widespread areas of the brain, including some of those responsible for generating some of the most common types of intractable seizures. In ways that are not completely understood, such stimulation seems to interfere with the electrical activity of cells responsible for producing seizures.

In 1994 trials of vagal nerve stimulation in human patients with intractable epilepsy were concluding in the United States, and the results appeared promising. Although the technology is sophisticated, the surgical technique is simple. The stimulator, a circular device about the size of a pocket watch, is inserted under the skin of the chest. A tiny wire is tunneled under the skin from the stimulator to the neck, where it is wrapped around the vagus nerve.

After implantation, the stimulator can be programmed by a small computer held against the chest. The intensity and frequency of stimulation can thus be changed as the condition of the patient warrants. Most patients have intermittent stimulation every 5 to 15 minutes throughout the day and night. Some people with epilepsy experience sensations that warn them of an impending seizure; by holding the programming computer against their chests to quickly activate the stimulator, they may be able to abort the attack.

The vagal nerve stimulator has the disadvantage of requiring a surgical procedure. Also, because the larynx (voice box) is stimulated, most patients feel slightly hoarse when the stimulator is operating. Serious complications are rare, however, and if vagal stimulation can be shown to be effective without the concomitant use of antiepileptic drugs, it would free patients from the chronic side effects of these medications. At this point the role of vagal stimulation in epilepsy treatment remains to be definitely proved. Continued trials of the process should provide some certainty.

—*Donna C. Bergen, M.D.*

Eye Diseases and Visual Disorders

Improvements in the treatment of eye diseases and visual disorders are occurring around the world. They range from the use of high-technology lasers that remove infinitesimally small amounts of tissue to low-technology public health programs that prevent blindness, which is so prevalent in the less developed world. In fact, a theme for eye care in the early 1990s could be "high-tech–low-tech."

The following brief survey of selected recent developments in preventing and treating eye disease provides a glimpse of the spectrum of problems that eye care specialists are faced with and some of the high- and low-tech solutions that are being employed. Several generalizations can be made: Early detection of eye disease through annual examinations often can prevent blindness in individuals at risk. Worldwide public health efforts are needed to wipe out preventable blindness. Advanced technology has facilitated sophisticated eye surgery that is improving the quality of life of millions of individuals.

Stunning advances in eye surgery

Modern eye surgery in the developed world has reached levels of high complexity. Ophthalmic surgeons use an operating microscope that magnifies the delicate tissues of the eye up to 16 times, enabling them to use tiny instruments and extremely fine sutures; for example, the nylon sutures that are now used to close incisions in the eye are only 15 to 20

μm (micrometers; a micrometer is one-millionth of a meter) in diameter, which is less than one-third the diameter of a human hair. Surgery inside the eye is often accomplished by insertion of fiber-optic lights and multifunctional instruments through one-millimeter (0.04-in) puncture wounds in the eye wall. Using the microscope to look through the pupil, the surgeon can manipulate tissues within the eye by using slender forceps and miniaturized scissors or lasers to remove or destroy fibrous tissue, abnormal blood vessels, or blood clots and restore the patient's eyesight.

Laser surgery of the eye continues to advance in scope and complexity. Argon lasers with wavelengths of 488 and 514.5 nm (nanometers; a nanometer is one-billionth of a meter), krypton lasers (531, 568, and 647 nm), and tunable dye lasers (577, 595, and 630 nm) are all used to treat glaucoma and diabetic retinopathy, an important complication of diabetes. These lasers work by photocoagulation—the heating of tissues that either kills the abnormal tissues or seals off abnormal blood vessels.

By using the mechanism of photodisruption—*i.e.,* creation of a small explosion that blasts a hole in the tissue through which the patient can see—Nd:YAG (neodymium:yttrium-aluminum-garnet) lasers (1,064 nm) can make openings in opaque tissue that sometimes forms in the lens capsule after cataract surgery. The argon-fluoride excimer laser (193 nm) can correct nearsightedness and astigmatism by the process of photoablation, which involves the removal of small amounts of corneal tissue. Holmium:YAG lasers (2.1 μm) can be used to treat farsightedness through a photothermal mechanism, which shrinks corneal tissue by heat and steepens the central cornea. There are many other new lasers with potential to cure eye disorders or correct visual problems. These include semiconductor diode lasers that can be as small and light as an audiocassette.

Surgery for refractive errors: a dream come true?

An estimated 25% to 30% of the human population is nearsighted, and nearly 50% of people worldwide need eyeglasses or contact lenses to correct their refractive errors. Refractive errors include nearsightedness (myopia), farsightedness (hyperopia), and astigmatism. Because so many people are affected by such errors and are dependent upon corrective lenses, there is strong motivation on the part of both patients and eye care specialists to seek methods of achieving normal vision without using external prosthetic devices.

Those with refractive errors have blurry vision because the light rays that enter the eye do not come to a sharp point of focus on the retina. In myopia the focal point of light falls in front of the retina; in hyperopia the focal point is behind the retina. The irregular curvature of the cornea in the astigmatic eye prevents light from focusing at any single point.

Currently, there are approximately 15 different types of surgery to correct these refractive errors—techniques known collectively as refractive surgery. Their increasing success is making a reality out of what was not very long ago little more than a dream. Most refractive surgery is done on the eye's most powerful focusing lens—the cornea—the clear tissue covering the front of the eye, which is the thickness of a credit card (about 550 μm) and the diameter of a dime (approximately 12 mm).

The most commonly used refractive surgical procedure is *refractive keratotomy,* which has developed gradually over the past 50 years. The surgeon uses a thin, exquisitely sharp microscopic diamond scalpel to make small incisions in the outer part of the cornea. To treat myopia, a radial pattern is used—like spokes on a bicycle wheel. The slight swelling of the cornea and pressure inside the eye that result from the incisions push the cornea into a new shape, which reduces or eliminates the nearsightedness. In patients

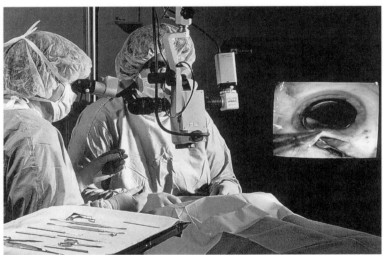

Ophthalmologists today routinely perform highly complex surgical procedures by using tiny instruments, extremely fine sutures, and an operating microscope that magnifies the delicate eye tissues up to 16 times.

with astigmatism, transverse (cross-wise, right-angle) incisions are made in the cornea to change the shape along specific meridians.

In the past, surgeons attempted to correct the entire refractive error in a single operation, but because patients' eyes heal differently, that approach was somewhat unpredictable. Therefore, in the 1990s surgeons commonly use a staged approach, in which an initial operation may be followed by one or two subsequent procedures to enhance the effect of the first procedure, fine-tuning the shaping of the cornea according to the individual's particular refractive error and visual needs. The success rate of the staged approach is good, with 50% to 60% of patients achieving near-perfect vision (20/20 or better) and 80% to 90% achieving vision 20/40 or better (the vision required for a driver's license), which frees them from the need to wear corrective lenses most of the time, although some may still need glasses for specific activities, such as driving at night. The major drawbacks of refractive keratotomy are (1) it causes a mild glare, which is seen around lights at night, (2) there is some fluctuation of vision from morning to evening, (3) an unsuccessful outcome occurs in approximately 10% of patients, and (4) there is a tendency for the eye to shift over a period of many years toward farsightedness, thus increasing the need for reading glasses.

The most recent widespread advance in refractive surgery is the use of an argon-fluoride excimer laser to reshape the cornea. On the basis of precise measurements of the eye and computer programs that determine the configuration of the laser beam and the number of laser pulses for the individual eye, the surgeon "sculpts" the cornea into the exact shape needed for proper focus of the eye. The tissue can be removed either from the surface of the eye (*photorefractive keratectomy*) or from beneath a thin protective flap of cornea (*keratomileusis*). Excimer laser surgery of the cornea can be extremely accurate because a single pulse of laser light removes approximately 0.25 μm of tissue without damaging the underlying tissue. The drawback of this procedure is that the healing of the cornea after treatment can be somewhat variable, thus decreasing the overall accuracy of the surgery. Still, approximately 50% to 60% of patients achieve 20/20 or better visual acuity, and 80% to 90% achieve 20/40 or better. The technology for excimer laser corneal surgery continues to change and improve. These lasers are used in most developed countries, although as of mid-1994 they were still under U.S. Food and Drug Administration investigation; therefore, in the United States they are presently used only in designated centers.

Refractive keratotomy and excimer laser corneal surgery are "patient friendly." They are done as outpatient procedures, require only eyedrops for anesthesia, allow the patient to see reasonably well without glasses within the first week, take only 5 to 15 minutes of actual surgical time, and involve only mild discomfort with proper postoperative medications.

A third type of refractive surgery does not involve shaping of the cornea but rather consists of the placement of a small lens, similar to a contact lens, inside the eye. The lens carries out the same focusing function as glasses or externally worn contact lenses but remains permanently in place. This type of lens is known as a phakic intraocular lens; it is placed in an eye that already has a normal crystalline lens (the phakos), so essentially the eye has two lenses after the surgery. Phakic intraocular lenses have been implanted for the past 40 years, but only in the early 1990s have the design and quality of the lenses improved to the extent that they might be used on a large number of patients. Therefore, intraocular lenses are currently under active investigation in many developed countries around the world.

Refractive surgery currently represents a high-technology aspect of ophthalmology, with glasses and contact lenses representing the traditional low-tech approach. However, some surgeons think that surgery to correct refractive errors might have an application in the less developed world, where access to glasses and contact lenses can be quite limited and many who have refractive errors must suffer blurry vision all the time. Procedures such as refractive keratotomy can be carried out by almost any surgeon who has some training and average skill and judgment, using instruments that cost only a few thousand dollars. A brief surgical procedure not only could restore the eyesight of people in less developed countries to near normal, greatly enhancing their quality of life, but also could contribute to the economic productivity and advancement of those countries.

Reducing the toll of preventable blindness

The number one cause of preventable blindness in the world is cataract, a gradual opacification of the crystalline lens inside the eye, which distorts images and causes vision to become blurry over a period of years, eventually resulting in blindness. In 1990 the World Health Organization (WHO) estimated that 13 million persons are currently blinded by cataract, the majority living in less developed countries.

In industrialized countries cataract surgery constitutes one of the largest medical expenses of governments. In the United States alone, approximately 1.5 million cataract operations are done each year. In less developed countries, on the other hand, blindness due to cataract has significant socioeconomic impact on individuals, families, and society. The 1990s have been designated the Decade of the Disabled, and one focal point of this WHO-sponsored program is the eradication of unnecessary blindness caused by cataract.

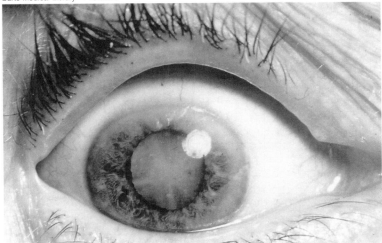

The vision of the eye at left is clouded by a cataract, an opacification of the eye's normally crystalline lens. Worldwide, cataracts are responsible for more preventable blindness than any other single cause. Surgery that removes the opaque lens and replaces it with a permanent intraocular lens implant can restore clear vision and is one of the most commonly performed operations in most developed countries. One of the goals set by the World Health Organization for the decade of the 1990s is to make cataract surgery increasingly available to people in all parts of the world. (The white spot is a reflection caused by the camera's flash.)

Most cataracts develop as a result of aging, and most commonly affect individuals over the age of 60. The cause of cataract is unknown, but genetic influences and exposure to solar radiation are among the suspects. Individuals living nearer the equator and working out-of-doors have a higher incidence of cataract than individuals living in more northerly or southerly climes who spend most of their time indoors. This has led some physicians to advise patients to shield their eyes and wear sunglasses that filter out ultraviolet rays when outdoors.

Although there is no sure way to prevent cataracts, ophthalmic surgeons have devised numerous operations to treat them. Unless a rare complication occurs, the surgery almost always improves the patient's vision. Cataract surgery poses two major challenges: the opaque lens must be removed from within the eye without permanently weakening the eye or distorting its shape, and the focusing power of the eye needs to be replaced by the implantation of an intraocular lens, which prevents the patient from having to use thick "Coke-bottle" glasses or contact lenses in order to see after surgery. The solution to the first problem was solved by the development of fine instruments that can work through small incisions (approximately four millimeters wide). Instruments such as the "phaco-emulsification tip" break the lens into fragments and aspirate them from the eye. Although there is not currently a laser that is used to remove cataracts, such instruments are under development and will enable surgeons to work through even smaller openings, which would maintain the strength and shape of the eyeball after surgery.

The solution to the second problem was the development of intraocular lens implants—six- to seven-millimeter-diameter disks of plastic or silicone that are placed inside the eye, decreasing the need for thick glasses. In the developed world, intraocular lens implants are used in over 95% of cataract operations. The design of intraocular lenses has become increasingly sophisticated. For example, there are now lenses that can be folded or injected into the eye through very small openings; there are also lenses that can provide more than one point of focus (multifocal intraocular lenses) so the recipient can see both near and distant objects clearly.

Many research scientists have set as their Holy Grail the search for methods or drugs that can actually prevent the formation of cataract. Currently, that search is being carried out intensively in molecular genetics and biochemistry laboratories.

The delivery of cataract surgery services where they are needed most constitutes a low-tech side of the cataract problem. In less developed countries, such as India and China, the number of patients with cataracts is increasing faster than the number of cataract operations performed each year. Reaching people who are without access to urban health care is an important challenge. The problem is being solved in many ways.

Numerous organizations are banding together under the aegis of the International Agency for the Prevention of Blindness to provide funds as well as an infrastructure for carrying out regional surveys that document the prevalence of cataract and determine the need for surgery. These organizations range from major institutions such as the National Eye Institute of the U.S. National Institutes of Health to small, nongovernmental organizations, such as the Christoffel Blindenmission, Helen Keller International, and Sight Savers. Through such organizations eye doctors volunteer their time and services in parts of the world where the need is great. Local paramedical teams are organized to identify high-risk populations and the individuals who already have cataracts. Once identified, these individuals are then taken to mobile camps or local clinics where volunteer physicians carry out high-volume cataract surgery. Patients with more complex problems can be transferred to secondary or tertiary care facilities.

This paradigm has worked especially well in some smaller countries—for example, Nepal. Larger countries such as India and China pose a much greater public health challenge that still needs to be met. In addition, surgeons face the quandary of needing to use inexpensive methods that enable them to remove cataracts quickly and efficiently, but the operation leaves patients without a focusing lens inside the eye. Afterward they require thick spectacles for useful vision. Often such spectacles are not available or are quickly lost; thus, patients' overall visual function is not greatly improved. On the other hand, placing an intraocular lens implant in the eye is expensive and more time-consuming and requires more sophisticated surgical techniques. Mass-produced, inexpensive lenses are now being used. During the Decade of the Disabled, efforts are being directed toward solving these problems concerning delivery of cataract services in the less developed world.

Sight-saving approaches to diabetic retinopathy

Approximately one-half of the estimated 12 million–14 million people in the United States who have diabetes mellitus develop diabetic retinopathy, a disorder of blood vessels within the retina and choroid, a vascular membrane at the back of the eye. The abnormal vessels develop small protrusions (microaneurysms); leak fat, proteins, and fluid into the most sensitive part of the retina (macular edema); may burst and cause bleeding inside the eye (retinal or vitreous hemorrhage); and sometimes grow uncontrollably inside the eye (neovascularization). Although people with diabetes who maintain near-normal blood sugar levels are at somewhat lower risk, diabetic retinopathy may still occur in any patient with either insulin-dependent or non-insulin-dependent diabetes, resulting in severe visual loss. In the U.S. alone it is responsible for an estimated 8,000 new cases of blindness per year.

An important low-tech public health challenge is making those who have the disease aware of the importance of having thorough eye examinations at least once a year. Early detection and early treatment of the disorder can prevent its progression, reducing the likelihood of more severe eye damage. To this end many ophthalmic and public health societies throughout the world have mounted public-awareness campaigns, such as the "Diabetes 2000" campaign of the American Academy of Ophthalmology and mass-media public-service announcements sponsored by the National Eye Institute's National Eye Health Education program.

At the same time, researchers have shown in prospective randomized controlled trials that early treatment of diabetic retinopathy with photocoagulation of the peripheral retina—a procedure that produces a few hundred tiny burns to stop the diseased tissue from producing factors that cause further damage in the eye—can effectively prevent progressive blindness. Similarly, using lasers to treat specific areas of hemorrhage or swelling can have a salutary effect on vision. Surgeons can also remove hemorrhages from within the eye by using the microsurgical techniques of vitrectomy. When a retinal detachment has occurred, vision can be effectively restored by vitreoretinal surgery, which mechanically eliminates the clear, jellylike substance known as the vitreous and reattaches the retina to its normal location in the eye by using compression straps around the eye or, more recently, expandable gases within the eye.

Macular degeneration: no solutions yet

Age-related macular degeneration (ARMD) is an important and growing public health problem; it affects

Diabetic retinopathy, a complication of diabetes that often results in blindness, is a disorder of the blood vessels within the retina and choroid. The abnormal blood vessels develop small protrusions that leak fat, proteins, and fluid into the macula, the most sensitive part of the retina; bleeding within the eye occurs if the blood vessels burst. Early detection and treatment can prevent progression of the disease process and reduce the likelihood of severe eye damage. Treatments for diabetic retinopathy include laser surgery, photocoagulation of the peripheral retina, and vitreoretinal surgery when the retina has become detached.

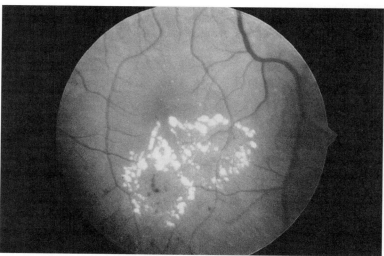

CNRI/Phototake

Voluntary nongovernmental organizations play a tremendously important role in providing essential eye care in less developed parts of the world, especially in remote areas. The goal is to reduce the toll of preventable blindness.

some 1.7 million persons in the U.S. alone and is the leading cause of legal blindness in older Americans. The macula is the very sensitive central part of the retina where the best vision resides. The entire macular region is only about five millimeters in diameter, so it is not surprising that a disease process in this small, highly sensitive area can have a generalized devastating effect on vision and cause functional blindness.

Because ARMD is so common, routine eye examinations of older individuals are essential; public health efforts need to be directed toward ensuring early detection. Another low-tech approach to the problem is the ongoing research into the role of nutrient supplements—and specifically whether antioxidant vitamins such as vitamin C or trace minerals such as zinc taken systemically can decrease the rate of occurrence or the severity of ARMD. Animal studies and some human trials have suggested that such supplements may be beneficial, but the results are inconclusive. At present the National Eye Institute is conducting the Age-Related Eye Disease Study—a 10-year investigation involving some 5,000 subjects aged 60 to 75—

which seeks more definitive answers to questions about the prevalence, severity, and treatment of macular disease.

Currently, there is no known effective treatment for ARMD. High-tech research is investigating the use of laser photocoagulation to seal off leaking blood vessels and vitreoretinal surgery to remove scar tissue from beneath the retina. Better understanding of the molecular genetics of ARMD may provide important solutions in the future.

—George O. Waring III, M.D.

Gastrointestinal Disorders

There have been numerous developments in the field of gastroenterology that have received considerable recent attention. The debate over the effectiveness of screening for colorectal cancer (cancers of the colon and rectum) has continued; at the same time, discoveries in molecular genetics have paved the way for accurate tests to identify persons at risk for inherited forms of the disease. Researchers have confirmed earlier findings on the role of a specific bacterium in the development of ulcers; the association of this same organism with stomach cancer is under investigation. There also have been refinements in the understanding of the different viruses involved in the serious liver disease hepatitis. A recent major outbreak in the United States of a relatively uncommon parasitic infection, cryptosporidiosis, has helped call attention to this potentially dangerous disease.

Colorectal cancer: reducing risk

Cancers of the colon and rectum are a major cause of illness and death in many Western countries. In the United States colon and rectal cancers are the third most common cancers in men and the second most common in women, and approximately 153,000 cases are diagnosed annually. Although colorectal cancer death rates have declined 7% in men and 30% in women over the past 30 years, it is estimated that some 56,000 people will die from this disease in 1994 in the United States alone. Researchers continue to identify risk factors, which increases the possibility that those at high risk might be able to reduce their vulnerability through dietary or pharmacological means or, at least, by undergoing regular screening. Because the vast majority of colon cancers arise from adenomatous polyps, which are benign, strategies to either prevent the development of such polyps or remove them before they become malignant are likely to be effective in reducing mortality. In fact, the results of a recent U.S. study have demonstrated the effectiveness of the latter approach.

The role of diet. The importance of dietary factors in gastrointestinal cancers is becoming increasingly recognized. Diets rich in fruits, vegetables, and high-fiber grains are particularly associated with lower rates of fatal colon cancer. Current recommendations for prevention of colon cancer include:

- reducing the consumption of both animal and vegetable fat to 25% of total calories (even lower than the 30% limit suggested in the general dietary recommendations accepted in the U.S.)
- increasing the intake of high-fiber foods, especially fruits and vegetables, to a daily total of 25 g
- avoiding obesity and increasing physical activity (balancing energy intake and expenditure)
- drinking only moderate amounts of alcohol
- abstaining from cigarettes and all other tobacco products
- consuming an adequate amount of calcium (at least 800 mg a day; low-fat dairy foods are among the most accessible sources)

Evidence of aspirin's benefit. Researchers also have raised the possibility that aspirin may help to prevent colorectal cancer. In an American Cancer Society study of 662,424 men and women, epidemiologists found that the risk of fatal colon cancer among persons using aspirin 16 or more times per month was approximately half that of nonusers; the trend of decreasing risk with increasing dosage was statistically significant in both men and women. The trend was not observed in users of acetaminophen (Tylenol, Datril, etc.). In a Swedish study of 11,683 persons with rheumatoid arthritis, a severe joint disease in which aspirin and nonsteroidal anti-inflammatory drugs (NSAIDs) are routinely used, it was observed that the arthritis patients had 30–40% lower rates of colon and rectal cancers. It has also been found in several studies that sulindac (Clinoril), another NSAID, inhibited the growth of polyps in patients with familial adenomatous polyposis (FAP), a hereditary disease that often leads to colon cancer.

The mechanisms by which aspirin and NSAIDs retard the growth of polyps and reduce the rate of colon cancer are not yet understood. It is known, however, that these drugs block the formation of prostaglandins, substances that are powerful intracellular regulators and that may regulate cell growth. Prostaglandins also play a role in immunity, inflammation, blood coagulation, protection of the stomach lining against acid, and tumor spread (metastasis). It is of interest to researchers that the apparent preventive effect of aspirin is not confined to colorectal cancer. Recent data have suggested that regular use of aspirin for 10 years or more is also associated with a 40% reduction in fatal cancers of the esophagus and stomach.

The optimum dose of aspirin for prevention of colorectal and other gastrointestinal cancers is not known. Several large-scale studies have begun to determine both the appropriate dose of aspirin and also its benefits, risks, and side effects. It is known, for example, that aspirin, because of its anticoagulant properties, can cause bleeding in the brain and in the stomach or other parts of the gastrointestinal tract.

Toward effective screening. Several national organizations in the United States advocate that everyone over age 50 undergo annual tests for occult (hidden) blood in the stool and sigmoidoscopic examination of the lower colon every three to five years. Results of well-designed studies of screening for occult bleeding offer promise of improvement in survival rates. While fewer than 50% of those with a positive test result turn out to have benign polyps or cancer, more than 75% of the cancers detected through such tests are at an early stage and thus more easily cured. A study at the University of Minnesota reported a 33% reduction in cancer mortality over a 13-year period in those who were screened annually for occult blood. Because of positive findings (*i.e.,* blood in the stool), 38% of those screened underwent the more invasive process of colonoscopy (an examination of the entire colon requiring the introduction, under sedation, of a fiberoptic device). Only 50% of the cancers diagnosed in this group were actually detected by occult blood testing, however; the remainder were discovered between tests, as symptomatic cancers. For this reason the study has engendered considerable controversy. Detractors have claimed that the decrease in mortality may be attributed more to the high percentage of colonoscopies performed than to screening for occult blood. However, preliminary data from studies under way in Europe confirm a decline in death rates in groups who have undergone screening.

With flexible sigmoidoscopy it is possible to examine the lower 60 cm (24 in) of the colon, where about 50% of benign and malignant tumors are found. (This procedure is less invasive and thus simpler than colonoscopy.) Two recent studies comparing the death rate from colorectal cancer in those who underwent flexible sigmoidoscopy with that of a control group who did not showed a 70% reduction in mortality from cancers within reach of the sigmoidoscope.

These findings have led to the suggestion that an efficient method for screening the entire U.S. population would be to offer a one-time colonoscopic examination to everyone at age 55. The exam presumably would help to separate those at low risk of colon cancer from those at increased risk (by virtue of the presence of adenomatous polyps or already existing cancer). Follow-up thus could be largely focused on the high-risk group—those with either benign or malignant tumors.

The expense of a nationwide colonoscopy screening program would be extremely high, however, and without a significant decrease in the cost, it is unlikely that the procedure could be made available on such a wide scale. Moreover, lack of compliance with screening recommendations would limit the scope of such a program. An alternative, less costly method, barium X-ray examination of the colon, is not sufficiently sensitive in the detection of small cancers and polyps larger than one centimeter (0.4 in), which are more likely than smaller lesions to be malignant.

Applications of molecular genetics. A range of genetic abnormalities have been identified in colorectal cancers. A gene on chromosome 5 is known to be crucial in the development of colorectal cancer in people with FAP. Once the specific mutations have been identified, scientists may be able to screen members of affected families at birth, pinpointing those individuals who carry disease-causing forms of the gene. An even larger high-risk group consists of those from families with a history of hereditary nonpolyposis colorectal cancer (HNPCC), a much more common cancer than FAP. In fact, HNPCC accounts for about 10% of all cases of colorectal cancer. Localization of the genes involved in HNPCC to regions of chromosomes 2 and 3 has provided confirmation of a genetic predisposition to this form of colorectal cancer within certain families. Here, too, it is extremely likely that an understanding of the genetic abnormalities will lead to screening for high-risk families. Identifying those who are at risk would allow regular screening to be limited to individuals who carry the defective genes, a measure that would reduce the costliness of screening programs. Those who are affected might employ preventive strategies, such as taking NSAIDs, at an early age before the onset of tumors, perhaps delaying the development of cancer or preventing it entirely.

The detection of genetic abnormalities may have other applications. For example, intestinal lining cells shed into the stool could be examined for the presence of specific mutations. Such a test might provide a much more effective screening tool than the occult blood tests currently in use. It has also been found that in certain tumors deletions of genes on chromosomes 17 and 18 indicate a poor prognosis independent of conventional methods for assessing disease progression. Molecular analysis of DNA taken from a tumor could thus be used to identify those patients who require intensive postsurgical chemotherapy or immunotherapy.

The ulcer "bug"

Helicobacter pylori (formerly called *Campylobacter pylori*) is a bacterium that is uniquely adapted to survival in the highly acidic environment of the stomach. It is also a known cause of gastritis (inflammation of the stomach). Its epidemiology is not well understood but, because there is a high prevalence of infection where sanitary conditions are poor and because the organism spreads within families, both oral–oral and fecal–oral spread are thought to be involved. The prevalence of *H. pylori* infection increases with age. It is estimated, for example, that approximately 60% of Americans are infected by the age of 60.

H. pylori grows in the mucus that overlies acid-secreting cells in parts of the human stomach. Infection with *H. pylori* causes the gastric tissue to become inflamed, which in turn leads to depletion of the protective layer of mucus. *H. pylori* also produces a toxin that damages the cells lining the stomach; the damage is exacerbated by ammonia that is produced by urease, an enzyme secreted by the organism. As an indirect result of the tissue injury, the production of the hormone gastrin within the stomach is increased. Gastrin then stimulates the stomach to increase the output of acid, which in turn may bring about additional injury to the stomach lining. After acute infection, *H. pylori* tends to remain in the stomach for many years. It is eliminated naturally only when significant damage

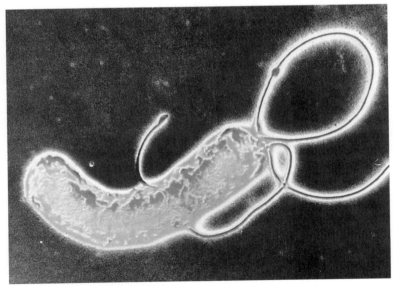

The link between the bacterium Helicobacter pylori *and ulcers, once a matter of some controversy, is now widely accepted. Ninety-five percent of patients with duodenal ulcers and 50–80% of those with gastric ulcers have evidence of* H. pylori *infection. Recent studies have demonstrated that eradicating the bacterium—by means of antimicrobial drugs (antibiotics)—reduces ulcer recurrence.*

to the acid-producing cells leads to decreased acidity and the subsequent overgrowth by other bacteria normally kept in check by stomach acid.

The diagnosis of H. pylori infection can be made by means of a biopsy of the stomach lining obtained via an endoscope; the tissue can then be examined under the microscope or, if necessary, grown in the laboratory. As an alternative, antibodies to the bacterium can be detected in the blood. A breath test that detects urease can also suggest the presence of H. pylori infection.

The link between chronic H. pylori infection and ulcers—controversial not so very long ago—is now well accepted. In the past decade it has been demonstrated that between 50% and 80% of patients with gastric ulcers and 95% of those with duodenal ulcers are infected. Furthermore, recent studies suggest that eradication of the bacterium reduces the recurrence of ulcers to very low rates. By comparison, traditional ulcer therapies, such as drugs to reduce or block acid secretion in the stomach, provided relief of symptoms but rarely a cure. On the basis of these findings—the high prevalence of H. pylori infection in ulcer patients and the proven effectiveness of antibiotic therapy—the U.S. National Institutes of Health (NIH) in 1994 issued a consensus statement on H. pylori and peptic ulcer disease. The expert panel convened by the NIH concluded that once the presence of the bacterium has been confirmed with appropriate tests, physicians treating ulcer patients should prescribe antimicrobial drugs as a matter of course.

A few years ago typical treatment for ulcers associated with H. pylori included a combination of either amoxicillin or tetracycline (antibiotics), bismuth (the active ingredient in Pepto-Bismol), and another antibiotic, metronidazole. A more recent regimen consists of a week's treatment with two drugs, amoxicillin and omeprazole (a potent inhibitor of acid secretion).

A possible association between H. pylori infection and gastric cancer is also under investigation. In studies in Japan, Colombia, China, and the United States (the latter conducted among Japanese Americans), it was shown that the prevalence of antibodies to H. pylori was significantly higher among those with gastric cancer than among controls. The finding does not establish a direct causal relationship between H. pylori and gastric cancer, but it is thought that the gastritis caused by H. pylori may in time lead to cellular changes in the stomach lining that progress to malignancy. Eradication of H. pylori in early adulthood (via antibiotics) and the development of a vaccine to enhance immunity against the bacterium are two strategies that might help prevent gastric cancer.

The many kinds of viral hepatitis

A considerable amount of new information has been gathered over the past five years concerning the role of different viruses in causing hepatitis. It is now believed that five viruses are responsible for acute or chronic hepatitis.

Hepatitis A virus (HAV). HAV is present in the bloodstream for about two to four weeks after infection, which occurs through fecal–oral transmission. Approximately 90% of those infected have no symptoms; in 10%, infection results in jaundice. The risk of liver failure is extremely low, and there is no risk of chronic infection. A vaccine to prevent HAV is being tested; it could be useful to travelers to regions where the virus is widespread and to others, such as military recruits or youngsters in day care, who are at high risk of infection.

Hepatitis B virus (HBV). HBV either is present in the bloodstream for about four to eight weeks after infection or becomes chronic. As in HAV, there are no symptoms of the acute infection in 90% of those affected; 10% develop jaundice. The risk of liver failure is 10 times higher, however, than with HAV. In about one-third of patients with chronic HBV infection, the liver shows a series of pathological changes that persist for several years. Initially, HBV replicates at a high rate; this is followed by a decrease in replication as the body's immunologic defenses take effect. A stage finally occurs in which the inflammation becomes much less evident.

Individuals who have chronic hepatitis caused by HBV infection are at high risk of developing cirrhosis (severe scarring of the liver), although the time between infection and the development of cirrhosis may be as long as 10–30 years. Patients with cirrhosis caused by HBV are also at risk of developing liver cancer (hepatoma), possibly as a result of interaction of HBV and other factors, such as dietary and environmental toxins.

HBV has infected more than two billion persons alive today, and the 350 million individuals who are chronically infected carriers of the virus are at risk of death from hepatitis, cirrhosis, and primary liver cancer (i.e., cancer that starts in the liver as opposed to cancer that has spread to the liver from another site). Primary liver cancer is the number one or two cause of cancer deaths in males in Asia (especially East Asia—China, Japan, Taiwan, Singapore, Korea) and sub-Saharan Africa. It is therefore vitally important to recognize that HBV infection can be prevented by a safe, relatively inexpensive vaccine. Although this vaccine has been available for a decade, it remains relatively costly; its use is thus beyond the means of many poor countries.

Since 1991 the U.S. Occupational Safety and Health Administration has required employers to provide hepatitis B vaccine to health care workers whose occupational exposure to blood or body fluids puts them at high risk for HBV infection. Recent studies of the effectiveness of the vaccine in this group have shown that the older an individual is at the time of vaccination, the poorer the response of the immune system. Other factors, such as smoking and increased body weight, also can affect the vaccine's capacity to stimulate immunity. As a result of these findings, it has been recommended that health care personnel be vaccinated early, preferably while they are in training. Further studies need to be done to determine the best course of action for those likely to respond poorly to the vaccine.

Hepatitis C virus (HCV). HCV infection was first recognized in the 1970s as so-called non-A, non-B hepatitis that resulted from blood transfusion. HCV is now known to be the major cause of transfusion-associated hepatitis. Infection may be short-lived or chronic. There are no symptoms in 95% of those with acute infections. Chronic infection occurs in 60–70% of cases, whether or not there is jaundice initially. Although more than 80% of patients with chronic disease show only mild evidence of inflammation, in 10–20% the infection results in cirrhosis over 10–30 years. Liver cancer develops in 15% of those with cirrhosis. A successful vaccine has not been developed. Some recent studies have indicated that the virus occasionally may be transmitted sexually as well as via blood.

Hepatitis D virus (HDV). HDV, also called delta agent, is a defective virus that can replicate only in the presence of HBV. In most instances infection with HDV occurs in patients who have previously had a chronic HBV infection. A recent study indicated that interferon alpha, already widely used to treat hepatitis B and C, is also effective against chronic HDV infection.

Hepatitis E virus (HEV). HEV occurs almost exclusively in Africa and Asia. Infection results in acute hepatitis and carries a high risk of liver failure in pregnant women. There is apparently no risk of chronic infection.

Cryptosporidiosis

Cryptosporidia are a group of parasitic protozoans that carry out their reproductive cycle within the small intestine of mammals and are ultimately excreted as oocysts in feces. Although cryptosporidium species have been recognized since the early 1900s, the organisms were not identified as a human pathogen until 1976. In recent years there has been increased recognition of one species, *Cryptosporidium parvum,* as an important cause of diarrheal disorders worldwide. A major outbreak occurred in Milwaukee, Wis., in April 1993, caused by contamination of the city's water supply. An estimated 350,000 persons were affected, indicating the potential public health threat of this parasite.

When *C. parvum* affects otherwise healthy individuals, it normally causes limited diarrhea. Among persons with AIDS and other immunocompromised patients, however, it can cause severe, unremitting diarrhea that lasts for more than a month and results in major loss of body fluid.

The infection is spread primarily in two ways, through water and directly from person to person. In the tropics, infection is more common in the warm and rainy months. Diagnosis is made through identification of oocysts in stool specimens. The way in which the cryptosporidium causes diarrhea is under study. It is thought that the parasite interferes with the delicate mechanisms of the small intestine, resulting in the malabsorption of sugars, vitamin B_{12}, and salts, but other factors may also be involved.

The best treatment for cryptosporidiosis has yet to be determined. Although several drugs have been tested, recent interest has focused on two oral antibiotics, paromomycin and azithromycin, and clinical trials are in progress.

—Bernard Levin, M.D.

A resident of Milwaukee, Wis., stocks up on bottled water. Authorities were not sure how it happened, but in April 1993 the city's water supply became contaminated with cryptosporidium, a parasite that can cause severe diarrhea. Outbreaks of cryptosporidiosis can pose a serious public health threat; in Milwaukee some 350,000 people fell ill.

Doors Opening for Children with Disabilities

by Gertrude M. Webb, Ed.D.

Less than 200 years ago, in both the United States and Europe, children whose intellectual, physical, or socioemotional behavior differed from what was considered normal were "warehoused." They were separated from general society; locked up in institutions located, like cemeteries, on the outskirts of communities; and housed in cells like criminals sentenced to life imprisonment. In these institutions children were at best socially looked down upon; often they were physically mistreated, and commonly they were labeled "mental idiots."

From warehousing to mainstreaming

In the United States, in the first half of the 19th century, parents, led by such educational reformers as Samuel Gridley Howe and Dorothea Dix, began demanding more humane treatment for their children who, having impairments, differed from the norm. The first schools for "deviant," or "handicapped," children addressed the needs of the physically impaired, primarily the deaf and the blind. Though such schools separated these children from their families and communities, the environments they provided were more protective of their pupils than the previous "warehouses." Among the most notable were the Perkins School for the Blind, established by Howe in Watertown, Mass., and the American School for the Deaf in Hartford, Conn. Both institutions emphasized *care* rather than custody and strove to help children cope with their impairments.

In 1869 handicapped children began to be returned to their own communities. The first class for the deaf in a public school was established in Boston, but then another 27 years passed before a class for mentally retarded children, in Providence, R.I., was established in a regular elementary school. After that, special classes that addressed the needs of the physically disabled, the visually impaired, and the deaf became more and more common in public schools throughout the United States. This trend—moving away from separation and isolation in faraway institutions—meant that youngsters with disabilities were attending schools in their local communities and living with their own families. Normal and disabled children began to know each other and each others' strengths and blessings as well as failings; often they realized that they were not so different from each other. Depending on the degree of family and community acceptance, the children either did well or did not thrive.

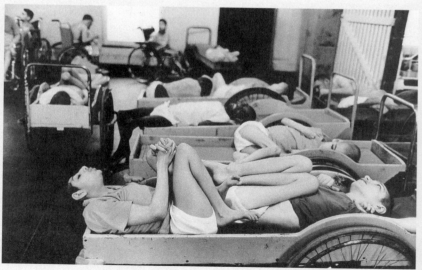

By the mid-19th century, treatment of the mentally and physically disabled had improved substantially in the U.S. This, however, was not the case as recently as the early 1970s at Willowbrook State School, Staten Island, New York City, the world's largest institution housing the mentally retarded and severely physically handicapped. Not only did children at Willowbrook not receive the kind of care that would have enabled them to develop to their fullest potential, they were subjected to conditions resembling those of "human warehouses" of the distant past.

Although special-class program designs within the public schools of home communities had their rewards and successes, they also had many problems. Nonetheless, they signaled a change in attitude on the part of society, which led the way to more respect and help for abnormal children. Along with this new understanding came a new and more respectful title for these children: *exceptional children*.

In the 1940s and '50s, professional groups such as the Council for Exceptional Children, parents groups such as the Association for the Retarded, and parent-professional groups such as the National Association for the Learning Disabled organized. Members educated themselves about the factors and forces that result in childhood disabilities. They funded programs and research and, perhaps most important, they became future-oriented, setting their sights on moving disabled children, both medically and educationally, toward normal functioning. These dedicated groups lobbied nationally and in every U.S. state calling for—and in some cases demanding—appropriate education for exceptional children.

In 1972 Massachusetts led in this effort by enacting Chapter 766 of the commonwealth's General Laws. The act created a design for identifying the disabilities of children by degree (mild, moderate, severe) and category (learning disabled, physically handicapped, mentally retarded, emotionally disturbed). Such refinements made it possible to establish appropriate programs that addressed the specific needs and problems of individual children. With the implementation of Chapter 766, the term *exceptional children* gave way to *children with special needs.* Moreover, in order that the children identified as having special needs would be effectively received in classrooms, the Massachusetts legislature, required teachers to undergo two years of special training. Colleges and universities throughout the state instituted or expanded special-education teacher-training programs.

Within the schools themselves a new classroom design, known as the "resource room," was created. In the resource room special educators taught children who were taken out of their regular classrooms for periods of remediation in their particular areas of weakness. The areas in need of remediation were identified in the so-called individual education plan (IEP) of each special-needs child. The IEP was designed by a team of educators, psychologists, social workers, and appropriate medical personnel who collaboratively assessed the child's level of functioning. The team then tailored an individualized program with specific strategies for achieving improvement within a specified time frame, which was agreed to by parents.

Massachusetts provided a model, but other states soon established special-education programs for more and more children. Seeing the benefits that individualized programming offered children with physical and mental disabilities, parents whose children had less severe problems began to request the same opportunities for their children. Soon the numbers of learning disabled children swelled in schools across the nation. In 1986 Madeleine Will, then assistant secretary of the Office of Special Education and Rehabilitative Services of the U.S. Department of Education, prepared a report entitled "Educating Students with Learning Problems—A Shared Responsibility," in which she called upon regular and special educators to work collaboratively to enable "hard-to-teach" students to achieve greater success in the regular classroom and thus to lower the numbers needing to be sent out of classrooms for special education—an approach that has come to be known as "mainstreaming."

A matter of rights

Over a period of several decades, national and societal concerns about the rights of minority groups in the U.S. culminated in congressional acts. The 1954 Supreme Court decision in *Brown* v. *Board of Education of Topeka* (Kan.) unanimously declared that racial segregation in public schools violated the 14th Amendment to the Constitution and that separate educational facilities were inherently unequal. The 1964 Civil Rights Act prohibited discrimination based on race, color, religion, or national origin and finally opened the door to equality for most Americans.

In a similar spirit, in 1973 Congress passed the Rehabilitation Act, which forbade discrimination against the disabled in education, employment, and housing and stipulated that persons with disabilities were to have access to public programs and facilities; section 504 of the act specifically required that modifications be made to public buildings to make them accessible to those with physical disabilities. Responding to increased parental and professional pressures, in 1974 the 95th Congress of the United States passed the Education for All Handicapped Children Act, mandating free and appropriate education in the least restrictive environment for special-needs children. This meant accommodating children with physical or mental impairments within regular schools to the fullest extent possible.

With the legislative changes came attitudinal changes. Regular educators who had never worked with slower children reacted with surprise. When they were given proper supports, they realized how *much* they could teach children with special needs. Teachers discovered new strategies that worked. For example, Margaret Dempsey, a teacher at the William Barton Rogers Middle School in Boston, discovered that when slower students were included in a group— *e.g.,* a reading group—they progressed notably. "Even if they were on the fringe at first," Dempsey learned, students almost always did much better than when left "sitting at their own desks totally baffled, doing nothing, and experiencing more failure." Other regular educators noticed that children with academic difficulties often demonstrated unique artistic, dramatic, and social abilities. Previously held myths and misconceptions about the special-needs child diminished as regular and special children learned together. As Mary Grady, a special-education teacher at Boston's Rogers Middle School, noted, when special-education students are integrated with regular students, labels disappear and so, too, does the stigma that is so often attached to having impairments.

Additional legislation followed. In 1986 Congress amended the Education for All Handicapped Children Act to include infants and toddlers. Amendments also added family-service and transition plans for adolescents and young adults. More and more, children with disabilities were seen as children first—children with the same basic needs as other children. Again, new respect brought a new designation. Children with disabilities were less often spoken of as "handicapped," "exceptional," or having "special needs"; the new and more accepted designation was *challenged* children. This emphasized the right of and need for children with disabilities to grow, to work, to love, to be loved—in other words, to be included as much as possible in the mainstream of life.

Celebrating diversity

During this period of evolution of civil rights legislation, neuropsychological, medical, and educational research—begun some 150 years earlier—continued investigating the role of the brain in learning processes. Better understanding of the contributions of the brain's left and right hemispheres to the thinking processes gave educators a new appreciation of those children whose prime way of learning was visual rather than language-based. Schools and society

had traditionally honored those who excelled in the language arts of listening, speaking, reading, and writing—primarily left-brain activities.

For generations those lacking language skills, who could not translate their ideas to written language or express themselves well verbally, were seen in schools as slow learners. Such were the demeaning educational experiences of the likes of Thomas Edison and Albert Einstein—and of many others whose true potential was *never* recognized. Those who exhibited strength primarily in right-brain activities—*e.g.,* visual organization, spatial conception—often excelled in the graphic arts.

Research into the functions of the brain's two hemispheres also led to a greater appreciation for individual uniqueness, so well expressed in the following lines attributed to Spanish-born cellist, conductor, and composer Pablo Casals (1876–1973): "Do you know who you are? / You are a marvel / You are unique. / In all of the world there is no other / exactly like you. / In the millions of years that have passed, / there has never been another like you. . . . / You may become a Shakespeare, a Michelangelo, a Beethoven. / You have the capacity for anything."

Educational practitioners had long valued the brain as the prime organizer of information. Teachers became aware that they could play a key role in the development (or diminution) of a child's learning capacities. Their verbal and nonverbal encouragement (or lack of it) could have a profound effect on children's self-images and their resultant learning, particularly on the progress or failure of those who learned "differently." Children who had been seen as slow learners were now seen as children who had individual ways of learning; though they differed from the norm, they deserved the chance.

The new appreciation for the special strengths of

Cameron Archibald (seated, holding book on his lap) gets on well in a regular classroom at the Emily Dickinson School in Redmond, Wash. Redmond is one of the cities in the U.S. that supports full inclusion of children with disabilities. Cameron suffers from seizures and must be tube-fed. The public school system pays for teacher training, extra aides, and special education teachers who can modify lessons for children with special needs. Like Cameron, many youngsters with physical or mental impairments, ranging from Down syndrome to autism, are flourishing both educationally and socially in regular classrooms.

Therese Frare—The New York Times

children with disabilities of all sorts coincided with the diversification of U.S. society, marked by increased immigration of people from the Middle and Far East, the islands of the Caribbean, South and Central America, and Africa. As children rubbed shoulders in schools with classmates from many different countries and cultures, diversity came to be celebrated and a part of the school agenda. Moreover, as differences began to be valued instead of demeaned, the nation became more accepting of those who differed physically, intellectually, and socioemotionally; "challenged" children came to be seen more and more as potential contributors to the human family.

Major steps forward

For 30 years Americans had struggled philosophically and legislatively for the civil rights of all Americans regardless of race, religion, color, socioeconomic status, or *disability.* Then, in 1990, the federal government spoke most clearly and emphatically in support of those rights when it legislated two all-encompassing laws for persons with disabilities, the Americans with Disabilities Act (ADA), followed three months later by the Individuals with Disabilities Education Act (IDEA), which amended the 1974 Education for All Handicapped Children Act.

The ADA clarified who could legitimately be categorized as disabled. The legislation defined a person with a disability according to a three-part formula as one who has a physical or mental impairment that substantially limits one or more of the major life activities, one who has a record of such impairment, or one who is regarded by others as having such an impairment. Responsibility for application of this definition fell largely on employers as they made judgments as to the usefulness and capabilities of prospective employees or current employees being considered for promotion. Discrimination based on negative attitudes ("I don't like fat secretaries") or generalized fears ("Some of my employees will quit if I hire a person with AIDS") was banned. The ADA also protected the rights of individuals with disabilities in a host of other situations: state and governmental public services, public accommodations (theaters, hotels, restaurants, shopping centers, grocery stores, clothing stores, banks, pharmacies, barber shops, hairstylists, zoos, museums, parks, schools, libraries, and so forth), public and private transportation, and telecommunications services.

It was not the intent of the law to create hardships for employers or to place severe restraints on programs or services. However, failure to make reasonable accommodations for the known physical or mental limitations of an otherwise qualified applicant or staff person was punishable. Employers were expected to make *reasonable* accommodations for individuals with disabilities. The Equal Employ-

In 1984 Mary Tatro went to the U.S. Supreme Court and won the right for her granddaughter Amber, who has spina bifida and needs a simple catheter procedure performed, to be accommodated in a public school. Tatro's case opened doors for thousands of other children with special needs.

ment Opportunity Commission, the courts, and the U.S. attorney general were empowered to enforce the ADA.

IDEA, in amending the Education for All Handicapped Children Act, dropped the use of the term *handicapped.* Rather, IDEA specifies that it applies to the "child/student/individual with a disability." This change in terminology importantly reflects the fact that a "disability" is just one aspect of an individual's being. IDEA included children from birth to age 21. It also added two new categories of disability to those already sanctioned by law—those of autism, often misunderstood as severe retardation, and traumatic brain injury. It also broadened the category designated "underrepresented" to include minority populations, the poor, and individuals with limited English proficiency as students eligible for special education and related services. IDEA further specified that Native American young people with disabilities were to be appropriately accommodated in tribally controlled schools on reservations.

To encourage states to identify and implement appropriate education for children with disabilities, the federal government offered financial assistance to states that came up with suitable plans. IDEA also empowered parents, giving them access to all records relevant to the identification, evaluation, and educa-

289

tional placement of their children and the right to an independent evaluation as well as opportunities for impartial due-process hearings if they believed that their child was not being effectively accommodated to receive a full education.

Mainstreaming, according to IDEA, means that schools must provide support personnel and supplementary services for children with disabilities within regular school programs. The law stipulates that a number of placement options are possible. A child may remain in the regular classroom all day and receive special instruction from a special-education teacher, be based in the regular classroom but leave to receive services in a special-education resource room, or receive the major portion of his or her education in a special-education class but join other students for some activities, usually nonacademic ones. There are, however, certain children whose disabilities may be so severe that no mainstreaming is possible.

"Inclusion": proponents and critics

As a result of the ADA and IDEA, public and private schools that had already been integrating children with disabilities with regular students strengthened programs already in place and introduced other programs that expanded the perimeters of mainstreaming. At the William Barton Rogers Middle School, a program called "Jericho"—a reference to the biblical battle in which the Israelites destroyed the walls of Jericho—has successfully "broken down the walls" between regular and special education within classrooms. In each of five classes in grades six, seven, and eight, half the students have mild to moderate learning disabilities, while the other half are regular students whose parents have approved their participation. After the program had been under way for nearly a year, teachers spoke of the students supporting each other and respecting each other's unique strengths to an extent they never thought possible. In essence, teachers and students alike were no longer aware of previous labels. Teachers point out that *all* students now know that their teachers have expectations of them.

This pursuit of healthy interaction between regular students and students with disabilities is reflected in the three-year "plan for excellence" that has been adopted by the Boston public school system. Nationwide, of the estimated 5 million students broadly defined as having impairments, approximately 1.6 million children with disabilities were "included" in regular classes in 1994; the Department of Education estimates that the number is growing by at least 100,000 a year. No formal federal policy exists that requires "inclusion," although the Department of Education strongly backs it.

Not all programs and schools have enjoyed the success that the Rogers school and other Boston-area

schools have had. Moreover, there have clearly been instances in which inclusion has *not* worked—either because the students could not adapt or because the teachers lacked the training, assistance, or services to handle the arrangements. Many teachers may support the concept but do not consider it realistic—at least yet. Some parents, students, and children who have experienced mainstreaming hold that it slows down normal classroom work. In some cases critics say that the idea of inclusion can never work and that it ultimately does more harm than good for those it is meant to help. As one educator has said, "In fact, the rights of some children are being violated by forcing them into the mainstream."

Triumphing thanks to technology

As IDEA and the ADA have been implemented, the technology industry has become a leading proponent of inclusion. Seeing the population of those with disabilities as a major and burgeoning market, engineers are designing and manufacturing "adaptive" and "assistive" aids with the potential to revolutionize the care and education of the physically and mentally disabled. These wonders of technology are giving students new independence and opportunities and are easing their transition into classrooms and society at large. From simple and cheap to highly sophisticated and costly, technological aids are greatly improving the abilities of youngsters with disabilities to communicate and to more fully participate in the regular classroom setting. Technologies include speech synthesizers and talking calculators and a wide array of other devices that facilitate listening, speaking, reading, and writing. Thanks to special switches on wheelchairs, even paraplegic and quadriplegic students can exercise greater control over their environments, both in and out of school. Previously confined to home or institutions, these children are now able to be active in ways that were never before possible.

Moreover, the latest assistive and adaptive aids are becoming increasingly available to the students who can benefit from them. In 1983 the Foundation for Technology Access (FTA) was started by a small group of parents and professionals in El Cerrito, Calif., in order to help youngsters with multiple disabilities obtain a quality education, aided by computers. There are now 45 FTA centers in 33 U.S. states and the Virgin Islands; each center has the most up-to-date computer technologies "for the sole purpose of giving children and adults with disabilities access to technology for learning, working, and playing." In 1992 the FTA helped at least 95,000 individuals directly and about 300,000 indirectly through educators and therapists who made use of its computer aids. The FTA is proving that "technology can be the great equalizer" and that "given the right tools, people with disabilities can learn like everybody else," says Jacquelyn Brand,

290

At the Oregon Research Institute in Eugene, five-year-old Christopher Cobbs, who has cerebral palsy, learns how to maneuver a specially designed wheelchair by using a virtual reality system. Once he has mastered it, he will be able to cross streets and navigate the hallways at elementary school. A revolution in technology has given hundreds of thousands of people with physical disabilities a new degree of mobility and independence that makes it possible for them to participate and succeed in ways they never could before.

the FTA's founder. "We would simply like to see people with disabilities reach their full potential. We need to see kids start school life with the tools they need to succeed." As the FTA continues to expand its resources, advocates of inclusion are learning, in Brand's words, "a great deal about disability and human potential."

Given the chance . . .

The efforts to ensure the rights of all individuals with disabilities continue. Writer Joseph P. Shapiro chronicles the history of this battle in the United States in *No Pity: People with Disabilities Forging a New Civil Rights Movement* (Times Books, 1993). He records the changes in America's attitudes and resultant governmental policies toward people with disabilities, which culminated in the landmark passage of the ADA. The book emphasizes that the disabled have rejected a paternalistic attitude toward them; what they really want, writes Shapiro, is a chance "to build bonds to their communities as fully accepted participants in everyday life."

Toward that end there have been important steps taken in legislation and the establishment of programs that ensure that schoolchildren receive a full and equal education despite their mental, physical, or learning disabilities. The efforts extend beyond primary and secondary education. Increasingly college-level programs make advanced learning possible for people with virtually every sort of disability. For example, at Curry College, Milton, Mass., the Program for Advancement of Learning (PAL) gives students with learning disabilities the chance to succeed. PAL characterizes its participants as "college-able, learning-disabled." Most of the PAL students are dyslexic and have language and reading difficulties. The program gives them "tools" to help them conquer their read-

ing and comprehension deficiencies so that they can handle college-level work that might otherwise defeat them.

Important court decisions in the wake of the ADA's passage have also broken down barriers. A learning disabled applicant to the Massachusetts state bar won the "right" to become a full-fledged member of the legal profession after the state's highest court ruled that he could take extra time to complete the bar examination. The court's decision was a signal to licensing boards for the legal as well as many other professions to make fair and reasonable accommodations for the disabled, as promulgated by the ADA.

Optimists believe the day will come when each American is recognized as worthwhile, and there will no longer be the need to fight for the civil rights of anyone. At that point society will have achieved a measure of success comparable to that suggested in the following parable:

A woman in search of the meaning of life visited a wise man in her village. "Can you tell me what heaven and hell are like?" she asked. "Come with me and I will show you," answered the wise man.

They set off down a path and came to a large house. In this house they found a large dining room with a great table set with all kinds of food from around the world. Seated at the table were dozens of people, all emaciated and hungry; they were each holding 12-foot-long chopsticks, which made it possible for them to feed themselves. "Surely this must be hell," the woman concluded. "Will you now show me heaven?" she asked.

The wise man led her farther down the path, and they came to another house. Again they found a large dining room and in it again a table piled with delicious foods from around the world. The people at the table were healthy, happy, and well nourished, but they too had only 12-foot chopsticks with which to eat. "How can this be?" asked the woman. "These people have 12-foot chopsticks but are happy and well-fed." The wise man smiled and then replied, "In heaven people feed each other."

Genetics

Geneticists around the world continued to sift through the human genome during the past year, discovering many new genes associated with human disease and, in a much-heralded accomplishment, producing the first physical map of the chromosomes. Several of the year's discoveries were controversial, including findings on genetic factors in aggressive behavior and sexual orientation, which added fuel to the "nature versus nurture" fire. The 1993 Nobel Prizes in two categories—physiology or medicine and chemistry—were awarded for discoveries that provided novel methods for gene exploration.

In addition to the disorders discussed in detail below, scientists identified the underlying genetic defects in three different inherited immunodeficiency syndromes, including a form of severe combined immunodeficiency similar to the disorder that afflicted the Houston, Texas, youngster who became known as the "bubble boy." Two disparate disorders resulting respectively from a deficiency or an excess of copper—Menkes' "kinky hair" syndrome and Wilson's disease—were discovered to be caused by defects in two surprisingly similar proteins whose function is to pump this essential trace element across cellular membranes. Other inherited diseases that succumbed to scrutiny were polycystic kidney disease, a disorder that affects one in 1,000; neurofibromatosis type 2, a potentially disfiguring nervous system disorder; multiple endocrine neoplasia type 2A (a tumor of the thyroid gland); Miller-Dieker lissencephaly (a malformation of the brain); hereditary hyperekplexia, a condition in which individuals are easily startled; and Canavan disease, a fatal syndrome of brain degeneration. Researchers at Duke University, Durham, N.C., discovered that one form of the blood protein apolipoprotein E is associated with late-onset Alzheimer's disease. Exceptionally interesting advances were made in cancer genetics with the identification of a new class of so-called mutator genes.

Landmarks and laureates

The 1993 Nobel Prize for Physiology or Medicine was awarded to U.S. scientists Phillip Sharp and Richard Roberts for their remarkable independent discoveries of so-called split genes in higher organisms. Until Sharp and Roberts published their findings in 1977, it had been assumed that the genetic "instructions," or code, for the structure of a given protein molecule consisted of a single unbroken linear sequence of nucleotides (the subunits that constitute DNA, the basic genetic material). This sequence, it was believed, was then transcribed into one continuous molecule of RNA, which acted as a messenger, carrying the instructions to the cell's protein-synthesis machinery. Bacterial cells, which had been studied exclusively up

until that time, show only this colinear organization. While analyzing the messenger RNA of a common mammalian virus, Sharp and Roberts realized that the corresponding gene consisted of a number of meaningful segments of DNA, now referred to as exons, separated by intervening irrelevant DNA sequences, or introns. The original RNA molecule includes both exons and introns, but the introns are discarded in a cutting-and-splicing process, much as a piece of film is edited. At first the rationale for "split" genes was a mystery, but eventually scientists realized that this arrangement provides both evolutionary and developmental flexibility.

The Nobel Prize for Chemistry was awarded to Kary B. Mullis of the U.S. and Michael Smith of Canada for the invention of two techniques that have revolutionized molecular biology. Mullis won for his brainchild, the polymerase chain reaction (PCR), a technique by

For their independent discoveries of discontinuities in the genetic sequences that serve as blueprints for protein structure, Phillip Sharp (below) and Richard Roberts (bottom) were awarded the 1993 Nobel Prize for Physiology or Medicine.

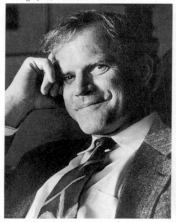

The 1993 Nobel Prize for Chemistry was awarded for contributions that had far-reaching implications for molecular genetics. Kary B. Mullis (far left) worked at the Cetus Corp. in Emeryville, Calif., when he invented the procedure known as polymerase chain reaction, or PCR, which enables scientists to create millions of identical copies of a single DNA sequence in a matter of hours. Michael Smith (left) of Vancouver, B.C., pioneered the technique of site-directed mutagenesis, a process by which DNA sequences can be altered in a purposeful, controlled manner.

which a single fragment of DNA can be amplified, or copied, exponentially by repeated rounds of DNA synthesis. Since its introduction, PCR has opened up previously unimagined possibilities for the study of evolution, forensic medicine, and medical diagnosis. The technique has become a key tool in the ambitious international effort to map the human genome. PCR has made it possible to identify the causative agent of a patient's viral or bacterial infection directly from a small tissue or blood sample. It has also been exploited in the search for the mutations underlying hereditary diseases.

Smith invented "site-directed mutagenesis," a way to convert one DNA sequence into another, slightly different, one. The method opened the door to an entirely new means of studying proteins. By systematically changing the amino acids that constitute a protein, researchers can determine what role each amino acid plays in the protein's structure or function. The method has found wide use in biotechnology, where scientists have sought to produce altered proteins that are more stable, more active, or more useful to medicine or industry than their natural counterparts—for example, hemoglobin variants that may serve as blood substitutes.

Charcot-Marie-Tooth disease: a mystery solved

Charcot-Marie-Tooth disease is the collective name of a group of hereditary nerve disorders, or neuropathies. The first cases were described in 1886 by two French physicians—the renowned neurologist Jean-Martin Charcot and his colleague Pierre Marie—and a British doctor, Howard Henry Tooth. The disorder affects the most distal (*i.e.,* endmost) muscles of the hands and feet and is characterized by progressive muscle weakness and atrophy (wasting). Some patients exhibit clawing of the hands and deformities of the feet that may require surgery. In most varieties of the disease, symptoms appear during the first decade of life or early in the second.

Charcot-Marie-Tooth disease, type 1 (CMT1), which affects about one in 2,500 individuals throughout the world, is now recognized as a primary defect in the peripheral nerves, which enervate (activate) the distal muscles. Over time, the myelin sheath that covers the nerves degenerates. This sheath is essential for the rapid conduction of the nerve impulse. Myelin is produced by a specific cell, the Schwann cell, which wraps its own lipid membrane around the nerve multiple times, much like a long muffler wrapped about the neck. The disease can be diagnosed by a test of nerve conduction velocity.

In recent years it has become clear that CMT1 is a genetically heterogeneous disorder, involving any one of probably four distinct genes. Most families exhibit an autosomal dominant inheritance pattern, meaning that only one copy of the defective gene needs to be inherited from an affected parent for the offspring to manifest the disease. Analysis of the patterns of transmission in several families showed that autosomal dominant CMT1 can be divided into three different categories, each associated with a different chromosome: CMT1A, linked to chromosome 17; CMT1B, linked to chromosome 1; and CMT1C, which remains to be mapped to a particular chromosome. A fourth type, CMT1X, shows what is known as a sex-linked pattern of inheritance, which means that women who are carriers of the defective gene are not affected, but their male offspring will have a 50:50 chance of inheriting the disease. The genetic defects in sex-linked disorders are always located on the X chromosome. The genes responsible for three of the four subcategories of CMT1 have now been identified, and mutations discovered in one of these were found to be responsible for yet another hereditary neuropathy.

The story began to unfold a few years ago when two groups of researchers, headed by P.I. Patel at Baylor College of Medicine, Houston, and Christine van Broeckhoven at the University of Antwerp, Belgium, made a remarkable discovery about CMT1A. Patients with this form of the disease were found to have a duplication of a small region of chromosome 17 to which CMT1A had been mapped, suggesting that having an extra copy of a gene located in that region gives rise to the illness. The investigation advanced when it was realized that a specially bred laboratory animal called the Trembler mouse had defects in the gene encoding a myelin protein of the peripheral nerves, called PMP-22, which is embedded in the compacted membranes of myelin that insulate the nerve fibers. The Trembler mouse has many of the symptomatic and pathological features present in human CMT1 disease. The murine condition also is inherited in an autosomal dominant fashion. In addition, the PMP-22 gene was found to map to a place on the murine chromosome that corresponds to the portion of human chromosome 17 on which the CMT1A gene is known to be located. These findings immediately suggested that CMT1A could arise from duplication of the PMP-22 gene, a hypothesis that was quickly supported by the work of four separate groups of investigators.

The discovery also raised some fascinating questions: How does duplication of the normal gene lead to the disease, and how is the duplication brought about? The former mystery is as yet unsolved, but the genesis of the duplication seems to be an error in recombination, the exchange of genetic material between paternally and maternally derived chromosomes that takes place during the normal development of germ cells (eggs and sperm). In the case of the duplication of chromosome 17, the two chromosomes are misaligned slightly during the recombination process, leading to the addition of a tiny fragment of DNA to one chromosome. The material added to the chromosome is identical to existing material—hence, duplication. Theoretically, misalignment also should lead to a deletion of the same tiny region of DNA in some people. Indeed, researchers found that patients with a different dominantly inherited neuropathy—called hereditary neuropathy with liability to pressure palsies—showed these predicted deletions.

Further exciting developments followed on the heels of these initial discoveries. The gene that encodes the major structural protein (protein zero, or P_o) of peripheral myelin was found to map to the same region of chromosome 1 as CMT1B. P_o is thought to be important for the compaction of myelin around the nerve. Suspecting its possible involvement in CMT1B, several groups of investigators tested this candidate gene and found a variety of mutations in CMT1B patients, confirming that the P_o gene is responsible for CMT1B. Similarly, a candidate gene for CMT1X emerged in the gene coding for connexin 32. Connexin 32, another structural protein, is used to assemble so-called gap junctions, channels that form between cells and through which small molecules are transported. It has now been established that mutations in this gene

Osteoporosis—the bone thinning that often leads to fractures— has long been linked to aging. In 1994 Australian researchers reported finding a gene that affects how the body uses vitamin D and thus influences the risk of bone erosion in later life.

are responsible for CMT1X. Interestingly, connexin 32 exists in myelin throughout the body, yet the clinical manifestations of CMT1X are limited to peripheral nerves.

Bone density: an inherited trait

In January 1994 a group of researchers in Australia announced that they had uncovered a genetic clue to the origin of osteoporosis. Diminished bone density is one of the major risk factors for osteoporotic fractures, which are a significant public health problem especially affecting postmenopausal women. A number of nongenetic factors influence bone density—for example, nutrition, smoking, and exercise—but genetic factors also have been suspected. Nigel A. Morrison, John A. Eisman, and their colleagues at the Garvan Institute of Medical Research in Sydney correlated one version of the vitamin D receptor gene—which they dubbed "b"—with increased bone density. Another version, designated "B," was associated with a lesser degree of density. Since genes exist in pairs, one inherited from each parent, everyone has two genes for the vitamin D receptor. The genes exert a codominant effect, however, so people with the Bb genetic endowment are more susceptible to osteoporosis than bb individuals but less susceptible than those with the BB genotype.

Vitamin D is required for the normal deposit of minerals in the bones and for calcium uptake from the digestive tract. The Australian scientists' data indicate that the vitamin D receptor gene contributes the bulk of the genetic influence on bone density in the individuals studied. Their findings also suggest that genetic testing could identify children at highest risk for developing osteoporosis in later life, so that preventive measures could be undertaken early.

Evidence for an "aggressiveness gene"?

The first identification of a genetic mutation leading to a behavioral trait was reported by investigators studying a large Dutch family. Certain male members of this family exhibit periodic outbursts of aggressive, sometimes violent behavior, usually brought on in response to anger, fear, or frustration. Affected individuals are also mildly mentally retarded. Instances of violence in the family history included one rape and several attempted rapes of sisters, physical attacks on non-relatives, and arson. Seeking information and help, the family reported these behaviors to geneticists in Leyden. The mild retardation and aggressive tendencies could be traced back through several generations, appearing only in males but transmitted through females. This sex-linked pattern of inheritance indicated that the gene responsible for these behaviors probably lies on the X chromosome.

By performing genetic linkage studies in this family (studies of chromosomal landmarks inherited with the aberrant behavior), scientists at the University Hospital in Nijmegen were able to pinpoint the genetic abnormality to a small region of the X chromosome. The affected individuals were found to have mutations in the gene that carries instructions for the synthesis of the enzyme monoamine oxidase A, which is responsible in part for the metabolism of certain neurotransmitters. This gene defect led to production of a defective enzyme too small to perform its function. The finding of a specific abnormality in an important enzyme suggests that drug therapies may be valuable for ameliorating the aggressive tendencies in the affected individuals. It remains to be seen whether mutations in the monoamine oxidase A gene might also be responsible for aggressive behavior in some people outside this family.

This discovery came on the heels of a widely publicized controversy over a scheduled National Institutes of Health-sponsored conference on genetic factors in crime. Organizers of the conference were forced to abandon their plans because of complaints that the research might impugn minorities, who make up a significant proportion of the U.S. prison population. Meanwhile, the National Science Foundation has reported plans to support research on potential biological factors associated with violent behavior.

Seeking clues to sexual orientation

Dean H. Hamer and colleagues at the National Cancer Institute set out to determine whether there might be a genetic basis for homosexuality. They began by interviewing 76 homosexual men to gather information about their genetic histories. The men reported higher incidences of homosexuality in maternal uncles than in paternal uncles and a higher incidence in cousins related through maternal aunts than in any other male cousins. These findings suggested an X-linked pattern of inheritance.

To home in on the region of the X chromosome that might be involved in male sexual orientation, the investigators performed genetic mapping studies on 40 pairs of homosexual brothers. They found that one particular region at the tip of the X chromosome was shared by both brothers more often than chance would have predicted; the region was shared in 33 pairs of brothers and not shared in only 7 pairs. Statistically speaking, the odds are 10,000 to one that this distribution occurred by chance.

Although this report captured the interest of both scientists and the general public, it must be emphasized that the result is only preliminary. No "gay gene" has yet been discovered. If there is such a gene,

By volunteering to participate in a genetic study, these gay brothers helped scientists isolate a region of the X chromosome that may be involved in male sexual orientation. It remains to be seen how other factors contribute to sexual preference.

Dennis Brack—Black Star

variations in it are almost certainly not the sole factor that determines homosexuality in men. In addition, such genetic variations may predispose rather than predestine an individual to homosexual orientation.

Insight into neurological disorders

The last few years have witnessed the discovery of genes for a number of inherited diseases characterized by a feature known as anticipation. *Anticipation* refers to more severe disease and an earlier age of onset in successive generations. A severe sex-linked form of mental retardation known as fragile X syndrome was the first of these disorders to be elucidated. The syndrome was found to result from an expansion of a repeated sequence of three nucleotides, or bases, in the gene's DNA. Huntington's disease and myotonic dystrophy, two dominantly inherited disorders that also exhibit anticipation, were later found to be caused by similar triplet repeats.

In the past year, researchers made inroads into two additional dominantly inherited neurological disorders that show anticipation. Their work cleverly capitalized on the hallmark of expanding triplet repeats. Harry T. Orr of the University of Minnesota and Huda Y. Zoghbi at Baylor College of Medicine, Houston, and their co-workers isolated the gene responsible for spino-cerebellar ataxia type 1 (SCA1), a neurodegenerative disease that causes weakness and lack of coordination. With time, SCA1 patients lose neurons in the cerebellum, brain stem, and spinocerebellar tracts. Orr and colleagues localized the disorder to a region of approximately 1.2 million bases of DNA on chromosome 6 and then surveyed this region of DNA for triplet repeats. They hit upon a repeat of the bases cytosine, adenine, and guanine (CAG), the same as that found in Huntington's disease, which expands from fewer than 36 repeats in normal individuals to more than 43 repeats in those affected by SCA1.

Meanwhile, a Japanese team focused on another neurological disorder, with the unwieldy moniker of dentatorubral-pallidoluysian atrophy, or DRPLA. This neurodegenerative disease is found mainly in the Japanese population and is characterized by varying combinations of muscle contractures, poor coordination, epilepsy, dementia, and jerky movements reminiscent of Huntington's disease. Lacking even the genetic map position of DRPLA, the scientists identified the DRPLA gene by searching for CAG triplet repeats in previously identified DNA sequences associated with brain function. Indeed, one such sequence exhibited an expansion of CAG repeats in all DRPLA patients tested, and those who developed the disease earlier had the greatest number of repeats.

The mechanisms by which expanding repeats cause disease are still being worked out and appear to be highly variable. In fragile X syndrome, for example, the number of repeats is increased a thousandfold in affected individuals, and the defective gene simply is not transcribed into messenger RNA. However, in all of the neurological disorders, the repeats consist of CAG triplets that change the structure of the gene's protein product. How this altered protein leads to the neurodegenerative diseases is not yet clear. Nor is anything yet known about the normal function of the proteins encoded by the SCA1 or DRPLA genes.

Anticipation characterizes two other neurological diseases, spinocerebellar ataxia type 2 and Machado-Joseph disease. As both of these inherited disorders have now been genetically mapped, it should not be long before the genes for these are also isolated.

Human Genome Project: the fourth year

In December 1993 a French research team completed the first physical map of almost the entire human genome. A physical map delineates the organization of genes and nucleotide sequences in the 23 pairs of human chromosomes, much the way a road map shows the relative positions of cities and towns.

Led by Daniel Cohen, a molecular biologist at the French Center for the Study of Human Polymorphism in Paris and the laboratory Généthon, the scientists first produced a collection of 33,000 cloned DNA

Disorders linked to triplet repeats				
disorder	chromosomal location	trinucleotide repeat*	normal number of repeats	number in affected persons
spinobulbar muscular atrophy	X	CAG	13–30	30–62
fragile X syndrome	X	CGG	6–54	50–1,500
myotonic dystrophy	19	CTG	5–37	44–3,000
Huntington's disease	4	CAG	9–37	37–121
spinocerebellar ataxia type 1	6	CAG	25–36	43–81
dentatorubral-pallidoluysian atrophy	12	CAG	8–25	54–68

*C=cytosine; A=adenine; G=guanine; T=thymine
Adapted from Joseph B. Martin, "Molecular Genetics of Neurological Diseases," *Science*, vol. 262, no. 5134 (Oct. 29, 1993), pp. 674–676; ©1993 AAAS

fragments of large sections of human chromosomes. These sections were grown in the laboratory in yeast cells as artificial chromosomes, also known as YACs. The trick then was to line up the YACs, reconstructing the organization of the original 23 pairs of chromosomes. The team accomplished this goal by mapping several types of signposts in human DNA, which then enabled them to identify overlaps between adjacent DNA segments.

So much information was generated in this project that the researchers could not publish their findings in the traditional journal form but instead are relying on electronic mail to distribute the details of their work. The data are likely to lead to the rapid discovery of more disease-related genes in the coming years.

—*Jane Gitschier, Ph.D.*

Health Policy

In his first state of the union address and again in a special address to the Congress on Sept. 22, 1993, U.S. Pres. Bill Clinton reaffirmed his campaign promise to revamp the nation's health care system. His pledge to make health care always available to everyone at affordable prices portended the most extensive proposal for health care reform ever devised by a presidential administration and the most substantively and politically complex issue ever to be addressed by the Congress. By the close of the first session of the 103rd Congress in November 1993, an additional half dozen other major proposals had been devised, and still others surfaced during the ensuing congressional session.

The main features of the major types of proposal that had been put forward by the close of 1993 are described below. Attempts to contrast details to any great extent would be futile because they change so frequently as a result of inevitable compromising and bargaining during the legislative process. By focusing on a few of the bills, however, the principal issues that constitute the health care reform debate can be well illustrated. Before turning to the specific bills, it is worthwhile to summarize the forces that gave impetus to the U.S. health care reform movement in the first place and the criteria that the president and others put forth by which to assess alternative proposals.

Pressures for reform

During the 1992 presidential election campaign, candidate Clinton singled out health care reform as the nation's most pressing domestic issue. He cited the rising costs of health care and the growing numbers of uninsured citizens as the most visible indicators of an industry in need of fundamental improvement. Analyses by the Congressional Budget Office had revealed that by the close of the century, spending for health care will consume nearly a fifth of the country's gross domestic product, and reports from the Bureau of the Census showed that nearly one-sixth of Americans were without health insurance.

These facts were not new; health services researchers at universities and government agencies had been tracking spending and insurance coverage trends since the 1960s, and the media had on occasion featured stories on these subjects. However, not until the 1991 special election for a U.S. Senate seat in Pennsylvania had health care reform been demonstrated to be a salient political issue in the minds of voters. In November 1991 Harris Wofford, a Democrat who had never held elective office, beat Richard L. Thornburgh, attorney general under Presidents Ronald Reagan and George Bush and former two-term governor of Pennsylvania. As Pennsylvania's secretary of labor and industry from 1987 to 1991, Wofford handled a steady stream of labor disputes that, in his words, "turned on the question not of wages but of who would pay for health benefits." It was that issue upon which he centered his Senate race and won the election. During that campaign and thereafter, polls and focus groups revealed that Americans nationwide were threatened by the prospect of losing their health insurance, an all-too-real possibility in an economy experiencing high unemployment and where most Americans under age 65 had insurance coverage through their jobs.

The Clinton campaign, in turn, linked the high and rapidly rising costs of health care and the large and growing numbers of uninsured citizens to other salient political issues. It argued that growing shares of businesses' revenues were being absorbed by health insurance fringe benefits, depriving workers of increased wages and causing prices of American products to be uncompetitive in international markets. Unemployment was characterized as being rooted at least in part in the high costs of health care, as potential employers refrained from hiring workers to escape having to absorb additional health care costs. Fear of losing insurance coverage was identified as a significant reason why many workers remained in jobs they wished to leave (so-called job lock), which resulted in inefficiencies in local labor markets.

Finally, the Clinton campaign joined health care reform to the issue of fairness, a quintessential American political theme. Respect for basic human rights, it was argued, demanded that the poor and near poor have access to health care equal to that of the country's better-off. Clinton repeatedly observed that the United States, with South Africa, stands virtually alone among industrialized nations in its failure to guarantee universal access to health care. That most employers provide at least some health insurance coverage for their workers while others provide little or nothing to their laborers was also cast in terms of unfairness. Those lacking insurance are less inclined to seek

Visiting towns across the U.S., Pres. Bill Clinton listened to the personal stories of Americans who, for one reason or other, lacked access to adequate health care. His campaign pledge to make affordable health care available to every American amounted to a call for the most drastic change in the U.S. health care system ever put forward by a president. Once the debate over health care reform was formally under way, he remained unwilling to compromise on the issue of universal coverage.

preventive services and care for illnesses during their early stages. As a consequence, when they do obtain care, it is likely to entail advanced and costly services, frequently rendered in hospital emergency rooms and other expensive sites. As the uninsured are unable to pay the costs of such services, those costs are borne by providers as "uncompensated care" and are ultimately incorporated into bills paid by the insured. This so-called cost shifting, the Clinton campaign argued, was yet another form of inequity to be remedied by insurance reform.

Popular public opinion favoring change was joined by many of the nation's most powerful interest groups. Though each group stressed the issues most dear to itself, a near consensus emerged in support of fundamental reform. Organized labor and the powerful American Association of Retired Persons (AARP) and other consumer groups weighed in for universal coverage and expansion of insurance benefits. Business groups and the nation's governors largely endorsed cost containment. Trade associations representing health care providers and insurance companies, historically opponents of radical change, voiced support for sweeping changes in the organization and financing of health care services.

Clinton seized upon these topics and sentiments, translating them into campaign promises to guarantee universal health insurance coverage, contain rising health care costs, and eliminate administrative waste and hassles. All of this was to be accomplished through some as-of-then-unspecified set of reforms labeled "managed competition." Editors of the *New York Times,* the *Wall Street Journal,* and other leading newspapers heralded managed competition as the policy of choice, as did the Jackson Hole Group, an assembly of government officials, academics, and spokespersons for prestigious large businesses, health care provider associations, and health insurance compa-

nies. The seeming consensus favoring managed competition was facilitated by the fact that few bothered to explicate the idea's particulars. Various conceptions of what managed competition might entail in practice coexisted among policy elites, while public opinion polls showed that only a minority of Americans were aware of any specific features contained in any of the various proposals being put forward.

Criteria for reform

In his special address to the Congress in September 1993, Clinton enunciated the following six principles that in his view should be addressed by health care reform legislation:

• universal coverage: a plan must cover all Americans, regardless of their health status, age, or income level

• cost containment: a plan must include demonstrably effective means of controlling the growth in health care spending

• simplicity: a plan must be administratively uncomplicated and eliminate much of the overhead in the existing U.S. system

• choice: a plan must afford all Americans free choice among health care providers

• quality: a plan must include demonstrably effective means of ensuring the quality of health care

• responsibility: a plan must induce families to participate in paying for their health care services and to adopt healthful lifestyles

These were to be the standards he would apply to bills developed in the Congress when deciding whether to sign health care reform legislation. The first of these—universal coverage—he subsequently set as the only "nonnegotiable" criterion.

The five proposals discussed below collectively span the political spectrum on many issues that constitute the health care reform debate. The first three proposals occupy the political center; the last two briefly discussed proposals stake out the political extremes: the liberal left and the conservative right.

The Health Security Act

The Health Security Act is the Clinton administration's bill, which was delivered to Congress on Oct. 27, 1993. The 1,342-page, 240,000-word document was the product of nearly nine months of deliberation by a task force of more than 500 experts led by the president's wife, Hillary Rodham Clinton. The bill is generally characterized as being a managed competition approach. That is, it relies on mixtures of government action and private-sector forces to reform the health care industry.

Like nearly all of the other major proposals, the president's bill has as a key ingredient insurance reform, which involves three major elements. First, the bill would prohibit "cherry picking"—*i.e.,* the practice by some insurance companies of offering insurance only to relatively healthy individuals. Under the president's plan all insurers would have to provide insurance to any person who wished to purchase it, regardless of his or her health status. Second, prices charged by insurers would be subject to government-imposed limits. Insurers would have to assess community rates; they could charge different prices to various groups on the basis of their ages but could not link prices to individuals' health status. Finally, government would define a set of standard benefits that all insurers would be required to include in their basic coverage. Insurers would be free to offer supplemental coverage for additional charges, but all would have to offer at least the standard benefits. These would be defined by a federal commission known as the National Health Board.

Health insurance reforms would ensure access to affordable health care to all working Americans and thereby diminish the numbers of uninsured as well as the problem of cost shifting. To augment the policy of universal access, the Health Security Act would expand the reach of government subsidies for the poor by broadening eligibility for the Medicaid program (the federally administered, state-financed system that pays for care for economically disadvantaged persons who meet state-determined eligibility criteria).

The president's program would be financed by savings that are projected in the federal Medicare program, which provides health care subsidies to the nation's elderly (those aged 65 and over), by selective increased taxes (*e.g.,* on tobacco products), and by cost sharing between employers and employees. This last provision, the so-called employer mandate, would require employers with a minimal number of employees to pay a portion (initially set at 80%) of their workers' insurance costs. The remainder would be paid by the employees themselves.

The Health Security Act specifies substantial expansions of benefits that would be covered beyond those ordinarily included in private health insurance plans. These include more extensive preventive care, such as immunizations and checkups, as well as more comprehensive mental health services and a phased-in program of long-term care for the disabled.

The president's plan would introduce new administrative elements into the health care industry. A key institutional innovation involves so-called Regional Health Alliances, which would carry out various administrative duties. Among other functions, the alliances would see to it that competing insurers and health plans complied with rules against cherry picking and would oversee competitors' advertising and enrollment practices. They also would serve as intermediaries between insurers and the public for the self-employed and families employed by small companies. The latter two groups would sign up for health care coverage through their Regional Health Alliance, which in turn would transmit the requisite information to the selected

THERE'S NO MISTAKE...ACCORDING TO THE NEW HEALTH-CARE LIST, THIS IS OUR NEW DOCTOR!

insurers or health plans. Alliances would thereby eliminate insurers' opportunities to select only the families they would prefer to enroll. Large, self-insured companies would not have to use alliances, being free to deal directly with insurers and health plans.

Cost containment would be accomplished in several ways. First, having eliminated competition among insurers based on cherry picking and benefit design, remaining insurers and health plans presumably would compete among themselves on the basis of the cost-effectiveness of the health care they provide. Second, Regional Health Alliances would be empowered to refuse to offer local health plans whose community rates were deemed to be excessive. Third, by offering more preventive care, health plans over time would be treating fewer persons with preventable diseases. Fourth, universal coverage would eliminate cost shifting and the inappropriate use of high-cost emergency rooms as points of first contact. Finally, if prices continued to rise, the federal government would impose ceilings on insurers' and health plans' rates.

The Managed Competition Act

The Managed Competition Act puts forth a proposal that, like the president's plan, relies on combinations of government regulation and market competition to remedy the nation's health care ills. This plan relies less on government action, however, and correspondingly more on market forces, prompting some to refer to the plan as "Clinton lite."

Introduced in the first session of the 103rd Congress by Rep. Jim Cooper, a Democrat, the Managed Competition Act of 1993 embodied principles and approaches devised by the Jackson Hole Group and endorsed by the Democratic Leadership Council, a group of moderate Democrats.

Advocates of the Managed Competition Act endorse all three elements of insurance reform described above—*i.e.,* guaranteed issue, community rating, and standard benefits. They argue that once these are in place, health care provider organizations will be strongly encouraged to compete among themselves on the basis of the cost-effectiveness of the services they render and the prices they charge. According to this theory, such incentives will lead health care plans to organize themselves into health maintenance organizations, which, evidence shows, provide a high quality of care at relatively low costs.

The Managed Competition Act would extend coverage to a larger number of low-income families than are currently covered by Medicaid. As in the president's approach, insurance reform and broadened government subsidies for the poor and near poor would greatly diminish the numbers of uninsured. Cooper contends that Americans would thereby have "universal access" to affordable health care coverage. Some might prefer to remain uninsured, but this group would likely be relatively small and would not contribute greatly to a cost shift, supporters of the Managed Competition Act argue. Proponents of this approach therefore see no need to impose employer mandates or any other form of mandate requiring people to purchase insurance coverage.

The Managed Competition Act would leave benefit decisions to a National Health Board, which would endorse services that had been shown to be effective. To assist in this function, the plan calls for expanded government-sponsored research into the effectiveness of medical care and the cost-effectiveness of alternative services and procedures. Such information would be freely available to health plans, which presumably would devise cost-effective ways of delivering services of proven worth. Additionally, health plans would be required to produce comparable information on the outcomes of the services they provided and their effects on the health of their members. Armed with such information, consumers could make informed choices among competing health plans.

U.S. Rep. Jim Cooper talks to senior citizens at a center for the elderly in his home state of Tennessee. Cooper, a Democrat, put forth one of the first alternatives to Clinton's Health Security Act. Cooper's more middle-of-the-road plan, relying less on government regulation and more on market competition than the president's plan, has been referred to as "Clinton lite."

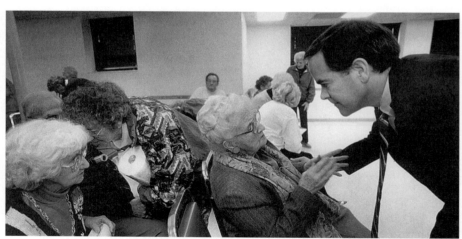

The Cooper plan would be financed principally by insurance premiums that would be paid by individuals or their employers and that might also entail member cost sharing through deductibles and coinsurance. Additionally, the plan's sponsors expect some savings to accrue to the Medicare program from the improved efficiencies created by market competition. The Managed Competition Act would set limits on the amounts of health insurance costs that employers would be allowed to deduct; thus, sufficient funds to finance extensions of coverage of the poor and near poor would be recouped.

This form of managed competition would create considerably fewer roles and responsibilities for government and, accordingly, require fewer new public administrative agencies than would the president's plan. Cooper supports the voluntary creation of health insurance purchasing cooperatives among small-business employers and the self-employed. These cooperatives would permit the latter groups to deal collectively with insurers and health plans and thereby to have a greater impact on the prices set by provider organizations and on the services they delivered. Finally, a National Health Board would be created to advise Congress and the administration on health benefit decisions, set health services research agendas, and make recommendations regarding other health policy matters.

The HEART Act

Also occupying the political center is the Health Equity and Access Reform Today (HEART) Act of 1993. Introduced by Sen. John Chafee, it is the most prominent Republican alternative to the two Democrat-initiated managed competition plans. Like the president's plan, HEART seeks universal coverage. While the president's plan would achieve this through employer mandates, Chafee's reform proposal would do so by so-called individual mandates. HEART would expand public coverage for the poor and near poor. Others would be required by law to purchase insurance coverage. The problem of some Americans' not being insured and its attendant cost shifting would thus be eliminated by legislative fiat.

Like the president's plan, HEART explicitly expands benefits to include preventive care, prescription drugs, and mental health and substance-abuse services. Chafee's approach includes the option of coverage for catastrophic care only, which would insure a more limited range of conditions with high deductibles and coinsurance. Further, HEART permits families to contribute before-tax income to medical savings accounts, which could be used to pay costs of health care.

HEART proposes financing mechanisms that are virtually identical to those of the Managed Competition Act. Thus, savings from the Medicare and Medicaid programs with private insurance premiums and cost

sharing are combined with changes in tax laws affecting employers' contributions to health insurance fringe benefits. Chafee's plan entails relatively little government involvement. A National Health Board would be established to make recommendations to Congress and the administration regarding health policy matters and would permit states to establish regional purchasing cooperatives.

The American Health Security Act

The American Health Security Act represents the most politically liberal proposal, recommending as it does the establishment of a single-payer health care system not unlike that found in Canada. This would, in effect, eliminate private health insurance altogether by making it illegal to sell insurance policies that covered benefits included under the government program. Government provisions, in turn, would be quite extensive, covering everything that would be included under Clinton's plan plus long-term care, hospice services, and dental care for persons under 18 years of age.

Introduced by physician and Democratic representative Jim McDermott, a former practicing psychiatrist from Washington state, the American Health Security Act would guarantee coverage to all Americans, financed by increased payroll and other taxes, including a $2-a-pack tax on cigarettes and a 50% excise tax on handguns and ammunition. Health care providers would be paid in accordance with government-imposed fee schedules and prohibited from billing patients directly; thus, there would be no deductibles or coinsurance. Government agencies would fully compensate providers for the services they rendered.

McDermott's bill evidences no preferences for how health care services should be organized; fee-for-service practices, small groups, and health maintenance organizations all would be permitted. All would be subject to government-imposed price controls, however. A National Health Board would oversee the operation of federal responsibilities, and counterparts would be established by the states.

The Comprehensive Family Health Access and Savings Act

Occupying the opposite political pole from the American Health Security Act is the Comprehensive Family Health Access and Savings Act. The Republican senator Phil Gramm, the plan's principal sponsor, believes that the health care industry requires only marginal repairs. His program therefore would make a few changes in the health insurance industry and thereafter rely almost entirely on market forces to reform health care delivery and financing. This approach would create no new government agencies.

Gramm's proposal would, however, effect two critical changes in the current U.S. system. First, it would require all insurers to offer coverage to all who ap-

Rep. Jim McDermott, a former practicing psychiatrist, had the backing of a committed group of liberal Democrats in his support for a single-payer, Canadian-style health care system that would eliminate private insurance entirely.

plied and guarantee renewal of policies. Second, like the Chafee plan, it would allow families to put pretax earnings into medical savings accounts and to use those moneys to cover health care expenses. The plan would not enforce other health insurance reforms required by the other major approaches. It would permit insurers to charge actuarially determined prices rather than community rates, and it would not require them to offer particular sets of benefits.

The Comprehensive Family Health Access and Savings Act would impose no mandates on either employers or individuals requiring them to purchase health insurance. On the other hand, the act would impose severe penalties on uninsured individuals who attempted to avoid paying the costs of the health services they used.

Politics

No one expected health care reform to proceed smoothly or quickly. By the close of 1993, seven major bills had been introduced, and several more were introduced in the first half of 1994. None of the major

bills described above had sufficient support in either the Senate or the House to be moved to passage. Interest groups pushed their favorite features and fought against the ones they dreaded. Meanwhile, the public remained largely ill-informed as to the particulars of specific bills.

Within the Congress, health care reform politics had become decidedly partisan. All 80 or so sponsors of McDermott's so-called Canadian plan were Democrats, and only one Republican senator, James M. Jeffords of Vermont, publicly endorsed the president's plan. The Managed Competition Act drew bipartisan support, as did the Chafee bill. Only a few legislators, all Republicans, lined up behind the Gramm proposal. If health care reform is to reflect a bipartisan consensus, as many believe it must, considerable compromising and bargaining remain to be accomplished.

The president's plan, as of mid-1994, appeared to have little prospect of being the gathering point for such bipartisan support. Business groups refused to endorse it because they considered it to rely excessively on government administration and regulation and because they believed that the mandate for employers to provide insurance to all employees would raise labor costs and contribute to unemployment. The politically influential AARP chose not to endorse the plan, preferring to take a "wait-and-see" posture. Labor groups, electing to support a more Canadian-like plan, gave only mild backing to the administration's bill. Some medical specialty groups, opposed to managed competition and the infringements it posed for them, joined forces with the Canadian approach. The stalwart American Medical Association was determined in its opposition to the president but offered no clear-cut endorsement of any existing proposal.

Through the first half of 1994, President Clinton was in no mood to make major concessions. Political realities prevented him from adopting features of the Canadian-style plan put forth by his fellow Democrats on the left, and he was unwilling to abandon his one nonnegotiable principle of universal coverage and accept in its place Representative Cooper's "universal access." On the other hand, Senator Chafee's support from his fellow Republicans, joined with his endorsement of universal coverage, tempted Clinton to seek alliances; these would come, however, only by the president's leaping over conservative and moderate members of his own party and liberal Republicans who supported Cooper's "pure" managed competition plan. Such was the political landscape as the second year of the health care reform legislative process proceeded; the fall 1994 elections promised to tell politicians and interest groups alike where the American electorate stood.

—*Thomas W. Bice*
and Thomas O. Pyle

302

Health Care in France: Saving the System

by Alexander Dorozynski

Aristotle distinguished two principles of equity: vertical equity, according to which people unequal among themselves are treated unequally, and horizontal equity, according to which equals are treated equally. These Aristotelian definitions were cited as guidelines for the provision of health care in Europe by economist Claire Lachaud at a 1993 meeting of the Council of Europe. Lachaud said that the financing of health care should follow the principle of vertical equity—the rich paying more than the poor—and the distribution of health care should be horizontally equitable; *i.e.,* those with equal needs should receive equal treatment whatever the income level.

This is not to say that Aristotelian equity has been achieved in all European health systems. It is, however, an ideal accepted by most people and their political representatives. At the same meeting, Geoffrey Podger, head of the International Relations Unit of the United Kingdom's Department of Health, noted:

It does seem exceedingly clear that health is perceived by the public generally as a moral rather than a market issue. Public opinion is generally not prepared to allow access to health care to be determined in the same way as access to high-quality housing or extravagant sport cars. In other words, if I am poor, it is considered acceptable, if regrettable, that I shall have neither an Alfa-Romeo nor a luxury condominium but not that I should be excluded from the possibility of a heart transplant.

Even if health care in Europe is not perceived as a market issue, it is nonetheless under economic constraints, with rising costs threatening to lead to the accumulation of huge public debts and to undermine the competitiveness of labor in a global economic market. Consequently, many countries are in the process of reforming their health systems. The most radical of these reforms are under way in Germany and in France, the two European countries where the costs of health care are highest. This report looks at the successes and failures of the French health system and at the changes it is presently undergoing.

The "glorious years": a system that worked

The French Sécurité Sociale was created in 1945 to be consistent in spirit with a form of democracy oriented toward solidarity. It guaranteed equal access to health care for all, provided basic old-age retirement pay and allocations to maintain large families, and gave the government the responsibility of protecting citizens—including disabled workers and the unemployed—against large out-of-pocket medical expenses. The Sécu, as it is familiarly called, was modified on numerous occasions, but during the first 30 years of its existence, corresponding roughly to the period known as the *trente glorieuses* (the "30 glorious years" of economic growth and low unemployment), it worked to the satisfaction of most users and providers.

The system was a mixture of public and private, leaving patients free to choose their physicians and physicians free to treat patients as they deemed appropriate (provided they did not exceed contractually agreed-upon fee limitations). Solidarity meant that in order for everybody to have access to the same level of health care and the same health care facilities, the wealthy subsidized the poor, the working generation subsidized the old and the young, and workers subsidized the unemployed.

A "hole" develops

In the mid-1970s increasing unemployment, the aging of the population, and the ever mounting costs of the country's generously provided health care started spelling trouble. Succeeding governments, faced on the one hand with a growing deficit on the Sécu's balance sheet and on the other with an electorate ready to defend the notion that rights previously granted (*les droits acquis*) should never be revoked, took seasonable measures to patch the holes that threatened to sink the ship. Fourteen rescue plans were drawn up, which included targeting of supply by imposing fixed rates for services and instituting measures to reduce demand, chiefly by increasing the share of copayments by individuals and their employers.

Those rescue measures had only temporary effects. The health insurance "hole" kept growing, reaching about F 20 billion (about $3.3 billion) in 1992 and F 30 billion ($5 billion) in 1993. The system's problems became so endemic that newspapers carried headlines about *le trou de la Sécu* ("the Sécu's hole")

303

Paying for health care: *la différence* (1990)

France	%	U.S.	%
hospital care			
out of pocket	6.8	out of pocket	5.0
the Sécu	89.9	government	54.7
private insurance	9.3	private insurance	34.9
complementary schemes	1.5	other private funds	5.4
physician services			
out of pocket	28.3	out of pocket	18.7
the Sécu	62.0	government	35.0
private insurance	8.6	private insurance	46.3
complementary schemes	1.1	other private funds	0.0
total personal health care expenditures			
out of pocket	18.8	out of pocket	23.3
the Sécu	74.0	government	41.3
private insurance	6.1	private insurance	31.8
complementary schemes	1.1	other private funds	3.6

Adapted from Jonathan E. Fielding, M.D., M.P.H., and Pierre-Jean Lancry, Ph.D., "Lessons from France—'Vive la Différence,' " *JAMA*, vol. 270, no. 6 (Aug. 11, 1993), pp. 748–756. Copyright 1993, American Medical Association

so that every reader would know of its depth. With the alarm thus sounded, it was time for radical steps to be taken. There was no question, however, of breaking up the Sécu's comprehensive health coverage. Indeed, the French people would take to the streets to defend their Sécu.

Despite its "hole," by the few objective criteria available, the French system compares well with that of the United States, which is also on the brink of major reforms. More than 99% of French citizens and residents are under the Sécu's umbrella, and by such standard measures of health status as infant mortality rates, life expectancy, and disease-specific mortality, France fares as well as or better than the U.S. Health care costs in France consume roughly 9% of gross domestic product (GDP). That is about 40% less than the cost of health care in the U.S., which does not cover or inadequately covers one-third of the population (about 35 million to 40 million people). But the cost of health care in France is higher than in other Western European countries; the figures for Spain, Portugal, Great Britain, and Denmark are 6% to 7%; 7% to 8% for Italy, Belgium, Norway, and Finland; and slightly over 8% for Germany and Sweden.

The Sécu's wide umbrella

The "package" offered by the system is reassuring. Its comprehensiveness is reflected in the fact that it follows employees from job to job through unemployment and to retirement, capping out-of-pocket costs below the level where they could cause excessive financial hardship and covering total costs in cases of severe and prolonged illness. Moreover, the system allows patients free choice of their physicians, covers care in both public and private hospitals, re-

imburses part of the costs of pharmaceuticals and dental care, and provides comprehensive maternity and infant care.

The Sécu pays for about three-quarters of total health care expenditures, the balance being shared between out-of-pocket expenses and supplemental health insurance reimbursements. Those with limited resources who have no supplemental coverage are fully or almost fully covered by social security. Solidarity between generations is reflected in the low contributions of retired people, who chip in between 1.4% and 2.4% of their retirement pay, and students, who pay a flat fee of F 865 (about $150) a year.

The person who pays the insurance, his or her spouse, a concubine, children under age 18, and parents (if they are dependent and live in the insured person's home) are all entitled to the full range of health insurance benefits. Recent legislation has extended the benefits to one individual of the same sex who is not related to the payer but has lived with him or her for at least a year. Thus, the new legislation de facto recognizes homosexual couples.

The Sécu is designed to protect people from the need to face health expenditures out of proportion to their incomes. One hundred percent reimbursement is limited to hospitalization for surgery or hospitalization for more than a month. For most hospital care the patient pays a flat out-of-pocket daily fee of F 55 (less than $10). The Sécu also reimburses 100% of the cost and installation of major prosthetic devices such as hip joints, pacemakers, and artificial limbs. Seventy percent of physicians' and dentists' fees are reimbursed, with the exception of fees to doctors in the so-called sector two—physicians who have been approved as "superior" by a local commission of peers and are allowed to negotiate prices with their patients "with tact and restraint." Sector-two physicians on the average charge about 30% more than their sector-one colleagues, but their patients are reimbursed only on the basis of a sector-one fee scale. As of 1990 the French government suspended entry into sector two but did not revoke the privilege from those who had it. (In 1991 sector two comprised roughly 34% of specialists and 15% of generalists.)

The Sécu reimburses the entire cost of prescribed pharmaceuticals that are considered to be indispensable (such as cancer drugs), 65% of the cost of necessary drugs (such as antibiotics), and 35% of nonessential, or so-called comfort, drugs (such as homeopathic medicines, many tranquilizers, antacids, and in some cases aspirin). It reimburses 65% of costs for prescribed hydrotherapy (spa treatment), including transportation and, for people with low incomes, up to F 600 (about $100) a day for hotel expenses. Hydrotherapy is a commonly prescribed form of treatment in France; in 1993 one in nine French citizens went to one of the 104 officially recognized spas. Spas are classified according to the diseases that are treated. For example, respiratory illnesses are treated at Saint-Honoré-les-Bains and La Bourboule, rheumatologic disorders are treated at Saint-Amand-les-Eaux and Aix-les-Bains, and digestive disorders are treated at Santenay-les-Bains and Vittel.

Most expenses connected with maternity, including comprehensive prenatal care, are fully reimbursed, and maternity insurance provides for prenatal and postnatal work leave that ranges from 16 weeks (for a first child) to 28 weeks (for the birth of twins to a woman who already has at least two children). There is also an allocation (of about F 3,600, or about $600) for "maternal rest" for a woman who adopts a child.

In most cases the patients pay their doctors directly and are later reimbursed, either by the general fund for employees (covering about 80% of the population) or by funds specific to farmers (covering 9% of the population) or to professionals and self-employed people (6%). The share of expenses that is not reimbursed is called the *ticket moderateur* because it is believed to moderate excesses in health care consumption. As noted above, however, a majority of French men and women (80%) have supplemental, or complementary, insurance, which may reimburse all or nearly all of the *ticket moderateur*. Complementary schemes include more than 7,000 mutual funds, usually linked with professions, and for-profit insurance companies. Mutual fund assessments are generally shared between employers and employees.

Satisfied patients and doctors

Both consumers and doctors are generally happy with this system. Consider a "typical" case. Jean-Jacques Gillon, who is 42 years old, is married, and has two children, lives in Paris and works as a typesetter. For several days he has been nauseated, so he visits his physician, Antoine Dupont. The doctor listens to Gillon's account of his symptoms, then examines him and diagnoses a gastrointestinal infection, for which he prescribes an antibiotic and vitamins.

Gillon pays a consultation fee of F 105 (about $18), and Dupont fills out a *feuille de maladie,* the prescription sheet that also serves as a receipt for the fee. Gillon takes the form to a pharmacy to have the prescription filled, paying F 65 for the antibiotic and F 40 for the vitamins. The pharmaceutical containers from which the pharmacist fills the prescriptions have removable stickers indicating the prices; the pharmacist places one of these from each of the two medications on the prescription sheet. Later Gillon mails the sheet to his local social security health insurance branch. A few days later he receives in the mail a computer printout indicating that 70% of the medical

Christian Vioujard—Gamma Liaison

Hydrotherapy at Vichy in central France is one of the forms of treatment covered under the wide umbrella of the Sécu. Patients are reimbursed at 65% for prescribed treatment for a wide range of medical conditions plus transportation; in some cases accommodation costs are also reimbursed. Vichy, the "queen" of French spas, gained fame for its healing mineral waters in the 17th century, when royalty and the illustrious flocked there to "take the cure" for any number of ills, ranging from digestive, skin, and rheumatic ailments to liver disorders and migraine headaches. In 1993 one in nine French citizens was treated at an officially recognized spa.

fee is reimbursed to him, as is 65% of the cost of the antibiotic. The vitamins, although prescribed, are not reimbursed at all. The money is transferred directly to his bank account.

Gillon is also a member of a nonprofit *mutuelle,* a complementary insurance scheme through his place of employment, to which he mails the Sécu's notice of reimbursement. A week or so later, he receives a notice that the remaining 30% of the doctor's fee and the remaining 35% of the cost of the antibiotic have been reimbursed by the *mutuelle*. That amount is also transferred to his bank account. Thus, the only expense that has not been fully covered is the F 40 for the vitamins.

Gillon earns a gross salary of F 1,650 a month plus a "13th-month" premium that he receives at the beginning of each year. His monthly pay after deductions amounts to F 1,320. Among the deductions, which do not include income taxes, F 800 a year goes to national health insurance, F 600 to retirement, F 45 to unemployment insurance, F 850 to supplementary retirement, F 140 to his supplementary health insurance, and F 380 to the "general social contribution," a recently imposed national "solidarity tax," which will be abolished if and when the current economic crisis ends. His contribution for health insurance amounts to 6.9% of his salary; his employer contributes about twice as much.

Gillon selected Dupont as his doctor because other members of his family had recommended him and because his office is conveniently located. He is pleased with his choice; the patient finds his doctor's "bedside manner" pleasant and feels that he is easy to talk to.

Dupont, a general practitioner, sees more than 100 patients a week. Like most doctors in France, he sets aside part of his time for visits to patients' homes. His annual income is about F 700,000; he nets about half as much. Because he is paid directly for services rendered, his paperwork is minimal—largely limited to filling out the *feuille de maladie*.

Dupont knows that German physicians earn nearly twice as much and American general practitioners about three times as much. But then, unlike his American colleagues, Dupont did not have to pay for his medical studies and did not start his career with a large debt. Nor does he have to pay the large sum American doctors pay for malpractice insurance; like most French doctors, he will probably never be sued by a patient, and if he is, and loses, the amount of damages will be paltry by comparison with sums awarded in the U.S. Like 70% of French physicians polled in 1993, Dupont does not think that practicing medicine is "financially interesting." Nonetheless, he makes a good living, his income has not been affected by the current economic crisis, and as a physician he is a highly regarded member of society (above bankers, lawyers, professors, and politicians).

Reacting to "hard times"

While patients like Gillon and doctors like Dupont do not, on the whole, have any major complaints about the health care system in their country, the French government and French employers are no longer happy with it. Unemployment and an increasing proportion of older people in the population have shrunk the Sécu's financial base, and in 1991 assessments had to be increased. The government then created a "generalized social contribution" of 1% on salaries. In 1994, when the Sécu's "hole" was expected to reach F 43 billion, this "hard times tax" was increased to 2.4%. By then employers contributed 12.8% and employees 6.8%—a total of 19.6% of gross salaries—to health insurance funds. Self-employed people paid 12.85% of their earnings. These increasing social contributions are increasing labor costs to the extent that France may lose its competitive edge in the global market.

According to the Organization of Economic Cooperation and Development, increased health expenditures did not appear to lead to better health for the French people. A new "plan" to rescue the ailing health insurance scheme therefore seemed to be urgently needed.

What was to be done with a system that, by the accretion of changes, reforms, and compromises and the maintenance of privileges and exceptions, had become a complex maze with myriad rules, regulations, and inconsistencies? For example, assessments are lower for civil servants and magistrates, and even lower for employees of the national power utility, EDF-GDF, than for the rest of the population. Assessments and reimbursements are, for historical reasons, higher in the northeastern *départements* of Alsace and Moselle. A puzzling example of the inconsistencies in the system is the wide range of prices that health professionals can charge for transportation. A country doctor who drives to visit a patient is allowed to charge F 2.50 per kilometer—which translates to about 60 cents per mile—but a nurse or orthophonist (one who provides special foot care) can charge only F 1.60. Professionals who walk (or ski) to visit their patients can charge much more: a doctor F 20 per kilometer, a nurse F 22, and an orthophonist F 7. But pity the pedestrian pedicurist, who, though his services have been prescribed by a doctor, gets but F 2.50 per kilometer.

Targeting excess

In 1993, the year that the right-wing government of Prime Minister Edouard Balladur took over, a liberal and immensely popular former health minister, Simone Veil, returned to the political scene. Veil, who had also served as a deputy to the European Parliament and who is best known for la Loi Veil, the law restricting smoking, became the new minister of social affairs, health, and urban affairs. Assisted by the physician-minister of health, Philippe Douste-Blazy, she began a process of reform that is by far the most radical France has seen so far. Rather than reviewing the entire system from top to bottom, the French government, under Veil's leadership, is tackling several fronts, all of which are believed to contribute to excessive consumption and high costs.

Too many physicians. Higher education in France is state sponsored, and any interested student can enroll in the first year of medical school. A year later a competitive examination limits the number of second-year enrollees. In the decade following the 1968 student "revolution," French medical schools swelled with students. In 1975 there were 8,600 second-year enrollees. From 1980 to 1992 the number of active physicians leaped from 115,904 to 174,907 and the physician-to-population ratio grew from 2.16 to 3.07 per 1,000. In response to the "glut," the number of second-year enrollments was gradually reduced to 3,500 in 1993, but the time lag between the decrease in enrollees and that of diplomas awarded means that many young doctors are still attempting to enter medical practice. Some young physicians barely eke out a living, and some medical graduates look for jobs in other fields.

Hospitals: costly, overused, substandard. In prosperous times many hospitals were built, often upon the initiative of local politicians, for whom hospitals represent prestige and jobs. Currently France has an estimated 50,000 excess hospital beds.

Hospitals in France must accept all emergency cases at any time of day or night. At the same time, however, many emergency wards are functioning below government standards, and in 1992 a scathing report by the National Consumers' Institute concluded that 200 of the 500 or so emergency wards in the country were inadequately staffed and equipped.

Public hospitals and some not-for-profit private ones receive global annual budgets to cover all services, including salaries of physicians and daily fees for in-patient services. This provides incentive to not discharge patients early but keep them hospitalized longer than needed. Since services, including ancillary ones such as laboratory tests and radiological examinations, are billed on a predetermined fee schedule, there is no competition based on price. These services tend to be overused and are often unnecessary. The new "Plan Veil" will attempt to reduce not only the overuse of hospitals but operating costs as well.

Doctor hopping. The French peculiarity of "medical nomadism," or doctor hopping, is the practice of patients consulting several physicians for the same condition, receiving several prescriptions, and then selecting whichever they think is most suitable to their case. Some patients have been known to see as many as 10 doctors in a single day for a single condition without informing any of them of previous visits. Doctor hopping costs patients nothing or next to nothing but weighs heavily on the health budget. It is hoped that this problem will be remedied by a mandatory medical record, to be established first for patients with at least two diseases requiring more than six months' medical follow-up. The record will have to be taken along by the patient if he or she chooses to consult another physician and still benefit from social security reimbursement. Each doctor will thus be informed of previous diagnoses and prescriptions. Doctors will be less likely to prescribe additional drugs and treatments. Moreover, the very existence of the record is likely to dampen the patient's enthusiasm for going from one doctor to the next.

Overprescription and overconsumption of drugs. The French are Europe's most avid consumers of pharmaceuticals, which represent, in spite of their comparatively low cost, nearly one-fifth of national health

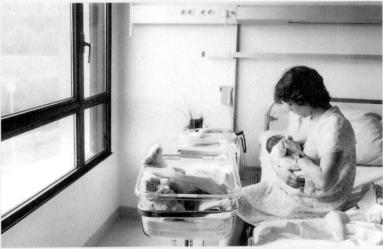

Shepard Sherbell—Saba

A maternity patient at the Robert Debré Hospital in Paris nurses her newborn, who boards in her private room. France has long recognized the importance of the health and proper care of the mother during and after pregnancy, and virtually all expenses connected with maternity, including comprehensive prenatal care and ample work leave before and after childbirth, are covered by the French health care system. The infant morality rate in France is low (6.7 deaths per 1,000 live births, compared with 8.5 in the U.S.). The rate of induced abortions is also substantially lower in France than in the U.S.

care expenditures. Home medicine cabinets are notoriously brimming with drugs, and surveys have shown that a patient's satisfaction with doctor's services is roughly proportional to the number of pharmaceuticals prescribed.

Medical committees have recently elaborated a series of *références médicales*—guidelines for physicians to follow in their prescription of pharmaceuticals and ordering of special examinations and laboratory tests for the most frequently diagnosed diseases. The guidelines specify, for instance, that a normal pregnancy requires no more than three ultrasonography examinations and that no more than one nonsteroidal anti-inflammatory drug for arthritis or one medication for a peptic ulcer should be prescribed at any given time. It is hoped that the guidelines will not only reduce overprescribing but also reduce the growing number of iatrogenic diseases caused by conflicting prescriptions—*i.e.,* conditions that are inadvertently induced by prescribed treatments. Douste-Blazy has said that the *références* are not meant to infringe on a doctor's decision in the handling of a particular case, but if a doctor systematically overprescribes, he or she will be subject to a fine. Sixty-five *références* had been elaborated by mid-1994, and more were in the process of being formulated.

Another measure the government is taking against overprescription of drugs is getting the pharmaceutical industry to reduce its advertising expenditures but allowing it to increase the prices of drugs. Pharmaceutical prices in France are negotiated between the manufacturers and the government.

The government also promises doctors that they will be rewarded for their help in controlling health care costs. At the time of the signing of the last contract by all but two of the major medical unions (Sept. 30, 1993), an increase of the basic GP's fee from F 100 to F 105 was authorized, and another increase may be forthcoming in 1995—provided health care costs are kept under control.

By the end of 1993, the growth of health care expenditures had started to slow down. After annual growth rates in the range of 6.6% to 9%, it was down to 5.7% for 1993. During the first three months of 1994, it appeared to be even further reduced, although precise figures are not available. Expenditures for pharmaceuticals and for laboratory tests have actually decreased. This was attributed to the publication of the *références médicales.* Although the legislation is not yet being enforced, the guidelines appear to have inspired a "fear of the gendarme" and reduced the number of prescriptions. Overall health care expenditures in 1993 stood at 8.9% of GDP.

Cost cutting: lessons from Germany?

It remains to be seen whether French doctors and patients will have the discipline that their German neighbors showed when their government reformed its public health insurance scheme after the cost of health care edged over 8% of GDP in 1992. During that year the 1,200 or so sickness funds financed by employees and employers ran a collective deficit of DM 9.5 billion (about $6.7 billion), largely attributed to excessive drug expenditures, which had risen by 9% in 1992.

Cost-cutting measures included setting limits on hospital budget growth, encouraging the retirement of doctors, and limiting the number of new practices. As a result, young doctors have found it difficult to make a living because of restrictions that do not allow them to set up their offices anywhere they want; rather, installation must be approved by health insurance funds. The tight rules are likely to be loosened in 1994 and 1995.

In December 1992 the German government set a limit on the total value of pharmaceuticals that doctors who are reimbursed by state-supervised sickness funds can prescribe to their patients, urged doctors to prescribe generic drugs, and set generic price reimbursement limits on brand-name products. Doctors were told that they would be faced with reductions in payments out of the state sickness funds if they did not curb prescriptions.

Results were almost immediate. Drug expenditures started falling and continued to fall throughout 1993. In March 1994 Horst Seehofer, the German minister for health, announced that 20% less had been spent on pharmaceuticals in 1993 than during the previous year. Furthermore, the health insurance scheme showed a surplus of DM 10 billion, and the ministry promptly urged health insurers to pass the savings on to consumers by lowering premiums. The main complaints about the curbing of drug prices have come from pharmacists and the powerful German pharmaceutical industry. Drug manufacturers now may have to cut back on research and development. The government, however, wants to go even further, requiring consumers to pay a larger share of the cost for drugs they use.

As of January 1996, Germans will be able to choose their insurance fund, whether private or public. The funds will thus be placed in direct competition with each other. Dental costs are also targeted. Patients will have to have an annual dental checkup; otherwise, their share of dental care costs will be increased.

Health policy experts in France and in many other countries, including the U.S., have wondered whether the German system, known as *Sozialmarktwirtschaft,* which matches acceptable equity with economic efficacy—at about half the U.S. cost—is exportable. It probably is not. As Podger, from the U.K., quipped at the Council of Europe meeting, "Good health care systems, like good wine, do not necessarily travel well from one country to another."

Focus on Health in a Changing South Africa

by Derek Yach, M.B.Ch.B., M.P.H.

In 1944 a government-appointed Commission on the Provision of an Organised National Health Service for All Sections of the People of the Union of South Africa reported on the state of health care in that country. Among other things, it found:

• a lack of coordination (health services were "disjointed and haphazard, provincial and parochial")

• a shortage of services (the unequal provision of hospital accommodation, then measured as a bed-to-population ratio of 1:304 for whites versus 1:1,198 for blacks)

• an unequal distribution of doctors-to-population in various regions of the country (one physician per 308 people in Cape Town, 1:22,000 in Zululand, and 1:30,000 in the northern Transvaal)

• inappropriate emphasis and priorities (with low priority going to preventive, ambulatory, and community-based services)

In its report, known colloquially as the Gluckman Report (for Henry Gluckman, a member of Parliament who served as the commission's chair), the commission proposed many reforms that were far-reaching and ambitious in scope. At the heart of the recommendations—and the only recommendation that was implemented to any extent—was the establishment of health centers as the basic unit for the delivery of care. These centers were to be modeled after the successful system that Sidney and Emily Kark had established in 1940 in the black rural community of Pholela in Natal province.

The Karks highlighted major threats to health, including the absence of adequate water and sanitation facilities, the poor state of education, and the fact that health services were mainly curative. At Pholela they initiated applied epidemiology research, school-based health programs, agricultural development, and improved hygiene. They stressed that "clinical services must be brought within the sphere of a broader social health scheme"—a truly revolutionary approach at the time. The achievements at Pholela still remain a shining example of highly effective health care delivery that specifically addresses and meets the health needs of poor, disenfranchised rural South Africans.

By the time the success at Pholela was reported, however, the National Party had become entrenched and the health center movement was being dismantled (some 40 health centers of an envisioned 400 had been established between 1945 and 1949). Most of the Gluckman Report's proposed reforms, in fact, were never realized.

Evolution of South Africa's health care

Racial fragmentation of health care expanded sharply after the National Party victory in 1948 with the cre-

In the rural community of Pholela in Natal province, a family doctor and community health worker make a home visit and speak with mothers about the preparation of nutritious meals. In the early 1940s a highly revolutionary community health program— one that considered health and health care delivery as part of the much broader social and economic picture—was established at Pholela by public health pioneers Sidney and Emily Kark. Today, as South Africa's health care reformers strive to establish a health system that will meet the needs of poor and disenfranchised rural populations, they are looking to the achievements made half a century ago at Pholela.

Sidney L. and Emily Kark

ation of 10 black homelands, each with its own health department. In 1983, in addition to a national Health Ministry, racially separate departments of health for whites, Asians, and Coloureds were introduced. This meant that for over a decade South Africa had 14 ministers of health!

Although for nearly half a century structural, functional, geographic, and racial fragmentation of health care increased, during that period extraparliamentary activity was devoted to ensuring that the key recommendations in the Gluckman Report would eventually form the basis of a future democratic, nonracially aligned national health service. In 1955 the Freedom Charter of the African National Congress (ANC) brought together 3,000 people to develop a broad strategy for establishing a democracy. Included in that strategy were demands for preventive health care services for all and free access to medical care at the time of need.

Racial fragmentation reached a peak in the late 1970s when the prominent black student activist Stephen Biko died in detention, apparently from a brain injury sustained in a scuffle with Security Police. (Police as well as white doctors were absolved of all criminal wrongdoing.) At the same time, there was growing community advocacy for improved health services for the black majority, which gave rise to several progressive nongovernmental organizations in the field of health. These organizations were characterized by a commitment to developing a national health service that redressed the racial and social inequities of the past and emphasized primary health care as the guiding philosophy.

Since February 1990, when fundamental sociopolitical reform started with the unbanning of the ANC, there has been movement in the direction of restructuring of all aspects of South African society, including the provision of health care. For the health sector, the creation of the National Health Forum in late 1993 represented the start of real transitional planning. With the April 27, 1994, election of a government of national unity, implementation of a five-year program of action aimed at redressing the effects of apartheid began.

The tragedy of history is that South Africa lost many talented public health professionals as the National Party unfolded its apartheid policies. Along with their emigration came the collapse of the idea of a national health service. Only now, five decades after the Gluckman Report was tabled, have the commission's ideas and recommendations been resurrected.

Health status: the legacy of apartheid

The legacy of apartheid (meaning "apartness") is that until 1991 the South African people were categorized as African (black, indigenous native, Bantu), Coloured (mixed race), white (European), and Asian (mainly Indian). Apartheid policies have been both a direct and an indirect cause of much death, disease, and misery. Studies have repeatedly indicated the long-term adverse impact of those policies on health—such that race is inextricably linked to people's prospects of survival and their quality of life. This situation is likely to remain for many decades. Thus, inequalities in South Africa will need to be analyzed by race for some time.

A prerequisite for the development of a rational health policy is the availability of high-quality data. In South Africa data are least available for the poorest sectors of the community. For example, 24.3% of all African deaths in 1985 were "ill-defined," and only 62% were certified by a medical practitioner. By contrast, 7.2% of deaths among the white population were ill-defined, while 86.4% were medically certified. Data reported by this author, therefore, should be regarded as suboptimal. Nonetheless, certain conclusions can be drawn from emerging trends. (In most cases, these data exclude 4 of the 10 designated African homelands—Bophuthatswana, Ciskei, Transkei, and Venda—which are currently self-administered and recognized by the South African government as independent states.)

Mortality. One of the most powerful indicators of the health status of a population is the infant mortality rate (IMR), the number of infants per 1,000 live births who die before their first birthday. Japan has one of the world's lowest IMRs (around 5), while for much of sub-Saharan Africa the figure is in the 80–120 range. In South Africa both race and regional variations exist. For example, the IMR of Africans (54.7) is 7½ times that of whites (7.3). Within regions there is less variability. When data are combined across regions for all races, it emerges that for the worst-off one-third of the population (Africans living in the three poorest regions of the country), 2 of every 25 children die before their first birthday.

A very specific measure of adult mortality is the percentage of people who die before their 60th birthday having survived childhood to age 15. Adult mortality for South African men is 38% and for South African women 25%; however, the rate for black South African men is 42%. (For comparison, the adult mortality figures for Japanese men and women, respectively, are 12% and 6%.)

Analysis of "excess mortality," or preventable deaths, has shown that there is an almost ninefold excess in the deaths of black South African children under the age of five years relative to the deaths of their white counterparts. Excess mortality in early childhood is predominantly due to diarrhea, acute respiratory infections and pneumonia, nutritional deficiency, and measles—all highly preventable.

Infectious diseases. South Africa's tuberculosis rates rank among the highest in the world and are a cause for grave concern. Approximately 100,000 new cases occur annually, of which 80,000 are reported. This figure has not varied much over the last few years. The rates are likely to increase, however, as the HIV/AIDS epidemic spreads. In late 1993 HIV-seroprevalence in male and female tuberculosis patients in Johannesburg hospitals was over 30%.

Diarrheal diseases, acute respiratory infections, and polio have shown substantial declines over the last decade. Measles is one of the most preventable diseases, but in 1992 a total of 19,000 cases was recorded. While immunization coverage for communicable childhood diseases has increased over the last decade, the national coverage (about 65–70%) is still below that of many poorer countries.

Typhoid rates were declining steadily, but a major outbreak (over 1,000 cases) in a slum area in 1993 reinforced the need for vigilance and control. With substantial rains after a long period of drought, along with increased migration and tourism to and from South Africa, there has been a quadrupling of malaria cases since 1992 (with over 10,000 reported cases in 1993). South Africa's currently effective malaria-control program will be placed under increasing pressure as a result of open borders, the increased resistance of the mosquito that carries the *Plasmodium falciparum* parasite, and poor preventive practices among travelers.

Nutritional status. Poor nutritional status of mothers is associated with low-birth-weight babies, whose subsequent growth and development are poor. Available nutritional status data (extrapolated from ad hoc surveys) indicate that 8–15% of the population is born weighing under 2.5 kg (5.5 lb) and about 25–40% of the population under age five has developmental delay or stunted growth. The Department of National Health and Population Development and the Department of Agriculture estimated that in 1990,

A direct and indirect consequence of apartheid is that the infant mortality rate for black South Africans is more than seven times higher than that for whites. A top priority of the new government is safeguarding maternal and child health.

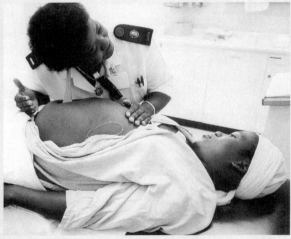

David Lurie—Katz/Saba

2.3 million South Africans were vulnerable with respect to their nutritional status. Although between 1965 and 1990 there were steady improvements in childhood nutritional status, the data are inadequate to identify whether there are specific communities that are still profoundly affected by malnutrition.

Iron deficiency anemia is thought to affect up to 25% of women in South Africa—the implications for pregnant women being profound. Improving the iron status of women is a complex issue, however, that will require more than just iron supplementation. Between 15% and 50% of children in rural areas are heavily infected with parasites—a situation that substantially contributes to childhood iron deficiency. A large proportion of female children are subsequently iron deficient during their childbearing years. Highly cost-effective measures to deworm whole populations and effectively break this cycle exist but have not been adequately applied.

Trauma and violence. Deaths from trauma are three times more common in South Africa than globally. The nation's violence mortality rate is the highest in the world (59.2 persons killed by violence per 100,000 deaths, compared with 9.6 in the U.S.). Motor vehicle deaths in South Africa rank fourth highest in the world (11.5 per 100 million km [62 million mi] traveled, compared with 1.1 in the U.S.). It is conservatively estimated by South Africa's Medical Research Council that the annual national cost of vehicular collisions in South Africa exceeds $2 billion (in direct costs alone).

Political strife accounts for about one-eighth of all violent deaths. In 1993 an estimated 3,500 South Africans died as a result of political violence. From the start of the transition process on Feb. 2, 1990, until early 1994, political violence killed over 10,000 people. Ongoing strife—ANC-Inkatha Freedom Party clashes, security force actions, right-wing (white) destabilization, and high levels of unemployment among black youths combined with no perceptible improvement in their living conditions—ensures further social disintegration and violence.

A disturbing recent trend is the increased use of guns in violent crimes of all types. In 1993 at Groote Schuur Hospital (the major Cape Town referral center), gunshot injuries accounted for about 100 of 600 trauma admissions per month, compared with about half that number in the two previous years. The impact of violence on health services has been extensively documented since 1986. Violence disrupts routine preventive, promotive, and curative services. The impact of violence on mental health has also been profound; in especially hard-hit communities, psychologists have documented a high prevalence of posttraumatic stress disorder, often necessitating individual, family, or communitywide counseling. In the African homeland of KwaZulu in the province of Natal, the destruction of property and concern over personal

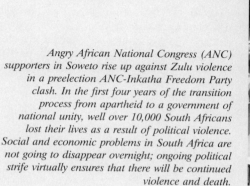

Angry African National Congress (ANC) supporters in Soweto rise up against Zulu violence in a preelection ANC-Inkatha Freedom Party clash. In the first four years of the transition process from apartheid to a government of national unity, well over 10,000 South Africans lost their lives as a result of political violence. Social and economic problems in South Africa are not going to disappear overnight; ongoing political strife virtually ensures that there will be continued violence and death.

and family safety have resulted in the displacement of about 100,000 people. Sustainable violence prevention will depend upon community-oriented programs that are innovative and holistic in their approach.

Mental health. On the whole the mental health status of South Africans has been much neglected. The poverty of good data reflects the fact that no communitywide surveys of mental health status have been done and that psychologists under apartheid stressed individual counseling as opposed to public health approaches. Under the new constitution more attention will be given to recognizing and preventing emotional disability, and in January 1994 the Psychology Association of South Africa reconstituted itself as a public health-oriented body. It is likely that a substantial mental health problem exists and that ongoing turmoil will continue to take a heavy psychological toll, with children and adolescents the most vulnerable.

AIDS and other sexually transmitted diseases. In 1992 AIDS accounted for only 0.6% of all deaths in South Africa. While AIDS is not currently a major cause of death or disease, by late 1993 there were an estimated 500,000 people in the country infected with HIV. Surveys conducted by the Department of National Health and Population Development showed that at the end of 1992 HIV-seroprevalence rates among women seeking prenatal care varied by region (from 0.7% HIV positive to 4.8%) and race (whites 0.09% and Africans 3%). About 18% of reported cases were among babies infected through vertical transmission (from mother to child). Key determinants of infection were migrancy and low social class. AIDS will pose a major threat to the health services and, importantly, to the economy by the end of the present century and well into the next. Mathematical projections estimate that in 2005 there will be 470,000 AIDS cases and 330,000 AIDS deaths—or 42% of all deaths that year—and that AIDS care may consume between 35% and 75% of the country's total health care budget.

The prevalence of sexually transmitted diseases (STDs) among women attending family-planning and prenatal clinics over the last decade has ranged 5–25% for syphilis, 4–12% for gonorrhea, and 5–16% for chlamydial infections. Moreover, a close link between HIV and other STDs is evident from recent data; HIV seroprevalence among STD clinic attenders in Johannesburg had reached 25% in black men and 16% in black women.

To date the government's response to AIDS has not matched the extent of the problem—the per capita investment in AIDS-control programs being only 18 cents. The Centre for Health Policy at the University of the Witwatersrand, Johannesburg, recommends that at least one dollar per capita be spent on controlling AIDS.

Determinants of health

The health status of individuals and populations is influenced by a wide range of factors. Some of these have had and will continue to have a profound effect on the health status of South Africans.

Economy and population growth. South Africa's economic performance over the last three decades has been extremely poor at a time when average population growth has been high—2.8% per annum. This hampers the ability of the state to provide social services, the ability of the private sector to generate much-needed jobs for the 400,000 new entrants to the labor market each year, and the ability of the land to support the people. In 1990 per capita gross domestic product (GDP) was $2,749. The distribution of wealth in South Africa, however, is highly skewed. For example, in 1990 black Africans constituted 95% of the 18 million South Africans living below the poverty level ($220 per month). In the future South Africa will need to give the highest priority to successful implementation of an economic development policy that targets the poor, reduces unemployment, and increases real economic growth. This must be combined with a population-control strategy. Importantly, the ANC has recognized that investing in health is crucial: "Health expenditure efficiently employed and effectively targeted is *not* a drain on economic resources but a positive guarantor of economic performance."

Water, sanitation, and housing. Worldwide the provision of adequate water, sanitation, and housing has been associated with substantial declines in death rates. Investments in water and sanitation are essential for public health. Government statistics estimate that, including the four homelands, 55% of the urban South African population of 26 million has good water and sanitation facilities, compared with 30–40% of the rural population. By some estimates less than 10% of the rural population has adequate sanitation services. About $3.9 billion in initial costs and $175 million in recurrent costs over a five-year period will be required for substantially improving sanitation. (Lower costs are possible if simpler technology is used.)

There is currently a significant demand for housing, with between 1.3 million and 3 million national housing units needed to accommodate 27% of urban dwellers presently living in nonpermanent structures. Only 42% of rural houses presently provide adequate health protection for their residents. The ANC recommends that state spending for housing rise to $1 billion by 1995, which would constitute 5% of GDP (compared with the present 2.1%). Innovative approaches to financing housing for blacks will be needed. Overcoming the housing shortage is seen as essential and must be addressed even before other needed health sector investments are allocated.

Urbanization and urban development. The new South Africa will inherit several problems of the "Apartheid City." These include spatial segregation of groups by race within cities; significant urban transportation costs, particularly for Africans (who travel an average distance of 37 km [23 mi] to their work, accounting for over 10% of their household income); wide disparities in income; and inefficient investments in infrastructures (due to "urban sprawl").

If current population trends continue, there will be about 50 million people in all of South Africa, including the homelands, by 2000, of whom more than half will be living in urban areas. By 1990 about 50% of Africans were urbanized, compared with about 90% for all other groups. By 2000 the fastest-growing metropolitan area, Durban-Pinetown, will have in excess of 5.5 million people, and greater Johannesburg will reach 10 million.

Urbanization holds the hope for overall improvements in health but carries with it many potential risks. Already common on the outskirts of big cities are squalid, overcrowded, and rodent-infested townships that have inadequate water and sanitation and high crime rates. Most urban-development planners have yet to incorporate a specific focus on health in plans for new townships. An improvement in the health of urban dwellers will not be possible until these apartheid-generated problems have been addressed.

Education. Literacy in South Africa has improved markedly over the last decade, especially among Africans. The 1990 nationwide adult literacy rate was 70%, with adults having an average of 3.9 years of schooling. However, the quality of African schooling remains low, and in 1993 only 38.2% of 360,000 African matriculants passed their exams.

School-based health programs in South Africa are virtually unknown. A greater emphasis on health education requires improvements in the overall quality of schooling. While school enrollment has increased steadily over the last few decades, the dropout rate (particularly among boys) is worrisome. Boys who drop out of school are far more likely to smoke, drink alcohol, use a variety of illicit drugs, and engage in violent acts and unprotected sex than are their school-going peers.

In 1990, 18 million South Africans were living below the poverty level—many on the outskirts of big cities in squalid, overcrowded townships with inadequate water and sanitation and high crime rates. Improvements in the health of the urban-dwelling black majority will depend on urban-development planning that incorporates a specific focus on health.

Ron Haviv—Saba

While the school enrollment has increased among Africans in South Africa and African literacy rates have improved over the past decade, the quality of schooling for the black majority remains low, and dropout rates, especially for male students, are high. In addition to raising the standards of education, school programs need to address health and lifestyle issues.

Fundamental curricular change is crucial to ensuring that healthy lifestyle habits are introduced from primary school on. Programs need to be geared toward preventing STDs and AIDS; preventing alcohol, tobacco, and drug abuse; controlling violence; and improving nutrition. Basic hygiene instruction and deworming programs also need to be considered part of the overall education program.

The long-term benefits of appropriate schooling on the mental health and general well-being of children cannot be overlooked. Since 1976 schoolchildren (particularly boys) have been increasingly involved in criminal activities. Psychologists foresee difficulties in the long term for reintegrating these children into society. In addition, innovative ways of reaching "hard to reach" children, especially those who do not attend school, will need to be pursued vigorously.

Energy. South Africa currently supplies in excess of 70% of Africa's installed electrical capacity. However, fewer than 10% of rural South African households and 50% of urban households have electricity. The provision of electricity holds many benefits for health. These include declines in respiratory diseases associated with the use of coal, wood, and dung stoves (a common cause of childhood deaths), a potential reduction in kerosene poisoning (responsible for 1,000 childhood deaths annually), improved literacy and learning through the provision of better lighting, greater access to the technological era afforded by the use of modern domestic appliances, and declines in fertility.

The provision of affordable electricity is seen as a high priority by major political players. However, health specialists point out that increased access to refrigeration and television could lead to sedentary living patterns and increased spending on new products that are not conducive to health. Refrigeration, for example, could alter patterns of food consumption and increase consumption of foods high in calories, fat, sugar, and salt; processed foods of low nutritional value; and alcohol. This could lead to an increased incidence of chronic diseases (*e.g.,* cardiovascular disease, diabetes, and alcoholism)—a trend that is already apparent in many urban communities.

Migration. Migration has profoundly influenced health in South Africa ever since the discovery of diamonds (1868) and gold (1886). The migrant labor system has long contributed to high rates of STDs (and now to increasing rates of HIV/AIDS) among rural residents. In the future the health implications of rural-to-urban migration will need to be addressed specifically. Since 1990 transnational migration has been accelerating rapidly. There are now approximately two million "visitors" to South Africa per year, mainly from the northern and northeastern bordering countries. The risk of transmission of a number of infectious diseases, of which malaria is the most obvious, is increasing at a time when tourism is being seen as a major future source of foreign exchange for the whole of southern Africa.

Addressing health problems

South Africa is beginning to address its many health problems. Some encouraging steps have been taken. Many more are needed.

Industry actions. In the past, certain industries have adversely affected health, and some are now actively pursuing new ways of contributing to health improvement. The oil industry, for example, has introduced child-resistant containers to prevent kerosene poisoning, and it supports efforts to reduce the lead content of gasoline produced and used in South Africa (current levels are among the highest in the world).

In South Africa, as in many countries, alcohol consumption not only is a major cause of motor vehicle injuries and deaths but also is associated with high homicide rates. "Drive safe" campaigns, which are being supported by the alcohol industry, are one example of the kind of responsible approach that needs greater support. The tobacco industry, however, is different. Its continued prosperity is simply not compatible with health. In 1990 there were an estimated 25,000 tobacco-related deaths in South Africa. The industry's powerful parliamentary lobby, its targeting of the black population, and its efforts to buy respectability by supporting sports and cultural events and sponsoring environmental projects make it a particularly tricky industry to control. Strong action (including effective legislation and increased taxation on tobacco products) will be required in the future, and these form part of the ANC's health policy.

Health services: reducing disparities. The health care sector plays an important role in improving the health status of populations, but the determinants of health mentioned above are often more important and have a longer-term impact both on the health status of the population as a whole and, more important, on the distribution of health within that population. Thus, strategies to reduce disparities in health status by race, region, and gender in South Africa will need to take a holistic approach.

The ANC has warned that the "private sector depends upon and crowds out the public sector." The private sector employs 50% of the country's 22,908 doctors, 80–90% of its dentists, 92% of its pharmacists, and 20% of its nurses. Further, it absorbs half of the total amount spent on health ($6.5 billion), mainly through private insurance received from the 21% of the population covered. It is estimated that the 50 million annual private health sector visits translate into annual per capita consultation rates of 6 for whites, 4 for Asians, 1 for Coloureds, and 0.3 for Africans.

Although there is an increasing trend toward a public-private mix in the health sectors—for example, 62% of private general practitioners in rural areas have an appointment in the public sector—over the last decade, health care expenditure has increased more rapidly in the private sector than in the public sector. Such spending, a reflection of government policy, distorts the distribution of resources available for care. While the overall percentage of the gross national product (GNP) spent on health care in South Africa (6.2% for 1990–91) is acceptable by worldwide standards, the distribution of spending reveals severe inequities.

The ANC believes that a defined program of health care services should be guaranteed for all South Africans at a total package cost of about $340 million per year, to be financed either through a guaranteed proportion of government expenditure or possibly with a percentage of a payroll tax being earmarked for the health system. There is, however, little room to maneuver in increasing the proportion of total government revenue going to the health sector because social spending has already increased markedly, defense spending has declined, and urgent increases in housing will be required. Such taxes could realistically raise about $500 million per year and would be a direct positive intervention for health as well.

Health personnel. In 1992 there were 22,908 registered medical practitioners in South Africa, of whom only about 1,000 (4.5%) were African. In the urban areas the ratio of general practitioners-to-population is 1:900, compared with 1:4,100 in rural areas. Eighty-two percent of physicians in the various medical specialties are concentrated in the three major metropolitan areas that constitute 38.2% of the total South African population (Greater Cape Town, Johannesburg-Pretoria, and Durban-Pinetown), as are 76% of dentists, 79% of psychologists, and 70% of pharmacists. Surprisingly, a majority of community health and preventive health specialists (79%) are concentrated in these metropolises. A more equitable distribution is seen among nurses and health inspectors.

Nurses constitute the largest group of health workers in South Africa. In 1992 there were 140,719 registered nurses and nursing school enrollees. Nurses serve as the backbone of the primary health care system, particularly in rural areas and urban townships. However, a nursing shortage is fast developing. Since 1984 the number of new nursing students has declined by 6% per year. Unattractive working conditions in the public sector, low salaries, and a lack of financial incentives are the reasons for the decreasing availability of nurses.

New initiatives for training health personnel are clearly needed. Some programs are already under way. In the western Cape for the last two years, winter and summer "short courses" have trained health systems researchers, community health workers, and women's health specialists, and in early 1994 the first students in a master's program in public health were enrolled. Initiatives to train public health workers have also begun in the northern and western provinces of Transvaal and Natal.

In South Africa 80% of patients consult a traditional healer before going to a professional nurse or medical doctor. Recently the potential for a health care partnership between African traditional healers and biomedical personnel was explored by the Medical Research Council. Traditional healers' methods were found to emphasize interpersonal relationships and promote group harmony, thereby decreasing vulnerability to illness. However, because the training of African traditional healers is not standardized, attempts at collaboration have been problematic. One exception is a recent initiative at Medunsa (the only black medical university in South Africa). Herbal medicines used by healers were analyzed in the university's laboratory, and therapeutically active ingredients as well as harmful agents were identified. There are now efforts under way to find traditional herbs that have antiviral potential and could be of relevance in the fight against AIDS. Other efforts have been directed to-

315

ward enlisting healers in the AIDS-control campaign—*e.g.,* in identifying HIV-infected patients and promoting safer sex practices. It is likely that a future health service will ensure that African traditional healers are drawn into some form of partnership with the newly evolving health ministries at both the national and provincial levels.

Future challenges

Six and one-half billion dollars is not buying the level of health for South Africans that one would expect. In fact, the World Bank in its *World Development Report 1993* ranked South Africa's health status relative to its financial status as among the worst in the world. *How* a country spends its resources rather than *how much* is spent determines health status. For well over half a century in South Africa, there has been an overemphasis on doing the wrong things and an underemphasis on doing the right things. Too great an emphasis has been placed on high-technology tertiary care such as excessive use of diagnostic technologies and the medical and surgical management of heart disease and cancer. Meanwhile, far too little emphasis has been placed on primary care and community-based disease prevention.

School-based programs for promoting safe sex, controlling tobacco and alcohol use, and deworming have been shown to be highly cost-effective yet are virtually unknown in South Africa. For adults smoking cessation, STD control and condom promotion, and aggressive tuberculosis-control programs are likely to result in vast health improvements and to be highly cost-effective yet have not been utilized to the degree that is needed. Among all cancer-screening programs,

ANC leader Nelson Mandela casts his vote on April 27, 1994. In January 1994, in anticipation of an election victory, the ANC issued a comprehensive health reform plan that specifically addresses apartheid-generated health problems.

Peter Turnley—Black Star

screening for cervical cancer is needed most but is presently inadequately funded.

All this results in an inefficient and wasteful health system and a high incidence of preventable deaths, disease, and disability. Correcting the balance will require strong political commitment to counter what have become strong vested interests.

Continued declines in many infectious diseases, particularly diarrhea and pneumonia, and the eradication or partial elimination of measles and polio are likely in coming years. By contrast, steady increases can be expected in a range of diseases associated with the aggressive marketing of tobacco and alcohol, increased consumption of high-fat diets, and continued high levels of air pollution. These include lung cancer, chronic lung disease, and heart disease. Already millions of South Africans have risk factors that predispose them to chronic diseases. For example, almost six million adults smoke, and over two and one-half million adults have blood pressure levels worthy of treatment. Cost-effective screening and prevention programs are likely to be the most beneficial in terms of curtailing the incidence of chronic diseases.

Funding, however, should not be transferred from childhood infectious disease control to the treatment of chronic diseases, which would increase inequities in health status. In their 1993 Nobel Peace Prize acceptance speeches, both Nelson Mandela and F.W. de Klerk identified the provision of child health and welfare services as a priority for the future.

Health for all is possible in South Africa. It will require national commitment and vision. Simultaneously, advantage must be taken of the unique opportunity that history has brought to restructure both the economy and the health sector. Anticipating victory in the April election, in late January 1994 the ANC published its preliminary health plan, with reforms based on the premise that "the mental, physical, and social health of South Africans has been severely damaged by apartheid policies and their consequences." Shortly after the election, the new health minister, Nkosezana Zuma, pledged that there would be rapid action on health under the new government. Immediate steps would include instituting nutritional feeding programs in schools, providing free health care for children under age six, and requiring stronger warnings on cigarette packages. Zuma also announced that tobacco use would be more actively discouraged and the excise tax on tobacco products increased.

Developing "healthy public policy" means considering at Cabinet level how every department of government can contribute to health. At the same time, public participation is crucial for implementing health interventions and ultimately for sustaining health. The emerging democratic focus augurs well for real participation of the South African people and for redressing inequities of the past.

Medical Education

The training of doctors was transformed at the beginning of this century when a scientific discipline was applied to the practice of medicine. As the century moves toward its close, concerted attempts are being made to establish reforms of a similar magnitude to align medical education with the changing health care needs of people throughout the world.

The single biggest piece of unfinished business of the 20th century, according to James Grant, executive director of the United Nations Children's Fund (UNICEF), is the extension of the basic benefits of modern science and medicine, now enjoyed by three-quarters of the world population, to the one billion people living in abject poverty in both the less developed and the industrialized worlds. Leaders in the field of medical education are in agreement that the present system needs to be changed radically if it is to meet that challenge. Medical education has been widely criticized for its insularity, its outdated learning methods, and an overrestrictive view of the role of the doctor.

The failings of the current system were identified in detail at the second World Conference on Medical Education, held over five days in August 1993 in the Scottish capital of Edinburgh. The first such conference had been held five years earlier in the same city. The most recent summit brought together 280 of the world's leading medical educators from 80 countries. The meeting was organized by the World Federation for Medical Education and sponsored by five of the United Nations agencies—the World Health Organization (WHO), UNICEF, the United Nations Development Program (UNDP), the United Nations Educational, Scientific and Cultural Organization (UNESCO), and the World Bank. The participation of these diverse agencies acknowledged that the medical profession alone cannot bring about the reforms that are required. Changes will also be needed in the economic, cultural, and political framework in which health professionals function.

The aim of the summit was to map out a path that medical schools around the world can follow to achieve reform. No single, clear route or global solution was offered because the problems are so diverse, as are the resources to deal with them. Annual health spending per capita in 1990, for example, was $5 in Zaire, whereas in Canada it was almost 400 times as much: $1,945. "We have to understand and respect the diversity of educational systems, the diversity of cultures and the diversity of economical ways and means to achieve the relevant quality of medical education as a precondition for improving health care," Adnan Badran, deputy director general of UNESCO, pointed out.

Redesigning the doctor

Despite the wide variations in the volume and quality of health care services throughout the world, common problems exist with the training of doctors. Delegates at the conference came up with a series of recommendations that were set forth in a report that concluded: "The doctor for the 21st century needs to be redesigned. Doctors have to be better providers of primary care; communicators; critical thinkers; motivated lifelong learners; information specialists; practitioners of allied economics, sociology, anthropology, epidemiology, and behavioral medicine; health team managers; and advocates for communities." Medical education, it added, "is faced with the urgent need to get its house in order, to diminish its weaknesses and expand its strengths."

One of the principal weaknesses arises from the way

Penny Tweedie—Panos Pictures

A sick child is attended at home in a village in Bangladesh; monsoon rains have prevented the mother from taking her baby to a clinic or hospital. Extending the achievements of modern medicine to the world's less privileged people and training more primary care doctors to work in rural and underserved communities are considered top priorities for medical education today.

medical education has developed as a hospital-based activity in which students are exposed to relatively rare conditions, often requiring expensive treatments. As a consequence, too many specialists are being produced when the most pressing need today is for doctors to work in and with local communities ministering to common problems. A report from the World Bank in 1993, "Investing in Health," emphasized the extent of misallocation of resources, particularly in less developed countries. Too much money is spent on expensive, high-technology health interventions, such as surgery for most cancers, while critical and highly cost-effective interventions such as the treatment of tuberculosis and sexually transmitted diseases remain underfunded. "In some countries a single teaching hospital can absorb 20% or more of the budget of the ministry of health even though almost all cost-effective interventions are best delivered at lower level facilities," the report said. Addressing delegates at the Edinburgh conference, George Psacharopoulos, senior human resource adviser to the World Bank, said medical schools should introduce more courses in public health and fewer in neurosurgery. He also called on governments to set limits on the number of specialists to be trained and to encourage doctors to move from urban areas to serve in more neglected rural communities.

Fitzhugh Mullan, an assistant U.S. surgeon general and one of the physicians who had worked on Pres. Bill Clinton's task force on health care reform, told the conference that fully two-thirds of doctors in the United States are specialists and that generalists would soon be in short supply. "We need to provide incentives and stimulants to reverse that trend," he said. He went on to describe measures that the president's task force was considering; included were incentives that would increase the number of doctors from minority groups and encourage doctors to practice in disadvantaged areas.

Another important issue that concerned the delegates at the conference was the nature of medical teaching, which too often focuses on treating episodes of illness when greater attention needs to be devoted to ways that physicians can establish partnerships with patients to prevent the occurrence of disease. The greatest medical challenges that doctors face today have to do with prevention of illness and management of chronic conditions rather than cures. The chronic diseases associated with an aging population and the emergence of newer problems such as AIDS require a different response from doctors than medical schools have been preparing them for. Hiroshi Nakajima, director general of WHO, spoke of the need for medical education to make a critical leap from a "disease" orientation to a "health" orientation: "New skills are required if graduates are to continue to justify the aim of medical education and the expectations of their

constituents. I choose the word *constituent* because the word *patient* carries the stigma of disease and dependency rather than the message of health and an individual's contribution to health."

Delegates also discussed the need for teaching methods to change. For too many students, learning is a passive process in which they are fed information via lectures attended by large groups. The world leaders in medical education agreed that the aim should be to create motivated self-learners by developing a system of problem-based, student-centered learning. The vast and rapidly accumulating amount of knowledge about human health and disease makes this a pressing requirement. It is impossible for students to learn in their four- to six-year training period all that they will need to know to carry out their practice effectively over their entire career. They need resources to allow them to update their skills and knowledge base constantly. V. Ramalingaswami of the All India Institute of Medical Sciences, New Delhi, said the curriculum also needs to be expanded beyond the traditional biomedical focus to include training in disciplines such as health economics, statistics, ethics, and social and behavioral sciences. Increasingly, doctors are having to manage budgets, decide who should get priority for treatment, and deal with the consequences of problems arising out of social conditions such as teenage pregnancy, domestic violence, and drug abuse. Doctors need new skills to adapt to their ever widening responsibilities.

Many other areas where action is needed were addressed. Some of the reforms that were called for in the conference's final communiqué were:
- more teaching to take place outside university hospitals
- better systems to be set up to ensure that adequate numbers of doctors are trained
- more primary care doctors and fewer specialists to be trained
- more attention to be devoted to preventive medicine
- the selection of medical students to take into account each candidate's social commitment as well as his or her academic ability
- lifelong learning to be promoted
- doctors' communications skills to be improved
- communities to participate in medical education
- doctors to be trained to work as part of a health care team
- the undergraduate curriculum to be broadened to include domains other than that of biomedicine.

Steps in the right direction

Positive changes are occurring in response to some of the problems. The Network of Community Oriented Educational Institutions for Health Sciences, a consortium of more than 80 medical schools throughout the world, has embraced change in many areas, including

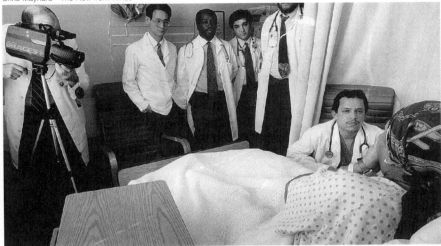

Residents at the Long Island Jewish Medical Center, New Hyde Park, N.Y., participate in a new academic program geared toward producing physicians who are advocates for and allies of patients as well as expert clinicians. The training doctors' interviews with patients are videotaped; later they will have the chance to evaluate their own communications skills.

developing non-hospital-based training programs. The progress, however, said the final report, "has been too fragmented, has left far too many medical schools untouched, and has failed to develop the necessary critical mass for consolidated change."

Several U.S. medical schools were cited for the teaching reforms they had introduced: Columbia University College of Physicians and Surgeons, New York City; University of Hawaii John A. Burns School of Medicine; Johns Hopkins University School of Medicine, Baltimore, Md.; University of Kentucky College of Medicine; University of New Mexico School of Medicine; Oregon Health Sciences University School of Medicine; and University of Rochester (N.Y.) School of Medicine and Dentistry. Among other innovations, the schools had added courses in ethics, epidemiology, and the history of medicine to their curricula. Lectures were deemphasized, and students were being introduced into clinical settings and to solving clinical problems in their first year, often in rural areas.

In South America the Kellogg Foundation has funded a series of initiatives, including one at the National University of Nicaragua in which individual students are assigned to a single city street in Léon. They are instructed to get to know the health needs of every resident and to work among the people to improve their health.

In the United Kingdom the General Medical Council, which oversees the quality of medical education, has called for large-scale changes to the curriculum. In its report "Tomorrow's Doctors," the council recommended that the factual content of the undergraduate course be reduced, greater emphasis be placed on encouraging students to teach themselves, and special-study modules be introduced that offer instruction in the social sciences and humanities. The report stressed the importance of students' developing qualities and attitudes that will make them good doctors.

These include an ability to cope with uncertainty, an awareness of personal limitations, and an ability to adapt to change.

Grant of UNICEF gave an example of what can be achieved by determined action. The commitment Third World countries have shown to immunization programs now means that in Calcutta, Lagos, Nigeria, and Mexico City much larger proportions of children are fully immunized by age two than in New York City, Washington, D.C., or the United States as a whole. He went on to emphasize the crucial part that medical education can play in improving the lives of people everywhere: "Physicians are cast in a key role at this crossroads in history. Improving their education and training and molding their motivations and value systems is tantamount to improving the health care of people." Grant cautioned, however, that powerful vested interests that stand to benefit from the status quo will oppose reform. "Forgive me if I am being too blunt," he said. "I believe that a specific barrier to reform of medical education is the inertia of the medical teachers themselves. In some cases, frankly, the medical establishment is a leading opponent of progressive reform."

A long way to go

The conference's report is to be used as a framework from which national and local changes can be constructed. That process was advanced at medical education conferences held in each of the six WHO regions—Africa, the Americas, the Eastern Mediterranean, Europe, Southeast Asia, and the Western Pacific—in 1994. Those conferences were attended by government officials as well as academicians and focused on how changes can be brought about in particular countries. Progress toward reform will be reviewed at the third World Conference on Medical Education, to be held in 1998.

Henry Walton, the president of the World Federation for Medical Education, has expressed great optimism for the future. Walton has said that although today many of the doctors produced by medical schools are not equipped to provide the health services that people need, a current of reform has begun to flow in medical education throughout the world that is already unstoppable. Despite the mounting momentum for reform, there is still a long way to go. An editorial in *The Lancet* in March 1994 expressed a more cynical view about any immediate prospects for meaningful reform: "The 'reforms' are seldom bold enough to depart from tradition and redefine the mission of medical education directly to address the needs of society today. Instead educational changes are incremental ones, driven more by a need to keep up to date and to persuade funders (public and private) that something is changing."

Anyone at the conference in Scotland who thought that the solutions to the problems of medical education would be simple or that their implementation could be speedy was advised otherwise by Daniel C. Tosteson, dean of Harvard Medical School, one of the U.S. schools that is helping forge new teaching methods: "Those of us who seek to change medical education and ultimately medical practice for the better should expect that change will be slow, require continuing labor, and will never end."

—*Bryan Christie*

Medical Technology

Medicine used to be defined primarily by the talents and personalities of the doctors who practiced it. But no more. Physicians have been joined by engineers, technicians, and scientists who create the wondrous tools, pharmaceuticals, and procedures that make medicine what it is today. Their innovations have unquestionably transformed the way doctors diagnose, treat, and prevent illness in patients. Today technologies such as lasers, recombinant gene therapies, and precision diagnostic imaging methods are an expected part of the health care system. Yet most of the marvels of medical technology were unheard of as little as a decade or two ago.

Diversity and pervasiveness

Medical technology encompasses many different fields of science, medicine, and industry. The technologies themselves range from "big-ticket" items like million-dollar magnetic resonance imaging (MRI) machines or thousand-dollar-a-dose drugs, such as interferon, for treating life-threatening diseases to simple, inexpensive home-test kits for pregnancy and cholesterol. Roughly 7,000 companies in the U.S. alone manufacture over 1,500 types of medical devices, and hundreds more products are presently in the testing phase. In the tradition of American entrepreneurship, some medical technology manufacturers are small "biotech" firms with only a single product or a modest output. On the other hand, corporate giants in the computer and electronics fields, such as Hewlett-Packard Co. and General Electric, have dozens of medical product subsidiaries. Moreover, a huge multinational pharmaceutical company, such as Pfizer, Inc., may spend billions to develop new drugs and own a laser company, an orthopedic implant manufacturer, and a dental supplies firm as well.

Medical technologies improve the quality of medical care and thus the overall health of the people who are served by them. New drugs, devices, and procedures often reduce patient pain, discomfort, and recovery time. At the same time, however, the expense of research, development, testing, and manufacture as well as the costs of buying equipment and training medical personnel to use it add significantly to health care costs. Yet certainly in the U.S., as well as in many other industrialized countries, both patients and medical providers demand the most technologically advanced health care.

Getting to the heart of a problem

Consider one of the recent innovations in heart surgery: the laser. The first successful heart surgery took place just four decades ago. But in the early 1950s, only the most skilled and daring surgeons were willing to try such an operation. Before there was even the most basic heart-lung machine, the patient's circulation had to be connected to that of another person. In the first such operation, the patient was a young boy with a congenital heart defect; his father lay on a gurney next to him in the operating room—his heart pumping blood through both their bodies. In the years since that operation, sophisticated surgical tools, computers, new drugs, and many new procedures have revolutionized heart surgery.

Cardiologists treating clogged coronary arteries have relied on two primary procedures—surgical bypass or balloon angioplasty. Now, however, a new method is being tested. At the San Francisco Heart Institute, doctors bend over the open chest of a patient with severe coronary artery disease and carefully aim a high-powered laser directly into the beating heart muscle. The operating theater is dark except for the quiet glow of a computer screen and a circle of bright lights just above the unconscious patient. One of the doctors touches a command button at the top of the screen, readying the 1,000-w laser beam for firing. Controlled by software and synchronized to the patient's own heartbeat, the powerful laser then fires in one-twentieth of a second, drilling tiny holes, literally between beats. Precise aiming and timing are the keys to this stunning new technology's success. Between beats the heart is gorged with blood, which acts as a backstop for the laser's energy, preventing it from drilling into other heart tissue.

When the laser is fired, puffs of white mist swirl around the barrel—not unlike the puff of smoke from an old-time revolver. Doctors watch an ultrasound monitor on which grainy blue and black pictures show blood flowing through the beating heart. The blood absorbs the laser's energy, creating a swirl of tiny bubbles, which rise as if in a glass of champagne, telling the doctors that their aim has been accurate. Oxygen-rich blood then flows through the minuscule tunnels drilled into areas of the heart that were previously starved for oxygen by blocked arteries. After the laser has done its work, the surfaces of the one-millimeter holes seal in just a few minutes, but the channels beneath the surface remain open indefinitely, enabling blood to circulate unobstructed.

The new cardiosurgical procedure that enables blood to flow directly into the patient's heart tissue, supplanting the blocked coronary artery, is called transmyocardial revascularization (TMR). The tool it relies on is known as the Heart Laser and was developed by PLC Systems in Massachusetts. Seven hospitals in the U.S. are testing TMR. Doctors performing the surgery are enthusiastic about its potential because it offers an alternative for patients whose coronary arteries are too diseased for conventional coronary bypass surgery or balloon angioplasty. Because the surgery avoids the arteries, it may eliminate the problem of restenosis, the tendency for arteries cleared by surgery or angioplasty to become clogged again.

Lasers and beyond

Laser use in modern medicine is continually expanding. The name *laser* is an acronym for "light amplification by stimulated emission of radiation"; one of the first to advance laser technology was Albert Einstein in 1917. Laser light is concentrated into a single, narrow beam traveling in one direction; most lasers generate tremendous heat, which can cut tissue or cauterize blood vessels. This limits bleeding during surgery, and the laser's pinpoint accuracy minimizes damage to surrounding tissue.

Already lasers are commonly used to treat ocular disorders such as advanced glaucoma and diabetic retinopathy, gastrointestinal bleeding, endometriosis, hemorrhoids, gallbladder disease, and growths in the mouth or nasal passages. They are even used to remove tattoos. At several U.S. medical centers, a new laser treatment is being tested to treat a common and annoying problem: snoring. The laser trims excess tissue from the tonsils, the soft palate, and the uvula—the triangle-shaped tissue that hangs below the palate. The outpatient operation is quick, requires little recovery time, and has been 80–85% successful. Lasers are also used in certain operations on the spine, breast, and brain. Each job may require a different type of laser—one best suited to the tissue being treated—and doctors have about a dozen medical lasers to choose from. Carbon monoxide lasers, for example, do not penetrate deeply into tissue because their beam is absorbed by water in the body, which makes them ideal for burning away surface lesions that might be cancerous. Other lasers make deep cuts in tissue, while some do not generate heat at all but turn tissue into gas by breaking chemical bonds. Heart Laser uses a single light-wave CO_2 laser.

Recent medical technology has also created a health revolution for the average citizen: home pregnancy tests, glucose meters that monitor the blood sugar of persons with diabetes, do-it-yourself blood pressure stations in drug stores and supermarkets, microprocessor-driven thermometers that detect fever almost immediately after being inserted in the ear, and slow-release patches that deliver drugs or hormones through the skin and often work faster, longer, and more directly and cause fewer side effects than medication taken in a pill form or by injection.

By mid-1994 the U.S. Food and Drug Administration (FDA) had approved over 600 biotech devices. Yet for every piece of medical technology that Americans (or people in other parts of the world who benefit from these devices) take for granted, dozens are still being refined. The Jarvik-7 artificial heart is a good example of a device that is currently available to surgeons but not yet the answer for heart-transplant patients. The device is primarily used as a bridge to transplantation but has also paved the way for a new generation of permanent artificial hearts. Countless other sophisticated technologies are undergoing tests that must satisfy the rigorous safety and efficacy requirements of the FDA before they can be approved for public use.

Patents, profits, and controversies

Biotechnology inventions constitute one of the fastest-growing segments of the patent market. The financial implications are enormous. Companies may spend hundreds of thousands of dollars to develop a new medical device, or millions in the case of most drugs, and they hope to earn that money back—plus a substantial profit. One way to help ensure large profits is to obtain exclusive rights to an invention through patents issued by the U.S. Patent and Trademark Office. For many research institutions, biotechnology has also become a clear way to produce profit from costly research and development. World-renowned institutions such as Harvard Medical School see a potential steady stream of income in commercializing the work done by their eminent scientists.

At a time when universities can no longer survive on endowments, they are forced to look for alternative funds. Medical technology offers a route to self-sufficiency. Not surprisingly, new legal and ethical questions are being raised by collaborations between academia and industry. How, for example, can universities like Harvard maintain academic integrity while being commercially competitive? Who should set research agendas—the medical school or the firm licensing the technology? Can research decisions be insulated from commercial considerations? Will academic and research groups honor the long-standing tradition of open exchange of ideas, or will they be more concerned with protecting trade secrets? Should state and federally funded university labs be able to license technologies to private firms?

Medical technology poses other problems and raises other questions as well. Nearly every innovation—whether a drug, a medical device, or a new procedure—requires costly research and development. Products regulated by the government are even more expensive because years of resources must be devoted to clinical trials. Pharmaceutical companies not only have to spend vast amounts of money to develop new products but, once they have the drugs in hand, must spend years conducting animal and then human trials to prove long-term safety and efficacy. The same is true for medical tools that will be used on humans. These costs are usually passed on to patients, clinics, and hospitals.

In the 1970s and 1980s, hospitals and clinics enthusiastically embraced medical technology as a means of gaining a competitive advantage. Insurance companies paid for the use of many emerging new technologies, so patients and doctors often had no qualms about the costs of sophisticated tests and procedures. A good example is the proliferation of diagnostic imaging devices such as computed tomography (CT) scanners and MRI machines. Hospitals everywhere bought these big-ticket items at great cost because having state-of-the-art technology helped attract physicians and patients.

Even beyond questions about costs, medical technology is not without controversy. For example, some doctors argue that lasers are no more efficient than standard surgical tools for operations involving large incisions.

Another innovation, the cochlear implant, a device for people who are profoundly deaf in both ears, has generated opposition from some in the deaf community. For one thing, the presently available models do not restore the normal ability to understand speech; most have been shown to be of only slight benefit in some people. Moreover, they are costly and cumbersome, and their effects on the social functioning of deaf people have not been studied.

Because some medical devices have been defective and caused injury, illness, or death in some users (Björk-Shiley heart valves and silicone-gel-filled breast implants, to name just two), some manufacturers are no longer making them. Fears of lawsuits have driven some manufacturers out of the business altogether.

New directions

Skyrocketing costs of medical care are now a major concern of everyone, and biotechnology firms are having to adjust. The need to reduce the costs of health care has spurred development of new kinds of biotech devices. Medicare and private insurance restrictions on hospitalization coverage have helped create a burgeoning market for technologies that are smaller, lighter, less expensive, and easier-to-use versions of hospital machines, which can be used in outpatient settings, and home-care devices that can be used by patients themselves (e.g., continuous infusion pumps that deliver drugs intravenously). Although less expensive, these new technologies still carry a significant cost. But despite costs, few would dispute the benefits of prosthetic devices that restore function or drugs that can thwart disease at the genetic level.

Innovative medical devices are not always revolutionary new tools. Often the equipment is designed to conduct routine tests or treat common illnesses faster, more thoroughly, and more efficiently. Ordinary diagnostic ultrasound, for example, can detect cysts on ovaries but cannot distinguish between tissues that are cancerous and those that are benign. A more sensitive probe, transvaginal color-flow Doppler ultrasonography, enables the physician to tell the difference between cancerous and benign growths by detecting the presence of tumor markers—specific protein molecules, or antigens, secreted by tumors or present on the surface of a cancerous growth's cells. Cancerous ovarian cysts have elevated levels of the antigen CA 125. The Doppler probe is sensitive to this tumor marker and thus can diagnose a malignancy much earlier than standard tests.

Sometimes lifesaving medical devices result from a mere fluke. A new tool for cardiopulmonary resuscitation (CPR) of heart attack victims was modeled on a common toilet plunger. In 1990 a 65-year-old Iranian immigrant with severe triple-vessel coronary disease was taken to San Francisco General Hospital after suffering a presumed heart attack. The patient had collapsed while watching television. His son had attempted to revive him with mouth-to-mouth ventilation but got no response. He then tried manual chest compressions, but his father remained unconscious, pulseless, and breathless. The son then remembered that his mother had revived her husband with a toilet plunger after a similar collapse. The son quickly got a plunger and proceeded to pump his father's chest for 10 minutes until he began to breathe on his own and move. Delighted with his success, the son recommended to the doctors at the hospital that a plunger be kept next to every bed in the coronary care unit. The doctors recommended that the son take a basic CPR course, but they could hardly argue with success.

Those physicians and colleagues at the University of California at San Francisco then began experimenting with a plunger technique on dogs. Eventually they devised a small, hand-held pump that both compresses and decompresses the chest. In traditional CPR a rescuer uses his or her hands to compress the victim's chest, forcing blood through the damaged heart. The hands, however, cannot decompress the chest as a plunger does. The new emergency rescue device that the San Francisco researchers developed is made of plastic and rubber and consists of three basic parts—a suction cup, a piston, and a horizontal handle. The suction cup is 6.5 cm (2.6 in) in diameter, the overall height of the device is 13.5 cm (5.3 in), it weighs only 0.7 kg (1.5 lb), and it enables the user to perform "active compression-decompression CPR." Known as the CardioPump and manufactured by Ambu International in Copenhagen, the new tool costs about $200. The user alternately pushes down and pulls up, forcing more blood through the coronary arteries and drawing vital air into the lungs. In preliminary trials the CardioPump has been a more reliable means of reviving victims than manual CPR.

Physicians as innovators

Medical technology is not a product only of vast medical corporations and institutions. Often new devices and techniques are dreamed up by those in the best position to know there is a need—doctors who work with patients every day. Many of their medical innovations are hardly "high-tech," but they are nevertheless clever solutions to obvious needs.

A group of scientists and physicians recently designed a special glove to protect against the risk of contracting AIDS or hepatitis from accidentally sticking themselves with used hypodermic needles or cutting themselves with scalpels. The glove is made of leather that has a pore size smaller than a needle point. An extra layer of leather covers the fingers that surgeons report they most commonly pierce: the thumb, index finger, and middle finger. Traditional surgical gloves made of rubber or latex are readily punctured.

Doctors often see ways to simplify procedures and reduce costs—methods that often elude medical equipment manufacturers. Naomi L. Nakao at Beth Israel Medical Center in New York City frequently performs surgery to remove polyps from the colon by lassoing the growth and then severing it with an electric current. Often, however, the detached polyp becomes lost inside a patient's body. Finally she and a partner, Peter Wilk, designed a net, or snare, that attaches to the lasso. Now when the polyp is cut away, it simply falls into the snare. While the need for the snare seems plain, it took doctors who routinely perform the surgery to appreciate it.

Searching for a way to solve one of the most common mistakes doctors make in treating ear infections

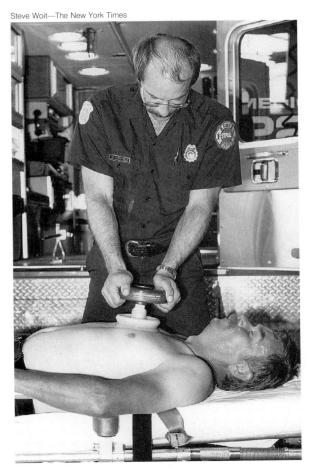

The CardioPump, a new emergency rescue device used by paramedics, was developed after physicians learned of a heart attack victim whom family members had revived at home with a common household toilet plunger.

among young children, Wilk and another colleague, James Cinberg, eliminated the need for knives to cut through infected eardrums. Inserting tubes in ears to drain bacteria-filled fluids and fight off chronic ear infections is among the most common pediatric surgical procedures. The two doctors knew that physicians often cut holes in the eardrum that are too big, which causes the tubes to fall out. Also, the knives had to be discarded after each procedure, generating a lot of waste. Wilk and Cinberg invented a plastic tube with its own cutting edge; a sharp edge pokes precisely the right size hole in the eardrum, allowing the doctor to push the drainage tube into place and leaving nothing to throw away.

While most medical technologies are designed to directly benefit children and adults, some new ideas are aimed at the unborn. William Cooper, head of the Christian Fertility Institute in Easton, Pa., is working on an artificial uterus that might nurture premature infants born in the second trimester of pregnancy. Most

Medical technology

who are born between four and six months' gestation do not survive because their lungs are so under-developed at that stage that they cannot breathe. The artificial uterus might allow doctors to suspend such a fetus in a liquid environment until its lungs matured. Cooper has designed a small chamber divided into upper and lower portions. The fetus would float in a synthetic amniotic fluid in the lower half, its umbilical cord reaching through to the upper section, where the placenta would be bathed with a solution of oxygen and nutrients. Doctors would be able to monitor progress and determine when the lungs had developed enough for the infant to be transferred to a traditional incubator. The invention first must be tested on other mammals such as primates to see if indeed it will work.

It was actually a group of medical residents at Columbia-Presbyterian Medical Center, New York City, who—while experimenting with a method of welding tissue with lasers—came up with a clever alternative for a surgical essential: stitches. They discovered that a mix of proteins and complex sugars made an easy-to-handle glue that bonded well to body tissue. The gelatinous adhesive is mixed with a green dye that absorbs laser light. After being applied to an incision, it is heated with the laser to solidify it. The seal is water-tight, but the adhesive remains flexible. Because the glue is organic, it does not inflame wounds, as stitches and staples sometimes do. Moreover, it spares the patient a return to the surgeon to have stitches removed; as the incision heals, the adhesive dissolves.

Creative computer solutions

Medicine would be in the Dark Ages without computers. Everything from modern medical imaging to hospital record keeping to assessing brain damage to designing drugs to diagnosing mental disorders de-pends on them. Countless procedures that were once rudimentary, time-consuming, or cumbersome have been transformed into quick and efficient computer-assisted techniques.

Early diagnosis and treatment are crucial to curing or halting the progression of breast cancer. Usually a surgical biopsy is done to reach a pathological diagnosis. Now, however, a new diagnostic refinement that relies on a computer program may help confirm or rule out a diagnosis of breast cancer without surgery. Adapted from software used to analyze shapes of geologic formations in the search for oil, the program evaluates the shape of nuclei in breast tissue samples. Cells from a suspicious lump are first removed in an office procedure called fine-needle aspiration. While this technique is less invasive than surgery conducted under anesthesia and requiring incisions, doctors have been reluctant to use it because the small amount of tissue retrieved often can be difficult to analyze accurately. Researchers who have experimented with the new computer program say it can more definitively analyze the nuclei from even a very few cells. Moreover, they believe that once cancer has been detected, the same software can be used to analyze lymph nodes sampled by needle aspiration to determine if the disease has spread.

Computers have been used to transform even that age-old standard tool of medicine: the stethoscope. Stethoscopes have now been devised with micro-processors that can automatically diagnose heart abnormalities. Such a computerized version, patented by Bloodline Technology, Inc., Incline Village, Nev., records heartbeats digitally, which are then analyzed and compared with some 25 different types of heart abnormalities stored in the computer's memory. If a close match is found, a readout flashes the name of the disorder and gives the reasoning behind the

Engineers at Fischer Imaging, Denver, Colo., teamed up with "Star Wars" technologists at Lawrence Livermore National Laboratory in California to develop a new method of X-raying women's breasts; they adapted a system originally used to detect defects in guided missiles. Initial testing indicated that the equipment could produce sharper images of breast tissue but exposed the woman to less radiation than conventional mammography. Because the research and development costs for sophisticated medical machinery can be enormous, joint ventures and "technology transfers" of this sort are becoming increasingly common.

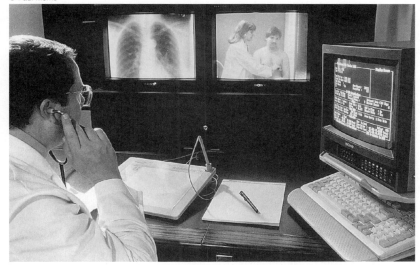

Telemedicine, utilizing satellite linkups and other advanced communications technologies, is a burgeoning new field that enables specialists at top medical centers around the world to act as long-distance consultants. Thus, a pulmonary expert in Boston can evaluate the X-rays of a patient in a medically underserved part of the world thousands of kilometers away and then prescribe and direct appropriate treatment.

choice. It might, for example, diagnose paroxysmal supraventricular tachycardia, which is an arrhythmia that causes a rapid and regular racing of the heart. The stethoscope thus becomes a computer consultant that doctors can turn to for a second opinion, and someday people with heart conditions might even have one at home to use to monitor their response to therapy.

Technology foresight

Taking ideas for medical technology from the drawing board to working prototypes to clinical research and finally to public use can be an expensive and lengthy process. In Europe, Japan, Australia, and New Zealand, governments are looking toward the future and forecasting their societies' health care needs well into the next century. The aim is to harness available resources to meet those needs while at the same time deriving the greatest economic benefit from investments in new technologies. The U.K., for example, announced in 1993 that industrialists and academics would explore technology partnerships focusing on improving the health and quality of life of an increasingly aging population.

In the U.S., with health care costs continuing to rise faster than the rate of inflation, public and private medical insurance plans are less and less willing to cover the costs of new technologies. Clearly, this will have an impact on the demand for new technologies as well as on incentives for research and development. Virtually all medical plans have standard clauses that exclude coverage for investigational or experimental tools or treatments, and the development of new drugs is increasingly based on cost-effectiveness studies. Such pressure to contain costs will continue as the baby-boom generation ages and more health care is needed.

At the same time, government policy makers and economic analysts see salvation in technology. Heading into the new century, medical technology, along with the computer and communications industries, will play a vital role in efforts to rejuvenate economic competitiveness and create jobs by harnessing high-tech brainpower.

—Sabra Chartrand

Mental Health and Illness

There have been numerous developments in mental health and illness during the past year. Among the major ones were the publication of a new diagnostic manual of mental disorders, the release of new information on the prevalence of psychiatric disorders in the United States, increasing use of new antidepressant medications, and continuing controversy about repressed memories of sexual abuse.

DSM-IV: new diagnostic "bible"

The fourth edition of the American Psychiatric Association's *Diagnostic and Statistical Manual of Mental Disorders,* abbreviated *DSM-IV,* was published in May 1994. Like its predecessors, the new manual is the official nomenclature of psychiatric disorders in the United States, but it also has considerable international influence.

The first *DSM* appeared in 1952 as the first official classification of mental disorders. The term *reaction* was used throughout, reflecting the psychobiological view that psychiatric disorders represented individuals' responses to psychological, social, and biological factors. *DSM-II* was published in 1968, dropping the term *reaction* and basing classifications on the mental disorders that were then included in the *International Classification of Diseases,* the officially recognized classification of medical conditions developed by the World Health Organization and used throughout the world. The third edition (*DSM-III,* published in 1980) signaled a revolution in psychiatric diagnosis because it included specific diagnostic criteria rather than general descriptions for each disorder. This led to a marked improvement in diagnostic reliability—notably, the likelihood that several different clinicians would reach the same diagnostic conclusions about a particular patient. That volume was used internationally and was translated into Chinese, Danish, Dutch, Finnish, French, German, Greek, Italian, Japanese, Norwegian, Portuguese, Spanish, and Swedish. A revised third edition (*DSM-III-R*) was published in 1987. The latter incorporated the latest information about psychiatric disorders, including refinements of the new approach to psychiatric diagnosis, changes in criteria for certain diagnostic categories, addition of some entirely new categories (*e.g.,* sleep disorders), and elimination of some previous categories (*e.g.,* egodystonic homosexuality).

The new fourth edition was produced by a 27-member task force and is based on extensive reviews of recent research and field trials that carefully evaluated the use of diagnostic criteria for specific mental disorders. The intention was to base the disorders that are included in the new nomenclature, as well as the criteria for diagnosing them, on empirical evidence (*i.e.,* verifiable data) rather than on assumptions or beliefs.

The manual stresses that it does not classify people; rather, it classifies disorders that people have. Thus, terms such as *schizophrenic* and *manic-depressive* are avoided. Moreover, a single individual can suffer from several different disorders, and there are important ways that persons with the same disorder may not be alike. Although the use of specific criteria has improved diagnostic reliability, application of the criteria requires professional clinical judgment; thus, the manual is not meant to be employed by lay or untrained individuals.

Mental disorder is defined in *DSM-IV* as follows:

a clinically significant behavioral or psychological syndrome or pattern that occurs in an individual and that is associated with present distress (*e.g.,* a painful symptom) or disability (*i.e.,* impairment in one or more important areas of functioning) or with a significantly increased risk of suffering death, pain, disability, or an important loss of freedom.

Behavior that deviates from social norms and conflicts that are primarily between an individual and society, on the other hand, do not constitute mental disorders "unless the deviance or conflict is a symptom of a dysfunction in the individual."

DSM-IV includes a number of important refinements based on recent empirical evidence, but for many disorders the diagnostic criteria are very similar to those of *DSM-III-R.* Perhaps the most important conceptual

change in the new manual is that the term *organic mental disorder,* previously used to cover disorders with an established "organic," or biological, cause (*e.g.,* dementia of the Alzheimer's type), has been dropped because it incorrectly implied that other mental disorders in the manual did not have biological causes. Similarly, to avoid perpetuating the notion that a dichotomy exists between "mental" and "physical" disorders, the term *physical disorder* has been replaced by *general medical conditions,* which are considered a part of a complete diagnostic assessment.

These changes in terminology reflect the extensive evidence that mental disorders frequently have a biological (often genetic) component and that illnesses commonly thought of as "physical" (*e.g.,* coronary heart disease) often involve psychosocial or behavioral factors. For example, stress, anger, and certain personality traits can be risk factors for heart disease, and clinical depression is common after acute myocardial infarction (heart attack). The members of the *DSM-IV* task force sought to avoid the implication that a mind-body dualism exists; the volume's introduction states that "there is much 'physical' in 'mental' disorders and much 'mental' in 'physical' disorders." The task force members lamented, however, that they were unable to find an appropriate substitute for the term *mental disorder.*

DSM-IV goes farther than did *DSM-III-R* in considering ethnic and cultural determinants of behavior. The task force paid special attention to the fact that the manual may be used to evaluate individuals from culturally diverse populations, including new immigrants, both in the United States and internationally. Clinicians need to avoid judging as psychopathologies normal variations in behavior, belief, and experience that are associated with an individual's cultural background. *DSM-IV* includes information about cultural variations in the clinical manifestations of disorders and provides an outline of cultural factors that clinicians should consider in the diagnosis. There is also a glossary of 25 specific "culture-bound syndromes." Examples are *boufée delirante,* a syndrome characterized by sudden outbursts of agitation and aggression, marked confusion, and psychomotor excitement that is observed in people from West Africa and Haiti; *dhat,* a folk diagnostic term used in India to refer to severe anxiety and hypochondriacal concerns, particularly about the discharge of semen; and *hwa-byung,* a Korean term for "anger syndrome," which is generally attributed to the suppression of anger and may manifest as fatigue, generalized aches and pains, appetite loss, fear of impending death, and other symptoms.

An important new addition to *DSM-IV* is the listing "Religious or Spiritual Problem" in a section called "Other Conditions That May Be a Focus of Clinical Attention." This section includes conditions such as bereavement and relational problems that are not at-

326

Included for the first time in the Diagnostic and Statistical Manual of Mental Disorders—*the diagnostic "bible" of psychiatry, used by clinicians around the world—are "religious or spiritual problems." The new volume (the fourth edition) recognizes that religious experiences, questions about faith, and personal spiritual "crises," while not psychopathologies in and of themselves, can have a profound effect on people's lives and therefore may be worthy of clinical attention.*

tributable to mental disorders but that may be a source of distress for which appropriate interventions may be of benefit. The inclusion of the religious or spiritual problem category emphasizes psychiatry's growing sensitivity to the importance of religious experiences in people's lives; it thus recognizes officially that such experiences can have their own validity and are not necessarily due to a mental disorder. As examples the manual includes "distressing experiences that involve loss or questioning of faith, problems associated with conversion to a new faith, or questioning of spiritual values that may not necessarily be related to an organized church or religious institution."

Perhaps the most controversial change in *DSM-IV* was the inclusion of criteria for "premenstrual dysphoric disorder"—in an appendix, along with other proposed categories that are deemed in need of further study before being included as official disorders, and as one of several examples of a "Mood Disorder Not Otherwise Specified." Even though premenstrual dysphoric disorder was not given the status of a separate, specific category in the official nomenclature, some feminist critics argued that its inclusion anyplace in *DSM-IV* could be used to mislabel and "pathologize" the experience of normal women. The criteria specify, however, that the condition should be diagnosed only if depressive symptoms severe enough to interfere with usual activities occur regularly in the last week of most menstrual cycles over a period of at least a year. Proponents of including this condition argued that it occurs in about 3% to 5% of women and deserves further attention and research and that it should not be confused with premenstrual syndrome, commonly called PMS, which is much milder, occurs much more frequently, and is not considered to be a mental disorder.

Another controversial diagnostic issue involving

women that received attention during the *DSM-IV* revision process concerned the occurrence of mood disorders shortly after childbirth. There is continuing disagreement about whether such disorders are unique and related to the hormonal changes that occur in pregnancy and during the postpartum period or whether the physical and emotional stresses of pregnancy and childbirth are similar to other sources of stress that can trigger mood disorders. The decision was not to give postpartum depression a separate category in *DSM-IV*. To facilitate further research in this area, however, diagnoses of major depression or bipolar disorder can be specified as occurring "with postpartum onset" if they occur within four weeks after the patient gives birth.

Prevalence of psychiatric disorders

The results of a landmark community survey of the prevalence of psychiatric disorders in the United States were published in the *Archives of General Psychiatry* in January 1994. The congressionally mandated National Comorbidity Survey (NCS), coordinated by the Institute for Social Research at the University of Michigan at Ann Arbor, was the first survey to administer a structured psychiatric interview to a representative national sample in the United States. A previous survey known as the Epidemiological Catchment Area (ECA) study had provided useful information on the prevalence of mental disorders but was based on results from only five specific sites.

From late 1990 to early 1992, trained personnel conducted detailed interviews with 8,089 individuals about psychiatric symptoms and risk factors. Those interviewed were selected to provide a representative sample of persons aged 15 to 54 years in the noninstitutionalized civilian population of the 48 coterminous states. Interview results were then assessed

Police try to prevent a woman from jumping off a London bridge. Recurrent thoughts of suicide are a characteristic symptom of a severe depression, and in up to 15% of cases such thoughts lead to action. A recent survey in the United States found that 17% of the population experience a major depressive episode in their lifetime—the incidence being highest among women. Despite the enormous public health impact of depression, a large proportion of sufferers do not receive treatment.

according to the *DSM-III-R* diagnostic criteria to determine the proportions of persons who met criteria for various disorders in the course of their lifetime and in the 12 months preceding the interview.

Nearly 50% of the respondents reported having at least one mental disorder in their lifetime, and close to 30% reported at least one mental disorder during the previous 12 months. The most common disorders and their lifetime prevalences were major depressive episodes (17%), alcohol dependence (14%), social phobias (13%), and simple phobias (11%). Consistent with previous risk-factor research, the NCS found that women had higher rates of mood and anxiety disorders, while men had higher rates of substance-abuse and antisocial personality disorders. Rates of most disorders declined with age and with higher socioeconomic status. Notably, only 42% of those who had experienced a mental disorder at any time in their lives had received professional treatment for it.

One of the many striking results of the NCS survey was that 14% of the population had a history of three or more disorders. This unfortunate group accounted for about 60% of the total disorders reported for the previous year and for about 90% of those disorders rated as causing severe impairment. The results of this carefully performed national survey indicate that a history of some psychiatric disorder is common among persons aged 15 to 54 in the United States; 48% had a history of at least one disorder in their lifetime, 29.5% in the previous 12 months. However, the major burden of mental disorders is concentrated in about one-sixth of the population, fewer than half of whom have ever received mental health specialty treatment.

Drugs for depression: too much of a good thing?

The NCS found that 17% of Americans between the ages of 15 and 54 experience an episode of major

depression in their lifetime and 10% have such an episode in the course of a year. These results, which suggest that up to 25 million people in the United States suffer from major depression every year, indicate how important depressive illness is as a public health problem.

Virtually everyone experiences occasional brief periods of feeling "down" and depressed—normal depressed mood. Deeper feelings of sadness and grief are normal after an important loss—for example, the death of a loved one. Major depression, however, is a clinical syndrome that must be distinguished from both normal depressed mood and normal bereavement.

The *DSM-IV* diagnostic criteria specify that a major depressive episode is characterized by persistent depressed mood or loss of interest lasting for at least two weeks and is associated with a characteristic set of symptoms including sleep or appetite disturbance, changes in activity level (psychomotor agitation or retardation), fatigue, feelings of worthlessness or inappropriate guilt, and diminished ability to think or concentrate. One other characteristic symptom can be fatal: recurrent thoughts of death or suicide (not just a fear of dying). Often such thoughts lead to action; up to 15% of persons who suffer from major depression actually kill themselves.

In addition to the suffering and distress experienced by persons with depressive illness—and by their families—the economic costs of depression are staggering. A recent study by the Massachusetts Institute of Technology estimated that the total cost of all types of depressive illness in the United States, including treatment costs and lost productivity, is $44 billion per year.

Given the profound public health impact of clinical depression, the importance of recognizing and treating it should be obvious. Fortunately, effective treatments

328

are available. Several types of psychotherapy (treatments centered on communication between a patient and a therapist) have been shown to be helpful. Hospitalization may be lifesaving for patients with severe degrees of impairment or at high risk for suicide.

Medications can also be highly effective in treating depression. Two classes of drugs, tricyclic antidepressants and monoamine oxidase inhibitors (MAOIs), have been widely used for decades and are effective for about 70% of depressed patients. Though the precise biological causes of depressive illness have not been established, it is generally accepted that antidepressant drugs work by correcting abnormalities in the functioning of brain neurotransmitter systems that regulate mood, particularly the norepinephrine and serotonin systems. The use of the above two classes of antidepressants unfortunately is complicated by the need for careful dose adjustments and also by the wide range of adverse effects that reflect the influence of these drugs on a variety of biological systems. Tricyclics may, for example, cause anticholinergic effects, such as dry mouth, constipation, difficulty with urination, and blurred vision (due to blocking of the neurotransmitter acetylcholine); autonomic nervous system effects (*e.g.,* dizziness, sweating, hand tremor); central nervous system effects (*e.g.,* sedation, "spacey" feelings, jitteriness); allergic effects (*e.g.,* skin rashes); and various other effects (*e.g.,* weight gain, impotence, inhibited orgasm). MAOIs may cause serious adverse effects if certain foods (*e.g.,* aged cheeses, sauerkraut, fava beans, all spoiled foods) are not avoided.

The availability of a new class of antidepressant drugs, the selective serotonin reuptake inhibitors (SSRIs), has been an important recent development for treatment of depression. Virtually all effective anti-depressant agents (including electroconvulsive therapy, a safe and effective treatment for severe depression) increase serotonin neurotransmission, but most such agents also affect other neurochemical systems. Fluoxetine (Prozac) was developed by scientists at Eli Lilly and Co. in 1972. Clinical trials began in 1976 in the U.S. The drug was marketed in Belgium in 1986 and approved by the U.S. Food and Drug Administration (FDA) and marketed as the first serotonin-selective antidepressant drug available in the United States in 1987. Because it did not require careful dose adjustments and, for most patients, had far fewer side effects than the other antidepressants, Prozac quickly became the most widely prescribed antidepressant. By 1993 about 10 million patients worldwide had received Prozac, and its 1993 sales amounted to $1.2 billion.

Some initial case reports raised the concern that fluoxetine might increase suicidal thoughts, or even actions, in depressed patients. Careful evaluations comparing large numbers of patients receiving fluoxetine, tricyclic antidepressants, or placebos did not find this effect. In the last several years, two additional SSRIs have been approved by the FDA and marketed in the U.S. for depression: sertraline (Zoloft) and paroxetine (Paxil). These drugs also have a low incidence of side effects. The main difference from Prozac is that they have shorter half-lives, which means that they are eliminated from the body sooner. Nefazadone (Serzone) is a fourth SSRI that has been approved in the U.S. but in 1994 was not yet on the market. Another new antidepressant drug, venlafaxine (Effexor), was approved in late 1993 and first marketed in the U.S. in early 1994. Venlafaxine acts on serotonin and norepinephrine, increasing levels of both in the brain. Like the SSRIs, it also has a low side-effect profile.

"Can't you give him one of those personalities in a bottle I keep reading about?"

Drawing by Lorenz; © 1994 The New Yorker Magazine, Inc.

The evidence to date indicates that although the SSRIs are effective antidepressants, they are no more effective than the previously available drugs as long as patients receive adequate doses of the tricyclics and MAOIs and can tolerate their side effects. Therein lies the advantage of the serotonin-selective drugs. Most patients need to take only one or two pills a day and experience few side effects; nausea, jitteriness, drowsiness, insomnia, and sexual dysfunction are among the most common. The newer drugs are also much less toxic if an overdose is taken. Like the other classes of antidepressants, SSRIs are generally effective in treating panic disorder. Unlike most of the other antidepressants—the exception being the tricyclic clomipramine (Anafranil)—the SSRIs are also of benefit in the treatment of obsessive-compulsive disorder, although Prozac is the only antidepressant thus far approved by the FDA for that use.

Concerns have been raised that the serotonin-selective antidepressants are being overused. There appear to be two aspects to such concerns. One aspect is the assumption that the sheer volume of prescriptions for these drugs is itself a problem. Ensuring appropriate use is an important issue for virtually all medications. Yet the evidence regarding the high prevalence of depressive illness, as well as other evidence that clinical depression continues to be both underrecognized and undertreated, suggests that a high volume of antidepressant prescriptions may merely reflect appropriate treatment for very common disorders.

The other aspect of concern about the extensive use of SSRIs reflects an uneasiness about the use of drugs to alter brain function and thereby change the temperament or personality of an individual. That concern was reflected in the book *Listening to Prozac: A Psychiatrist Explores Antidepressant Drugs and the Remaking of the Self* (Viking, 1993) by psychiatrist Peter Kramer, which quickly became a best-seller. Kramer describes patients who experienced marked improvements in traits usually thought of as enduring aspects of personality, such as shyness, hypersensitivity, and overcautiousness, presumably as a result of taking Prozac. Although the patients experienced these changes as very positive for their lives, should there be concern about using a drug to change the "self"? Some believe the potential to change the self suggests a *Brave New World* scenario similar to that foretold by the British novelist Aldous Huxley.

While certainly provocative, the questions and concerns that have been raised may be premature, based as they are on the assumption that a person's "normal" personality can be changed to something else by a drug. Some forms of depression can be very chronic, and effective treatment may produce what seems like a personality change. Moreover, placebo effects can be very powerful, particularly when bolstered by expectations and beliefs shared by a particular culture.

More research and experience are needed before it is known whether the serotonin-selective antidepressant drugs can produce personality changes that are distinct from their effects on depression, anxiety, and obsessions and whether such effects, if they do occur, are a beneficial extension of control over the self or a threat to what makes each person uniquely human.

Repressed memories of abuse: true or false?

One of the most controversial issues in the mental health field in the past few years has been the increasing number of adults who believe they have recovered previously repressed memories of sexual abuse during childhood. These memories, dating back decades, are recovered during therapy, sometimes with the aid of hypnosis, and usually involve alleged recurrent in-

In 1993 a former seminary student filed a lawsuit against Chicago's Joseph Cardinal Bernardin alleging that the priest had sexually abused him 17 years earlier. The charges were dropped four months later—the accuser acknowledging that his memory of the experience, recovered under hypnosis, may not have been reliable.

Barry Thumma—AP

Eileen Franklin Lipsker is escorted out of court after testifying that 21 years earlier she had seen her father molest and murder a childhood friend. The memory of that traumatic event, Lipsker claimed, had remained repressed in her mind for two decades. It suddenly came back to her one day in 1989 as she watched her own daughter draw pictures; she was struck by how similar her daughter's red hair and blue eyes were to those of her friend of long ago. She later recalled that she, too, had been sexually abused by her father. A psychiatrist, called by the prosecution as an expert witness, played an important part in convincing the jury that recovered memories can be accurate. The father was found guilty of first-degree murder.

cidents of sexual abuse by a parent or other relative. Sometimes the individuals claim to have been victims of and witnesses to organized satanic cult rituals that may have involved human sacrifice. These patients have had no previous recollections of such events but become convinced that the repressed trauma is the source of present emotional troubles and the psychological problems for which they sought therapy.

Individuals who recover such memories are often encouraged to confront the alleged abuser. Some may then sever their relationship with that person or even pursue legal action. The accusers are typically adults, and many have forbidden their parents to have any contact with grandchildren. The accused parents may adamantly deny the charges, protesting that they are the victims of false accusations.

This highly charged area has become a matter of controversy for mental health professionals and for the public. The controversy has been heightened by a number of widely publicized lawsuits, including a $10 million suit filed in November 1993 against Chicago's Joseph Cardinal Bernardin. Stephen Cook, aged 34, a former seminary student from Philadelphia, alleged that he had been sexually abused 17 years earlier by Bernardin, then the archbishop of Cincinnati, Ohio, and by another Catholic priest, the Rev. Ellis Harsham. Cook's allegations apparently were based on memories recovered under hypnosis, and Bernardin vigorously denied the charges. Four months after the suit was filed, Cook announced that he was dropping the charges against Bernardin because he had come to believe that his memories about the former archbishop were not reliable. (Cook continued his suit against Harsham, who he claims had molested him over a period of many years; the case was later settled out of court.) That the Bernardin case represents a much larger trend is indicated by the recent forma-

tion of an organization, the False Memory Syndrome Foundation, by people claiming to have been falsely accused of abuse. In less than two years the group has grown to about 7,000 individuals and families.

With controversies of this kind, there is a tendency to jump to conclusions and take sides on the basis of a few examples. The complexity and importance of the problem, however, call for careful evaluation on a case-by-case basis. Some general points can inform such evaluations. Sexual abuse of children appears to be more common than most people would like to believe, although quantification of its extent is difficult. Certainly complaints or hints from children about such abuse demand immediate attention and evaluation. Further, there is evidence that some children cope with abuse psychologically by developing at least partial amnesia toward it (so-called source memory defects). On the other hand, efforts to enhance or recover memories should be undertaken only by properly trained professionals who are qualified to diagnose and treat mental disorders. Studies have shown that hypnosis does not increase the accuracy of memories but can enhance the individual's conviction that a memory is accurate. This can be a very unfortunate combination in a sensitive area like sexual abuse. Troubled persons seeking help and explanations for their problems are particularly vulnerable to suggestion. Memories of abuse that arise only during therapy, particularly under hypnosis, need external corroboration before being deemed authentic.

The tragedy of childhood sexual abuse demands attention. Its victims should receive appropriate treatment, and prevention should be instituted whenever possible. On the other hand, the tragedy of creating new victims of false accusations also needs attention and prevention.

—Richard M. Glass, M.D.

331

Making Sense of Schizophrenia

by Shôn W. Lewis, M.D.

Schizophrenia remains one of the strangest and most devastating illnesses known to humankind. It is a strange disorder because its symptoms arise out of disturbances in the higher workings of the brain. It is devastating because in three-quarters of cases the sufferer is left with lifelong psychological deficits that limit the ability to function independently and derive satisfaction from life.

Schizophrenia was first recognized as an illness distinct from other mental disorders in the second half of the 19th century by the German psychiatrist Emil Kraepelin. Kraepelin called the condition *dementia praecox,* or premature dementia. The Swiss psychiatrist Eugen Bleuler first coined the name *schizophrenia,* which literally means "split mind," although the popular notion of split personality has nothing to do with schizophrenia as it is understood today.

Striking symptoms

Schizophrenia usually shows itself first in early adult life, developing slightly earlier in men than in women. It can come on suddenly but more typically develops over a period of several months. The most striking symptoms are those involving abnormalities of perception, language, and belief. The disturbances of perception take the form of hallucinations, which are most commonly auditory and characteristically complex, such as a chorus of voices talking to or about the sufferer. In rare cases schizophrenic patients experience visual, tactile, and even olfactory hallucinations. Disturbances of language often mean that the affected individual speaks or writes incoherently, making vague statements and linking together seemingly unrelated ideas. The disturbances of belief are unshakable and often extremely bizarre delusions, frequently involving beliefs about elaborate plots, which have no basis in reality. The individual may, for example, have ideas about external forces interfering with or controlling his or her thoughts and actions. The sudden onset of florid (typical) symptoms is seen in the following case:

For two weeks John, a 20-year-old college student, had been feeling uneasy when in public. He had the impression that people had started to look at him strangely. Certain news items on the radio had acquired a special significance and seemed loaded with a particular meaning for him. One morning, as he was buying a newspaper, the way the storekeeper handed him his change suddenly convinced John that the man was the devil. All the events of the

previous two weeks suddenly fell into place. John was convinced that his classmates were machines constructed by the storekeeper to spy on him and insert alien thoughts into his mind. Even miles from the campus, he could hear his fellow students talking about him and repeating his thoughts. John became sure that these voices were being transmitted through "detectors" housed in electric appliances in his apartment. Later he sent one of his professors a note that contained a string of jumbled and confused ideas. The professor made urgent enquiries only to discover that John had left school, leaving no forwarding address.

Another persuasive account of florid symptoms—which are often referred to as "positive" symptoms, as distinct from the apathy and self-neglect of "negative" symptoms—comes from the novel *The Ordeal of Gilbert Pinfold* by the British writer Evelyn Waugh. The protagonist, a passenger on a cruise ship, believes he can hear other passengers discussing him when he is alone in his cabin. Gradually, he becomes convinced that the whole ship is conspiring to deceive him.

For a long time, two hours perhaps, Mr. Pinfold lay in his bunk listening. He was able to hear quite distinctly not only what was said in his immediate vicinity, but elsewhere. He had the light on, now, in his cabin and as he gazed at the complex of tubes and wires which ran across his ceiling, he realised that they must form some kind of general junction in a system of communication. Through some trick or fault . . . everything spoken in the executive quarters of the ship was transmitted to him. . . . That alone could explain the voices.

As mentioned above, in addition to "positive" symptoms, schizophrenia usually involves the development of more subtle but longer-lasting "negative" symptoms, including social withdrawal, loss of motivation, and loss of normal emotional expressiveness. Consider the following case:

Lisa had been shy as a child and had had few friends. After leaving high school she worked in a series of menial jobs, living with her parents. At age 22 she became increasingly withdrawn and confided to a co-worker that her neighbors had begun to experiment on her during the night. Over a course of months, she became convinced that the neighbors had replaced parts of her body with aluminum replicas and were able to control her actions. She was hospitalized in the psychiatric ward for two months, and her delusions decreased in response to drug treatment. While she was in the hospital, however, her grooming and hygiene deteriorated; upon discharge, she took to wearing grubby clothes and not washing for days on end. She spoke little, was irritable, and did not return to work. She would sit in front of the television for most of the day and had lost interest in the few things in life that she had previously enjoyed. Six months later she suffered a relapse of positive symptoms.

It is the characteristic mix of positive and negative symptoms that constitutes the basic criterion for the contemporary diagnosis of schizophrenia.

How common?

Schizophrenia is surprisingly common, affecting nearly one in every 100 individuals. It is also surprisingly widely distributed around the world, occurring at similar rates in both developed and less developed countries with broadly similar symptoms. The course of the disorder varies. One in six or so patients will suffer a single episode and recover completely. At the other end of the spectrum is another one in six who continues to suffer persistent symptoms despite all attempts at treatment. For most patients, however, the severity of the illness lies between these two extremes and is marked by persistent mild negative symptoms, punctuated with recurrent bouts of florid symptoms. This state of affairs effectively precludes a full recovery to previous levels of functioning. A better long-term outcome is likely with a later age of onset, good social adjustment before the start of the illness, relatively swift onset with early treatment, and minimal negative symptoms. Sadly, one in 10 people with schizophrenia will kill himself or herself.

Insights into cause

Despite the frequency of schizophrenia and its devastating consequences to both the sufferers and their families, there has been relatively little research into the cause until recently. Paradoxically, general ideas about the cause have come full circle since schizophrenia was first recognized. At that time it

A drawing by a 25-year-old diagnosed with schizophrenia reveals the confused and frightening inner world of those who suffer from this much-studied but still not fully understood mental disorder.

seemed natural to assume that the affliction was a disease of the brain. The first major autopsy study of the brain in schizophrenia was actually performed by the German neuropathologist Alois Alzheimer, a student of Kraepelin's, and the first to describe the form of dementia later named for him, Alzheimer's disease. The study was inconclusive.

With the rise of psychoanalysis in the first half of the 20th century, it became fashionable to view schizophrenia not as a brain disease but as a condition resulting from adverse childhood experiences. Various sociological and political explanations for schizophrenia were expounded by so-called antipsychiatrists such as Thomas Szasz and R.D. Laing in the 1960s, who saw the disorder as an understandable psychological reaction to what would today be termed dysfunctional families. Although these ideas reflected the mood of the times, they clearly focused the blame on the parents, a viewpoint for which there is no scientific support. Since then, increasing research has reestablished that schizophrenia has its origins not in poor parenting or troubled families but in a distinct disorder of the brain.

One of the strongest clues to the cause of schizophrenia has been known for many years: the disease tends to run in families. Just because an illness runs in families, however, does not automatically mean it is genetic; children can learn patterns of behavior from their parents as well as inherit them; infectious diseases also can be transmitted within families. Convincing evidence of genetic transmission has come from twin studies. It is known that if one member of a pair of identical twins develops schizophrenia, the likelihood of the other twin's developing schizophrenia is 45–50%; if the pair are nonidentical, however, the risk of the second twin's being affected is only 10%. Since identical twins share all their genes and nonidentical twins share no more than other siblings, this difference in rates is strong evidence for the existence of a genetic factor. Conclusive evidence has come from adoption studies, in which adopted children of schizophrenic mothers are followed as they grow up; despite being raised from infancy in normal households, these individuals still have a 10-fold higher risk of having schizophrenia, compared with adoptees whose biological mothers were not schizophrenic.

Although genetics clearly plays a part, the mechanism is not likely to be straightforward. First, schizophrenia is far too common a disease to be the work of a single faulty gene; illnesses caused by single-gene defects are always rare. Schizophrenia is more likely to have the complex genetics of other common so-called multifactorial disorders such as coronary heart disease and diabetes. In such conditions there may be several different genes at work in different families. In addition, it is possible that some cases of schizophrenia are inherited and others the

333

result of nongenetic processes. Such a pattern would fit with the observation that a small percentage of schizophrenia cases cluster in a few families, whereas in most cases there is no apparent family history of the disorder. Some authorities have proposed that there might be both familial and sporadic subtypes of the disorder. Close study of the families of schizophrenia sufferers has revealed another curious pattern: often several relatives of affected individuals have a characteristic type of eccentric personality that has come to be known as schizotypal personality. Perhaps these family members are carriers of the genetic defect but do not have full-blown schizophrenia.

Another puzzle about the genetics of schizophrenia is how a disease that carries a biological disadvantage can persist through the generations. Given that affected individuals often do not have children, one would expect the disease to disappear after a very few generations. There are several possible explanations for why it has not. One is that although those who suffer from schizophrenia are at a biological disadvantage, unaffected carriers might have some subtle advantage. Such an effect is known to be the reason for the persistence of certain other genetic diseases. Sickle-cell anemia is the classic example. There is no direct evidence for this in schizophrenia, however, although some experts have proposed that family members may possess greater than average creativity. Other possible explanations for schizophrenia's persistence are that it involves several genes, that fresh mutations are common, or that environmental factors are at least as important as genetics. Furthermore, some researchers have pointed to the possibility that schizophrenia is a relatively new disease and, on the basis of epidemiological surveys, one whose incidence might already have peaked. Again, direct evidence for this hypothesis is difficult to pin down.

Despite all these uncertainties, the existence of a gene or genes predisposing individuals to schizophrenia is likely, and recently developed and highly sophisticated molecular genetic techniques are being applied to search for them. Although promising, this approach has not yet yielded conclusive results. Reports of schizophrenia genes located on chromosome 5 and chromosome 11 have emerged over the past five years but have not been fully substantiated. The quest continues.

Clues from brain imaging

The invention some 23 years ago of computed tomography (CT) marked the arrival of a remarkable new tool for research into brain diseases of all types. Detailed images of the living brain can be obtained painlessly and noninvasively by means of CT. Within a few years of its inception, CT was being used to compare the brains of schizophrenic patients with those of healthy volunteers. It soon became clear that in schizophrenia there were often minor enlargements of the fluid-filled spaces, known as the cerebral ventricles, located deep inside the brain. These changes were seldom dramatic, however, and were too subtle to enable a diagnosis to be made on the basis of a CT scan. Nonetheless, they were crucial in establishing beyond reasonable doubt that schizophrenia is indeed a disease of the brain.

At first these anatomic changes were thought likely to be progressive, as is the case in degenerative brain disorders such as Alzheimer's disease. However, as CT studies became more sophisticated, it was apparent that enlargement of the ventricles could be seen even in young, first-episode patients, and if the same patients' brains were scanned again several years later, the enlargement remained but had not progressed. The static nature of these physical abnormalities implied that they were probably present even before the disease started. The question arose: Could these structural differences represent some early neurodevelopmental abnormality?

Enlargement of the fluid-filled cavities called cerebral ventricles is apparent in a magnetic resonance imaging scan of the brain of a person with schizophrenia (far right) when it is compared with the brain scan of his normal twin (right). Because such anatomic differences can be seen early in the course of the disease and do not appear to progress over time, many authorities speculate that they represent an early neurodevelopmental abnormality.

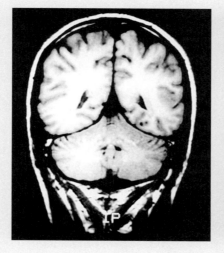 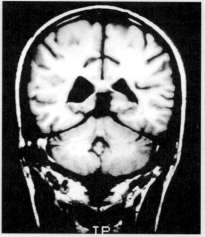

Photographs, Max Agvilera-Hellweg

Further progress came with the advent of another innovation in medical imaging, a process called magnetic resonance imaging (MRI), which produced extremely detailed pictures of the structure of the brain. MRI scans revealed that in many schizophrenic patients there were seemingly developmental abnormalities in the structure of parts of the brain deep in the temporal lobes, where much of the filtering and processing of thought and emotion occur. At the same time, new postmortem studies of the brains of schizophrenic patients revealed that brain cells in some regions showed a pattern of disorganization that could be explained only as a disturbance in the way cells came together early in brain development. These changes were found particularly in the gray matter of the cerebral cortex, which is formed during the first months of fetal life from immature cells migrating outward from their origin deep in the brain. The explanation now most favored is that some interruption of this normal process of nerve cell migration occurs before birth in the brains of people who later develop schizophrenia. Thus, many investigators have turned their attention to factors that could affect fetal brain development.

Prenatal influences

Several research studies over the past 10 years have claimed to show that the rates of obstetric complications during pregnancy and delivery are higher than expected in the births of children who later develop schizophrenia. These studies usually look at the rates of recorded complications in the birth records of adult schizophrenic patients; these are compared with complication rates among a nonschizophrenic control group. Although not all studies agree, the findings collectively seem to indicate that rates of obstetric complications in general are higher in the histories of people with schizophrenia. How to interpret this finding is still being debated. Certainly, problems during pregnancy and birth are not a major cause of schizophrenia, although it is likely that they do contribute in a minority of cases. It is still unclear which particular complications of pregnancy are the important ones.

Another prenatal risk factor that has been investigated is a history of maternal influenza infection in mid pregnancy. The evidence supporting this theory is intriguing but by no means conclusive. It rests on observations that there are unexplained spikes in the incidence of schizophrenia 20 years or so after major flu epidemics. The notion of influenza as a possible risk factor does tie in with the well-established finding that there is a slight but definite excess of late winter and early spring birthdays among people in whom schizophrenia develops. This pattern is typical of diseases attributed to prenatal exposure to a virus, a prime example being congenital rubella. Early exposure to an infectious agent is unlikely to be a major cause of schizophrenia in general, but it illustrates one plausible mechanism by which fetal brain development could be disrupted. A recent study has also suggested that severe maternal malnutrition might be a risk factor.

Brain functioning

Whatever the exact mechanism, be it a genetic influence or some form of intrauterine brain damage or a mixture of the two, most researchers now agree that schizophrenia is likely to be the end result of problems "wired into" the brain at an early stage. Why such a very early fault should give rise to dramatic symptoms 20 years after the fact requires explanation. In fact, the 20-year gap before the onset of symptoms is more apparent than real. For instance, when researchers examine the school reports of schizophrenic patients and normal peers, they find more frequent descriptions of abnormal behavior (such as withdrawal), undue social anxieties, and a slightly lower intellectual capacity in the former. These anomalies are subtle, but recent studies of large cohorts of individuals followed from birth confirm that the small proportion who develop schizophrenia show a wide range of minor behavioral problems, some appearing quite early in childhood.

Different parts of the brain mature biologically at different rates. Those parts controlling fundamental functions such as movement and perception are already well-developed at birth. The last brain systems to mature do not do so until adolescence. These are the areas, particularly areas of the frontal cortex, that mediate the highest forms of abstract and complex thinking. It may be that it is only when these areas become fully connected and come "on-line," so to speak, that the typical disturbances of higher thinking such as delusions and hallucinations start to appear.

Just which brain areas are responsible for delusions and hallucinations is currently of great interest. One way of addressing this question is to use a type of brain imaging that reveals brain *function* rather than brain *structure*. The two main functional imaging techniques are single photon emission tomography (SPET) and positron emission tomography (PET). Both rely on the injection or inhalation of mildly radioactive isotopes that are taken up for short periods by the brain tissue. By monitoring the concentration of radioactive substances, scientists are able to chart the small but measurable increases in blood flow and metabolism that accompany activity in a particular brain region. Normal perception, cognition, and movement all involve detectable metabolic and circulatory changes in the specific brain region involved.

The hypothesis in schizophrenia is that the abnormal perceptions and thought patterns will show up as areas of abnormal activity on functional brain imaging. Early work in this field suggests that individual symptoms do correlate with unusual patterns of activity in particular brain regions. For example, patients with active auditory hallucinations will show increased activity in the area of the left hemisphere involved in the processing of speech. Positive symptoms in general seem to be correlated with abnormal levels of activity in deep temporal lobe structures, particularly on the left side of the brain. On the other hand, negative symptoms seem to correlate with reduced function in the frontal cortex. This latter finding ties in with the long-standing observation made by many clinicians that the negative symptoms of schizophrenia resemble the symptoms shown by patients who have neurological injury to the frontal lobe. As well as creating images of regional brain activity, functional imaging can provide information about the presence or absence of receptors for particular neurotransmitters (chemicals that carry nerve impulses from cell to cell). This approach has been used to test one of the cornerstone theories of neurotransmitter abnormalities in schizophrenia, the so-called dopamine hypothesis.

Rise and fall of the dopamine hypothesis

The bridge between genes and brain structure, on the one hand, and thought and behavior, on the other, is the complex system of neurotransmitters in the human brain. Abnormality in the action of one or more neurotransmitters is likely to be involved at some level in generating symptoms in schizophrenia. The particular neurotransmitter that has been implicated is dopamine. The dopamine hypothesis of schizophrenia was first put forward in the early 1960s and was based on two clinical observations made at that time. The first was that amphetamines (stimulant drugs), which caused a massive increase in brain dopamine levels, could very closely mimic the symptoms of schizophrenia if taken in sufficiently large amounts. The second observation was that the early antipsychotic drugs such as chlorpromazine (Thorazine) produced side effects that resembled the symptoms of Parkinson's disease, a condition known to result from a deficiency of dopamine. That antipsychotic drugs did indeed block dopamine receptors was later confirmed in the laboratory. The hypothesis posited that schizophrenia results from an overactivity of dopamine in particular brain systems, and this notion has been highly influential, particularly in directing the search for better drugs for the treatment of schizophrenia.

There have always been certain issues that the dopamine hypothesis cannot easily explain, however. One is that antipsychotic drugs, even those with potent affinities for dopamine receptors, failed to work in up to one-quarter of patients. Another is that even when the drugs did work they never worked immediately, usually taking at least a week or two for effects to occur. Third, although these drugs were usually effective in treating positive symptoms, they had little or no effect on negative symptoms, which in many

ways were the most troublesome features of the disorder. But it was the unexpected emergence of one particular drug, clozapine (Clozaril), that finally forced a radical reappraisal of the dopamine hypothesis.

The clozapine revolution

Until the development of clozapine, all drugs for treating schizophrenia had very similar profiles in terms of effectiveness and side effects. This is not surprising since the dopamine hypothesis was directing pharmaceutical research, and specific dopamine-blocking agents were thus developed. Clozapine, a completely new kind of drug, first appeared in the late 1970s but was quickly abandoned in widespread clinical practice because it produced a rare but severe side effect, a potentially fatal blood disorder. In the late 1980s, however, reports of its unusual effectiveness in patients who did not respond to other antipsychotics led to a reappraisal of clozapine. It was shown to have several advantages: it was significantly superior to any existing drug in the treatment of resistant positive symptoms; it did not have any of the parkinsonian side effects associated with other drugs; and it actually improved negative as well as positive symptoms.

While the toxicity of clozapine limits its use to patients in whom symptoms persist despite conventional treatments, it is effective in improving up to half of such cases, occasionally dramatically. A rush of scientific research has sought to elucidate the property of clozapine that makes it so much better than other drugs. It blocks a range of different neurotransmitter activity, not just that associated with dopamine, so the search for its secret is complicated. It may well be that its effect in blocking another neurotransmitter, serotonin, is critically important.

Breakthroughs anticipated

It is an exciting time in schizophrenia research. Recent advances in brain imaging and molecular genetics, along with new understandings of the likely neurodevelopmental origins of the disorder, should result in a major breakthrough in understanding the cause of the disorder before the end of the century. Already the emergence of clozapine, the first major advance in drug treatment in 30 years, is leading to new insights into the brain systems involved. This research is likely to give rise to a new generation of more effective drugs with fewer side effects.

Alternatives to drug treatment are also emerging. Innovative forms of psychological treatment—such as cognitive behavioral therapy—quite unlike traditional forms of psychotherapy, have demonstrated that some schizophrenic patients can be trained to think themselves out of their symptoms. With better understanding of schizophrenia and improved treatments on the horizon, the outlook for those affected by this destructive illness is more promising today than ever before.

336

Obesity

Obesity is a serious chronic condition that affects over one-third of the adult population of the United States. Obesity is not a single disease, and it may have many causes, so some scientists define obesity as a syndrome (collection of diseases). Obesity is associated with numerous medical complications, and the social penalties for being obese in the U.S. are severe. About half of all Americans are on a diet at any given time, and dieters spend over $30 billion to $50 billion annually on efforts—usually unsuccessful—to lose or control their weight. This report explores some of the causes of, the medical and social problems associated with, and current and future treatments for this huge problem.

Defining obesity

Scientists differ about how obesity should be defined, but most would agree that it consists of an excess accumulation of adipose (fat) tissue. Attempts to define obesity in understandable terms have led health professionals to focus on weight and to use terms such as *ideal, desirable,* or *healthy* body weight to describe people who are *not* obese.

Many define obesity as a weight that is more than 20% over "desirable" weight, as specified in the widely used 1983 Metropolitan Life Insurance tables (or as weight greater than 30% over the "ideal" body weight, obtained from the original 1959 Metropolitan Life Insurance tables); these weights are considered important because they are associated with lower life expectancy. The tables came from surveys of selected groups of people who bought life insurance. Some health professionals believe that those groups may not be representative of the general population; therefore, they define obesity according to a body mass index (BMI). BMI is calculated by dividing weight in kilograms by the square of height in meters. A "healthy" weight is said to be a BMI of 18–24; a BMI of 27 or above is considered "obese."

All of these definitions are flawed because they do not measure excess body fat, only excess weight. Although there are sophisticated laboratory methods for measuring excess body fat, there are no simple methods of doing so among the general population. Until such means are developed, measures of body weight will continue to be used.

Seeking the causes

In the past, obesity was most often viewed as a behavioral problem; obese people were thought to have a lack of self-discipline, which led to excess weight. Most people assume that those who are obese simply eat too much, and numerous studies have shown average food intakes of obese people to be higher than those of lean people. A major study conducted by Steven W. Lichtman and colleagues from the Obesity Research Center of St. Luke's-Roosevelt Hospital Center in New York City, the results of which were published in the *New England Journal of Medicine* (Dec. 31, 1992), found that obese subjects consistently underestimated their daily food intake and overestimated their activity levels. So-called diet-resistant obese subjects (those with a history of not being able to lose weight in spite of dieting and exercising) estimated their average daily caloric consumption at 1,028 calories, but the actual average was 2,081. The subjects believed they were spending, or burning, an average of 1,022 calories per day but were actually expending no more than 771 calories in physical activity.

It is erroneous, however, to assume that all obese people eat too much. Many lean people eat more than obese people, yet they do not become fat. Conversely, many obese people eat fewer calories than do some lean people yet continue to weigh much more. Moreover, if obese people reduce their caloric intake to match that of lean people, they do not necessarily become lean. Studies in animals show that some animals that are genetically obese must eat about half of what their lean siblings eat to weigh the same amount. These differences do not appear to be due to a difference in activity levels.

Over the last 100 years, caloric intake in the U.S. has gone down, but the incidence of obesity has gone up. These facts have led to a reevaluation of the causes of obesity, and recent evidence suggests that there are important genetically determined biochemical differences in obese people that distinguish them from lean people. About 20 genes have been found so far that contribute to body weight or body fatness, but little is known about how these work to cause obesity. Moreover, genetic differences account for only about 25% to 40% of the variation between obese and nonobese people. This means that the environment accounts for a large proportion of the problem. Most scientists now believe that genetic susceptibility and the environment of Western civilization interact to produce obesity.

While relatively little is known about the genetic mechanisms that cause people to be obese, a great deal is known about changes in the environment that lead to obesity. The two major differences between Americans today and their leaner ancestors are the amount of fat in the diet and the level of activity in their daily lives. In earlier times the percentage of calories that people derived from fat was lower, while activity levels were higher.

Scientists postulate that when people (or animals) switch from a low-fat to a high-fat diet, the fat must be burned or it will be stored as adipose tissue. Fat is the most energy-rich food in the diet (nine calories per gram, compared with only four calories per gram for protein and carbohydrate). People differ in their ability to burn fat, and obese people tend to store fat until their increasing obesity causes biochemical changes that allow the excess fat intake to be burned. Exercise, or increased muscular activity, causes fat to be burned; with the development of labor-saving devices, however, people have become less active, thus compounding the problem of obesity. The United States probably has the highest prevalence of obesity of any industrialized country in the world, but there have also been significant weight increases among people in other industrialized parts of the world where muscular work has decreased and at the same time the availabilty of palatable food has increased—*e.g.,* among people in Western Europe, Canada, and Australia and in the white population of South Africa.

Obesity is associated with many changes in hormone levels in the body, and it is difficult to determine if these changes cause obesity or are due to obesity. With increasing fatness, the body's insulin levels rise, and obese people have a tendency to become diabetic. Obese diabetics have high levels of plasma insulin and are said to be "resistant" to the action of insulin. This insulin resistance is associated with many of the medical complications of obesity (discussed below). The levels of adrenaline and noradrenaline, major hormones of the sympathetic nervous system (SNS), are altered in obesity. Research scientists have shown that obese laboratory animals do not increase their SNS activity appropriately when stimulated, and since the SNS helps control energy expenditure, this may play a role in causing the animals to be fat. The same appears to be true in people.

Much research today is focused on hormones that affect food intake and body weight; *e.g.,* cholecystokinin (CCK), neuropeptide Y, galanin, and enterostatin. When humans or animals are given injections of CCK, food intake is decreased initially. However,

with continued CCK administration, this effect wanes. CCK is a natural body hormone secreted by cells lining the small intestine; it stimulates contraction of the gallbladder and triggers the release of enzymes from the pancreas. Neuropeptide Y stimulates food intake when injected into animals (rats were found to continue eating until they could hold no more food), and there is some evidence that concentrations of neuropeptide Y in certain areas of the brain differ between the lean and obese. More research is needed, however, to determine whether this particular hormone plays an important part in causing obesity.

Galanin, a brain peptide, and enterostatin, a peptide produced in the stomach, pancreas, and brain, are hormones only recently discovered in the body and are causing much excitement among scientists. Galanin apparently increases the preference for fat in the diet, while enterostatin appears to lower preference for dietary fat. Consequently, injections of galanin lead to weight gain, and injections of enterostatin result in weight loss. Obese rats have high levels of galanin in certain areas of the brain, but when the hormone is blocked in the brain, dramatic weight loss occurs. Thus, scientists postulate that this substance promotes intake of fatty foods, leading to obesity.

Other research focuses on energy expenditure in obesity. While obese people are less active than lean people, the extra weight causes increased energy expenditure when they are active. Basal metabolic rate (BMR), the minimal amount of energy required for the body to maintain itself at rest, appears to be similar among obese and lean people when differences in fat and lean tissue are taken into account. However, some scientists have found that obese people or animals may not increase their energy expenditure to the same extent that lean subjects do when they eat, exercise, or are exposed to the cold. Other studies

At the Children's Research Center at Yale-New Haven Hospital, New Haven, Conn., investigators are studying the metabolic alterations in obese children. By measuring a young subject's oxygen consumption and carbon dioxide production (a method known as indirect calorimetry), they are able to calculate his metabolic rate. Obese children tend to have high levels of plasma insulin and to become resistant to its action, which places them at risk for a number of medical complications. Those who appear to be at greatest risk are those who have greater amounts of upper-body intra-abdominal fat, as opposed to lower-body subcutaneous fat.

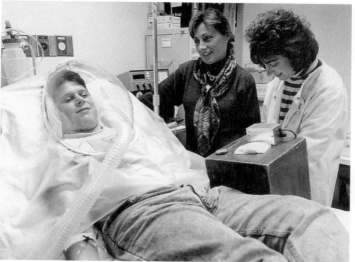

Courtesy of Sonia Caprio, M.D., Yale-New Haven Hospital; photograph, Rob Lisak

suggest that obese people may return to baseline BMR more rapidly after such stimuli than do their lean counterparts. A lower BMR and lower activity level allow greater storage of energy as fat and less fat breakdown. This helps explain the fact that some obese people can eat the same amounts as lean people yet weigh more. Also, despite the fact that most obese people eat more than lean people, even when they reduce their caloric intake to that of lean people, they remain heavier. Consistently eating less than "normal" amounts is very difficult, which helps explain why so many obese people fail to stick to diets that radically reduce caloric intake and why they rarely are able to maintain long-term weight loss.

Medical complications

Obesity is associated with an increased incidence of life-shortening conditions, including diabetes, high blood pressure, high blood fats, heart disease, strokes, sleep apnea, and some types of cancer. Obesity also contributes to numerous conditions that reduce the quality of life, including degenerative arthritis, gout, gallbladder disease, and decreased fertility. Several of these problems appear to be caused by the syndrome of insulin resistance. With increasing obesity, muscle, fat, and liver tissue become less able to transport glucose across the cell membranes, leading to a high amount of sugar in the blood, or diabetes. The way the body handles fats consumed in the diet as well as fats that are manufactured by the body is altered, leading to the buildup of cholesterol and triglycerides in the bloodstream and arteries. Insulin resistance appears to alter the functioning of the SNS, and this may lead to hypertension. These three conditions are major risk factors for the development of atherosclerosis—narrowing of the arteries that results in reduced blood flow—and this in turn increases the risk of heart attack and stroke.

Insulin resistance and its attendant complications occur more frequently in obese people whose excess adipose tissue is localized to the upper body. With so-called male-pattern obesity individuals have a high waist-to-hip ratio (measure of the waist at its smallest point divided by the circumference of the hips at their widest point), whereas with "female-pattern obesity" people carry more fat on their hips and thighs. (These two body types are also described as "apples" and "pears," respectively.) Waist-hip ratios of greater than 0.95–1.0 in men and greater than 0.8 in women are associated with excess risk. Recent studies show that upper-body fat deposited within the abdominal cavity (visceral fat) is associated with greater risk than fat beneath the skin (subcutaneous fat).

Sleep apnea is a complication of obesity that in many cases is not recognized but may be life-threatening. With increasing obesity an individual finds it more and more difficult to breathe, especially while sleeping, and some obese people have periods during sleep when they stop breathing. The oxygen level in the blood drops, and the carbon dioxide level rises. This alerts the brain, and the person must wake up to start breathing again. Some unfortunate people may wake up as many as 600 times in a single night! Without a good night's sleep, sleep apnea sufferers become confused and sleepy during the day, have severe nightmares, and even develop hallucinations. The excess carbon dioxide buildup is thought to lead to high blood pressure, and eventually some of these people develop congestive heart failure. If this cardiac condition is left untreated in its end stages, the mortality rate is about 70% in five years.

Fortunately, weight loss improves or even cures most of these conditions. Some studies show that even modest weight loss may produce dramatic improvements in risk factors associated with obesity.

Social consequences

As dramatic as the medical complications are, they are insignificant in the minds of many obese people compared with the massive social penalties they pay for being obese. A fat person generally has a harder time than a lean person meeting people, making friends, finding a job, getting promoted, and being accepted into college or graduate school.

Prejudice and discrimination toward the obese start in early childhood. One study that evaluated children's preferences for playmates found that obese children were the least preferred playmates among children with a variety of other disabilities (*e.g.,* confined to wheelchairs or with facial disfigurements). A study reported in the Sept. 30, 1993, issue of the *New England Journal of Medicine,* conducted by Steven L. Gortmaker and colleagues at Harvard Medical School, Harvard School of Public Health, and the New England Medical Center, found that the social and economic consequences of being overweight in adolescence were significant—in fact, more severe than the consequences associated with many other chronic physical conditions. The investigators followed a group of adolescents over a period of seven years into early adulthood and found that compared with lean adolescents, obese adolescents completed fewer years of school, were less likely to get married, had lower household incomes, and were more likely to live in poverty.

Other studies have found that obese adolescents and adults have a poorer self-image and score higher on depression indexes than do lean people (although clinical depression is not more common in obese people). Self-image, symptoms of depression, and overall quality of life improve with significant weight loss.

Treating obesity

There are several approaches to treating obesity, and new ones are continually being sought.

Glenn Osmundson—Providence Journal-Bulletin

The social penalties for being obese are severe. Bonnie Cook of Rhode Island, who weighs 145 kg (320 lb), was denied a job at a state institution because of her weight—the employer contending that her obesity was self-imposed and therefore should not be considered a disability. In November 1993 the United States Court of Appeals for the First Circuit ruled unanimously that in denying Cook a job the employer had in fact discriminated and that such an action was in violation of the 1973 Rehabilitation Act. This was the first federal court decision in which workplace bias linked to obesity was deemed illegal.

Diet and exercise. Standard treatment of obesity is based on behavioral methods—namely, those of diet, exercise, and altered lifestyle. Unfortunately, success rates are quite low. Only about 3% or fewer have lost weight and maintained the loss after five years. This is true for diets alone, exercise alone, or a combination of both. Most treatment programs produce short-term weight loss, but long-term maintenance is difficult, and even the most successful programs report only very modest long-term loss. The most commonly recommended diet reduces calories and is low in fat and high in fiber. The typical American diet contains about 38% of calories as fat and only about 12 g per day of dietary fiber. Carefully controlled studies in human subjects show that reducing the fat content of the diet, even if calories are kept constant, results in weight loss. However, fat added to food improves the taste, while added fiber increases the work of chewing and swallowing. Thus, many people prefer tasty, low-work, high-calorie diets.

Very low-calorie diets. Many commercial programs initially use so-called very low-calorie diets (VLCDs), often relying on prepared liquid formulas that contain about 400 to 800 calories per day and result in very rapid weight loss. The public enthusiasm for VLCDs peaked in the 1980s. These diets are not as dangerous as was once feared, but recent studies have shown that weight loss on VLCDs is not much different from that on higher-calorie diets (800–1,000 calories), and risks with the latter are theoretically lower. Although VLCDs initially cause more rapid weight loss (loss after 12 to 16 weeks averages 20 kg [44 lb]), usually there is a greater rate of weight regain when the diet is stopped. A few studies suggest that compared with higher-calorie diets with similar weight losses over time, VLCDs may reduce the tendency to develop diabetes and hypertension months after the diets have

ended. More research is needed to confirm these results and to determine if a VLCD might be indicated in some patients with these conditions.

Drugs. Because long-term success is poor with standard treatments, attention is turning to more aggressive treatments such as the use of drugs. The obesity drugs currently available in the U.S. are: benzphetamine, dextroamphetamine, diethyl-propion, fenfluramine, mazindol, methamphetamine, phendimetrazine, phenmetrazine, phentermine, and phenylpropanolamine. All of these drugs are adrenergic agents—*i.e.,* they stimulate nerve fibers in the autonomic nervous system, which stimulates the heart, smooth muscles, and glands—except fenfluramine, which stimulates the neurohormone serotonin. How they work is not entirely clear. Adrenergic drugs appear to reduce appetite and thereby reduce food intake. They may regulate the way the body uses energy, increasing the metabolic rate. Some scientists speculate that adrenergic drugs bring on early satiety, thus making people feel "full" more quickly.

Fenfluramine, by increasing serotonin activity in the brain, results in a reduction of food intake initially, producing weight loss, but studies in rats show that intake returns to normal. Nonetheless, weight remains lower, suggesting that serotonin produces alterations in metabolic rate. Studies of effects on metabolic rate in humans who take fenfluramine have had conflicting results. Thus, the basic mechanisms of action of this drug are not yet clear.

There are few studies that have used combinations of obesity drugs. One recent study used half doses of fenfluramine and phentermine, along with a standard diet and exercise program. At the end of 34 weeks, women lost as much as 14% of their body weight and men as much as 25%. The drugs were continued for periods of up to 3.5 years, and subjects maintained a modest weight loss for as long as they remained on the drugs. This study supports the theory that obesity is a chronic disease that requires continuous treatment. This and other studies show that complications of obesity are markedly improved in patients who take obesity drugs, although this may be due to weight loss per se and not specifically to the drugs.

Laws in many U.S. states prohibit prescribing obesity drugs for longer than 12 consecutive weeks because of the potential for abuse and addiction (with dextroamphetamine and methamphetamine in particular). If laws are to be changed, more research must be done to determine the safety and efficacy of combinations of drugs given for many years.

A thigh-reducing cream? In 1993 a great deal of publicity was given to a report that a cream containing aminophylline, a chemically modified form of theophylline, a drug most commonly used to treat asthma, would reduce the size of the thighs if applied daily. The rationale behind this treatment was that aminophylline diffuses through the skin and causes breakdown of fat in the localized area. The magnitude of the effect in 12 women studied was not great—thigh size was reduced 1.3–3.8 cm (½ to 1½ in) over five weeks—and the thighs rapidly enlarged again if use of the cream stopped. The rapid increase in thigh diameter raised the possibility that the cream may work simply by dehydrating the skin. Most experts agreed that this cream would have limited usefulness and would have to be used continuously to be effective. There are no data on whether the effect continues over the long term.

Fake fats. Another substance that is being tested for potential use in obesity is Olestra, a fat substitute. Olestra is a sugar molecule that has six fatty acid molecules attached. It is said to have a "mouth-feel" of real fat, but its structure makes it indigestible by the human intestine. Because the substance is heat stable, it can be used for cooking; it can also be used in margarines, salad dressings, and even ice cream. Although this substance was discovered many years ago and has undergone extensive testing, the U.S. Food and Drug Administration (FDA) has not yet decided that it is safe for humans to consume, and it has not been released for use by the public. The product has received a great deal of publicity and its release is eagerly awaited by the public. However, it would substitute for only a modest amount of the fat in the average American diet and is not likely to promote major weight loss.

Surgery. At the extreme end of treatments for obesity are surgical procedures. In 1991 a consensus conference held at the National Institutes of Health concluded that surgery may be justified for massively obese individuals refractory to other treatments. Vertical banded gastroplasty (VBG) and gastric bypass surgery are the two most commonly used types of surgery for obesity in the United States. Both involve dividing the stomach into a small upper pouch and a large lower pouch.

With VBG a one-centimeter (0.4-in) band of Marlex, a type of plastic mesh, placed between the upper and lower pouches produces a mechanical obstruction to the passage of food; the very small capacity of the upper pouch limits food intake. Once this small amount of food has passed through the obstruction, it is processed and digested normally by the body. With gastric bypass the stomach is completely divided, and a section of the small intestine is pulled up and connected to the upper pouch. Thus, food passes from a very small upper pouch directly into the small intestine. The lower stomach and duodenum (the first part of the small intestine) do not receive food. Gastric bypass is associated with rapid passage of food, especially liquids, into the lower small intestine; this results in what is called the "dumping syndrome," which produces abdominal cramping and sometimes diarrhea. Weight loss correlates with the extent of dumping.

With both of these operations, weight loss persists for many years. Both procedures produce nausea and vomiting if too much food is consumed, and the dumping syndrome associated with gastric bypass may produce considerable discomfort. These effects tend to lessen with time; their role in reducing food intake undoubtedly produces much of the early weight loss. Studies indicate that gastric bypass is superior to VBG for long-term weight loss and weight maintenance. VGB, on the other hand, is easier to perform and has fewer side effects. Mortality risk in both operations is low—less than 1% when performed by an expert surgeon.

Is weight loss always healthy?

As noted above, obesity is associated with a number of medical complications that are thought to lead to serious illness and early death. Many of these complications, such as high blood pressure, diabetes, high blood fats, and sleep apnea, improve with weight loss, and scientists have thus assumed that weight loss would improve long-term health and lead to a lower death rate. However, a number of epidemiological studies have recently challenged this view and have shown that weight loss in some cases appears to be associated with a *higher* death rate.

Epidemiological studies look at a population over time and try to determine the factors associated with disease or death. None of the studies that show an increased death rate with weight loss was specifically designed to look at this question, and there are other potential explanations for the results. For example, people who have cancer and some other serious diseases generally lose weight; thus, it would not be surprising that weight loss is associated with a higher death rate. There are also suggestions that weight loss, at least in some segments of the population, may be associated with lower death rates when it is voluntary. More research, specifically designed to answer these questions, is needed.

Directions for future research

The availability of many new molecular biology and genetics techniques holds great promise for uncovering the causes of obesity and determining why some people develop complications that shorten life span. It may be possible in the future to identify individuals who are genetically "destined" to become fat. Since obesity in adulthood is so difficult to treat, preventive measures for high-risk individuals, started in childhood, may result in less weight gained with aging. It may be possible, for example, to determine key genetic differences between lean and obese people and then to insert the gene or genes that will make the biochemistry of the obese person more like that of a lean person.

These approaches could produce long-term success, which is so lacking in efforts to treat obesity now. In the interim it seems likely that increased attention will be focused on pharmacological treatments. The success of the one combination-drug regimen that has been tried will lead to the study of other regimens. After many years of neglect (the last new obesity drug was approved by the FDA in 1972), the National Institutes of Health and other research agencies are supporting obesity research, and pharmaceutical companies are greatly increasing the funds spent on developing new obesity drugs. Already, new drugs that promote energy expenditure by increasing metabolic rate or that block fat from being absorbed by the body are under study. One aim is to develop drugs that will have fewer side effects and less potential for abuse than currently available agents. Meanwhile, the food industry is working to develop new fat-free foods and fat substitutes that will allow people to decrease their fat intake without sacrificing taste quality.

On the surgical front, there is research to determine the mechanisms of action of the existing procedures for treating obesity. Since surgery produces the best results of all current treatments for obesity in terms of long-term weight loss, determining why and how this occurs—determining the roles of malabsorption of nutrients, food aversion, decreased intake, and altered metabolism—may provide insights that can be used for new drug or diet development.

Finally, research is needed to answer these questions: Is weight loss necessarily "healthy"? Does it prolong life? Studies looking at health effects, cost benefit, and effects on death rate must be carefully designed to determine if it is in fact wise for society to be spending the large amounts of money currently being spent on weight reduction.

—Richard L. Atkinson, M.D.

Osteoporosis

Osteoporosis (literally, "porous bone") is a thinning of the bones that occurs with aging. In the U.S. alone, it affects some 25 million people, four out of five of them women, and is responsible for at least 1.2 million fractures per year.

The criteria for defining osteoporosis have undergone two important modifications in the past few years. In 1994 an expert panel of the World Health Organization (WHO) agreed upon normal standards for bone mass and, by the same token, standards for what should be judged abnormal. The bone mass of the

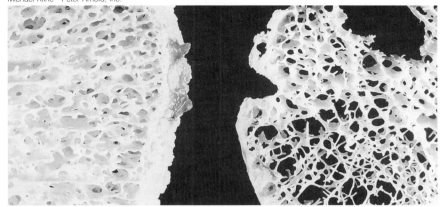

The three-dimensional lattice-like structure of normal bone (far left) depends on its many vertical and horizontal connections for strength and weight-bearing capacity. Osteoporotic bone (left), which has lost these connections, may be unable to withstand even the ordinary stresses of daily living and is readily subject to fracture.

"healthy young adult" is considered the norm for people of all ages. Even so, a certain amount of variation exists among healthy young persons. The degrees of individual variation in bone density, as they cluster around the average, are termed *standard deviations.* With bone density, as with other characteristics that vary from person to person—such as height, weight, and blood pressure—the range from one standard deviation above the average to one standard deviation below includes about two-thirds of all normal values. For bone mass the WHO panel designated all values more than one standard deviation below the young adult average as *osteopenia,* meaning "shortage of bone." They further defined all values more than 2.5 standard deviations below the average as *osteoporosis,* whether or not fractures have occurred. In taking this approach the WHO panel explicitly classified about one-sixth of ostensibly normal *premenopausal* women in developed countries as having bone mass values low enough to place them at significant risk for fracture.

Another definitional sea change took place at the International Consensus Conference on Osteoporosis in Copenhagen in 1990. The assembled experts agreed that osteoporosis is "a disease of excessive skeletal fragility due both to decreased bone mass and to microarchitectural deterioration of bone tissue, with consequent increased risk of fracture." This approach shifted the emphasis of the definition from reduced bone density to fragility and its consequences (fractures); moreover, it changed the status of low bone mass from a synonym for the disease to a risk factor. Thus, low bone mass (osteopenia or osteoporosis, in the WHO scheme) is now viewed primarily in relation to the risk for fracture, just as high blood pressure is considered a predisposing factor for stroke.

Academic as these refinements might seem, they herald important changes in the approach of scientists to understanding, preventing, and treating osteoporosis. The Copenhagen definition not only relegates low bone mass to the status of a risk factor for fracture,

but it recognizes *microarchitectural deterioration* as another, equally important factor. Microarchitectural deterioration encompasses two processes, loss of trabecular connections and accumulated "fatigue damage." What these processes entail is explained below.

The skeleton as a structure

Bony tissue in the vertebrae and at the ends of the long bones is not solid but instead consists of a three-dimensional lattice of bony plates and spicules, collectively called trabeculae, or trabecular elements. Vertically oriented trabeculae ordinarily carry most of the weight of the body, and horizontally oriented trabeculae brace the vertical structures and keep them from buckling under the load. Loss of connections among these lattice elements greatly weakens the structure out of all proportion to the actual loss of bone tissue. One reason why spinal fractures are so much more common in women than in men is that women have a greater tendency to lose these critical trabecular connections.

So-called fatigue damage occurs when any structural material—steel, wood, concrete—is subjected to regular use; bone is no exception. All structures bend very slightly under ordinary use; repeated bending eventually produces ultramicroscopic tears in the basic fabric of the material. As these tiny tears accumulate over time in bone, they weaken it. One of the functions of the bone-remodeling process—the normal cycle of bone deposition and resorption—is to detect and replace these damaged regions. But when that process fails for any reason, damage accumulates, and bone becomes so weak that a fracture can occur with relatively little force.

Bones already weakened by reduction in density or loss of trabecular connections are particularly susceptible to fatigue damage because they bend more than normal bone does in ordinary use, and fatigue damage therefore accumulates more rapidly in them than in normal bone. Some scientists now believe that one of the factors contributing to hip fracture, an extremely

343

common fracture in elderly people, is an accumulation of precisely such unrepaired fatigue damage in the upper end of the femur (thigh bone).

Hip fracture reconsidered

The emphasis on fractures in current definitions of osteoporosis, and on the circumstances and characteristics that put a person at risk for fracture, also reflects the growing realization of the importance of falls in the elderly and specifically the *way* in which old people fall. Recent studies have shown that young people absorb some of the energy of a fall and protect their bones, both by reflex twisting of the body, which causes them to land on soft parts, and also by using their arms to break the fall. The elderly commonly have much slower reflexes than the young, and when older people fall they often slump to the floor sideways, thus striking the vulnerable bone at the side of the hip.

Physicians have known for a long time that hip fractures are more common in excessively thin individuals than in normal-weight or overweight people. This is partly because very thin people have bones that are more fragile but also because they have less padding in the form of fat tissue. These observations have led to experiments in which hip pads of various kinds have been placed into undergarments designed to be worn by elderly people at high risk of hip fracture. While there are problems of practicality and cost with these protective garments, studies have shown clearly that hip fracture risk can be greatly reduced by this simple intervention. Possibly the same protection could be achieved, somewhat more feasibly, by padding the environment in which old people live (and fall).

Measuring bone mass: improved techniques

Methods for measuring bone mass have advanced enormously in recent years. Technically speaking, bone mass is bone *mineral* content, but because mineral (primarily calcium but also phosphate and carbonate) makes up two-thirds of the weight of bone—a proportion that does not change appreciably in osteoporosis—mineral content is a useful index of the total amount, or mass, of bone. (The remaining one-third of bone mass consists of organic material, primarily the protein collagen.)

The mineral content of bone is measured by a narrow beam of radiation (in the X-ray region of the electromagnetic spectrum) passed back and forth across the body. Mineral absorbs the X-ray energy, and measurement of how much of the beam is absorbed indicates how much mineral is in the beam's path. Bone mass can be conveniently measured in the entire skeleton, as well as in the spine, at the hip, and at the wrist or heel. Many techniques are used. The most common are dual energy X-ray absorptiometry (DEXA) and single photon absorptiometry (SPA); both

are available at most major medical centers. The dual energy instruments are used for thicker body parts such as the spine or hip, while SPA is used mainly for measurements at the wrist and heel. Since bone loss in osteoporosis tends to be generalized, any site is about as good as any other for assessing bone mass. With the instruments now in use, measurement time is five minutes or less at any one site.

When mineral content is expressed per unit area of the shadow cast by the bone as the beam passes across it, the resulting value is a measurement of *bone mineral density*. If all bones were the same size, content and density would vary in parallel; however, people who are big-boned often have lower bone-density values than their small-boned counterparts. This is because their bony material is spread over a larger volume. In terms of susceptibility to fracture, the actual amount of bone a person has (mass) is probably more important than how densely it is packed.

A method of bone measurement similar in concept to DEXA and SPA but different in execution is radiographic absorptiometry. No specialized equipment is required; instead a conventional X-ray is taken of the patient's hand, with a calibration standard on the X-ray film alongside the hand. The resulting X-ray is processed by computer programs that measure the amount of mineral in certain finger bones.

Another method, currently under development, uses ultrasound. The transmission of a pulse of ultrasonic energy through a solid material is a well-established technique used by engineers to assess the integrity of such structures as steel beams and bridge piers. Sound-wave transmission is influenced not only by the mass density of the material (as are the absorptiometric methods) but also by internal voids and discontinuities—precisely the types of defects present in osteoporotic bone as a result of trabecular disconnections or accumulated fatigue damage. Scientists do not have as much clinical experience assessing bone mass with the ultrasonic methods as with absorptiometry, but early results are promising. The ultrasound instruments have the additional advantages of being cheaper and more portable than absorptiometry instruments and do not involve any radiation exposure.

Heredity's influence

It has commonly been assumed that heredity is somehow involved in osteoporosis, that having had a mother, aunts, or grandmothers with osteoporosis places a woman at greater risk of developing the condition herself. However, since families share lifestyles and eating habits as well as genes, the precise contribution of heredity to bone thinning has been uncertain. Recent studies have provided solid evidence pointing to two distinct roles for genetics—influencing how much bone people have and determining key differences in the shapes of certain bones.

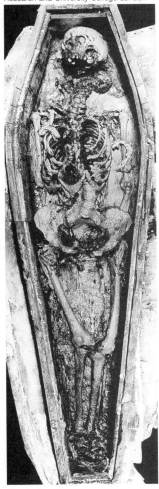

The removal of this and 86 other skeletons from the crypt of an 18th-century London church undergoing restoration gave medical researchers an opportunity to compare the bone density of present-day women, both young and old, with their counterparts of two centuries ago. An X-ray technique was used to measure bone density in the femurs (thighbones) of only well-preserved skeletons. The results indicated that by comparison the modern women not only had greater bone loss before menopause, they also had higher rates of bone loss after menopause.

Studies of adult twin pairs have shown that identical twins are more alike in their bone density than are fraternal twins, even late in life, when factors such as exercise, diet, and illnesses have had a chance to exert their influences. These findings have been greatly amplified by the discovery of differences in a key gene that appears to contain the blueprints for the cell receptor to which the active form of vitamin D attaches in various tissues. While it is not yet known how the gene influences bone mass, individuals who have two copies of the form of the gene designated b have been found to have denser bones than individuals who carry both forms (Bb), and the latter have an advantage over people whose genetic endowment is BB. Furthermore, when fraternal twins inherit the same forms of the gene, their bone densities differ no more than do those of identical twins.

Because there is substantial overlap in bone values between groups of individuals with different forms of the gene, scientists believe that environmental factors, such as diet and exercise, may influence expression of the gene. Therefore, having a less advantageous form of this gene does not necessarily condemn a person to having fragile bones. It does, however, suggest that an individual may need to pay more attention to factors that influence bone health—such as postmenopausal hormone replacement and a high-calcium diet—than does a person who has the "good" form of the gene.

Scientists have long been puzzled by the fact that certain Asian peoples, such as the Japanese, have rates of hip fracture only about half that of persons of northern European extraction—even when they have lived in the U.S. for years. In old age the bone density of these Asians is just as low as that of Caucasians, and they lose bone with age at about the same rate. It turns out that the difference in fracture risk is due largely to subtle differences in the shape of the upper end of the femur, where hip fractures occur. Relative to body size, the neck region of the femur is longer in Caucasians. Engineering analysis shows that a long neck segment is inherently weaker than a short segment. So, given the same bone mass and the same force of impact in a fall, Caucasians are more likely than Asians to suffer hip fracture.

Bone mass: the peak is the point

It is generally agreed that the amount of bone people have in old age depends on both the amount they had at their adult peak and the rate at which they lose bone as they age. While there are undoubtedly individuals who lose bone more or less rapidly than others, for most people bone loss in later life proceeds at a fairly uniform rate. Thus, the *peak* amount of bone people have is the major determinant of how much will be present in old age.

In the 5–15 years following menopause, women typically lose an average of about 15% of their bone mass. (Thin women lose somewhat more and heavy women somewhat less.) However, if a woman starts in the upper quintile of normal peak density values, she can sustain that 15% loss and still end up with as much bone as, or more than, the average woman has before menopause. On the other hand, the same 15% loss in a woman starting in the lower quintile of normal premenopausal values will place her at high risk for fracture immediately after menopause.

This realization has shifted scientific attention in recent years from the factors that affect bone loss to the factors that influence accumulation of bone mass during growth. One of these is heredity. Of the environmental factors, the most important seems to be calcium intake, although level of physical activity during childhood and adolescence is also vital. Until recently it had been assumed that the calcium intake of people in the industrialized nations was typical of what humans had always eaten or, because of easy access to dairy products, perhaps even higher. However, studies of humankind's closest primate relatives (chimpanzees) and of human societies of hunter-gatherers, both observed in their natural habitats, have made it clear that the human diet was once far richer in calcium than it is today—perhaps as much as four to five times richer.

While the need for calcium during growth has never been seriously questioned, the issue of how much is optimal has recently been reexamined. The recommended dietary allowance (RDA) for calcium is currently 800 mg/day up to age 10, 1,200 mg/day from age 11 to 24, and 800 mg/day thereafter. These recommendations assume that calcium is absorbed very efficiently by the body during the phases of most rapid growth. At the time of publication of the most recent RDAs (1989), calcium absorption had never been adequately tested in children or adolescents, so the assumption of efficient absorption was only a guess. However, recent studies using stable isotopes of calcium have shown that calcium-absorption efficiency in adolescents is about the same as in adults—which is lower than had been presumed. Hence, the premise on which the RDA for children and teens was based is now known to be incorrect, and the RDAs must be considered to be too low.

The question of what constitutes optimal calcium intake has been approached in another way by a retrospective analysis of studies of calcium balance published over the past 70 years. *Balance* is a measurement of the difference between intake and output, or, in other words, the amount of calcium the body is

able to retain on any given intake. Positive balance almost always means bone gain, and negative balance bone loss. Taken together, these studies show that adolescents do not reach the limit of their ability to retain calcium until intakes exceed 1,600 mg/day, not the 1,200-mg/day figure established by the RDA.

These somewhat theoretical arguments have been buttressed by recent controlled trials of calcium supplements in children and adolescents, which have shown that calcium intakes above the RDA do, in fact, augment bone gain during growth. Finally, studies in women in the third decade of life (well after they have stopped growing in height) have shown that young adults are still adding bony material to their skeletons—that is, consolidating the bone mass built during growth. Available evidence indicates that the window of opportunity for increasing bone mass closes at about age 30. Exercise has a positive influence on this third-decade gain, but calcium intake has an even stronger effect.

When the above insights are combined with the realization that the typical U.S. teenage girl currently consumes less than half of the current, probably inadequate, RDA for calcium, it seems an inescapable conclusion that many individuals, particularly young women, are failing to achieve the peak bone mass their genetic endowment would predict and that they are therefore placing themselves at a greatly increased risk of osteoporosis later in life. It is in part for this reason that osteoporosis has sometimes been called "a pediatric disease that waits until old age to express itself." Current evidence suggests that the optimal calcium intake during childhood may be as much as 1,100 mg/day, during adolescence 1,500 mg/day, and for the third decade 1,100 mg/day. As a reflection of the growing awareness that current standards are too low, a 1994 consensus conference convened by the National Institutes of Health issued new recommendations very close to those cited above (*see* table).

Another condition that can prevent the achievement of peak bone mass is the eating disorder anorexia nervosa. Young women with this problem are excessively thin yet have a distorted body image that leads them to believe that they are overweight. They starve themselves to the point where they have many endocrine as well as nutritional deficiencies, including absence of normal ovarian function. Such women, even those as young as in their 20s, nearly always have much lower than normal bone mass measurements and often suffer typical osteoporotic spine fractures. Some recovery of bone mass is possible if normal weight can be attained and ovarian function reestablished, but this does not often happen. The other major eating disorder, bulimia, which is characterized by a compulsive binge-and-purge cycle, is not associated with significant abnormalities of the bones.

Young women athletes may also fail to achieve their

Calcium recommendations: in need of revision?		
age group	RDA (mg/day)	optimal intake* (mg/day)
birth to 6 months	400	400 (250 if nursing)
6 months to 1 year	600	600
1 to 10	800	800
11 to 24	1,200	1,200–1,500
adult men		
25 to 50	800	800
51 to 65	800	1,000
over 65	800	1,500
adult women		
25 to 50	800	1,000
over 50	800	1,500 (1,000 if taking estrogen)
pregnant and nursing	1,200	additional 400

*conclusions of the June 1994 National Institutes of Health Consensus Development Conference on Optimal Calcium Intake

Although these college students have probably reached their full height, they are still building skeletal bone. For women in their 20s, physical activity and an adequate calcium intake are vital for the achievement of peak bone mass.

peak bone mass. Often they are so thin that normal ovarian function is suppressed and they become estrogen deficient. Consequently, they may suffer bone loss that appears, in many respects, like that associated with menopause. Some of them may even experience the vertebral fractures typical of postmenopausal osteoporosis. The occurrence of osteoporosis in these young women is sometimes interpreted to mean that while exercise is generally good for bone, too much can be harmful. However, in this situation it is probably not the exercise per se but the low amount of body fat and the estrogen deficiency (coupled in many instances with inadequate calcium intake) that should be blamed. Other men and women who have comparable exercise programs, but who follow diets that are adequate to support both body weight and strenuous training, do not experience premature bone loss.

Treatment: no easy answers

A combination of high calcium intake, adequate vitamin D level, a vigorous exercise program, and hormone replacement therapy following menopause could probably prevent 50–75% of all osteoporosis.

Treatment of established osteoporosis, especially after fractures have occurred, is more problematic. This is partly because once the damage has been done, there is no good way to reverse it and partly because there are so few medications that strengthen bone.

In the U.S. today only two agents, estrogen and calcitonin, have been approved by the Food and Drug Administration (FDA) for treating osteoporosis. Both are hormones. Estrogen, the female hormone lost at menopause, is very effective in preventing bone loss while it is being taken, but it does not restore bone lost before the start of hormone replacement or prevent further loss once estrogen therapy is discontinued. Likewise, calcitonin, a hormone that reduces bone destruction, can stabilize bone mass but does not restore lost bone to any appreciable extent. Both estrogen and calcitonin act by suppressing bone remodeling. Another class of compounds, bisphosphonates, also suppresses remodeling. One of this group (etidronate) has been approved in some European countries, and several others are being studied in the U.S.

Perhaps more promising is fluoride, also approved in Europe for treating osteoporosis but not in the U.S. Fluoride is the only agent known that stimulates new bone deposition. It is capable of restoring spinal bone density to fully normal levels (although it does not seem to be able to restore lost trabecular connections in the interior of vertebral bodies). The cost of getting a new drug through the FDA approval process is enormous, however, and fluoride is not patentable; thus, it seems unlikely that this promising agent will be developed in the U.S. in the near future.

Many contributing factors, many interventions

Osteoporosis is increasingly being viewed as a multifactorial disorder. Fractures occur not simply because bone mass is subnormal but also because the bone has been weakened in other ways (such as defective remodeling and loss of trabecular connections), because elderly people fall in such a way as to jeopardize the most vulnerable bony regions, and because these individuals have inadequate soft-tissue padding over bony prominences, as well as for many other reasons. Each of these factors, in turn, has many contributors of its own. Low bone mass is most often a reflection of failure to reach the maximum possible mass during growth, and this in turn is most often due to inadequate calcium intake.

The realization of its multifaceted nature makes osteoporosis in a sense more complex than was once thought. At the same time, this very complexity provides medical science a great many more vantage points from which to attack the problem. Clinically, these translate into multiple opportunities to intervene effectively to prevent fractures, which remain the sole important consequence of this disorder.

—*Robert P. Heaney, M.D.*

Worn Out, but Why?

by Alex Poteliakhoff, M.D.

Many individuals of enormous accomplishment owe their success as much to their boundless energy as to their particular talents or genius. Consider Napoleon, a supreme leader in war, who, whether for good or ill, changed the map of Europe in his short lifetime. On Dec. 1, 1805, the eve of his victory at Austerlitz, he not only issued detailed battle plans to his generals but dictated a scheme for the establishment of a girls' boarding school near Paris. And when others flagged during prolonged sessions of the Council of State, Napoleon, ever animated and sharp-witted, would chastise: "Come, sirs, we have not earned our stipends."

Another example of one with remarkable energy is the giant among 20th-century artists, Pablo Picasso, who on the occasion of his 80th birthday danced a flamenco on the dinner table. Of course, he also astonished the world with his prodigious output of paintings, sculpture, ceramics, poetry, and even plays; a cascade of continuously evolving styles; and numerous romances extending well into old age.

However, there are also those who have gained recognition and renown only in the face of a lifelong struggle with chronically low energy and virtually constant exhaustion. Two examples come readily to mind. Charles Darwin enjoyed normal health while working as a naturalist on the surveying expedition of the HMS *Beagle* (1831–36). But some four years after his return to England, he experienced the onset of disabling fatigue, which forced him to lead a secluded life. Though he could work no more than two to three hours a day, with the support of his sympathetic family and his own iron self-discipline, Darwin gave the world the concept of evolution and revolutionized scientific thinking about human development.

While still a young woman in her 30s, Florence Nightingale led a group of nurses to minister to the British troops in the Crimean War. At the military hospital in Scutari, Turkey, she introduced sanitation; reduced the incidence of typhus, cholera, and dysentery; and tended the sick and wounded day and night. Upon her return to England, Nightingale organized humane and efficient medical services for all the armed forces, dictated new concepts of hygiene for hospitals throughout the world, inaugurated training for nurses and midwives, and helped to reform workhouses. But all of this was accomplished by a gaunt,

debilitated invalid; "Crimean fever" had reduced the formerly vigorous woman to a state of chronic fatigue. Nonetheless, even while confined to her couch year after year, she set new standards for hospital care and established nursing as a respected profession.

Dedication and determination enabled Darwin and Nightingale to triumph over fatigue. Yet how many others have forfeited their ambitions and dreams not because they lacked ability but because their lives were blighted by perpetual tiredness and lack of vitality? No wonder the poorly understood syndrome variously known as chronic fatigue syndrome (CFS), postviral fatigue syndrome, and even Florence Nightingale disease attracts so much popular attention and has become the subject of endless scientific study.

The purpose of this report is to explore in detail the nature of fatigue and to review some of the research that has sought its causes. The discussion focuses *not* on CFS but on fatigue as a broader phenomenon. To begin, it is necessary to consider the complex process by which biological energy is generated.

Where energy comes from

Fatigue is a symptom, an expression of any of a large number of underlying disturbances. These disturbances may be due to a distinct disease, such as tuberculosis or cancer, or they may be brought on by a viral infection or by stress, either physical or psychological. A full explanation of the processes responsible for fatigue has so far eluded the scientific world. Of all the scientists, however, it is the physiologist who is most at home with this subject. The mechanism of muscle fatigue is well mapped out, whereas the causes of postviral fatigue and the fatigue associated with stress and depression are poorly understood. In order to elucidate what *is* known about fatigue, it is useful to look at biological energy—what it is and where it comes from.

The eminent British physiologist Ernest Starling, who lived at the turn of the last century, neatly described energy, derived from the breakdown of food, in terms of calories required for work and maintenance of body temperature. More recently, with the advent of molecular biology, scientists have begun to look at the whole energy "chain of command," each "link" of which—from the brain to the various organs—must carry out its specific function. At each stage in the chain, energy is used. This energy is derived primarily from high-energy phosphates such as adenosine triphosphate (ATP), a compound first discovered in the early 1930s and later found to be present in all types of cells. ATP is a source of energy for muscle contraction and for the transport of molecules across cell membranes in many organs.

In order for a muscle to contract, the chemical energy in foods must be converted into mechanical energy, and the body has a very complex and sophisticated way of doing this. Starches, fats, and, to a lesser extent, proteins provide the calories. First, the body digests these substances, breaking them down into their respective constituents: sugars, free fatty acids, and amino acids. Then, because direct combustion of these substances is too robust and crude to be of use, their energy is channeled into the production of ATP, which permits a controlled and finely adjusted use of energy.

There are two processes, or pathways, by which the energy of foodstuffs is released for duty in muscles: aerobic and anaerobic. The anaerobic (*i.e.,* non-oxygen-requiring) process, which is simpler and quicker, but less efficient, than the aerobic one, provides immediate energy. Glucose is broken down into lactic acid, and adenosine diphosphate (ADP) is converted to ATP. The slower, more efficient aerobic process can be sustained almost indefinitely. Breakdown products of glucose (lactate and pyruvate) and fats (free fatty acids) provide the energy to, once again, convert ADP to ATP.

"Links" in the energy chain

The energy chain of command starts with signals from the brain in the form of electrical impulses. In order to travel across the gaps between nerve cells, these signals are converted into chemical energy in the form of compounds called neurotransmitters. In depression—a disorder characterized, at least in part, by a pervasive feeling of exhaustion—there appears to be a deficiency of certain neurotransmitters. Drugs that alleviate depression act to make these essential chemicals—*e.g.,* serotonin—more available, thus improving cell-to-cell communication.

The brain, having assessed the body's need for energy, will act through one of two systems: the self-governing autonomic nervous system (ANS) or the endocrine (hormonal) system. To bring about an immediate surge of energy, the sympathetic part of the ANS—the part concerned with preparing the body to react—causes the neurotransmitter norepinephrine to be secreted at nerve endings or stimulates the adrenal glands to pump epinephrine and norepinephrine into the bloodstream. These rapidly acting hormones prepare the subject for the classic "fight or flight" response and mobilize glucose as a source of energy.

The hypothalamus, a structure located at the base of the brain, directs and governs the endocrine system. In the hypothalamus several releasing factors are produced, the function of which is to stimulate the pituitary gland. The pituitary, in turn, acts on a number of subsidiary glands to regulate such processes as sexual activity, growth, metabolism, and energy. The releasing factors of particular interest in connection with energy and fatigue are, first, corticotropin-releasing hormone (CRH), which, through the pituitary, acts on the outer portion (cortex) of the adrenal glands to produce cortisol, the "stress hormone"; second, thyrotropin-releasing hormone, which, again through the pituitary, stimulates the thyroid gland to produce

Although each will be remembered for making enormous contributions, the 19th-century nursing pioneer Florence Nightingale and the protean 20th-century artist Pablo Picasso were diametric opposites on the stamina scale. Nightingale struggled daily against debilitating fatigue; Picasso (shown here at 76) overflowed with physical and creative energy.

(Left) Keystone © EB, Inc.; (right) Rene Burri—Magnum

hormones that control the rate of metabolism (the rate of oxygen consumption and energy use); and, third, gonadotropin-releasing hormone, which results in the secretion of testosterone, the male hormone associated with aggressiveness.

Hormones produced as a result of the activity of the hypothalamus and pituitary gland are spoken of as "first messengers." They travel to the surface of target cells in the various organs and tissues. The message is then communicated to the interior of the cell by another substance, cyclic adenosine monophosphate (cAMP), the so-called second messenger, which is manufactured from ATP. The end result is the specific activity of that cell. In the case of the cells of the adrenal cortex, for example, after the first messenger, the pituitary hormone adrenocorticotropin (ACTH), reaches the cells' surfaces, cAMP takes over, and the cells then produce the required product, cortisol.

Only the basic structures and functions of the energy chain of command have been described here, leaving out many other complex pathways and mechanisms. Still, this rough outline should be enough to allow a consideration of the pathological processes that might result in a shortage or absence of energy. There is no simple, single-factor explanation for fatigue; the crux of the problem may lie in the brain, the endocrine glands, or the muscles.

Aging and illness: something in common

A look at two very different conditions may help to further elucidate the nature of fatigue. The first is a rare and disabling illness, Addison's disease, in which damage to the adrenal glands results in a deficiency of cortisol. The second is a common and universal condition—namely, old age.

The cardinal symptom in Addison's disease is an overwhelming fatigue; giving the patient a cortisol-like drug can alleviate this. The obvious inference is that cortisol plays a key part in energy processes in the body. Indeed, in addition to helping inhibit inflammation and maintain blood pressure, cortisol ensures a supply of glucose, fatty acids, and amino acids, all of which may be used as fuel. Whereas the adrenal hormone epinephrine helps the individual to cope with short-term stress, cortisol is essential for adaptation to longer-term stress.

As is the case in Addison's disease, a major hallmark of old age is a loss of energy. Much of what is known of the underlying physiological processes in aging comes from studies in animals. For example, physiologist Joseph Meites at Michigan State University has found that the concentration and turnover of catecholamines (epinephrine-like hormones that serve as neurotransmitters) in the brain are lower in old rats than in their younger counterparts. Other researchers have found that if the adrenal cortex of young and old animals is stimulated with ACTH, the output of cortisol

is lower in older animals than in younger ones. In human studies a Japanese scientist found that one of the thyroid hormones is somewhat reduced in elderly people, no doubt leading to a slowing down of mental and physical activity. Studies of human aging have established that loss of activity of muscle enzymes such as creatine kinase (necessary for the production of ATP) between ages 65 and 85 is partly responsible for the 35% decline in muscle strength that occurs during those years.

Depression and fatigue: connected?

It appears from this and other evidence that the symptom of fatigue may arise from abnormalities at any point along the energy chain of command. As has already been noted, depression seems to be characterized by a deficiency of neurotransmitters. There is also evidence of a lack of hypothalamic releasing hormones in CFS and in some forms of depression. As long ago as 1978, it was reported in the journal *Psychosomatic Medicine* that gonadotropin-releasing hormone, given intravenously to healthy male volunteers, brought about an increase in alertness, a decrease in fatigue, and increased speed of performance. It is this releasing hormone that results, among other effects, in the production of testosterone. In another experiment, involving patients with depression due to a stressful life event, researchers found that an injection of hypothalamic releasing factor relieved the depression and restored the subjects' energy and drive.

This author has also investigated hormonal levels in fatigue. In one study, published in 1981 in the *Journal of Psychosomatic Research,* blood cortisol levels were measured in people who complained of constant tiredness. The subjects, patients seeking care at a primary health clinic because of chronic fatigue—that is, fatigue of at least a month's duration, not due to any significant underlying disease—were found to have lower levels of blood cortisol than controls. It was of interest that the patients were found to have experienced more stressful life events in the preceding year than had controls.

The painstaking research of Mark A. Demitrack and colleagues at the National Institute of Mental Health in Bethesda, Md., confirmed the association of chronic fatigue and impaired cortisol output. Over the past several years, it has become increasingly recognized that an important element in chronic fatigue is diminished activity of the hypothalamic-pituitary-adrenal (HPA) axis.

In summary, human fatigue appears to be related to abnormalities of structure or function in one or more "links" in the energy chain of command. Shortage of fuel—*i.e.,* food or calories—is unlikely to play any significant part in long-lasting, debilitating fatigue. In fact, the symptoms of hypoglycemia (low blood sugar)—faintness, sweating, hunger, and trembling—

are quite different from the lethargy and torpor, both physical and mental, that most often characterize chronic fatigue.

Acute fatigue: not purely subjective

Defining and distinguishing different types or degrees of fatigue is a necessary step in examining the nature of this elusive symptom. First, there is acute fatigue, or fatigue of the moment. It may be either physical or mental. Acute fatigue is considered to be physiological in origin and harmless. Indeed, most of the time it does no damage to the body. It deserves study for three good reasons. One is that an understanding of *acute* fatigue may help to explain *chronic* fatigue. The second is that, logically, any chronic fatigue state must start with an acute phase; thus, prevention of excessive acute fatigue should help to prevent the chronic condition. Last, acute fatigue may occur in the presence of chronic fatigue, thus exacerbating illnesses consequent to chronic fatigue. Acute fatigue may be divided into grades as follows: grade 1—a little tired, work efficiency is not impaired; grade 2—very tired, work efficiency is impaired; and grade 3—extremely tired, the need to rest is imperative.

Hypothalamic-pituitary-adrenal axis

+ = enhances   − = inhibits
CRH = corticotropin-releasing hormone
5-HT = serotonin
NE = norepinephrine
IL-1 = interleukin-1 (a cytokine)

Adapted from Seymour Reichlin, M.D., "Neuroendocrine-Immune Interactions," *New England Journal of Medicine*, vol. 329, no. 17 (Oct. 21, 1993), pp. 1246–53

This author conducted an experiment to discover whether there are measurable physiological indicators of acute fatigue. The subjects were healthy hospital medical staff, doctors and nurses. Twice a day, at 9:30 AM and 5:30 PM, each subject ranked his or her state of fatigue according to the above grades. At these times researchers measured the resistance of tiny capillaries in the skin of the forearms of the study participants; also, blood was drawn and analyzed in order to get an eosinophil count (eosinophils are a type of specialized white blood cell). Capillary resistance (CR) rises and falls in harmony with the level of cortisol in the blood, so the CR measurement can be used as an index of cortisol level. An inverse relationship exists between blood cortisol levels and the number of circulating eosinophils.

In subjects who reported acute fatigue in the evening, CR was lower and the eosinophil count was higher than in those who claimed to be less tired or not tired. It should be emphasized that all the subjects were physically healthy and working; *i.e.,* not labeled as suffering from chronic fatigue. The results suggest that acute fatigue is probably linked to a lower output of cortisol at the end of the day—whether as a cause or as an effect—and that the symptom of fatigue is not merely psychological but has a demonstrable physical basis.

These findings were supported by research carried out in 1987 at the Salk Institute for Biological Studies, La Jolla, Calif., where investigators subjected rats to electric shocks four times a minute over a period of five hours. The stress induced in the animals produced an initial surge of ACTH and cortisol, but the levels of these hormones dropped significantly as stress continued. This decline, brought on by extreme stress, could be analogous to the smaller drop in cortisol levels seen in human subjects at the end of a moderately stressful day.

The consequences of chronic fatigue

Some years after his work on acute fatigue, this author studied hospital outpatients suffering from chronic fatigue. The purpose of the research was to determine which diseases, if any, were linked to chronic fatigue, to learn about the subjects' sleep habits, and to see whether the patients had actual muscle fatigue. The degree or intensity of fatigue, whether mental or physical or both, was graded on the basis of the subjects' capacity for work and social activity. Seventy-four patients with chronic fatigue were compared with an equal number of nonfatigued patients matched for age and sex. It was found that both groups spent an equal amount of time in bed, but those with persistent fatigue experienced a poorer quality of sleep, with periods of insomnia for which they compensated by taking daytime naps and getting extra sleep on weekends. Muscle strength was basically the same in both groups, but forearm muscles tired more quickly in those with chronic fatigue.

The most significant finding, however, was that rheumatic diseases—those characterized by pain and inflammation in muscles or joints—were fairly common in the chronically fatigued patients but absent in controls. There were seven cases of rheumatoid arthritis (RA) in the chronically fatigued group, nine cases of prolapsed ("slipped") disks in the neck or lumbar spine, and another nine cases that included fibromyalgia (a syndrome marked by persistent muscle pain and tenderness), frozen shoulder (a condition of severe pain and stiffness), and rarer rheumatic diseases. On average, the onset of fatigue had preceded these conditions by a period of 12 months, which strongly suggests that chronic fatigue was a major factor in their development, not just a symptom caused by them. The reason this finding is important is that RA and related diseases are autoimmune disorders, and research on chronic fatigue has uncovered tantalizing links between persistent, long-lasting tiredness and activation of autoimmune processes.

Immunity gone awry

Immunity is, in general, a protective device. Once an individual has been in contact with a specific infectious organism, the cells of the immune system will "remember" the offending organism and organize a defense to protect against any repetition of infection. Under certain circumstances, however, the immune response can become an enemy, producing antibodies that attack and destroy the body's own tissues (autoantibodies).

Interestingly, studies of people suffering from CFS show some evidence of immunologic dysfunction, and this has drawn the attention of some authorities away from the possible viral origins of CFS to the probable autoimmune consequences of the condition. One such expert is Stephen E. Straus, chief of the Laboratory of Clinical Investigation at the National Institute of Allergy and Infectious Diseases in Bethesda. Straus noted in 1992 that because cortisol is a potent suppressor of immune responses, reduced cortisol levels might allow the immune system to remain overactive. Overstimulation of immunity could, in turn, account for the higher-than-normal antibody levels seen in some CFS patients.

A thorough investigation of immune activation in CFS was conducted by Alan L. Landay in the department of immunology at Rush-Presbyterian-St. Luke's Medical Center, Chicago, and colleagues. They found that CFS patients had reduced levels of a particular kind of immune system cell, the suppressor T cell, the function of which is to prevent activation of antibody-producing B cells. Loss of these particular T cells could pave the way for production of harmful autoantibodies. The researchers concluded that im-

mune activation is indeed a feature of CFS in many cases. In another study, scientists at the University of Washington identified many autoimmune antibodies in CFS patients. Twenty-nine percent of the subjects had antithyroid antibodies, and 36% had anti-smooth-muscle antibodies. In a similar study conducted by this author, involving a small series of general practice patients, autoantibodies were found twice as often in chronically fatigued patients as in controls.

Cortisol and similar substances, when given by injection, often produce clinical improvement in patients suffering from RA, and this fact has prompted researchers to look for lower-than-normal blood cortisol levels in these patients. No clear-cut results were seen until a team of West German researchers reported their findings in 1990 in the *Journal of Rheumatology*. They had divided their patients into three groups based on the extent of disease activity—low, medium, and high. They found that even patients with low disease activity had consistently lower 24-hour cortisol levels than healthy controls. This research provides additional evidence that a diminished output of cortisol may permit activation of an autoimmune process. Moreover, clinicians have long noted a profound fatigue at the onset of RA, and the presence of specific autoantibodies, termed rheumatoid factors, in the blood of RA patients makes it an acknowledged autoimmune disorder. As long ago as 1936, the noted British rheumatologist Philip Ellman observed that RA was often preceded by stressful life events, which, in turn, are likely to lead to chronic fatigue.

Stress and exhaustion

Little has so far been said on the subject of stress in connection with CFS. When the disorder occurs in epidemic form, as was the case in an outbreak near Lake Tahoe, Nev., in the mid-1980s, viruses of one kind or another are almost certainly responsible. However, when CFS occurs sporadically, the cause is less obvious. Sometimes there is evidence of viral infection, while in other cases the precipitating factor appears to be a stressful event such as being in an automobile collision or experiencing the death of a loved one.

According to the classification devised by the renowned authority on stress Hans Selye, an individual's response to a stressful situation may be adequate, excessive, or inadequate. In the last case, the person struggles to cope but becomes exhausted. Scientists studying exhaustion in various groups of people—mountain climbers, airline pilots, and victims of post-traumatic stress disorder—have repeatedly demonstrated low blood cortisol levels. On the basis of this finding, it might be expected that symptoms of chronic fatigue, coupled with inadequate function of the HPA axis, would be seen in shift workers, airline crews, soldiers suffering from battle fatigue, and others coping

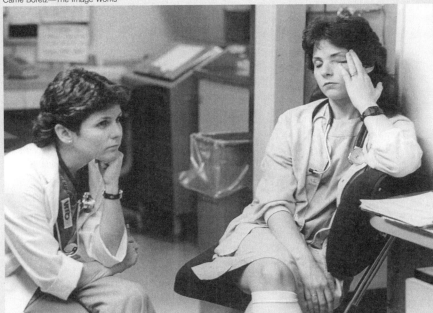

Hospital staff routinely work long hours, have rotating work schedules, and suffer from chronic sleep deprivation. Scientists who study fatigue are finding evidence that people subjected to this kind of stress have disturbances in functioning of the hypothalamic-pituitary-adrenal axis.

with overwhelming anxiety, sleep deprivation, and similar stresses. However, a great deal of further research will need to be done to confirm this supposition.

New perspective on stress and disease

The interconnectedness of the brain, the seat of mental and emotional activity; the endocrine system; and the immune system is now widely accepted, and a new science—psychoneuroimmunology—has emerged that focuses exclusively on this complex interrelationship. Through its control of the ANS, the releasing hormones of the hypothalamus, and the various pituitary hormones, the brain modulates the immune system. In turn, the immune system, when activated by bacteria, viruses, allergens, or other agents, produces a group of chemical messengers called cytokines, some of which exert a powerful effect on the brain. Cytokines have the capacity to influence behavior, sleep, wakefulness, appetite, and other cerebral activity. In particular, they stimulate the production of CRH, which activates the pituitary-adrenal axis to produce cortisol. The intimate connections between the brain, the endocrine system, and the immune system undoubtedly permit physical and mental stress to have a profound influence on autoimmune processes. If the response of the HPA axis to stress is poor, as apparently is the case in CFS, the immune system may escape from control and allow the production of harmful autoantibodies.

If further research confirms that persistent exhaustion is indeed a precursor of autoimmune disease, then preventive steps could be taken. Susceptible individuals might be identified, and safe means of intervening in the autoimmune process could be devised. Strategies also could be developed for prevention. If an individual's family history suggests a predisposition to autoimmune disease, that person might take greater care to avoid becoming chronically fatigued. Should an autoimmune ailment develop, treatment could include both specific, curative measures and general measures to combat fatigue.

An intriguing treatment possibility is suggested by experimental use of cAMP, the second messenger in the energy chain, in such conditions as psoriasis and RA. In one Chinese study psoriasis patients were given cAMP and a similar compound, either intramuscularly or intravenously; 80% showed some degree of improvement. In 1988 Russian researchers reported finding a deficiency of cAMP in patients with RA. They also found that papaverine, a substance that inhibits phosphodiesterase (the enzyme that destroys cAMP) and therefore increases the availability of cAMP, possessed marked antiarthritic properties in rats with experimentally induced arthritis. The investigators suggested that cAMP insufficiency might play a part in the causation of RA. Papaverine, which has antispasmodic properties, is probably not the answer to treating RA in human patients, but these findings point to the possibility of using an alternate method to increase blood levels of cAMP.

As the nature of fatigue continues to unfold, its role in a large area of human illness becomes more apparent, and the prospects for intervention become ever more real. The future may hold not only relief from chronic states of low energy and tiredness but also effective treatments for a variety of diseases.

353

Pediatrics

A number of recent developments have had a significant impact on the health and health care of infants, children, and adolescents. For example, the prophylactic use of anti-inflammatory agents such as cromolyn sodium and corticosteroids has markedly reduced the number of emergency room visits and hospitalizations of children with asthma, the most common chronic pediatric illness. Newer forms of medical imaging, such as ultrasonography, computed tomography, and magnetic resonance imaging, are increasingly being applied to the diagnosis of children's ailments. Rapid advances are also being made in organ transplantation for children. Improved procedures for fetal surgery allow some anatomic defects to be corrected before birth. The outlook for children with cancer continues to improve; for example, the cure rate for most types of Wilms' tumor, a malignancy of the kidneys, is now 90%, and that for acute lymphocytic leukemia is around 75%. Only 35 years ago 95% of these childhood cancers were fatal.

The 1990s almost certainly will be remembered as the decade in which molecular biology made the transition from the laboratory to the bedside. More than 200 genetic conditions, including such disorders as Duchenne muscular dystrophy, cystic fibrosis, and fragile X syndrome (a major cause of mental retardation), can now be diagnosed by means of recombinant DNA technology. In the next several years, breakthroughs in gene therapies for some childhood disorders can be expected.

This report looks specifically at three areas in which the health and well-being of children are being (or could be) improved. These include the development of new vaccines, the use of surfactant to treat respiratory distress syndrome in newborns, and the wider adoption of an effective but still underused injury-prevention device—the bicycle helmet.

Defeat of a disease

In sharp contrast to the acclaim that accompanied the development of vaccines against poliomyelitis, a recent vaccine triumph has gone largely unheralded by both health care professionals and the general public. With the advent of a vaccine that provides immunity against *Haemophilus influenzae* type B (Hib), a serious infectious illness in children has virtually disappeared. Not long ago the *H. influenzae* organism was the leading cause of invasive bacterial disease in children under age five.

There are two basic types of *H. influenzae* bacteria, those with and those without a polysaccharide capsule around the cell wall. The unencapsulated bacteria, which regularly colonize the respiratory tracts of children, ordinarily are not dangerous. Depending on a child's age and the season of the year, 60–90% of children may carry the organism. When a youngster has a cold, however, and the tiny eustachian tube connecting the middle ear and nose becomes blocked, unencapsulated *H. influenzae* organisms may produce a middle ear infection. Encapsulated organisms, on the other hand, present a much more serious health threat. In children less than five years of age, the polysaccharide capsule of the encapsulated *H. influenzae* allows the bacterium to elude the immature immune defenses. In these young children—and especially in those under two years of age—*H. influenzae* can cause pneumonia, meningitis (inflammation of the membranes that surround the brain), septic arthritis (toxic inflammation of the joints), cellulitis (inflammation of connective tissue), and epiglottitis (a frightening condition in which the airway becomes occluded).

Before the Hib vaccine became available, an estimated one in 200 youngsters who were infected with Hib developed invasive disease. Nearly all of these cases occurred in children under 5 years of age, and two-thirds occurred in those less than 15 months of age. The death rate for meningitis, the most common of these infections, was between 3% and 6%. From 20% to 30% of children who developed meningitis suffered permanent neurological effects such as deafness and brain damage. Research carried out as early as 1933 showed that the reason for this unique age-dependent susceptibility was that the blood of young children lacked or had insufficient amounts of a bactericidal (bacteria-killing) factor.

The first vaccines against Hib were developed in the 1970s. They consisted of purified polysaccharide (polyribosyl-ribitol phosphate; PRP) derived from the capsule of the encapsulated Hib organism. Testing in Finland showed that the vaccine was effective in children over 18 months of age but not in younger children. The product was licensed by the U.S. Food and Drug Administration (FDA) in April 1985 and is recommended for administration to children between 18 and 24 months old. Since most serious Hib infections occurred in babies too young to receive the PRP vaccine, another product was developed that linked, or conjugated, the PRP polysaccharide with a protein capable of producing an immune response in young infants. Several conjugate vaccines were licensed in late 1987, initially for use in 18-month-olds. The recommended age for Hib vaccination was reduced to 15 months in April 1990 and then lowered again shortly thereafter to 2 months. Depending on the particular product used, either three or four doses of Hib vaccine are recommended. At the end of 1993, the U.S. Centers for Disease Control and Prevention (CDC) estimated that approximately 60% of U.S. children had received three doses of the vaccine.

The effect has been dramatic. According to the CDC, the age-specific incidence of Hib disease among children under five years of age decreased from 37

per 100,000 in 1989 to less than one per 100,000 in 1992. The National Bacterial Meningitis Reporting System's statistics reflect an equally impressive decline in meningitis due to Hib—an 82% drop in cases between 1985 and 1991. At one major U.S. children's hospital in 1992, samples of cerebrospinal fluid from children with meningitis revealed that the prevalence of infection due to *Streptococcus pneumoniae* and *Neisseria meningitidis,* the other two most common causes of bacterial meningitis in children, had remained stable, but no cases were attributed to *H. influenzae.*

Vaccines: progress and problems

Fewer than 200 cases of measles were reported in the United States in 1993, an all-time low. However, unlike the smallpox virus, which has been eradicated from the globe, the measles virus persists, and outbreaks can be expected in communities with low immunization rates. A long-awaited varicella (chicken pox) vaccine was expected to be approved by the FDA in 1994. Unlike the clear health benefits of immunization for Hib, or even measles, the advantages of the varicella vaccine are apt to be more economic than medical. Varicella rarely causes severe illness in healthy children, but it does require that they stay home from school or day care, often making it necessary for parents to miss work.

The availability of a new vaccine—even one that is much-needed and highly effective—can present a different kind of problem, however. Each new vaccine product means an additional two or three injections for every child. Current recommendations in the U.S.,

for example, call for 12 injections of four different vaccines to be given by age two. Given that 30% of U.S. children are not fully immunized by age two, anything that would simplify the schedule of recommended immunizations would be a step in the right direction. Vaccine preparations that can be combined, as well as less painful methods of administration, are urgently needed.

Some of the problems surrounding the immunization situation in the U.S. stem from the lack of a coherent policy. Although federally funded vaccines are available for some U.S. children, the health care system does not ensure that vaccines are available to all. Further, when families see a number of different health care providers, it is difficult to keep children on schedule with the many inoculations they need in early life; a computerized system that would track childhood immunization seems long overdue.

Saving the lives of newborns

In developed countries the risk of dying before reaching adulthood—*i.e.,* during infancy, childhood, and adolescence—is greatest during the first few days after birth, the neonatal, or newborn, period. Deaths during this period are most apt to be associated with prematurity, and the major cause of death is respiratory distress syndrome (RDS), or hyaline membrane disease. Among U.S. infants born weighing less than 2,500 g (5.5 lb), the incidence of RDS is approximately 56 per 1,000, whereas the incidence in full-term infants weighing more than 2,500 g is only 2 per 1,000. Until very recently half of all infants with RDS died. The survival rate is now over 90%, however, thanks in large measure to the development of surfactant, a detergent-like substance that lowers the surface tension of the lining of the lung.

The oxygen needs of fetuses are met by the umbilical blood supply, which mediates exchanges between the fetal and maternal blood circulation. At the moment of birth, infants depend on their previously fluid-filled lungs to fill immediately with air so that oxygenation of the blood can take place in tiny sacs (alveoli) in the lungs. The change from liquid-filled to air-filled alveoli requires an agent for reducing surface tension, without which the surfaces of the alveoli would stick together. In fact, it is the function of type II pneumocytes, cells in the lining of the lungs, to synthesize and secrete just such a substance, called surfactant. Like other specialized body cells, however, type II pneumocytes are not fully functional if an infant is born too early. As a consequence, the lungs of premature babies synthesize an insufficient amount of surfactant and tend to remain in their collapsed state following birth. One way to appreciate the role of surfactant in lowering surface tension is to blow into a container of plain water; at best one or two bubbles appear and quickly burst. If detergent is added to the water, however, the surface tension is reduced, and blowing into the water produces a multitude of bubbles.

In addition to preventing the alveoli from inflating properly, the high surface tension of the premature infant's lungs causes fluid and protein to leak into the alveoli and form a protein-containing film, or hyaline membrane. Untreated, the condition progresses in severity over the first two to three days of life. In infants who survive, the type II pneumocytes eventually multiply and produce enough surfactant to allow the lungs to expand and oxygenate the blood.

The existence of a natural detergent-like substance that lowers surface tension in the lungs has been known for nearly 40 years. It was also clear to scientists that making up for a deficiency of surfactant would improve the preterm infant's chances of survival. But the road from concept to practical application was a long and tortuous one. As with most biomedical advances, many years were devoted to basic research before animal studies could be carried out; then small pilot studies in humans needed to be done, and finally came acceptance of the new treatment as a standard in the care of newborns. In 1980 a group of Japanese investigators led by T. Fujiwara reported the first successful treatment of hyaline membrane disease with an artificial surfactant. They used a lipid substance, containing about 1% protein, extracted from the lungs of cows. It was enriched with dipalmitoylphosphatidylcholine (DPPC) and phosphatidylglycerol. Subsequent clinical trials of surfactant confirmed and amplified the initial observations of the Japanese scientists.

Two types of surfactants are currently in use: synthetic and natural. The synthetic products are composed principally of DPPC along with agents added to enhance adsorption (adhesion) of the surfactant to the alveolar surfaces. The natural surfactants are obtained from the lungs of animals, usually calves. The substance is administered directly into the lungs through an endotracheal tube. Surfactant is used in two ways. In one approach a single dose is administered prophylactically to premature infants before signs of respiratory distress develop. The other approach, called "rescue" therapy, is to administer surfactant only when and if symptoms develop.

Treatment of premature infants with surfactant requires considerable expertise and should be undertaken only by specialists in neonatology. Surfactant therapy is not without complications, including the potential to cause bleeding into the lungs; this is the reason some physicians prefer not to initiate treatment until symptoms are apparent.

Various studies have shown that the use of surfactant reduces deaths from RDS by between 30% and 70%. Considerably more important to infant survival than any medical therapy, however, is prevention of premature births in the first place. Prematurity is linked to poverty and also to the growing incidence of out-of-

wedlock pregnancy. In the U.S., for example, one-fifth of all white infants and two-thirds of black infants are now born to single mothers, many of whom are still in their teens. Neonatal intensive care units are sure to remain full until these socioeconomic factors have been adequately addressed.

Bicycle helmets: not just for "nerds"

The well-being and survival of children are affected more by the environment in which they live and by their behavior than by the health care they receive. Injuries remain a plague of the young, killing more Americans aged 1–34 than all diseases combined. Injuries cause almost half of the deaths of U.S. children between the ages of one and 14 and nearly four-fifths of the deaths of persons aged 15–24.

Head trauma is generally the most serious form of injury. While only 12% (approximately three million) of trauma admissions to U.S. hospitals per year involve head injuries, they constitute 75% of all trauma fatalities. More disturbing is the fact that approximately 75,000 head-injury victims per year end up with permanent disabilities. The greatest challenge in trauma prevention, therefore, is reducing the number and severity of head injuries.

One such strategy is the wearing of protective helmets in activities—such as bicycling—where the likelihood of striking a hard surface or object is high. In the U.S. alone, bicycling injuries among children

That bicycle helmets reduce young cyclists' risks of head injury is well accepted by public health authorities. Now kids themselves are coming to recognize that they can ride safely and still be "cool."

and adolescents account for more than 400,000 emergency department visits and from 500 to 600 deaths per year. The majority of children admitted to hospitals with traumatic coma have either been struck by an automobile (40%) or been passengers in an automobile involved in a collision (24%); however, approximately 10% of pediatric traumatic coma victims have been riding bicycles.

The case for children's wearing protective helmets while riding bicycles is compelling. One study of injuries among bicycle riders experiencing a crash showed that safety helmets reduce the risk of head injury by 85%. Evidence notwithstanding, until very recently the idea of wearing bicycle helmets had not caught on with parents or with children. Most parents were unaware of the magnitude of bicycle-related head trauma, and many did not realize the degree of protection afforded by helmets. In addition, helmets were expensive, ranging between $40 and $60, approximately two-thirds the cost of a bicycle. For children an important factor was social; wearing helmets was not considered a "cool" thing to do. Because so few children wore them, those who did were often regarded by their peers as "nerds" or "sissies."

In the summer of 1986 in the Seattle, Wash., area, a campaign was launched to induce as many schoolchildren as possible to wear bicycle helmets. Parental awareness was raised through educational materials distributed by physicians and hospitals. Parents and children alike were targeted by public service ads and a profusion of stories in the print and broadcast media about the young victims of cycling injuries. The real-life messages from injured children themselves and their parents seemed to carry more weight than statistics and warnings. Seattle stores cooperated by lowering the price of helmets, and helmet manufacturers and bicycle shops offered discount coupons for purchasing helmets. A precedent was set when a large retail chain offered helmets for $19.95. The "nerd factor" was combated by the involvement of prominent sports figures and the rewarding of helmet wearers with free tickets to baseball games and coupons for french fries at fast-food chains.

The results of the campaign were impressive. Between 1986 and 1994, the percentage of schoolchildren in Seattle wearing helmets while riding bicycles increased from 3% to 59%. During the same period, bicycle-related head injuries in 5–14-year-olds who were members of a large Seattle-area health maintenance organization decreased by 66%. Similar campaigns have been carried out in other communities, and a steadily increasing number of mandatory local laws have accelerated the trend to universal bicycle helmet usage.

Before Aug. 18, 1967, when the career of Boston Red Sox star player Tony Conigliaro was effectively ended when he was hit in the head by a pitched ball, helmets were rarely worn by batters in professional baseball. Now their universal use is unquestioned, and the same can be predicted for bicycle helmets.

A long way to go

While exciting medical developments and treatment advances such as those discussed above continue, the fact remains that all too many children in the world do not enjoy good health or health care. Despite the fact that the United States is one of the world's wealthiest countries, over a fifth of its children now live in poverty. As mentioned previously, teen pregnancy and premature birth are serious problems. Homelessness, academic underachievement, and child abuse are rampant. The ready availability of firearms contributes to the rising rates of suicide and homicide among children and adolescents. Solving such difficult problems will require extraordinary energy and commitment not only on the part of pediatricians and parents but on the part of society at large.

—Abraham B. Bergman, M.D.

Pharmaceuticals

If the past year in the field of pharmaceuticals were to be characterized, it would undoubtedly be called the "year of the brain." During 1993 alone more new products for the treatment of neurological disorders reached the market than in any other year in the past 13. The Food and Drug Administration (FDA)—the federal agency that authorizes the marketing of new pharmaceuticals in the U.S.—approved six new agents for the treatment of neurological conditions ranging from multiple sclerosis (MS) and epilepsy to Alzheimer's disease and schizophrenia.

Overall, the FDA approved a total of 25 new drug compounds in 1993 and 11 in the first eight months of 1994. (A table listing these new drugs appears on pages 360–361.) The agency also cleared five significant biological products, or biologics, a category that includes serums, toxins, allergenic products, blood and blood components, vaccines, and the like. These included treatments for MS and cystic fibrosis (CF) and two new vaccines. The average review time of 26.5 months for the products approved in 1993 was the lowest in at least 14 years. Of the biologics, the approval times of the new therapies for MS and CF stand out; they were approved within 12 months of submission of their marketing applications.

Review times are expected to continue to decrease as the FDA proceeds with the revamping of its drug-approval process under the User Fee Act, passed by Congress in 1992. The act, which requires drug companies to pay scheduled fees to the agency, mandates specific time limits for review of new pharmaceutical products: 6 months for so-called priority approvals and 12 months for products in the standard approvals category. Priority drugs are those for life-threatening or serious illnesses for which no adequate alternatives exist; standard drugs are those that offer some therapeutic gains over products already marketed and those with little or no advantage over existing products.

Three of the products approved in recent months represent significant medical breakthroughs as the first treatments for disorders that previously had no approved therapies: interferon beta-1B (Betaseron) for ambulatory MS patients, tacrine (Cognex) for mild to moderate dementia due to Alzheimer's disease, and dornase alfa, or DNase (Pulmozyme), for CF. Although these therapies are not cures, they may provide relief from the incapacitating symptoms of these serious disorders.

MS breakthrough

In the summer of 1993, the FDA approved interferon beta-1B, a recombinant form of the naturally occurring immune system modulator beta interferon, for the relapsing-remitting form of MS, which affects about 30–40% of the approximately 350,000 MS patients in the U.S. MS is a progressive autoimmune disease of the nervous system; its hallmark is patchy destruction of the myelin sheath that insulates nerve fibers in the brain and spinal cord, resulting in disruption of nerve signal transmission. Relapsing-remitting MS is characterized by recurrent attacks of neurological dysfunction—vision problems, lack of motor coordination, tremors—followed by partial or complete recovery. The new treatment has not been tested or approved for the chronic, progressive form of MS, which can lead to complete paralysis.

In clinical studies interferon beta-1B given every other day over a two-year period was found to reduce the frequency of annual exacerbations of MS by 31%. Twenty-five percent of patients in one trial were completely free of exacerbations at the end of two years, compared with 16% of those who took a placebo. Patients receiving the drug also had fewer hospitalizations for exacerbations. In addition, lesions (areas of destroyed myelin), which were measured by magnetic resonance imaging, had been reduced 1% by drug therapy at the end of two years; by comparison, lesions increased by 17% in patients who took a placebo. Those who continued on interferon beta-1B for a third year in the studies showed some reduction in exacerbations, but the results were not as conclusive as those for the first two years.

The drug is self-injected by MS patients at home, much as people with diabetes administer their own insulin. Potential side effects include pain or swelling at the injection site, flulike symptoms (fever, chills, muscle pain), and menstrual disorders. Laboratory tests may reveal a low white blood cell count and increased liver enzyme levels (a sign of toxicity).

Pregnant women must be cautioned about the drug's potential for inducing abortion. Because interferon beta-1B sometimes causes depression and suicidal thoughts, patients with signs of depression must be monitored closely.

Owing to the limited availability of the drug, not all MS patients who stand to benefit from interferon beta-1B will be able to receive it immediately. Initially, the drug was being distributed to patients through a novel lottery system set up by the marketer, Berlex Laboratories Inc. Between September 1993 and the spring of 1994, over 100,000 patients were certified by their doctors as eligible and were assigned a lottery number. By April 1994, 50,000 MS patients were receiving the drug.

Under the Berlex "Equal Access Program," once a patient's number comes up, he or she is given an identification/credit card to present at a participating pharmacy. After receiving a supply of the drug, patients have 55 days to obtain insurance reimbursement and pay the pharmacy; a 12% finance charge is assessed after the 55-day period. (A year's supply of the drug costs close to $10,000.) The manufacturer, Chiron Corp., expects to be making enough interferon beta-1B by the end of 1995 to treat 100,000 MS patients. This unique system is one example of the strategies now being employed by biotech and pharmaceutical firms to ensure equitable distribution of high-priced, high-tech therapies of which supplies are limited.

Alzheimer's disease: help for some

Tacrine (Cognex) was approved by the FDA in September 1993 for treating symptoms of Alzheimer's disease, a degenerative brain disorder estimated to affect four million people in the U.S. alone, causing 100,000 deaths annually and resulting in health care costs of $70 billion–$90 billion. Alzheimer's disease is characterized by destruction of the cholinergic neurons—the nerve cells that make acetylcholine, a neurotransmitter that carries nerve impulses in the brain. Tacrine apparently improves cognitive function by slowing the degradation of acetylcholine and thus increasing the available amount of the neurotransmitter. The drug may become less effective as the disease progresses and the number of functioning cholinergic neurons declines.

In clinical trials tacrine showed a small but clinically meaningful benefit for some patients. The fact that patients showed a wide range of responses to the drug was attributed to several factors, including the variability of tests used to measure cognitive and behavioral functions. A number of patients were unable to tolerate the therapy and withdrew from the trials (see below). Twenty percent of those who completed clinical trials showed a modest improvement on assessment scales that measure such abilities as memorizing words and drawing pictures. In a study of 653 patients who took up to 160 mg of tacrine per day (a dosage shown by an earlier trial to be beneficial) for 30 weeks, 23–42% were rated as improved on the basis of interview assessments, compared with 17–18% of placebo-treated patients. The product information provided for physicians notes that tacrine does not stop the dementing process, but it can improve some patients' abilities to perform everyday activities.

About 70% of those enrolled in the tacrine trials dropped out, mostly because they showed signs of liver damage. Clinical data suggest that more than 80% of these patients can resume tacrine therapy without further problems. A March 1994 survey indicated that 50,000 people were taking the drug. Because of tacrine's potential to cause liver damage, patients must undergo weekly blood monitoring of liver enzyme levels for at least the first 18 weeks of therapy. After that, monitoring needs to be done only once every three months. Weekly monitoring should be resumed for at least six weeks each time the dosage is increased.

Improved anticonvulsants

Ending a 15-year period in which no new antiepileptic drugs were marketed in the U.S., the FDA approved two such agents, felbamate (Felbatol) and gabapentin (Neurontin), in 1993. Because people with epilepsy often become resistant to or intolerant of their therapies, there is always a need for new anticonvulsant drugs. In the U.S. alone the number of those with refractory epilepsy is estimated to be about 625,000 to 750,000.

Felbamate was approved for use alone or in combination with other antiepileptic drugs in adults with epilepsy and as adjunctive therapy (i.e., in combination with other drugs) for seizures associated with Lennox-Gastaut syndrome (a rare but severe form of epilepsy) in children. The promise of this new treatment took an unexpected turn in the summer of 1994, however, when the FDA and Carter-Wallace, the company that markets felbamate, received 10 reports of the blood disorder aplastic anemia in persons taking the drug. Two of the 10 patients died. Carter-Wallace immediately sent letters to 240,000 physicians, warning them to discontinue use of felbamate unless the drug was absolutely necessary to control seizures. While this announcement of a serious side effect caused great concern, many physicians and epilepsy patients decided to continue felbamate therapy with close monitoring. After further evaluation, the FDA could decide to remove the drug from the market altogether or strictly limit its use.

Gabapentin, the second new epilepsy drug, has the major advantage over existing agents of not affecting the metabolism of commonly coadministered antiepileptic drugs. It was approved for use as adjunctive therapy in the treatment of partial seizures in adults with epilepsy.

Drugs for psychiatric conditions

New drugs have become available for the treatment of depression and schizophrenia. Venlafaxine (Effexor), a drug that blocks the reuptake of two neurotransmitters, serotonin and norepinephrine, is considered the first of a new class of antidepressants. Unlike the older classes of these drugs—the tricyclics and the monoamine oxidase inhibitors—venlafaxine apparently does not carry the risk of cardiac complications such as heart attack, palpitations (extremely rapid heart rate), abnormal heartbeat, and hypertensive crises. The drug appears to have a side-effect profile similar to that of the newer antidepressants fluoxetine (Prozac), sertraline (Zoloft), and paroxetine (Paxil), all of which selectively inhibit the reuptake of serotonin. However, unlike these other agents, venlafaxine has been associated with sustained increases in blood pressure. It is recommended that those taking the drug undergo regular blood pressure monitoring and that dose reduction or discontinuation of the medication be considered if blood pressure is affected.

December 1993 saw the approval of risperidone (Risperdal), a drug that blocks dopamine and serotonin receptors in the brain, for the treatment of schizophrenia. Previously, the most significant advance in schizophrenia treatment had been clozapine (Clozaril), introduced in 1989. While it produces dramatic improvements in some patients, clozapine has a major drawback, a rare but life-threatening side effect called agranulocytosis (a serious decrease in white blood cells, which impairs the patient's ability to fight infections). While risperidone does not appear to have this adverse effect, in approving the drug the FDA cautioned that until long-term data can be collected, it should not be portrayed as being safer than other antipsychotic treatments. Moreover, risperidone may cause muscle spasms and involuntary movements of the head and limbs, troublesome side effects also reported with many older antipsychotic agents and a major reason why many patients simply stop taking their medication. In the clinical trials of risperidone, however, the noncompliance rate was slightly lower than is common with other antipsychotics.

A "first" for CF

CF is the most common fatal genetic disease of Caucasians. In the U.S. alone some 30,000 children and young adults are affected. The disorder is characterized by the production of viscous mucous secretions in the lungs and gastrointestinal tract. People with CF generally have difficulty breathing and suffer from repeated bouts of respiratory infection throughout their lives. The resulting lung damage usually leads to death at an early age (the median age of survival is 28).

Until recently, the main treatments for CF were intravenous antibiotics for the associated infections and

(continued on page 362)

Drug compounds approved by the FDA in 1993 and early 1994 *

generic name (brand name)	manufacturer	use	major side effects
priority approvals			
aprotinin (Trasylol)	Miles	reduction of blood loss during coronary artery bypass surgery	serious allergic reaction, kidney dysfunction, heart attack, closure of leg vein grafts
cladribine (Leustatin)	RW Johnson	hairy cell leukemia	decrease in blood neutrophil, red blood cell, and platelet counts, fever, infection, fatigue, nausea, rash, headache, injection-site reactions
cysteamine (Cystagon)	Mylan	nephropathic cystinosis (hereditary metabolic disorder)	nausea, vomiting, loss of appetite, sleepiness, rash
enoxaparin (Lovenox)	Rhone-Poulenc Rorer	prevention of deep vein thrombosis after hip replacement	hemorrhage, decrease in blood platelets, reduction of red cell hemoglobin, fever, swelling, nausea, local irritation, pain
felbamate (Felbatol)	Carter-Wallace	antiepileptic`	loss of appetite, vomiting, inability to sleep, nausea, headache, dizziness, sleepiness; several reports of aplastic anemia (including two deaths)
gabapentin (Neurontin)	Warner-Lambert	antiepileptic	fatigue, sleepiness, dizziness, loss of muscular coordination, involuntary rapid eyeball movement, tremor
imiglucerase (Cerezyme)	Genzyme	long-term enzyme replacement in Type 1 Gaucher disease	headache, nausea, abdominal discomfort, dizziness, rash
indium In-111 pentetreotide (OctreoScan)	Mallinckrodt	adjunct for diagnostic imaging of neuro-endocrine tumors	dizziness, fever, facial redness, headache, low blood pressure, changes in liver enzymes, joint pain, nausea, sweating, weakness
iobenguane sulfate (I 131 MIBG)	CIS-US	adjunct for diagnostic imaging of pheochro-mocytomas and neuroblastomas	transient marked high blood pressure, fever, chills, low blood pressure
levocabastine (Livostin)	Iolab	seasonal allergic conjunctivitis	mild occular stinging and burning, headache
levomethadyl acetate (ORLAAM)	BioDevelopment Corp.	opiate dependence	weakness, bodily discomfort, slow heart rate, abdominal pain, constipation, joint pain, inability to sleep, nervousness
perflubron (Imagent GI)	Alliance	enhancement of MRI (bowel)	oily and/or bad taste, nausea and/or vomiting, diarrhea, abdominal fullness, excessive gas, abdominal pain, difficulty swallowing
rimantidine (Flumadine)	Forest Labs	influenza A	nausea, vomiting, loss of appetite, dry mouth, abdominal pain, inability to sleep, dizziness, headache, nervousness, weakness
risperidone (Risperdal)	Janssen	schizophrenia	inability to sleep, anxiety, sleepiness, involuntary movement, headache, dizziness, excessively rapid heart rate, nasal inflammation, constipation, diarrhea, nausea, weight gain, sexual dysfunction
salmeterol xinafoate (Serevent)	Glaxo	asthma	respiratory infection, nasal and pharyngeal inflammation, excessively rapid heart rate, palpitations, hives, rash, bronchospasm, headache, tremor, nervousness
stavudine (Zerit)	Bristol-Meyers Squibb	HIV infection	functional disturbance in peripheral nervous system, elevated liver enzymes
strontium Sr-89 (Metastron)	Medi-Physics	pain relief in bone cancer	bone pain (rare); one case of fatal blood poisoning following decrease in white blood cell count

*through August 15, 1994

tacrine (Cognex)	Warner-Lambert	dementia due to Alzheimer's disease	elevated liver enzymes, nausea and/or vomiting, diarrhea, indigestion, muscle pain, loss of appetite, loss of muscular coordination
tacrolimus (Prograf)	Fujisawa USA	prevention of organ rejection in liver transplantation	tremor, headache, diarrhea, high blood pressure, nausea, kidney dysfunction, high potassium level, low magnesium level, excess uric acid, high blood sugar
trimetrexate glucuronate (Neutrexin)	U.S. Bioscience	*Pneumocystis carinii* pneumonia	blood, liver, kidney, and gastrointestinal toxicities

standard approvals

acrivastine/pseudo-ephedrine (Semprex-D)	Burroughs Wellcome	seasonal allergic rhinitis	sleepiness, inability to sleep, nervousness, headache, dry mouth
budesonide (Rhinocort)	Astra USA	allergic and nonallergic rhinitis	nasal irritation, pharyngeal inflammation, increased cough, nosebleed, dry mouth, indigestion
calcipotriene (Dovonex)	Bristol-Myers Squibb	psoriasis	burning, itching, skin irritation, skin redness, dry skin
cisapride (Propulsid)	Janssen	nocturnal heartburn due to gastroesopha-geal reflux	headache, diarrhea, abdominal pain, constipation, nausea
famciclovir (Famvir)	SmithKline Beecham	acute herpes zoster (shingles)	headache, nausea, fatigue, diarrhea
fenofibrate (Lipidil)	Fournier	high cholesterol	infections, pain, rash, weakness and/or fatigue, headache, indigestion, flulike symptoms
fluvastatin (Lescol)	Sandoz	high cholesterol	upper respiratory infection, headache, indigestion, diarrhea, back pain
gadodiamide (Omniscan)	Sterling	enhancement of MRI (central nervous system lesions)	nausea, headache, dizziness
granisetron (Kytril)	SmithKline Beecham	prevention of nausea and vomiting associated with cancer therapy	headache, weakness, sleepiness, diarrhea, constipation, fever, high blood pressure
lodoxamide tromethamine (Alomide)	Alcon Labs	eye disorders (*e.g.,* vernal keratitis)	transient ocular burning, stinging, or discomfort, ocular itching, blurred vision, dry eye, tearing and/or discharge
loratadine (Claritin)	Schering	seasonal allergic rhinitis	headache, sleepiness, fatigue, dry mouth
perindopril erbumine (Aceon)	RW Johnson	hypertension	cough, dizziness, headache, weakness, upper respiratory infection, nasal inflammation, lower extremity pain, swelling
piperacillin/tazobactam (Zosyn)	Lederle	moderate to severe piperacillin-resistant infections	diarrhea, headache, constipation, nausea, inability to sleep, rash, vomiting
rocuronium bromide (Zemuron)	Organon	adjunct to general anesthesia	prolonged neuromuscular block, irregular heart-beats, abnormal EKG, excessively rapid heart rate, nausea, vomiting, asthma, hiccup, rash
torsemide (Demadex)	Boehringer Mannheim	hypertension; edema (swelling) associated with congestive heart failure or kidney or liver disease	headache, excessive urination, dizziness, nasal inflammation, weakness, diarrhea
venlafaxine (Effexor)	Wyeth-Ayerst	depression	weakness, sweating, loss of appetite, vomiting, dizziness, anxiety, abnormal ejaculation, male impotence

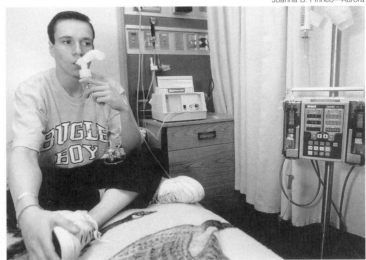

The first drug specifically for the symptoms of cystic fibrosis became available in the U.S. in December 1993. Dornase alfa (Pulmozyme), a recombinant form of a naturally occurring enzyme, is inhaled into the lungs, where it cuts through the thick mucous secretions that obstruct patients' airways. Those who used the new drug in clinical trials reported significant improvements in such symptoms as coughing and shortness of breath.

(continued from page 359)

so-called percussion therapy—pounding on the chest and back to relieve mucous congestion in the narrow pulmonary airways. In December 1993, however, the FDA approved a new biological product, dornase alfa (Pulmozyme), as the first treatment specifically for CF symptoms. Dornase alfa is a recombinant form of deoxyribonuclease, a naturally occurring enzyme that is capable of cutting through the mucus that accumulates in the lungs of people with CF. Patients treat themselves at home, using an inhaler to administer the medication. While this new therapy does not reverse the progression of the disease, it provides some improvement in pulmonary function.

In clinical trials it was found that dornase alfa decreased the risk of respiratory infections by close to 30%. Daily treatment for 24 weeks also increased patients' lung capacity by about 5%. Those receiving the drug reported having more energy and experiencing less breathlessness and fewer episodes of coughing; they also spent fewer days in the hospital than did patients in a control group. Long-term studies are under way to see if the improvement in pulmonary function persists over time. Reported side effects included voice alteration, sore throat, laryngitis, rash, chest pain, and conjunctivitis (inflammation of the mucous membranes of the eye).

A product of biotechnology, dornase alfa took approximately five years from scientific conception to market, half the time it usually takes for a drug to become commercially available. The cost of a year's supply is around $10,000. The manufacturer, Genentech Inc., has a program to provide financial assistance to those who are not able to pay for the drug. Dornase alfa is also being studied for the treatment of chronic bronchitis, a much more common and widespread condition than CF.

Old drugs, new uses

Several pharmaceutical products already on the market were approved for additional uses during the past year. The antihypertensive agent terazosin (Hytrin) was approved as the second drug specifically for the relief of urinary symptoms associated with benign enlargement (hypertrophy) of the prostate gland. The first was finasteride (Proscar), approved in 1992. Two members of the class of antihypertensives called angiotensin-converting enzyme (ACE) inhibitors received approval for use as adjunctive therapy in the management of congestive heart failure: quinapril (Accupril) and lisinopril (Prinivil; Zestril). Another already available ACE inhibitor, captopril (Capoten), was approved for the treatment of dysfunction of the heart's left ventricle following a heart attack as well as for prevention of kidney damage (nephropathy) as a complication of diabetes. The ACE inhibitor enalapril (Vasotec) was approved for use in preventing congestive heart failure in asymptomatic patients who have weakening of the left ventricle.

In the spring of 1994, the cancer drug paclitaxel (Taxol) was approved for treatment of breast cancer patients who fail to respond to first-line chemotherapy or who relapse after chemotherapy. Paclitaxel was originally approved at the end of 1992 for the treatment of patients with ovarian cancer who fail to respond to platinum-based chemotherapy agents.

New over-the-counter pain remedy

At the beginning of 1994, a version of naproxen (Naprosyn; Anaprox), a prescription nonsteroidal antiinflammatory drug widely used for treating arthritis and other types of inflammation, was approved for over-the-counter (OTC) use. Marketed under the name Aleve, the new OTC product has been approved for temporary relief of minor aches and pains, including headache, toothache, and menstrual cramps, and for reducing fever. The recommended daily dose is 600 mg. Higher-strength versions of the drug continue to be available by prescription only.

A catastrophic trial

Pharmaceutical development does not always proceed without problems. It is estimated that only 20% of drugs being developed clinically by pharmaceutical companies ever reach the consumer. Often, research is halted in early stages when it becomes clear that the compound lacks efficacy or produces undesirable side effects. Sometimes the risks of a drug become evident only when it moves from pilot studies to more advanced clinical testing. Such a situation occurred in the summer of 1993 with FIAU, or fialuridine, a drug that showed great promise for the treatment of chronic hepatitis B virus infection.

Pilot studies had shown that FIAU strongly inhibited replication of the liver-damaging hepatitis B virus in patients with chronic infection. A clinical study, which had begun in March 1993 and was to run for six months, was halted in late June when one patient suddenly developed symptoms of liver failure and died. Subsequently, 4 more patients—out of a total of 15—died, and others suffered serious, sometimes long-term, side effects. Trials of FIAU were terminated immediately. Laboratory studies revealed that the drug essentially stops DNA synthesis in the mitochondria, cellular organelles that are partially responsible for energy production in the human body.

An FDA advisory committee convened to evaluate the FIAU clinical trial found that the researchers may have acted too hastily, moving the drug into advanced studies on the basis of insufficient data. Questions were also raised by Congress and consumer groups as to whether the researchers ignored some early signs of toxicity and failed to heed patient complaints of minor but potentially related side effects. The FIAU catastrophe led an FDA task force to recommend updating of the agency's regulations regarding the reporting of adverse events associated with experimental drugs. Later a National Institutes of Health report exonerated the scientists of any wrongdoing and said the incident served as a reminder of the risks inherent in human experimentation.

MedWatch: monitoring drug safety

Even after rigorous premarket safety testing, drugs are occasionally found to have unanticipated, sometimes serious, adverse effects. Temafloxacin, an antibiotic approved in 1992, was withdrawn from the market four months later following 50 reports of adverse reactions, including three deaths. A drug for heart failure, flosequinan, released in March 1993, was taken off the market the following July because of deaths and

hospitalizations among those taking it. To improve the tracking of serious events associated with drugs and medical devices already on the market, in June 1993 the FDA launched the MedWatch program. This initiative is meant to increase health professionals' awareness of such events and encourage reporting. "There simply is no way that we can anticipate all possible effects of a drug or device during the clinical trials that precede approval," said FDA Commissioner David A. Kessler in an address to health professionals. One adverse event occurring in one of 1,000 subjects in a clinical trial might be missed; that same event could occur in many patients once the drug was on the market and being taken by many thousands.

Under the MedWatch program, health professionals receive a "Desk Guide to Adverse Event and Product Problem Reporting," which includes case studies, descriptions of serious adverse events and product problems, and instructions for reporting by computer modem and FAX. The simplified reporting procedure now requires only a single form.

One of the catalysts for establishing an improved, streamlined reporting system was the lack of good data on the incidence of autoimmune disorders in the recipients of silicone breast implants—a deficiency blamed largely on poor reporting of such cases. A goal of MedWatch is to prevent similar problems in the future. Many health professionals simply do not think to report adverse events, or they are hesitant to file a report out of fear that their identity will be released in court cases. The FDA has issued a proposed regulation that would protect the identities of both reporting physicians and patients.

Fulfilling a main objective of MedWatch, the FDA has already seen a 40% increase in voluntary reporting of serious adverse drug events. Under a new, broader definition of "serious," such events include death, life-threatening condition, hospitalization, disability, congenital anomaly, or medical intervention to prevent permanent damage. Currently, 70% of voluntarily reported adverse drug reactions meet these criteria.

During the first year of the program, the agency received over 7,500 voluntary reports regarding drugs, biologics, devices, and nutritional supplements; 55% of these reports concerned serious events or effects. The incidence of aplastic anemia associated with felbamate was picked up via MedWatch. Another problem identified by the new reporting system concerned the occurrence of intestinal stricture and blockage in CF patients receiving pancreatic enzyme products. In response to these reports and similar reports in the U.K., in February 1994 the FDA asked manufacturers to remove these compounds from the market. Clinical studies may be necessary before such products can be sold in the future.

*—Carol Nicholson
and Danielle Foullon*

Special Report

ALS: Patterns and Progress

by Geoffrey Dean, M.D.

Amyotrophic lateral sclerosis (ALS) is a progressive degenerative disorder of the nervous system. In the United States it is often called "Lou Gehrig's disease," after the celebrated New York Yankees baseball player who brought the disease to popular attention when it forced him to retire in the late 1930s. The condition was first accurately described in 1865 by the renowned French neurologist Jean-Martin Charcot of the Salpêtrière Hospital in Paris. Charcot observed patients with marked wasting, or atrophy, of the muscles (amyotrophy) and wasting of the nerve fibers in the lateral columns of the spinal cord, causing this part of the cord to become hardened, or sclerosed. He therefore called the disorder *la sclérose laterale amyotrophique*. In France the disorder is often known as *la maladie de Charcot* ("Charcot's disease"). In the United Kingdom, Ireland, and most Commonwealth nations, it is called motor neuron (or neurone) disease (MND).

ALS is characteristically a disorder of late middle life, although it can occur at a younger age. It affects men more frequently than women—in a ratio of about 3:2. While ALS is typically perceived as a rare disease, the annual incidence in Europe and North America is about two cases per 100,000 people, similar to the incidence of multiple sclerosis (MS). There is a greater public awareness of MS, however—probably because MS patients survive considerably longer on average, so at any one time there are considerably more people suffering from MS than from ALS.

Function—and dysfunction—of motor neurons

The symptoms of ALS are due to the death of one class of nerve cells, the motor neurons, whose function is to send electrical impulses along the nerve fibers from the brain to the muscles. These electrical instructions are not sent directly but travel via a biological relay system. The upper motor neurons (UMN) carry the impulses from the cerebral cortex to the bulb, or brain stem, where they are relayed by the lower motor neurons (LMN) to the muscles that control the head and neck, in particular the muscles involved in speech and swallowing. Other neurons send nerve fibers from the cerebral cortex down the lateral columns of the spinal cord, to be relayed in the anterior horn cells of the spinal cord to the nerves that carry instructions to the muscles of the trunk and limbs.

In ALS both UMN and LMN are involved, but often one group predominates. The symptoms vary according to the part of the nervous system affected, and the condition can be divided into subgroups according to the motor neurons that are most affected. When the symptoms primarily affect the head and neck, the resultant conditions are known as pseudobulbar (predominantly UMN) and bulbar palsy (LMN). When the trunk and limbs are most severely affected, the conditions are known as primary lateral sclerosis (predominantly UMN) and spinal muscular atrophy (LMN). In pseudobulbar palsy, besides difficulty with speech and swallowing, symptoms include inappropriate crying and laughter, and in bulbar palsy there is marked wasting of the tongue and muscles of the face. UMN involvement results in rigidity of movement of the limbs, and LMN involvement results in wasting of the muscles.

Other disorders besides ALS may affect the motor neurons. The poliomyelitis virus, for example, damages motor neurons in the anterior horn cells of the spinal cord and can cause paralysis in one or more limbs. There are also a number of relatively uncommon motor neuron diseases that are genetically determined, the majority inherited as autosomal recessive disorders (*i.e.,* an abnormal gene must be inherited from each parent for symptoms to occur). Werdnig-Hoffmann disease, the most frequent of these disorders, causes marked weakness and floppiness of affected infants, evident from birth; victims seldom survive more than one or two years. There are in addition inherited juvenile forms of motor neuron disease, such as Kugelburg-Welander syndrome, which progresses relatively slowly. An adult-onset form of spinal muscular atrophy that affects only the LMN is also genetically determined and is a relatively more benign disorder than ALS.

Onset and progression

The first evidence of ALS is usually an insidious asymmetrical weakness first noticed in one of the limbs, in many cases the hand. This weakness is followed by marked atrophy of the muscles involved, and the affected muscles display spontaneous, localized twitchings (fasciculations). As more and more muscles become involved, the disorder takes on a symmetrical distribution and includes the muscles of chewing and swallowing and those that control movement of the face and tongue. Fasciculations are often marked in the tongue. Involvement of the muscles of breathing may lead to death unless respiration is assisted mechanically. More often, however, death results from pulmonary infection.

Throughout the progression of the disease, the patient's awareness and intellectual ability remain intact, as does control of urination and defecation. The course of the illness is generally relentlessly progressive, but those who develop it in their 20s or 30s generally live longer than those whose first symptoms appear when they are over 50. (In cases of inherited, or familial, ALS, symptoms often appear at a younger age, between 30 and 50. Survival in such cases is usually two to three years from the onset of symptoms.)

A study of life expectancy in ALS (MND) was conducted recently by this author and Michael Goldacre in the Oxford Health Board Area, a region of south-central England with a population of just over two million. Data were provided by the Oxford Record Linkage Scheme, a system that consolidates information from all hospitals in the area and also includes records of the cause of death on all death certificates. The mean life expectancy after a firm diagnosis of MND was found to be just over one year. While survival time from the onset of symptoms varies, normally it is not more than three years.

Strange epidemic in Guam

The cause of ALS is unknown, but major clues uncovered during the past several decades are providing a better understanding of the disease. The first of these clues came to light in 1945 when neuropathologist Harry M. Zimmerman of Montefiore Medical Center and Hospital, Bronx, New York City, went to Guam to study medical problems threatening U.S. troops occupying the island. Zimmerman found that ALS, known

on the island as *lytico* (a contraction of *paralytico,* derived from the Spanish *paralítico,* "paralyzed" or "palsied"), was unusually common among the indigenous people, the Chamorros. In fact, in one village, Umatac, the incidence of ALS was more than 100 times greater than had been reported anywhere else in the world. In this village of about 800 inhabitants, a quarter of all deaths were from ALS. Zimmerman also observed a disorder that combined parkinsonism (muscular rigidity and tremor similar to that occurring in Parkinson's disease) and dementia of the type that occurs in Alzheimer's disease. Some Chamorros were affected simultaneously by ALS and this parkinsonism-dementia complex.

Considerable research has been undertaken to determine the cause of these strange afflictions in Guam. They have also been observed in two villages in the Kii Peninsula in Japan and in some coastal villages in New Guinea, although relatively few people are affected in these localities. In all three places the seed of the cycad plant, or false sago palm, was used either as food, as a medicine, or as a poultice applied to the skin. The disorder does not seem to be genetic in the Chamorros, nor appear to have an infectious origin.

In the early 1960s Marjorie Grant Whiting, a research nutritionist working with epidemiologist Leonard T. Kurland, who was then in charge of the ALS study in Guam sponsored by the U.S. National Institute of Neurological and Communicative Disorders and Stroke, suggested that ALS in Guam might have a dietary cause. The Chamorros use the starchy cycad seed to make a flour known as *fadang,* which in turn is used to make tortillas. The seeds are first dehusked and then are washed repeatedly, each time in fresh water, to remove potentially toxic substances, a process that indicates the Chamorros' awareness of the risk of illness associated with the seeds. Whiting and Kurland hypothesized that the shortage of food during World

Brown Brothers

Retiring from professional baseball, Lou Gehrig is overcome by emotion as he bids his fans and teammates farewell. The New York Yankee slugger was forced to end his career after being diagnosed with ALS. The disorder has since been widely referred to in the U.S. as "Lou Gehrig's disease."

War II, when Guam was occupied by the Japanese, may have led to many Chamorros' using flour made from unwashed seeds.

Because ALS-like symptoms could not be produced in the laboratory in rats fed a diet that included cycad, for a time there was some doubt that cycads were truly the cause of the syndrome. However, in 1986 Peter S. Spencer, then director of the Institute of Neurotoxicology at the Albert Einstein College of Medicine, Bronx, and now at the Oregon Health Sciences University, produced an ALS syndrome in monkeys by feeding them β-N-methylamino-L-alanine (BMAA), a toxic substance isolated from the cycad. Spencer theorized that the severity of the disease depended on the amount of toxin ingested, and some of the Chamorros may have had higher intakes of BMAA than others.

The U.S. virologist D. Carleton Gajdusek, a co-recipient of the 1976 Nobel Prize for Physiology or Medicine for his work on slow viruses, speculates that the key to the strange disorder in Guam may lie in a mineral imbalance, in particular a diet deficiency in calcium and magnesium coupled with a high intake of aluminum. However, other authorities, including Kurland, dispute the occurrence of this mineral deficiency. Researchers who have autopsied the brains of ALS patients have detected abnormally high levels of aluminum, just as have been observed in the brains of patients with Alzheimer's disease.

Since the 1950s the incidence of ALS in Guam has declined dramatically, although the disease remains more common there than in Europe or North America. Today the Chamorro people eat a much more varied diet, and they are keenly aware of the dangers of insufficiently washed cycad. Another possible explanation for their susceptibility to ALS could be an underlying genetic factor, as yet undiscovered, that makes the Chamorros highly sensitive to the toxin contained in the cycad.

Variable incidence: clue to causation?

It used to be thought that the incidence (rate of new cases per year) of ALS was more or less the same throughout the world, with the exception of Guam and the few villages in Japan and New Guinea. Now, however, there is good evidence that ALS incidence is changing in the Western world and that it varies among different populations. A marked increase in deaths from ALS has been reported in many countries, including the U.S, the United Kingdom, France, Canada, Japan, Finland, and Sweden, in the past 20–30 years. It has been suggested that the increased mortality from ALS in the U.S. might simply reflect an increase in the number of neurologists and, therefore, in the likelihood that ALS will be diagnosed. In England, however, where there has not been a comparable rise in the number of neurologists, a similar increase in ALS mortality has occurred.

Moreover, death rates from ALS in the Western world are likely to reflect very accurately the numbers who develop the disease; in more than 80% of those diagnosed as having ALS (or MND), the disease is mentioned on the death certificate in the United Kingdom, Ireland, and North America. By comparison, among white South Africans of European descent, the mortality from ALS is only half of that in England and Wales. This is not a result of underdiagnosis or poor record keeping; white South Africans have good medical care, and when ALS occurs, it is listed on the death certificate in over 80% of patients (generally as "motor neuron disease"). The prevalence of MS among white South Africans is also low, only one-fifth

U.S. neurotoxicologist Peter S. Spencer (far right) visits with local residents in a part of New Guinea that was formerly the focus of an unusually high incidence of ALS. It was Spencer who in the mid-1980s theorized that a toxic substance contained in cycad seeds might be a cause of this neurodegenerative disorder. Spencer went on to demonstrate that such a substance could indeed produce ALS-like symptoms in monkeys.

of that in England and Wales, suggesting that an environmental factor may be involved in both diseases.

Further evidence of the variability of occurrence of ALS in different populations comes from studies conducted in the United Kingdom. Neurophysiologist Marta Elian of Oldchurch Hospital, Essex, England, and this author have shown that male Asian immigrants to England and Wales have half the risk of dying from ALS that is seen, after correction for age, in the general population of those countries; female Asian immigrants have one-fifth the risk. In all probability, both genetic and environmental factors are involved; therefore, it is not surprising that the incidence of ALS varies in different populations and places.

Polio, trauma, and other factors

As noted above, the paralysis that occurs in poliomyelitis also results from the death of motor neurons. Some of those who had paralysis due to acute poliomyelitis as children or young adults develop an ALS-like syndrome, sometimes called postpolio syndrome, later in life. One explanation for this condition might be that many of their neurons were destroyed during the acute attack of polio and, with aging, additional numbers of neurons have died. In a 1988 survey Christopher Martyn of the British Medical Research Council's Environmental Epidemiology Unit found a correlation between areas in England that had a high prevalence of paralysis due to polio 40 years earlier and those with a high mortality from ALS in the 1980s. However, if virus-induced damage to the motor neurons were responsible for the subsequent development of ALS, it could be expected that deaths due to ALS would now be declining because such a large proportion of the population has been immunized against the poliovirus. Instead, there has been a rise in deaths from ALS.

Other factors that have been suspected as affecting the risk of developing ALS are trauma (ALS occurs after fractures more often than can be explained by chance) and prolonged exposure to insecticides or solvents. No occupation appears to carry an elevated risk of ALS, although it has been noted in the United Kingdom that more than the expected number of workers in the tanning industry die from ALS. More research is needed into the possible relationship of ALS and occupational exposures.

Intriguing findings

In November 1993 an international meeting of scientists involved in research on ALS-MND convened in Chantilly, France. The focus of the meeting was the remarkable advances that have recently occurred in the understanding of some factors that may cause at least some forms of ALS.

Familial ALS (FALS) affects approximately 10% of ALS patients and is genetic in origin. The disorder is inherited as an autosomal dominant characteristic;

J.A. Tainer and E.D. Getzoff, The Scripps Research Institute, La Jolla, California

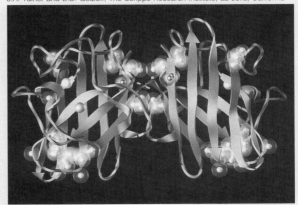

Using the technique of synchrotron crystallography, scientists have revealed the molecular structure of superoxide dismutase, an enzyme that removes harmful free radicals from the body. Some people with ALS have abnormal forms of this enzyme.

if a person carries the defective, or mutated, gene, on average, 50% of his or her children will inherit it. For several years Teepu Siddique, a neurologist at Northwestern University Medical School, Chicago, and others had been searching for the gene or genes that are responsible for FALS. In 1993 Siddique, along with Robert H. Brown and Daniel Rosen of Massachusetts General Hospital in Boston, demonstrated that one familial variant of ALS is linked to a gene on chromosome 21. The gene carries the instructions for synthesis of the enzyme superoxide dismutase (SOD1), which acts as a scavenger, removing from the body unstable molecules, called free radicals, that can damage nerve cells. Different families with FALS have different mutations of the SOD1 gene.

Subsequently, Wim Robberecht and colleagues at University Hospital Gasthuisberg, Leuven, Belgium, found that in some FALS families individuals who carry the gene mutation for FALS have much less SOD1 activity in their blood than those who do not carry the gene. Moreover, low blood levels of SOD1 can be detected years before the onset of clinical ALS. Nonetheless, defects in the gene for SOD1 do not completely explain ALS; low SOD1 levels are present in only a proportion, perhaps one-quarter, of all FALS patients, and SOD1 levels are not low in those with sporadic (*i.e.*, nonfamilial) ALS.

It has also been suggested that low levels of SOD1 may lead to a high level of glutamate. Glutamate is a neurotransmitter vital to normal neuronal functioning; when present in excess, however, it can cause the death of motor neurons. Other clues have been found relating ALS to glutamate. One comes from studies showing that after oral administration of glutamate, ALS patients have higher blood levels of the neurotransmitter than do healthy controls. Another is the similarity in chemical structure of glutamate and

Patrick Guis—Gamma Liaison

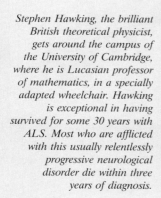

Stephen Hawking, the brilliant British theoretical physicist, gets around the campus of the University of Cambridge, where he is Lucasian professor of mathematics, in a specially adapted wheelchair. Hawking is exceptional in having survived for some 30 years with ALS. Most who are afflicted with this usually relentlessly progressive neurological disorder die within three years of diagnosis.

BMAA, the substance linked to the ALS-parkinsonism-dementia syndrome that occurs in Guam.

Stanley Appel, at the Baylor College of Medicine, Houston, Texas, has found evidence that the sporadic form of ALS may be caused by an excessive influx of calcium into motor neurons, resulting in biochemical changes that ultimately lead to cell death. The one conclusion that can be drawn from these various avenues of research is that ALS is probably a disorder that has more than one cause.

While research on families with FALS is of great importance to the further understanding of the disease, it also creates ethical and psychological dilemmas. When scientists discover either a mutation in the SOD1 gene or low SOD1 blood levels in individuals from FALS families who have not yet developed any ALS symptoms, they have strong evidence that the mutated gene has been inherited. Such evidence presents the same dilemma that doctors must face when they have patients from families with Huntington's disease and other serious inherited disorders for which genetic tests are available. Should individuals who undergo such tests, or who take part in family studies, be told that they have inherited the gene and are therefore likely to develop the disease—even though they are now symptomless?

Certainly, people should not be told that they carry the gene responsible for FALS—or any other serious disorder—unless they wish to know, and they should be told only after they have had expert counseling and fully understand the implications of their decision. It is an extremely difficult decision, involving not only the prospect of a debilitating disease and an early death but crucial life choices such as whether to marry and have children. On the other hand, those who have not inherited the gene can be reassured that they and their children have been spared.

Making a correct diagnosis

Because the underlying process in ALS is at present untreatable, it is extremely important that the diagnostic evaluation rule out any other, potentially remediable causes of motor neuron dysfunction. Many people experience occasional muscle twitching very similar to the fasciculations of ALS. Indeed, most medical students and doctors, including this author, have at some time experienced such twitching and worried that these benign occurrences might be the first symptom of ALS.

Specific clinical findings, which can be detected by a neurologist, make a definite diagnosis possible. These include abnormally brisk, or exaggerated, reflexes and an abnormal Babinski reflex (*i.e.,* the big toe flexes upward rather than downward when the sole of the foot is stroked). LMN involvement is seen in the wasting of the muscles, which is often especially evident in the thenar and hypothenar eminences—the groups of muscles in the hand that control the thumb and little finger. Electromyography (EMG) is a very useful aid in the diagnosis of ALS. A needle is inserted in the muscle to be studied while the muscle is at rest and during contraction; the electrical activity in the muscle is amplified and visually displayed. The EMG can record fasciculations and other abnormal spontaneous movements (fibrillations) that occur in muscle fibers deprived of nerve signals.

Other conditions that produce ALS-like symptoms must be excluded; for example, compression of the cervical spinal cord by a tumor or by bony growths projecting into the spinal column. Treatable disorders that can mimic ALS include chronic lead poisoning and overactivity of the thyroid gland. Rare biochemical disorders can be excluded by the appropriate laboratory tests. As already mentioned, an ALS-like syndrome can also occur as a late effect of poliomyelitis.

Treatment: mostly supportive

While there is as yet no treatment that has any influence on the underlying pathological process in ALS, much can be done by the patient's doctor, family, and friends to make life as comfortable and free from anxiety as possible. Aids such as wheelchairs, hoists, and special typewriters can be used to help overcome disability. If the muscles controlling speech are severely affected, a voice synthesizer can be used. Controlled by a slight movement of a finger, this device can produce spoken words and sentences from typed signals. Stephen Hawking, the British theoretical physicist and author of *A Brief History of Time,* among other books, who has survived with ALS for three decades, uses a voice synthesizer to deliver his papers and lectures. His long survival with ALS is, however, quite unusual.

In some patients the intravenous administration of thyrotropin-releasing hormone may improve muscle tone, and trials are being undertaken to assess other treatments, such as the use of riluzole, a substance that blocks glutamate receptors. As yet, no treatment has been shown to make a convincing difference, although there is great hope for the future.

A great fear of ALS patients is that they will choke to death. They can be reassured that with the use of proper feeding techniques and appropriately textured

Despite the limitations imposed by being connected to a respirator via a tracheostomy tube, Jacob Javits, the former U.S. senator from New York who died of ALS in 1986, managed to remain mobile and active during his last years.

George Gardner

foods, this will not happen. Eventually, though, it may be necessary for a feeding tube to be placed directly into the patient's stomach via a small surgical incision in the upper abdomen.

Once the respiratory muscles are severely affected, the question arises of whether to institute mechanical ventilation. In Europe, the United Kingdom, and a number of other countries, such heroic interventions are resorted to less readily than in the U.S. However, most U.S. insurance plans cover the cost of ventilator-assisted respiration for only a very limited time, usually not more than six months.

Artificial ventilation is carried out through a tube placed in the trachea; the tube is attached to a machine that inflates the lungs with air. Such treatment requires day and night care either at home or in a nursing home or hospital. It is costly, requires a secure electricity supply, and can place a great strain on the family and its resources. While on the respirator, the patient can generally be taught to speak as he or she exhales. Total paralysis may develop, but the patient remains fully conscious and intellectually unimpaired. The problem then arises of deciding when to turn off the respirator.

Coping

Although there is every hope that the cause of ALS will be found and good methods of prevention and treatment developed, at present the disease is uniformly progressive. For most patients life expectancy after a firm diagnosis is not much longer than a year. Some may have such familial support and financial strength that they will wish to extend their lives as much as possible even if they are totally paralyzed. Others may wish to ensure—via written instructions—that their lives are not prolonged.

Much assistance can be provided by voluntary support organizations such as the ALS and MND societies. They can help people obtain wheelchairs, hoists to help patients move from bed to a chair or into the bath, and special typewriters and voice synthesizers. Often they can help patients and their families obtain nursing and social services. They are also invaluable sources of psychological support. For many patients a belief in God and the power of prayer and the support of their family, friends, and religious community provide great comfort.

Meanwhile, research continues apace. In June 1994 scientists at Northwestern University announced that they had developed a mouse genetically engineered to be susceptible to ALS. With this first animal model of the disease, the testing of new therapies can be accelerated. Such developments offer real hope for the future. It is only a matter of time before the concerted international research effort solves the puzzle of what the English actor David Niven, who died of ALS in 1983, called "this bloody disease."

369

Physical Fitness

Turn to fiction—TV commercials and print ads—and ours is a country of tennis players, joggers, skiers and weight lifters. Turn to fact, however, and ours is a nation of people who seldom get off their duffs. That's why the Federal Centers for Disease Control and Prevention, along with assorted doctors and exercise experts, faced up and recently issued a new prescription for physical fitness.

How lovely to think of silent suburbs flocked with residents on evening strolls along the verges. How welcome a city's nighttime streets could be if they held more ordinary people than predators. And how pure the air that isn't laced with the fumes from the car left behind in the garage. The Government's advice is more than a prescription for better health. It's a blueprint for a better place.

—*New York Times,* Aug. 18, 1993

Many of the advantages of regular exercise have been appreciated since the days of the ancient Greeks. It is not news, therefore, that a physically active lifestyle offers substantial health benefits. However, it is only recently that this impression has been supported by convincing scientific evidence; numerous recent studies have shed much new light on the types and amounts of physical activity that are needed for maintenance of good health. This evidence indicates that physically active persons are likely to accrue a wide range of specific health benefits and, indeed, are likely to live longer than their sedentary counterparts. Health experts hope that this new information provides a much-needed boost to efforts to promote the public health through positive lifestyle changes, including increased physical activity.

Physical activity and physical fitness

Perhaps the best-documented benefit of regular physical activity is an enhancement of physical fitness. Appropriately selected physical activity programs produce improvements in each of the key components of physical fitness—cardiorespiratory endurance (*i.e.,* "aerobic" fitness), muscular strength, flexibility, and coordination. While each of these aspects of physical fitness is known to decline with age, these functional capacities decline more slowly in physically active persons than in the sedentary. This suggests strongly that regular exercise may be a powerful way to maintain a high level of function and independence into older age. Encouragingly, recent studies have shown that marked improvements in physical fitness can be attained even by persons in their eighth and ninth decades of life!

Nearly two decades ago the accumulating evidence of the benefits of regular physical activity on physical fitness led experts to issue guidelines on recommended exercise—an "exercise prescription." This prescription specified a *mode, intensity, duration,* and *frequency* of activity. The prescribed mode of exercise was "aerobic" exercise (*i.e.,* exercise that involves rhythmic movements using large muscle groups). The

recommended level of effort (intensity) for performing that activity was in the range of 40% to 85% of individual capacity (*i.e.,* maximal heart rate, measured as heartbeats per minute, which for healthy adults is estimated by subtracting age in years from 220). The duration for that activity was 15–60 minutes (usually 30 minutes or more) and the frequency three to five days per week. In the intervening years these guidelines were widely disseminated to the public, and they have been extensively utilized in structured exercise program settings. To the extent that the guidelines have been followed, they have paid off; probably millions of Americans have applied the prescription and as a result have experienced profound improvements in their physical fitness.

Current activity status of American adults

While many Americans have become more physically active, most adults in the United States remain far less physically active than is recommended by experts. Surveys of the U.S. population indicate that physical activity levels among adults improved somewhat dur-

Loss of vim and vigor is not inevitable with the passing of the years. Indeed, there is ample and growing evidence that regular exercise offers a powerful way to maintain vital functional capacities and independence—in spite of one's age.

Charles Gupton—Stock, Boston

370

ing the 1960s, '70s, and early '80s. The best available evidence, however, suggests that the activity habits of American adults have not improved further over the past decade.

What is particularly alarming is that even with past improvements only a small minority of adult Americans are active at the level recommended in the traditional exercise prescription. A recent survey done by the U.S. Department of Health and Human Services as part of the "Healthy People 2000" initiative showed that 22% of U.S. adults fit into the "regular, moderate, or vigorous" activity category, but only 10% exercised vigorously for 30 or more minutes on three or more days per week; that 54% were irregularly active; and that 24% were sedentary.

Exercise for disease prevention

From a public health perspective, the fact that such a small fraction of Americans are regularly physically active is especially worrisome because physically inactive persons are now known to be at markedly increased risk for premature development of several highly prevalent chronic diseases. These include coronary heart disease (CHD)—the number one killer of American adults—high blood pressure, adult-onset diabetes (non-insulin-dependent diabetes mellitus [NIDDM]), osteoporosis, cancers of the breast and colon, and anxiety and depression.

Preventing coronary heart disease. The strongest evidence linking physical inactivity to disease is that for CHD—the most prevalent of the cardiovascular diseases and the major killer in most industrialized nations. Numerous large-scale epidemiological studies and many smaller investigations have demonstrated that there are important physiological benefits to the cardiovascular system from regular physical activity and that an active lifestyle reduces by about one-half the likelihood that a person will develop CHD.

Preventing diabetes. It is well known that the physiological effects of exercise include an increased rate of transfer of glucose (sugar) from the blood into the cells of the body. It is also known that regular exercise can play an important role in maintenance of an appropriate body weight. Hence, it has long been thought that exercise might play a role in preventing NIDDM, a disease that is common in obese persons and that involves an impaired ability to clear glucose from the bloodstream.

Two important studies, both conducted by JoAnn Manson and colleagues at Harvard Medical School, have confirmed that regular participation in exercise can reduce the risk for the development of diabetes. Both studies involved following a large number of persons—females in one study and males in the other—for a period of years. Over 87,000 female participants in the Nurses' Health Study were followed prospectively for eight years. Women who reported participat-

"It's part of the company's new emphasis on health and fitness."

ing in vigorous exercise at least once per week were one-third less likely to become diabetic than their sedentary counterparts. This relationship between exercise and avoidance of diabetes remained significant even after controlling for body mass index, a reliable measure of body fatness. In a subsequent study of male physicians, over 21,000 subjects in the Physicians' Health Study were monitored for five years. As was found in the study of women, men who exercised vigorously at least once per week were about one-third less likely than physically inactive men to develop diabetes during the period of observation. Again, as was found with women, this relationship persisted after statistically controlling for body fatness.

Taken together these two studies provide strong evidence that physically active persons, as contrasted with sedentary persons, are less likely to develop NIDDM. This observation is particularly important because NIDDM afflicts some 12 million persons in the U.S. and is a major cause of cardiovascular disease, kidney failure, and blindness. It is also noteworthy that in both of the aforementioned studies, only modest levels of physical activity were needed to produce important health benefits. In both studies persons who exercised more frequently than once per week experienced some added benefit, but the greatest benefit was associated with being somewhat active rather than sedentary. Substantial documentation exists to support the conclusion that regular physical activity reduces risk for development of high blood pres-

371

sure, certain cancers, osteoporosis, and probably the mental health problems of depression and anxiety as well. Preliminary evidence also suggests that it can reduce the pain of arthritis and increase resistance to infection.

Physical inactivity: the public health burden

As evidence documenting the health risks of a sedentary lifestyle has mounted, public health authorities have become increasingly interested in quantifying the overall burden to public health associated with physical inactivity. The results of two important studies published in recent years have quantified, in very stark terms, the price that American society pays for its lack of physical activity.

In one of these studies, Robert A. Hahn and colleagues from the U.S. Centers for Disease Control and Prevention (CDC) in Atlanta, Ga., examined national statistics on the death rates from nine chronic diseases (including coronary heart disease, stroke, lung cancer, breast cancer, and diabetes). These investigators made use of population surveys showing the prevalence of physical inactivity and epidemiological studies demonstrating the relative risks that physically active and inactive persons had of dying from the various diseases. The conclusion derived from their analyses was that over 250,000 deaths per year in the U.S. can be attributed to physical inactivity.

In a somewhat similar investigation, J. Michael McGinnis of the U.S. Office of Disease Prevention and Health Promotion and William Foege, executive director of the Carter Center in Atlanta, performed an extensive search of the biomedical literature in order to identify the major nongenetic factors contributing to death in the United States. Their results indicated that diet and physical inactivity, considered together, account for an estimated 300,000 deaths per year, which was second only to tobacco-related deaths at 400,000 per year.

How much activity for health?

It now seems irrefutable that physical activity reduces chronic disease risk, but a central question is: How much and what types are needed to provide this important health benefit? As noted above, the traditional exercise prescription (*i.e.,* continuous aerobic activity for 30 or more minutes on three to five days per week) is known to provide important *fitness* benefits. Those who meet this standard are also expected to derive the health benefits of an active lifestyle. Since it is clear that so few adults adhere to this type of exercise program, it needs to be asked whether the traditional prescription is the only one from which disease-prevention benefits can be derived. Recent studies are very encouraging.

Several large-scale epidemiological studies published in the past few years show with remarkable

consistency that sedentary persons are at markedly greater disease risk than are persons who are at least moderately physically active. Higher levels of habitual activity result in progressively greater benefits and reduced risks. However, there is a clear "diminishing returns" effect. This means that from the standpoint of public health promotion, much more would be gained from motivating the sedentary to become moderately active than from moving the already somewhat active into a higher activity bracket. It is important to note that physical activity status in the studies that support this conclusion was based on *total* activity, including moderately intense activities accumulated in short bouts interspersed throughout the day.

Exercise and longevity

Some of the strongest evidence supporting the health benefits of physical activity has come from the work of Ralph Paffenbarger and his colleagues, who for several decades have been studying the health habits and disease experiences of the male alumni of Harvard College. Early investigations by Paffenbarger's team showed that men who maintained a physically active lifestyle during adulthood were less likely to develop coronary artery disease, high blood pressure, and certain cancers. More recent studies showed that physically active men, contrasted with their inactive counterparts, were at lower risk of death from "all causes," which is to say that regular physical activity was associated with increased longevity.

In 1993 Paffenbarger's team reported in the *New England Journal of Medicine* a finding that, from the perspective of public health promotion, may be the most important information yet to emerge from the Harvard Alumni Study. If a physically active lifestyle is associated with reduced disease risk, it would be logical to hypothesize that sedentary persons who become active would experience reduced risk for development of disease. As logical as that may seem, this hypothesis had not been directly tested until Paffenbarger and colleagues showed the effects on death rates of *changing* certain health behaviors. Having observed over 10,000 men for an average of nine years each, they found that becoming moderately physically active was associated with a 23% reduction in risk of death as compared with alumni who remained sedentary. These findings provide important support for the implementation of public health programs to promote moderate physical activity in adults who are currently sedentary.

A new prescription

As a result of these recent findings, experts have reexamined the traditional exercise recommendations. On the basis of such a review, the CDC and the American College of Sports Medicine (ACSM), in cooperation with the President's Council on Physical Fitness and Sports, issued a new recommendation in July 1993. That recommendation is that every American adult accumulate 30 minutes or more of moderate-intensity physical activity on most, and preferably all, days of the week.

This new "prescription," though in some ways similar to the traditional exercise guidelines, is an important departure in two major ways. First, "moderate-intensity" physical activity is sanctioned. This means that persons who are unable or unwilling to engage in more vigorous forms of exercise (*e.g.,* jogging, cycling, swimming) should feel encouraged to take part in more moderate forms of activity. Examples are brisk walking (5–6 km/h [3–4 mph]), bicycling for transportation or pleasure (less than 16 km/h [10 mph]), golf (carrying clubs or pulling a cart), table tennis, or mowing the lawn (with a power mower). These are activities that a much larger proportion of the population is likely to do on a regular basis. Although it should

Those who are reluctant, unmotivated, "too busy," or otherwise unlikely to exercise are among those likely to benefit from the new "exercise prescription," which sanctions "moderate-intensity" activities that are engaged in for short periods at various times of day, including yard work and other chores.

Phyllis Picardi—Stock, Boston

not be hard for the vast majority of people to find "moderate" activities that are enjoyable and can be accomplished in a normal day, some activities were evaluated and considered to be "too light"—*i.e.,* too low in intensity—to provide important health benefits. These included slow walking (at only 2–3 km/h [1–2 mph]), light stretching exercises, golf (using a motorized cart), fishing (sitting), light carpet sweeping, and mowing the lawn (using a riding mower).

The second departure is that physical activity can be accumulated in short bouts throughout the day. This should be helpful to persons who have difficulty finding major blocks of time for activity. For example, one might accumulate 30 minutes of physical activity by walking briskly for 10 minutes from a parking place to one's office in the morning, reversing that path in the afternoon, then doing 10 minutes of active yard work in the evening.

The new exercise guidelines therefore recommend that people make activity part of their way of life rather than something they force themselves to do. As Steven Blair, an epidemiologist at the Cooper Institute for Aerobics Research, Dallas, Texas, and an exercise expert, has said, "We made a mistake saying that exercise had to be intense and continuous."

Acting on the new recommendation

As indicated above, nearly 80% of American adults do not currently meet this new recommendation. However, the potential benefits to the public health are enormous. Thus, although implementing the recommendation will be a massive undertaking, it is critical that institutions and organizations such as schools, public health departments, work sites, and recreation departments identify ways in which their constituents can be encouraged to become more physically active. Because increased physical activity would be one of the most viable and economical forms of disease prevention, the ACSM has recommended that under the health care reform package that is eventually adopted in the U.S., physicians be reimbursed for giving exercise counseling.

At its most fundamental level, of course, physical activity is a personal behavior—one that each individual makes his or her own decisions about. Therefore, the American public will be a physically active one only when more adults choose physically active pursuits over the sedentary pursuits that have become so attractive and common. In simple terms this means more stair climbing and fewer elevator rides, more walking and bicycling and less automobile driving, more gardening and lawn mowing and less television watching, and more playing of basketball and soccer and less playing of video games. A physically active lifestyle is enjoyable, energizing, and, as has now been shown by research, lifesaving as well!

—*Russell R. Pate, Ph.D.*

Rheumatology

Rheumatology is the medical specialty that treats arthritic and inflammatory disease involving the connective tissues, blood vessels, and various organ systems. Most of the common rheumatic disorders are either degenerative—for example, osteoarthritis, in which bone and cartilage deteriorate—or inflammatory. The latter category can be further subdivided into metabolic conditions—such as gout, caused by an excess of uric acid—and autoimmune disorders—for example, rheumatoid arthritis and systemic lupus erythematosus (lupus), which arise when the immune system goes awry and attacks the body's own tissues. Other rheumatic syndromes, such as rheumatic fever and Lyme disease, are caused by infectious agents. Finally, there is a category of rheumatic disorders, including fibromyalgia and polymyalgia rheumatica, for which the cause is unknown.

There have been numerous developments and some significant progress in the field of rheumatology in the past few years. These include several new treatment approaches—especially important because established therapies for many rheumatic disorders are less than satisfactory.

Promising treatment for joints

Rheumatoid arthritis (RA) is the most common inflammatory disease of joints, frequently resulting in irreversible damage. Conventional treatments involve the use of drugs that are only partially effective and occasionally produce toxic side effects. Sometimes the toxicity is universal and unavoidable, as in the loss of calcium from bone that results from the use of steroids. In other instances the side effects are rare but quite serious when they do occur, as in the liver or lung damage that may be caused by methotrexate. These liabilities have been a major stimulus to the search for more effective and safer treatments for the disease.

Because RA is an autoimmune disease and therefore involves abnormal stimulation of immune responses, suppressing the immune system is a logical goal of treatment, particularly if it can be done in a way that paralyzes the offending components of immunity but leaves the others unimpaired. Antigens—proteins recognized by the body as foreign—stimulate the immune system to act. In an autoimmune disease, even normal constituents of the body seem to be capable of acting as antigens.

During the past few decades, experiments in animals have demonstrated methods for suppressing the responses to certain antigens. Unfortunately, most of these are quite complex and involve features that make them impractical for use in human patients.

Recently, however, researchers treating people with severe RA announced the results of a successful experimental therapy called *oral tolerance,* which involves the relatively simple process of orally administering the specific antigens believed to have caused the disease. It takes advantage of the human body's unique ability to suppress immune responses to foreign proteins ingested via the digestive system, without which virtually all foods could potentially trigger an immune reaction.

This trial could not have been attempted if other investigators had not already done work to identify specific autoantigens (the body constituents that stimulate autoimmune reactions). Scientists studying autoimmune diseases had found that by immunizing susceptible species of animals with certain autoantigens, they could produce disorders similar to those that affect humans. For example, immunization with myelin basic protein (MBP), a substance found in brain matter, provokes a disease similar to multiple sclerosis (MS) in certain animals, and type II collagen,

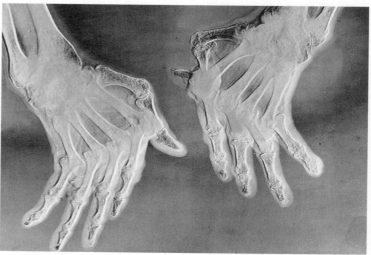

The damage to joints caused by rheumatoid arthritis (RA) can be severe and debilitating, as this X-ray shows. Because conventional treatments—which aim primarily to relieve symptoms—are less than satisfactory and often have unwanted side effects, researchers have long sought a means of blocking the underlying autoimmune process. An innovative approach called oral tolerance shows promise for accomplishing this objective.

the major structural protein in cartilage, appears to create a condition similar to RA. Subsequently, it was shown that "feeding" these very substances to the susceptible animals suppressed autoimmunity, blocking the development of the diseases. The next step was to see if oral tolerance would work in humans.

The initial attempt involved isolating MBP from the brains of cows and administering it in capsule form to patients with MS—an autoimmune neuromuscular disease. After a year of treatment, the expected immunosuppressive effect was apparent, and there was evidence of clinical benefit—for example, a reduction in the number of severe attacks—in some patients. Moreover, there were no side effects from the therapy. Shortly thereafter, an orally administered form of type II collagen, purified from the cartilage of chicken breastbones, was tested in volunteers with RA. The study lasted only three months and, like the MS trial, involved only a small group of patients. Many of the RA patients experienced improvements such as reductions in joint pain and swelling. Again, no toxicity was noted.

Because both MS and RA are long-term diseases, the findings of these initial trials should not be overstated. At present, however, it can at least be said that some patients with these autoimmune conditions can be helped by an approach that employs oral tolerance. A much larger, multicenter study of the treatment was scheduled to begin in late 1994. In addition to examining the therapy's benefits, researchers were hopeful they would be able to identify the immunologic mechanisms that make it work. Knowing such pathways could enable them to make the approach more effective or more widely applicable.

Other treatment developments for RA

A number of traditional treatments for RA, including therapy for the juvenile form of the disease, are being refined. New drugs have been introduced, and some physicians have begun to try potent combinations of drugs. Researchers continue to investigate the role of diet both as a cause and as a method of treating the disorder; at the same time, RA has become a principal focus of biotechnology-based therapies.

Minocycline therapy. The tetracycline derivative minocycline may prove to be a relatively safe and effective treatment for RA. The first evidence of the benefit of using tetracycline in RA began with anecdotal and somewhat controversial claims made in the 1960s, when antibiotic treatment was tried on the theory that RA might be caused by a bacterium. Subsequently, minocycline was shown to work in animals that had a disease much like human RA.

Recently, the National Institutes of Health (NIH) sponsored a large-scale multicenter, one-year trial of oral minocycline, and the results, which were reported in the fall of 1993, suggested that the original claims

for the drug were correct. A group of over 100 patients who received minocycline in the NIH study showed evidence of clinical improvement—e.g., decrease in joint pain and swelling—and favorable changes were also seen in the laboratory tests used to measure the severity of the disease. Equally important, most patients tolerated the drug well, and no serious side effects were noted. Although not yet approved by the U.S. Food and Drug Administration (FDA) for treatment of RA, minocycline is marketed for other uses (e.g., skin, respiratory, and urinary infections; sexually transmitted diseases; fevers caused by ticks and lice) and is therefore available to rheumatologists. It may be that more effective tetracycline-based drugs can be developed in the future. Studies comparing minocycline with methotrexate in the treatment of RA and evaluations of minocycline in disorders such as scleroderma and lupus are also needed.

Increasingly aggressive therapies. The experiences with oral tolerance and minocycline suggest that approaches to treating RA that are more benign than current therapies may be emerging. At the same time, aggressive treatment strategies have also been pursued. The rationale for an aggressive approach is the evidence that for many patients RA is far from a benign disorder. Severe RA shortens life expectancy and leads to other illnesses, such as infections, and a need for joint surgery.

The aggressive approach to treating RA has been pioneered largely by individual physicians seeking better ways to manage patients whose disease is starting to become severe. Such treatment usually consists of the administration of a combination of drugs with disease-modifying properties. The list of medications is formidable and includes such potent drugs as azathioprine (also used to prevent rejection after organ transplants) and methotrexate (an early cancer chemotherapy agent subsequently used for RA). Rheumatologists using combinations of up to four drugs report that their patients experience improvement without obvious toxic side effects. Controlled studies are needed to determine whether combination therapy does in fact have added benefits for the management of severe RA. Until such studies can be done, most rheumatologists urge caution, as long-term health hazards have not been assessed, and the cost of such therapy is considerable.

Dietary modification. Many people who suffer from RA report changes in their symptoms related to diet. There is, however, only meager scientific evidence to support such claims. Although a few studies do show a connection between sensitivity to milk and other dairy products and disorders similar to RA, for most patients eliminating dairy foods has no effect on joint discomfort. Likewise, avoiding foods from plants of the nightshade family (such as tomatoes) has no clear impact.

Recently, however, it has been suggested that there may be biologically plausible explanations for the beneficial effects of dietary changes in RA, though such approaches may not be practical. Perhaps the most persuasive evidence comes from Norwegian studies of extreme caloric deprivation, sometimes total fasting, or abstaining from solid foodstuffs, often for a period of a few weeks. Participants in these studies reported subjective signs of improvement. Other clear-cut data show that severe malnutrition seriously compromises the immune system as well as the body as a whole, which might explain the benefits of fasting in RA.

A perhaps more feasible approach comes from a study using a strict lactovegetarian diet, which excludes eggs as well as all forms of meat but includes dairy foods. While it was difficult to meet nutritional needs with this diet (for example, some patients experienced serious weight loss) there were indications of improvement in symptoms of RA over several months. Additional research into the relationship of nutrition and the immune system is needed to identify modifications that might be both helpful and practical.

Methotrexate for juvenile RA. Juvenile rheumatoid arthritis (JRA) is a condition similar to the adult disease but one that occurs in children. Traditional treatments have been ineffective and frequently have interfered with normal growth or produced permanent crippling. A collaborative U.S.-Russian trial has now shown that low-dose methotrexate therapy is an effective treatment for patients with JRA. This is an important achievement that should help many children with this serious disease, at least until better therapies can be developed.

Innovations through biotechnology. The field of biotechnology, which has spawned such innovative products as chimeric proteins and monoclonal antibodies, has also furnished many investigative biological products for the treatment of RA. In fact, because disease activity is easily measured in RA and because a successful treatment would have enormous commercial potential, RA has been singled out as a prototypical target for biological interventions.

On the whole, at least thus far, results have been disappointing. All of the treatments that have been tried require injections, produce side effects such as flulike symptoms, and vary in effectiveness. Some products that have had the greatest immunologic impact (for example, producing pronounced changes in the levels of various immune system cells) have not yielded relief of symptoms.

Exercise for osteoarthritis: a second opinion

Osteoarthritis is an age-related degenerative process that frequently affects the knees, hips, and lower spine. Neck pain and swelling and discomfort at the fingertips or the base of the thumb may occur as well. Both heredity and obesity make a person susceptible to the disease. Because use of the involved joints is painful, avoiding physical activity has been standard treatment. It seemed logical to suppose that there would be further deterioration of a damaged joint when it was stressed. Now, however, it appears likely that this approach has been wrong.

Several studies have shown no convincing association between regular jogging or running—activities that place considerable stress on certain joints—and the early development of osteoarthritis of the hip or knee. In addition, after adjusting for obesity, investigators have been unable to correlate excessive work-related use of a joint with the subsequent development of the disease. Recently, a carefully conducted prospective trial showed that a regular, supervised walking program can be quite helpful for patients who already have osteoarthritis of the knees. Some of the benefits shown by this study might have been related to weight reduction, which in turn relieves stress on the joints, but it is probable that the improvement was also a function of increased strength and flexibility. A heightened sense of well-being and fitness may have contributed as well. At the very least, the exercise was

Contrary to the long-held notion that weight-bearing physical activity may further harm joints damaged by osteoarthritis, recent evidence shows that people with arthritic knees actually benefit from a regular walking program.

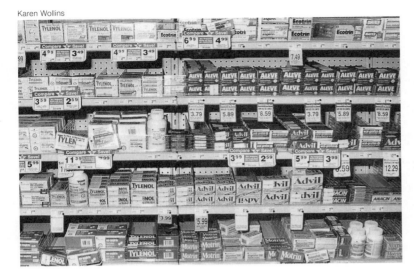

A plethora of nonprescription drugs for arthritis pain can be found in any supermarket or drugstore. The newest remedy to become available over the counter is the nonsteroidal anti-inflammatory drug naproxen, sold under the brand name Aleve.

not deleterious, even though it involved weight bearing as well as motion. Because of the many benefits of physical activity, virtually all patients with osteoarthritis should be strongly encouraged to exercise regularly within the limits of their tolerance. Advisable activities include walking, calisthenics, swimming, bicycling, and other aerobic activities.

Relieving pain but sparing the stomach

The pain in virtually all forms of arthritis responds at least partially to aspirin and to nonsteroidal anti-inflammatory drugs (NSAIDs), such as ibuprofen and naproxen. These drugs can, however, produce side effects that on occasion are serious. In particular, they are apt to upset the stomach when used on a sustained basis. If the irritation becomes severe, it may result in ulceration and even hemorrhage.

Much of the effectiveness of NSAIDs in relieving joint inflammation, as well as their capacity to irritate the stomach, has been ascribed to the fact that they inhibit the secretion of prostaglandins (a family of potent chemicals released by white blood cells and cells lining the joints). Prostaglandins amplify inflammation within a joint, but they also contribute to a normal regulatory process in the stomach by helping to modulate the secretion of mucus. Thus, when NSAIDs interrupt the production of prostaglandins, joint pain may be relieved but the stomach lining loses part or all of its mucous coating, making injury from stomach acid, irritant foods, or the drugs themselves likely.

Over the years, pharmaceutical firms have made major commitments to developing NSAIDs that do not have such harmful gastric effects, but only limited progress has been made. Some recently introduced NSAIDs, such as the prescription drugs nabumetone and oxaprosen, have weaker prostaglandin-inhibiting properties but seem to be capable of alleviating pain. Although they may be safer drugs for treating arthritis,

it is too early to draw firm conclusions. Because they are taken only once a day, these drugs are certainly more convenient for patients who must take NSAIDs on a regular basis.

One way of overcoming the stomach injury caused by NSAIDs is to use so-called cytoprotective agents. The most effective of these agents are prostaglandin-like substances that replenish the supplies of natural prostaglandins depleted by NSAIDs. On the basis of preliminary evidence that it decreased the number of NSAID-related abnormalities in the stomach, the drug misoprostol has been widely used for this purpose. A large trial called the MUCOSA study has now been completed and has shown that misoprostol does indeed decrease the risk of gastrointestinal bleeding in patients who take NSAIDs on a prolonged basis. Misoprostol, however, frequently causes diarrhea and is an expensive medication.

Another way to avoid gastric irritation in arthritis treatment is to use an analgesic (*i.e.,* pain-relieving) drug that does not affect prostaglandin secretion at all. This is, in fact, the case with the over-the-counter drug acetaminophen, which was overlooked for years by rheumatologists, who preferred anti-inflammatory drugs because they believed such drugs forestalled additional joint damage. Recently, questions about the effectiveness of NSAIDs in preventing joint injury have led to increased use of acetaminophen for mild joint pain.

In 1994 the FDA approved a form of the NSAID naproxen (under the brand name Aleve) as a new over-the-counter medication. The agency had done the same with ibuprofen (Motrin, Nuprin, Advil) a number of years earlier. While naproxen has been shown to be an effective and safe drug, it has not been shown to be superior to ibuprofen. Further, there are questions about its potential to accumulate in the body. Various NSAIDs are eliminated from the body at dif-

377

ferent rates, and most depend on the kidney and liver for proper excretion. Because naproxen stays active in the body for a longer period of time than ibuprofen, pain relief lasts longer; in the elderly or in patients with kidney or liver disease, however, the drug could accumulate to a toxic level. Physicians must therefore monitor patients with chronic illnesses who use Aleve.

The search for other treatments

Polymyositis/dermatomyositis (PM/DM) is a systemic connective tissue disease characterized by degenerative changes in skeletal muscles (polymyositis) and often in the skin (dermatomyositis). It is a rare but serious, and sometimes fatal, disorder. The muscle weakness produced by the inflammation may be progressive and usually requires extensive use of steroid and immunosuppressive drugs. Further problems may arise from these drugs, and some patients do not respond to them. There is new evidence, however, that gamma globulin, given intravenously in high doses, can help treat DM and PM in both adults and children. Although preparation of the amounts of gamma globulin needed for treatment is currently prohibitively expensive (a single course of treatment may cost from $5,000 to $10,000), the discovery of gamma globulin's potential effectiveness is seen as a step toward new treatment methods for PM/DM. The hope is that cost-effective adaptations of this regimen can be found.

A procedure called photophoresis is being tried as a treatment for scleroderma, a disease characterized by gradual hardening (sclerosis) and scarring of the skin and certain internal organs. The procedure involves the ingestion of a short-acting photosensitizing drug, the removal of blood followed by its exposure to a light source, and then the return of the treated blood to the patient. In theory, this process selects and removes or changes the activity of the immune system cells that incite scleroderma. Studies show that photophoresis is probably safe, although it is invasive and extremely expensive. It has not yet been determined whether the procedure is effective.

Rheumatological complications of HIV

In the past few years, HIV has been associated with several autoimmune diseases not previously considered to be related to other pathogenic processes. Reiter's syndrome, a disorder marked by inflammation in the joints, the gastrointestinal and genitourinary tracts, and the eye, has developed in many patients with HIV infection. Others have developed inflammatory processes similar to those that occur in Sjögren's syndrome, a disorder characterized by dryness of the mouth and eyes and not thought to be primarily viral in nature. Inflammation of blood vessels (vasculitis) also has been described in those with HIV infection.

These associations suggest that autoimmune diseases may in some instances be attributable to in-fectious agents. In some diseases of animals, the immune system cells called lymphocytes fail to undergo the normal process of programmed cell death (apoptosis). This failure has been linked to the presence of a retrovirus; the abnormal lymphocytes live longer and, as they accumulate, symptoms like those of autoimmune disease emerge. Researchers are now asking if HIV may be capable of producing a similar pattern in humans.

Foreign substances and immunity

One of the principal controversies in rheumatology today concerns the role of implants in triggering autoimmune disorders. The uncertainties surrounding this subject have been amply demonstrated in the contradictory testimony presented at hearings on the possible health risks of silicone-gel-filled breast, testicular, and penile implants. Silicone is an oil-based compound used in a gel form in implants. Over time, it is apt to leak from these implants. Some women with silicone-gel breast implants have experienced local discomfort and have developed fibrous tissue around the implant, an indication of inflammation and scarring.

In animal studies the use of silicone-like oils as vehicles for vaccines is associated with a stronger immune response than is elicited by other forms of delivery. Evidence seems to be mounting that the introduction of silicone into the human body may have a similar effect on the immune system. Whether the process indeed causes an immunotoxic reaction remains to be determined. Nonetheless, the fact that some implant recipients have developed conditions similar to RA and lupus was sufficiently alarming that the FDA recommended an end to the routine use of silicone-gel breast implants for cosmetic purposes. Whether the symptoms of these disorders will abate with removal of the implant is not yet known. Complicating matters, residual silicone that has leaked from implants into breast tissue cannot be surgically removed. The precise risk of autoimmune diseases' arising from implants remains unknown, however. A recent study from the Mayo Clinic in Rochester, Minn., found no association whatsoever.

The injection of bovine collagen to remove wrinkles and scars has been associated with an increased incidence of dermatomyositis. A high proportion of these cases have shown evidence of an immune response to collagen, suggesting that the foreign substance was a stimulus for the development of the disease. At present, however, the number of cases is too small to determine whether there is a definite link. Perhaps the best advice for anyone considering such procedures is to remember that no foreign substance introduced into the body has been proved conclusively to be entirely safe. Even though the risks may be small, prospective patients should carefully consider the actual long-term benefit of mainly cosmetic procedures.

Fibromyalgia: new theories, new acceptance

Fibromyalgia is an enigmatic disorder that is best characterized as a widespread lowering of the pain threshold at soft tissue sites throughout the body. The cause of this rheumatic disease remains unknown—a situation that both adds to the frustration of sufferers and produces a great deal of consternation on the part of physicians who must diagnose and treat the problem. Many physicians have had doubts that the symptoms patients describe actually exist. Moreover, in some cases psychosomatic elements may be present, compounding the difficulty of diagnosis and treatment and adding to the controversy that surrounds this poorly understood condition.

Recently, rheumatology experts have begun to study the disease systematically, and some progress has been made. Formerly called fibrositis, the disorder has been officially renamed fibromyalgia (*myalgia* meaning "muscle pain"), since there is no evidence of inflammation (as would be indicated by the suffix *itis*). There are limited data to suggest that the disorder may arise from a deficiency of the neurotransmitter serotonin in peripheral nerves or even in the nervous system itself. Although this serotonin-deficiency hypothesis still needs to be verified, it at least suggests that a plausible explanation of the problem, which has thus far been lacking, will be found with further investigation. It is also important for patients that the disease be clearly distinguished from chronic Lyme disease and chronic fatigue syndrome, both of which share some symptoms with fibromyalgia.

Fibromyalgia continues to be a contentious illness, and some physicians remain skeptics. Nonetheless, other musculoskeletal pain syndromes are well accepted by medical science, even though they too are based solely on subjective reports by patients who have no physical evidence of abnormality. Polymyalgia rheumatica, for instance, is a recognized syndrome in which the patient's complaints of widespread pain *are* accepted by physicians despite the lack of clear signs. Until it is better understood, this should also be the case with fibromyalgia.

—*David E. Trentham, M.D.*

Skin Cancer

Skin cancer, the world's most common form of cancer, is also one of the most treatable and preventable. Both cutaneous melanoma—cancer of pigment-producing cells (melanocytes) in the skin—and nonmelanoma skin cancer (NMSC)—cancer of the so-called barrier-producing cells that manufacture keratin, the tough protein that is the skin's major constituent (keratinocytes)—represent growing public health problems. Both health professionals and the general public have critical roles to play in the prevention and early detection of skin cancer.

Alarming rates: causes and patterns

Skin cancer rates are rising. In the United States alone, there are at least one million new cases a year, a number equal to that for all other forms of cancer combined. At least one in six Americans (and possibly as many as one in three) will suffer from skin cancer in his or her lifetime. Approximately 90,000 new cases of melanoma, the most dangerous type of skin cancer, occur each year worldwide, and in the U.S. the incidence of melanoma is increasing faster than that of any other kind of cancer. The world's highest NMSC and melanoma incidence rates occur in Queensland, Australia, where melanoma alone is the third most commonly diagnosed malignancy. Skin cancer can also kill; in the U.S. it causes about 9,000 deaths a year. The deaths are often of young adults, and most of them are due to metastatic melanoma (that which has spread outside of the skin to other parts of the body).

While skin cancer occurs in all human populations, Caucasian adults carry the highest risk. White adults, especially those with light complexions, who burn easily and tan poorly after sun exposure, have higher skin cancer rates than people with darker pigmentation. Persons of Celtic or Anglo-Saxon background are particularly vulnerable. Specific associated host or genetic factors include light eye color, light hair color, and a tendency to freckle.

Increasing human exposure to sunlight—ultraviolet (UV) radiation—in the 20th century seems to be responsible for the extraordinary rise in skin cancer rates. Experiments have shown that the UV portion of sunlight, which represents less than 5% of the total solar energy reaching the Earth, is the major culprit. Differing patterns of exposure to UV radiation may account for different types and degrees of skin cancer. The risk of NMSC, for example, is directly proportional to cumulative UV radiation over many decades, and over 90% of NMSC occurs in maximally sun-exposed body areas. In addition, distinctive DNA mutations, or "fingerprints," attributable to UV rays in human NMSC tumors support a causative role for sunlight. In contrast, intermittent harsh recreational sun exposure, such as blistering sunburns in childhood and adolescence, appears to increase the risk of developing melanoma during adult life. Longer UV rays (UVA), with wavelengths of 320–400 nm (nanometers; billionths of a meter), and shorter UV rays (UVB), with lengths of 290–320 nm, are often considered separately because of their different properties. While UVA reaches the surface of the Earth in greater quantity, UVB is more biologically active in the skin and therefore more readily causes redness, burning, tanning, and DNA mutations. Artificial sources of UV radiation exposure (such as sunlamps and sun beds) require further investigation, as they represent increasingly common exposures that pose potential risks.

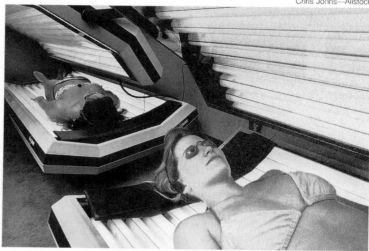

The incidence of skin cancer is rising at alarming rates. Though all populations are affected, Caucasian adults—especially those with light-colored hair and eyes, who have a tendency to freckle and burn easily— are at highest risk. Increased exposure to sunlight and depletion of the stratospheric ozone have contributed to the present skin cancer epidemic. Personal behavior is also an important factor. Artificial indoor tanning devices, which constitute a growing source of ultraviolet-light exposure, undoubtedly further increase the skin cancer risk.

Stratospheric ozone depletion, which is causing increased amounts of UVB radiation to reach the Earth's surface, may serve to exacerbate the skin cancer problem. The stratosphere, a region roughly 16 to 48 km (10 to 30 mi) above the surface of the Earth, is rich in ozone (O_3), a highly reactive form of oxygen. Ozone absorbs UV radiation, prevents it from reaching the Earth's surface, and remits the energy as heat. Inert chlorofluorocarbons (CFCs), produced by industry and used in insulating materials and as refrigerants and aerosol propellants, are increasing in the atmosphere at a rate of 5–7% a year. CFCs can initiate a series of chemical reactions that ultimately deplete ozone.

In 1985 researchers documented an Antarctic ozone hole, enhanced and exacerbated by the polar vortex, a huge air mass trapped locally by prevailing winds blowing in a circular pattern. More recent data document ozone loss in other geographic areas, resulting in an increase in UV radiation reaching the Earth. The United Nations Environment Program predicts that a 10% ozone depletion over Europe and North America would increase the incidence of NMSC by 26%.

Other risk factors for skin cancer deserve mention. Environmental factors have been linked to NMSC, including ionizing radiation (X-rays) and arsenic exposure, as have certain medical treatments (*e.g.,* psoralen and UVA [PUVA] treatment) and certain genetic disorders (*e.g.,* nevoid basal cell carcinoma syndrome). Higher-than-average numbers of moles and the presence of atypical moles are markers for persons at high risk for melanoma. In addition, those with a family history of melanoma are at increased risk, suggesting an as-yet-unidentified inherited predisposition.

Melanoma

Malignant melanoma, the most serious form of skin cancer, can be fatal when it spreads from the skin to other body organs. Fortunately, the prognosis improves dramatically when the cancer is diagnosed and treated at an early stage. Persons with early melanomas confined to the skin can be cured by simple surgical excision of the lesion. On the other hand, melanoma that spreads to regional lymph nodes or other organs generally leads to death. While overall five-year melanoma survival rates in the U.S. have risen from 49% (in the early 1950s) to 82% (in the early 1990s), death rates over the same time period have also risen by nearly 150% because melanoma is occurring more and more frequently. Hence, the prevention and early recognition of melanoma are critical to saving lives.

Melanoma can occur anywhere on the skin. The back (in both men and women) and lower legs (in women) tend to be favored sites. Early recognition is possible because melanoma has distinctive features. These telltale signs are designated by the letters *A, B, C,* and *D:*

- *A* for asymmetry
- *B* for border (irregular)
- *C* for color (black or multicolored)
- *D* for diameter (greater than 6 mm [0.25 in])

As cutaneous melanoma is a visible tumor, it should be more easily discovered in an asymptomatic phase than other types of cancer. Interestingly, some studies have found that men are less likely than women to notice melanoma. Of 213 melanoma patients studied, 66% of the women detected their own lesions, whereas only 42% of the men did. Among the men, 23% said lesions were first spotted by their wives, 30% by a medical professional, and 6% by someone else (*e.g.,* another family member or friend). Among the women, only 2% of their melanomas were first detected by their husbands; 22% reported that lesions were spotted by a medical professional, and 9% reported they were first noticed by someone else.

Any new mole or one that changes in size, shape, or color—i.e., that has A, B, C, or D features—may in fact be melanoma and therefore should be medically evaluated without undue delay. Further, anyone who discovers a potential melanoma should not irritate the spot by poking or probing. Nor should one attempt self-treatment with topical salves or ointments until the lesion has been evaluated by a professional.

Persons at high risk for melanoma may benefit from having regular skin examinations by a skin diseases expert. Such exams have resulted in detection of earlier tumors in people who have relatives with melanoma. Because white men aged 50 and over have a greater risk of dying from melanoma than any other segment of society, they would likely benefit from special education and early detection efforts.

Nonmelanoma skin cancer

NMSC occurs on maximally sun-exposed areas such as the head, neck, and hands in 90% of cases. The two most common NMSC subtypes, basal cell carcinoma and squamous cell carcinoma, generally invade locally, metastasize (spread) infrequently, and are associated with high cure rates. Basal cell carcinoma classically appears as a pearly, translucent, raised skin lesion, sometimes with a central depression and visibly dilated blood vessels. Squamous cell carcinoma is a gritty plaque, often with a pink or red base. Treatment options for NMSC include destructive modalities such as freezing the tumor, electrodesiccation and curettage, surgical excision, or radiation.

While NMSC metastasis is uncommon, recurrence occurs frequently. Recurrence rates vary between 5% and 40% for basal cell carcinoma and between 0.5% and 23% for squamous cell carcinoma, depending on the initial treatment modality and the number of years of follow-up. Most recurrent cancerous basal cell lesions develop in the same location within 3

years after removal of the primary lesion, but up to a quarter will recur as much as 5 to 10 years later. Risk factors for recurrent NMSC include age greater than 70 years, anatomic location (especially lesions on skin folds or the central portion of the face), large size (lesion diameter greater than 2.5 cm [one inch]), lesions not easily differentiated, and lesions arising from a chronic wound.

A study reported in 1992 by researchers at Dartmouth Medical School, Hanover, N.H., found that patients with prior NMSC also have a substantially increased risk of developing a new skin cancer—in either the same part of the body or another part. Overall the estimated risk of developing a new NMSC is 35% after three years and 50% after five years. Generally the new tumor is of the same cell type as the previous one but is distinctly not a recurring tumor. The Dartmouth researchers found that among 1,805 subjects with a history of NMSC, the risk of a subsequent tumor was highest for men, people aged 60 and over, and those who had had several previous skin cancers. The difference between recurring and new lesions may not always be apparent.

Highly preventable cancers

Skin cancer prevention efforts have focused on the identification and education of susceptible individuals to reduce excessive exposure to UV radiation. Prevention programs stress the importance of minimization of sun exposure and elimination of harsh sun reactions, such as sunburn. Personal protection guidelines stress avoiding sun exposure during peak UVB hours (10 AM–2 PM), wearing broad-brimmed hats and protective clothing (tightly woven fabrics, shirts with long sleeves, long pants, etc.), using sunscreen, staying in the shade, being aware of photosensitizing medications that can exacerbate effects of even minimal sun exposure, and avoiding suntan parlors.

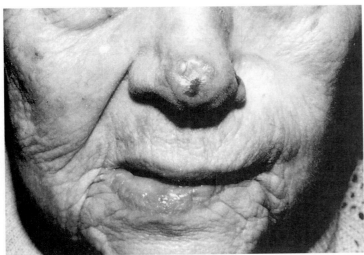

A typical basal cell carcinoma (such as the one shown here on the nose) appears as a pearly, translucent, raised nodule with a central depression. These nonmelanoma skin cancers occur most often on sun-exposed parts of the body, spread to other parts of the body relatively rarely, and are highly curable, especially if recognized and treated early.

Courtesy of Howard K. Koh, M.D., and Barbara Gilchrest, M.D.

Little Miss Coppertone, who for decades unabashedly exposed herself on the beach (right)— and paid the consequences— is now "sun smart." In the summer of 1994 she wisely began covering up in the midday sun (far right) and at the same time helped promote the daily ultraviolet radiation index that the U.S. National Weather Service began to make available for television, radio, and newspaper weather forecasts.

Moderate sun exposure permits the skin to make vitamin D and promotes a sense of well-being. Hence, using common sense in the sun is the key. Because people receive most of their UV light exposure before adulthood, children and adolescents should be targeted in public health efforts. Parents can help instill "safe sun" habits in youngsters at an early age.

Recent studies indicate that regular and consistent use of the sunscreens and sunblocks that are available today can protect against both UVA and UVB rays. Sunscreens, which absorb UV light through invisible chemical agents such as para-aminobenzoic acid (PABA) and PABA esters or non-PABA compounds are ranked by their sun protection factor (SPF); a sunscreen with an SPF of 10 allows an individual to be exposed to 10 times more sunlight before skin reddens than without protection. Sunblocks, such as zinc oxide, the opaque white ointment that lifeguards often use on their noses, physically block UV light. A recent study in Australia found that regular use of sunscreens prevented the development of solar (actinic) keratosis, a precursor of squamous-cell carcinoma; thus, by implication, regular sunscreen use could possibly reduce the risk of NMSC.

Most experts recommend the liberal application of sunscreens of at least SPF 15 (with reapplication after swimming or sweating) to block out most of the harmful rays of the sun. Projections suggest a 78% reduction in the lifetime risk of skin cancer for individuals who regularly use sunscreens during the first 18 years of life. However, the precise role that sunscreens play in preventing skin cancer, particularly melanoma, awaits further research. The Food and Drug Administration is currently considering revised labeling for sunscreens that would state that regular use may reduce the chance of skin cancer and other skin damage.

It is hoped that behavior change—*i.e.,* fewer hours of sunlight exposure, more sunscreen use, and less determination to obtain a tan—will lead to reduced skin cancer rates in the future. Unfortunately, only a minority of teenagers currently use sunscreens and other sun protection regularly. Only half of U.S. adults regularly use sunscreen, even during intentional exposures, and only a quarter regularly use a product with the recommended SPF of 15 or above. Moreover, surveys suggest that a suntan is still viewed as attractive and healthy by most Americans. By contrast, in Australia a strong coalition of health care, government, and school officials, with major support from the media, has started to make an impact. Public awareness of the sun's potential to damage the skin has increased and, more important, sun-seeking behavior has been altered.

Preservation of stratospheric ozone, essential to life on Earth, should be another part of the global strategy for future skin cancer control. Attempts to combat ozone depletion thus far have included national and international bans against CFCs. The U.S. banned the use of CFCs in hair sprays and other aerosols in 1978. In 1987 the Montreal Protocol on Substances That Deplete the Ozone Layer, ratified by more than 50 countries, called for a 50% reduction of CFCs worldwide by the turn of the century. In 1990 this goal was upgraded to a total phaseout of CFCs by the year 2000. Increasing use of hydrochlorofluorocarbons as CFC substitutes, recycling CFCs from automobile air conditioners, and replacing CFCs used in making foam insulation are other measures that will reduce ozone depletion.

In June 1994 the U.S. National Weather Service began issuing a daily "UV index" to warn people of the need for sun safety. It is hoped that this will be another way of raising sun awareness.

Skin cancer is common but preventable. With continued prevention, education, and early-detection efforts, there should be fewer cases and fewer deaths from skin cancer in the future.

—*Howard K. Koh, M.D., and Barbara A. Gilchrest, M.D.*

Meta-analysis: Nuisance or New Science?

by Steven N. Goodman, M.D., Ph.D., and Kay Dickersin, Ph.D.

Meta-analysis? For most nonscientists, who think of *analysis* as a word that describes all of the ways that scientists sift, summarize, and interpret data, it may be surprising to learn that there is a new discipline that purports to do more. Meta-analysis is not some arcane, hypertechnical form of analysis but rather a set of techniques designed to do what most people thought scientists had been doing all along—combining results from many experiments to come up with a synthesis of all data on a specific scientific question.

The term *meta-analysis* was proposed in 1976 by the U.S. educational psychologist Gene V. Glass, who defined it as "the statistical analysis of a large collection of analysis results from individual studies for the purpose of integrating the findings." However, the term was not widely accepted until relatively recently. For many years a vigorous debate was conducted in the biomedical literature over the appropriateness of numerous other descriptors, such as "overview," "data pooling," "literature synthesis," "systematic review," and "quantitative review." In 1989 the issue was essentially settled by the National Library of Medicine (NLM) when it introduced meta-analysis as a new medical subject heading. Later, in 1993, the NLM—the world's largest medical research library, which publishes *Index Medicus,* a cumulative index of the literature of medicine—established "meta-analysis" as a formal publication type.

Origins of the method

Although the recognition of meta-analysis as a scientific method, if not an actual discipline, is fairly recent, the process itself has a long history. Data pooling goes at least as far back as the work of British statistician Karl Pearson in the late 19th and early 20th centuries, although the practice of synthesizing research data, at least on an informal basis, has certainly been in existence as long as such data have been generated. Pearson's "meta-analysis" consisted of an averaging of five estimates of the correlation between inoculation for typhoid fever and death from the disease. The results led him to conclude that the vaccine was not highly effective. Work on combining results of separate studies was done by a number of influential U.S. and British statisticians long before the current surge in activity.

After Glass's introduction of the term *meta-analysis,* many social scientists started pursuing such studies. Subsequently, meta-analysis was "discovered" by medicine, public health, and health services research, and over the past 10 years the field has seen a rapid expansion. In 1986 there were only 21 citations using the word *meta-analysis* in MEDLINE, the NLM's electronic database, which indexes essentially all biomedical journal articles. Since then, the number has more than doubled each year. Meta-analysis of epidemiological data has only recently become commonplace, although one of the earliest meta-analyses, published almost 30 years ago, examined the association between prenatal X-ray exposure and childhood cancer risk. There are now at least two medical journals that publish mainly meta-analyses, and a number of "meta-meta-analyses" have appeared—evaluating the quality of meta-analyses themselves!

Usefulness in medical practice

In biomedical research meta-analysis has been most widely used to evaluate the efficacy of medical treatments—in particular those treatments that have been assessed in carefully controlled experiments on humans, known as clinical trials. It is not possible to appreciate why there has been an explosion of interest in meta-analysis without understanding what preceded it.

In the past a doctor who wanted to determine the best treatment for a particular patient could turn primarily to one of three written sources: (1) reports of original research on that topic, (2) a "review" article in a medical journal that summarized the current knowledge on the subject, or (3) a textbook. None of these was the perfect source of information. It is a rare research article that reports results so definitive that a physician could, with confidence, immediately give the treatment to a patient. In addition, many clinical experiments that examine therapies with moderate benefits study too few patients to be able to discern that modest effect statistically. A so-called negative study—one that shows no statistically significant effect—rarely proves that the treatment has no clinically meaningful benefit. Finally, practicing physicians often do not have the time to retrieve all the research reported in the literature or the skills to critically assess the validity of the results.

For these reasons many physicians have come to depend on review articles and textbooks, which provide a synthesis of the research by experts in a particular clinical field. Yet these sources have their own problems. Often, authors do not provide a truly comprehensive summary of the published research but instead emphasize those studies that are most consistent with their own practice preferences or studies that other scientists may judge to be methodologically weak. Even if the research literature is well represented in a review, it is hard to know how to weigh the results of those studies showing a treatment benefit against those that find no benefit. It was for these reasons that scientists began to examine ways of providing reviews that were systematic and comprehensive and could present a proper quantitative measure of the totality of evidence in a given field.

The qualitative component

A properly conducted meta-analysis has two components, qualitative and quantitative. The qualitative part involves first carefully defining the medical or biological question that will be addressed and then devising a literature search strategy that will find all clinical trials that pertain to this question. Typically, the search is restricted to clinical experiments that are randomized (*i.e.,* treatments are assigned to the study participants on the basis of chance) and controlled (*i.e.,* there is at least one control group to compare with the treatment group). Such experiments are known as randomized controlled trials. Finding such research often is not

easy: studies with similar objectives may be coded with different keywords in electronic databases such as MEDLINE; some are published only in abstract form; and some are never published at all. Typically, investigators depend on multiple sources of information to identify these trials—bibliography searches, interviews with investigators in the field, surveys of researchers, personal contacts, and so forth.

But even when all of the relevant trials can be identified, the work is not over. Clinical trials can vary widely in design. Because different trials use different criteria when enrolling patients, measure somewhat different endpoints, administer the treatment somewhat differently, and measure or report other relevant patient factors differently, the matter of deciding which studies should or can be included in the meta-analysis is not simple and straightforward. There are several examples of meta-analyses on the same topic that combined disparate groups of studies and came up with somewhat disparate conclusions. In a properly done meta-analysis, all of the most important features of the research in an area should be laid out clearly for the reader. In addition, most meta-analysts try to assess the quality of the reported trials and point out the ways in which research in that field is deficient and could be improved. This qualitative component of meta-analysis is often its most useful contribution, but it is also the component that is most likely to be inadequate.

After determining the trials that will be included, the meta-analyst must decide whether to use only the summary data published in the literature or to contact the original investigators and attempt to obtain the more detailed original data on each patient. Original data offer the tremendous advantage of allowing the

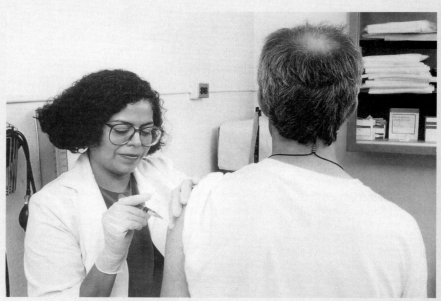

An AIDS patient receives an injection as part of a controlled clinical trial. Such trials provide data that, in turn, are used in making critical medical decisions. By combining the results from many trials, meta-analysis broadens the base of the decision-making process. The ultimate goal is improved patient care.

meta-analyst to statistically "adjust" for individual patient differences, as well as to conduct analyses that may not have been reported in the published paper. However, obtaining such information is extremely labor-intensive, and the original investigators may no longer have the data or may be unwilling to share them. Thus, the vast majority of meta-analyses currently reported in the medical literature are derived solely from published summaries.

The quantitative component

The second component of a meta-analysis is the quantitative one. Estimates of treatment benefit are combined into a single "best guess," which usually has a higher degree of precision than any of the contributing experiments. Before this step can be taken, however, the meta-analyst must ensure that the trials are similar enough that their results can be pooled. This is done with a standard statistical tool, a test of homogeneity. If the trial results are determined by this test to be too disparate to have occurred by chance, they are usually not combined. Rather, an effort is made to explain their differences. Thus, the oft-repeated claim that meta-analysis can resolve "conflicting" trial results is not true and is based on the simplistic notion of statistical conflict; *i.e.,* that trials conflict when one trial is statistically significant and another is not. In fact, two trials showing exactly the same treatment effect may differ in their degree of "statistical significance" only because one trial has more subjects than the other. Meta-analysis shows that these trials do not conflict but rather provide different degrees of evidence for the observed effect.

This component then mathematically combines the selected trials. The mathematics are not difficult, and standard formulas are employed. Estimates of the effects seen in all of the contributing studies are averaged, using a "weighting factor" related to their precision; because large studies produce the most precise estimates, they get the most weight. The results of this pooling are usually displayed in a graphlike format as a series of parallel horizontal lines with a symbol (*e.g.,* a circle, square, or triangle) near the center of each, representing the observed effect of a particular study, and the length of the line representing the imprecision in that estimate of effect (namely, the confidence interval). The pooled effect is also represented by a symbol located near the center of a line. Typically, the symbol (the pooled estimate) lies roughly in the middle of the other symbols (the individual estimates), and the line (the pooled confidence interval) is shorter than any of the others. Figure 1 (page 387) shows the results of one large meta-analysis that evaluated the drug tamoxifen in the treatment of early breast cancer.

Another part of the quantitative meta-analysis is a search for subgroups of studies (or of patients) that show a degree of effect from the treatment in question different from others. The sensitivity of the overall effect arrived at, or the summary result, to a variety of biological and methodological assumptions can thereby be explored. In some circumstances the summary result may not be the most useful number for a doctor. When using the results of a meta-analysis to make decisions about treating Mr. Smith, the doctor may want to focus on the single trial or subset of trials conducted in patients most like Mr. Smith. The initial qualitative component of a meta-analysis should present enough information about the patients and interventions in each study that the doctor can decide which trials are most relevant to his or her patient. Typically, however, the pooled estimate from all the trials is the best one to use. While the degree of benefit may vary somewhat from one patient to another, it is very unusual for a treatment to be on average beneficial in some and actually harmful in others.

Apples and oranges?

It should not be hard to see why such a method might generate controversy. Among the most often heard criticisms are that meta-analysts are combining "apples and oranges" and that the resulting summaries have an undeserved aura of objectivity and authority. Proponents of meta-analysis counter that the combined trials are chosen to be "similar enough" on important characteristics that the resultant summaries should be interpretable and valid. In most cases this is a reasonable claim, but just how reasonable is a matter of scientific judgment.

Another cavil arises from the seemingly automatic nature of the process. One outspoken critic of meta-analysis has complained that "the study of previous studies is being reduced to a routinized task of coding relegated to a research assistant, upping output per author-month by suppressing any role for wisdom." There is some truth in this charge; meta-analyses vary in quality, and the poorer ones do the discipline no credit. But as will be demonstrated in the example described below, a properly done meta-analysis takes considerable effort and is as likely to depress "author output" as to increase it.

Another objection to meta-analysis has come from those who conduct the clinical trials, who sometimes resent their years of tremendous effort being reduced to an easily calculated "effect size," with the consequent elevation of the meta-analyst to the level of an expert in the field. In the past the large, carefully conducted clinical trial was regarded as the "gold standard" of clinical research. To some extent it still is. It is rare to find groups of small trials with patients, methods, and outcomes similar enough that their combination could improve upon a single large trial's ability to reveal internal patterns that might be clinically meaningful. The suggestion that medical research should move toward many small trials, the results of which would then be subjected to meta-analysis, threatens the acknowledged benefits of larger trials. But it is also clear that the combination of many well-done trials can lead to conclusions that are on a firmer foundation than those based upon a single well-conducted trial. The optimal balance between small trials, large trials, and meta-analyses is not yet a settled issue and is likely to be debated for years to come.

How it works: an example

One of the most prominent exponents of meta-analysis is Richard Peto, a biostatistician at the University of Oxford. Peto and his colleagues perform a particular type of meta-analysis that entails the collaboration of numerous individual investigators. As noted above, meta-analyses are usually based on data presented in published articles. The Oxford group has chosen instead to get its data directly from the investigators. This allows them to examine the actual data rather than depend on extrapolating information from published graphs or tables.

Peto, who refers to meta-analyses as "overviews," starts by contacting all of the investigators involved in the original studies that he and his group have identified as relevant for inclusion. Some of the studies might have been conducted many years earlier, and some might be fairly recent. Most of the study results are available in the published literature, although some are unpublished. The collaborative group then holds a meeting and agrees to a set of ground rules, including which individual patient data from each of the studies will be used and which members of the group will be credited as authors of the meta-analysis.

One of the best-known series of meta-analyses using individual patient data is that produced by the Oxford-based Early Breast Cancer Trialists' Collaborative Group, whose members include researchers at hospitals, universities, and other institutions around the world. This series comprises more than 100 separate analyses concerning treatment for early breast cancer; it includes analyses related to surgery (mastectomy versus lumpectomy), radiation (radiation versus no radiation), and chemotherapy (cytotoxic chemotherapy versus no chemotherapy; tamoxifen treatment versus no tamoxifen). Because individual patient data have been made available from each study, the group has been able to perform all its analyses specifically comparing subgroup populations, such as older versus younger women, as well as women who differed in other ways.

Subgroup analyses often are not possible in meta-analyses that rely solely on published data. Even in a research area where most investigators consider a certain type of subgrouping important—for example, grouping by age—different researchers may choose to organize their data differently. In breast cancer studies, for example, one investigator might analyze data comparing women over 50 with those under 50, while another might compare postmenopausal women with premenopausal women. The original data from each study include the actual age of each woman, however, allowing the meta-analysts to use any age cutoff they choose in framing their analysis and still include data from all studies.

Figure 1, adapted from a report by the Early Breast Cancer Trialists' Collaborative Group, published in the British journal *The Lancet* in 1992, shows the effect of tamoxifen (a drug that blocks estrogen receptors) on deaths in women with early breast cancer. The outcome measure is a figure called the *odds ratio*—approximately equal to the risk of breast cancer in those on tamoxifen divided by the risk in those who did not take the drug. If tamoxifen had no effect, the odds ratio between it and a placebo would be equal to 1.0. If tamoxifen was protective, the odds ratio would be less than 1.0. The result of each clinical trial is indicated in Figure 1 by a single horizontal line. The line represents the 99% *confidence interval* (in most meta-analyses, 95% is used) around the "best guess" of each trial, which is indicated by a black square, the size of which is proportional to the sample size of each trial. The confidence interval is the range of estimates of effect (*i.e.,* odds ratios) that is judged by convention to be statistically compatible with the observed effect for that trial. If an interval includes an odds ratio of 1.0, then by definition that trial has not ruled out a zero benefit, and its observed effect is deemed "nonsignificant" even if, on the other side of the interval, it also does not rule out a large benefit.

As can be seen in Figure 1, few of the single trials provide a "definitive" result; almost every confidence interval crosses the solid vertical line that indicates equivalence (*i.e.,* odds ratio = 1.0). (The dashed vertical line represents the pooled result.) The presentation of the data from all trials on the same figure allows one to reach a summary conclusion by using both statistical (formal) and visual (informal) methods of interpretation. The combined analysis presented in Figure 1 indicates that the odds of death for women with breast cancer were smaller for those who took tamoxifen than for those who did not—*i.e.,* women on tamoxifen survived longer—even though few of the individual trials could claim to show this.

An advantage of this type of presentation is that it allows the reader to judge the available data with and without certain studies. For example, it has recently been revealed that a clinic participating in breast cancer studies under the National Surgical Adjuvant Breast and Bowel Project (NSABP) submitted falsified data. Today one might, therefore, decide to recalculate the combined odds ratio, either formally or informally, without NSABP results; omitting the two NSABP studies from the meta-analysis would have a negligible effect on the overall results.

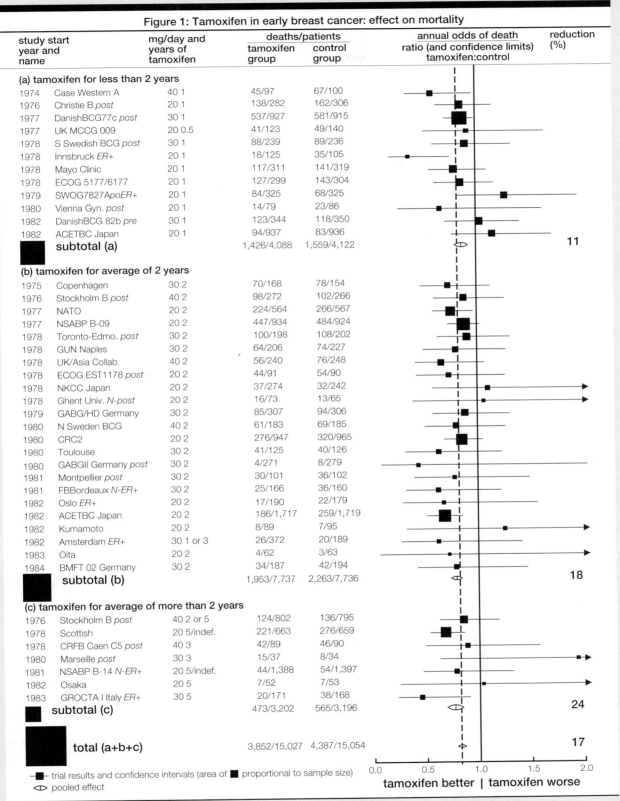

Figure 1: Tamoxifen in early breast cancer: effect on mortality

study start year and name	mg/day and years of tamoxifen	deaths/patients tamoxifen group	control group	annual odds of death ratio (and confidence limits) tamoxifen:control	reduction (%)
(a) tamoxifen for less than 2 years					
1974 Case Western A	40 1	45/97	67/100		
1976 Christie B *post*	20 1	138/282	162/306		
1977 DanishBCG77c *post*	30 1	537/927	581/915		
1977 UK MCCG 009	20 0.5	41/123	49/140		
1978 S Swedish BCG *post*	30 1	88/239	89/236		
1978 Innsbruck *ER+*	20 1	18/125	35/105		
1978 Mayo Clinic	20 1	117/311	141/319		
1978 ECOG 5177/6177	20 1	127/299	143/304		
1979 SWOG7827ApoER+	20 1	84/325	68/325		
1980 Vienna Gyn. *post*	20 1	14/79	23/86		
1982 DanishBCG 82b *pre*	30 1	123/344	118/350		
1982 ACETBC Japan	20 1	94/937	83/936		
subtotal (a)		1,426/4,088	1,559/4,122		11
(b) tamoxifen for average of 2 years					
1975 Copenhagen	30 2	70/168	78/154		
1976 Stockholm B *post*	40 2	98/272	102/266		
1977 NATO	20 2	224/564	266/567		
1977 NSABP B-09	20 2	447/934	484/924		
1978 Toronto-Edmo. *post*	30 2	100/198	108/202		
1978 GUN Naples	30 2	64/206	74/227		
1978 UK/Asia Collab.	40 2	56/240	76/248		
1978 ECOG EST1178 *post*	20 2	44/91	54/90		
1978 NKCC Japan	20 2	37/274	32/242		
1978 Ghent Univ. *N-post*	20 2	16/73	13/65		
1979 GABG/HD Germany	30 2	85/307	94/306		
1980 N Sweden BCG	40 2	61/183	69/185		
1980 CRC2	20 2	276/947	320/965		
1980 Toulouse	30 2	41/125	40/126		
1980 GABGII Germany *post*	30 2	4/271	8/279		
1981 Montpellier *post*	30 2	30/101	36/102		
1981 FBBordeaux *N-ER+*	30 2	25/166	36/160		
1982 Oslo *ER+*	20 2	17/190	22/179		
1982 ACETBC Japan	20 2	186/1,717	259/1,719		
1982 Kumamoto	20 2	8/89	7/95		
1982 Amsterdam *ER+*	30 1 or 3	26/372	20/189		
1983 Oita	20 2	4/62	3/63		
1984 BMFT 02 Germany	30 2	34/187	42/194		
subtotal (b)		1,953/7,737	2,263/7,736		18
(c) tamoxifen for average of more than 2 years					
1976 Stockholm B *post*	40 2 or 5	124/802	136/795		
1978 Scottish	20 5/indef.	221/663	276/659		
1978 CRFB Caen C5 *post*	40 3	42/89	46/90		
1980 Marseille *post*	30 3	15/37	8/34		
1981 NSABP B-14 *N-ER+*	20 5/indef.	44/1,388	54/1,397		
1982 Osaka	20 5	7/52	7/53		
1983 GROCTA I Italy *ER+*	30 5	20/171	38/168		
subtotal (c)		473/3,202	565/3,196		24
total (a+b+c)		3,852/15,027	4,387/15,054		17

■— trial results and confidence intervals (area of ■ proportional to sample size)
⬦ pooled effect

0.0   0.5   1.0   1.5   2.0
tamoxifen better | tamoxifen worse

Adapted from Early Breast Cancer Trialists' Collaborative Group, "Systemic Treatment of Early Breast Cancer by Hormonal, Cytotoxic, or Immune Therapy," *The Lancet*, vol. 339, no. 8784 (Jan. 4, 1992), pp. 1–15

**Figure 2: Cumulative meta-analysis:
trials of thrombolytic therapy**

year	cumulative randomized controlled trials	patients	odds ratio
1960	1	23	
	2	65	
1965	3	149	
1970	4	316	
	7	1,793	
	10	2,544	
	11	2,651	
1975	15	3,311	
	17	3,929	
	22	5,452	
1980	23	5,767	
	27	6,125	
	30	6,346	
1985	33	6,571	
	43	21,059	
	54	22,051	
	65	47,185	
	67	47,531	
1990	70	48,154	

favors treatment   favors control

Adapted from Elliott M. Antman, M.D., *et al.,* "A Comparison of Results of Meta-analysis of Randomized Control Trials and Recommendations of Clinical Experts," *JAMA,* vol. 268, no. 2 (July 8, 1992), pp. 240–248. Copyright 1992, American Medical Association

Keeping doctors up-to-date

Recently an international collaborative effort called the Cochrane Collaboration started an important trend in meta-analysis. It is identifying and organizing randomized clinical trials in all areas of medicine so that meta-analyses can be done. The group intends that these meta-analyses be updated continuously; the results will be available electronically, via networks or on diskette. The project that served as a model for this effort was the Cochrane Pregnancy and Childbirth database (based on the Oxford database of Perinatal Trials), which has already accomplished this goal in the field of perinatology (the study of newborns) and is now being used worldwide.

Several Boston researchers (Joseph Lau, Elliott M. Antman, Thomas C. Chalmers, and their colleagues) have termed this technique of regular updating *cumulative meta-analysis*. It enables a cumulative estimate of a treatment's effect to be recalculated with each new trial that is performed. A cumulative meta-analysis is shown in Figure 2, representing the results of trials testing the efficacy of drugs that dissolve blood clots (thrombolytic drugs) versus other treatments for patients who have just had a heart attack. The first trial, conducted around 1960, was small (23 patients)

and showed a positive effect for the thrombolytic drug, but since the 95% confidence interval included 1.0, this positive association did not exclude chance as an explanation. If one had conducted a meta-analysis 13 years later, however, in 1973, one would have seen good evidence of the efficacy of thrombolytic treatment, based on the combined evidence from 10 trials. Because scientists generally repeat an experiment a number of times to make sure that their findings are reliable, additional trials carried out in the late 1970s would have been justifiable, but by 1986 the results from more than 40 trials were available, and by 1990 data from 70 trials had been published. If an ongoing meta-analysis had been carried out as these trials were being performed, it would have shown that by the mid-1980s there was already compelling evidence to support the efficacy of thrombolytics. This observation could have led much earlier to a halt to new studies and a recommendation that this treatment be widely employed—perhaps saving both money and lives.

What is curious is that trials continue to be done, even now, testing the effectiveness of thrombolytic therapy. One reason may be that these drugs still are not as widely used as they should be, and investigators may assume that some physicians are waiting for yet more positive evidence. Another reason may be that investigators and clinicians alike have not kept up-to-date with the available evidence. In a 1990 survey of medical textbooks, Antman and his colleagues found that the books were inconsistent in recommending the use of thrombolytics after a heart attack, though the evidence supporting this therapy was overwhelming. Moreover, some texts continued to recommend treatments that had been shown to be ineffective; several published as late as the mid-1980s made no mention of thrombolytic therapy.

Patients: the ultimate beneficiaries

With increasing use of computers, groups such as the Cochrane Collaboration will be able to keep medical information up-to-date by using methods such as cumulative meta-analysis. There is a developing movement to establish research registries in a large number of fields so that physicians, meta-analysts, and even the general public can have access to all of the completed and ongoing experimentation in a particular condition or with a specific treatment. This movement, although still in its infancy, is growing rapidly. At present, most of the activity is concentrated in the fields of AIDS and cancer research.

In the future, doctors will probably be able to use a computer to find the latest information regarding treatment for any medical condition, and meta-analysts may be able to do comprehensive searches at the keyboard with confidence. Patients will be the ultimate beneficiaries, however, in that they will be able to feel assured of getting the very best care.

Smoking

No possible claim can be made for cigarettes as enhancers of life on any level. . . . They should be regarded as the vile little marauders that they are, possessing no merit and vast lethal capacity, needing to be banished with the passion that we banish any other product that we innocently adopt only to discover that it endangers our lives.

—William Styron, novelist and former smoker, *The Nation*

By the time the now-famous 1964 document *Smoking and Health: Report of the Advisory Committee to the Surgeon General of the Public Health Service* was issued, it was well established that cigarette smoking was a major health risk. Today it is known with overwhelming scientific certainty that smoking substantially increases the risks for cancer, heart disease, emphysema, stroke, and other chronic conditions.

Not just your everyday epidemic

Currently, one in every five deaths in the United States is caused by tobacco use, including more than one-third of all cancer deaths. In fact, tobacco use is responsible for more than 400,000 deaths annually, more than the combined total from motor vehicle crashes, drug abuse, alcoholism, homicide, suicide, and AIDS—each of which is a major public health epidemic in its own right. Yet, despite this enormous public health burden, cigarettes and other tobacco products remain among the most available, least regulated, and most profitable products in U.S. society.

Once regular tobacco use has been adopted, an individual finds it difficult, if not nearly impossible, to stop using it because of a combination of physical, psychological, social, and environmental factors that are, to a large extent, directly manipulated by the tobacco industry. Recent research into and revelations about the complex and dynamic nature of the relationship between nicotine addiction and tobacco industry practices have fueled the public health efforts to achieve substantial reductions in tobacco use before the turn of the century. This report, although not an exhaustive review of the subject of smoking, addresses several major developments that have led to a state-of-the-art model of tobacco control.

Tobacco: profile of a killer

Contrary to the image portrayed by the tobacco industry, not everybody smokes. In general, the proportion of people who smoke has been declining for the past several decades. National Cancer Institute (NCI) data for 1992 indicate that fewer than 25% of U.S. adults smoke. Also, for the first time, more adult males had quit smoking (28%) than smoked (27%). However, not all demand for tobacco is declining. The U.S. production of smokeless tobacco (chewing or "dipping" tobacco or moist snuff) increased by 83% between 1981 and 1993. Smokeless tobacco, like cigarettes, is highly addictive and causes cancer and other dis-

From Andrew A. Skolnick, "Kid Stuff . . . ," *JAMA*, vol. 271, no. 8 (Feb. 23, 1994), pp. 578–579. Copyright 1994, American Medical Association

An estimated five million Americans are users of smokeless tobacco. Like cigarettes, smokeless tobacco products contain nicotine and are addictive as well as cancer-causing. Like candy cigarettes, Big League Chew shredded bubble gum is packaged to look like the "real thing" and to make tobacco use seem not only acceptable but desirable to very young children.

eases—particularly of the mouth and digestive system. Of the five million current users of smokeless tobacco, an estimated 6% are males aged 12 to 18 years.

Tobacco use among youth continues to be a serious public health concern. According to Surgeon General M. Joycelyn Elders' 1994 report *Preventing Tobacco Use Among Young People,* more than three million young people (approximately 16% of those aged 12 to 18) are regular smokers. Youths constitute a strategically important market to the tobacco industry—as "replacements" for smokers who die or quit each year. As much as 90% of all long-term tobacco use begins before high school graduation. In fact, without new teenage smokers, cigarette use would quickly become a social anachronism.

Men who smoke are 22 times more likely to die of lung cancer than those who do not smoke, and women who smoke are 12 times more likely to die of lung cancer than nonsmoking women. In the U.S., smoking accounts for 20% of all deaths and 30% of all cancer deaths. In fact, lung cancer, 87% of which is smoking-related, is now the leading cause of cancer death in both sexes; in 1986 it replaced breast cancer as the leading cause of cancer deaths among both white and black women. Among black men, lung cancer death rates rose sharply after 1950 and are now higher than the rates for white men. Both these trends coincide with increased tobacco industry marketing to women and minority groups. The NCI predicts that the lung cancer death rate for men will peak before the year 2000 and then begin a decline. Among women, however, the rate will probably increase well into the next century.

Tobacco-related death and disease are not confined only to smokers but include their nonsmoking spouses, children, and others exposed to so-called passive, or second-hand, smoke. In 1993 the U.S. Environmental Protection Agency (EPA) classified environmental tobacco smoke (ETS) as a group A carcinogen—*i.e.,* one of a select group of toxic substances known to cause cancer in humans—and found it to be responsible for 3,000 lung cancer deaths annually in nonsmokers. Other researchers calculate that when heart disease deaths and deaths from other cancers are included, mortality attributable to ETS is probably close to 53,000 annually. The EPA also found that between 150,000 and 300,000 serious respiratory ailments in young children—many of which are severe enough to require hospitalization—are caused each year by passive smoke.

In effect, the tobacco industry has brought on one of the most deadly epidemics in modern America. Worldwide, tobacco may be responsible for more than three million deaths each year. Nevertheless, in the U.S. alone, the industry spent $5,230,000,000 in 1992—an increase of nearly $600 million over the previous year—to advertise and promote cigarettes. These contradictions pose an unprecedented challenge to the public health community. This challenge, however, has not gone unanswered. Moreover, it is now being met not only with increased understanding but with effective tools for change.

Fighting Goliath

Despite the magnitude of the problems caused by tobacco use, there has been no uniform, comprehensive, or aggressive national strategy to deal with it. Rather, the response has consisted of a patch-work of dedicated public and private organizations and individuals working to stem the tide of tobacco-related death and disease. Though the resources of the antitobacco forces pale in comparison to those of the industry, many of these public health efforts have been remarkably effective. The federal government's effort to control tobacco has been channeled into research, dissemination of information, and formulation of policy. Funding for smoking-related research has been made available from several federal agencies. For example, between 1984 and 1993, the NCI funded more than 100 studies costing more than $300 million. Since 1963 the surgeon general's office has released 23 scientific reports on smoking and health, addressing topics that have included the connection between tobacco use and cancer (1982), involuntary smoking (1986), nicotine addiction (1988), and tobacco use among youth (1994). Federal policies have included requiring health warnings on cigarettes (1965), banning tobacco advertisements on the broadcast media (1970), prohibiting smoking on commercial domestic flights (1989), and increasing the federal excise tax on cigarettes from 16 to 24 cents (1990).

Despite these efforts, as already noted, tobacco is still one of the least regulated consumer products. That may soon change, however, with the recent public disclosure that the tobacco industry "doses" cigarettes with nicotine, which has led the Food and Drug Administration (FDA) to consider imposing the first serious regulations on tobacco products. In February 1994 FDA Commissioner David A. Kessler said the revelations about the addition of nicotine to tobacco products could provide "a legal basis on which to regulate these products under the drug provisions" of the law. Such an action would have far-reaching ramifications for the manufacture and sale of tobacco. In effect, any tobacco products found to contain enough nicotine to be addicting could be banned.

In early 1994, when it was disclosed that the tobacco industry "doses" its products with nicotine, David A. Kessler, commissioner of the Food and Drug Administration, lambasted industry officials and charged that cigarette manufacturers create and sustain addiction. Such manipulation of nicotine levels could provide a legal basis for imposing strict regulations that would effectively remove cigarettes from the over-the-counter market.

AP/Wide World

Although federal policies on the whole have been modest, many state and local governments have seized the initiative. Nearly every state has enacted laws restricting youth access to tobacco and smoking in public places, workplaces, and schools. A few, most notably California and Massachusetts, have raised state excise taxes on tobacco by 25 cents per pack and used at least some of the revenue for public health education and prevention programs. In 1994 Michigan raised the tobacco excise tax by 50 cents, an act that will not only provide funds for local public education and other needs but save thousands of lives each year—by encouraging current smokers to quit and discouraging youth from starting.

Many local governments have taken aggressive action to reduce smoking. Nationwide by 1993 there were more than 540 local ordinances passed to regulate tobacco use, including several that completely eliminated smoking in restaurants and workplaces and required licenses of all enterprises that sell tobacco products. Nonetheless, few state or local public health authorities have had any permanent resources (staff, funds, materials) for tobacco control—certainly none that were comparable to the tobacco-promotion resources.

The important efforts of nongovernmental voluntary health agencies, groups, and individuals should not be overlooked. Since 1977 the American Cancer Society (ACS) has annually sponsored the Great American Smokeout to foster community-based activities that encourage smokers to stop smoking for at least 24 hours and to show them that they can quit permanently. On Smokeout day in 1992, an estimated 3.3 million smokers did not smoke, an estimated 7.5 million reduced the number of cigarettes they smoked, and an estimated 1.5 million gave up smoking for three to five days following the Smokeout. Moreover, on that day alone, 9.7 million packs of cigarettes were *not* smoked, which meant that $17.8 million was *not* spent on cigarettes. The ACS, the American Lung Association, and the American Heart Association have been instrumental in informing the public of the dangers of tobacco and have formed the Coalition on Smoking OR Health, a Washington, D.C.-based organization, to advocate smoking-control policies at the national level. Added to these are the researchers, advocates, community leaders, and volunteers who have taken up the cause of tobacco control. Included are groups such as Doctors Ought to Care (DOC), Stop Teenage Addiction to Tobacco (STAT), Americans for Nonsmokers' Rights, and Group Against Smoking Pollution (GASP), to name only a few. In the past few years, many more groups have sprung up in communities across the country; each has served to reinforce community concerns about smoking-related diseases and to protect smokers and nonsmokers from tobacco use.

Even when taken together, these efforts do not represent a single, coordinated strategy. However, when they are combined with the results of research, they provide a practical model of a public health strategy that can be systematically applied toward tobacco control through the decade of the 1990s and beyond.

ASSIST: getting serious about smoking control

The American Stop Smoking Intervention Study for Cancer Prevention (ASSIST) is the largest, most comprehensive public health antismoking project ever undertaken in the United States. In October 1991, following a yearlong national competition involving 37 states, 17 state health departments were awarded federal government contracts to be part of this landmark program. These states—Colorado, Indiana, Maine, Massachusetts, Michigan, Minnesota, Missouri, New Mexico, New Jersey, New York, North Carolina, Rhode Island, South Carolina, Virginia, Washington, West Virginia, and Wisconsin—have a combined population of 91 million people, or slightly more than a third of the total U.S. population; 23 million are children and adolescents; slightly more than 10 million are African-Americans, and 7 million are Latinos or belong to other ethnic groups; and nearly 20 million are regular tobacco users.

ASSIST has major support from the NCI, whose financial outlays will exceed $120 million over the seven-year project period (1991 through 1998). The ACS is providing more than 800,000 volunteers through 1,000 local units and some $25 million to $30 million for local staff, materials, volunteers, and in-kind support. As the leading national voluntary health organization for cancer research and services, the ACS has identified smoking prevention as one of its top four priorities. When the thousands of other health and social service agencies that have joined state and local tobacco-control coalitions are added in, ASSIST represents one of the most formidable community-based public health programs ever put together. Furthermore, because ASSIST is a demonstration project and not a controlled trial, the major portion of the fiscal resources provided to the states will be used in direct support of smoking-control interventions at the community level. It is precisely because of this community-based approach that ASSIST, as a major science-based intervention model, is uniquely capable of having a major impact on tobacco use among adults and youth.

Evolution of the project. The community approach evolved over decades of scientific investigation. Research carried out in the 1980s and early '90s focused on a wide array of smoking interventions—school programs, programs at health facilities, self-help methods, and mass media campaigns. Since the same programs do not work for everyone, researchers looked at interventions aimed at special groups such

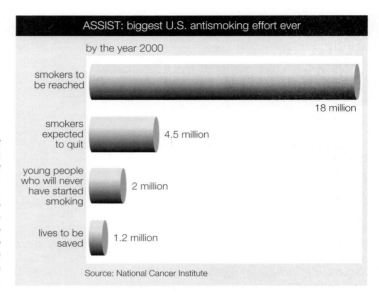

ASSIST: biggest U.S. antismoking effort ever

by the year 2000

smokers to be reached — 18 million

smokers expected to quit — 4.5 million

young people who will never have started smoking — 2 million

lives to be saved — 1.2 million

Source: National Cancer Institute

Begun in 1991, the American Stop Smoking Intervention Study for Cancer Prevention (ASSIST) is the most comprehensive antismoking project ever undertaken in the U.S.; 17 states, with a combined population of 91 million, have been awarded government contracts to participate. ASSIST's ultimate goal is to save lives; specifically, the aim is to reduce smoking prevalence in the participating states to 15% by the year 2000. If that goal is achieved, the project will have been one of the most cost-effective interventions in modern public health history.

as minorities, youth, women, and heavy smokers. To assess the combined effectiveness of these and other strategies when integrated into a community framework, the NCI launched the Community Intervention Trial for Smoking Cessation (COMMIT). COMMIT studied more than one million people in 11 cities in 1988–93 in the largest such randomized trial ever attempted. It has provided the NCI with years of practical experience in working with communities to reduce tobacco use. As early findings from this research emerged, the NCI began plans to implement a large-scale demonstration project that would reduce smoking by the turn of the century. In recognition of the need for a strong community base and access to volunteers and local organizations, the linkup with the ACS was formed. This process culminated in ASSIST.

Goals. ASSIST addresses tobacco use (cigarettes and other forms) among adults and youth, with the aim of accelerating the downward trend in tobacco consumption. Specifically, ASSIST aims to reduce smoking prevalence in participating states to 17% by 1998 and to 15% by 2000. The NCI predicts that over the entire project period 18 million smokers will be reached, 4.5 million smokers will stop smoking, 2 million young people will have been prevented from starting to smoke, and 1.2 million lives will be saved. The ASSIST goals coincide with the health-promotion and disease-prevention objectives for the nation established by the U.S. Public Health Service in 1990 as part of its Healthy People 2000 campaign.

During the first 24 months of the project (phase I), each of the 17 states conducted a detailed site analysis and needs assessment that looked at the distribution of tobacco use among the population (by age, gender, and geographic area), the economic burden of tobacco use (in terms of excess hospital use, days lost from work, and premature deaths), and the social and political climate for enforcing laws and establishing policies governing tobacco. Following these assessments, each state developed its own comprehensive five-year plan. Among the strategies proposed in these plans are: demonstrating to education and labor leaders the effectiveness of policies prohibiting smoking in schools and workplaces and educating communities about the colossal impact of tobacco advertising on the health of residents.

In the intervention phase (phase II), which began in October 1993 and will continue through 1998, sites will implement their plans. State programs will make use of the mass media to reach the public and will institute proven interventions in workplaces, health care settings, schools, churches, and other community institutions. As just one example, states will provide training for doctors, dentists, and other health care providers to make smoking-cessation counseling a routine part of their practices. Research shows that these health professionals can have a dramatic influence on their patients and that those who use special techniques are up to six times more effective in helping patients quit than those who simply advise against smoking. The Centers for Disease Control and Prevention (CDC) has found that if all primary care providers offered brief counseling to all of their patients who smoke, an additional one million persons could be helped to stop smoking each year. Health professionals should ask patients whether they smoke, advise against it, point out the substantial health benefits of not smoking, provide assistance (*e.g.,* distributing self-help materials; establishing a quitting date; in some cases prescribing nicotine replacements such as patches or gum), and provide support through follow-up. Detailed guidelines have been provided for communities to ensure that

392

all interventions selected are consistent with current scientific knowledge.

Although identifying and instituting appropriate intervention strategies are integral components of the project, ASSIST places most of its emphasis on the strategic use of the media and the adoption and implementation of policies that support nonsmoking as the accepted community norm. Major interventions include increasing the comprehensiveness of school health education, reducing minors' illegal access to tobacco products, protecting nonsmokers from exposure to ETS, restricting or eliminating advertising and promotion of tobacco products (particularly ads and promotions aimed at children and youth), increasing state excise taxes on tobacco, and making smoking-cessation resources widely available in the community.

Grass roots action. One of the most important features of ASSIST is its "grass roots," or community, base. Research and experience in tobacco control show that community involvement is essential. Programs that include community representatives in planning and implementation are more likely to be adopted, or "owned," by the community and thus will have important access to community resources, such as volunteers, local group leaders, and local media.

In 1990 the "Uptown Coalition," formed by church leaders and residents of an inner-city community in Philadelphia, thwarted a massive tobacco industry campaign introducing Uptown, a cigarette aimed at the African-American population. The coalition's efforts resulted in the withdrawal of the product one month after initial test-marketing. The Uptown ad campaign drew the wrath of Louis Sullivan, then secretary of health and human services, who said that "Uptown's message is more disease, more suffering, and more death for a group already bearing more than its share of smoking-related illness and mortality." This example and many other successful actions on the part of communities provided strong evidence that such coalitions work.

The number of community organizations that have joined ASSIST coalitions is already more than 3,000 and is expected to grow even larger as ASSIST moves through the intervention phase. These organizations receive ASSIST funds and will provide the long-term capacity for community-based smoking control that to date has been so lacking. Furthermore, with the involvement of community volunteers and advocates, this continued effort can accomplish change at a fraction of what it would cost the federal government.

Nationwide impact. ASSIST's impact will extend well beyond the 17 funded states. The ASSIST model will provide a base of experience from which other programs and initiatives, in other states and nationally, can draw. ASSIST's aggressive policy-based intervention approach already has been instrumental in shaping both the California and Massachusetts statewide tobacco-control programs, which, as noted above, are supported by funds from increased state cigarette excise taxes. And drawing on the ASSIST experience, the CDC in 1993 launched the Initiatives to Mobilize for the Prevention and Control of Tobacco Use (IMPACT) program. IMPACT provides funding (about

A smoker indulges in a cigarette outside the Department of the Treasury in Washington, D.C. Although some states have adopted more aggressive strategies than others to restrict smoking, most have enacted laws that prohibit or limit smoking in public places, workplaces, and schools; nationwide, cigarette smoking is increasingly becoming an out-of-doors activity.

Paul Hosefros—The New York Times

$5 million annually) for smoking control in the remaining states and the District of Columbia. Taken together, ASSIST programs and other initiatives that the ASSIST model has or will have stimulated represent the first time that there has been anything close to a coordinated, nationwide program for tobacco control.

Trial and error

As with most successful public health efforts, the current state-of-the-art approach to tobacco control developed over many years of trial and error. Some of the earliest tobacco-control efforts focused on persuading current smokers to quit and keeping new smokers from starting by providing information about the risks of smoking. The 1964 U.S. surgeon general's report and the antitobacco public service announcements aired on television and radio during the late 1960s increased awareness of smoking as a major public health problem and had an initial impact on reducing cigarette consumption. Clearly, however, these strategies were not sufficient—especially in light of the industry's intense campaigns to promote smoking and to confuse the public about smoking risks.

The limited success of the early antitobacco efforts forced a shift in focus to changing the behavior of individuals—so-called assisted strategies (e.g., clinic programs, behavior therapy, nicotine patches, acupuncture) that would help smokers overcome their addiction in spite of environmental influences. (Environmental influences include the distribution of free cigarettes, massive tobacco advertising campaigns, tobacco-industry sponsorship of sporting and arts events, and acceptance of smoking in restaurants, offices, and other public places.) This approach had problems, including low participation rates, high cost, and the limited potential to reach large numbers of people.

Then, as now, most smokers (close to 90%) attempted to and eventually quit using tobacco without benefit of an "assisted" strategy. Abstinence rates after 12 months for persons using self-help methods vary from 8% to 25%. Assisted methods produce success rates of between 20% and 40%. The more intensive (and costly) the program, the more successful it is likely to be. However, except for heavy smokers or those who already have early symptoms of tobacco-related disease (shortness of breath, smokers' cough, poor circulation), assisted programs are unlikely to reach the majority of smokers. Alternatively, a simple counseling message from a health care provider can reach much larger numbers. Smoking-cessation rates based on encouragement from a physician or other health professional generally vary from about 4% to more than 20%, depending on the intensity of the message, supportive therapy, and follow-up.

Changes in the social environment, such as the declining social acceptability of smoking, are directly associated with declining tobacco use. Strategies that clearly have had an impact are: raising the price of tobacco products through excise taxes; reducing access of minors to tobacco products; making schools, health care facilities, restaurants, workplaces, and other public places smoke-free; and restricting advertising and promotion.

In California a modest 25-cent rise in the state cigarette excise tax (enacted by referendum in 1988) increased the total cost from $1.75 to $2 per pack; this resulted in a 13% to 17% decline in cigarette consumption in the first year, and by 1994 there had been a 28% statewide reduction. In Canada a $3 hike in tobacco taxes (raising the total cost to nearly $6 per pack) resulted in a 60% decline in tobacco consumption among youth. In general, experience indicates that for every 10% increase in the cost of cigarettes, there is a 4% drop in consumption. On the basis of these experiences, U.S. Pres. Bill Clinton has proposed, as one of the ways to help pay for health care

The tobacco industry spends $4 billion a year to promote its products. As of August 1993, New York City no longer allowed cigarette ads on its 4,268 outdoor phone booths. In 1992 the city received $322,000 in revenues from those ads alone.

Andrea Mohin—The New York Times

reform, raising the federal excise tax on cigarettes by 75 cents to 99 cents a pack. But many health activists propose raising the tax by $2 a pack in the hope of reducing the number of smokers by 7.6 million and saving nearly two million lives. According to one conservative estimate, it would take more than 400,000 typical quit-smoking clinic programs to achieve the same result.

As the focus of smoking control expanded beyond information and the individual to include the environment, researchers also began to recognize that smoking initiation and cessation are dynamic processes with multiple stages. As a result, it became evident that smoking could be addressed at several stages. Hence, the current state of the art in tobacco control combines various environmental changes with various types of programs directed at specific groups of individuals. It is now quite apparent that no single approach is best for all smokers, no single channel will reach everyone, and no single time is "right" for everyone to attempt to quit. As the NCI stated in its 1991 document *Strategies to Control Tobacco Use in the United States: A Blueprint for Public Health Action in the 1990's:* "A comprehensive smoking control strategy is characterized by the delivery of persistent and inescapable messages to quit or not start smoking coupled with continuously available support for individual cessation efforts provided through multiple channels and reinforced by environmental incentives for nonsmokers." Persistent and inescapable messages are such things as broad restrictions on smoking in public places, well-enforced laws governing sales of tobacco to youth, and the elimination of advertisements depicting smoking as a normal, healthy, social behavior.

Making a difference

Since the intervention phase of ASSIST began in the fall of 1993, important achievements have been made. The Rhode Island General Assembly, at the urging of community groups, enacted a ban on smoking in public schools specifically aimed at protecting students and teachers from involuntary exposure to smoke. The *Seattle Times,* the major daily newspaper in Seattle, Wash., initiated a policy to refuse any further tobacco-product advertising, saying that it could no longer in good conscience provide a forum for promoting such inherently dangerous products.

Even tobacco-belt states have had remarkable successes. Despite a 1992 state "smokers' rights" law that threatened to prohibit counties from restricting smoking in public places, 58 counties and 153 municipalities in North Carolina passed regulations that protect citizens from exposure to second-hand smoke. Elsewhere in the tobacco belt, the discrepancy between more than 400,000 premature deaths per year and an estimated 260,000 jobs directly dependent upon

tobacco farming and manufacture is growing increasingly unacceptable. Health advocates have proposed setting aside excise tax revenues to help tobacco growers switch to nonlethal crops.

The ultimate goal of tobacco control is to save lives. Overall, ASSIST expects to prevent as many as 1.2 million premature deaths, including more than 400,000 cancer deaths (primarily from lung cancer). Moreover, with more than four million adult quitters and more than two million youth prevented from becoming addicted as a result of its initiatives, at a cost of roughly $130 per life saved over the course of the project, this may be one of the most economical and effective interventions in modern public health history.

—Robert Marshall, Jr., Ph.D.,
and Donald R. Shopland

Transplantation

Organ transplantation has been one of the success stories of surgery over the past 30 years. Because the body's immune system tends to reject a transplant, immunologists at first doubted that the grafting of organs would ever be possible. Effective ways of controlling rejection were found, however, and surgeons have developed techniques for transplanting virtually all organs and tissues apart from the brain and spinal cord. The difficulty in transplanting the latter is the absence of a way to connect nerves after they have been cut in the central nervous system; at the other extreme, corneas, which are not nourished by blood and thus are not subject to rejection, have been transplanted since the beginning of the 20th century. The exact number of transplants done worldwide each year is not known, but it is certainly in excess of 100,000 kidneys, 30,000 each of livers and hearts, and several thousand each of lungs and pancreases. Most transplants are performed in North America, Europe, and Australasia, but increasingly countries in other parts of the world are starting organ-transplantation programs.

There are two basic types of transplants. One is a living graft, in which the tissues or cells must survive and function in the recipient, as with the transplant of a kidney, liver, heart, or lung, for example. The other, known as a dead, or "scaffold," transplant, involves the grafting of a structure, such as an arterial wall or a bone, into which living cells from the recipient can infiltrate and colonize. All grafts of vital organs require living cells, and the organs must therefore be removed from donors whose cells are still alive.

A graft may be transplanted in the same individual, as is the case with skin grafts and other procedures in plastic surgery; this is called an autograft. A transplant from an identical twin, known as an isograft, is biologically the same as an autograft. Grafts from individuals of the same species who are not identical twins are called allografts; they may be from living relatives—for instance, from parent to child—or from the bodies of completely unrelated individuals. A graft from one species to another is called a xenograft. When the graft is between closely related species, as with a baboon and a human, it is known as a concordant xenograft; a discordant xenograft is one between distantly related species, such as a pig and a human.

Although the surgery for an organ graft may have been performed perfectly, the body recognizes the new organ as foreign tissue and reacts against it as if it were invading viruses or bacteria. The body's extremely efficient defense against foreign tissue, called the immune reaction, is carried out by white blood cells called lymphocytes. Certain lymphocytes can kill bacteria and viruses—as well as grafted tissue—by direct contact or by toxic action; others kill by means of antibodies secreted into the blood. In order to control this immune response so that a graft can be protected, it is necessary to treat transplant patients with drugs and special antilymphocyte antibodies, called immunosuppressive agents. However, because the body's immune reaction is such a basic, vital force, controlling it with drugs tends to produce unwanted side effects. Moreover, complete inhibition of immune defenses results in the patient's becoming susceptible to even mild infections that would normally be resisted. In this respect the transplant recipient's compromised immunity is not unlike that of a person with AIDS.

Thirty years after the introduction of effective immunosuppression, rejection and the side effects of immunosuppressive drugs are still responsible for the majority of graft failures and patient deaths following transplantation. Nonetheless, the overall results of organ grafting have improved steadily, and the majority of patients now survive for more than five years after receiving a transplant. The number of donor organs available for transplantation purposes is not sufficient to meet the demand, however, raising certain ethical problems. Partly for this reason, there has been an upsurge of interest in the transplantation of organs from other animals to humans and in the prospects of transplanting cells rather than whole organs. Such developments raise hopes for a relatively simple therapy for patients with diseases that cannot now be treated.

Immunosuppression

The immune system that protects humans from the bacterial, viral, and fungal hazards of the environment is extremely complicated. There are several different cellular components of this system. They include cells that engulf foreign material (macrophages), others that produce antibodies that can act from a distance (B lymphocytes), and so-called killer cells that act locally (T lymphocytes, or T cells). All of these components arise from nonspecialized stem cells in the bone marrow. Lymphocytes are the main agents in the rejection of a graft, with the T cells playing an especially promi-

nent role. Thus, most research in graft rejection is aimed at interfering with T-cell function or with killing T cells directly.

Several powerful agents acting at different stages of T-cell activity can be used for this purpose. The best known are the corticosteroids, the antileukemic drug azathioprine, and cyclosporine, a proteinlike substance derived from an earth fungus. Other drugs, including the agent FK-506 (tacrolimus; Prograf), discovered by Japanese scientists in the late 1980s, are currently being evaluated. In addition, antibodies directed against lymphocytes can be produced in the serum of animals. In this procedure animals are injected with human lymphocytes to produce antibodies against them, and the animal serum, which now contains the antibodies, is then injected into humans as an immunosuppressant. It is now also possible to create monoclonal antibodies, which are produced by a clone of discrete cells directed at a specific target. In theory, monoclonal antibodies are more likely to be effective and are less toxic than the cruder antilymphocyte serum. Monoclonal antibodies can be effective, however, only if it is known exactly what their target should be, and at present scientists' knowledge of how lymphocytes act is still incomplete.

The main trigger of the immune reaction, and hence the rejection of grafts, is what are known as transplant antigens. These antigens, the substances in a transplanted organ that actually stimulate the immune response of the host, differ from one individual to another. In fact, each person has a complex mosaic of antigens that is unique. Matching of antigens between donor and recipient, insofar as this is possible, thus helps lessen the odds that a transplanted organ will call forth a strong immune response and be rejected.

In the recipient only a small fraction of T cells respond (determined by the specific antigens of the grafted organ), but once stimulated this small population reproduces in a clonal manner to a huge number of cells. Some immunosuppressive drugs are specific inhibitors of this proliferation; cyclosporine and FK-506, for example, block the formation of the signal to proliferate. Monoclonal antibodies can also be used to "blindfold" or kill specific T cells. A massive onslaught against T cells, however, although now possible, leaves the patient in a vulnerable state, unable to mount a defense against a viral or other infection. With T-cell suppression there is also a danger that B lymphocytes will develop into tumors in response to normally harmless viruses. The goal, therefore, is to limit the immunosuppressive attack to just those T cells capable of responding to the antigens of the donor organ in question.

Every organ has, in addition to its normal, functioning cells, "passenger" cells derived from bone marrow. Some of these cells have the ability to attack the immune system of the transplant recipient, or host. The

Transplantation researchers have shown that "chimerism," in which donor-organ cells migrate into the host's body and host cells infiltrate and survive in the transplanted tissue, plays an important part in graft tolerance. The process gets its name from Chimera in Greek mythology, a fire-breathing monster composed of different animal parts.

importance of this two-way immunologic response—*i.e.,* of cells from a graft against the host and cells from the host against the graft—occurring without rejection has been shown by Thomas E. Starzl and colleagues at the University of Pittsburgh, Pa. These researchers have detected passenger cells from the donor organ scattered widely in the recipient's body, where they remain viable for many years. Thus, when an organ is transplanted, passenger cells pass out of the organ into the recipient, and cells derived from the bone marrow of the recipient pass into the organ. After a few weeks the organ consists of a mixture of donor and recipient cells, and the recipient also has a mixed-cell constitution. This cell exchange is called chimerism, after Chimera, the creature in Greek mythology made up of parts of different animals. When only a few cells emigrate from the donor organ, the condition is called *microchimerism;* in bone marrow transplants *macrochimerism* occurs.

In organ grafting, cells derived from the bone marrow of the donor can thus be said to engage in an immunologic battle with similar cells in the recipient. It is possible that a stalemate in this conflict may result in a balance between, or mutual coexistence of, graft and host. At first, such peacekeeping may require low dosages of immunosuppressive drugs. After a time, a truce may persist without drug treatment, which is, of course, a great boon to patients. Such a state is called "operational tolerance" and occurs frequently in the recipients of liver grafts. Some liver-graft recipi-

ents in the University of Pittsburgh transplant program have been off all immunosuppressive medication for more than 10 years without experiencing rejection. It seems that such tolerance is partly explained by the migration of cells derived from bone marrow to and from the graft; that is, by microchimerism. The donor liver cells secrete transplant antigens into the blood, which probably results in specific suppression of the recipient's aggressive tendencies against the graft. When kidneys have been transplanted together with the liver from the same donor, there is a very low incidence of rejection, the liver apparently protecting the kidneys. Such observations have led some researchers to wonder if it may be possible to mimic the operational-tolerance effect of the liver without actually transplanting it.

It has been shown by Paul Terasaki and his colleagues at the University of California at Los Angeles Tissue Typing Laboratory that an exact match in transplant antigens between donor and recipient, although desirable, is not always necessary. Some mismatches appear to be permissible, while others inexorably result in rejection. It is conceivable that a limited number of artificially produced transplant antigens combined with a short course of powerful immunosuppression might be used to select and inactivate only those T cells that would react against the organ graft. This might produce operational tolerance, so that the patient would not have the high risk of infection and other major side effects associated with long-term treatment with immunosuppressive drugs.

Nonetheless, the ability to control rejection varies greatly from one type of transplant to another. For example, skin transplants, unless done as autografts, have always been the most difficult to protect from rejection. The reason for this remains unclear. Likewise, the rejection of intestines and lungs, also tissues that are exposed to the environment, has been difficult to overcome. In these latter cases, however, and particularly with intestinal transplants, there has been progress in understanding the factors involved, and grafts done at a number of centers are now functioning well several years later. Use of FK-506 seems to be an important element of the successful intestinal transplants performed by University of Pittsburgh surgeons.

In biological systems there are usually alternative pathways that offer flexibility of response and help individuals to survive in a hostile environment. This characteristic is reflected in the extreme complexity of the immune system in humans. Undoubtedly it will be some time before the complex interactions and mechanisms of the immune system are understood sufficiently to allow operational tolerance to be achieved in all allograft recipients. Nevertheless, the fact that operational tolerance is possible suggests that this goal will eventually be reached.

Developments in xenografting

In all, there have been more than 30 attempts at xenografting in the 20th century. One of the first widely publicized cases took place in California in 1984 and involved an infant, known to the public as Baby Fae. She lived for 20 days after surgeons replaced her congenitally deformed heart with a heart from a young baboon. Partly because of the shortage of organs for transplantation, there is intense work under way to understand and control the rejection responses that occur when organs are transplanted across species. It is well known that grafts between closely related species, *i.e.,* concordant xenografts, can sometimes be maintained by powerful immunosuppression; this is the case, for instance, in grafts from a mouse to a rat or from a monkey to a baboon.

The closest animal relative of humans is the chimpanzee but, partly because the chimpanzee is an endangered species, it is not considered acceptable as an organ donor. However, baboons, more distantly related to humans, have been used recently as liver donors in the Pittsburgh program. The two patients who received these grafts in 1992 and 1993 were given powerful immunosuppressants, but both died, one after 70 days and the other after 26 days. This outcome was disappointing and gave rise to the additional concern that organs from one species may not function appropriately in another; for example, the proteins produced by a baboon's liver may not be able to maintain a human in good health. Another difficulty in using primate donors is that many primate species carry potentially dangerous viruses. Moreover, some people have strong feelings against removing organs from defenseless creatures that are relatively closely related to the human species.

For these and other reasons, researchers have searched for a more satisfactory animal donor. The pig is currently a popular candidate. It can be kept free of diseases that might be dangerous to humans; its organs can be obtained at appropriate sizes for humans; and pigs are relatively easy to work with surgically. Because pigs are easy to breed, their use in transplantation is not likely to be as controversial as the use of primates.

Research is in progress involving genetic engineering to produce acceptable grafts from pigs. A concordant xenograft reacts in a manner similar to an allograft; a graft between distantly related species (*e.g.,* a pig and a human) behaves quite differently. In a discordant xenograft the capillary circulation in the organ is destroyed instantly, a reaction that has proved to be difficult to understand and overcome. The protein in the blood called complement is normally in an inactive, dormant state but can be activated, for instance, in response to an infection caused by invading bacteria. In such circumstances the complement becomes a lethal chemical that kills the bacteria. Each species has circulating in the blood anticomplementary proteins that hold complement in check. The human protein that inactivates complement depends on genes present in the nucleus of the cell. A scientific team in Cambridge, England, has incorporated one of these genes into the DNA of pigs in the embryo stage to produce so-called transgenic pigs; that is, pigs with a human gene that prevents activation of complement. The researchers anticipate using organs from a third generation of transgenic pigs in clinical trials in 1996.

An attempt in California in 1992 to transplant a pig liver to a human was not successful; the organ did not come from a transgenic pig. Although the transplant

Baboon-to-human liver transplants in Pittsburgh, Pa., drew widespread protest (right). British scientists have produced the first laboratory-bred "transgenic pigs," whose organs are likely to be more suitable—morally and immunologically—for human transplantation; the sow (below) is a second-generation transgenic pig.

DID THE BABOON CONSENT ?

ANIMALS ARE NOT OURS TO EXPERIMENT ON

(Left) IMUTRAN, Cambridge, England; (right) AP/Wide World

was undertaken as an emergency measure, it was widely criticized.

The almost instantaneous destruction of discordant xenografts has prevented long-term studies. If, however, this initial, explosive reaction can be controlled, it will be possible to determine the next hurdle that needs to be overcome. The intensive activity in this area suggests that further attempts at xenografting may soon be made. Enthusiastic scientists believe that xenografting will become a practical procedure in the next two or three years; less optimistic ones, including this author, feel it unlikely that xenografts will supplant allografts within the coming decade.

Cell grafting

In the treatment of some diseases, it is necessary to transplant whole organs. In others it should be possible, at least in theory, to transplant only certain cells. For example, it has been thought that diabetes might be treated by transplantation of the islets of Langerhans and associated cells that produce insulin. Attempts to do so, however, have been disappointing since it is difficult to extract the islets from the pancreas and, when extracted, they do not function well. Attempts to use adrenal cells from fetal tissue in the treatment of Parkinson's disease have also not as yet fulfilled researchers' hopes.

Bone marrow, the jellylike substance found inside virtually all bones, was one of the first cellular grafts to be tried in humans and is now the treatment of choice for leukemia and several other malignant and nonmalignant blood disorders. In this graft bone marrow is aspirated from, or sucked out of, the donor's pelvic bones through a needle. It is then filtered to remove any small bone or fat particles; further processing is needed only if the patient and donor have different blood types. The filtered marrow is then injected into the recipient's bloodstream, and the cells "home" to the recipient's marrow, where they grow. In order for the graft to "take," the recipient's diseased blood cells must first be destroyed by radiation or drugs. It may eventually become possible to transplant other functioning cells; for example, liver cells for treatment of patients with liver failure. Apart from bone marrow, however, cell grafting is at an early stage.

Genetic engineering has now made it possible to "transfect" cells—*i.e.,* insert genetic material from normal cells into abnormal cells to produce normal cells that replicate in the recipient—*e.g.,* provide the critical pancreatic enzymes that are missing in patients with cystic fibrosis or the blood coagulation factor that is missing in patients with hemophilia. The vital gene is incorporated into the nucleus of the cell to be transplanted via a viral or plasmid vector. The transfection of genetic material is similar in principle to the technique described above to create transgenic pigs, although in this procedure it is only the patient who receives the cells and who benefits from them. The advantage is not passed to the next generation as an inherited gene. Although cell transplantation is still in a very preliminary stage (the first international meeting of cell-transplantation researchers took place in Pittsburgh in June 1992), the applications of molecular biology to this field are likely to lead to new forms of therapy in the next few years.

Ethical issues

In North America, Western Europe, and Australasia, organ donation has relied predominantly on two types of sources. The first is altruistic donation, in which relatives of a person who has died from brain trauma or hemorrhage give permission for organs to be used for transplantation or individuals indicate prior to death their wish to have organs used for transplant (either by carrying a donor card or discussing the matter with relatives). The second is the donation of a kidney or part of a liver by a close blood relative, usually a parent, or by other living donors emotionally involved with the recipient but not a blood relative; for example, a spouse.

By far the most common source of organs is cadavers with brain stem destruction but in whom vital functions of the lungs and heart are maintained mechanically, thus allowing the blood to be oxygenated and the tissues to continue living. In certain countries, however, it is difficult to obtain organs from the dead because of the belief that the body should be intact in the next life. Some countries have various legal restraints; in Japan, for example, until recently there was a law against removing organs from a dead person if the heart was still beating. In the past in the United States and elsewhere, prisoners donated organs, and organs were sometimes removed from bodies after execution; the latter practice is currently widespread in China.

Because donations do not provide enough organs for the large number of patients needing transplants and because organs from cadavers are illegal or otherwise difficult to obtain in some countries, a third source has developed. It consists of organs purchased from poor people unrelated to the recipient. With improving results in transplantation, a person whose life depends on a transplant may be prepared to pay money for an organ. The commercial purchase of organs has been made illegal in many countries, however, and a doctor involved in an organ transplant for which the donor has been paid may be barred from practicing and face other punishment. Some countries now monitor transplantation. In the United Kingdom, for example, a legal document certifying the donor's death (including the criterion of brain death) must be signed by the surgeon removing the organs, and a similar certificate must be signed by the surgeon performing the transplant.

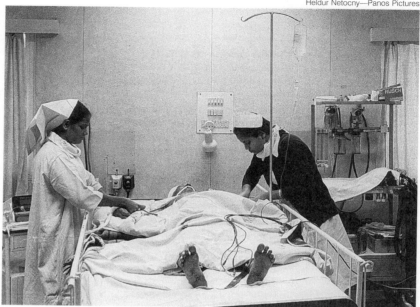

In June 1994 the Indian Parliament passed the Transplantation of Human Organs Bill, which deals with two important ethical issues. Brain stem death was made the criterion for certification of death. Previously, doctors in India could not legally remove organs for transplantation until the heart had stopped beating. Now they can retrieve organs after two independent neurologists and doctors who are not part of the transplant team have certified a patient's brain stem death. The bill also outlaws trade in human organs, a practice that had been rampant. The new bill is expected to make more organs available for transplant as well as to halt the selling of organs by poor people.

There also have been reports, usually unconfirmed, of pressure being put on people to donate organs, of people being kidnapped so that organs could be removed, or of organs being removed without permission in the course of another operation. There have even been allegations of murder in order to obtain organs for transplantation. It has been suggested that organized criminals, with doctors in their pay, might remove organs in one institution, produce false documents for the organs, and then export them to another institution, possibly in a different country. Allegations also have been made that the criterion of brain death has been ignored so that organs could be removed prematurely from donors who did not in fact suffer permanent and irreversible destruction of the brain stem.

Such practices and allegations are disturbing because they can undermine the confidence of the public in the ethics of organ transplantation. The International Transplantation Society has produced guidelines for ethical practice in transplantation and recommendations for legislation and certification procedures similar to those in place in the U.K.

Because organ grafting is so expensive, questions have been raised as to the appropriateness of transplanting organs, especially when budgets for health care are limited. Even in wealthy countries, where most transplants are done, priorities for treatment must be established. Further, in order for organ transplants to be performed with good results, it is necessary to have a well-developed medical infrastructure—*i.e.,* well-equipped operating rooms and intensive care facilities, surgeons available to remove organs from donors, and laboratories to test donors for cancer or viruses such as HIV or hepatitis. Even so, there are dangers involved. The detection of disease in the donor may sometimes be difficult; transmission of HIV from donors incubating the virus before a test has proved positive is possible, and cancer cells may reside in an organ without there being history of cancer in the patient. Even if artificial lungs, kidneys, hearts, or livers were to become available, it is unlikely that they would, in the short term, remove the need for biologically functioning grafts and, furthermore, the cost of artificial organs would be enormous.

Other difficult ethical questions that have been raised are: Who should receive a transplant when resources are so scarce? What consideration should be given to the patient's age and the nature of the disease? Should organs donated in one country be used in another where organ donation is prohibited or not practiced? Should a patient receive an organ graft for self-inflicted injuries; for example, should a transplant be done on one whose liver has been destroyed by alcoholism? Should a patient whose first transplant is rejected receive a second organ, or should an available organ go to someone who has not yet had a transplant?

It is likely that as immunosuppression improves and grafting becomes more effective and less dangerous, nonvital body parts such as the thyroid and adrenal glands, limbs, and reproductive organs will be transplanted. Grafting of such body parts as testes and ovaries especially will raise important new ethical issues; for example, the sperm and ova from these organs will be those of the donors, who, rather than the recipients of the grafts, will be the true biological fathers and mothers of any progeny.

—*Sir Roy Y. Calne*

SOUND INFORMATION ABOUT MATTERS OF HEALTH

HEALTHWISE

Vegetarianism Comes of Age

by Virginia Messina, M.P.H., R.D., and Mark Messina, Ph.D.

The word *vegetarian* was used for the first time in England in 1839. It came not from the word *vegetable,* as people often think, but from the Latin *vegetus,* which means "whole, sound, and lively." But there were vegetarians long before the mid-19th century. The Greek philosopher Pythagoras of the 6th century BC was a vegetarian, as were his followers. Disagreements about meat eating are recorded in the letters of Paul in the New Testament, indicating that some members of the early Christian church were vegetarians.

Meatless eating became popular in England in 1847, when the first Vegetarian Society was formed. Around that time several groups in the United States also advocated a vegetarian diet. The American transcendentalist philosopher Henry David Thoreau and others who pursued a utopian society shunned animal flesh. So did the members of the new Seventh-day Adventist Church, founded in the 1860s. One famous church member, John Harvey Kellogg, a physician, spent much of his life experimenting with meat substitutes, although he is best remembered for promoting cereal products as breakfast foods, which his brother W.K. Kellogg, founder of the cereal company, marketed.

More than a full century later, vegetarianism enjoyed a new surge of support with the burgeoning of interest in natural foods and health in the 1960s, and another revival came in the 1980s with the increased public concern for animal welfare. A 1991 Gallup Poll found that there were 12 million adult vegetarians in the United States, and the number of people interested in meatless eating is growing rapidly. One leading magazine for vegetarians, *Vegetarian Times,* reported an increase in circulation from 158,000 in 1990 to 250,000 in 1993.

Many types, many reasons

There are several different types of vegetarian eating patterns. *Lacto-ovovegetarians* avoid all animal flesh, including meat, poultry, and fish, but do eat other animal products such as eggs and dairy foods. *Lacto-vegetarians* exclude eggs but include dairy products, while *ovovegetarians* eat eggs but not dairy foods. *Vegans,* or strict vegetarians, eat no animal foods; they avoid animal flesh, dairy products, and eggs and frequently do not use nondietary products of animal origin such as leather and wool.

Macrobiotic diets are based on the ancient Chinese cosmological principles of yin and yang and are largely vegetarian, although some may include fish. This type of diet varies according to climate, season, and personal needs but consists mainly of whole grains and vegetables, including sea vegetables (arame, hijiki, kelp, nori, wakame), with smaller amounts of legumes and some fruits. Bean and vegetable soups are popular macrobiotic dishes.

People who consume only limited amounts of animal flesh sometimes refer to themselves as *semivegetarians*. Often these people are in a transition stage and will eventually adopt a totally meatless or even vegan diet.

People choose vegetarianism for a variety of reasons. Concern about the effects of animal agriculture on the environment is one reason for avoiding meat. Compared with the cultivation of plant crops, the raising of livestock requires far more land, water, and natural resources such as petroleum. Animal agriculture also produces more pollution. And because of the need for vast open spaces for grazing, the raising of meat animals contributes to loss of forests. Concerns about world hunger also influence some people to adopt a vegetarian diet. Because plant foods are produced more efficiently, they can play a key role in feeding impoverished populations.

Still others opt for vegetarianism because of concerns about animal welfare. Animal rights activists have been particularly critical of the conditions to which animals are subjected on modern-day factory farms. Many vegans refuse to eat eggs and dairy foods because they feel that hens and dairy cattle are not treated humanely.

These days perhaps the most popular reason for choosing a vegetarian diet is health. There is increasing epidemiological evidence that vegetarians have a much lower incidence of many of the chronic diseases that plague those who consume typical Western, meat-centered diets.

Health benefits: the evidence

Populations whose diets are largely plant-based have lower rates of heart disease, hypertension (high blood pressure), obesity, and other conditions associated with the diets of affluent, industrialized nations. For example, the Tarahumara Indians of Mexico eat a diet based on corn, beans, and squash. Traditionally, these people have been known for their incredible athletic stamina. Popular sports of this group require participants to run up to 320 km (200 mi) over a period of several days. The Tarahumara also have very low rates of heart disease and hypertension. Rural South African black populations also eat a near-vegetarian diet, based primarily on locally produced grains. Perhaps because of the high fiber content of their diet, they rarely suffer from intestinal diseases and have an extremely low rate of colon cancer.

In a recent series of studies that examined the dietary habits in people of China, it was found that those who lived in urban areas and regularly ate meat had much higher incidences of colon and breast cancer than did rural Chinese who ate a more traditional plant-based diet. Similarly, in the United States members of the Seventh-day Adventist Church—approximately 50% of whom are vegetarian—have lower rates of heart disease, cancer, diabetes, and other chronic diseases than do other Americans.

In general, studies have shown that compared with meat eaters, vegetarians have lower rates of heart disease, colon, lung, and breast cancer, diabetes, obesity, hypertension, gallstones, and kidney stones. While many lifestyle factors may contribute to risk for these diseases, including exercise habits and tobacco and alcohol use, diet is thought to play a major role. The following is a brief review of some of this research.

Heart disease. In a British study of dietary patterns and heart disease conducted in 1988, vegetarians were found to have a 24% lower risk of heart disease than people who ate meat. Those who were vegans had a 57% lower risk.

There are many reasons why vegetarians have low rates of heart disease. One is that vegetarian diets are typically low in both saturated fat and cholesterol, two dietary components that raise blood cholesterol levels. Vegetarians of all ages have been shown to have lower cholesterol levels than their meat-eating counterparts. Moreover, when meat is added to the diet of vegetarians, their blood cholesterol levels increase. Vegetarians also eat substantial amounts of soluble fiber, which is known to help lower cholesterol levels. (Soluble fiber is found in cooked dried beans, oats, brown rice, barley, fruits, and many vegetables.) Animal protein itself may raise blood cholesterol levels. Numerous studies conducted over the past 25 years indicate, for example, that replacing animal protein in the diet with soy protein lowers blood cholesterol levels, even if the fat content of the diet remains the same.

Compared with meat eaters, vegetarians also consume more antioxidants, substances such as vitamin C and beta-carotene that repair cellular damage at the molecular level. Recent theories suggest that antioxidants, which are found largely in plant foods, help to prevent atherosclerosis (obstruction of blood flow due to fatty deposits in the arteries). In fact, there is now evidence that very low-fat vegetarian-style diets, in combination with other health measures, actually reverse existing atherosclerosis.

With the emphasis today on reducing fat in the diet, it is important that those who are considering becoming vegetarians know that "meatless" is not necessarily synonymous with "low fat." For example, some people erroneously think of tofu—because it is a vegetable product and has no cholesterol—as being fat-free. In fact, a serving of tofu contains more fat than an equivalent amount of skinless white-meat chicken. However, most of the fat in tofu is polyunsaturated, whereas most of the fat in chicken is saturated. Many frozen vegetarian entrées also contain more fat than would be expected in a meatless dish.

Cancer. According to the American Dietetic Association, vegetarians are at lower risk than nonvegetarians for colon, breast, and lung cancer. Among Seventh-day Adventists, for example, death rates from cancer are about half those of the general U.S. population. One recent study showed that meat eating is more closely associated with colon cancer than any other dietary factor, and another found that the saturated fats in red meat were strongly linked to risk for prostate cancer.

Vegetarians eat less total fat than omnivores, and fat is thought to be a factor that raises the risk of some kinds of cancer. The high fiber intake of vegetarians probably also contributes to the lower incidence of colon cancer in this group. The plentiful amounts of antioxidants consumed by vegetarians may also offer protection against cancer. A variety of compounds called phytochemicals are found only in plant foods and may help to protect against cancer. While these are not nutrients, they appear to have important physiological effects. There may be hundreds of phytochemicals in plant foods, and since vegetarians base their diets on plant foods, they may be more likely than omnivores to reap the health benefits of these substances. Soybeans, for example, are rich in

Dishes served at the Zen Palate, a vegetarian eatery in New York City, show the unmistakable influence of classic Chinese cuisine. Vegetarian meals are an increasingly popular option for people dining out.

phytochemicals called isoflavones, which are being intensely studied for their role in cancer (and heart disease) prevention.

Meat may also contain substances that directly raise the risk of cancer. Meats that are cooked at high temperatures, especially those cooked on the grill, form cancer-causing compounds such as heterocyclic amines.

Diabetes. Vegetarians have lower rates of non-insulin-dependent diabetes, which is the most common type of diabetes, than do omnivores. This may be because vegetarians as a group are leaner than nonvegetarians, and obesity is a major risk factor for this form of diabetes. A high intake of complex carbohydrates and fiber, which is typical of vegetarian diets, also improves glucose metabolism and may help to lower blood glucose levels. Diabetics are at especially high risk for heart disease and related complications; the low intake of saturated fat and cholesterol in the vegetarian diet may help prevent these conditions in those who have diabetes.

Hypertension. Vegetarians typically have lower blood pressures than meat eaters, at least in part because on average they are slimmer. Also, vegetarians may have a higher intake of potassium, which is associated with reduced blood pressure. As far back as the 1920s, researchers observed that adding meat to the diets of vegetarians significantly raised their blood pressure within just a few weeks.

Kidney stones and gallstones. Vegetarian diets may help to protect against kidney stones. Diets high in animal protein cause increased amounts of calcium, oxalate, and uric acid—the three main components of kidney stones—to be excreted in the urine. One group of British researchers has suggested that people with a tendency to form kidney stones should follow a vegetarian diet.

Obesity, high cholesterol intake, excess calorie intake, and a lack of dietary fiber all are associated with the formation of gallstones. It not surprising, then, that vegetarians have a lower incidence of these stones than meat eaters. In one study, 25% of the women who ate meat had a history of gallstones, compared with only 12% of vegetarian women.

Meeting nutrient needs

Vegetarian diets are actually closer to the current dietary recommendations than other types of eating patterns. The "Food Guide Pyramid" issued in 1992 by the United States Department of Agriculture (USDA) stresses the importance of making plant foods the foundation of the diet. A vegetarian eating pattern also makes it easier to meet the latest *Dietary Guidelines for Americans,* issued jointly by the USDA and the Department of Health and Human Services in 1990, which emphasize that most Americans should consume more complex carbohydrates (found only in plant foods) and less fat. The World Health Organization also recommends that people in less developed nations avoid adopting meat-centered, high-fat Western dietary habits.

As a result of the considerable evidence implicating dietary factors in disease causation, vegetarian diets are gaining respect among health professionals. Leading professional organizations, such as the American Dietetic Association, are producing educational materials on vegetarian diets, and vegetarian dishes are becoming more common on restaurant and school cafeteria menus.

Most health professionals now agree not only that vegetarianism is a healthy choice but also that vegetarian diets can significantly improve health. Still, any dietary pattern requires some consideration to ensure that all nutrient needs are met. Specific nutrient concerns for vegetarians are as follows:

Protein. Protein-containing foods are essential for providing amino acids, the chemical building blocks for the manufacture of new proteins for body tissues. Humans have specific needs for 20 different amino acids. Eleven of these can be synthesized in the body; the remaining nine must come from food and are therefore considered essential in the diet. The nutritional quality of a protein source is based upon the amounts of the essential amino acids it contains. Eggs and soybeans, for example, provide high-quality protein.

In the past, nutrition experts expressed concern about the quality of plant proteins and the ability of a plant-based diet to provide the essential proteins. The old way of thinking held that vegetarians needed to eat particular combinations of plant foods at each meal in order to get exactly the right amino acids in the right proportions. This practice was known as protein combining. More current thinking is that people need only eat a variety of protein-rich foods *throughout the day* in order to safely meet protein requirements. In fact, when people eat a variety of plant foods and consume a sufficient amount of calories, the body's protein needs are very easily met. Moreover, the amount of protein necessary for normal body functions is much lower than was once thought, and most Americans considerably exceed the recommended daily allowance. (*See* table below.)

While dairy products and eggs are excellent sources of protein, vegans can get adequate amounts of protein by eating legumes, nuts and seeds, and soy-based foods. (The table on page 407 contains a list of foods acceptable in a vegetarian diet that are good sources of protein.)

Iron. Although iron-deficiency anemia is common throughout the world, vegetarians, even including premenopausal women, are no more likely than meat eaters to be iron-deficient. Concerns about the adequacy of iron intake in the vegetarian diet stem from the fact that the iron in meat, called heme iron, is more easily absorbed than the iron in plant foods, called nonheme iron. However, a number of factors increase the amount of nonheme iron the body can absorb from foods; for example, consuming a food rich in vitamin C at the same meal. Furthermore, when the amount of iron in the diet is low, more of that iron is absorbed. Vegetarians who consume moderate amounts of iron in foods such as beans and leafy green vegetables and also consume vitamin C-rich foods can easily meet their iron needs.

Recently, high levels of iron in the blood have been linked to increased risk for both heart disease and cancer. There may be some advantage to consuming moderate but sufficient levels of dietary iron, making plant sources of iron a good choice.

Calcium. Many foods are rich in calcium. In fact, most Americans who eat dairy products actually get only 50% of their calcium from those products, while the rest comes from plant foods. The calcium provided by most plant sources—with a few exceptions (spinach, beet greens, rhubarb, and Swiss chard)—is absorbed as well as that provided by milk.

Calcium is important for the health of bones. Bones are dynamic and are constantly releasing and absorbing calcium. In the early part of life, as the skeleton is growing, more calcium is deposited in bone than is released. As people age, however, the bones start to lose more calcium than they absorb. The calcium is excreted via the urine and feces primarily, but it is also lost through the skin. If the loss becomes severe, bones can weaken and are more easily broken. This condition is called osteoporosis, a disease of thin, porous bones.

People who develop their bone mass to the maximum extent have the lowest risk of developing osteoporosis. Therefore, adequate calcium is very important early in life, when bone mass is still increasing. However, avoiding bone loss later in life is important, too.

There is some evidence that animal protein in the diet actually increases the excretion of calcium from the body. In clinical studies, people who eat large amounts of protein lose more calcium through their urine than do people who eat small amounts of protein. Moreover, animal protein has a greater effect on calcium excretion than plant protein. Therefore, the lower overall protein content of a vegetarian diet and its inclusion of only plant protein may help to conserve calcium.

Since vegans do not eat dairy foods, they typically have a lower calcium intake than either lacto-ovovegetarians or omnivores. However, there is currently no good information about whether vegans have better or worse bone health than people in these other groups. Vegans may actually have lower calcium requirements because they do not eat any animal protein. This hypothesis is supported by epidemiological studies that show that in many populations where calcium intake is very low, bone health is actually better than in groups where calcium intake is high. There could be many reasons for this, including genetics, physical

U.S. protein consumption: more than enough				
age group	males		females	
	RDA (g)	average (g)	RDA (g)	average (g)
7–10	28	71	28	71
11–14	45	92	46	66
15–18	59	122	44	63
19–24	58	113	46	64
25–30	63	113	50	64
31–39	63	99	50	63
40–49	63	95	50	62
50–59	63	89	50	56
60–69	63	79	50	54
70+	63	69	50	49

Sources: National Research Council; Second National Health and Nutrition Examination Survey, 1976–80

How much calcium a day? recommended daily intake (mg)				
	United States*	United Kingdom	Japan	World Health Organization
children	800	600	400	450
adolescents	1,200	700	900	650
adults	800	500	600	450
pregnant women	1,200	1,200	1,000	1,100
*based on current RDA				

activity, low protein intake, or other nutritional factors. It is clear that many factors affect a person's need for calcium. (The table above shows that the recommended daily intake of calcium varies considerably from one country to another.) Plant foods that are rich in calcium include various kinds of greens, legumes, and soy-based products. (*See* table, page 407.)

Zinc. Zinc is particularly important for the synthesis and degradation of DNA, the genetic material. Children and pregnant women appear to be more vulnerable than men to zinc deficiency. The zinc content of typical vegetarian diets is similar to or slightly lower than that of meat-based diets. However, zinc absorption from foods varies considerably depending upon a number of factors. For example, fiber and substances called phytates, both of which are abundant in plant foods, can inhibit the absorption of zinc

A whole-wheat-crust pizza topped with plenty of fresh vegetables makes a nutritious—and fun—meal for family members of all ages. Those who eat no animal products can substitute soy cheese for cheese made from milk.

Karen Wollins

and other minerals in foods. Therefore, the amount of zinc absorbed by vegetarians may be lower than that absorbed by meat eaters. Nonetheless, zinc deficiency is rare among vegetarians. Good sources of zinc include whole grains, legumes, seeds, nuts, and dairy products.

Vitamin B_{12}. Vitamin B_{12} is found predominantly in animal foods. Lacto-ovovegetarians can generally get plenty of this nutrient from the eggs and dairy products they eat. Vegans, however, may be at risk for deficiency. Surprisingly though, vitamin B_{12} deficiency is not at all common among vegans. Since the need for this nutrient is extremely small, and since excess B_{12} is stored in the liver, people who adopt a vegan diet may not show deficiency symptoms for as long as 20 years. Also, because B_{12} is produced by microorganisms living in the soil, root vegetables that are contaminated with the microorganisms may be a source of this nutrient for vegans. Finally, many vegans use products that are fortified with B_{12}. Soymilk and imitation meat products are often fortified. Some brands of nutritional yeast are good sources of this nutrient. However, sea vegetables and fermented soy products such as tempeh and miso are not reliable sources of vitamin B_{12}, as they may contain a type of the vitamin that is not used by the human body. Breast-fed infants of vegan mothers are at highest risk for vitamin B_{12} deficiency. All vegans should be sure to consume fortified foods, or they may need to take a B_{12} supplement. Symptoms of B_{12} deficiency include anemia and irreversible neurological impairments.

Vitamin D. Vitamin D is needed for proper bone formation. Eggs and fish oils are among the few natural sources of this nutrient. While milk does not naturally contain any vitamin D, all milk sold in the U.S. is fortified with it. Also, many breakfast cereals, breads, and other foods are fortified with vitamin D. Because the vegan diet is generally devoid of vitamin D, most authorities recommend that vegans eat some fortified foods or take a vitamin D supplement.

Humans can make all the vitamin D they need when their skin is exposed to the sun. For light-skinned individuals in temperate climates, exposing the arms and face to the sun three times a week for 20 minutes will produce adequate vitamin D. Dark-skinned persons, those who live in northern climates, and people who live in smoggy areas need somewhat more exposure. Using sunscreen is important for protecting against skin cancer, but it can reduce vitamin D synthesis; with sunscreen an individual therefore needs more exposure.

Feeding the whole family

Vegetarian diets are healthy for all age groups. In order that the nutrient needs of certain groups are met—for example, the very young and the elderly—some special planning may be necessary.

Pregnancy. Pregnant women need more of all of the essential nutrients. Consuming enough calories to provide for adequate weight gain is especially important during pregnancy. Several studies show that pregnant vegetarians have healthy diets, gain an appropriate amount of weight, and deliver healthy babies. In fact, one study of vegan women showed a greatly reduced incidence of toxemia, a serious blood disorder that can occur as a complication of pregnancy.

Infants and toddlers. Studies indicate that vegetarian infants who are fed according to current dietary guidelines grow and develop well. All infants should receive breast milk or infant formula during the first year of life. Breast-feeding is usually the best choice for all infants and is especially beneficial for vegan babies, although the latter may also be fed a soy-based infant formula such as Isomil, Nursoy, Prosobee, and Soyalac. Infants younger than one year of age should not be given cow's milk or regular soymilk. Children under age two do not need to be on low-fat diets, and those eating lacto-ovovegetarian meals should have whole, not low-fat, milk.

Infants can begin to eat solid foods between five and six months of age. First feedings for all infants are infant cereals mixed with breast milk or formula. Barley or rice cereals are good first choices. After the introduction of cereal, babies can begin to eat pureed fruits and vegetables. Higher-protein foods are generally introduced into babies' diets at around eight to nine months of age. Good choices for vegetarian infants include thoroughly cooked pureed legumes, pureed tofu, cottage cheese, and smooth nut butters. Breast-fed infants, vegetarian or not, usually need a vitamin D supplement beginning at about three months and an iron supplement beginning at about six months. If the mother's diet is not adequate in vitamin B_{12}, then the baby may also need a B_{12} supplement.

Preschoolers. After the rapid growth of the first year or two of life, both growth and appetite slow down in preschoolers. Picky eating habits are typical in this age group whether the child is a vegetarian or not. Young children have relatively high nutrient needs, however, so it is important to make sure they consume an adequate amount of food. Snacks can help. Because youngsters this age have a limited capacity for food, vegetarian children may need to eat some

A balanced vegetarian diet: many foods to choose from	
necessary nutrients	**good sources**
protein	dairy products, dried beans, peas, and lentils, eggs, grains, nuts, seeds, soy foods (tofu, tempeh, soymilk, soy protein)
iron	beans, blackstrap molasses, dried fruits, grains, green leafy vegetables, potatoes, prune juice, soy foods
vitamin C	asparagus, broccoli, brussels sprouts, cabbage, cauliflower, cantaloupe, cranberries, grapefruit, honeydew melon, kale, kiwi fruit, mango, orange, papaya, peppers, pineapple, potatoes, snow peas, strawberries, sweet potatoes, tangerine, tomatoes, watermelon
calcium	dairy products, almonds, beans (black, great northern, garbanzo, kidney, navy, and pinto), blackstrap molasses, bok choy, broccoli, greens (collard, turnip, and mustard), kale, sweet potatoes, soybeans, soymilk, sesame seeds, tahini (sesame seed butter), tempeh, tofu, English muffins
zinc	dairy products, whole grains, legumes, cashews, pecans, soy nuts, sunflower seeds
vitamin B_{12}	dairy products, eggs, nutritional yeast
vitamin D	eggs, fortified milk, fortified cereal products

refined foods such as refined grains and cereals, as their high-fiber diet tends to be very filling. Different preschoolers will have their own food preferences. Foods that are likely to appeal to many in this age group are peanut butter, flavored soymilk, milkshakes made of plain soymilk blended with fruit, macaroni dishes, and foods made with blended tofu, such as tofu-stuffed pasta shells.

School-age children. The same guidelines used to plan meals for adults can be applied to meals for children aged 6 to 12, but portions should be smaller. School lunches can be a major challenge for vegetarian families, especially for those that follow a vegan diet, as many schools do not offer strict vegetarian entrées. The best choice may be to pack bag lunches. Sandwiches for vegetarian children can include cheese, meatless deli slices (found in natural foods stores), peanut butter and sliced bananas or other fruits, or spreads made from tofu or beans. (Many of the recommended cookbooks in the list on page 408 include ideas for vegetarian sandwiches.)

Children are especially partial to foods they can prepare themselves or grab for quick snacks. Snacking can be a nutritious habit when the snacks are healthy ones. The following are a few ideas for vegetarian snacks that may be especially appealing to children: dried fruit and nut mix; rice cakes spread with almond butter; peanut butter and sliced bananas on crackers; cinnamon toast; English muffin pizzas; raw vegetables with dips made from blended tofu or low-fat cottage cheese; frozen fruit bars; oatmeal cookies; soymilk-fruit shakes; frozen banana chunks; dairy or soy yogurt or low-fat cottage cheese mixed with fruit.

Adolescents. Vegetarianism is growing more in popularity among adolescents than any other age group. Adolescents have extremely high nutrient and calorie needs. Since teen diets often include liberal amounts of snack foods and fast foods, a vegetarian diet can help to point adolescents toward more healthful, lower-fat dietary habits. Vegetarian versions of foods that are popular with teens are easy to make. For example, teens might enjoy milkshakes made with soymilk, pizzas topped with soy cheese and vegetables, spaghetti with vegetable or marinara sauce, or chili made with beans or soy protein (a product with a texture similar to that of cooked ground beef; available in natural foods stores). A growing number of imitation meat products are available, including vegetarian hot dogs and veggie burgers. Good vegetarian snack items for teens include trail mix, dried fruits, pretzels, and various sandwiches.

All adolescents need to make a special attempt to consume adequate amounts of calcium and iron. Teens who do not want to include dairy products in their diets should opt for one of the calcium-fortified soymilks or other fortified nondairy "milks" and should also be sure to eat other plant foods that are rich in calcium.

Older adults. Senior citizens are becoming increasingly interested in meatless meals. Many older people make dietary changes for health reasons—to help lower blood cholesterol or blood pressure and to control non-insulin-dependent diabetes. Although the nutrient needs of the elderly remain high, calorie needs tend to decrease with aging. Therefore, making good food choices is especially important. For people who have trouble chewing certain foods, items such as stewed fruit, well-cooked vegetables, some refined grains, cooked breakfast cereals, and nut butters can be good choices. Several over-the-counter products, food enzymes in tablet or liquid form, can help to make beans (and other high-fiber, complex-carbohydrate foods) more digestible for people who have a problem with them.

FOR FURTHER READING:
Periodicals
Vegetarian Gourmet
2 Public Avenue
Montrose PA 18801-1220

Vegetarian Journal
PO Box 1463
Baltimore MD 21203

Vegetarian Times
PO Box 570
Oak Park IL 60303

Vegetarian Voice
PO Box 72
Dolgeville NY 13329

Veggie Life
PO Box 57159
Boulder CO 80322-7159

Cookbooks recommended especially for beginning vegetarian cooks
Gelles, Carol. *The Complete Whole Grain Cookbook.* New York: Donald Fine, 1989.
Goldbeck, Nikki. *Nikki & David Goldbeck's American Wholefoods Cuisine.* New York: New American Library, 1983.
Lemlin, Jeanne. *Quick Vegetarian Pleasures.* New York: HarperPerennial, 1992.
The Moosewood Collective. *Moosewood Restaurant Cooks at Home.* New York: Simon and Schuster/Fireside, 1994.
Robertson, Laurel, Flinders, Carol, and Ruppenthal, Brian. *The New Laurel's Kitchen.* Berkeley, Calif.: Ten Speed Press, 1986.
Wasserman, Debra, and Mangels, Reed. *Simply Vegan.* Baltimore, Md.: The Vegetarian Resource Group, 1991.

Cookbooks for all vegetarian cooks
D'Avila-Latourrette, Brother Victor-Antoine. *This Good Food.* Woodstock, N.Y.: Overlook Press, 1993.
Elliot, Rose. *The Complete Vegetarian Cuisine.* New York: Pantheon Books, 1988.
Katzen, Mollie. *The Moosewood Cookbook,* rev. ed. Berkeley, Calif.: Ten Speed Press, 1992.
Saks, Ann, and Stone, Faith. *The Shoshoni Cookbook.* Summertown, Tenn.: Book Publishing Company, 1993.
Sass, Lorna J. *Recipes from an Ecological Kitchen.* New York: William Morrow and Co., 1992.
Thomas, Anna. *The Vegetarian Epicure.* New York: Knopf, 1972.
Vitell, Bettina. *A Taste of Heaven and Earth.* New York: HarperPerennial, 1993.

Comprehensive guides to nutrients in foods
Netzer, Corrine T. *The Corrine T. Netzer Encyclopedia of Food Values.* New York: Dell Books, 1992.
Pennington, Jean A.T., ed. *Bowes and Church's Food Values of Portions Commonly Used,* rev. ed. New York: Perennial Library, 1989.

Wrists at Risk

by William J. Anderson, M.D.

Traditionally, work-related injuries due to stress and strain were considered to occur almost exclusively in industrial settings. The only workers thought likely to be affected were manual laborers who perform repetitive or forceful hand actions—for example, meat packers who hack through thousands of pounds of beef each day or assembly-line workers who are perpetually turning screwdrivers and torque wrenches.

Perhaps the first description of the disabling effects of mechanical stress on those engaged in physical labor came from the Italian physician Bernardino Ramazzini, author of the first comprehensive treatise on occupational diseases, *Diseases of Workers* (1760):

Manifold is the harvest of diseases reaped by certain workers from the craft and trades they pursue. All the profit that they get is fatal injury to their health, mostly from two causes. The first and most potent is the harmful character of the materials they handle. The second, I ascribe to certain violent and irregular motions and unnatural postures of the body, by reason of which, the natural structure of the vital machine is so impaired that serious diseases gradually developed therefrom.

Today medical science has a much better understanding of the effect of mechanical stress and work on the human body and, in particular, on the musculoskeletal system. But despite increasing knowledge about work-related musculoskeletal injuries, their incidence has continued to rise. Moreover, repetitive stress injuries (RSIs), as they are often called today, have been reported with increasing frequency not only in factory workers but also among data entry clerks, telephone operators, newspaper reporters and editors, and many types of computer users.

A new "epidemic"?

According to U.S. Department of Labor statistics, in 1982, 18% of all occupational injuries were due to repetitive stress; by 1989 this figure had risen to 49%. Carpal tunnel syndrome (CTS), a repetitive stress disorder marked by pain in the wrist and hand, has been labeled by some as "the epidemic of the '90s." In one study of editors and writers at the *Los Angeles Times,* 40% said that they experienced pain in the hand and wrist caused or exacerbated by prolonged periods spent typing on computer keyboards. Similar problems have been reported among newsroom personnel at *Newsday,* the *New York Times,* and the wire service Reuters.

CTS is a major cause of absenteeism in the U.S. and a major source of claims for workers' compensation. It is estimated that the average company with high risks for CTS will pay $250,000 a year in compensation for every 100 employees. In 1988 surgery to treat CTS accounted for $15.5 million in Medicare expenditures. Clearly, CTS and other RSIs have high costs for industry, government, health care agencies, and the individuals who are affected.

Is this indeed a new "epidemic"—*i.e.,* are carpal tunnel syndrome and other, similar conditions in fact more prevalent today—or are these disorders simply being diagnosed and reported more frequently than in the past? The answer is both.

Several factors may have contributed to increased reporting of upper-extremity RSIs. They include increased awareness of these occupation-related syndromes among members of the medical community, reduced tolerance for discomfort on the job and increased tendency of workers to report such discomfort to medical personnel, and increased attention to health and safety in the workplace, coupled with encouragement of early reporting of muscle and joint symptoms. Factors responsible for an actual rise in the incidence of RSIs include the increased pace of work in today's workplaces, pressure for improved productivity in response to outside competition, and greater use of vibrating power tools. Perhaps most significant, however, is the advent of the computer. This major technological advance, which is credited with making office work faster and more efficient, has also transformed the nature of the work people do with their hands and arms. Thus, while fewer of to-day's workers are experiencing traumatic injuries due to strenuous effort and force, changes in workplace design and the physical demands of work are con-tributing to an increase in RSIs.

Understanding overuse injuries

By definition, RSIs involve damage, whether temporary or permanent, to the soft tissues of the human body as a result of repeated exertion. The tissues primar-ily involved are muscles, tendons, nerves, and blood vessels. RSIs go by many different names—repetitive strain or repetitive motion injuries or disorders, cumu-lative trauma disorders, overuse disorders, and, most recently, work-related musculoskeletal disorders, the official designation of the World Health Organization. These terms are often used interchangeably, however, and basically mean the same thing.

In order to understand RSIs, it is necessary to have a fundamental knowledge of biomechanics. The terms *work capacity* and *work tolerance* are frequently used to describe the ability to perform sustained, dynamic work over a specific period of time. When a per-son undertakes a particular job, the body adapts to the demands of the required tasks. With incremental increases in work intensity, the musculoskeletal sys-tem increases its function to match the demand. This response of increased function to match increased demand continues until the musculoskeletal system reaches a maximum capacity beyond which it cannot safely increase output.

On the basis of observations of skilled workers in different jobs situations, engineers have identified so-called normal times needed for performing specific jobs. In recent years, however, it has been recognized that physical attributes such as strength, flexibility, and endurance may vary greatly among individuals—especially with regard to gender and age—thus calling into question the value of "normal times" as predictors of the time required for a specific person to perform a specific job. Since each individual's muscles and tendons have a maximum performance capacity, or a threshold of resistance to damage, excessive de-mands on the musculoskeletal system over time will inevitably result in pain and injury.

RSIs develop when the same movement is per-formed over and over, sometimes many thousands of times a day. For example, a computer operator is likely to spend many hours at the keyboard, sit-ting in the same position and doing the same task without breaks or variation. Working in this fashion allows no time for stressed tissues of the arms and hands to recover. If the person's leisure-time activi-ties also include repetitive finger or wrist motions—as are typical in needlework and gardening—the risk of developing an RSI may be increased. The more the hands and wrists are overworked, the worse the symptoms will be.

Anatomy of a problem

CTS is the most common injury due to repetitive stress. An understanding of the anatomy of the wrist makes it clear why this part of the body is particularly vulnerable to the effects of overuse.

The wrist joint is formed by two rows of bones called the carpal bones (from *karpos,* the Greek word for "wrist"). The carpal tunnel is a small passage al-most completely surrounded by the carpal bones. On the palm side of the hand, the tunnel is enclosed by a tight band of fibrous tissue called the transverse carpal ligament. Through the tunnel run nine tendons, several blood vessels, and the median nerve. The latter is a soft structure filled with fibers that carry elec-trical signals (nerve impulses) back and forth between the hand and the spinal cord. The tendons, known as finger flexor tendons, are rodlike structures that move the fingers. They transmit forces from muscles in the forearm to the fingers and enable the fingers to close to make a fist.

The vulnerable wrist

palm side of hand

median nerve

carpal tunnel

median nerve

transverse carpal ligament

blood vessels

muscle

finger flexor tendons

carpal bones

tendons

cross-section of wrist

During movements of the fingers and wrist, the finger flexor tendons rub against the walls of the carpal tunnel and the median nerve itself. Although the tendons are lubricated by a special tendon lining and by synovial fluid, frequent rates of movement, especially in combination with forceful gripping, may cause swelling of the tendons or the sheaths that surround them. Because there is little room for expansion within the tight confinement of the carpal tunnel, the result of swelling is that the softest tissues, the median nerve and its blood vessels, become compressed, or "pinched." This pressure causes the numbness, tingling, and pain in the wrist and hand that are the primary symptoms of CTS. As the pressure on the nerve gets worse, affected individuals may lose control of some of the hand muscles, causing them to drop objects that they attempt to hold or pick up. They may also wake up at night with aching in the hand that makes them want to shake or rub it.

Repeated, forceful gripping or grasping motions—as in the use of wire clippers, pliers, and power drills—can also cause CTS as a result of the stress exerted over the base of the palm, where the median nerve is protected only by the 3-mm (0.1-in)-thick transverse carpal ligament. Leaning the wrists on a desk or table while operating a computer can also place excessive pressure on the median nerve and may result in inflammation of the tendons and tissues surrounding the nerve.

Not all cases of CTS are the result of work-related injury or use of the hands. Illness that causes tissue inflammation—*e.g.,* arthritis, gout, hypothyroidism, diabetes mellitus—may affect the median nerve within the carpal tunnel. In severe diabetes, for example, disease-related damage to the small blood vessels disrupts the supply of nutrients to the nerve. Swelling and bleeding associated with a fracture of the wrist can also put undue pressure on the median nerve. Pregnancy, menstruation, menopause, use of oral contraceptives, and hysterectomy with removal of the ovaries are associated with changes in metabolism that can result in fluid retention or thickening of the tendons and tendon sheaths, which, in turn, can contribute to CTS.

Diagnosis

Carpal tunnel syndrome is most commonly diagnosed by an orthopedic surgeon or a specialist in hand surgery. While the family doctor or internist may see that numbness and pain are a problem, he or she may not recognize that the cause is CTS as opposed to arthritis of the wrist joint or some other type of hand or wrist ailment.

The diagnosis is made on the basis of the patient's medical history, a physical examination, and, sometimes, X-ray and laboratory and electrical studies. During the physical examination, the physician may test the sensation of each finger by rubbing an object such as a pencil or a piece of cotton across the patient's fingers and asking whether the sensation feels "normal." The doctor may also tap on the base of the patient's palm at the level of the wrist to see if the median nerve is sensitive or under pressure. This may cause a sensation something like an electric shock to shoot into the patient's fingertips. The patient may be asked to bend the wrist for 20–60 seconds to see if the symptoms get worse. In many cases grip and pinch strengths will be measured by the physician, and X-rays of the wrist will be taken to see if there are any skeletal causes for the CTS—such as old fractures or osteoarthritis.

Occasionally, the doctor will order electrodiagnostic studies. One of these is the nerve conduction study, which measures the speed of the electrical signals along the nerve as it passes through the carpal tunnel. Another is the electromyogram, which involves placing electrodes into the hand and forearm muscles for a brief period of time to see how healthy the muscle is. The health of the muscle provides an indication of the soundness of the nerve that runs through it.

Nonsurgical treatment

If CTS is the result of a non-use-related problem or a medical condition, the specific treatment is aimed at that underlying problem, whether it be diabetes, thyroid disease, or another cause. Women who are pregnant or breast-feeding may find that their symptoms disappear once they give birth or cease lactating and lose the excess fluid and weight accumulated during pregnancy.

If the syndrome is a result of overuse of the wrist and hand, either in work or in recreation, then avoiding or reducing the activity responsible will often rapidly alleviate the symptoms. Frequent resting of the hand and stretching exercises (*see* below) for the hands, elbows, shoulders, and neck muscles will decrease symptoms over a period of time. A detailed history—the first step in diagnosis—is crucial to discovering whether repetition, excess of force, awkward posture, or uncomfortable position of the wrist or arms is contributing to CTS.

Almost everyone with CTS of short duration or those with minimal symptoms can be treated without surgery. Resting the wrist by wearing a splint or brace at night not only provides support for the wrist and relieves overworked wrist structures and tendons but also helps prevent reinjury while these tissues and the median nerve are healing. In addition, the brace will prevent repeated stress against the palm, which can further irritate and damage the median nerve. The best kind of brace is one that has a metal bar supporting the wrist and palm side of the forearm. These can be bought at most drug or medical supply stores. Although it is not difficult to get a brace that fits the individual properly, it is important that he or she understand the condition being treated and its degree of severity. Therefore, before proceeding with self-treatment using a brace, it is best to consult an orthopedist or hand surgeon to ensure that splinting is the correct treatment in that particular case.

Anti-inflammatory drugs, including aspirin and other over-the-counter medications, are very effective in reducing tendon-sheath swelling within the carpal tunnel; some of these medicines may actually increase the lubrication of the tendons as they slide through the sheaths, thereby reducing friction. Splinting or bracing the wrist, as well as taking anti-inflammatory drugs, results in relief of symptoms in over half of the people with CTS. However, since anti-inflammatory medicines may have side effects such as gastrointestinal distress and may be contraindicated for certain people, it is important to seek professional advice about taking any such medications.

Nutritional supplements such as vitamin B_6 and the "healing vitamins," C and E, may be helpful in relieving the symptoms of CTS, especially where there are no associated systemic diseases (such as diabetes) or injuries (for example, a wrist fracture). Because too much vitamin B_6 can be harmful, the doctor should be consulted about the dosage that will be most beneficial.

Injections of anti-inflammatory drugs, such as a soluble steroid, are sometimes useful either alone or in combination with other treatments. Injecting this type of medicine directly into the carpal tunnel can act directly to reduce the swelling of the tendons and alleviate the inflammation and irritation of the median nerve. It is important to emphasize that carpal tunnel syndrome may be related to a combination of factors, including overuse at work and play and various medical problems. Therefore, combining several different treatments may be the most effective approach.

Surgery: last resort

If a person continues to have symptoms of CTS despite nonsurgical treatment and changes in activities involving the hands, the doctor may recommend surgery. Although there are many variations of carpal tunnel release procedures, the two basic approaches involve either open surgery or a minimally invasive (endoscopic) technique. The goal of both is the same—to decompress the carpal tunnel by severing the transverse carpal ligament, thus releasing pressure within the carpal tunnel. Both are outpatient procedures with a total operating time of often less than 20 minutes, and both involve a local anesthetic (with or without intravenous sedation).

Open carpal tunnel release was first performed in 1927 at the Mayo Clinic in Rochester, Minn. This procedure is the time-honored operative treatment for severe CTS. The operation involves a two- to three-centimeter-long incision in the mid palm, between the two muscular areas at the base of the palm. Once the skin, underlying connective tissue, and transverse carpal ligament have been cut, the surgeon uses special instruments called rakes to spread apart the surgical opening, thus allowing a clear view of the nerve, blood vessels, tendons, and bony structures of the carpal tunnel. Using loupe magnification attached to eyeglasses, the surgeon then examines the anatomy of these structures, looking for narrowing or constriction of the nerve or excessive thickness of tendon lining. The surgeon will also gently retract, or pull aside, the nerve and tendon and inspect the bony side of the carpal tunnel to see if there are any abnormal bony spurs or tumors protruding into the carpal tunnel from the bony side. In addition, many surgeons release the tourniquet that is preventing blood flow to the hand and measure the amount of time it takes for the blood vessels within the nerve in the carpal tunnel area to fill. If the blood vessel fills quickly and the nerve turns uniformly pink, it is an indication that the artery supplying the blood probably did not sustain permanent damage from prolonged pinching or pressure. If this is the case, the prognosis is good. By contrast, the surgeon may see the nerve filling with blood up to the anatomic area of the carpal tunnel, from which point the nerve may remain white, indicating damage to the artery and a poorer outlook for complete recovery.

Following the operation, most surgeons will apply a plaster dressing similar to a half cast to support the patient's wrist until the sutures are removed 10 to 14 days later. The patient is encouraged to keep the wrist elevated for the first two or three days after the surgery but is strongly encouraged to straighten and flex the fingers frequently to minimize swelling and stiffness. Four to five days after surgery, the patient may start using the hand to lift light objects and assist the "free" hand with activities of daily life. (In general, bilateral surgery is not recommended because the free hand is needed for performing basic functions.) The plaster dressing is usually removed about seven days after surgery, and a removable wrist splint is placed on the hand and wrist. The sutures are removed about 14 days after surgery.

During the next four to six weeks, the patient gradually increases hand activity; the wrist splint is worn periodically during this time for support. The patient's occupation will determine when he or she can return to work. Office work can usually be resumed two to three weeks after the operation, providing the person limits the pace of work and takes frequent breaks. Those whose jobs require heavy and forceful gripping may not be able to return to work for three to four months. Open carpal tunnel release is successful in relieving symptoms in 70% to 95% of cases.

In the mid-1980s a new approach to carpal tunnel release surgery was developed, using endoscopic

Fast, efficient optical scanners enable supermarket checkers to ring up the price of each item with a flick of the wrist. However, the constant repetition of this motion can result in pain or even disability.

technology. (Endoscopes are fiber-optic devices that can be used to view the interior of body cavities.) The advantages of endoscopic carpal tunnel release over open surgery are less pain during and after the procedure and faster healing, allowing an earlier return to work. There are two basic approaches to endoscopic release: single and double portal. In both cases the surgeon uses visual and palpable landmarks in the hand and wrist to determine safe locations for the incisions, thus avoiding injury to structures such as the median nerve, ulnar nerve, and arteries. The double-portal technique requires two one- to two-centimeter-long incisions in the forearm just above the wrist and another incision one centimeter long in the mid palm. A slotted, small-diameter tube is carefully passed into the carpal tunnel through one of these incisions (the choice depends on the specific instrument and technique being used) to protect important surrounding nerves, blood vessels, and tendons. An endoscope is inserted into one end of the slotted tube, and a series of scalpel blade assemblies are introduced through the other end. Using the endoscope to view the interior structures, the surgeon inspects and severs the transverse carpal ligament. For the single-portal tech-

nique, a three-centimeter-long incision is made on the palm side of the forearm just above the wrist. This incision allows passage of a device that contains the endoscope and a retractable knife blade. The blade is gradually advanced until the transverse carpal ligament has been divided in two. The entire assembly is then slowly withdrawn.

There are specific and important contraindications to the use of the endoscope in carpal tunnel release surgery. Endoscopic techniques are not used in cases where there is inflammatory or infected tenosynovitis (involvement of the tendon sheaths), anatomic abnormalities (posttraumatic or congenital), or any condition that interferes with the surgeon's ability to get a clear view of the relevant structures. Endoscopic surgery also is not appropriate in patients who have had previous unsuccessful carpal tunnel release surgery. The patient must be informed beforehand that the endoscopic procedure may need to be converted into an open surgery if any difficulties are encountered.

Surgeons require substantial training and experience to become proficient in the endoscopic procedures. Although preliminary results of a multicenter study suggest that complication rates for endoscopic carpal tunnel release are comparable to those for open techniques, a controlled prospective study has yet to be done to determine if any differences exist in the results of the two operative approaches or between the two endoscopic techniques.

Prevention

People who use—or overuse—their hands in any repetitive action may be able to prevent CTS from developing. The following are some suggestions.

● Taking regular work breaks or periodically resting the hands and arms may be very effective in preventing the tendons from swelling and eventually causing CTS. Every 20 to 30 minutes, people should put down their tools or sit back from the computer keyboard and relax their hands by gently shaking them and performing the stretching exercises described below. This exercise routine takes only two to three minutes, but if done regularly throughout the day, it can give the tendons and muscles a chance to catch up to the job demands. If possible, one should walk around the room and give the entire musculoskeletal system a brief break.

● Alternating the actions done with the hands is an effective way of giving them a rest while continuing to work. One way to do this is to have workers at risk for CTS change or rotate tasks at regular intervals or, for those working at a computer, to switch from the keyboard to a mouse. This not only allows variation of hand activities but also creates an opportunity to stretch and relax the whole body.

● Resting the wrists on a specially designed (ergonomic) wrist pad *while* typing can actually make the carpal tunnel compression problem worse. A "wrist rest" is exactly that: a place to rest the wrists when the person is *not* typing. A better alternative is to remove the hands from the keyboard entirely and briefly rest them on the lap or thighs.

• Keeping the wrists in a straight, or neutral, position parallel to the floor while typing is important. The keyboard should be flat and at or just below elbow level, and the computer keys should be a comfortable distance from the body. The wrists should never be excessively angulated. A wrist brace may help to maintain the straight alignment.

• Checking the position of the body, arms, and forearms periodically while performing any seated task—whether at home or at work—can prevent unnecessary overloading of the upper body or shoulder muscles. The upper arms should be held close to the body and the forearms slightly inclined down or parallel to the floor. The chair should be adjusted so that the feet are flat on the floor.

What people do *before* and *after* using their hands is often just as important as what they do while working with them. Some very simple exercises to stretch the muscles and tendons and maintain maximum flexibility can help prevent CTS. Many people feel stiff when they first get up in the morning, and their muscles and tendons may feel "brittle." After a warm shower, however, the connective tissues are more elastic and flexible. This is the best time to do the following warming-up and stretching exercises for the hands, wrists, forearms, elbows, and shoulders.

Wrist extension. With the wrist extended (forearm parallel to the ground, wrist bent, fingers pointing upward), gently press back on the fingers with the other hand. Hold for 10 seconds and relax. Repeat five times.

Wrist curl. With the wrist flexed (forearm parallel to the ground, wrist bent, fingers pointing downward), use the other hand to press gently on the back of the flexed hand. Hold for 10 seconds. Repeat five times.

Finger stretch. Make a tight fist with the hand and then release, spreading the fingers as far apart as possible. Hold for 10 seconds. Repeat five times.

Shoulder roll. From a relaxed position, raise the shoulders upward toward the ears, roll shoulders backward, and return to relaxed position. Repeat five times. Reverse direction of roll.

Neck relaxers. Tilt the head gently to one side (ear toward shoulder) and then to the other, stretching the muscles in the side of the neck.

Sitting up straight and facing forward, gently turn the head as far as possible to the right and look over the right shoulder. Reverse and look over left shoulder.

Return to forward-facing position. Slowly bring the chin to the chest, then raise the chin up as far as possible, taking care not to overextend the neck. Repeat each neck stretch several times.

The exercises should be done gently and slowly, with care taken not to stretch more than feels comfortable. Spending a total of 10 to 15 minutes doing these stretching exercises before work in the morning or before going out to work in the garden can make the difference between an injury-free and an injury-prone day.

Finally, at least one scientific study suggests that a program for increasing muscular strength in the wrist, hand, and forearm can prevent overuse disorders. Since each individual's starting point or physical condition is different, people should always consult their own doctor before beginning a program of progressive resistance exercise. Moreover, any specific conditioning program such as weight lifting should be designed and supervised by a competent professional trained in exercise physiology, physical therapy, or upper-limb biomechanics and physiology. If these kinds of strengthening regimens are not performed properly, they can actually cause more problems than they relieve.

Toward an injury-free future

In hopes of decreasing the incidence of CTS among office workers, many companies are busily attempting to change the traditional positioning of the hands and fingers on the keyboard. One innovative design splits the keyboard into three parts—one for the right hand, one for the left, and one for the numeric keypad—all of which separate, rotate, and tilt to any number of positions to avoid the rigid and stressful position of the hand, arms, and shoulders while maintaining the standard layout of the letters. Another experimental keyboard is split in two, and the halves are angled for a more natural hand position. Perhaps the most elaborate solution is a keyboard that arranges its keys on two vertical planes, so that the palms of the hands face each other as they would if one were playing a concertina. Side-view mirrors assist in keeping track of hand placement. In the most radical departure from tradition, one manufacturer has eliminated keys altogether and developed a prototype machine that consists of two padded hand rests with individual finger wells, similar to the holes in a bowling ball. Each finger operates five separate switches by pressing down or flicking forward, backward, left, or right. The company says that the system can be learned in less than 15 hours.

Two major drawbacks of these "user-friendly" keyboards are their high price and the scanty biomechanical and physiological data supporting their claims of preventing or reducing repetitive strain disorders. Until ergonomic engineering finds definitive solutions to the problems of rapid, repetitive motions, worker awareness and active programs for prevention will remain the best defense against overuse injuries.

Getting the Upper Hand on Exercise

by Barry A. Franklin, Ph.D.,
and Frances Munnings

Most physical fitness programs emphasize lower-body aerobic exercise, with activities such as running, walking, and bicycling. This type of exercise is fine—as far as it goes. To be comprehensive, a fitness program should provide a workout for the whole body, and it should increase muscle strength as well as aerobic (*i.e.,* cardiorespiratory) capacity.

"Armed" for exercise

Indeed, many of the activities of daily living—raking leaves or carrying groceries, for instance—require muscular endurance and aerobic fitness in the upper and lower body. Many recreational activities depend as much, if not more, on work of the upper body as of the lower body: tennis, golf, swimming, canoeing, baseball, and gardening among them. The same is true of many occupational activities: carpentry, painting, machine-tool operation, assembly-line work, and housecleaning. One occupation—orchestra conducting—relies almost entirely on sustained upper-body work and, interestingly, orchestra conductors are noted for their longevity. Arturo Toscanini was nearly 90 when he died, and Leopold Stokowski and Paul Paray reached their 90s. All continued conducting into their final years. Some suggest that this longevity is related to job satisfaction; others believe that regular upper-body exercise has something to do with it.

Some persons may be unable to perform lower-extremity exercise; for them upper-body exercise may be the only exercise possible. For example, those who have peripheral vascular disease (blockage of the blood vessels in the lower extremities), orthopedic problems, or disabling arthritis may have difficulty walking—no less walking briskly—but they can achieve cardiorespiratory fitness through upper-body exercise. The same is true of paraplegics and amputees.

Almost invariably, strength-training programs—that is, progressive resistance exercise regimens such as lifting weights or performing routines on circuit-training machines at health clubs—systematically exercise every major muscle group, including the upper-body muscles. Likewise, endurance programs (*i.e.,* aerobic training to decrease heart rate and blood pressure and increase oxygen intake and utilization) should include

arm exercise as well as leg exercise. Furthermore, it is not difficult to incorporate upper-body aerobic exercise into a training program.

First, one needs to have an understanding of some basic exercise principles. Then one needs to find the right upper-body exercises for one's own personal program. Finally, one needs to make a conscientious effort to *do* them on a regular basis—ideally, three times per week.

Rationale for upper-body endurance training

Aerobic exercise training brings about favorable cardiovascular, respiratory, and metabolic adaptations. For the most part, these adaptations are largely specific to the muscles that are trained. Physiologists refer to this concept as "training specificity."

A well-documented effect of regular endurance exercise training is a lower heart rate at rest and during exertion at a given workload. This is important from a clinical standpoint because it reduces the work of the heart. One widely publicized Scandinavian study showed that regular leg training achieved by pedaling a cycle ergometer (stationary cycle) caused a substantial decrease in the heart rate during leg exercise at low and high workloads but not when arm exercises were performed. Conversely, a program that focused on arm training using a cycle ergometer adapted for arm cranking resulted in a marked reduction in the heart rate during arm work, whereas heart rate reductions during leg exercise were small. These findings imply that a substantial portion of the conditioning re-

415

Exercising on a machine that simulates cross-country skiing provides a vigorous total-body workout. It strengthens and tones major muscle groups while building a stronger heart and lungs, thereby increasing cardiorespiratory endurance.

sponse can be attributed to adaptations in the specific trained muscles.

Because training benefits show little or no transfer from one set of limbs to another, it is important not to restrict exercise training to the legs. Persons who rely on their upper extremities for occupational or recreational activity especially should train their arms as well as their legs. Their conditioning programs should incorporate types of muscle effort that correspond to those required for their daily activity. Such tailoring of an exercise program to one's specific needs will help maximize the conditioning effect because training benefits will carry over into everyday life.

Safety considerations

In the past, arm exercise training for persons with heart disease was prohibited because it was assumed to be unsafe. This caution stemmed from isolated medical reports of cardiovascular complications during some forms of upper-body work (*e.g.,* hammering nails or changing a flat tire). Researchers had also shown that arm exercise at below the maximal heart rate provoked higher heart rate and blood pressure responses than leg exercise, presumably resulting in greater demands on the heart.

Numerous recent studies, however, suggest that upper-body work is far less hazardous than was once presumed. Arm exercise generally fails to elicit electro-cardiographic evidence of ischemia (insufficient blood supply to the heart muscle), cardiac rhythm irregularities, blood pressure abnormalities, or chest pain (angina). Moreover, it appears that the upper extremities adapt to regular exercise in the same manner as the lower extremities. In other words, arm training and leg training result in comparable improvements in upper- and lower-body fitness when exercises of equivalent intensity, frequency, and duration are used for both sets of limbs.

Designing a program

Four factors should be considered when an upper-body aerobic exercise program is set up: heart rate, workload, equipment, and method.

Heart rate. When physiologists measure the heart rate during arm and leg exercise, they consistently find that the maximal heart rate is slightly lower during arm work than during leg work. Thus, prescribing the intensity of arm exercise based on a maximal heart rate that was obtained during an exercise stress test—for example, on a treadmill or stationary bicycle—may yield a training heart rate that is too high. As a general rule, the heart rate for leg training should be reduced by 10 to 15 beats per minute for arm training.

Workload. Specially designed arm ergometers that are secured to a stationary platform and use bicycle handgrips over the pedals are particularly useful for upper-extremity training. These are most likely to be found in clinical settings, such as a physiology laboratory or a cardiac rehabilitation facility, although many health clubs have them as well. Using an ergometer, one determines the mechanical resistance, or workload, for leg pedaling or arm cranking by multiplying the weight applied (in kilograms) by the distance this weight moves per revolution (in meters) by the number of revolutions per minute. This is usually expressed as kilogram-meters per minute (kgm/min). Some equipment manufacturers express the workload in Watts (1 Watt = 6 kgm/min). Because the distance the applied weight moves per revolution does not change, workloads are augmented by increases in the weight applied, the revolutions per minute, or both.

When determining the workload for arm training, it is important to recognize that although maximal physiological responses are generally greater during leg exercise than during arm exercise, the heart rate, blood pressure, and oxygen consumption during arm exercise are greater for any given workload. Therefore, an appropriate workload for leg training will generally be too high for arm training. Appropriate workloads for arm training are approximately 50% of those used for leg training. In other words, a person using 300 kgm/min (50 Watts) for leg pedaling would use 150 kgm/min (25 Watts) for arm cranking, and the physiological responses to these workloads would be similar.

Equipment. As noted above, ergometers specially adapted for arm exercise can provide an excellent upper-body aerobic workout. Other, more widely available equipment especially suitable for upper-body training includes rowing machines, wall pulleys, and shoulder wheels. Often people use a metronome with these devices to standardize the work intensity to a set rate of movements. In other words, they perform the arm work to the cadence, or rhythm, established by the metronome.

Many commercially available exercise devices provide both upper- and lower-body exercise. These include simulated cross-country ski machines and some treadmills and stationary cycles. Certain models of cycle ergometers enable one to exercise arms and legs separately, using the arm levers only or the pedals only, or to exercise the upper and lower extremities together, using the levers and pedals simultaneously. Another popular machine found at many health clubs simulates vertical ladder climbing and provides a vigorous workout for both the arms and legs.

One innovative device, the Playbuoy® arm exerciser, is designed for two people. It can be used to strengthen and aerobically condition the upper body, improve coordination and timing, and have fun. The Playbuoy consists of a plastic buoy (similar to a buoy on a swimming pool lane divider) that is fitted over two 6.1-m (20-ft) waxed ropes, at the ends of which are four plastic handles. Standing about six meters apart and each grasping a pair of handles, the partners shuttle the buoy back and forth over the span of the ropes. They do this by alternately separating and bringing together the ropes by shifting the positions of the handles. By changing the arm positions and varying the spread of the ropes, different upper-body muscle groups are exercised. Beginners, deconditioned people, and the elderly may want to shorten the ropes, which makes the workout somewhat less rigorous.

Hand-held 0.45- to 1.4-kg (1- to 3-lb) weights can also be used for a good upper-body aerobic workout. A very popular approach, which incorporates upper- and lower-body exercise, is to carry weights and vigorously swing the arms while walking briskly. This combination produces significantly greater increases in heart rate, oxygen consumption, and calorie expenditure than does walking at comparable speeds without arm movement. In fact, walking at a comfortable pace combined with arm-weight swinging provides an aerobic workout comparable to that from moderately paced jogging while it also provides an upper-extremity workout.

One does not necessarily need to use "specialized" equipment to get a good upper-body workout. The equipment used in quite a few popular sports and recreational activities provides excellent upper-extremity training—e.g., racquets used in racquetball, squash, or tennis; oars used in canoeing; poles used in cross-country skiing; and clubs used in golf. Of course, one would need to play tennis or golf, go cross-country skiing, or canoe on a regular basis (two to three times a week) in order to achieve a training effect.

According to *U.S. News and World Report* magazine, the "latest fitness craze" is so-called aerobic boxing—and both women and men are doing it. This popular form of exercise not only builds strength in the upper body but also provides excellent cardiorespiratory conditioning. A total-body aerobic boxing workout typically begins with light stretching followed by 10 minutes of calisthenics and jumping rope, then proceeds to 15–20 minutes of vigorous boxing activity that includes punching a punching bag, shadowboxing, lunging, and ducking. The routine ends with stretching exercises such as squats and push-ups. So, investing in a pair of boxing gloves and a punching bag might not be a bad idea!

Karen Wollins

Having some fun and getting some exercise, a couple tries out the Playbuoy®, a lightweight, plastic-and-rope arm exerciser that provides a surprisingly vigorous upper-body aerobic workout. Beginners may want to start with the ropes shortened several meters.

Getting the upper hand on exercise

Not all exercise for the upper body requires equipment. Various types of calisthenics can provide a vigorous workout that involves all the major muscle groups in the upper body. While swimming can do the same, especially if various strokes are used, the actual amount of energy expended is highly dependent on the individual swimmer's skill and efficiency.

Method. As already indicated, various methods, or activities, can be used to gain upper-extremity aerobic benefits. The most important factor in selecting the right one is to choose a form of exercise one enjoys. Whatever method one chooses, one must consider four aspects: mode, frequency, intensity, and duration.

● *Mode.* Exercise should be continuous and rhythmic in nature. People who enjoy an exercise that involves only or primarily the legs—*e.g.,* walking, hiking, jogging, or bicycling—should find a way to add upper-body exercise to their programs. As noted above, they might do this by carrying and swinging weights while walking or by using equipment such as a cross-country skiing machine or a bicycle ergometer that has pedals and arm levers.

● *Frequency.* Ideally, one should exercise three times a week. Twice may not be adequate, and studies show that more than five sessions do not confer additional aerobic benefits. Moreover, the incidence of injury increases markedly with too-frequent sessions.

● *Intensity.* A popular way to establish the intensity of exercise is to directly measure the maximal heart rate (heartbeats per minute) by doing a graded exercise test. The basic way to estimate the maximal heart rate in healthy men and women is to subtract one's age from 220. However, the variance for any given age is considerable—plus or minus 10 beats per minute.

Exercise should be done at 70% to 85% of measured or estimated maximal heart rate. However, for arm exercise alone, the heart rate should be about 10 to 15 beats per minute lower than the rate for leg exercise.

Another popular method for regulating exercise intensity uses the so-called Borg scale to rate "perceived exertion." The scale consists of 15 grades from 6 to 20—6 being rest and 20 being maximum effort. In between are descriptive "effort ratings" at every odd number, from "very, very light" at 7 to "very, very hard" at 19. The ratings are based on one's overall feeling of exertion and physical fatigue and tend to correspond quite well to metabolic changes such as heart rate and oxygen consumption during exercise. (One should not overemphasize any one factor, such as arm or leg fatigue or shortness of breath.) Among healthy young individuals, one's personal effort rating on the Borg scale generally approximates one-tenth of the actual heart rate response. Exercise rated as 11 to 15, between "fairly light" and "hard," is appropriate for aerobic conditioning and corresponds to 70% to 85% of maximal heart rate (or 60% to 80% of the

maximal oxygen consumption). Ratings greater than this generally indicate an exercise intensity that is too high, regardless of the heart rate response.

Yet another way to regulate intensity, which is especially appropriate for beginning exercisers, is to use the "talk test" to gauge the strenuousness of a workout. Anyone who is too out of breath to carry on a conversation comfortably during exercise is probably working too hard.

● *Duration.* Each exercise session should last 20 to 60 minutes, depending on intensity and on whether upper- and lower-body exercises are done separately or combined. High-intensity sessions can be shorter, low-intensity sessions longer. It should be emphasized, however, that the benefits of exercise are cumulative. Recent studies have shown similar training effects in subjects who completed three 10-minute bouts of moderate-intensity exercise per day and in those who performed one "long" exercise bout of 30 minutes.

Longer periods of exercise are appropriate when the exercise itself uses the arms and the legs—*e.g.,* cross-country skiing—but if one is concentrating on arm exercise alone, the time should be shortened to perhaps 10 to 15 minutes. Persons who use their upper extremities extensively in their occupational or recreational activities might want to devote up to half of the exercise session to upper-body work.

Total fitness

There is no doubt that regular exercise such as brisk walking, jogging, bicycling, or working out on a treadmill, exercise bicycle, or stair-climbing machine provides many substantial health benefits—from lowering the risk of cardiovascular disease, osteoporosis, and diabetes to burning calories and contributing to weight loss. Exercise may even increase longevity. Yet because the body's physiological adaptations to regular exercise are largely muscle specific, aerobic exercise programs that are restricted to leg training, though beneficial in many respects, are necessarily limited in scope. Moreover, such programs fail to consider that many occupational and recreational activities use both the upper and lower extremities.

It is perhaps relevant to note that those who do not like to exercise or doubt that it has benefits frequently challenge the very concept of "fitness." "Fitness for what?" they ask. Exercise enthusiasts respond, "Fitness for life." Yet most physical-conditioning regimens are improperly designed to enhance a person's capacity to perform activities required for daily living. *Total* exercise programs should include both aerobic and resistance (*i.e.,* strength-building) components. The aerobic portion, like the resistance portion, should involve both upper and lower extremities. Only then does exercise provide total fitness.

Say No to Drugs (in Pregnancy)

by Bruce D. Shephard, M.D.

The advisability of taking drugs during pregnancy is a subject of concern for patients and physicians alike; neither wants to take the chance of exposing the growing fetus to a substance that may be harmful. The risk of a birth defect from exposure to most drugs in early pregnancy is actually quite small, probably on the order of 1% or less. However, a few drugs—called teratogens—are known to cause defects consistently. These include certain sex hormones (especially androgens) and some chemotherapy agents used to treat cancer. For perspective, it is helpful to keep in mind that major birth defects occur in only approximately 2–3% of *all* pregnancies and that among these defects only 2–3% are thought to occur as a result of exposure to a teratogenic drug. Such exposure therefore accounts for perhaps one birth defect in every 1,500 pregnancies.

The lesson of thalidomide

Worldwide attention became focused on the potential for drug-induced birth defects following the thalidomide tragedy of the late 1950s. The drug thalidomide was prescribed widely in Europe as a sedative, and for a time its capacity to cause severe limb deformities went unrecognized. Between 1959 and 1962, however, several thousand babies in West Germany and several hundred in Great Britain were born deformed. The infants of some U.S. women were also affected. The drug caused malformations in approximately one in three infants exposed to it during early pregnancy. As a result of the thalidomide experience, in 1962 the U.S. Food and Drug Administration (FDA) established that, prior to marketing, any drug must be shown to be safe and effective for its intended use; as a standard part of safety testing, new drugs are administered to pregnant animals. Such tests help to screen out drugs that could be harmful to the human fetus.

Today, despite the lesson of thalidomide, there is a certain casualness about drug use during pregnancy. There are a number of reasons for this attitude. First, rather than causing major, obvious malformations, drugs, like various environmental toxins, may be quite subtle in their effects—*e.g.*, causing only a minor anomaly such as a tiny skin growth. Other effects may be behavioral (such as a learning disability) and therefore more difficult to attribute to a drug. Also, a drug's effects may become evident only in the long term, as in the case of DES (diethylstilbestrol), a group of hormonal drugs formerly widely prescribed to prevent miscarriage. After 30 years of use, it was shown that DES was associated with a small risk of vaginal cancer in adolescent females who were exposed in utero (*i.e.,* before birth).

Another factor that affects attitudes toward drug use during pregnancy is that most birth defects do not have a single identifiable cause, either genetic or environmental. The majority of defects are thought to be multifactorial in origin—that is, due to a number of possibly interacting causes—making the study of teratogenicity all the more complex. Finally, the risk of a given drug's causing a specific birth defect is hard to quantify, and extremely large numbers of patients are needed to produce statistically significant data. For the pregnant woman, however, talk of statistical significance is irrelevant—an adverse outcome has a 100% significance.

Fetal vulnerability

The teratogenic period—the time when birth defects are most likely to occur—is fairly well established in humans. This period is from approximately the second to the eighth week of fetal development (corresponding to the 4th to 10th weeks following a woman's last menstrual period, assuming a regular 28–30-day

419

Considered safe during pregnancy	
drug	symptom
acetaminophen (Datril, Tylenol)	pain
Kaopectate	diarrhea
laxatives: some mild stimulants (e.g., Milk of Magnesia, Senokot, Dulcolax); some bulk laxatives (e.g., Metamucil); some stool softeners (e.g., Colace, Surfak)	constipation
antacids*	heartburn
diphenhydramine (Benadryl)	itching; insomnia
chlorpheniramine (Chlor-Trimeton)	hay fever; sinus congestion
*avoid those containing aspirin	

cycle). Before this time, exposure to a teratogen usually causes an "all or none" effect—either the fetus is unharmed or a miscarriage occurs.

While most fetal organ formation takes place during the first three months of pregnancy, some development does continue after the first trimester. For example, the female genital system, including the uterus and vagina, does not completely form until well into the fifth month. The fetal brain continues its development throughout pregnancy. Moreover, drug-related alterations in fetal biochemistry and physiology may occur in the second half of pregnancy even after the fetus is fully formed. For example, the antibiotic tetracycline may impair bone development when exposure occurs after the 20th week of pregnancy. When taken in the second half of pregnancy, warfarin and aspirin, which act as blood thinners in the adult body, may cause internal bleeding in the fetus. Tranquilizers and other drugs affecting the central nervous system may cause lethargy or decreased sucking in the newborn or may have a delayed impact in the form of subtle behavioral disturbances. Until a few decades ago, it was widely believed that the placenta acted as a barrier, protecting the fetus from substances in the maternal circulation. Today, however, it is recognized that most drugs easily cross the placenta and reach the fetus to some degree.

Patterns of maternal drug use

The use of medications during pregnancy appears to be increasing. A 1992 study sponsored by the World Health Organization and involving 14,778 women from 22 countries found that 86% of the women had received drugs during pregnancy, with an average of 2.9 prescriptions each. The researchers who conducted the study concluded that on the basis of current knowledge, overall drug prescribing went beyond what was medically justifiable. Earlier studies (from the 1970s and 1980s) had reflected only a slightly lower frequency of medication use, showing 50–90% of women taking at least one prescription drug during each pregnancy. One survey of a suburban Baltimore, Md., population of 22,752 mothers who were pregnant between 1981 and 1987 found that 68% had used at least one prescription or nonprescription product (excluding illicit drugs and multivitamins). Medication use was found to be more common among women who were married, white, better educated, and/or older; had a higher income; or had received early prenatal care. Among the most commonly used medicines were analgesics such as acetaminophen, antihistamines, decongestants, and antibiotics.

Similar findings were reported in a study of 4,186 pregnant women from New Haven, Conn.; 66% used at least one drug during their pregnancies, and women who regularly used caffeine, alcohol, and cigarettes were the most likely to use a prescription or nonprescription drug. That study also found that higher socioeconomic status was a predictor of women who were more likely to use drugs during pregnancy, suggesting perhaps that more affluent women may be better able to afford medications or less willing to tolerate pregnancy symptoms. A number of authorities point out that in most Western countries, once pregnancy has been confirmed, there is a tendency to regard alleviation of its discomforts and symptoms as a relatively harmless practice. This is especially true where data linking specific drugs to birth defects are lacking.

Another possible factor influencing drug prescribing and use during pregnancy is the growing number of drugs available, both prescription and nonprescription. Every year 500 new drug products are introduced. Over-the-counter (OTC) drugs, because they do not require a prescription, are often considered harmless by those who take them. These drugs, especially, are likely to be used during the period after conception but before a woman realizes she is pregnant. (During this time before the first missed period, home pregnancy tests may not yet show a positive result.) So-called recreational drugs such as marijuana also may be used during this time by women who are unaware that they are pregnant.

A rational approach: some guidelines

Because much remains unknown about the effects of drugs on the unborn baby, a woman needs to make the most informed decisions she can about her use of medications before and during pregnancy. The following are some general guidelines.

● Women who are trying to conceive would be wise to avoid the use of drugs—prescription, OTC, and recreational.

● Women who are pregnant should avoid the use of medication throughout pregnancy—and especially in the first three months—unless prescribed by a doctor.

Many pregnancy symptoms can be relieved by means of nondrug therapy. For example, morning sickness may be alleviated by dietary changes, stress reduction, and limitations on activity.

● When medication must be used, it is best to choose the least potent form of the drug whenever possible. For example, less medication is absorbed by the body from a decongestant inhaler than from an oral form of the same drug.

● Women should be informed about any drug they take at any time, but this is especially true during pregnancy. They should know the benefits, risks, and alternatives to use of the drug in question. The table below lists the potential risks and benefits of selected medications for chronic conditions such as diabetes, high blood pressure, or epilepsy. If a woman takes a prescription drug, she should know its FDA pregnancy classification. A drug's classification is indicated in manuals such as the *Physician's Desk Reference* and in the patient package literature that comes with most prescription drugs. This classification system was established to provide a rough guide to a prescription drug's likelihood of being teratogenic. Drugs in categories A, B, and C are the safest. Category D drugs—those in which there is evidence of human fetal risk but benefits may outweigh risks—are seldom indicated during pregnancy. Category X drugs—those in which a demonstrated human teratogenicity clearly outweighs benefits to maternal health—are never indicated. It is always preferable to choose a category A drug over a B, or a B over a C, if possible. Also, it is usually better for the doctor to prescribe a well-known drug, such as penicillin or ampicillin, over a newer version of the same drug, such as piperacillin or mezlocillin, as the newer products have had less opportunity to be studied. Many communities have a teratogen information service that can advise women about a given drug. Such information is reassuring, and often these services are a more objective source than articles in the lay media or even the *Physician's Desk Reference,* which may be somewhat out of date or include overly cautious language. To find out how to contact a teratogen information service, women should consult a perinatologist or the obstetrics-gynecology department of a university medical center.

● When considering taking any drug, women should discuss the decision with their physicians. This is the best way to get a balanced perspective on the risks and benefits of a given drug. Some medications may have appropriate "off label" uses—that is, uses that are not specified in the FDA-approved package labeling. The use of aspirin to treat the complication of pregnancy called preeclampsia is one such example. Another is the use of terbutaline, an asthma drug, to prevent preterm labor. Discussion with the physician may also provide reassurance when there has been inadvertent drug exposure in early pregnancy. For example, several recent studies have not found any link between oral contraceptives and birth defects, a reassuring fact for women who conceive despite taking birth control pills. On the other hand, exposure to a few drugs in early pregnancy—for example, the acne drug isotretinoin (Accutane)—is a matter of significant concern. In such instances a woman may want to discuss with her doctor the option of pregnancy termination. Such a decision can best be made if the woman fully understands the known facts as they affect her individual circumstances.

Substance abuse

Substance abuse during pregnancy may include cigarette smoking, alcohol use, abuse of prescription

Treating medical conditions during pregnancy: benefit versus risk	
condition	comment
asthma	continue most medications such as theophylline and aminophylline; avoid drugs containing iodides, which may cause fetal goiter; avoid steroids such as prednisone and triamcinolone unless advised by physician; safety of cromolyn has not been established, but it has not been reported as a teratogen in humans
high blood pressure	continue medications under physician supervision
diabetes	avoid all oral medication; use insulin only (higher dosage of insulin usually needed during pregnancy)
seizures	phenytoin (Dilantin) and other anticonvulsant drugs have been associated with increased risk of fetal malformation, but the benefits of most of these drugs in preventing seizures usually outweigh risks; use of a single drug at the lowest possible dosage presents the least risk; consultation with a neurologist may be advisable
hypothyroidism (thyroid hormone deficiency)	dosage of thyroid hormone should be monitored frequently to determine need
heart problems (congestive heart failure, coronary heart disease, arrhythmias)	digoxin and propranolol appear to be safe

or nonprescription drugs, or the use of illicit drugs such as marijuana or cocaine. Most of these drugs readily cross the placenta. The harmful effects of alcohol—apparent as fetal alcohol syndrome—are perhaps the most well-known birth defects associated with drug abuse. In general, the adverse impact of other forms of drug abuse may be due to nutritional deficiencies and fetal growth problems secondary to the drug abuse rather than to the direct effect of the drug on fetal development. Interactive effects on the fetus of various combinations of drugs are generally unknown. Some of the more common street drugs and their risks during pregnancy are discussed below.

Marijuana and hashish. Birth defects following exposure to marijuana and hashish have been found in animals but not in humans. Impaired fetal growth has been reported in humans, however. Marijuana also contains chemicals that may be carcinogenic to the mother and may cause lung damage similar to or worse than that caused by cigarette smoking.

Heroin and other narcotics. Heroin addiction is highly dangerous to the fetus and may be associated with preterm labor, growth problems, and a fatal syndrome of narcotic withdrawal following birth. The incidence of sudden infant death syndrome (SIDS) is increased 10-fold among infants whose mothers use narcotics. Maternal complications of narcotic use include hepatitis and AIDS, which are especially prevalent among those who inject drugs.

Cocaine. A central nervous system stimulant, cocaine is associated with contractions of the uterus, which may lead to preterm labor or bleeding complications due to premature detachment of the placenta from the wall of the uterus (abruptio placentae). Cocaine use is associated with a high rate of birth defects (as high as 10%), as well as with increased rates of miscarriage, stillbirth, and growth retardation. Maternal complications of cocaine include seizures, heart attacks, and high blood pressure.

Hallucinogens. Very little is known about the capacity of LSD and phencyclidine (PCP; angel dust) to cause birth defects in humans, but such defects have been found in animals. These drugs are known to produce psychotic episodes in the mother.

Amphetamines. Amphetamines, often used as stimulants for staying awake or as diet pills, have been linked to fetal heart defects. In the mother, amphetamines may cause high blood pressure or irregular heartbeat.

Tranquilizers. Minor tranquilizers of the drug group known as benzodiazepines, such as diazepam (Valium) and others, have been linked to isolated cases of birth defects. Other studies have not confirmed this risk. Excessive use of minor tranquilizers in pregnancy may be associated with a withdrawal syndrome in the infant after birth, characterized by loss of muscle tone, irritability, and impaired body temperature regulation.

Alcohol. Fetal alcohol syndrome (FAS) is a distinct pattern of congenital physical and mental abnormalities. When first described in the 1970s, FAS was found in infants born to women who drank heavily during their pregnancies. Since then it has been identified even in offspring of moderate drinkers. Elements of this syndrome may include some or all of the following: low birth weight, poor coordination, facial deformities, heart defects, hyperactivity, and mental retardation. In the U.S. the full syndrome occurs in about one to three of every 1,000 live births. FAS ranks with Down syndrome and spina bifida as a major cause of mental retardation. Because the fetus metabolizes alcohol more slowly than the adult, the drug persists longer in the fetus than in the mother. The minimum amount of alcohol consumption required for causing FAS—or a less severe condition called fetal alcohol effect—is unknown; therefore, it is recommended that women abstain from alcohol throughout pregnancy and the preconception period. Mothers who breast-feed also should avoid alcohol, as the alcohol level in the milk is similar to that in the mother's blood.

Tobacco. Cigarette smoke, which has been described as the most common "known harmful exposure" in pregnancy, imposes serious risks to both mother and baby. Fetal and infant mortality rates are increased by more than 50% in first-time mothers who smoke more than one pack per day during pregnancy. Cigarette smoking can retard fetal growth as well as increase the risk of low birth weight, stillbirth, and maternal complications such as abruptio placentae. Smoking reduces the fetal oxygen supply by as much as 50% owing to the action of the carbon monoxide in smoke, which displaces oxygen from the bloodstream. The offspring of smoking mothers also have higher rates of SIDS and pneumonia than do babies of nonsmokers.

The relationship between smoking and birth defects is unclear. Some studies show an increased risk of cleft palate, heart defects, and the deformities known collectively as neural tube defects. A 1990 investigation found an association between smoking and *minor* birth defects in the infants of mothers over 35; minor birth defects are associated with a greater chance of psychomotor problems in later childhood.

A study published in February 1994 showed that nicotine from secondhand smoke even reaches the fetuses of nonsmoking women who are routinely exposed to cigarette smoke. The researchers did not investigate whether in utero exposure to passive smoking had an effect on the babies' health.

Caffeine. Research conducted in the early 1980s prompted the FDA to advise pregnant women to avoid caffeine. These studies suggested a correlation between high caffeine consumption and the risk of miscarriage, prematurity, and low birth weight. However, they did not control for other factors that might affect pregnancy outcome, such as smoking and alcohol use, and have not been uniformly confirmed by subsequent research. For example, a multicenter study, conducted under the auspices of the National Institute of Child Health and Human Development and published in February 1993 in the *Journal of the American Medical Association,* found no increased risk of miscarriage or low birth weight with moderate caffeine consumption when other factors such as smoking were taken into account. The investigators studied the effects of moderate caffeine intake only, defined as three cups of coffee, five 12-oz cans of caffeine-containing soft drinks, or seven cups of tea. On the other hand, just 10 months later the same journal published the results of Canadian research that came to the opposite conclusion. The Canadian investigators found that consumption of one and a half to three cups of coffee per day doubled a woman's risk of miscarriage, and drinking more than three cups tripled the risk. At the present time there is no consensus on what constitutes a "safe" level of caffeine consumption during pregnancy.

Drugs and breast-feeding

Breast-feeding is increasing in the United States. Of the women who gave birth in 1991, 60% breast-fed, compared with only 22% in 1971. While the nutritional

Contraindicated during breast-feeding	
drug	**comment**
bromocriptine	suppresses lactation
cocaine	causes cocaine intoxication
cyclophosphamide	possible immune suppression; unknown effect on growth or association with cancer
cyclosporine	possible immune suppression; unknown effect on growth or association with cancer
doxorubicin*	possible immune suppression; unknown effect on growth or association with cancer
ergotamine	vomiting, diarrhea, convulsions (with dosages used in migraine medications); 1/3 to 1/2 therapeutic blood concentration found in infants
lithium	1/3 to 1/2 therapeutic blood concentrations found in infants
methotrexate	possible immune suppression; unknown effect on growth or association with cancer
phencyclidine (PCP)	potent hallucinogen

drug is concentrated in human milk

and immunologic benefits of breast-feeding have been well documented, less is known about the risks to newborns from maternal drug ingestion. Reasons for the lack of data are that most of the research has been done in animals only, that many studies have used outdated methodologies, and that human studies have largely focused on a drug's capacity to produce side effects, such as drowsiness, in the nursing infant rather than measuring the infant's blood level of the drug in question.

It is well known that most drugs readily transfer from the maternal blood circulation into the breast milk. However, quantitative data on specific drugs are lacking. The concentration of a given drug in breast milk varies with the size and frequency of dosage and the drug's own metabolic characteristics. In general, the infant usually ingests less than 1–2% of the total maternal drug dose. However, the concentration of a drug in the newborn is also influenced by the maturity of the infant; higher drug levels are found in preemies than in babies born at term. Only a very few drugs are known to be harmful to the breast-fed infant. They are listed in the table, left.

Breast-feeding is not necessarily contraindicated in mothers who require certain medications. The following are some guidelines that may be helpful in making the decision whether to take a particular drug while breast-feeding.

● Consider avoiding the drug altogether, especially if it is being taken for relief of minor symptoms, such as the discomforts of a cold. However, it is usually advantageous to use pain medication following childbirth, as pain may actually inhibit the milk "letdown" reflex, making breast-feeding more difficult.

● If it is necessary to take medication for a transitory problem, stop breast-feeding temporarily and express the milk from the breasts until drug therapy has been completed. This approach may be appropriate for a short course of antibiotics or for medications taken in association with dental work or minor surgery.

● In some cases it is advisable to continue taking a drug but still all right to breast-feed. If possible, take the medication just *after* nursing, so that the drug's concentration in the breast milk is minimized. Avoid long-acting (extended-release) drugs and those with long half-lives, such as certain antidepressants and some tranquilizers (*e.g.,* diazepam).

● When an acute condition such as a bacterial infection or a medical indication such as high blood pressure makes medication use necessary, the drug should be taken, and the decision whether to continue breast-feeding should be based on the benefits and risks—as it is with medication use at other times. This is an important decision to discuss with the physician. In most cases breast-feeding can continue or need be discontinued for only a short time.

Active Vacations: Exercise Your Options

by Joe Sweeney

Art and Annie just got home from their vacation. *Some vacation!* They spent most of the week cooped up in their car, driving the length of California visiting Disneyland, Knott's Berry Farm, and virtually every other tourist attraction in the state. As usual, they tried to fit three weeks of travel into one. The pace was hectic, the food fattening, and the lines at all the tourist sites long. By the time they arrived home, Art and Annie were exhausted, stressed, and, to their dismay, several pounds heavier than when they set out.

When Maria and Michael needed a vacation, they opted for a five-day bicycle tour of New England. They slept in comfort in picturesque accommodations and spent their days pedaling through the countryside, enjoying fresh air, delightful scenery, and invigorating exercise. Picnic lunches and other conveniences, including bike maintenance and repair, were taken care of by the trip leaders. At night they joined the other trip participants in relaxing and delicious meals of homemade soups, garden-fresh salads, seafood caught that day, and home-baked pies made with just-picked berries. At the end of their trip, Michael and Maria were rested and refreshed. Their muscles felt toned, and they were pleased to find their clothes fitting a little less snugly around the waist.

Many people think of an "active vacation" as unrelenting physical exertion, perhaps resembling boot camp or a training regimen for a triathlon. In fact, a physically oriented vacation that matches an individual's preferences and fitness level can result in a memorable, remarkably relaxing, thoroughly rewarding, and possibly even life-changing experience.

Today, as more and more people make health and fitness greater priorities in their lives, active vacations are growing in popularity. The following will look at some of the many options for active getaways, point out the benefits of an active versus a sedentary holiday, and offer tips on selecting the right trip and then preparing for it properly.

Endless possibilities

There are so many different kinds of active vacations that just about everyone—including those with limited time, money, or experience—should be able to find the right trip. Whether a person has two weeks or two

days, there is bound to be a suitable choice. Many active vacation plans offer one-week programs. Some trips span 10 to 12 days, and a few last up to three weeks. However, there are also shorter four- or five-day getaways. In addition, weekend adventures are sometimes offered as an introduction to or preparation for a subsequent longer trip.

The choice of activities is equally varied. Bicycle tours are available all over the U.S. and most of Europe. Some popular destinations include the San Juan Islands of Washington state, the Redwood forests of northern California, the Kona Coast of Hawaii, the canyon lands of Utah (via mountain bike), and the French, English, and Italian countrysides.

Hiking tours are leaving footprints in the Cascades of Washington and Oregon, the Sierras of California, the Rockies of Colorado, and several mountain ranges in the eastern United States. In the winter, cross-country skiers can travel from inn to inn on ski tours of the Northeast. The more adventurous traveler may choose to trek the Alps of Switzerland or even more exotic destinations such as Thailand and Nepal.

The number of fitness resorts and health spas has surged over the past decade, as has their range of offerings. Many of these resorts provide balanced fitness programs with well-instructed classes. A relaxed atmosphere, good fellowship, and nutritious, low-fat "spa cuisine" are additional benefits.

Water sports enthusiasts can immerse themselves in rafting, kayaking, canoeing, snorkeling, swimming, or windsurfing adventures or combinations of the above. Lovers of the outdoors who wish to keep their feet dry might choose to explore the forests, the meadows, or the deserts on wilderness trips that center on backpacking, horseback riding, bird-watching, or photography.

Also increasing in popularity in the environmentally conscious 1990s are ecology-oriented vacations. Working as part of a team, often alongside experienced scientists, group members may study wild-

424

flowers in the Rocky Mountains, observe the habits of dolphins off the coast of Hawaii, help save the rain forests in Central America, join an archaeological dig in Wyoming, or track mountain lions in the wilderness of Idaho. Although such expeditions are actually "working" vacations, participants derive enormous satisfaction from donating time, muscle, and brainpower to worthwhile projects—all in the name of the environment. Accommodations range from tents to dormitory-style housing to well-equipped lodges. Pampering usually is not on the agenda, but travelers do learn much about the planet—and themselves.

Trips for everyone

Many touring companies and fitness resorts offer outings or sojourns for particular groups of people. For example, a bike-touring company might set aside a few tours a year for singles only. A walking-tour operator might offer an excursion reserved for seniors. There are also active vacation opportunities geared for families. Some family bicycle tours offer discounted rates for children, and some rafting trips allow a child to ride free with each adult who pays. Anyone planning such a trip should be sure to inquire about the minimum age requirement, however.

There are backpacking trips for women only, and some fitness resorts feature "couples" weeks and "men only" weeks each year. While the vast majority of spa guests are female, it is a myth that a fitness resort is not a suitable destination for a man. Consider the example of Larry:

After a lot of pleading, Linda finally persuades her husband, Larry, to go with her to the fitness resort she has been visiting annually for years. Larry dreads the prospect. He knows he will play no golf, watch no television, and eat no steak for seven agonizing days. On the first morning of their vacation, Linda gets Larry up at 6 AM to join her on a sunrise mountain hike. Huffing and puffing up the steep ascent, Larry quickly loses his ability to protest verbally, much to Linda's relief. Despite his own discomfort—or perhaps because of it—Larry is impressed by the strength and stamina displayed by several guests, some of whom are clearly older than he. His attitude about this "fitness stuff" begins to change.

Although the 9 AM stretch session presents a formidable challenge for his little-used muscles and inflexible joints, Larry stands noticeably taller and seems more relaxed by the end of the class. Then, in the casually competitive 10 AM volleyball game, he feels right at home. He may not be ready to admit it publicly, but he has had more fun on the court than he usually has sitting in front of the TV watching his favorite team.

As the week progresses, so does Larry. By the fifth day he scales the mountain without stopping to catch his breath. That afternoon, during a stretching class, he touches his toes for the first time in a decade. The dull ache he often feels in his lower back has disappeared. His mind is calmer. He has not called his office in three days, and he feels no guilt. At the end of the trip, Larry is amazed not only that he has survived a whole week with no alcohol, no red meat, and no ice cream but also that he really has not missed them. As they are packing to go home, Larry says he wishes they could stay another week!

Another myth about active holidays is that they are contests of strength, fortitude, and ability to endure discomfort—a vacation fit only for the "jock" who wants to test his or her mettle. In fact, there are trips designed for many different levels of exertion and virtually every degree of experience.

Michael and Maria, the couple who went on the bicycle trip, were not old hands at long-distance cycling, nor were they seeking an especially strenuous physical challenge. They picked the bike tour because they thought it would be relaxing. Being city dwellers, they knew they would relish the clean air and unspoiled beauty of the New England countryside. After looking over the literature from several tour operators, they chose a trip that covered short daily distances and stopped at night in comfortable, well-appointed inns and guesthouses. The tour company provided bikes, helmets, trip leaders, and a support van that was always ready to rescue pooped pedalers or perform on-the-spot bike repairs.

Trip members were free to set their own pace, with no pressure to keep up and no competition to see who could finish first or ride farthest. Each day an easy-to-read map atop the handlebar bag guided riders to a pleasant spot where tour leaders had laid out a picnic lunch. The leisurely pace allowed plenty of time to stop and enjoy the scenery, chat with local residents, and browse in the art galleries and craft shops that dotted the landscape. By midafternoon every rider had reached that day's destination, usually with plenty of time left for a swim, hike, or nap before dinner. Meals were hearty, abundant, and companionable. With their tireless leaders to look after lunches, luggage, and flat tires, Michael and Maria enjoyed a worry-free week.

Activity's benefits

The human body is designed for movement. Therefore, when people are active on a regular basis, their bodies function more efficiently than when they are continually sedentary. As many people now know, a consistent exercise routine can increase muscle strength and improve muscle tone, flexibility, posture, coordination, and energy level. Regular aerobic workouts increase metabolism (the rate at which the body burns calories). Physical activity also helps to reduce stress, blood pressure, body fat, and, ultimately, the risk of heart disease. What some people do not know is that many of the above benefits can be realized during a single week by the person who takes an active vacation. Even more important, however, is that one physically active week, by providing a strong dose of momentum, can point an individual toward a healthier lifestyle and provide the needed motivation for making long-lasting changes in exercise habits.

On the other hand, vacationers who are confined to a car or bus seat for hours at a time, day after day, will probably experience low energy and lethargy. Upon returning home, their listless bodies tend to continue to do what they have been accustomed to doing— namely, very little. The person who takes an inactive vacation will therefore tend to remain inactive after the holiday.

An added physical benefit of an active vacation is the effect on body fat and dietary habits. Companies that lead exercise-oriented tours know the importance of supplying high-quality "fuel" to provide energy for tour participants. Meals will probably be high in complex carbohydrates—fruits and vegetables, whole wheat breads and cereals, beans, rice, and pasta— and low in fatty foods. As a result of the exercise and the high-energy/low-fat diet, people returning home from an active holiday may notice that their clothes fit a little looser—even though they have eaten more than usual during the trip. Certainly they have probably eaten differently than they usually do, and they may find themselves making long-term changes in eating habits as a result.

The effects of activity extend far beyond the physical, however. Such accomplishments as shooting a series of rapids, scaling a mountain, or completing every set and repetition in a rigorous weight-training class engender a strong sense of satisfaction. That feeling is particularly great in a given individual if physical triumphs are rare or nonexistent in that person's everyday life. This pride in achievement, a very significant by-product of exercise, can lead to enhanced self-esteem and confidence and can foster a sense that life's greatest challenges are perhaps more manageable than they appeared before.

Whereas the "inactive" vacationer may be exposed to many of life's common stressors—traffic jams, crowds, ringing telephones, blaring TVs, long waits in slow lines—the active trip participant can escape these pressures, finding an environment that contains few such reminders of everyday life. For instance, as the river-raft enthusiast helps maneuver the craft between boulders the size of hippos, he or she is highly unlikely to be distracted by any thoughts of problems back at the office. The mental diversion, together with the physical exercise, helps clear the clutter from a person's brain. The mind becomes more relaxed, and the individual is better able to think clearly. On returning home, the active vacationer will have a sense of mental or emotional refreshment as well as physical reinvigoration.

An active vacation may also be an experience of intellectual and social growth. A Chinese proverb says: "I hear and I forget. I see and I remember. I do and I understand." While the main activity of the car, bus, or cruise ship traveler is observing, the active vacationer not only sees but hears, smells, and feels the culture and climate of the region and becomes totally immersed in the environment.

The relationships formed during an active vacation are often unique. People connect, bond, and develop strong ties when they share each other's moments of struggle and sweat, exploration and discovery, growth and learning. Plato said, "We learn more about a person from an hour of play or games than from a year of conversation."

The "right" vacation

Selecting the vacation that matches an individual's interests, fitness level, and budget is essential to enjoyment of the total experience. The following are some important considerations.

Choosing the activity. If cycling is a person's consuming passion, then a bicycle tour is obviously the trip to select. For people whose interests are varied

Catering to adventurous cross-country skiers, a remote hostelry in the Purcell Mountains of British Columbia is accessible only on foot or by air. Led by experienced guides, guests of the lodge spend their days exploring the nearby forests, mountains, and alpine meadows. Evenings, they join other guests for an excellent family-style meal, enjoy some old-fashioned fiddle music, or soothe sore muscles in the sauna just outside the lodge.

Bill Ballenberg

and many, a fitness resort is usually a smart choice. With a broad range of activities—from tennis to tai chi, weight training to water aerobics, and hiking to yoga—a health spa can satisfy even someone with the most discriminating of tastes. If a couple cannot agree on any single activity that appeals to both, a spa vacation is a wise move; she can do her thing while he does his.

If a person is traveling alone but seeks the safety and camaraderie of a group setting where he or she will not be the "odd person out," just about any activity-oriented tour or fitness resort will suffice. Most active vacations welcome and regularly include single travelers.

If one's objective is to combine exercise with a week of being pampered, it is wise to make sure camping is not on the agenda. However, an easy, short-distance bike or walking tour featuring deluxe accommodations and first-class meal service can spoil a person quite nicely. Some luxury spas "do it all" for their guests, even assigning each one a personal fitness instructor for the duration of the stay. That instructor consults with the guest and creates his or her personal daily workout routine. Massages, facials, pedicures, and other such services may be included in the luxury spa package. Of course, people should expect to pay a premium price for this kind of coddling.

Determining the level of challenge. Before signing up for a trip, the potential participant should carefully examine the literature provided by the operator or outfitter. If the trip is suitable for the inexperienced, whether rafting, sailing, horseback riding, or whatever, the tour brochure will indicate this. Each tour's level of difficulty also will be indicated in the trip brochure. For example, a bicycle tour featuring 32 to 40 km (20 to 25 mi) per day on flat terrain might be described as easy-to-moderate. A rafting trip will rate the difficulty or class of rapids that will be encountered. A walking or hiking tour will list the average distance to be covered each day and the elevation change. For example, an easy hike would involve minimal elevation change and walking or hiking on well-groomed trails or backcountry roads; good walking shoes will be recommended for such a trip. A moderate hike includes more elevation change and options for more-challenging hikes on one or more days; in this case lightweight hiking boots would be called for. An advanced hike features mountainous terrain with some steep ascents and descents; sturdy hiking boots will be strongly recommended for this kind of endeavor. An advanced hike is suggested for the experienced hiker, but it could be enjoyed by the novice who is adventurous and athletically inclined and is in excellent physical condition.

People who are eager to increase their fitness level might select a trip geared toward a level of endurance that is clearly above theirs—but within reach. It is crucial, however, that they have the time and motivation to train and prepare adequately for the event. On the other hand, people at just about any fitness level can find appropriate instruction and activities at most health resorts and spas.

An injury or other physical limitation need not inevitably keep a person from participating in an active vacation; however, some adjustments to the plan may be in order. For example, a person who makes arrangements to go on a hiking tour and then injures a knee or develops a back ailment might elect to postpone or cancel that holiday. Long downhill stretches, in particular, would put considerable pressure on the knees or back and could aggravate an existing condition. The person with a shoulder problem would be wise to skip a planned rafting or kayaking trip since the shoulder muscles play a vital role in maneuvering the vessel. Once again, a spa or resort would make sense as an alternative. There, activities could be designed to avoid aggravating the injury, and stretching, yoga, and massage might help the healing process and safely increase range of motion in affected joints. Water aerobics and leisurely walks would provide some exercise, but not too much. Classes in back care would teach correct sitting, standing, walking, and lifting postures and include exercises to strengthen and stretch the back. The spa guest with physical limitations will have plenty of time to rest, recuperate, and read a book or two.

People with chronic medical conditions need not rule out active holidays. Most trip operators clearly designate physical problems that would prevent a person from participating, and the reservation form is usually accompanied by a questionnaire that helps to identify special requirements such as the availability of refrigeration for insulin or other perishable medications. If a person is unsure about the wisdom of a strenuous activity or remote destination, he or she should consult both the trip operator and a physician.

Knowing what to expect. Will the week feature first-class lodging and haute cuisine or camping under the stars, with chuck-wagon stew and campfire coffee? Are the trip participants expected to help with cooking or to clean up? Can the tour operator accommodate special dietary needs? Is there plenty of free time each day?

Before making a decision about a trip, the potential participant should have a good idea what a typical day is like. Again, this information is usually provided in the brochure. For example:

Kayaking adventure—typical day's schedule
Daily: 4–6 hours spent in kayak, 2–3 in morning and 2–3 in afternoon; route chosen to see as much as possible of local flora and fauna, both aquatic and terrestrial

Morning: breakfast at 7:30 AM; break camp and load supplies and equipment into support craft (guests help); off the beach by 9 AM; paddle till lunchtime

Afternoon: lunch; paddle; set up camp (guests help); opportunity for hiking, swimming, or relaxation

Evening: dinner around campfire; short kayak outing from camp before dark; retire to tent for the night

Fitness resort—typical day's schedule
Daily: three vegetarian meals; as much exercise or relaxation as desired—all activities optional; massages and other services available by appointment; exercise classes are coed

6:30 AM: morning hike

7:30 AM: breakfast

9 AM, 10 AM, and 11 AM: 45-minute classes, including (but not limited to): low-impact aerobics, stretching, water aerobics, weight training, volleyball

12 noon: lunch

1 PM: nutrition lecture

2 PM, 3 PM, and 4 PM: several classes offered, including (but not limited to): yoga, circuit training, tai chi, step aerobics, meditation, back care

5 PM: rest or attend workshops on subjects from poetry writing to wreath making

6 PM: dinner

8 PM: movie, lecture, or slide presentation

Financial considerations. Another important item of information found in the trip brochure is the cost of the vacation. While some active holidays are more expensive than their sedentary counterparts, many are not. Then again, at first glance a spa vacation or a cycling or walking tour might appear quite costly, but because the price often includes all meals, equipment, transportation, instruction, activities, and tips, it can be an extremely good value. The prospective holiday planner should consider that even if an active vacation involves significant monetary investment, it also may be an investment in one's long-term mental and physical health.

How to prepare

The trip brochure will include a list of important items *not* supplied by the tour operator. The list should be studied carefully and added to if necessary. Key items to consider are: appropriate and comfortable clothing and footwear, sun protection, an extra pair of prescription glasses, medications, first aid supplies, and reading material. Even common over-the-counter drugs—aspirin, nasal spray—may be unavailable in remote destinations. Therefore, travelers who plan to canoe a wild river or aid in a bird-banding expedition in the rain forest of Costa Rica need to give extra thought to preparedness. Running out of film or not having warm-enough clothes could spoil the vacation. Running out of a prescription drug or losing one's only pair of glasses could necessitate costly alterations in vacation plans.

428

Hikers exploring Alaska's Glacier Bay National Park encounter a formidable obstacle in the form of the rushing Tatshenshini River. Is this what the trip brochure meant when it assured participants of being "immersed in the outdoor experience"?

Many questions need to be answered before one embarks on the trip: What will the climate be like? How cool will it be in the evening? How hot will it get during the day? Are extra changes of clothing needed in case of capsizing? What about a waterproof camera? Are athletic shoes adequate for all activities at the spa, or should one pack walking shoes or lightweight hiking boots?

The key is to pack all the essential items but avoid taking anything that will be available on site. It is easier and often cheaper for a person to rent a bicycle from the tour company for the duration of the outing than for the person to pack and ship his or her own bike. Equipment such as bike helmets and canoe paddles are usually supplied free of charge by tour operators. If prospective participants are unsure about whether certain items will be available, they should not hesitate to call or write to find out. Finally, any new equipment purchased for the trip should be tested well ahead of time. Shoes, in particular, should be broken in ahead of time. The first day of a weeklong backpacking trip is the *wrong* time to discover that the new pair of hiking boots does not fit properly.

Getting in shape

A magical thing happens when a trip deposit has been mailed and a financial commitment made: people suddenly become motivated to train for the upcoming event. Since any activity is more enjoyable for the person who is well-conditioned—and therefore not likely to suffer injuries—it adds to the pleasure of the vacation if one is fit to participate.

It is a good idea to begin training as early as possible, ideally a few months ahead of time. People who have not been exercising should always consult a doctor before starting a new workout program. The person who is planning a cycling trip should spend some time on a bike. Hiking and walking are the appropriate preparation for a trekking adventure.

People who are not already active should begin slowly and build gradually, starting with as little as 10 to 20 minutes of exercise every other day and adding 5 minutes to the routine every two weeks. This very conservative approach has some great benefits; since the initial workouts are so brief, it is very easy to find the time for them, and the risk of injury or excessive fatigue is minimal. If one initiates the routine well in advance of the vacation, one can build up to substantial workouts.

Injuries caused by too much activity too soon are common, and carelessness or unbridled enthusiasm certainly sets the stage for a training injury. The worst scenario is when a last-minute injury occurs to a person who is mentally, emotionally, and financially committed to an active vacation. Unfortunately, this happens all too often. The best advice is to proceed slowly and carefully.

Investigating the possibilities

One of the best sources of information about healthy outdoor adventures is the advertisements in the back pages of natural history, outdoor, cycling, walking, and photography magazines (see list, page 430). Many such special interest publications include a card that one can send postage-free to request brochures and information on particular trips. There are also magazines and books that boast complete listings of fitness resorts throughout North America or even around the world. Resorts are categorized according to theme, activities offered, type of accommodations, diet, cost, and more. Travel agents can be excellent sources of information, and some agents specialize in adventure travel or spa vacations.

Health clubs and exercise studios in one's hometown may have tour literature available and instructors who are knowledgeable about fitness vacations. The yoga instructor will undoubtedly know about yoga retreats, and one who leads walking clinics may be familiar with trekking adventures. Local cycling, canoeing, sailing, walking, and other interest-oriented groups can provide information on specific kinds of tours. So can organizations such as the Sierra Club and the Audubon Society. Friends who have experienced active vacations are terrific sources. They will be happy to describe their exploits in tremendous detail and with great enthusiasm. Getting them to *stop* talking about their adventures will be the challenge.

Not everyone is interested in a "packaged" trip organized and run by a commercial tour operator. Some prefer to design and plan their own active adventures, researching suitable sites, making necessary reserva-tions themselves, and renting any equipment they do not already own. Both types of trips have advantages and drawbacks. When a family or a group of friends create their own itinerary, they must expect to devote plenty of time and effort to advance planning and coordination, but they may be able to organize a less expensive trip than one run by a tour operator, and they know in advance who their travel companions will be. As anyone who has ever vacationed with a relative or good friend knows, however, familiarity is not a guarantee of compatibility. Moreover, since the people one meets on an active holiday are bound to have similar interests, they usually do not remain strangers for long.

Moving experiences

Like Art and Annie, who came home from their California auto trip feeling pooped and plump, many people are tired of taking "holidays" that leave them exhausted, stressed, and, frankly, in need of a vacation. There is little chance of that happening with a stimulating "active vacation." More than likely, the participant will return feeling rested, refreshed, and exhilarated.

At the very least a physically oriented holiday will be memorable. Probably it will be a lot of fun. Better yet, it may be a catalyst for a healthy and permanent

While floating down a steamy tributary of the Amazon River in South America, ecology-minded travelers learn the secrets of the local flora and fauna from their naturalist guide.

Kevin Schafer—Special Expeditions

lifestyle change. And chances are that when it comes to planning the next vacation, the choice will be for *another* moving experience.

Adding activity to business travel

Unfortunately, not all trips are for pleasure. Business travel can be extremely enervating and is usually very sedentary—long hours in the cramped quarters of a plane seat followed by long hours spent sitting in meetings. The following are some tips for making that next business trip a more active—and generally healthier—event.

• When making a plane reservation, order a special meal. Most airlines have low-fat fruit or seafood plates and vegetarian meals available by request in advance.

• Choose a hotel that has its own fitness facilities.

• Pack workout gear, appropriate shoes, and an audiotape or videotape of a routine that can be performed in a hotel room. Take or buy fruit and bottled water for healthy snacks in the room.

• Inquire about the most pleasant—and safest—routes for running or walking. Many hotels can provide maps of recommended routes.

• Keep a pair of walking shoes in a briefcase or carry-on bag and go for short, nonstop walks between meetings or airplane flights. Do not try to elevate the heart rate, just stand tall and walk to release tension, reduce backache, and clear the mind.

• Use stairs instead of elevators and escalators whenever possible.

• Order wisely from restaurant menus, choosing baked, broiled, or steamed foods instead of fried, breaded, or creamy dishes. Drink more water and fewer alcoholic beverages.

• Schedule fitness activities. Enter exercise times in a daily planner in red ink. With a written reminder, one is more likely to keep workout appointments.

• If a one-on-one meeting is planned, suggest a walk. The physical movement, relaxed atmosphere, and absence of interruptions may make for a highly productive session.

• Recognize exercise not as an interruption in important business matters but as an aid to problem solving. Physical activity can stimulate creative thinking; the solution to a persistent problem might just surface during a workout.

Sources of information

The following are periodicals that regularly contain advertisements for and information about active and adventure travel.

Bicycling
Rodale Press, Inc.
33 E. Minor Street
Emmaus PA 18098
1-800-848-4735

Canoe and Kayaking Magazine
PO Box 7011
Red Oak IA 51591
1-800-678-5432

Earthwatch
(environmental expeditions)
PO Box 403
Watertown MA 02272
1-800-776-0188

EcoTraveler
PO Box 469003
Escondido CA 92046
1-800-334-8152

Escape
PO Box 5159
Santa Monica CA 90409
310-392-5235

Natural History
American Museum of Natural History
Central Park West at 79th Street
New York NY 10024
1-800-234-5252

Outdoor Photographer
(photographic travel and workshops)
Box 57213
Boulder CO 80322

Outside
Box 5300
Boulder CO 80322
1-800-678-1131

Sierra
Sierra Club
730 Polk Street
San Francisco CA 94109

Smithsonian
Smithsonian Associates
900 Jefferson Drive
Washington DC 20560
1-800-766-2149

TravelFit
Prestige Publications, Inc.
4151 Knob Drive
Eagan MN 55122

The Walking Magazine
PO Box 56561
Boulder CO 80322
1-800-678-0881

Through Children's Eyes

by Joelle Mast, Ph.D., M.D., and Barbara Ladenheim, Ph.D.

When babies are born their vision is immature. How well they will see when they grow up depends on many factors, including heredity, their early visual environment, and, equally important, the early detection and treatment of visual problems. An undetected visual deficit can delay all aspects of development, placing a child not only at an educational disadvantage but also at a social disadvantage. Correcting poor vision at a young age can benefit the individual's later visual development. Moreover, certain treatments are more effective when started early than if delayed.

Because parents are the ones who are most likely to notice a possible vision problem at an early stage, it is important for them to understand the steps in normal visual development, know how to spot potential difficulties, and be informed about when and how infants' and young children's vision should be screened.

Visual function: multifaceted

How well a person sees depends on the interplay of several aspects of visual function. The ability to distinguish fine detail is a measure of the function called *visual acuity*. Strictly speaking, acuity refers to the smallest high-contrast stimulus an individual can detect—*e.g.,* the smallest line of letters he or she can read on the Snellen eye chart, the most commonly used test of visual acuity.

How dark an object must be to be perceived against a slightly lighter background is a measure of *contrast sensitivity*. A person's contrast sensitivity threshold is the smallest difference in contrast that he or she can detect—for example, the smallest perceptible difference between white and a very pale gray.

Everyone's two eyes differ slightly in the visual information they receive. One can demonstrate this disparity by holding up one finger and looking at it while alternately closing one eye at a time. The finger will appear to move slightly because each eye sees it from a different viewpoint. The visual system uses this disparity to perceive the depth of objects in space—a visual function called *stereopsis*.

Other aspects of visual function include the ability to differentiate between objects on the basis of their hue (*color vision*) and the ability to detect movement of objects in space (*motion perception*).

Normal development in infancy. During the first year of life, the visual system undergoes rapid development at all levels. The eyeball increases in size, the fovea (a region of the retina) and central visual pathways mature, and nerve-cell connections in the cerebral cortex of the brain increase. In terms of function, acuity, contrast sensitivity, color vision, and stereopsis approach adult levels.

Contrary to popular belief, infants do see at birth, and their motor control of eye movements is surprisingly good. However, both the structure and the function of their visual system are immature. Different visual functions mature over the first months of life, each at its own rate. Although different testing procedures may indicate adult levels in one or another function at different ages, the relationships between functions are consistent among all infants. For example, stereopsis matures before acuity.

Infants have very limited ability to focus—that is, to accommodate the lens of the eye to discern distant objects. Their accommodation is best at distances of 20–75 cm (1–3 ft). In addition, the infant's retina (the sensory membrane that lines the eye) is immature. This is especially true of the foveal region, which is the center of the visual field and the source of maximum visual acuity. Depending on the test used, the average newborn has a visual acuity that corresponds to a Snellen acuity of 20/200 to 20/400, which may seem very low compared with the adult visual norm of 20/20. (An acuity of 20/20 means that at a distance of 20 ft a person can see what the average adult can see from 20 ft. An acuity of 20/200, therefore, means that the infant can see clearly at 20 ft what an average adult is able to see from 200 ft.)

Possibly because of their accommodative limitations, infants direct their attention to nearby objects.

431

Through children's eyes

At close distances (within 75 cm), their level of visual acuity allows them to pick out facial features and expressions. Thus, nature has equipped the immature visual system so that newborn babies can see their mothers' faces when nursing. Acuity develops rapidly during the first six months of life, reaching a Snellen equivalent of 20/20 to 20/150, depending on the test used. Certainly by the end of the first or second year of life, the child's visual acuity reaches adult levels.

The contrast sensitivity of the newborn is also lower than that of an adult. Thus, there is a physiological reason why newborns prefer looking at objects that display a high degree of contrast. This preference can be a source of mild consternation to parents, who typically desire to make eye contact with their babies. Because there is usually a sharp line of contrast between the hair and the forehead, the newborn's eyes tend to seek out the hairline when looking at another person's face. As the parent moves the baby about in an attempt to establish eye contact, the infant constantly redirects its attention to the hairline. Fortunately, this tendency is short-lived. Contrast sensitivity matures more rapidly than acuity, and levels similar to those of adults are reached by 10–12 weeks of age.

Color vision is another function that is immature at birth, although infants can make discriminations based on hue as early as one month of age, and there is evidence that differential sensitivity to light of different wavelengths is present earlier. An infant's color vision approximates that of an adult by three months of age. Owing to early immaturity of an infant's contrast sensitivity and color vision, a high-contrast black-and-white mobile would be more likely to capture a newborn's attention than one in muted pastels.

Critical periods of development. While an infant's vision is developing, there are critical periods during which appropriate visual stimulation is necessary for normal development to proceed. Specific functions of cells in the brain are determined at this time. For example, the information received by the brain from each of the two eyes must be equivalent in subject matter and clarity. If the information coming from the eyes is too discrepant, binocularity, or stereopsis, will not develop. Images from the eyes can be discrepant because of weakness in the muscles responsible for eye movement or poor vision in one eye. In addition to lack of binocularity, a discrepancy of vision between the eyes can lead to a suppression of vision in the "weaker" eye. Suppression in turn causes amblyopia (also called "lazy eye"), which is the loss of vision in an eye due to disuse. If the suppressed eye is not stimulated during its critical period, cells in the brain do not develop normally, and permanent visual loss results.

Fortunately, the human visual system is most amenable to treatment during this period of early development. Visual function can be improved by provision of adequate stimulation. This capacity for permanent change in function as a result of a change in the stimulus environment is called *plasticity,* but the plasticity is limited to a critical period. It is therefore crucial to identify abnormalities of visual function as early in life as possible so that corrective measures can be taken while the infant's eyes still retain the capacity for change.

Both the American Academy of Pediatrics and the American Academy of Ophthalmology recommend that by six months of age all infants have their eyes examined by a physician and that they receive regular vision screening throughout the early childhood years. This is especially critical for those children at high risk for visual problems. Children at risk include those with a family history of ocular abnormalities such as amblyopia, retinoblastoma (a hereditary tumor of the eye), or congenital cataracts. Others with a high incidence of visual deficits are infants born prematurely and children with multiple physical disabilities, especially neurological impairments. In many states it is now mandated that vision screening be available to all infants and children who have developmental delay.

What parents should watch for

child's age	newborn	2–3 months	6–7 months	1–2 years	preschool	school
sign of a possible problem	•poor eye contact •white spot in pupil •poor fixation •jerky eye movements	•not reaching for objects •not following objects past midline	•not bringing objects to midline •consistent eye turning	•head tilting	•holding toys close	•holding books close •trouble seeing chalkboard

Recognizing potential problems

Parents are frequently the first to detect an abnormality in an infant's or a young child's vision. It is important for them to be alert to behavioral signs of vision deficits.

By one month of age, infants should look at, or fixate on, high-contrast objects. As mentioned above, very young babies may direct their gaze to an adult's hairline if that is an area of high contrast. The eyes of a newborn may follow an object as it moves from the side of the body to the midline of the body but not past the midline. By two months, however, most babies are able to follow movement past the midline and will smile responsively. By three to four months, infants will track an object as it moves in a 180° trajectory and will reach for an object offered within their grasp.

In addition to failure to reach the above developmental milestones, other clues that may signal a potential vision problem include jerky or random eye movements, head cocking, consistent outward or inward deviation of an eye, squinting, closing one eye in sunlight, frequent tearing of the eyes when the baby is not crying, and apparent discomfort in bright light (photophobia). It should be noted that many infants appear slightly cross-eyed because the bridge of the nose is wide or because they have prominent epicanthic folds (skin folds at the interior corner of the eye). When there is any question of abnormality, professional evaluation should be sought.

Visual abnormalities of childhood

Visual deficits are common in children; as many as 25–30% have some visual impairment. At least 10% of children need corrective lenses by age 10. Deficits in color vision affect up to 10% of boys and 0.5% of girls. Between one and four years of age, both astigmatism and anisometropia (see below) increase in incidence, thus increasing the risk of amblyopia.

When parents ask, "How well does my baby see?" they are usually asking about acuity. Abnormalities of acuity are frequently due to refractive error such as *myopia* (nearsightedness), *hyperopia* (farsightedness), or *astigmatism* (unequal curvature of a refractive surface of the eye, leading to distortions in vision). These are abnormalities of the structure of the eyeball or the cornea (the transparent covering of the eyeball). Less common but serious eye conditions that physicians look for are amblyopia, strabismus, cataracts, glaucoma, retinopathy of prematurity, and retinoblastoma.

As noted above, the brain needs to receive information from the two eyes that is equivalent in clarity and subject matter. Differences in clarity can occur if the refractive power of the eyes is unequal, a condition termed *anisometropia*. Differences in subject matter result from misalignment of the eyes, a condition known as *strabismus*. When information from the

two eyes differs, the brain may suppress information from one eye. If this suppression continues, amblyopia may result. Treatment consists of patching the dominant eye. The younger the child, the quicker and more effective the treatment. While patching produces some recovery of acuity in children up to eight years of age, other visual functions have shorter periods of plasticity. Stereopsis is typically lost if amblyopia and strabismus are not treated by one year of age. Strabismus (also called heterotropia or squint) results from an imbalance among the eye muscles; it can be surgically corrected. Diminished acuity and other refractive errors can be remedied with corrective lenses.

Cataracts, or opacities (clouding) of the lens, are an uncommon but important cause of blindness in childhood. Causes of cataracts in infants and young children include congenital infections, trauma, metabolic disorders, and some chromosomal abnormalities. Early surgical removal of cataracts and treatment of any coexisting amblyopia can result in significant recovery of vision.

Retinopathy of prematurity (ROP), formerly called retrolental fibroplasia, is a disorder of the retina that is strongly associated with prematurity and low birth weight. It is characterized by proliferation of blood vessels in the retina, which can lead to retinal detachment and blindness. One or both eyes can be affected. An important cause of ROP is exposure to high levels of oxygen in neonatal nurseries. It may also be associated with diabetes and some other infant conditions. Early treatment of ROP with cryotherapy, which freezes the outer edge of the developing retina, from which new vessels grow, is effective in a majority of infants.

Retinoblastoma is a tumor of the retina that occurs in approximately one in every 20,000 births. Although rare, it is one of the six most common tumors of childhood. Early detection and treatment result in a cure rate of over 85%. Because genetic factors play a part in the disease, children who have parents or siblings with a history of retinoblastoma should be evaluated by an ophthalmologist.

Common vision assessment tests

The pediatrician or family physician is usually the first health professional to examine an infant's eyes. If he or she finds any signs of abnormalities, the infant should be referred to an ophthalmologist for a full evaluation of eye health.

The first eye exam should be performed by the primary care provider at birth. It should include an inspection of the eyes and a test of the pupillary reflex (contraction of the pupil in response to light entering the eye). By one month of age, most infants, when alert, will fixate on a high-contrast toy or light. In examining a one-month-old the physician inspects the pupils, checks fixation, assesses the red reflex, and tests for misalignment of the eyes. The red reflex represents light reflected back from the retina, which is what causes the red reflections often seen in the eyes of subjects in flash photography. To evaluate the red reflex, the physician looks at the baby's eyes through an ophthalmoscope. A difference in the two eyes or absence of the reflex is found with cataracts, retinal disorders, and tumors such as retinoblastoma. A test of the corneal light reflex, also known as the Hirschberg test, is used to check for strabismus. A penlight is held at arm's length from the infant. When the baby's eyes fixate on the light, the position of the light reflected on the cornea is noted. The reflection should fall on corresponding points on the two eyes. If an eye deviates inward, the reflection in that eye will be displaced laterally in the direction of the ear. If an eye is turning outward, the reflection will be displaced laterally toward the bridge of the nose.

By two months of age, infants will follow, or track, a moving object in all directions. Most physicians therefore add tracking to the exam for babies this age. By four to six months, when visual attention span is longer, the cover/uncover test can be added. In this test the child is shown an object, and then, while both eyes are fixated on the object, one eye is covered. If the uncovered eye moves, it was not fixating with binocular vision, and strabismus is present. If the covered eye moves when the covering is removed, this suggests a latent tendency toward strabismus in

that eye. If a child strongly objects to having one eye covered, this may be an indication of significant visual loss in the other eye.

Some clinicians also perform the Bruckner test, in which the child is told to look at the light of the ophthalmoscope. With fixation of the eyes, the pupils constrict, leading to a dimming of the red reflex. While unequal dimming is supposed to indicate strabismus or anisometropia, the test is not very reliable, especially in infants; therefore, most primary caregivers do not use it.

Older children have their acuity screened in the pediatrician's office (by the doctor or nurse) or at school (by the school nurse or a volunteer from an organization such as the Lighthouse for the Blind). Typical screening tests include the Allen test, which uses schematic drawings of common objects, called optotypes (*see* illustration), or the "tumbling E" test, in which the child is asked to indicate the direction that the "arms" of capital E's in different positions are pointing.

Recent advances in vision screening

Despite the frequency of visual problems in children, formal screening of visual acuity rarely is done prior to age three or four. This is the earliest age at which children are able to cooperate with traditional acuity tests. A survey of pediatricians found that 33% screen their young patients for acuity when they reach three years of age, 66% screen patients at four years, and 75% screen at five years. Because of delays in screening, many cases of anisometropia go undetected, and amblyopia results. In a nationwide survey conducted by the American Academy of Pediatrics of 7,754 children aged 3–5 years, 8% failed acuity screening, and 5% failed binocular vision screening.

The impact of poor vision on the ability to learn and, ultimately, to function in society may be magnified in children who have developmental disabilities such as motor or cognitive impairment. It is therefore critical to assess the visual abilities of these youngsters at an early age so that treatment can be undertaken and appropriate intervention begun in their educational and rehabilitation programs.

As mentioned above, the standard acuity tests used for adults and older children cannot be administered successfully to children under the age of three. Tests such as the Hirshberg test, which can easily be performed with infants, provide information about the health and movement of the eyes, but they do not give an indication of how well an infant sees. Therefore, assessing acuity in babies and toddlers has always been problematic.

Over the past 20 years, however, vision researchers have devised methods by which infants who cannot talk or read an eye chart can communicate what they do or do not see. These methods have enabled scien-

A series of different-sized optotypes—schematic representations of familiar objects—is sometimes used to test the visual acuity of school-aged children.

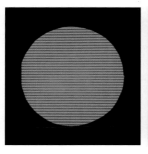

Visual evoked potential testing is one method of assessing visual acuity in infants. Electrodes attached to the baby's head (far left) record activity in visual areas of the brain; (middle and left) the stimuli, different-sized stripes, are displayed on a video screen.

tists to learn a great deal about the visual capabilities of infants. What these methods have in common is that they are quick and noninvasive and take advantage of behaviors that are already in the infant's repertoire, primarily the preference for high-contrast patterns. In certain tests it is enough for the infant to fixate momentarily on the relevant display. In others the display must be interesting enough to hold the baby's attention for several seconds. Thus, the challenge vision researchers face is to develop tests that hold the attention. In the past decade, techniques that achieve this goal have moved from the laboratory into clinical practice. Some of these are described below.

Acuity cards. Acuity card techniques are a relatively recent application of the preferential looking procedure, used for research purposes for many years, which takes advantage of an infant's propensity to look at high-contrast patterns. Variations of these tests allow vision care specialists to assess acuity in normal infants, those at risk for visual or neurological disorders, and those with known or suspected disorders. In each case infants can be evaluated using both eyes together or one eye at a time, thus enabling the examiner to identify any differences in acuity between the eyes.

In one such test the infant is shown a series of rectangular cards, 24.5 × 56 cm (10 × 22 in), on which a 12.7-cm (5-in) square field of black and white stripes is set against a homogenous gray background. The size and spacing of the stripes are different on each card, and the background of each is matched for luminance to the stripes on that card. In the center of the card is a pinhole that allows the examiner, standing behind the card, to watch the baby's eyes. The striped field is placed asymmetrically on the background; therefore, the examiner can change its position relative to the viewer (the infant) by rotating the card.

As the test proceeds, the infant eventually will see a card on which the stripes are too small and close together to be clearly distinguishable from the background. By observing the baby's looking behavior, an experienced examiner can determine at what point the infant can no longer see the stripes clearly. An acuity measure is derived from the size of the smallest stripes the infant is able to see at a specified distance. A Snellen equivalent can be derived, although it is not identical to a true Snellen score. Charts like the Snellen chart evaluate *recognition* acuity; *i.e.*, the smallest letters that can be identified. The acuity card procedure tests *resolution* acuity; *i.e.*, the smallest stripes that can be seen clearly. Acuity cards can also be used to test contrast sensitivity. The infant is shown a series of cards similar to those described above except that the striped field on each card has a different degree of dark-light contrast. The examiner can tell when the degree of contrast has become too small for the baby to perceive it.

Acuity testing can be administered in a few minutes and is quite reliable. Occasional rewards, such as the sight of a small, noisy toy, may help to keep the young subjects from becoming bored. The tests are appropriate over a range of age groups, and they can be used with both normal children and children with disabilities. They are also useful for assessing the efficacy of medical interventions to correct vision problems.

Photorefraction. With the procedure known as photorefraction, refractive error (myopia, hyperopia, and astigmatism) can be evaluated without the use of drugs to dilate the pupil of the eye. Since photorefraction literally provides a picture of the eyes when in use, valuable information can be obtained about the function of the eyes as they work together. It is, therefore, especially valuable for screening for disorders that may lead to amblyopia.

In photorefraction, flash photographs are taken of the patient's eyes as he or she looks at a specified target, usually a bright, colorful, high-contrast picture or toy. In the resulting photo the flash is reflected back from the retina—as in the "red-eye" phenomenon in some amateur photos. Analysis of the reflection provides information about refractive error.

In addition to assessing refractive error, photorefraction, sometimes referred to as photoscreening, can detect differences in refraction between the eyes, deviation of the eyes, and inappropriate focusing. It is particularly suited for use with infants and children because it is quick, requires minimal cooperation, and does not necessitate dilation of the eye. Photorefractive techniques are increasingly being recognized by infant vision specialists as a primary tool for vision screening.

The "sweep-VEP" technique. Visual evoked potential (VEP) testing analyzes activity in the visual areas of the brain in response to visual stimulation. "Sweep" refers to the presentation of a series of different stimuli in a very short period of time, an improvement over traditional transient visual evoked potential testing, in which hundreds of presentations of the same stimulus are necessary to obtain reliable information. Since, in the traditional method, each stimulus is separated from the next by a significant period of time, each test can take up to several minutes. The sweep-VEP procedure, with its capacity to present many stimuli in a matter of seconds, is a particularly useful method for testing infants, whose attention span can be extremely short.

In sweep-VEP testing, electrodes are placed on the infant's head, and brain activity is recorded while the baby watches a display on a TV-like screen. Acuity is tested with a stimulus consisting of light and dark stripes. The size of the stripes is decreased in discrete steps during a test that typically lasts from 6 to 10 seconds. When the stripes become too small to be seen clearly, the brain will not give a consistent response to the stimulus. As in the acuity card procedure, an acuity measure is derived from the size of the smallest stripes that lead to the appropriate evoked response from the brain. The tester can evaluate contrast sensitivity and more complex functions by changing the nature of the visual stimuli.

The innovative methods described above have been used successfully for several years to assess patterns of visual development in infants and young children. They depend on a minimal level of behavioral response—the ability to attend to a visual display—and give an indication of "functional" vision. Having been specifically designed for use with nonverbal subjects, they are appropriate for testing of both normal and developmentally disabled infants and children.

Each of the procedures described above focuses on a different aspect of vision. Photorefraction assesses the optical status of the eye and the positioning of the eyes relative to each other. Sweep-VEP testing checks whether the visual pathway from the eye to the primary visual cortex is intact. Acuity cards go a step farther, assessing the infant's behavioral response to specific visual information. It should be noted that the sensitivity and reliability of these tests are dependent upon the methodology used and the experience of the examiners. In experienced hands the combination of tests can provide valuable insight into visual function in very young children.

436

The importance of early assessment

The human visual system undergoes most of its development during the first six months of life. Ideally, all infants should be screened during this period. If parents notice that a baby is having a visual problem, they should be sure to voice their concerns to their primary physician. Although most children do not have their first vision screening until they are about to enter school, pediatric specialists (physicians, nurses, nurse practitioners, physicians' assistants, and others) are becoming increasingly aware of the importance of examining ocular health at birth and screening visual function as early as six months of age. Youngsters who fail regular pediatric or specialized screenings, those who are in specific risk categories, and those who have obvious problems such as visible cataracts, severe strabismus, lack of fixation, or poor tracking should be referred to a pediatric ophthalmologist for further evaluation and treatment.

Since certain problems do not manifest themselves until a child is older (for example, acuity deficits as a result of myopia), all youngsters should be retested periodically. Reevaluation at different ages enables the examiner to determine whether different aspects of the visual system are developing appropriately. Abnormalities may indicate neurological problems.

The goals of early vision assessment are not limited to detection of treatable conditions, however. Knowledge of a child's visual deficits can avert or minimize social and educational consequences of impaired vision. It is helpful, for example, for a teacher to know that a youngster cannot answer questions about the picture he or she is holding because the child cannot see it, not because he is inattentive. With knowledge of existing problems, therapists can modify materials or therapy programs to accommodate a patient's specific visual deficits. For example, a teenage girl with severe motor limitations was considered functionally blind and not a candidate for a therapy program. Testing with sweep-VEP and acuity cards showed that she did have vision but of low acuity. As a result, she was placed in a rehabilitation program that offered visual therapy.

The American Academy of Pediatrics is currently revising its guidelines for screening vision in children. Unfortunately, even though specific guidelines were published as recently as 1986, many preschool-aged children were not being routinely screened. And even when screenings were taking place, follow-up care was insufficient. The new guidelines will be specific about the tests to be used and their administration and interpretation. Nonetheless, the success of such screening programs lies in the availability and implementation of follow-up care. Detection of visual problems at an early age is meaningful only when it leads to appropriate treatment.

Nutrition for the Later Years

by Marcia H. Magnus, Ph.D.

The population of the U.S.—like that of most industrialized countries—is getting older. One of every eight Americans is now age 65 or older, and by the year 2030 the figure will be one in five. Although older Americans currently make up only 12% of the population, they account for 36% of health care costs, 30% of hospital costs, and 30% of all drug prescriptions. Nutrition is particularly important among this age group; 85% of older people suffer from diseases that could be prevented or treated by appropriate eating habits. Furthermore, physicians often overlook or misdiagnose poor nutritional status in their elderly patients.

Nutrient needs of the aging body

With increasing age come numerous bodily changes that influence an individual's nutritional requirements. Although these changes occur at different rates in different people, by age 70 the kidneys and lungs lose on average about 10% of their weight, and the liver loses 18%; skeletal muscle mass diminishes by as much as 40%. Between the ages of 51 and 75, metabolism (the rate at which the body burns calories) decreases by 10%, and after age 70 by 20%. This slowing of metabolism translates into a reduced need for calories in older people, and leads to an increase in body fat and a decrease in muscle mass. Moreover, with age the body's ability to absorb and use most nutrients declines. Along with these biological changes often comes a heightened concern about psychosocial issues that are associated with aging, such as deteriorating body functions, loss of loved ones, and reduced social opportunities for maintaining self-esteem. These, in turn, may ultimately have an impact on nutritional status.

Every day the human body needs approximately 55 nutrients—including water, calories, carbohydrates, fats, proteins, vitamins, and minerals—all of which are essential for normal body function and physical well-being. Despite their slowing metabolism and reduced caloric needs, older adults generally need the same amount of nutrients as younger adults. It is therefore critical for older people to choose so-called nutrient-dense foods—those that pack a maximum of nutrition into a minimum of calories. Furthermore, since the elderly tend to suffer from a greater number of diseases, and in particular chronic diseases, than younger adults, it is even more important that older people choose foods with high nutrient value.

Certain age-related changes—such as diminished secretion of digestive juices and slower movement of food through the intestines—adversely affect the body's ability to absorb and use nutrients. Sensory perception—taste, smell, and vision—also declines with age, although in varying degrees from one individual to another.

Deficiencies and excesses

The average elderly person needs about 1,800 calories a day, although individual needs vary depending on body size and level of physical activity. Older adults who are not physically active need fewer calories on a daily basis than their active counterparts. Studies show that many older adults do indeed eat fewer calories than younger persons and that sedentary, homebound elderly individuals eat fewer calories than reasonably healthy older people living on their own or in institutions.

The need for dietary protein is 0.8 g per kilogram of body weight (one kilogram = 2.2 lb), and protein should provide 12–14% of a person's total caloric intake. Studies of the diets of older Americans have shown that most get adequate amounts of protein, perhaps owing to the fact that the need for protein does not increase with age. Men of all ages usually consume more protein than women, whites more than blacks, and people who are under 75 years old usually consume more than those over 75.

When it comes to total fat and saturated fat, many older people eat more than is recommended; again, men eat more than women. At the same time, most older adults fail to consume recommended amounts of polyunsaturated fat, which is considered to be more "heart-healthy" than saturated and monounsaturated fat. Many of the elderly need to add to their

437

diets more low-fat sources of protein—low-fat dairy foods, fish and poultry, and vegetable protein—while cutting back on meat, which is high in both total and saturated fat.

While many older people do not eat enough complex carbohydrates, they often eat too much sugar in the form of sweets. Approximately 55% of a person's total caloric intake should come from simple and complex carbohydrates. Simple carbohydrates include the sugars found in fruits and milk; sources of complex carbohydrates include vegetables, whole-grain breads and cereals, and peas and beans.

For people of any age, a diet that is high in sodium, total fat, saturated fat, and cholesterol contributes to heart disease, certain cancers, diabetes, and obesity. Among older adults, however, these conditions are aggravated by declining levels of physical activity and the aging body's decreasing ability to absorb nutrients. Oftentimes, the diets of older adults not only contain excessive amounts of fat, cholesterol, and sodium but also are lacking in fiber and complex carbohydrates.

Defeating deficiency

Dietary surveys of the eating habits of older Americans reveal both negatives and positives. For example, some 30% of people aged 65 and over skip meals almost daily, and only 3% of those between ages 55 and 74 eat the minimum recommended servings of fruits and vegetables. On the other hand, one-third of older adults regularly eat whole-grain products, and compared with other adults, this age group drinks fewer soft drinks (which have no nutritional value).

Some surveys indicate that even though many older Americans do not eat enough of certain nutrients, clinical deficiency symptoms are rare in this group, occurring in only 5% of those whose diets fail to meet the recommended dietary allowances (RDAs; nutritional standards that specify the amount of any given nutrient needed to maintain good health). Other studies find a higher percentage of deficiency symptoms among older adults. Still other research indicates that among some subgroups of older adults, vitamin B_6, zinc, calcium, fiber, and water are the nutrients most likely to be underconsumed.

Vitamin B_6. Vitamin B_6 helps the body make use of nutrients; it is also necessary for production of red blood cells. Symptoms of deficiency include dermatitis (skin irritation), irritability, mental confusion, nervousness, anemia, and insomnia. Older adults appear to need more vitamin B_6 than their younger counterparts. Good sources include navy beans, potatoes, watermelon, salmon, and bananas.

Zinc. Studies have shown that many older people, particularly those in poor health and those of low socioeconomic status, are deficient in zinc. Deficiency symptoms include delayed wound healing, dermatitis, loss of the sense of taste, and impaired immune response. Many seniors would probably benefit from a zinc supplement that provides 100–150% of the RDA. (The RDA for zinc is 12–15 mg/day.) However, excess zinc intake interferes with immune function, so it is important not to take too much. Good dietary sources of zinc are oysters, crabmeat, beef, fish, and poultry.

Calcium. Perhaps the most common misconception of older adults about diet is that milk and other dairy products are strictly for babies and children. Dietary surveys consistently show that most elderly people do not consume enough calcium, thereby increasing their risk of osteoporosis (thin, brittle bones). Moreover, the adult RDA for calcium—800 mg/day—may not be sufficient to enable many older adults to maintain strong, healthy bones. Good sources of calcium include low-

Recommended dietary allowances for older adults*		
nutrient	men aged 51 and over	women aged 51 and over
vitamin A	1,000 RE[†]	800 RE
vitamin D	200 IU	200 IU
vitamin E	10 IU	8 IU
vitamin C	60 mg	60 mg
vitamin B_6	2 mg	1.6 mg
vitamin B_{12}	2 µg	2 µg
folate	200 µg	180 µg
calcium	800 mg	800 mg

RE=retinol equivalent
IU=international unit
evidence suggests that nutrient needs change with advancing age and may not be the same in the 60s as in the 70s and later decades of life
[†] *1 RE=6 µg beta-carotene*

Source: National Academy of Sciences-National Research Council, 1989

Nutrient-dense foods like fruits and vegetables are the best choices for older adults, who have the same nutrient needs as younger adults but require fewer calories. In addition to packing a maximum of vitamins and minerals into a minimum of calories, these foods are excellent sources of fiber, which is lacking in the diets of many seniors.

fat milk, other low-fat dairy products, green leafy vegetables, canned salmon (with soft, edible bones), and canned sardines (with bones).

Fiber. Many older people consume about one-third the amount of fiber, or roughage, they need. Although it is not digested, fiber is particularly important for this age group because it holds water, binds excess cholesterol, and has a softening effect on the stools, making elimination easier.

Water. Too often the vital need for water is overlooked by the elderly. The normal thirst mechanism diminishes with age and, as a consequence, many older adults simply do not feel thirsty. Still others try to cut down on their intake of liquids because they are affected by incontinence (which usually can be effectively treated). Many nursing home caregivers indicate that one of their biggest problems is persuading residents to drink enough fluids. With inadequate water intake, dehydration can occur easily; symptoms of dehydration such as dizziness and concentrated urine are often undetected by elderly individuals themselves or by those who care for them. Older adults need to drink six to eight cups of water a day (including coffee and tea but excluding fruit juices).

The RDAs for older adults are generally considered to be adequate except that, according to some studies, the level set for vitamin B_6 (1.6–2.0 mg/day) appears to be too low. Other research suggests that the RDA for riboflavin (1.2–1.4 mg/day) may be too low and that for vitamin A (800–1,000 RE [retinol equivalents] per day, or 4,000–5,000 IU [international units]) too high.

The current RDAs, which were issued in 1989, define nutrient needs for all older adults in a single age category—over 51 years. There is, however, increasing evidence that nutrient needs change over the ensuing decades. Preliminary data suggest that the nutrient needs of a 60-year-old are different from those of an 80-year-old or a 90-year-old. Nevertheless, until the current RDAs are revised, they remain the best and most authoritative guidelines available.

Who needs supplements?

Approximately 33–69% of older adults use vitamin and mineral supplements as a form of "nutritional insurance" to meet the nutrient needs their diets may not provide. Many of those who use supplements, particularly those who take large doses of individual vitamins or minerals, do not need them, and in some cases these supplements may actually be harmful. On the other hand, many elderly people who do not currently use supplements should, in fact, take them. Subgroups of the elderly population that would benefit from a multivitamin supplement include *all* women, the oldest old, persons in poor health, and those who live alone, lack social support or mobility, or have insufficient money for food.

To avoid the toxic side effects associated with certain vitamins and minerals, it is best to choose a supplement that has a large number of nutrients. These multivitamin products are also the most effective, as the different nutrients work together. A safe, effective supplement contains 100–150% of the RDA for each particular nutrient. Studies have shown that such supplements improve immunity in elderly people and decrease their risk of infection. Supplements that greatly exceed the RDAs should be used only when prescribed by health professionals for specific, diagnosed conditions.

Although vitamin E deficiency is rare among older adults and there is no scientific evidence of a need for supplementation, many in this age group take vitamin E supplements on the assumption that this vitamin retards the aging process. In fact, the single most important lifestyle factor that may retard the aging process is physical activity.

Chronically ill adults and the institutionalized elderly, who are likely to have minimal exposure to sunlight, may be deficient in vitamin D, which people need in order to get maximum benefit from calcium. However, a vitamin D supplement is recommended only when a blood test indicates that the individual's level of the vitamin is below normal.

Poor nutrition: contributing factors

For people of any age, many factors may contribute to poor eating habits and consequently inadequate nutrition. Among the elderly, in particular, five factors can be singled out as contributing to poor nutrition: social isolation, medical conditions, medications, poverty, and oral health problems.

Solitary existence. Approximately 33% of older adults live alone, and these seniors are more likely to have nutritional problems than those who live with spouses or other relatives. Many elderly people who live alone have transportation problems that make it difficult for them to shop for food. Some have inadequate facilities for storing food. Another problem for many is planning and cooking one-person meals.

Certain subgroups of the elderly are more likely to live alone—and to skip meals—than others. Although more than 60% of older men live with their wives, only 30% of older women live with their husbands. Older adults who live alone, particularly men, are more likely to skip meals than those who live with family or friends. Daily contact with others is an important morale booster and can improve meal frequency.

Poor health. It is not uncommon for older people to have multiple health problems and physical disabilities that make it difficult for them to eat healthy diets. Approximately 80% are afflicted with osteoarthritis and, for them, varying degrees of joint pain make food shopping and preparation—and even feeding themselves—a challenge. Dietary restrictions for treating such diet-sensitive conditions as high blood pressure, high blood cholesterol, and diabetes may seem

An elderly woman navigates her kitchen with the aid of a walker. Physical disabilities make the preparation of food as well as shopping for it a trial for many older adults and are a significant reason for poor nutrition in this age group.

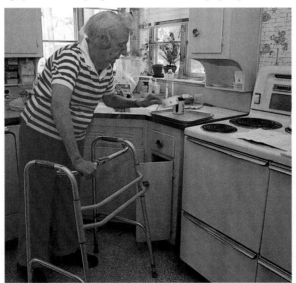

C.C. Duncan—Medical Images Inc.

burdensome, even overwhelming, to elderly people. Altering long-standing eating habits or having to give up favorite foods may make meals more of a chore than a pleasure.

Older adults who have disabilities that prevent or restrict movement often find it hard to take care of their most basic daily needs—dressing, bathing, walking. These people may have difficulty in shopping for and preparing food. According to surveys, approximately 4% of noninstitutionalized older Americans and 17% of those over age 85 report that they cannot either shop for or fix their own meals because of a health or physical problem. In another survey more than 30% of a group of homebound elderly persons reported difficulty in shopping or cooking for themselves.

Drug effects. Over half of older people take at least one medication daily, and many of those who have multiple conditions may take six or more drugs a day. Cardiovascular medications such as diuretics are the most widely used, followed by medicines to treat arthritis, neurological disorders, and respiratory and gastrointestinal conditions. The elderly also commonly take over-the-counter antacids, laxatives, and analgesics. All of these drugs can produce side effects that have an impact on nutritional status. Self-prescribed vitamin and mineral supplements that exceed the RDAs often produce toxicity—the more the supplement exceeds the RDA, the more likely this is to occur. And like other nutrition-related conditions, symptoms of vitamin and mineral toxicity are commonly overlooked or misdiagnosed in this age group.

Studies have shown that 4–5% of adults over 60 have a physical condition that interferes with their appetite. Many prescription drugs alter the sense of taste (*e.g.,* the anticonvulsant phenytoin); some drugs stimulate the appetite (*e.g.,* certain antidepressants and tranquilizers), while others decrease it (some antihypertensive drugs). Many medications diminish the older person's ability to perceive one or more of the taste sensations (bitter, sweet, salty, and sour); still others leave an aftertaste in the mouth. These effects may be only temporary if the drug is needed to treat an acute condition. On the other hand, alterations of taste sensation may be of long-term or even lifetime duration if the ailment being treated is a chronic condition. The cardiac medication digoxin, for example, one of the five most commonly prescribed drugs, causes nausea and loss of appetite.

Side effects of nausea and vomiting, a particular problem with anticancer drugs, can, if unchecked, lead to protein-calorie malnutrition (a deficiency of both protein and calories that may affect as many as 60% of older adults). Many drugs interact with nutrients in food, resulting in unwanted weight losses and gains, nutritional deficiencies, and reduced effectiveness of medications. These harmful effects are more common among those elderly people who take drugs for chronic (compared with acute) conditions and among those who use multiple medications.

Economic factors. More than 25% of U.S. elderly have incomes below or just barely above the poverty line. Older adults who are below the poverty line are at higher nutritional risk than those who have adequate incomes. Almost 33% of African-American and 23% of Hispanic elderly are poor, compared with 11% of whites. Studies of economically needy seniors indicate that the majority do not have enough money to buy the food they need, and 38% have skipped meals because they could not afford groceries.

Problems with chewing and swallowing. Oral health can have a profound impact on food intake. Having decayed and missing teeth, having no dentures or ill-fitting ones, and having sensitive teeth and gums all interfere with the pleasure of eating. An alarming 40% of people aged 60–70 and 62% of those over age 70 have no teeth at all. Persistent dental problems force many older adults to avoid foods that are fibrous and crisp, while gum disease may make it unpleasant for them to eat foods that are very hot or cold. Because of degenerating bone tissue in the aging jaw, dentures that initially fit well may become loose. Dentures should be refitted every two years.

While poor dental health interferes with the ability to chew, xerostomia, or dry mouth, makes it difficult for many elderly people to lubricate and swallow food. Approximately one in five older adults suffers from this condition, which is characterized by severe reduction in the amount of saliva produced.

An estimated 30–40% of the institutionalized elderly have difficulty swallowing, a problem they may attempt to solve by changing their eating habits. Some limit the type and quantity of food and liquids, which leads to protein-calorie malnutrition and dehydration. Many believe that their repeated bouts of coughing and choking when eating and drinking are unavoidable consequences of advancing age. Being in an upright position while eating, eating food that has an appropriate consistency, and eating in an unhurried atmosphere are particularly important for older people who have difficulty swallowing.

Poor nutrition: warning signs

Many of the warning signs of poor nutrition in older adults are the very factors that contribute to the poor nutrition. Nevertheless, as previously noted, the condition is often misdiagnosed or overlooked by physicians. Physical signs include recent unintended weight loss, tooth loss, poorly fitting dentures, dry mouth, and difficulty swallowing. Long-term use of multiple medications and mental confusion may also signal poor eating habits.

Psychosocial signs of poor nutrition include bereavement; depression, loneliness, or living alone; being homebound and having little exposure to sunlight;

and increased use or abuse of alcohol (which often replaces food). Economic indicators of poor nutrition include low socioeconomic status, lack of money for groceries, inadequate housing and kitchen facilities, and homelessness. Food-related signs include having a disability that interferes with shopping, meal preparation, or eating; skipping of meals and snacks; not drinking fluids; wasting or rejecting food; having insufficient stock of food at home; eating inadequate amounts of fruits and vegetables; lacking knowledge

Determine your nutritional health: a checklist

Read the statements below. Circle the number in the yes column for those that apply to you or someone you know. For each yes answer, score the number in the box. Total your nutritional score.

	yes
I have an illness or condition that made me change the kind and/or amount of food I eat.	2
I eat fewer than two meals per day.	3
I eat few fruits or vegetables or milk products.	2
I have three or more drinks of beer, liquor, or wine almost every day.	2
I have tooth or mouth problems that make it hard for me to eat.	2
I do not always have enough money to buy the food I need.	4
I eat alone most of the time.	1
I take three or more different prescribed or over-the-counter drugs a day.	1
Without wanting to, I have lost or gained 10 pounds in the last six months.	2
I am not always physically able to shop, cook, and/or feed myself.	2
total	

Total your nutritional score. If it is:

0–2 Good! Recheck your nutritional score in six months.

3–5 You are at moderate nutritional risk. See what can be done to improve your eating habits and lifestyle. Your office on aging, senior nutrition program, senior citizens center, or health department can help. Recheck your nutritional score in three months.

6 or more You are at high nutritional risk. Take this checklist with you the next time you see your doctor, dietitian, or other qualified health or social service professional. Talk with him or her about any problems you may have. Ask for help to improve your nutritional health.

Remember that warning signs *suggest* risk but do not represent diagnosis of any condition.

Nutrition Screening Initiative, a project of the American Academy of Family Physicians, the American Dietetic Association, and the National Council on the Aging, Inc.

about nutrition; and having none of the traditional "comfort foods" that increase interest in eating. Identification of these warning signals is crucial to preventing or solving nutritional problems.

Identifying those at risk

In 1990 the American Academy of Family Physicians, the American Dietetic Association, and the National Council on Aging joined in developing the Nutrition Screening Initiative, a five-year effort to increase public and professional awareness of the importance of nutrition to the health of older Americans. The initiative is supported by 25 other professional organizations. A major focus of the program has been the development of screening tools for use in assessing nutritional risk in the elderly.

One such tool is the "Determine-Your-Nutritional-Health" checklist, a simple test that can be used by seniors, their friends, or family members to evaluate their individual risk of poor nutrition (see checklist, page 441).

Possible scores on the checklist range from 0 to 21. Those with higher scores are more likely than low-scorers to have low nutrient intakes (below the RDAs) and be at risk for poor health. These individuals may need further, more detailed assessment of their nutritional status.

A score above 6 on the checklist indicates a definite need for a more thorough assessment. Dietitians, home health aides, health and social services professionals, physicians, and other medical professionals use the "Level 1 screen" to identify those elderly individuals who, because of a significant change in body weight, should be immediately referred for "Level 2 screening." Those who do not have a quantifiable nutritional deficit severe enough to warrant more intensive assessment are referred to such services as the congregate meal program, Meals-on-Wheels, shopping or transportation assistance, dietary counseling, or economic assistance programs.

The Level 2 screen helps physicians and other medical professionals identify those with more serious nutrition-related problems such as protein-calorie malnutrition, obesity, high blood cholesterol, and osteoporosis. It calls for measurement of height and weight, laboratory tests, cognitive and emotional status assessment, an evaluation of chronic medication use, and physical examination for clinical signs of nutrient deficiencies.

Since its inception the Nutrition Screening Initiative has distributed more than 300,000 copies of the "Determine-Your-Nutritional-Health" checklist and 22,500 screening manuals for professionals nationwide. The effort has led to the establishment of nutrition screening programs for older adults in a variety of settings. In one large screening program, which assessed the health and nutritional status of 2,052 Medicare bene-

ficiaries in New England who were aged 70 or older, researchers found that 24% were at high nutritional risk. More comprehensive evaluations of the numerous screening programs conducted under the initiative will be carried out in the future.

Help for those who need it

By the early 1970s it was becoming clear that many Americans over age 60 could not afford adequate diets, were unable to prepare adequate meals at home, had limited mobility, or were isolated and lacked incentive to prepare and eat food alone. In response, Congress in 1972 passed federal legislation to provide nutrition programs to redress these problems. By 1992 approximately 2.7 million older adults were participating in congregate meal programs, dining regularly in social settings such as community or recreation centers, senior citizens centers, and churches. Most centers offer noonday or dinner meals on weekends. Studies show that on those days when older persons participate in a congregate meal program, they are better nourished than nonparticipating counterparts of similar age and background.

In 1992 nearly 800,000 older adults received more than 94 million home-delivered meals through the Meals-on-Wheels program. For the homebound elderly this single hot meal, delivered five days a week, is their main source of food. Not surprisingly, recipients have more adequate intake on days when food is delivered than on nondelivery days. For many of them the Meals-on-Wheels driver is their only human contact during the course of the day.

In addition to congregate and home-delivered meals, a wide range of other nutrition services caters to the needs of older adults. These include food stamps, food-shopping assistance, community food-distribution programs, and emergency food services (soup kitchens, food pantries). Despite the availability of these many programs, however, only 22% of eligible older adults take advantage of them. And although the federal nutrition programs are mandated to target seniors who are in greatest social and economic need, some groups—ethnic and linguistic minorities and the homeless elderly, in particular—are generally underserved.

Local social services agencies for the aged in most localities have comprehensive lists of such nutrition-related services. Other reliable sources of nutrition information for the elderly include registered dietitians at local hospitals, the American Dietetic Association (1-800-877-1600), the American Institute for Cancer Research (1-800-843-8114), and local offices of the U.S. Department of Agriculture Cooperative Extension Service, the American Diabetic Association, the American Cancer Society, and the American Heart Association.

Working up a Cold(-Weather) Sweat

by Barry A. Franklin, Ph.D.,
and Frances Munnings

Perhaps unfortunately, not all people who live in northern climates are able to follow the birds and go south for the winter. Those who stay home must contend with snow, ice, and cold weather—unless, of course, they are willing to hibernate.

For some, however, wintertime is not all bad. Many Northerners love the cold and snow and actually look forward to winter. In fact, many Southerners flock to the North to enjoy outdoor winter sports: downhill and cross-country skiing, skating, sledding and tobogganing, and even ice fishing. These winter athletes welcome cold temperatures, and the more snow, the better.

Then again, not all people who live in the North are winter-sports enthusiasts. Other outdoor exercisers such as joggers and walkers may find that keeping up their fitness program is a challenge when the temperature drops, the wind blows, and snow starts to fall. Winter also presents added challenges to those who are just going about their everyday activities. A walk to the corner store or the bus stop may be a feat in itself. Furthermore, there is the added—and, for many, unwelcome—chore of shoveling snow.

Whether one loves it or hates it, cold weather is stressful. This is true even for healthy, fit people. It is even more stressful for persons with asthma and emphysema because cold air may trigger spasms in the airways of the lungs. Cold air also places increased stress on the cardiovascular system, which can be especially dangerous for those who have heart disease. Roads, sidewalks, and exercise trails can be treacherous in winter. Often an innocent-looking patch of snow has a less-innocent patch of ice under it. And when it snows, visibility is often compromised. Needless to say, bruises and broken bones just add to the stress of winter. Other not-uncommon cold-weather hazards are frostbite and hypothermia.

Fortunately, these winter stresses can be minimized. What it takes is a little knowledge of the hazards and some planning to prevent problems. Some useful information and commonsense precautions for those who exercise in the cold and those who exert themselves shoveling snow follow.

Stress on the cardiovascular system

Exertion in the cold, especially snow shoveling, stresses the cardiovascular system. Cold air triggers physiological responses in everyone. As already noted, however, the cold is much more stressful for persons who have heart disease. It is also considerably more taxing for those who are not accustomed to exercise than for those who are physically fit and healthy.

Physiological mechanisms. Two physiological mechanisms increase cardiovascular stress. First, inhalation of cold air may cause a reflex spasm, or constriction of the heart's (coronary) arteries. It may also increase the volume of blood pumped with each heartbeat. In a person whose heart vessels are clogged with cholesterol, the added stress may provoke symptoms of cardiac oxygen deficiency (myocardial hypoxia) and chest discomfort (angina pectoris).

Second, cold triggers a reflex to conserve body heat. When body temperature drops, the blood vessels in the skin constrict. This shunts the blood to the internal organs, where it is needed to keep vital organs at normal temperature. However, when the blood vessels constrict, blood pressure increases, forcing the heart to work harder. In addition, more oxygen is required by the heart muscle. While these increased demands on the heart are unlikely to cause symptoms in a person whose circulatory system is healthy, those who have heart disease and are not in good physical condition may experience ischemia (obstruction of arterial blood flow to the heart), angina, or both.

This constriction also decreases loss of body heat through the skin. Because vasoconstriction reduces the volume of blood exposed to cold, it affects the insulative properties of subcutaneous tissue. Cold

443

weather causes the skin to become cooler, decreasing the difference between the air's temperature and the temperature of the skin; heat loss is thereby reduced. Fingers, toes, the nose, and ears generally have good ability to vasoconstrict. The scalp and face, however, have little or no ability to vasoconstrict and therefore are sites of considerable heat loss.

Signs of trouble. In the most extreme cases, physical exertion can provoke myocardial infarction (a heart attack). Many people mistake the symptoms of a heart attack for indigestion. In fact, 25% of all heart attacks are not recognized. The following symptoms demand prompt action even though all symptoms may not be present:
● uncomfortable pressure, fullness, squeezing, or pain in the center of the chest lasting two minutes or more
  ● pain that spreads to the shoulders, neck, or arms
  ● severe pain in the chest and arms
  ● breathlessness
  ● light-headedness, dizziness, fainting, or sweating, often with nausea
  ● palpitations or other unusual heart rhythm irregularities

If any of these symptoms occur, one should stop the activity at once and sit or lie down. Even if the symptoms abate, it is usually wise to get help. Either the person with symptoms should be driven promptly to a hospital, or an emergency rescue service should be called.

Frostbite: the risks

Frostbite is the most common cold-weather injury. It occurs when the temperature of the skin drops below 33.8° C (93° F) and ice crystals form in the cells of the skin and tissues. The hands, feet, ears, and nose are the parts of the body that are most vulnerable. At below-freezing temperatures flesh freezes quickly—in about a minute. Frostbite also occurs in milder temperatures if exposure is prolonged.

When making decisions about outdoor activity, one should dress according to the windchill temperature, not the temperature alone. Wind removes the layer of air surrounding the body that the body usually is able to warm. Windchill factor is the measure of this effect. Put another way, windchill is the measure of how cold the air actually feels on exposed skin. (The table below shows the effects of wind on temperature.) It is interesting perhaps, but not reassuring, to know that winds higher than 40 mph have little additional effect on the temperature!

Needless to say, persons who go outdoors when the windchill factor is extremely low need extra protection. This is just as true for those who are waiting a few minutes for a bus as for those who do prolonged exercise in the cold.

Recognizing frostbite. In the earliest stages, frostbite causes tingling, burning, and redness of the skin. This is followed by the skin's becoming grayish yellow or white and feeling firm or waxy. Next, the skin feels very cold and numb, and pain disappears. In some cases blisters may appear. If frostbite is superficial, the exterior of the affected area will be white and frozen, and it will feel soft and resilient when the skin is depressed. In deep frostbite the frozen part feels woody.

What to do immediately. Self-treatment may be adequate for the most superficial frostbite, but generally it is wise to see a doctor whenever frostbite occurs. Many problems can accompany frostbite, including infection of the damaged skin. Also, a doctor can determine how much tissue damage has occurred and what treatment is appropriate. Frostbitten skin often looks more injured than it really is; a trip to the doctor can therefore be reassuring.

Before one sees a doctor, however, self-treatment is necessary. While still outdoors, the frozen part, if

wind speed (in mph)	When the wind blows . . .					
	actual temperature in degrees F (degrees C)					
	30 (−1.1)	20 (−6.7)	10 (−12.2)	0 (−17.8)	−10 (−23.3)	−20 (−28.9)
	how cold it feels					
calm	30 (−1.1)	20 (−6.7)	10 (−12.2)	0 (−17.8)	−10 (−23.3)	−20 (−28.9)
10	16 (−8.9)	4 (−15.6)	−9 (−22.8)	−24 (−31.1)	−33 (−36.1)	−46 (−43.3)
20	4 (−15.6)	−10 (−23.3)	−25 (−31.7)	−39 (−39.4)	−53 (−47.2)	−67 (−55)
30	−2 (−18.9)	−18 (−27.8)	−33 (−36.1)	−48 (−44.4)	−63 (−52.8)	−78 (−61.1)
40	−6 (−21.1)	−21 (−29.4)	−37 (−38.3)	−53 (−47.2)	−69 (−56.1)	−86 (−65.6)

directly exposed, should be covered with clothing or some other material. Hands and fingers should be held close to the body or even in the armpit. Persons who have symptoms of frostbite should get indoors as quickly as possible and remove any wet or restrictive clothing.

Next it is important to warm the affected area as rapidly as possible. Towels soaked in warm water are helpful, or the affected part can be immersed in water that is between 40° and 42° C (104° and 107° F)—warm but not hot. If water is not available, blankets or other cloth should be used. The person should not rub the affected area because that could increase tissue damage. Hot stoves, radiators, heat lamps, and heating pads should not be used for rewarming, as they may burn the skin. One can take aspirin or a similar analgesic to relieve pain during the rewarming process. Once sensation begins to return and skin starts to become pink, medical attention should be sought.

During and after rewarming, it is important that the frostbitten person *not* drink alcohol. If toes or feet have been frostbitten, the person should not walk; after rewarming, toes should be wiggled and feet elevated. Extreme care should be taken that frostbitten skin is not refrozen after it has thawed.

Hypothermia: deceptive and dangerous

Hypothermia is not as common as frostbite but is more dangerous—and it can be fatal. While frostbite affects the extremities, hypothermia has a profound effect on the cardiovascular and central nervous systems.

Hypothermia means "low temperature." It occurs when core body temperature decreases from its normal 37° C (98.6° F) to 35° C (95° F) or lower. In mild cases of hypothermia, people can rewarm themselves by shivering. However, if core temperature continues to fall, serious circulatory problems develop, and death is likely.

Hard to recognize. One factor that makes hypothermia especially dangerous is that persons may be unaware that it is occurring and therefore may not take the necessary steps to prevent its becoming fatal. Falling body temperature affects circulation and decreases blood flow to the brain, causing the person to become confused. Outdoor exercisers and snow shovelers may especially be at risk because the rigorous nature of their activity has warmed them and they may not feel the cold. It is easy to develop hypothermia, especially when one is tired and sweaty. After prolonged outdoor exercise one should cool down indoors.

What to do. Because it is not always easy to tell when the body temperature is dropping, the cold-weather exerciser or snow shoveler should heed the following symptoms:
- shivering, the body's attempt to generate heat
- numbness

- muscle weakness
- drowsiness
- sleepiness
- disorientation or slurred speech

Because hypothermia can be life-threatening, the individual who suspects it or a companion should call for medical help. While waiting for assistance, they should make an attempt to raise body temperature by removing wet clothing and warming the body with blankets.

Other cold-weather problems

Less-common cold-related problems are cold urticaria and Raynaud's phenomenon. Those who are affected by these conditions will need to take special precautions when undertaking any cold-weather endurance activity. In some cases, outdoor exercise may be contraindicated.

Cold urticaria. About 1% of the population is allergic to cold. Fortunately, most cases are mild. Persons who suffer from cold urticaria break out in itchy hives when they exercise or exert themselves in the cold. In severe cases of cold urticaria, excessive amounts of histamine are released into the bloodstream, and the person experiences swelling of the windpipe, wheezing, fainting, or shock. Antihistamines may prevent the problem, but persons who have severe symptoms generally should avoid exercising in cold weather or shoveling snow, or they should at least consult a physician before they do so.

Raynaud's phenomenon. About half a million Americans experience Raynaud's phenomenon, which is an exaggerated response to cold. In most cases the problem occurs in people who are otherwise healthy; in some cases, however, it may be an indication of a rheumatic disorder. Women are affected by Raynaud's phenomenon more often than men. Stress and emotional upset as well as cigarette smoking, caffeine intake, and certain medications are thought to aggravate the problem and may trigger attacks. Most often the parts of the body that are affected are the hands and feet. The constriction of blood vessels associated with exposure to cold causes the extremities of the Raynaud's phenomenon sufferer to turn white from loss of circulation, then blue as oxygenated blood returns, then red when the vessels dilate and blood surges back.

The key to comfort for people who suffer from Raynaud's phenomenon is to protect their extremities especially well. They should take extra care to wear socks that keep their feet warm and good ski mittens whenever they are exposed to cold, even if the temperature seems relatively mild. Commercially available pocket warmers may also help. For an unfortunate few, no matter what they do to protect themselves from the cold, outdoor exercise and snow shoveling may simply be too painful.

Preparing for cold-weather exercise

Whenever it is cold outside, the exerciser should prepare first. There are certain measures that will increase safety and prevent an outdoor workout from being overly taxing.

Warming up. It is a good idea to warm up before going outside, even if heavy exercise is not on the agenda. When muscles and joints are cold, an injury is more likely to occur—especially after a slip or fall. Further, a warm-up reduces the initial chill and enables one to exercise outdoors more comfortably. Warming up also aids performance in those who are running or doing other vigorous exercise.

To warm up, one should do some initial stretching exercises and then run in place, jump rope, or ride a stationary bicycle for a few minutes. The stretching should focus on the muscles of the limbs and the torso and should be done gently, with each stretch position held for about 15 seconds. Once outdoors, one should start to exercise slowly and then gradually increase intensity.

Dressing properly. The basic idea in dressing for outdoor exercise in cold weather is to keep the wind out and allow moisture to escape. Wearing several layers of clothing is important for two reasons. First, the different layers act as insulators because they trap heat. Second, one can take off the outer layers as the body warms up (even in the cold, exercise generates a lot of body heat).

The layer next to the skin should be capable of wicking moisture from the skin to the outer clothing layers. Polypropylene does this well; cotton, however, soaks up the moisture and keeps it next to the skin. Wool is good for the middle layer because it keeps the body warm even when wet. Many fabrics, when wet, will actually draw heat away from the body and pass it into the air. The outer layer should be wind- and water-resistant. Wearing a zippered outer layer rather than a pullover makes it easier to either open the garment partly or remove it altogether as one gets warmer. Gore-Tex and similar fabrics that "breathe" will allow perspiration and heat to escape. Nylon may be too air permeable, and polyurethane is likely to cause retention of sweat and promote chill. (For those reasons polyurethane has been banned from use in apparel for downhill skiing competition.) It is always important to change wet clothing, especially gloves and socks. If skin or clothing gets wet, the body loses heat much faster.

The head loses heat more easily than other parts of the body. As noted above, vasoconstriction shunts blood from the skin to the organs to conserve body heat, but in the scalp vasoconstriction is inefficient, so more heat is lost. In fact, up to 40% of heat loss is from an uncovered head, so it is important to wear a hat, hood, or scarf for protection. This is good advice even for persons who are just running errands.

Heat is lost quickly from hands and feet, too. Wearing more than one pair of socks may help, but not if it makes shoes too tight. Tight shoes will reduce the blood supply to the feet and make them even colder. Some people get around this problem by wearing larger shoes than they normally wear. Shoes that are one full size larger than one's usual size will accommodate extra socks. Gloves and mittens should not be worn tight-fitting either. Mittens are generally warmer than gloves, as they allow more circulation in the fingers.

Wearing a mask will help to counteract the effects of inhaling cold air. The mask should fit over the nose and mouth and ideally will cover the neck, thus also protecting these areas from frostbite. Cold-weather masks sold at pharmacies work well, as do ski masks, scarves, or bandannas. Men who jog or stay outdoors for prolonged periods in cold weather should wear extra layers of clothing to protect the genital area, as penile frostbite has been reported in the medical literature.

To avoid slippery surfaces it is wise to walk or run on trails that are plowed or shoveled regularly. Many winter runners as well as fitness walkers wear shoes that provide traction, with treads similar to those on hiking shoes.

Some advice for outdoor exercisers stays the same no matter what the weather. If exercising after dark (or on winter mornings before sunrise), one should wear reflective clothing, and carrying a flashlight will not only make the exerciser visible but also illuminate the path.

Another precaution that outdoor exercisers should take is to shield eyes from sunlight, which can be extremely bright in winter, especially if reflected off snow. Sunglasses or goggles will protect eyes from damaging ultraviolet rays. Wearing sunscreen on any exposed parts of the face is also a good idea; sunburn is just as possible in winter as in summer. Lotion and lip balm will help protect the face and lips from windburn and from dryness and chapping, which are common in winter.

Energy and fluid needs: what to eat and drink. Keeping the body warm takes extra energy, so it is necessary to take in more calories when exercising in the cold. Exercisers should take along extra snacks if they are cross-country skiing or doing any activity that keeps them outdoors for long periods of time.

It may be less apparent in cold weather than in warm weather that one is perspiring, but winter exercisers also need to drink plenty of liquids to replace the fluid lost in sweat and in warming the air they breathe. When a person becomes dehydrated, blood flow to the skin decreases, increasing susceptibility to cold injury.

Additional calories and an adequate fluid intake are important, but caffeine, alcohol, and tobacco should

incorrect

correct

The safe way to shovel snow: dress comfortably in clothes that are protective in the cold and wind, warm up first, start slowly, use arms and legs, keep knees bent, lift small loads, push or sweep snow if possible, and take frequent breaks.

be avoided. Caffeine and nicotine constrict blood vessels and cause dehydration. Alcohol blocks the normal response of shivering; dilates the blood vessels of the skin, causing heat loss; and impairs judgment.

Snow shoveling: risks and tips

Snow shoveling is a strenuous activity. It involves pushing, lifting, turning, and throwing—*i.e.,* upper-extremity exercise and isometric exertion. Persons who shovel snow not only are vulnerable to frostbite and low back pain but are also at increased risk for a heart attack or a potentially fatal cardiac rhythm irregularity. Over a two-day period in 1992 in metropolitan Detroit, Mich., for example, 17 people died while shoveling snow.

The heart, which is already working harder than usual because of the cold weather, has additional demands imposed on it by the rigorous nature of the upper-body exertion. These added demands make snow shoveling a cardiovascularly stressful activity for anyone, but some people are more likely than others to suffer a heart attack while shoveling. This includes those who have a sedentary lifestyle and exert themselves excessively when not in condition; cigarette smokers; those who are overweight; and those who have high blood pressure, elevated blood cholesterol, or a heart condition.

Energy expenditure. One of the first things to keep in mind about shoveling snow is that it takes a lot of energy. The energy expended depends on the weight of the snow and the shoveling rate. Physical exertion requires oxygen. This means that for any given task, the fit person works at a lower percentage of his or her maximal capacity to take in oxygen. Such exercise capacity is often described in terms of workload units known as metabolic equivalents, or METS. (One MET is equal to the amount of oxygen required for sitting at rest; very light work, such as desk work, amounts to 2 METS; a slow walk is approximately 2–3 METS; speed walking or heavy gardening would be 5–6 METS; jog-

ging may be 7–9 METS; and fast running or heavy labor is 10 METS or more.) If 10 shovelfuls of snow are removed a minute, the oxygen consumption will range from 6 to 15 METS. For persons who are not accustomed to strenuous activity or cardiac patients whose exercise capacity may be only 6 to 8 METS, this requires maximal, indeed Herculean, efforts.

It helps to compare snow shoveling with other activities. A 70-kg (154-lb) man lifting a weight of 4 kg (8.8 lb)—the weight of the snow and the shovel combined—exerts about the same amount of energy as would be required for playing singles tennis or for light downhill skiing. Increasing the weight to 6.2 kg (13.6 lb) makes the energy exerted comparable to that of playing basketball or handball or running 8.9 km/h (5.5 mph). Shoveling wet snow takes even more energy. A single shovelful may weigh 10.1 kg (22.5 lb). At a rate of 10 shovelfuls per minute, shoveling wet snow is as strenuous as running 14.5 km/h (9 mph) for the same time period.

Added cardiac stressors. Several other factors contribute to the cardiac stress of snow shoveling. These include the following:

● *Arm effort required for heavy lifting.* The heart does not work as efficiently during arm work as it does during leg work. At a given workload, oxygen consumption, caloric expenditure, heart rate, and blood pressure are greater during arm work than during leg work.

● *Upright posture.* Exercising in an upright position, especially when the legs move very little, can cause pooling of blood in the lower extremities and a decrease in the blood returning to the heart. The heart compensates by increasing the heart rate and thus working harder. These added stresses occur while the oxygen demands of the heart are already high from the exercise itself.

● *Cold exposure.* Breathing cold air can cause a reflex spasm, or transient narrowing of the coronary arteries, which thereby increases the cardiac work.

• *Valsalva maneuver.* A common physiological reaction to lifting a heavy weight, such as a shovelful of snow, is to hold the breath with the mouth closed. Holding the breath produces increased pressure in the chest area and hinders the return of blood to the heart, causing an increase in blood pressure. (Cardiologists sometimes instruct patients to do this during the course of a physical examination because it can help distinguish various kinds of heart murmurs.) However, persons shoveling snow should avoid such a maneuver, known as the Valsalva maneuver, especially if they have heart disease.

• *Isometric effort.* An isometric contraction is one in which there is muscle tension but little or no movement. When a person strains to lift a heavy load of snow, such a contraction may occur. Although the volume of blood pumped by the heart per minute (cardiac output) rises, blood flow to the muscles is impaired (probably because of reflex vasoconstriction and sustained muscle contraction). These responses cause a disproportionate rise in blood pressure.

In a recent study carried out by the Cardiac Rehabilitation Department at William Beaumont Hospital, Royal Oak, Mich., investigators monitored the physiological responses of 10 unconditioned but healthy young men while they shoveled wet, and therefore heavy, snow. The researchers found that the heart rate and blood pressure of most subjects catapulted to dangerously high levels—levels that were comparable to or higher than the maximum values achieved by the same subjects during exhaustive treadmill exercise testing. Moreover, after only two minutes of shoveling, heart rate responses of most subjects exceeded the upper limit commonly prescribed for safe exercise training.

Another study measured the stress of shoveling snow of relatively light weight in men with known heart disease and men in good health. Those with coronary disease paced themselves better so as not to overload their cardiovascular capacity, whereas the healthy controls were more likely to impose excessive demands on their cardiovascular systems.

Shoveling safely. Because of the added stress it places on the heart, snow shoveling can pose problems even for those who are fit. One can reduce these stresses by taking the following steps:

• Warm up first and start gradually.

• Pace the work by alternating exercise and rest, and take frequent breaks.

• Use the arms and legs, not just the arms, when lifting, and keep knees slightly bent.

• Lift small loads more often, rather than large loads, and use a short shovel with a small scoop.

• Whenever possible, push or sweep the snow rather than lifting it.

• Dress in layers; wear clothing that is protective in the wind.

• Wear a cold-weather mask to avoid inhaling cold air or exposing the face and neck to cold and a hat to prevent heat loss from the head.

• Avoid large meals, alcohol, and tobacco, which place added stress on the heart and blood vessels, before and after shoveling.

Who should not shovel. Elderly persons and persons who have heart disease or high blood pressure simply should not shovel snow. Those who are over 40 and have other major coronary risk factors (*e.g.,* cigarette smoking, elevated blood cholesterol, and sedentary lifestyle) should consult a physician before shoveling snow.

For some, an alternative to shoveling snow may be to use a snowblower. One should keep in mind, however, that operating a snowblower requires some exertion, and the operator must cope with the elements just as the shoveler must.

Staying in and staying fit

Understandably, some people simply do not want to brave the cold for exercise; others are hampered by one of the cold-weather problems described above. Fortunately, good alternatives exist, so no one has to give up fitness when the mercury plummets.

One increasingly popular indoor activity is shopping-mall walking. Most cities have indoor malls. Some malls even sponsor walking clubs, especially for senior citizens, and some open early so that walkers do not have to contend with crowds of shoppers.

Another good choice is to join a health club; most offer winter membership or pay-by-the-month plans. The exercise options at health clubs are vast: jogging and walking courses; treadmills; exercise bicycles of all sorts; rowing, stair-climbing, and cross-country-skiing machines; strength-training machines and weight-lifting equipment; aerobics classes; swimming; and racquet sports.

Sometimes it is easier to stay home and exercise, in which case one can easily devise a well-rounded winter fitness program. Home exercise equipment comparable to that offered in a health club is one possibility. (Good equipment is likely to cost several hundred to several thousand dollars.) Exercise videos are abundant and can be purchased or rented. With a little imagination and ingenuity, one can even devise a strength-training routine using weights from the kitchen cupboard: cans of food, bags of rice or beans, bottles of vinegar, and so forth.

The winter exercise challenge

There is no need to move to the Sunbelt to stay fit—or get fit—in winter. With proper motivation, and by knowing the risks and taking a few precautions, everyone who lives in the frigid North *can* meet the cold-weather exercise challenge.

Keeping Healthy on Campus

by Carol L. Otis, M.D.,
and Roger Goldingay

Every year 14.5 million students enroll in 3,400 U.S. institutions of higher learning. These students have unique health and social services needs that are critical to their success. Many are leaving home for the first time and will be responsible for making their own health decisions without the benefit and experience of a parent's advice.

Most of those enrolled in colleges and universities today are not the traditional 18–22-year-old college students. They come from diverse ethnic and socio-economic backgrounds. More than half are over age 24. Many are single parents, and growing numbers are people with disabilities. Many work part-time, or they are returning to school from the job market to either start or complete their education. Also, there are over 400,000 international students enrolled in U.S. universities and colleges.

Often residing in communities a long way from home and lacking familiar support systems, today's students are not unlike a migrant population faced with a cultural environment that is foreign, fiercely competitive, and often frightening. While there are exciting new opportunities, there are also new demands and pressures. Furthermore, compared with prior generations, today's students are at greater risk in terms of their health and safety. Rates of sexually transmitted disease (STD), suicide, and substance abuse are especially high in this group. Students may lack the experience, skills, and financial resources to gain access to health care, and an ill-informed decision may have significant personal consequences.

Families and students themselves invest substantially in a college education. Proper health care must be regarded as a foundation for success. Given the nature of the educational environment in this fast-paced and changing world and the fact that today's schools are not ivory tower institutions acting in loco parentis, how can students and their families best prepare for the health challenges of university life?

College bound

All college-bound students need to plan for health care *before* starting school. They should thoroughly investigate the health care services available at their intended institution and inquire about prematriculation health requirements. They may need a preadmission physical examination and a statement of health from their private physician. They may need certain pre-college vaccinations as well as records of previous immunizations. The college may also require students to furnish a record of their complete health history. Further, the school is likely to want proof of medical insurance. Not surprisingly, it may take a month or more to complete the medical exam, have the required tests and vaccinations, obtain the necessary records, and then get all the paperwork to the university.

Insurance concerns. University students are among the most underinsured segments of the U.S. population. A survey in California indicated that up to 30% of full-time students had no coverage and another 30% had incomplete or inadequate coverage. The reasons are many. Most students are covered by their parents' policies. That plan, however, may have a substantial deductible that must be met before a student is covered, or it may require a student to receive care from a designated managed care provider in his or her hometown. Further, students are usually covered by their parents' policies only up to age 22 or 23, even if they remain full-time students. Some insurance carriers are now reviewing their policies on reimbursement for dependents and lowering the age for students' coverage. Students therefore need to review with the university any medical insurance requirements before attending school. Those who have private insurance should verify each year that coverage is adequate to meet their evolving needs and will supplement what the institution offers for emergency care, episodic care, dental care, and optometry needs. They also need to confirm that their insurance transfers to another state if they are attending an out-of-state institution.

Keeping healthy on campus

It is very important that students have all the information and forms necessary to be covered by their insurance. Too often a student ends up in the emergency room late at night with no personal knowledge of his or her coverage, and precious time is wasted tracking down the needed information during a crisis.

If family insurance plans are lacking or inadequate, students should investigate insurance available through the university. Although there is no centralized insurance carrier that covers colleges, most have negotiated a group coverage plan, usually at lower rates than an individual can obtain. Consistent with the low rates, however, most such plans offer limited benefits. These plans may provide coverage only for after-hours care, surgery, or hospitalization that is not part of the student health service. Approximately 7% of university-offered plans cover accidents only. Another 58% place a $5,000 to $10,000 cap on maximum benefits. Only 15% of plans offer up to $100,000 coverage. Also, certain preexisting illnesses and psychiatric and dental care may be specifically excluded. In selecting a plan students should consider underlying personal medical and dental needs, where routine and specialized medical, vision, and dental care will be obtained and where prescriptions will be filled.

Medical records. When a student relocates to another community for college, he or she should take along and understand all necessary medical documents. This would include a personal health history with information about prior surgery, hospitalizations, immunizations, current medication usage, and allergies. If the student has a chronic medical condition or has had recent surgery, he or she should take along all relevant records, including physicians' statements, operative notes, and X-rays. The latter are particularly important in cases of orthopedic problems that will be followed by a different doctor.

Students should also take prescriptions for contact lenses, eyeglasses, and medications, including those that may be used episodically such as antihistamines for seasonal allergies or asthma medications in case of an attack.

Usually students who are minors (under age 18) will need to take along parental or guardian consent forms for treatment. They should also carry in their wallet names and phone numbers of persons to be contacted in case of emergency.

Going prepared. Students with a chronic medical condition such as diabetes, asthma, or hypertension need to plan for routine and urgent care. They should establish a relationship with a physician in the college environment and have all necessary records there as well as at home to ensure the best continuity of care.

Dental needs also should be considered in advance. Are routine dental visits to occur at home or away? Is there any indication that major dental work is needed in the near future? Dealing with an infected tooth or impacted molars during the school term can be very inconvenient and may cause important classroom and study time to be lost.

Students should make sure they have ample amounts of all medications they take on a regular or occasional basis as well as supplies such as insulin syringes, or they should verify that the same brands are available in the new community. It is wise to look into the cost of prescription medications. Most health services have a pharmacy that offers lower prices than off-campus pharmacies; it may have a limited inventory, however, so drugs may need to be ordered, or it might not carry certain medications that a student takes or needs. Also, campus pharmacies may not be available for after-hours prescription filling, and they may not accept prescriptions from doctors who are not on the university health service staff. Sometimes

Going away to college offers many exciting new opportunities, and most students are healthy when they get there. But newfound freedom combined with communal living, eating, and learning can pose health risks. Moreover, college students often lack the expertise and resources to get proper health care when they need it. All college-bound students need to plan ahead in order to stay healthy and make the most of campus life.

health plans will pay for medications only it they are purchased at specific sites.

Finally, when students leave for college, they should take a personal first aid-medical kit. Ingredients will vary from person to person. Having certain supplies on hand enables self-treatment for minor emergencies and common illnesses (*e.g.,* a lacerated finger, an irritated eye, a swollen knee after a fall, indigestion, or a bad cold). Having such a kit can save an inconvenient trip to a doctor or pharmacy when one is not feeling well or is pressed by schoolwork.

The college health service

The majority of U.S. college students have some form of health care available through the school. Approximately 1,600 of the 3,400 institutions of higher learning have a health service on the campus. Vocational or technical schools often do not have services, but most two- and four-year colleges provide on-site health care. The service may range from a one-person first aid center to a large health service offering full-service care including X-rays and laboratory tests, pharmacy services, and in-patient hospital care. Many health services employ nurse practitioners, and many are nurse-directed centers offering acute care with referrals to outside physicians or other providers for other needs.

The model college health service, as defined by the American College Health Association (ACHA), is one that provides affordable, convenient, quality health care linked to the educational mission of the university. Unique and important to the college health service is that it includes and values student involvement and offers creative outreach programs for prevention and health education.

How can students and prospective students determine the adequacy and quality of the health service at the college of their choice? They should investigate the type and breadth of services available. Many campus orientations include a visit to the health facility, which is best made prior to needing its services. It is wise to check to see if the facility is currently accredited or plans on being accredited by either the Accreditation Association for Ambulatory Health Care, Inc. or the Joint Commission on Accreditation of Healthcare Organizations. As of June 1994, about 70 U.S. university health services had received accreditation, and many more were in the process of becoming accredited. Another way to ascertain quality is to find out whether the campus clinicians are affiliated with a local medical or nursing school or are board certified in their medical specialty. Nurse practitioners and physicians' assistants are licensed by state organizations. Nurses may also have specific certification in college health nursing by the American Nurses Association. A health service's membership in the ACHA is an indication of its commitment to meeting the unique health needs of

college students. In June 1994, 910 institutions were members; in addition, many college health service personnel were individual ACHA members.

At some centers one can choose a primary care health provider. The majority of campus health services have a strong health education department staffed by individuals trained in public health. They also may offer "wellness" classes and train students to be peer health counselors.

Health problems

Students are generally healthy. Their most common medical problems are acute infections, skin disorders, and musculoskeletal injuries. Students need prompt, convenient, and accessible care for these problems in order to minimize the impact on their studies.

Acne, affecting 70–80% of young adults, tops the list of skin problems among college students. Acne is caused by blocked oil ducts in the skin, and the tendency to have acne is inherited. Because the treatment for acne focuses on control, young people should be under regular clinical care. Close to half of U.S. college health services have dermatologists on staff. Others can refer students with troublesome acne and other skin problems to outside specialists.

The majority of infectious illnesses experienced by college students are viral. Upper respiratory infections, sore throats, eye infections (conjunctivitis), influenza, and gastroenteritis ("stomach flu") are all miseries familiar to a large majority of college students. Such infections are passed from sufferer to sufferer via aerosol droplets from sneezing or coughing or via contaminated hands and eating surfaces. Crowded classrooms, dormitory living, and new strains of viruses carried by students from different parts of the country (or the world) compound the likelihood of infection.

College students need to learn self-care for these common maladies. Preventive strategies include frequent hand washing, not sharing utensils, and maintaining general health. Basic self-care includes increasing rest and fluids, maintaining proper nutrition, and treating symptoms. Students should seek medical care if they have (1) fever over 38° C (101° F), (2) persistent pain in a sinus, the chest, or the abdominal area, (3) sore throat and a prior history of strep throat, (4) yellow or green sputum or nasal drainage, (5) signs of dehydration (*i.e.,* feeling dizzy or scant urine production), (6) blood in stools or sputum, or (7) an illness lasting more than one week.

One of the most dreaded infections of college students is infectious mononucleosis, also know as "mono" or "the kissing disease." Mono is transmitted in ways similar to the common cold and not necessarily by kissing. Although feared, mono is most often a mild illness similar to other viral sore throats. Surveys show that about 50% of entering college freshmen have been previously exposed and have antibodies to

451

the virus; 80% of college graduates have evidence of exposure. At least half of those infected never know they have the illness.

Mononucleosis, which is caused by either the Epstein-Barr virus or cytomegalovirus (both herpesviruses), infects the lymphoid tissue in the lymph glands, throat, and abdomen. Usually it is experienced as a mild sore throat with fever. In 1–12% of cases the infection causes more significant problems such as chronic fatigue, nausea, abdominal pains, vomiting, rash, jaundice, or associated strep throat, which result in a loss of school time. With proper rest, nutrition, and control of symptoms, most people recover in one to six weeks. Because those who are infected produce specific antibodies against the responsible viruses, in most cases they will not get the infection again.

Some childhood viral diseases can infect college students who were not immunized or did not get the disease as a child. In particular, college campuses have experienced significant outbreaks of measles and mumps. Measles can be a serious disease in young adults, sometimes accompanied by pneumonia. Mumps can cause inflammation of the testes and subsequent sterility.

The vaccination to prevent these childhood diseases (known as MMR, for measles, mumps, and rubella) was first used in the 1960s. As children who received this vaccine approached college age, it was discovered that a booster dose was needed to augment the initial childhood series. As of 1989, boosters have been recommended or required for most high school and college students. Rates of both illnesses have since declined, though such outbreaks still occur. In March 1994 students at Rutgers University in New Jersey came down with measles, and all students and faculty at the New Brunswick and Piscataway campuses were required to have measles immunizations.

Chicken pox can infect young adults who did not have the illness as children. Whereas childhood chicken pox is usually mild, in young adults it can be a more severe illness causing pneumonia and other problems. Because it is highly contagious, affected students are quarantined to their rooms, not allowed to attend class, or sent home during the approximately two weeks of infectious skin rash. When the recently approved chicken pox vaccine becomes available, college-bound young adults who never had the illness as children may be targeted for vaccination.

With the influx into the United States of students from all over the world, the student population at large may be at risk for other infectious diseases. Tuberculosis (TB) and hepatitis B are the two receiving the most attention. Some schools have mandatory testing of foreign students for TB and offer skin testing as a screening test to others. TB is spread via aerosol droplets from the coughs and sneezes of people with an active infection.

Hepatitis B, a viral illness causing inflammation of the liver, can be prevented by vaccination. It is endemic in certain areas of Asia and is transmitted in the same manner as the AIDS virus (HIV)—*i.e.,* via sexual or blood contact. Many students entering health care professions are required to have the vaccination before attending school. The vaccine is given in a series of three injections spread out over a six-month period. Although it is not currently universally recommended for all young adults, the ACHA strongly recommends it for college students.

College students are also prone to the stomach flu, a viral infection causing the miseries of nausea, vomiting, and diarrhea. Most cases are self-limited and usually last just a few days. Other forms of gastroenteritis that are not infrequent on campus are bacterial food poisoning from improperly cooked food and infections transmitted by food handlers. Hepatitis A, a less serious liver infection than hepatitis B, is one of the viruses that can be transmitted by those who are involved in the preparation of food. Hepatitis A may produce symptoms such as fatigue, loss of appetite, muscle aches, fever, nausea, vomiting, and abdominal pain, but it may also be asymptomatic. In cases of large outbreaks of such foodborne or food-related illnesses, public health officials or the student health service will attempt to contact all exposed individuals and offer specific treatment.

Sexual health

Surveys show that the proportion of young Americans who have had premarital sexual intercourse has increased steadily since the 1960s. A survey conducted in 1991 indicated that 78% of females and 86% of males had had intercourse by age 20. Not only are heterosexual intercourse rates increasing, so is the number of sexual partners young people have. A 1993 survey reported in the *Journal of American College Health* found that 65% of college-bound adolescents had had intercourse the year before they started college. Thirty percent of these sexually active teens had two to three partners in that year, and 16% had six or more partners. Sexual relationships of young adults are often ones of "serial monogamy"—*i.e.,* they have sexual relations with only one partner at a time, but after that relationship ends, they move into a sexual relationship with another person.

A study of undergraduates at a southeastern U.S. university looked at increasing rates of heterosexual intercourse from 1973 to 1988. Among male students rates increased from 72.3% in 1973 to 91.7% in 1988. The rates for female students were 63% in 1973 and 88% in 1988. The same survey indicated that the numbers of both men and women having casual intercourse with more than one person also increased significantly. Accompanying the high rates of sexual activity are unwanted pregnancy, sexual violence (rape

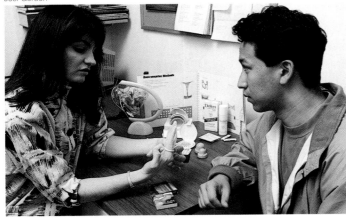

Most freshmen have had sexual experiences before starting college. Although well-informed about the risks of "unsafe sex," they often do not use contraceptives or take advantage of the confidential counseling services that most schools offer.

and other forms of sexual assault), and STDs. No nationwide figures are kept on the rates of pregnancy or abortion, but these are significant problems for college students. Most health services provide birth-control information. Many have on-campus services that provide contraceptives of all types, pregnancy testing, morning-after pills, and pregnancy counseling. Others provide off-campus referrals for these services.

STDs are the hidden epidemic on college campuses. These diseases differ in their incubation periods, symptoms, and health consequences, but all share a common mode of transmission—unprotected sexual contact. The most prevalent infections are human papillomavirus (HPV), also known as genital warts, or condyloma; chlamydia; nongonococcal urethritis; herpes; gonorrhea; molluscum contagiosum (a viral skin infection that can affect the genitals); syphilis; and HIV.

HPV infection is caused by viruses that are transmitted during genital contact. A report published in the *Journal of American College Health* in 1993 found that 34% of visits by men to a college STD clinic were for HPV. It is estimated that 80% of sexually active young adults have been exposed to the virus. The person infected with HPV may not have visible lesions or know that he or she carries the virus but can still spread the virus to others. The incubation period may range from weeks to months. Manifestations of the virus are visible warts, abnormal Pap smears in women, and precancerous lesions in affected tissues in men and women. Some but not all strains of HPV are associated with cervical cancer in women. Treatment (electrocauterization, cryotherapy, laser or surgical excision) can destroy visible lesions, but complete eradication of the virus often is not possible. Those who are known to be infected need to rely on abstinence or use of condoms during any genital contact to prevent transmission of the virus to a partner.

Chlamydia trachomatis is an obligate intracellular parasite that infects the urethra, cervix, uterus, and fallopian tubes in women and the urethra and epididymis in men. Surveys have reported prevalence rates of chlamydial infection as high as 5% to 20% among students attending STD clinics or receiving routine gynecologic care. Many cases are asymptomatic and thus can be readily spread to unsuspecting partners. Infection can result in pelvic inflammatory disease in women and permanent scarring and infertility in both sexes. Treatment with antibiotics (*e.g.,* tetracycline, doxycycline, or erythromycin) in the acute stages is usually effective. Preventing transmission of the infection is achieved through abstinence or the use of condoms during sexual activity.

Dramatically increasing rates of sexual activity and STDs have raised major concerns about the transmission of HIV among college students. The ACHA, in conjunction with the Centers for Disease Control and Prevention, in Atlanta, Ga., has conducted several seroprevalance studies among university students. The initial survey was done in 1988 and '89 at 19 institutions. Blood specimens were collected anonymously from students who had had blood drawn for routine medical purposes during visits to campus health services. Of nearly 17,000 samples taken, 30 (or 0.2%) were positive for HIV. The risk was greatest among older students and men. Similar surveys conducted in 1989 and '90 and in 1991 and '92 found similar rates. These results showed that rates of infection among college students were lower than the rates for other groups known to be at high risk. The potential for further spread of infection, however, was considered significant; thus colleges may be sitting on a time bomb.

Campuses have responded to the challenge of HIV by offering education and prevention programs. Most colleges encourage condom use and make condoms readily available to all students. Many campus health services offer confidential and/or anonymous HIV testing. Infected students have access to confidential health care either on campus or by referral.

Keeping healthy on campus

Surveys of sexual health knowledge indicate that students are well-informed about STDs, HIV, and their modes of transmission and about "safer sex" to prevent infection. Studies examining sexual behavior, however, have repeatedly found that students do not translate this knowledge into appropriate personal, preventive behavior. Too often the assumption of college students is that "it can't happen to me." Some may be embarrassed to purchase or use condoms or lack the skills to negotiate condom usage with a new partner. The reasons most often cited for spurning condom use are inconvenience, reduced sensation during sexual intercourse, likelihood of breakage, and expense. Health educators use a variety of strategies to teach about and encourage safer sex behavior.

Substance abuse

Alcohol is the most popular and most abused drug on campus; 75–96% consume it. A 1993 survey found that one in three college students drink to get drunk; notably, 35% of college women drink to get drunk (up from 10% in 1979). The same survey found that 42% of college alcohol users are binge drinkers— *i.e.,* having five or more drinks on a single occasion (compared with 33% in the general population).

Alcohol is a cofactor in accidents, violence, unwanted or unplanned sexual contact, and emotional and academic problems. A 1989 study reported in the *Journal of American College Health* found that 25% of all deaths of college students were alcohol-related. In a survey conducted at Tulane University, New Orleans, La., 70% of students reported having had unplanned sexual intercourse while under the influence of alcohol. In 1987 a study published in *Journal of Counseling Psychology* found that 55% of college men and 53% of college women involved in acquaintance rape were under the influence of alcohol at the time.

Only 13% of college students use cigarettes daily, compared with 26% of the population at large, but many still consider that rate too high. Joseph A. Califano, Jr., president of the Center on Addiction and Substance Abuse at Columbia University, New York City, has advocated the banning of all advertising, distribution, and sales of tobacco products on college campuses: "By eliminating smoking on campus, we can save thousands of lives and billions of dollars."

The use of smokeless tobacco is increasing on campuses. In a 1989 study 22% of college men and 2% of college women at 72 different institutions reported using smokeless tobacco—either chewing it or "dipping" it (rubbing on the teeth and gums); 18% of these also smoked cigarettes, compared with 14% of nonusers of smokeless tobacco. Smokeless tobacco is associated with health risks such as tooth erosion, gum inflammation, and oral cancer. Like cigarette smoking, it is a physically addicting habit that is difficult to break and may lead to a lifelong addiction.

Alcohol, which more than 75% of college students imbibe, is by far the most popular recreational drug on campus; it is also the most abused. A 1993 survey found that one in three students drinks to get drunk.

Marijuana is the illegal drug most commonly used by young adults—college students and nonstudents—with rates of use estimated to be around 35% in 1989. Studies of college students show they have lower daily usage rates than age-matched peers who are not in school (1.8% versus 4.8%).

The U.S. Department of Health and Human Services recently issued a report on illicit drug use by young adults. From 1985 to 1989 use of substances other than marijuana was 19% for those in college, compared with 24% for high school graduates not in college. Seventeen percent of college students annually report experimenting with cocaine; an estimated 4% are regular users.

Recognizing the serious nature of substance abuse, most campuses have instituted high-profile outreach and treatment programs, or they provide referrals for prevention and treatment. Many have chapters of Alcoholics Anonymous, Al-Anon (a self-help program for families of alcoholics), and SADD (Students Against Driving Drunk) either on campus or in nearby communities. Some campuses receive funding to create alcohol and drug-free living environments and activities, such as alcohol-free parties. In 1989 Congress passed the Drug Free Schools and Communities Act. That legislation requires, as a condition for receiving federal funds, that all institutions of higher learning certify that they have adopted and implemented a program to prevent unlawful possession, distribution, and use of illicit drugs and alcohol on campus. Under the act, colleges must distribute printed information on standards of conduct and legal sanctions for and health risks of drug and tobacco use as well as list counseling resources.

Mental health

Stress is a ubiquitous factor in the life of any college student. Students typically have too much to do in too little time with too much riding on the outcome. Often students find themselves overextended, overcommitted, and sleep-deprived.

The most significant mental-health risk associated with college stress is that of suicide. Risk factors include a recent failure in schoolwork, problems in a romantic relationship, social isolation, depression, substance-abuse problems, and intoxication at the time. Suicide is now the third leading cause of death for the young-adult college-aged population. Nationwide, 50,000 people between the ages of 15 and 24 attempt suicide each year; one in 10 is successful. However, a 1994 review of suicide among college students found that the rate of successful suicides among college students is only one in 10,000, lower than the rate for age-matched nonstudents.

Most campuses are aware of the pressure on students. Many have or provide referrals to counseling centers, and some offer clinics or classes in time management, coping with test anxiety, and stress reduction. The most important thing a student can do to prepare for the stress of college is develop skills for managing stress. This includes learning effective time-management skills, finding ways to build self-esteem, and establishing realistic goals. Many students have a life of all work and no play, which contributes to stress. Exercise and relaxation can be critical to staying in balance and allowing "the batteries to recharge." One important way to reduce stress is to avoid becoming overcommitted; this means learning to say "no." Students should establish a support network comprising friends, family, and counselors. This is especially true if they are at college away from home. On campus it is usually beneficial to cultivate new friends and join study groups or clubs to reduce the anonymity of a new or large school. Students who feel overwhelmed by stress, depression, or anxiety should ask for help from friends, family, professors, and counselors.

Injuries: common and preventable

Automobile collisions are the major cause of death in the 15–24-year-old group (followed by homicide, suicide, cancer, and AIDS). Use of alcohol and other drugs and nonuse of seat belts are major cofactors. Riders of motorcycles, mopeds, and bicycles are also at significant risk of injury. A study at the University of Wisconsin found that during the previous year a quarter of all student bicyclists had been injured while riding, with head injury being the greatest risk. Most injuries are preventable. With the goal of decreasing unintentional injuries and deaths by 20% by the year 2000, many U.S. states have passed mandatory seat belt- and helmet-use laws.

Injury due to trauma is among the top five reasons why students visit a health center. Most injuries are mild musculoskeletal strains or sprains. Proper initial diagnosis and treatment are important in reducing further injury.

Eating patterns and risks

During the years at college, young adults develop their own lifestyles. Dietary habits and physical activity patterns established at this time can help or hinder academic performance and have a significant impact on both current and future health. However, for a host of reasons, students often adopt lifestyle habits that are not the most conducive to health.

Financial factors, academic pressures, busy schedules, and peer pressure may lead students to make unhealthy food choices. Confronted with dormitory food, supplemented by candy bars on the run and late-night

Richard Pasley—Stock, Boston

Hungry students at Johns Hopkins University, Baltimore, Md., take a meal break. Campus food seems to be gaining a better reputation. Many college dining halls offer a wide variety of choices, including vegetarian selections and meals that are low in fat, low in calories, and "heart healthy." With a little effort, students can maintain a balanced diet and even avoid the proverbial freshman-10-pound weight gain.

pizza, many students gain weight, commonly known as the "freshman 10 pounds." Proper nutrition and physical activity can prevent weight gain and reduce the risk of developing diabetes, hypertension, heart disease, and possibly even cancer. Most campuses have nutrition services that students can take advantage of; some offer individual dietary counseling, and many have access to computerized programs for diet analysis. In recent years campus food services have begun offering "heart-healthy" meals with many low-calorie, low-fat, low-sodium selections, and most have been willing to post information about the nutritional content of the food they serve.

During their young adult years, women have different nutritional needs from those of men. They need nearly twice the amount of iron (18 mg/day, whereas men need only 10 mg/day) to prevent anemia. Anemia is a low red blood cell count, usually due to inadequate iron intake in the diet. An estimated 25–40% of women are affected by anemia during their reproductive years; as a result of menstrual blood losses, women are more prone to it than men. Symptoms include fatigue, poor concentration, and impaired athletic performance.

Women of college age need ample calcium in their diets on a daily basis in order to maximize bone mineral content and prevent osteoporosis (bone thinning and consequent fractures). The late teens and early 20s are a time of skeletal consolidation for women, so having adequate calcium intake is crucial. Many authorities now think that optimal calcium intake for young women may be as high as 1,600 mg a day.

Both iron and calcium can be obtained from foods. Foods high in iron include liver, red meats, egg yolk, green leafy vegetables such as spinach, dried fruits (raisins, apricots, prunes), dried beans and peas, blackstrap molasses, and enriched cereals. Calcium-rich foods include dairy products (milk, ice cream, yogurt, cheese, cottage cheese), canned sardines and salmon (with bones), spinach, broccoli, kale, collard and mustard greens, oysters, and oranges. Women who do not eat enough of these foods may need to take supplements.

While women have higher needs for certain nutrients than men, they usually take in too few calories to meet their daily needs. Society places great pressure on young women to be slim, and most college-age women are very weight conscious. Whether or not they are truly overweight, a majority of college women report they are dieting in an attempt to lose weight. Chronic dieting produces hunger, which often leads to splurging. This pattern, known as "yo-yo dieting," can become a way of life and lead to the development of eating disorders. Owing to the increased pressures from their sport to be unrealistically lean, athletic women are at especially high risk for eating disorders. Surveys have indicated that between 20%

and 60% of female college athletes regularly engage in harmful eating practices.

Disordered eating occurs along a continuum of severity. Common weight-control practices include chronic dieting, using diet pills, fasting, and binge eating followed by vomiting or taking diuretics and laxatives. Such practices can harm physical and mental health. The eating disorders of anorexia nervosa and bulimia nervosa have their peak prevalence among women aged 15 to 24. These chronic medical and psychological disorders are among the most common serious illnesses for women in this age group. Early recognition and treatment appear to offer the most hope for control and recovery. Most colleges are aware of the prevalence and serious nature of these problems, and many have peer support groups and professional counselors to help students overcome their dangerous and health-jeopardizing behaviors.

A time for healthy transition

College students are a unique population with their own unique health risks and health needs. For many students the college years are ones of change, experimentation, personal and social upheaval, and growth. The separation from parents is important to the personal development that occurs in late adolescence and young adulthood. This phase is one of new independence, experimentation, and development of individual and sexual identity. It is also one in which peer pressures are strong and risk taking is likely. Often the new independence is accompanied by a sense of invincibility or immortality. At this time in life, young people may dream their greatest dreams, but they may not realistically assess their limits. The risk-taking behavior that results can jeopardize health.

With proper preparation and motivation, students *can* adequately prepare for the health needs and challenges of the college environment. Adopting health-promoting lifestyle habits and taking preventive steps to avoid illness and injury are the best ways for students to ensure that they will stay healthy during these most important years of their lives. The changes and development that occur during these years are also critical to future health and success. As physician Richard Keeling, past president of the ACHA, has said, "Without the wholeness of health, students cannot achieve their goals."

FOR FURTHER INFORMATION:

American College Health Association, PO Box 28937, Baltimore MD 21240-8937; (410) 859-1500.

Otis, Carol L., and Goldingay, Roger. *Campus Health Guide.* New York: College Entrance Examination Board, 1989.

Rowh, Mark. *Coping with Stress in College.* New York: College Entrance Examination Board, 1989.

Hemophilia

by Ruth Andrea Seeler, M.D.

The mode of inheritance of the blood-clotting disorder known as hemophilia has been recognized since antiquity. The Talmud, the ancient compendium of Jewish tradition, states that if a woman's first two sons died from hemorrhage after circumcision, her third son—and male infants born to her sisters—should not undergo the ritual. A full appreciation of the specific pattern of transmission did not come until the 19th century, however. In 1803 a Philadelphia physician, John Henry Otto, recorded a "hemorrhagic disposition" in some but not all of the male descendants of a New Hampshire woman. Otto noted that the woman's daughters, although not affected by the condition, were nonetheless able to pass it on to their sons. That women could be carriers of the disorder was observed by another U.S. physician, John Hay, in 1813. It was not until the early 20th century that the hereditary mechanism in hemophilia was explained, as a result of the work of U.S. biologist Thomas Hunt Morgan.

The problem in hemophilia is that one of the coagulation factors—proteins that cause the blood to clot—is deficient in either amount or activity. The normal coagulation system relies on a complex, delicately balanced sequence of many proteins and their inhibitors. The system must react by quickly forming a blood clot whenever a blood vessel is injured, thereby preventing the person from literally bleeding to death. Yet it must not form clots too easily, as this would cause strokes and heart attacks. The clotting factors are known by number according to their order of discovery; some were later found to be duplicates, so not all of the numbers are used in the current system. The numbering of the factors is unrelated to their sequence of activation in the clotting process.

Origin, incidence, and severity

Many genes, located on several different chromosomes, control the synthesis of the numerous coagulation factors. However, the genes of particular clinical significance—those responsible for hemophilia A (factor VIII deficiency) and hemophilia B (factor IX deficiency)—are both located on the X, or female, chromosome.

In their normal complement of genetic material, women have 23 pairs of chromosomes, one pair of which consists of two X chromosomes (so named because they are roughly X-shaped). Men have 23 pairs, one of which consists of an X and a Y. If a woman has a defective gene for a particular clotting factor on one of her X chromosomes, she is likely to have a normal, functioning counterpart to that gene on her other X chromosome. She is a carrier of hemophilia but is not affected by the disease. On the other hand, every son she bears has a 50-50 chance of inheriting the X chromosome with the defective gene. And since in males the X chromosome is paired with a Y, a son who receives a defective gene on the X chromosome lacks a normal counterpart to carry out the function of the defective gene (*i.e.,* to produce clotting factor). He will, therefore, have hemophilia. The daughters of a woman who carries a gene for hemophilia have a 50-50 chance of being carriers themselves and, if they are, of passing the disease on to their male offspring. The sons of a man with hemophilia will not be affected, but all of his daughters will be carriers. (This is known as an X-linked recessive pattern of inheritance.)

Hemophilia A occurs in approximately one in every 10,000 live male births, while hemophilia B occurs in only one in 40,000 live male births. About one-third of hemophilia cases are due to a recent mutation rather than to an inherited defect. Therefore, hemophilia sometimes occurs in families that have no prior history of it. The incidence is the same in all races and all areas of the world.

Individuals who have little or no activity of a clotting factor are classified as having *severe* hemophilia;

457

when there is 2–5% of normal clotting activity, the disease is said to be *moderate;* a patient with *mild* hemophilia has clotting function that is 5–15% of normal. A majority of those with factor VIII deficiency have severe disease, whereas close to 50% of those with factor IX deficiency have mild cases. Only individuals with severe hemophilia suffer spontaneous, unprovoked bleeding into the joints (hemarthrosis). Males with mild and moderate cases of hemophilia bleed only after trauma, surgery, dental extraction, and other causes of internal or external injury.

Enormous progress is being made in the understanding of hemophilia at the molecular genetic level. This involves determining the sequence of the subunits that make up the normal gene and identifying those sequences associated with abnormal function of the gene. Scientists now know that no single genetic defect is responsible for either hemophilia A or hemophilia B, and the gene sequence associated with disease may vary from family to family. Once the specific defect of the factor VIII gene is known for a particular family with a history of hemophilia A, it is possible to test all females in the family to determine whether they are carriers. Also, it is possible to test an unborn child to determine its sex and, if the fetus is a male, to see if it has inherited the defect in question. However, as noted above, in about 33% of patients with hemophilia, the disease is a result of a recent mutation, and there is no family history to suggest a need for genetic testing.

Treatment: current practice, future prospects

While effective therapy for bleeding episodes is available in the form of coagulation factor replacement, it must be administered every time there is an injury. For a child with severe hemophilia, this could mean one or two infusions a week—or between 50 and 100 a year. In those with mild or moderate disease, the number of infusions averages one or two a month.

In order to free patients from the need for repeated infusions, scientists have long sought a way to enable the hemophiliac's body to make its own clotting factor. One method currently being explored is so-called gene therapy—*i.e.,* insertion of a normal gene for clotting factor into the cells of the hemophiliac. Only a few years ago such treatment seemed no more than a dream. Today it is a top-priority goal of the National Hemophilia Foundation to develop a successful gene therapy by the year 2000.

The major biotechnical problems are finding the best way to insert the normal gene into the DNA of the cells of an affected individual and then figuring out how to ensure that the new gene will function. In order to be effective, the gene must be inserted into the appropriate body cells. In the case of factor VIII hemophilia, the cells in question are those lining the blood vessel system; in factor IX disease, the target

would be liver cells. The gene for factor IX is approximately 10 times smaller than that for factor VIII and therefore may be the first one chosen for human gene therapy, even though there are fewer severe factor IX than factor VIII hemophiliacs.

Contrary to one of the persistent myths about the disease, hemophiliacs do not bleed any faster than other people. Rather, because their blood clots at a slower rate, they tend to bleed for a longer time. The bleeding ceases only when so much blood has accumulated in the tissues that pressure from the tissue swelling causes the blood vessel to collapse. As mentioned above, hemophiliacs who have severe disease are prone to spontaneous hemarthroses. With repeated episodes of bleeding into a joint, the iron in the red blood cells causes a severe irritation and proliferation of the joint lining. Repeated hemarthroses eventually result in severe arthritis. The factors that determine the extent of joint destruction are the number of hemarthroses and the amount of blood that accumulates in the joint.

Coagulation factor concentrates, which first became available in the late 1970s, have made possible prompt, efficient therapy for bleeding episodes and offer the possibility for young hemophiliacs to reach adulthood without incurring joint destruction. The key to preventing permanent damage is rapid recognition of a joint bleed before there is obvious pain, noticeable tissue swelling, and the consequent decreased motion of the joint. Consideration is now being given to recommending prophylactic infusion of clotting factor three times a week, beginning in infancy, for those with severe disease to prevent joint damage.

The availability of clotting factor concentrates has, in fact, revolutionized hemophilia care by putting therapy directly into the hands of the patient or his family. The concentrate comes in the form of a white powder that is available in varying potencies to accommodate patients of different height and weight. Required dosage varies for different kinds of injuries. At the first sign of a bleed, the patient or parent reconstitutes the factor with sterile water and infuses it into a vein.

Most parents master the infusion technique by the time an affected youngster is four or five years old, and boys learn to self-infuse by the time they reach age seven or eight. Because the powdered factor is stable and easy to transport, families may travel freely and enjoy vacations without having to worry, as they once did, about rushing to the emergency room in a strange city for a blood transfusion or being unable to find a doctor who has experience in treating hemophilia.

Today factor preparations in the United States are manufactured so as to be free of HIV and hepatitis C virus. U.S. children with hemophilia who were born after 1985 have not been exposed to HIV through treatment with clotting factor. When concentrates are

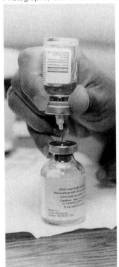
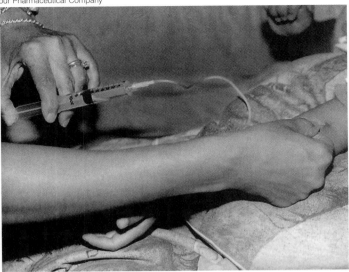

The availability of clotting factor concentrate makes it possible for hemophilia patients and their families to treat bleeding episodes immediately and at home. First, sterile water is added to the powdered concentrate (far left). The reconstituted factor is drawn into a syringe and then slowly infused into a vein in the patient's arm (left).

manufactured, plasma from many thousands of persons goes into each batch of factor concentrate. In the late 1970s and early 1980s, however, no tests existed to screen donor blood for HIV and hepatitis C. Thus, between 1979 and 1982, the vast majority of hemophiliacs—perhaps up to 90%—who received concentrate were exposed to HIV. The tragic consequences are now obvious in the large numbers of hemophiliacs who became infected with HIV; moreover, some of these men transmitted the virus to their wives, and some children were then infected in utero. As a result of this earlier tragedy, AIDS is currently the leading cause of death in people with hemophilia.

It was not until after the AIDS virus was isolated in the mid-1980s that it was found to be exquisitely heat sensitive, and by early 1985 all factor concentrates were being routinely subjected to heat treatment (which effectively killed HIV but did not eliminate the then-unidentified hepatitis C virus). Tragically, those hemophiliacs who were coinfected with HIV and hepatitis C died from liver failure along with complications of HIV infection.

In 1990 Congress passed the Ryan White Act to help hemophilia treatment centers provide care to hemophiliac AIDS patients and their families. The legislation was named for an Indiana teenager who acquired AIDS from contaminated clotting factor and died in 1990 at the age of 18. After his diagnosis, White's family was forced to leave their hometown because of prejudice about AIDS. White helped educate people about the nature of AIDS and, more important, that the disease could not be transmitted through casual social contact with an infected person.

Living with hemophilia: the challenges

Although hemophilia exists from the moment sperm and egg unite, parents are often unaware that a new-

born has a bleeding disorder. The first symptoms may be puzzling, spontaneous bruises on the baby's arms, trunk, and thighs or mouth bleeds related to teething. As the infant becomes a toddler and starts to walk and fall, hemarthroses begin to occur. The frequency of joint bleeds increases as the youngster grows and becomes increasingly active. The frequency decreases when he becomes old enough to take care to avoid minor injuries—usually not until adulthood. Even then, however, spontaneous hemarthroses continue to occur.

Despite these ever present risks, this generation of hemophiliacs can look forward to happy, productive lives. They should be able to grow to adulthood without fear of developing chronic, disabling arthritis. Sports participation is important for most males, and hemophiliacs are no different. While it would be unrealistic for them to expect to be football players or to engage in other contact sports (karate, boxing), they should be able to run, play, ride a bike, cross-country ski, and do the vast majority of things that boys and young men do.

Some young boys are very coordinated and athletic, while others have little or no sports ability. Swimming is an excellent activity for youngsters with hemophilia. Older boys often do well with weight training; building and maintaining excellent musculature can help protect the joints from injury. In school, boys with hemophilia can participate in soccer, softball, tag football, and other team sports. In the teen years most are able to play tennis, volleyball, and racquetball (with protective goggles). Basketball may be safe in high school as a casual form of recreation but is not a good idea at the varsity level, where it can involve rough contact. Some physicians allow their well-coordinated patients to play baseball but recommend that they play the outfield, where they are less likely than infielders to collide with base runners. Some hemophiliacs infuse clotting factor on a prophylactic basis and become adept at the potentially dangerous sport of downhill skiing.

Owing to stunning advances in biotechnology, there are now devices that can deliver coagulation factor concentrate on a continuous basis. These are small pumps, worn on the belt, that infuse a constant amount of factor all day long, or at least during the 12 or so hours a day that a person is active. Continuous infusion of factor may become commonplace within the next five years.

The coagulation factor molecules are too large to be injected subcutaneously (under the skin) or intramuscularly, as is the practice for insulin or antibiotics. Coagulation factor must therefore be injected directly into the patient's bloodstream. The continuous-infusion pump requires an implanted venous access device; *i.e.,* an indwelling catheter (tube) from one of the veins to the surface of the body.

Youngsters with hemophilia should receive all routine childhood immunizations. When these children develop an infection, however, they should be given oral antibiotics rather than intramuscular antibiotic shots. An injection that goes deep into muscle will cause a muscle bleed unless coagulation factor replacement is also administered.

Parents need to be cautioned that anytime a child with hemophilia sustains a blow to the head or the abdomen, a wait-and-see approach should *not* be taken. Rather, the youngster should immediately be given a preventive infusion of clotting factor. The most common bleeding-related cause of death in hemophiliacs is bleeding into the head following a relatively minor injury. Simple scrapes and bruises do not require coagulation factor replacement. Because of its anticoagulant property, aspirin should never be given to children—or, for that matter, taken by adults—with hemophilia.

Another problem for those with severe hemophilia is the development of an immune response to clotting factor. As explained above, patients with hemophilia A make an abnormal form of factor VIII. Depending upon how abnormal that protein is, the body may treat normal factor VIII as a foreign protein and make an antibody to destroy it. This is a natural immune response. For example, when a child is infected with the measles virus or is given measles vaccine, the body recognizes the virus or vaccine as a foreign protein and makes an antibody against it, thus preventing subsequent measles infection. However, if a hemophiliac makes an antibody against factor VIII, this antibody, called an inhibitor, essentially renders normal factor VIII infusions useless.

Therapy for patients with inhibitors is a daunting challenge, but significant progress has been made in the past 10–15 years. When the amount of the inhibitor is low, it may be overcome by large doses of clotting factor, now possible with the existence of pure concentrates. Another approach, called immune tolerance induction, is to give small amounts of factor every day to train the immune system to become tolerant of it. Other approaches include infusing large amounts of concentrates that intervene in the coagulation process at some point other than the one at which the defective factor works.

Fortunately, there are now specialized hemophilia centers that are experienced in the management of these difficult patients. It is currently estimated that about 10% of severe hemophiliacs will develop inhibitors. (Patients with mild or moderate hemophilia rarely develop inhibitors because their coagulation factor, although not normal, differs less from normal factor VIII and IX than the coagulation factor of those with severe disease.) Hemophilia centers routinely test patients with severe hemophilia for inhibitors when they are seen for checkups. However, many seek help at a center precisely because regular factor replacement therapy is no longer effective in stopping a bleeding episode.

Support and resources

As is the case with many other chronic diseases, hemophilia support groups can be instrumental in helping patients and families adjust and cope. Support groups are excellent sources of information, and they help members stay current with advances in treatment. All families with hemophilia should belong to a local chapter of the National Hemophilia Foundation. (The address of the national headquarters is: Soho Building, 110 Greene Street, Suite 303, New York NY 10012; phone: 212-219-8180.) The foundation can recommend resources and advise families on all aspects of care and treatment. It also publishes a list of more than 20 camps in the U.S. for hemophiliacs.

A particularly useful book written by an experienced parent expressly for others facing the same situation is *Raising a Child with Hemophilia: A Practical Guide for Parents* by Laureen A. Kelley, which is available from: Armour Pharmaceutical Co., Educational Publications, 920A Harvest Drive, Blue Bell PA 19422.

FOR FURTHER INFORMATION:
The Hemophilia Handbook. The Georgia Chapter of the National Hemophilia Foundation. 30 Perimeter Center East, Suite 100, Atlanta GA 30346.
AIDS and Hemophilia: What Everyone Needs to Know/ El SIDA y la hemofilia: Lo que todos necesitamos saber. Northern California Hemophilia Foundation; reprinted by the National Hemophilia Foundation, 1989.
Jones, Peter. *Living with Hemophilia,* 3rd ed. New York: Oxford University Press, 1991.

PosturePerfect

by Mary Pullig Schatz, M.D.

Good posture is an asset. It is energy-efficient, allows optimum circulation of blood to and from the vital organs, and reduces muscle strain. The body language of good posture conveys self-confidence, competence, and control: someone with good posture is more likely than someone who slouches to make a first impression of being effective, efficient, and credible. Consider the connotations of such descriptions as "He is a fine, upstanding man" and "She has regal bearing."

The subject of posture makes many people feel uncomfortable, however, as they look at themselves and see much room for improvement. In fact, at the very mention of "posture," most people immediately sit up straighter! But how long does it take before they lapse back into their usual round-shouldered slump?

Many people have not-so-fond memories of how, during their adolescent years, they were constantly badgered by parents and teachers about slouching. As young adults, however, they probably forgot all those admonitions. Years later if they think about their posture at all, they wonder why it has deteriorated—and why they are not as tall as they used to be.

Unfortunately, even if one heeds the exhortations of well-meaning relatives and teachers to stand up straight and "keep your shoulders back," good posture is not assured. Some people take that advice too literally, adopting a rigid, upright position, raising their shoulders toward their ears—a practice that can lead to chronic neck pain in later years. By adulthood, tissues and self-image have been molded by years of poor posture, and improvement does not happen overnight. Still, people do not have to simply accept poor posture. Patience, persistence, attention to alignment, and some simple corrective exercises can make a significant difference.

Improvement in posture begins with awareness—people striving for better posture would do well to become posture observers. They should be aware of

their own posture at various times of day and in various situations and note how their emotions influence their stance. They should also pay attention to how other people carry themselves, and while noticing others' posture, they will be reminded of their own determination to stand straighter.

The stress factor

In the most common type of poor posture, the upper back is abnormally rounded and the head is held forward. The muscular imbalances associated with this "head forward" stance include weak, overstretched, and overworked muscles in the upper back, overworked neck muscles, and shortened muscles in the upper front chest. This kind of posture can lead to neck and back strain and can even cause tension headaches.

Stress serves to exaggerate postural strain by increasing muscle tension. Muscles that are already irritated, tense, or overworked by poor posture are most vulnerable. These overtaxed muscles send additional signals of stress throughout the body, further increasing overall muscle tension. Using gentle yoga stretches for postural reeducation can help break this self-perpetuating stress cycle. The brain perceives a slow, gentle stretching of a muscle as the opposite of muscle tension. Whereas a tense muscle sends emergency signals to the entire body, the natural biofeedback from yoga stretches and improved posture signals a state of well-being.

Straight talk about curves

Before attempting to correct poor posture, it is helpful to understand a bit about the anatomy of the spine, as it is the configuration of the spine and its muscles that constitutes so-called posture. Although folk wisdom dictates that one should have a "straight" back, what appears straight in good posture is actually a properly curved spine. The natural curves of

461

the spine—cervical (neck), thoracic (upper back), and lumbar (lower back)—are vitally important, allowing it to act as a shock absorber during the jolts the body receives when walking, running, or riding in a moving vehicle. These normal curves lie in the front-to-back plane of the body. Too much or too little curve in any of these areas can lead to dysfunction, pain, and even disease. When the curves are right, the opposite is true: mobility, comfort, and health—and, of course, the visible result of beautiful posture.

Every joint in the body is controlled by at least two sets of muscles: the flexors, which bend a joint, and the extensors, which straighten it. In addition, some joints (including those of the spine) have rotator muscles that twist, turn, or rotate the bones. Good posture can exist only when the flexors, extensors, and rotators are in proper balance, allowing each joint to function efficiently. An intelligent program of stretching and strengthening can restore balance to the muscles and will gradually bring about positive postural changes.

The normal spine

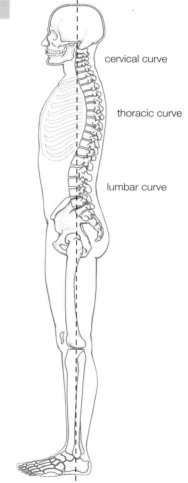

cervical curve

thoracic curve

lumbar curve

(Above and opposite page) Illustrations copyright © J. William Myers.
Adapted with permission from *Back Care Basics: A Doctor's Gentle Yoga Program for Back and Neck Pain Relief.* Copyright © 1992 by Mary Pullig Schatz, M.D. Rodmell Press, Berkeley, California

However, simply embarking on an exercise routine to correct stooped shoulders or strengthen the back muscles is not enough to bring about a permanent improvement in posture. It is also essential that the person with poor posture change his or her self-image, because feelings about the self are translated into the way people carry themselves. If people hold on to mental pictures of themselves as individuals who habitually slouch or slump, corrective exercises will have only limited value.

Posture and daily activities

Every activity—sleeping, working, driving, eating, walking, watching TV—has an effect on posture and can either prolong the status quo or contribute to the goal of improved posture. To be most effective, therefore, postural improvement work must not be confined to exercise time but should be incorporated into a new way of life. If poor posture is maintained while one is at work, commuting, sleeping, and watching television, 30 minutes of therapeutic exercise will not make up for all those hours of destructive movement patterns.

One should move consciously and deliberately, mindful of how the posture is being affected. Walking "tall" is important; leaning forward or walking in a stooped position is, of course, to be avoided. Also to be avoided is habitually crossing the arms in front of the chest. An alternative is to stand with them crossed behind the back, each hand holding the opposite elbow, or, if shoulder flexibility is limited, to gently grasp the opposite forearm or hand.

Desk jobs

Sitting at a desk all day can be a real postural challenge; a little time spent arranging one's work space to facilitate good posture is well worth the effort. A variety of chairs and many other aids—back cushions, document holders—are available to help people achieve a correct, comfortable sitting posture.

Chairs are very important. A so-called kneeling chair, where the seat is slanted forward and the body weight is on the posterior bones at the bottom of the pelvis (the ischial tuberosities, or so-called sitting bones) and the shins, is fine for keeping the spine erect in tasks that require leaning forward slightly (such as sewing or writing) or maintaining an erect posture (such as using a microscope) but not for tasks in which it is usual to lean back slightly (such as typing or computer work). A chair with an adjustable back and an adjustable lumbar support would be more suitable for the latter activities. The seat of the desk chair should be at a height that allows the feet to rest flat on the floor, with the knees and hips bent at a 90° angle. The lumbar support should be adjusted specifically for the individual's back.

Work surfaces and materials should be arranged at a proper height. Computer screens should be at eye level so that the head does not have to be held in an awkward position, and the keyboard should be placed low enough for the hands to rest comfortably on the keys without making it necessary to lift the shoulders. A stand-up desk or an elevated work surface, such as the top of a file cabinet, might be a suitable alternative to sitting or at least provide occasional relief to overworked muscles and joints.

A common practice of office workers is to prop the telephone receiver between the shoulder and the ear to free the hands. This causes muscle strain, which one can relieve by alternating ears or, better yet, if the job requires a lot of telephoning, using a headset or speaker phone.

Practice makes perfect

The following pointers, activities, and exercises will enable people to improve their posture and to maintain that improvement.

Evaluating alignment. A friend can help one to check body alignment. To do this a plumb bob or a small weight is tied to one end of a string, and the other end is attached to the ceiling or the top of a door frame so that the string hangs straight with the weight suspended just above the floor.

To evaluate alignment from the side, stand so that the string is about 2.5 cm (one inch) in front of the center of the anklebone. When viewed from the side, the plumb line should appear to bisect the body, passing upward through the centers of the knee joint, hip joint, and shoulder to the opening of the ear. If the head and shoulders are in front of the line, one has the "head forward" stance—one of the most common posture problems. This posture is often reflected by an increase in the thoracic curve.

If the center of the knee joint is behind the line, the knees may be hyperextended (overstraightened). One should also use the line to see if the lower back curve appears normal, increased (swayback), or decreased (flat back).

When one stands with the back to the plumb line, the string again should appear to bisect the body, passing through the center of the back of the head, the center of each vertebra, the cleft of the buttocks, and points midway between the knees and midway between the heels. Minor variations are insignificant. If an area of misalignment is painful, however, then it is probably significant and may be related to scoliosis, an abnormal sideways bend in the spine.

Posture check. Whenever possible, a few seconds should be devoted to a quick posture check. Take a long, slow deep breath, drawing the air into the abdomen and allowing the lungs to expand fully; try consciously to breathe into and expand the upper back. As the air is gently and smoothly exhaled, the posture can be checked and adjusted. The body should become more erect—though the chin should

not be lifted and the shoulders should be relaxed. Any number of daily activities can serve as a cue for a posture check—for example, when picking up the telephone, stopping at a stoplight, stepping into an elevator, or checking the time.

Walking for good posture and health. Walking helps strengthen the muscle groups that stabilize and protect the spine. It also offers an excellent cardiovascular workout. Because it is a low-impact aerobic activity, walking is an ideal exercise for people with posture problems; skeletal misalignments can be greatly magnified by the momentum generated in high-impact activities such as jogging and aerobic dancing.

A healthy walking posture encourages the natural spinal curves. The spine should not be held rigid but should be allowed to move sinuously from front to back in response to the movements of the legs. Viewed from the side, a walker's ear, shoulder, and hip should be in alignment. In contrast to a forward-leaning posture or one where the head juts out in front of the shoulders, this alignment allows the weight of

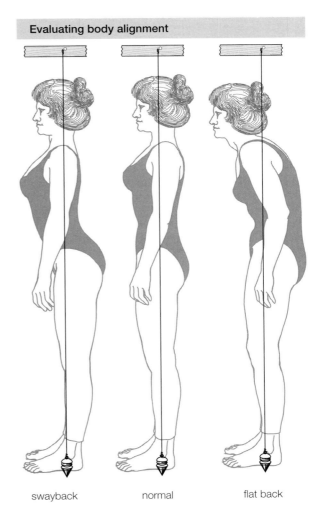

Evaluating body alignment

swayback   normal   flat back

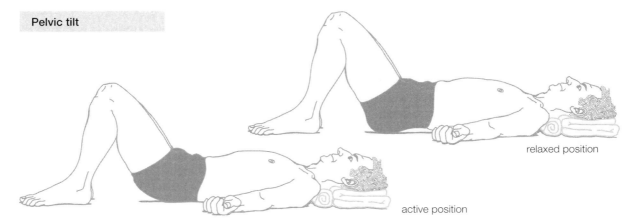

relaxed position

active position

the body to be properly balanced and avoids over-working the back muscles. Imagining that the top of the head is moving up rather than forward and imagining being suspended by a helium balloon will help a person assume more natural spinal curves and will lessen the tendency to lead with the chin. Walking with a bag of beans on the top of the head, letting the head push up against the weight as if it were a crown, is a useful exercise.

The muscles of the shoulders and upper back should be as relaxed as possible, but the shoulders should not be allowed to round forward. Nor should the shoulders be pulled rigidly back. The breastbone should be lightly lifted, but the lumbar spine should not be overarched.

Standing tall. A useful exercise is to stand erect with bare feet parallel to each other, 8–12 cm (about 3–5 in) apart, directly under the hips. Become aware of the weight distribution on the bottoms of the feet. Is there more weight on one foot than the other? Is there more weight on the heel or the ball of each foot? The weight should be equal on the two feet and distributed evenly between the heels and the balls of the feet.

Activating the legs. In order to gain the leg and buttock strength and stability needed to support good posture, one needs to learn how to activate the muscles above and below the knee. To do this, stand with the feet parallel. Keeping the upper body erect, bend the knees so that they move out directly over the feet. The knees should not come together or splay apart, nor should the lumbar curve increase.

Inhale; then exhale and slowly begin to straighten the legs by pushing the heels into the floor while straightening the knees. Again, do not let the knees come together or separate but keep them moving parallel to each other; imagine that someone is pressing into the backs of the knees trying to keep them from straightening. The knees should not be hyper-extended; be sure to stop the backward motion of the knee joint at a normal straight-leg position. If possible, one should have a friend describe the exact position

of the knees, or one can check it in a mirror. People who habitually hyperextend their knees may feel as though their knees are bent when they assume a normal straight-leg position.

When doing this exercise one should be aware of the feeling of the muscles working in the calves and thighs as the legs are straightened. Once the straight-leg position has been attained, maintain the activity of the muscles—without actually moving the legs—for 30 to 60 seconds. During this time one should concentrate on one's balance and alignment, focusing on distributing the weight evenly on the bottoms of the feet and attempting to lengthen the body upward from a point in the center of the top of the head—but without raising the chin. Note that each leg is active and straight but the knees are not locked. Feel the pull of gravity on the feet, and visualize the body's connection to the Earth; imagine the body as a mountain with a broad solid base or a tall tree with deep roots and a crown of leafy branches reaching toward sunlight. Throughout this exercise one should breathe smoothly and easily: with each inhalation there is a sense of the mountain or tree growing taller; with each exhalation one enjoys his or her new height.

Sitting tall. Choose a sturdy chair with a firm, flat seat. The height of the chair should be such that when the buttocks are resting on the forward third of the seat, the thighs can be parallel to the floor and the knees exactly over the ankles. If the seat is so high that the feet cannot touch the floor, some books or a wooden block can be placed under the feet. If the seat is so low that the knees are higher than the hip joints, a folded blanket can be put on the seat. Without these adjustments, the sitting position will create stress in the lower back and make good posture difficult. Practicing this pose with a beanbag on the top of the head can help one to lengthen the spine upward without tilting the chin.

Concentrate on sitting on the "sitting bones," not the tailbone or sacrum. Make sure that the weight of the body remains equally distributed between the right and left sides. To avoid slumping, allow the breast-bone to gently lift, but do not overarch the lower back. It may prove helpful to imagine that roots extend from the sitting bones down toward the center of the Earth, while the top of the head reaches for the sky. With each inhalation and exhalation, feel lightness in the spine as it elongates upward from its steady base. Keep the chin level, neither elevated nor lowered, and relax the neck and shoulder muscles, with the shoulders dropping away from the ears. Sit in this position, concentrating on the breathing and alignment, for one to three minutes at least once a day. Better yet, do it as often as possible during the course of the day.

Kneeling backbend

passive variation

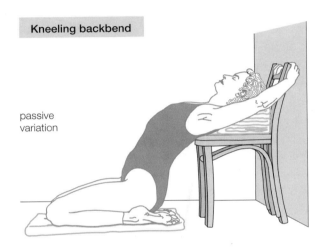

active variation

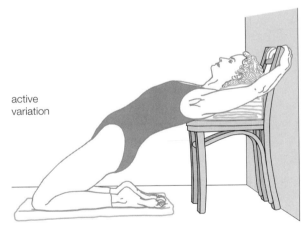

resting position

(Opposite page and above) Adapted with permission from *Back Care Basics: A Doctor's Gentle Yoga Program for Back and Neck Pain Relief.* Copyright © 1992 by Mary Pullig Schatz, M.D., Rodmell Press, Berkeley, California

Pelvic tilt. Lie on the back with the knees bent and the feet parallel on the floor. Place a folded towel behind the head and a rolled-up towel behind the neck. Inhale deeply, letting the abdomen expand. While exhaling, press the lower back into the floor by pulling in the navel and contracting the abdominal muscles. Inhale as before. Exhale again and drop the navel and lower back toward the floor, at the same time pressing the shoulders, elbows, and head into the floor without allowing the shoulders to round forward. Repeat slowly at least 10 times, and work toward being able to hold the active position for 10 to 20 seconds.

Kneeling backbend. Place a sturdy chair so that its back is against a wall, and put a neatly folded blanket on the seat with enough hanging over the front edge to pad it. Place two or three folded blankets in a stack on the rear of the seat. With the knees hip-width apart and cushioned by a blanket, kneel in front of the chair facing away from it. There are passive and active variations of this exercise. To do the former, lean back so that the edge of the chair seat presses just below the shoulder blades. Let the head rest on the blankets. (If necessary, fold the blankets to make them higher.) Grasp the back of the chair so that the elbows point to either side. If the knees tend to separate, fasten a belt around the upper thighs. Breathing quietly, hold the pose with the buttocks resting on the heels for 20 seconds to several minutes, giving the front chest muscles a chance to relax and lengthen. Then bend forward and rest the torso on the thighs and the forehead on the forearms for a few moments to release any tension in the back.

In the active variation, one lifts the hips while pressing the knees, shins, and feet into the floor. While holding the position, breathe naturally and quietly—do not hold the breath. Then rest again with the torso on the thighs and the forehead on the forearms.

FOR FURTHER INFORMATION:
Kendall, H.O., Kendall, F.P., and Boynton, D.A. *Posture and Pain.* Malabar, Fla.: Robert E. Kreiger Publishing Co., 1985.
Schatz, Mary Pullig, M.D. *Back Care Basics: A Doctor's Gentle Yoga Program for Back and Neck Pain Relief.* Berkeley, Calif.: Rodmell Press, 1992; telephone 1-800-841-3123.

Back Designs (1045 Ashby Avenue, Berkeley CA 94710; telephone 510-849-1923) is a good source for furniture and aids to help improve posture and protect the back.

Rockport Walking Institute (220 Donald Lynch Boulevard, Marlboro MA 01752; telephone 1-800-343-9255) can provide information on walking physiology, shoes, walking as a hobby, walking vacations, and a walking magazine.

FROM THE PAGES OF THE 1994
ENCYCLOPÆDIA
BRITANNICA

Medical Update from the 1994 Encyclopædia Britannica

The editors of the *Medical and Health Annual* have included this section in order to share with readers articles that have been either revised or rewritten by distinguished scholars for the most recent printing of *Encyclopædia Britannica.* The following is a newly revised portion of the article The Development of Human BEHAVIOUR, which offers an in-depth look at a complex and fascinating topic in the field of human psychology. This is in keeping with the *Annual*'s goal of providing the broadest possible picture of "health." (Like all *Encyclopædia Britannica* articles, this selection uses British spellings.)

The Development of Human Behaviour

Human beings, like other animal species, have a typical life course that consists of successive phases of growth, each of which is characterized by a distinct set of physical, physiological, and behavioral features. These phases are prenatal life, infancy, childhood, adolescence, and adulthood (including old age). Human development, or developmental psychology, is a field of study that attempts to describe and explain the changes in human cognitive, emotional, and behavioral capabilities and functioning over the entire life span, from the fetus to old age.

Most scientific research on human development has concentrated on the period from birth through early adolescence, owing to both the rapidity and magnitude of the psychological changes observed during those phases and to the fact that they culminate in the optimum mental functioning of early adulthood. A primary motivation of many investigators in the field has been to determine how the culminating mental abilities of adulthood were reached during the preceding phases. This essay will concentrate, therefore, on human development during the first 12 years of life.

Theories of development

The systematic study of children is less than 200 years old, and 90 percent of its research has been published since the mid-1940s. Basic philosophical differences over the fundamental nature of children and their growth have occupied psychologists during the 20th century. The most important of such controversies concerned the relative importance of genetic endowment and environment, or "nature" and "nurture," in determining development during infancy and childhood. Most researchers now recognize, however, that it is the interaction of inborn biological factors with external factors, rather than the mutually exclusive action or predominance of one or the other force, that guides and influences human development. The advances in cognition, emotion, and behaviour that normally occur at certain points in the life span require both maturation (*i.e.,* genetically driven biological changes in the central nervous system) and events, experiences, and influences in the physical and social environment. Generally, maturation by itself cannot cause a psychological function to emerge; it does, however, permit such a function to occur and sets limits on its earliest time of appearance.

Three theories of human development have been dominant during the 20th century, each addressing different aspects of psychological growth. In retrospect, these and other theories seem to have been neither logically rigorous nor able to account for both intellectual and emotional growth within the same framework. Research in the field has thus tended to be descriptive, since developmental psychology lacks a tight net of interlocking theoretical propositions that reliably permit satisfying explanations.

Psychoanalytic theories. Sigmund Freud's psychoanalytic theories were influenced by Charles Darwin's theory of evolution and by the physical concept of energy as applied to the central nervous system. Freud's most basic hypothesis was that each child is born with a source of basic psychological energy called libido. Further, each child's libido becomes successively focused on various parts of the body (in addition to people and objects) in the course of his emotional development. During the first postnatal year, libido is initially focused on the mouth and its activities; nursing enables the infant to derive gratification through a pleasurable reduction of tension in the oral region. Freud called this the oral stage of development. During the second year, the source of excitation is said to shift to the anal area, and the start of toilet training leads the child to invest libido in the anal functions. Freud called this period of development the anal stage. During the period from three through six years, the child's attention is attracted to sensations from the genitals, and Freud called this stage the phallic stage. The half dozen years before puberty are called the latency stage. During the final and so-called genital stage of development, mature gratification is sought in a heterosexual love relationship with another. Freud believed that adult emotional problems result from either deprivation or excessive gratification during the oral, anal, or phallic stages. A child with libido fixated at one of these stages would in adulthood show specific neurotic symptoms, such as anxiety.

Freud devised an influential theory of personality structure. According to him, a wholly unconscious mental structure called the id contains a person's inborn, inherited drives and instinctual forces and is closely identified with his basic psychological energy (libido). During infancy and childhood, the ego, which is the reality-oriented portion of the personality, develops to balance and complement the id. The ego utilizes a variety of conscious and unconscious mental processes to try to satisfy id instincts while also trying to maintain the individual comfortably in relation to the environment. Although id impulses are constantly directed toward obtaining immediate gratification of one's major instinctual drives (sex, affection, aggression, self-preservation), the ego functions to set limits on this process. In Freud's language, as the child grows, the reality principle gradually begins to control the pleasure principle; the child learns that the environment does not always permit immediate gratification. Child development, according to Freud, is thus primarily concerned with the emergence of the functions of the ego, which is responsible for channeling the discharge of fundamental drives and for controlling intellectual and perceptual functions in the process of negotiating realistically with the outside world.

Id and ego

Although Freud made great contributions to psychological theory—particularly in his concept of unconscious urges and motivations—his elegant concepts cannot be verified through scientific experimentation and empirical observation. But his concentration on emotional development in early childhood influenced even those schools of thought that rejected his theories. The belief that personality is affected by both biological and psychosocial forces operating principally within the family, with the major foundations being laid early in life, continues to prove fruitful in research on infant and child development.

Freud's emphasis on biological and psychosexual motives in personality development was modified by the German-born American psychoanalyst Erik Erikson to include psychosocial and social factors. Erikson viewed emotional development over the life span as a sequence of stages during which there occur important inner conflicts whose successful resolution depends on both the child himself and his environment. These conflicts can be thought of as interactions between instinctual drives and motives on the one hand and social and other external factors on the other. Erikson evolved eight stages of development, the first four of which are (1) infancy: trust versus mistrust, (2) early childhood: autonomy versus shame and doubt, (3) preschool: initiative versus guilt, and (4) school age: industry versus inferiority. Conflicts at any one stage must be resolved if personality problems are to be avoided.

Erikson's theory

Piaget's theory. The Swiss psychologist Jean Piaget took the intellectual functioning of adults as the central phenomenon to be explained and wanted to know how an adult acquired the ability to think logically and to draw valid conclusions about the world from evidence. Piaget's theory rests on the fundamental notion that the child develops through stages until he arrives at a stage of thinking that resembles that of an adult. The four stages given by Piaget are (1) the sensorimotor stage from birth to 2 years, (2) the preoperational stage from 2 to 7 years, (3) the concrete-operational stage from 7 to 12 years, and (4) the stage of formal operations that characterizes the adolescent and the adult. One of Piaget's fundamental assumptions is that early intellectual growth arises primarily out of the child's interactions with objects in the environment. For example, Piaget believed that as a two-year-old child repeatedly builds and knocks down a tower of blocks, he is learning that the arrangement of objects in the world can be reversed. According to Piaget, children organize and adapt their experiences with objects into increasingly sophisticated cognitive models that enable them to deal with future situations in more effective ways. The older child, for instance, who has learned the concept of reversibility, will be able to execute an intelligent and logical search for a missing object, retracing his steps, for example, in order to determine where he may have dropped a set of keys. As children pass through successive stages of cognitive development, their knowledge of the world assumes different forms, with each stage building on the models and concepts acquired in the preceding stage. Adolescents in the final developmental stage, that of formal operations, are able to think in a rational and systematic manner about hypothetical problems that are not necessarily in accord with their experience. Piaget's theory is treated in greater detail below in the sections on cognitive development in infancy and childhood.

Learning theory. A more distinctively American theoretical view focuses primarily on the child's actions, rather than on his emotions or thinking. This point of view, called learning theory, is concerned with identifying those mechanisms that can be offered to explain differences in behaviour, motives, and values among children. Its major principles stress the effects of reward and punishment (administered by parents, teachers, and peers) on the child's tendency to adopt the behaviour and values of others. Learning theory is thus directed to the overt actions of the child, rather than to inner psychological states or mechanisms.

Learning is any relatively permanent change in behaviour that results from past experience. There are two generally recognized learning processes: classical and instrumental conditioning, both of which use associations, or learned relations between events or stimuli, to create or shape behavioural responses. In classical conditioning, a close temporal relation is maintained between pairs of stimuli in order to create an association between the two. If, for example, an infant hears a tone and one second later receives some sweetened water in his mouth, the infant will make sucking movements to the sweet taste. After a dozen repetitions of this sequence of the tone followed by the sweet water, the infant associates the sounding of the tone with the receipt of the sweetened water and will, on subsequent repetitions, make sucking movements to the tone even though no sugar water is delivered.

Classical and instrumental conditioning

Instrumental, or operant, conditioning involves creating a relationship between a response and a stimulus. If the experiment described above is changed so that after the tone is heard, the infant is required to turn his head to the right in order to receive the sweetened water, the infant will learn to turn his head when the tone sounds. The infant learns a relation between the response of turning his head and the subsequent receipt of the sweet taste. This set of relations is referred to as instrumental conditioning because the child must do something in order to receive the reward; the latter, in turn, makes the infant's head-turning response more likely in future occurrences of the situation. Rewards, such as praise and approval from parents, act as positive reinforcers of specific learned behaviours, while punishments act as negative reinforcers and make the future performance of such behaviours less likely to occur. Scientists who believe in the importance of these principles use them to explain the changing behaviour of children over the course of development.

Development in infancy

Conception occurs when the sperm from the male penetrates the cell wall of an egg from the female. Human development during the 38 weeks from conception to birth is divided into three phases. The first, the germinal period, lasts from the moment of conception until the time the fertilized egg is implanted in the wall of the uterus, a process that typically takes 10 to 14 days. A second phase, lasting from the second to the eighth week after conception, is called the embryonic period and is characterized by differentiation of the major organs. The last phase, from the eighth week until delivery, is called the fetal period and is characterized by dramatic growth in the size of the organism.

Prenatal development is extremely rapid; by the 18th day the embryo has already taken some shape and has established a longitudinal axis. By the ninth week the embryo is about 2.5 centimetres (one inch) long; face, mouth, eyes, and ears have begun to take on well-defined form, and arms, legs, hands, feet, and even fingers and toes have appeared. The sex organs, along with muscle and cartilage, also have begun to form. The internal organs have a definite shape and assume some primitive function. The fetal period (from about the second month until birth) is characterized by increased growth of the organism and by the gradual assumption of physical functions. By the 20th week the mother can often feel the movements of the fetus, which is now about 20 centimetres long. By the 32nd week the normal fetus is capable of breathing, sucking, and swallowing, and by the 36th week it can show a response to light and sound waves. The head of the fetus is unusually large in relation to other parts of its body because its brain develops more rapidly than do other organs. The seventh month is generally regarded as the earliest age at which a newborn can survive without medical assistance.

THE NEWBORN INFANT

By definition, infancy is the period of life between birth and the acquisition of language approximately one to two years later. The average newborn infant weighs 3.4 kilograms (7.5 pounds) and is about 51 centimetres long; in general, boys are slightly larger and heavier than girls. (The period of the newborn covers the first five to seven days, which the infant normally spends recovering from the stresses of delivery.) During their first month, infants sleep for about 16–18 hours a day, with five or six sleep periods alternating with a like number of shorter episodes of wakefulness. The total amount of time spent sleeping decreases dramatically, however, to 9–12 hours a day by age two years, and, with the cessation of nocturnal feedings and morning and afternoon naps, sleep becomes concentrated in one long nocturnal period. Newborns spend as much time in active sleep (during which rapid eye movements occur) as in quiet sleep, but by the third month they spend twice as much time in quiet as in active sleep, and this trend continues (at a much slower rate) into adulthood.

Reflexes of the newborn		
	effective stimulus	description
Blink reflex	bright flash of light	infant closes eyelids tightly
Sucking reflex	put index finger into infant's mouth	infant begins to suck
Rooting reflex	tickle infant at corner of the mouth	infant turns head toward side of stimulation
Licking reflex	put sugar water on infant's tongue	infant licks lips
Pursing reflex	put sour-tasting drops on infant's tongue	infant purses lips and may blink
Grasp reflex	put finger or pencil against infant's palm	infant's fingers flex and enclose object
Babinski reflex	gently scratch side of infant's foot	infant bends big toe upward and spreads small toes
Stepping reflex	hold infant upright with feet on the floor and move him forward	infant extends legs as if walking
Moro reflex	produce sudden loud noise near infant's head	infant quickly extends arms and brings them together in the midline
Withdrawal reflex	prick sole of infant's foot with pin	infant flexes leg and withdraws from pin

Inherited reflexes

At birth the infant displays a set of inherited reflexes, some of which serve his very survival. An infant only two hours old typically will follow a moving light with his eyes and will blink or close them at the sudden appearance of a bright light or at a sharp, sudden sound nearby. The newborn infant will suck a nipple or almost any other object (*e.g.,* a finger) inserted into his mouth or touching his lips. He will also turn his head toward a touch on the corner of his mouth or on his cheek; this reflex helps him contact the nipple so he can nurse. He will grasp a finger or other object that is placed in his palm. Reflexes that involve sucking and turning toward stimuli are intended to maintain sustenance, while those involving eye-closing or muscle withdrawal are intended to ward off danger. Some reflexes involving the limbs or digits vanish after four months of age; one example is the Babinski reflex, in which the infant bends his big toe upward and spreads his small toes when the outer edge of the sole of his foot is stroked.

The newborn baby can turn his head and eyes toward and away from visual and auditory stimuli, signaling interest and alarm, respectively. Smiling during infancy changes its meaning over the first year. The smiles that newborns display during their first weeks constitute what is called reflex smiling and usually occur without reference to any external source or stimulus, including other people. By two months, however, infants smile most readily in response to the sound of human voices, and by the third or fourth month they smile easily at the sight of a human face, especially one talking to or smiling at the infant. This social smiling, as it is called, marks the beginning of the infant's emotional responses to other people.

COGNITIVE DEVELOPMENT

Perception.   Research shows the achievement of extraordinary perceptual sophistication over the first months of life. The fetus is already sensitive to stimulation of its skin, especially in the area around the mouth, by the eighth week of intrauterine development. Judging from their facial expressions when different substances are placed on their tongues, newborn infants apparently discriminate between bitter, salty, or sweet tastes; they have an innate preference for sweet tastes and even prefer a sucrose solution to milk. Newborns can also discriminate between different odours or smells; six-day-old infants can tell the smell of their mother's breast from that of another mother.

Much more is known, however, about infants' ability to see and hear than about their senses of touch, smell, or taste. During the first half-year of life outside the womb, there is rapid development of visual acuity, from 20/800 vision (in Snellen notation) among two-week-olds to 20/70 vision in five-month-olds to 20/20 vision at five years. Even newborn infants are sensitive to visual stimulation and attend selectively to certain visual patterns; they will track moving stimuli with their gaze and can discriminate among lights that vary in brightness. They show a noticeable predilection for the sight of the human face, and by the first or second month they are able to discriminate between different faces by attending to the internal features—eyes, nose, and mouth. By the third month, infants can identify their mothers by sight and can discriminate between some facial expressions. By the seventh month, they can recognize a particular person from different perspectives—for example, a full face versus a profile of that face. Infants can identify the same facial expression on the faces of different people and can distinguish male from female faces.

Visual abilities

Newborns can also hear and are sensitive to the location of a sound source as well as to differences in the frequency of the sound wave. They also discriminate between louder and softer sounds, as indicated by the startle reflex and by rises in heart rate. Newborns can also discriminate among sounds of higher or lower pitch. Continuous rather than intermittent sounds and low tones rather than high-pitched ones are apparently those most soothing to infants.

Even young infants show a striking sensitivity to the tones, rhythmic flow, and individual sounds that together make up human speech. A young infant can make subtle discriminations among phonemes, which are the basic sounds of language, and is able to tell the difference between "pa," "ga," and "ba." Furthermore, infants less than one year old can make discriminations between phonemes that some adults cannot because the particular discrimination is not present in the adult language. A distinction between "ra" and "la" does not exist in the Japanese language, and hence Japanese adults fail to make that discrimination. Japanese infants under nine months can discriminate between these two phonemes but lose that ability after one year because the language they hear does not require that discrimination.

Sensitivity to speech

Determinants of attention.   Both movement and contrasts between dark and light tend to attract an infant's attention. When an alert newborn is placed in a dark room, he opens his eyes and looks around for edges. If he is shown a thick black bar on a white background, his eyes dart to the bar's contour and hover near it, rather than wander randomly across the visual field. Certain other visual qualities engage the infant's attention more effectively than do others. The colour red is more attractive than others, for example, and objects characterized by curvilinearity and symmetry hold the infant's attention longer than do ones with straight lines and asymmetric patterns. Sounds having the pitch and timbre of the human voice are more attractive than most others; the newborn is particularly responsive to the tones of a mother's voice, as well as to sounds with a great deal of variety. These classes of stimuli tend to elicit the most prolonged attention during the first 8 to 10 weeks of life. During the infant's third month a second principle, called the discrepancy principle, begins to assume precedence. According to this principle, the infant is most likely to attend to those events that are moderately different from those he has been exposed to in the past. For instance, by the third month, the infant has developed an internal representation of the faces of the people who care for him. Hence, a slightly distorted face—*e.g.,* a mask with the eyes misplaced—will provoke more sustained attention than will a normal face or an object the infant has never seen before. This discrepancy principle operates in other sensory modalities as well.

Judgment.   Even infants less than one year old are capable of what appears to be complex perceptual judgments. They can estimate the distance of an object from their body, for example. If an infant is shown a rattle and hears its distinctive sound and the room is then darkened, the infant will reach for the rattle if the sound indicates that the object can be grasped but will not reach if the sound indicates that it is beyond his grasp.

More dramatically, infants will also reach for an object with a posture appropriate to its shape. If an infant sees a round object in the shape of a wheel and hears its distinctive sound and also sees a smaller rattle and hears its sound, he will reach in the dark with one hand in a grasping movement if he hears the sound of the rattle but will reach with both hands spread apart if he hears the sound associated with the wheel.

The four-month-old infant is also capable of rapidly learning to anticipate where a particular event will occur. After less than a minute of exposure to different scenes that alternate on the right and left side of their visual field, infants will anticipate that a picture is about to appear on the right side and will move their eyes to the right before the picture actually appears. Similarly, infants only five to six months old can detect the relation between the shape of a person's mouth and the sound that is uttered. Thus, they will look longer at a face that matches the sound they are hearing than at one where there is a mismatch between the mouth's movements and the sound being uttered.

Infants develop an avoidance reaction to the appearance of depth by the age of 8 to 10 months, when they begin to crawl. This discovery was made on the surface of an apparatus called the visual cliff. The latter is a table divided into two halves, with its entire top covered by glass. One half of the top has a checkerboard pattern lying immediately underneath the glass; the other half is transparent and reveals a sharp drop of a metre or so, at the bottom of which is the same checkerboard pattern. The infant is placed on a board on the centre of the table. The mother stands across the table and tries to tempt her baby to cross the glass on either the shallow or the deep side. Infants younger than seven months will unhesitatingly crawl to the mother across the deep side, but infants older than eight months avoid the deep side and refuse to cross it. The crying and anxiety that eight-month-olds display when confronted with the need to cross the deep side are the result of their ability to perceive depth but also, and more importantly, their ability to recognize the discrepancy of sitting on a solid surface while nevertheless seeing the visual bottom some distance below. Both nervous-system maturation and experience contribute to this particular cognitive advance.

Finally, infants create perceptual categories by which to organize experience, a category being defined as a representation of the dimensions or qualities shared by a set of similar but not identical events. Infants will treat the different colours of the spectrum, for example, according to the same categories that adults recognize. Thus, they show greater attentiveness when a shade of red changes to

yellow than when a light shade of red merely replaces a darker shade of the same colour. Five-month-old infants can tell the difference between the moving pattern of lights that corresponds to a person walking and a randomly moving version of the same number of lights, suggesting that they have acquired a category for the appearance of a person walking. By one year of age, infants apparently possess categories for people, edible food, household furniture, and animals. Finally, infants seem to show the capacity for cross-modal perception—*i.e.,* they can recognize an object in one sensory modality that they have previously perceived only in another. For example, if an infant sucks a nubby pacifier without being able to see it and then is shown that pacifier alongside a smooth one, the infant's longer look at the nubby pacifier suggests that he recognizes it, even though he previously experienced only its tactile qualities.

Memory.   Infants make robust advances in both recognition memory and recall memory during their first year. In recognition memory, the infant is able to recognize a particular object he has seen a short time earlier (and hence will look at a new object rather than the older one if both are present side by side). Although newborns cannot remember objects seen more than a minute or two previously, their memory improves fairly rapidly over the first four or five months of life. By one month they are capable of remembering an object they saw 24 hours earlier, and by one year they can recognize an object they saw several days earlier. Three-month-old infants can remember an instrumental response, such as kicking the foot to produce a swinging motion in a toy, that they learned two weeks earlier, but they respond more readily if their memory is strengthened by repeated performances of the action.

By contrast, recall memory involves remembering (retrieving the representation, or mental image) an event or object that is not currently present. A major advance in recall memory occurs between the 8th and 12th months and underlies the child's acquisition of what Piaget called "the idea of the permanent object." This advance becomes apparent when an infant watches an adult hide an object under a cloth and must wait a short period of time before being allowed to reach for it. A six-month-old will not reach under the cloth for the hidden object, presumably because he has forgotten that the object was placed there. A one-year-old, however, will reach for the object even after a 30-second delay period, presumably because he is able to remember its being hidden in the first place. These improvements in recall memory arise from the maturation of circuits linking various parts of the brain together. The improvements enable the infant to relate an event in his environment to a similar event in the past. As a result, he begins to anticipate his mother's positive reaction when the two are in close face-to-face interaction, and he behaves as if inviting her to respond. The infant may also develop new fears, such as those of objects, people, or situations with which he is unfamiliar—*i.e.,* which he cannot relate to past experiences using recall memory.

Piaget's observations.   As stated previously, Piaget identified the first phase of mental development as the sensorimotor stage (birth to two years). This stage is marked by the child's acquisition of various sensorimotor schemes, which may be defined as mental representations of motor actions that are used to obtain a goal; such actions include sucking, grasping, banging, kicking, and throwing. The sensorimotor stage, in turn, was differentiated by Piaget into six subphases, the first four of which are achieved during the initial year. During the first subphase, which lasts one month, the newborn's automatic reflexes become more efficient. In the second subphase, the infant's reflex movements become more coordinated, though they still consist largely of simple acts (called primary circular actions) that are repeated for their own sake (*e.g.,* sucking, opening and closing the fists, and fingering a blanket) and do not reflect any conscious intent or purpose on the infant's part. During the third phase, lasting from the 4th to the 8th month, the infant begins to repeat actions that produce interesting effects; for example, he may kick his legs to produce a swinging motion in a toy. In the fourth subphase, from the 8th to the 12th month, the

The visual cliff

Perceptual categories

Recall memory

child begins coordinating his actions to attain an external goal; he thus begins solving simple problems, building on actions he has mastered previously. For example, he may purposely knock down a pillow to obtain a toy hidden behind it. During the fifth subphase, covering the 12th to 18th months, the child begins to invent new sensorimotor schemes in a form of trial-and-error experimentation. He may change his actions toward the same object or try out new ones to achieve a particular goal. For example, if he finds that his arm alone is not long enough, he may use a stick to retrieve a ball that rolled beneath a couch. In the final subphase of infancy, which is achieved by about the 18th month, the child starts trying to solve problems by mentally imagining certain events and outcomes rather than by simple physical trial-and-error experimentation.

The child's actions thus far have shown progressively greater intentionality, and he has developed a primitive form of representation, which Piaget defined as a kind of mental imagery that can be used to solve a problem or attain a goal for which the child has no habitual, available action. An important part of the child's progress in his first year is his acquisition of what Piaget calls the idea of "object permanence"—*i.e.*, the ability to treat objects as permanent entities. According to Piaget, the infant gradu-

Object perma-nence

ally learns that objects continue to exist even when they are no longer in view. Children younger than six months do not behave as if objects that are moved out of sight continue to exist; they may grab for objects they see but lose all interest once the objects are withdrawn from sight. However, infants of nine months or older do reach for objects hidden from view if they have watched them being hidden. Children aged 12 to 18 months may even search for objects that they have not themselves witnessed being hidden, indicating that they are capable of inferring those objects' location. Show such a child a toy placed in a box, put both under a cover, and then remove the box; the child will search under the cover as though he inferred the location of the toy.

Vocalizations. The first of the two basic sounds made by infants includes all those related to crying; these are present even at birth. A second category, described as cooing, emerges at about eight weeks and includes sounds that progress to babbling and ultimately become part of meaningful speech. Almost all children make babbling sounds during infancy, and no relationship has been established between the amount of babbling during the first six months and the amount or quality of speech produced by a child at age two. Vocalization in the young infant often accompanies motor activity and usually occurs when the child appears excited by something he sees or hears. Environmental influences ordinarily do not begin to influence vocalization seriously before two months of age; in fact, during the first two months of postnatal life, the vocalizations of deaf children born to deaf-mute parents are indistinguishable from those of infants born to hearing parents. Environmental effects on the variety and frequency of the infant's sounds become more evident after roughly eight weeks of age. The use of meaningful words differs from simple babbling in that speech primarily helps to obtain goals, rather than simply reflecting excitement.

PHYSICAL GROWTH AND DEVELOPMENT

A child's first year is characterized by rapid growth of body and brain: healthy, well-nourished children experience an almost 200 percent increase in height between birth and one year. Every normal, healthy infant proceeds through a sequence of motor development that occurs spontaneously and requires no special training. The infant can reach for and grasp an object by about the 4th month and can grasp a small object between his thumb and forefinger by the 10th month. By 4 months of age most babies are able to sit up for a minute or so with support, and by 9 months they can do so without support for 10 minutes or more. Most babies begin crawling (*i.e.,* moving with one's abdomen in contact with the floor) between 7 and 10 months and are creeping on hands and knees adequately at the end of that time. By 10 months an infant can pull himself up to a standing position by holding onto an external support (*e.g.,* a piece of furniture), and by 12 months he can stand

up alone. He is able to walk with help by 12 months and can walk unaided by 14 months. By 18 months, with exposure to stairs, the average child can walk up and down them without help, and by his second birthday he can run, walk backward, and pick up an object from the floor without falling down.

EMOTIONAL DEVELOPMENT

Emotions are distinct feelings or qualities of consciousness, such as joy or sadness, that reflect the personal significance of emotion-arousing events. The major types of emotions include fear, sadness, anger, surprise, excitement, guilt, shame, disgust, interest, and happiness. These emotions develop in an orderly sequence over the course of infancy and childhood.

Even during the first three or four months of life, infants display behavioral reactions suggestive of emotional states. These reactions are indicated by changes in facial expression, motor activity, and heart rate and of course by smiling and crying. Infants show a quieting of motor activity and a decrease in heart rate in response to an unexpected event, a combination that implies the emotion of surprise. A second behavioral profile, expressed by increased movement, closing of the eyes, an increase in heart rate, and crying, usually arises in response to hunger or discomfort and is a distress response to physical privation. A third set of reactions includes decreased muscle tone and closing of the eyes after feeding, which may be termed relaxation. A fourth pattern, characterized by increased movement of the arms and legs, smiling, and excited babbling, occurs in response to moderately familiar events or social interaction and may be termed excitement. In the period from 4 to 10 months, new emotional states appear. The crying and resistance infants display at the withdrawal of a favourite toy or at the interruption of an interesting activity can be termed anger. One-year-old infants are capable of displaying sadness in response to the prolonged absence of a parent.

Early emotions

Finally, infants begin displaying signs of the emotion of fear by their fourth to sixth month; a fearful response to novelty—*i.e.*, to events that are moderately discrepant from the infant's knowledge—can be observed as early as four months. If an infant at that age hears a voice speaking sentences but there is no face present, he may show a fearful facial expression and begin to cry. By 7 to 10 months of age, an infant may cry when approached by an unfamiliar person, a phenomenon called stranger anxiety. A month or two later the infant may cry when his mother leaves him in an unfamiliar place; this phenomenon is called separation anxiety. It is no accident that both stranger and separation anxiety first appear about the time the child becomes able to recall past events. If an infant is unable to remember that his mother had been present after she leaves the room, he will experience no feeling of unfamiliarity when she is gone. However, if he is able to recall the mother's prior presence and cannot understand why she is no longer with him, that discrepancy can lead to anxiety. Thus, the appearance of stranger and separation anxiety are dependent on the improvement in memorial ability.

The appearance of fear

These emotions in young infants may not be identical to similar emotional states that occur in older children or adolescents, who experience complex cognitions in concert with emotion; these are missing in the young infant. The older child's anger, for example, can remain strong for a longer period of time because the child can think about the target of his anger. Thus, it may be an error to attribute to the young infant the same emotional states that one can assume are present in older children.

Attachment. Perhaps the central accomplishment in personality development during the first years of life is the establishment of specific and enduring emotional bonds, or attachment. The person to whom an infant becomes emotionally attached is termed the target of attachment. Targets of attachment are usually those persons who respond most consistently, predictably, and appropriately to the baby's signals, primarily the mother but also the father and eventually others. Infants are biologically predisposed to form attachments with adults, and these attachments in turn form the basis for healthy emotional and so-

Parent-
child
interaction

cial development throughout childhood. Infants depend on their targets of attachment not only for food, water, warmth, and relief from pain or discomfort but also for such emotional qualities as soothing and placating, play, consolation, and information about the world around them. Moreover, it is through the reciprocal interactions between child and parent that infants learn that their behaviour can affect the behaviour of others in consistent and predictable ways and that others can be counted on to respond when signaled.

Infants who do not have a particular adult devoted to their care often do not become strongly attached to any one adult and are less socially responsive—less likely to smile, vocalize, laugh, or approach adults. Such behaviour has been observed in children raised in relatively impersonal institutional surroundings and is shared by monkeys reared in isolation.

The social smiling of two-month-old infants invites adults to interact with them; all normal human infants show a social smile, which is, in fact, their first true sign of social responsiveness. The social smile is apparently innate in the human species. At about six months of age infants begin to respond socially to particular people who become the targets of attachment. Although all infants develop some form of attachment to their caregivers, the strength and quality of that attachment depends partly on the parents' behaviour to the child. The sheer amount of time spent with a child counts for less than the quality of the adult-child interaction in this regard. The parents' satisfaction of the infant's physical needs is an important factor in their interaction, but sensitivity to the child's needs and wishes, along with the provision of emotional warmth, supportiveness, and gentleness are equally important. Interestingly, mothers and fathers have been observed to behave differently with their infants and young children: mothers hold, comfort, and calm their babies in predictable and rhythmic ways, whereas fathers play and excite in unpredictable and less rhythmic ways.

One significant difference has been detected in the quality of infants' attachment to their caregivers—that between infants who are "securely" attached and those who are "insecurely" attached. Infants with a secure attachment to a parent are less afraid of challenge and unfamiliarity than are those with an insecure attachment.

During the first two years of life, the presence of targets of attachment tends to mute infants' feelings of fear in unfamiliar situations. A one-year-old in an unfamiliar room is much less likely to cry if his mother is present than if she is not. A one-year-old is also much less likely to cry at an unexpected sound or an unfamiliar object if his mother is nearby. Monkeys, too, show less fear of the unfamiliar when they are with their mothers. This behavioral fact has been used to develop a series of experimental situations thought to be useful in distinguishing securely from insecurely attached infants. These procedures consist of exposing a one-year-old to what is known as the "strange situation." Two episodes that are part of a longer series in this procedure involve leaving the infant with a stranger and leaving the infant alone in an unfamiliar room. Children who show only moderate distress when the mother leaves, seek her upon her return, and are easily comforted by her are assumed to be securely attached. Children who do not become upset when the mother leaves, play contentedly while she is gone, and seem to ignore her when she returns are termed insecurely attached–avoidant. Finally, children who become extremely upset when the mother leaves, resist her soothing when she returns, and are difficult to calm down are termed insecurely attached–resistant. About 65 percent of all American children tested are classed as securely attached, 21 percent as insecurely attached–avoidant, and 14 percent as insecurely attached–resistant. All other things being equal, it is believed that those children who demonstrate a secure attachment during the first two years of life are likely to remain more emotionally secure and be more socially outgoing later in childhood than those who are insecurely attached. But insecurely attached–resistant children are more likely to display social or emotional problems later in childhood. The development of a secure or insecure attachment is

Secure and
insecure
attach-
ments

partly a function of the predictability and emotional sensitivity of an infant's caregiver and partly the product of the infant's innate temperament.

Temperament.   Individual infants tend to vary in their basic mood and in their typical responses to situations and events involving challenge, restraint, and unfamiliarity. Infants may differ in such qualities as fearfulness, irritability, fussiness, attention span, sensitivity to stimuli, vigour of response, activity level, and readiness to adapt to new events. These constitutional differences help make up what is called a child's temperament. It is believed that many temperament qualities are mediated by inherited differences in the neurochemistry of the brain.

Most individual differences in temperament observed in infants up to 12 months in age do not endure over time and are not predictive of later behaviour. One temperamental trait that is more lasting, however, is that of inhibition to the unfamiliar. Inhibited children, who account for 10–20 percent of all one-year-old children, tend to be shy, timid, and restrained when encountering unfamiliar people, objects, or situations. As young infants, they show high levels of motor activity and fretfulness in response to stimulation. (They are also likely to be classified as insecurely attached–resistant when observed in the "strange situation.") By contrast, uninhibited children, who account for about 30 percent of all children, tend to be very sociable, fearless, and emotionally spontaneous in unfamiliar situations. As infants, they display low levels of motor activity and irritability in response to unfamiliar stimuli. Inhibited children have a more reactive sympathetic nervous system than do uninhibited children. Inhibited children show larger increases in heart rate in response to challenges and larger increases in diastolic blood pressure when they change from a sitting to a standing posture. In addition, inhibited children show greater activation of the frontal cortex on the right side of the brain, while uninhibited children show greater activation of the frontal cortex on the left side.

Inhibited
and
uninhibited
children

These two temperament profiles are moderately stable from the second to the eighth year; studies reveal that about one-half of those children classed as inhibited at age two are still shy, introverted, and emotionally restrained at age eight, while about three-quarters of those children classed as uninhibited have remained outgoing, sociable, and emotionally spontaneous.

Development in childhood

LANGUAGE

The capacity for language usually emerges in infants soon after the first birthday, and they make enormous progress in this area during their second year. Language is a symbolic form of communication that involves, on the one hand, the comprehension of words and sentences and, on the other, the expression of feelings, thoughts, and ideas. The basic units of language are phonemes, morphemes, and words. Phonemes are the basic sounds that are combined to make words; most languages have about 30 phonemes, which correspond roughly to the sounds of the spoken letters of the alphabet. Although one-month-old infants can discriminate among various phonemes, they are themselves unable to produce them. By 4 to 6 months of age, however, infants usually express vowellike elements in their vocalizations, and by 11–12 months of age they are producing clear consonant-vowel utterances like "dada" and "mama."

Virtually all children begin to comprehend some words several months before they speak their own first meaningful words. In fact, one- to three-year-olds typically understand five times as many words as they actually use in everyday speech. The average infant speaks his first words by 12–14 months; these are generally simple labels for persons, objects, or actions; *e.g.,* "mommy," "milk," "go," "yes," "no," and "dog." By the time the child reaches his 18th month, he has a speaking vocabulary of about 50 words. The single words he uses may stand for entire sentences. Thus, the word "eat" may signify "Can I eat now?" and "shoe" may mean "Take off my shoe." The child soon begins to use two-word combinations for

Growth in
vocabulary

making simple requests or for describing the environment: "Want juice," "Daddy gone," "Mommy soup." These simple statements are abbreviated versions of adult sentences. "Where is the ball?" becomes "where ball?"; the sentence "That's the ball" becomes "that ball." These early two-word combinations consist mostly of nouns, verbs, and a few adjectives. Articles (a, an, the), conjunctions (and, or, but), and prepositions (in, on, under) are almost completely absent at this stage. In their telegraphic sentences, children usually place the subject, object, and verb in an order that is correct within certain broad limits for their native language. For example, an American child will say "want ball" rather than "ball want" for a sentence meaning "I want the ball."

In the few months before the child's second birthday, there is a major increase in the size of his vocabulary and in the variety of his two- and three-word combinations. By two years of age a child's comprehension vocabulary contains an average of about 270 words. By the end of the second year, he understands interrogatives such as "where," "who," and "what," and by three years of age he can correctly interpret the respective use of the words "this" or "that" and "here" or "there," as well as the terms "in front of" and "behind." By three years of age children are learning at least two new words a day and possess a working vocabulary of 1,000 words.

Children in their second and third years sometimes use words as overextensions; "doggie," for instance, may refer to a variety of four-legged animals as well as to dogs, and the word "daddy" may be used in reference to all men. This occurs simply because, although the infant detects the differences among various types of animals, he has only one word ("dog") in his vocabulary to apply to them. Overextensions are more common in speech than in comprehension, however; the child who uses the word "apple" for all round objects has no difficulty pointing to an apple in a picture illustrating several round objects. Other words are underextended; that is, they are defined too narrowly. Some infants will use the word "car" to refer only to cars moving on the street but not to cars standing still or to a picture of a car.

Syntax and grammar

Children learn the rules of syntax (*i.e.*, the grammatical rules specifying how words are combined in a sentence) with very little explicit instruction or tutoring from adults. They begin to flesh out their noun-verb sentences with less critical words such as prepositions, conjunctions, articles, and auxiliary verbs. Children follow a typical sequence in their acquisition of grammatical rules, depending on the language they are learning to use. In English, a child first masters the grammatical rules for the present tense (*e.g.*, "I want") and begins to use the present progressive ending ("-ing") and the plural. This is followed by mastery of the irregular past tense ("I made," "I had"), possessives (my, mine, his), articles (a, an, the), and the regular past tense ("I walked," "he stopped"). These successes are followed by mastery of the third person present tense ("he goes") and auxiliary verbs ("I'm walking," "we're playing").

Deaf children learning sign language from deaf-mute parents show in their signs the same course of development that is apparent in the speech of children with normal hearing. Deaf, like hearing, children make their first signs for objects and later display signs for more complex ideas like "Mommy eat" or "Daddy coat."

By the middle of the third year, children tend to use more sentences containing four, five, or six words, and by the fourth year they can converse in adultlike sentences. Finally, five- and six-year-olds demonstrate metalinguistic awareness—*i.e.*, a mastery of the complex rules of grammar and meaning. They can differentiate between sounds that are real words and those that are not—*e.g.*, they regard "apple" as a word but reject "oope" as a word. They can tell the difference between grammatically correct and incorrect sentences and will make spontaneous corrections in their speech; that is to say, if a child makes a speech error, he recognizes it and will say the phrase or sentence correctly the second time.

A major disagreement among theories of language acquisition is their relative emphasis on the role of maturation of the brain, on the one hand, and of social interaction, on the other. The most popular view assumes that biological factors provide a strong foundation for language acquisition but that infants' social interaction with others is absolutely necessary if language is to develop. The special biological basis of language is supported by the fact that deaf children who are not exposed to a sign language invent a symbol system that is similar in structure to that developed by hearing children. But interaction with other people is also crucial. Even during the first year, children's production and perception of speech sounds are increasingly shaped by the linguistic environment around them, reflecting their exquisite sensitivity and susceptibility to human speech. Indeed, the amount and variety of verbal stimulation is a critical factor in language development, as is the adult caregivers' sensitivity to an infant's own vocalizations; mothers who ask questions and encourage their infants' vocal responses have children who show a more advanced language development.

COGNITIVE DEVELOPMENT

The mental activities involved in the acquisition, processing, organization, and use of knowledge are collectively termed cognition. These activities include selective attention, perception, discrimination, interpretation, classification, recall and recognition memory, evaluation, inference, and deduction. The cognitive structures that are involved in these processes include schemata, images, symbols, concepts or categories, and propositions. A schema is an abstract representation of the distinctive characteristics of an event. These representations are not photographic copies or visual images but are more like schematic blueprints that emphasize the arrangement of a set of salient elements, which supply the schema with distinctiveness and differentiate it from similar events. The child's ability to recognize the face of another person is mediated by a schema, for example. Young children already display a remarkable ability to generate and store schemata. Another type of early cognitive unit is the image; this is a mental picture, or the reconstruction of a schema, that preserves the spatial and temporal detail of the event.

Cognitive structures

Symbols represent the next level of abstraction from experience; they are arbitrary names for things and qualities. Common examples of symbols are the names for objects, letters, and numbers. Whereas a schema or image represents a specific experience, such as a sight or sound, a symbol is an arbitrary representation of an event. The letter *A* is a symbol, and children use schemata, images, and symbols in their mastery of the alphabet. Symbols are used in the development of higher cognitive units called concepts. A concept, or category, may be thought of as a special kind of symbol that represents a set of attributes common to a group of symbols or images. The concept represents a common attribute or meaning from a diverse array of experiences, while a symbol stands for a particular class of events. Concepts are used to sort specific experiences into general rules or classes, and conceptual thinking refers to a person's subjective manipulations of those abstract classes.

Jean Piaget tried to trace specific stages in children's progressive use of symbols and concepts to manipulate their environment. According to Piaget, two of the four stages of cognitive development occur during childhood: the pre-operational stage (2 to 7 years), in which the child learns to manipulate the environment by means of symbolic thought and language; and the concrete-operational stage (7 to 12 years), in which the beginnings of logic appear in the form of classifications of ideas and an understanding of time and number. An important structure in Piaget's theory of cognitive development is the operation, which is a cognitive structure that the child uses to transform, or "operate on," information. Children learn to use operations that are flexible and fully reversible in thought; the ability to plan a series of moves in a game of checkers and then mentally retrace one's steps to the beginning of that sequence is one such example of an operation.

The concrete-operational stage

It is important to make a distinction between the knowledge and skills a child possesses, called competence, and the demonstration of that knowledge in actual problem-solving situations, called performance. Children often possess knowledge that they do not use even when the occasion calls for it. Adapting to new challenges, according to Piaget, requires two complementary processes. The first, assimilation, is the relating of a new event or object to cognitive structures the child already possesses. A five-year-old who has a concept of a bird as a living thing with a beak and wings that flies will try to assimilate the initial perception of an ostrich to his concept of bird. Accommodation, the second process, occurs when the information presented does not fit the existing concept. Thus, once the child learns that the ostrich does not fly, he will accommodate to that fact and modify his concept of bird to include the fact that some birds do not fly.

One of the central victories of cognitive development occurs during ages five to seven and, according to Piaget, marks the child's entry to the concrete-operational stage. This is the ability to reason simultaneously about the whole and about part of the whole. For instance, if an eight-year-old is shown eight yellow candies and four brown candies and asked, "Are there more yellow candies or more candies," he will say that there are more candies, whereas a five-year-old is likely to respond incorrectly that there are more yellow candies.

A child who has reached the concrete-operational stage is able to solve several other new kinds of logical problems. For example, a five-year-old who is shown two balls of clay of the same size and shape will tell an adult that they have the same amount of clay, but, when the experimenter rolls one of the balls into a long but thin sausage, the five-year-old will tend to say that the untouched sphere has more clay in it than the sausage-shaped object does. A seven-year-old, however, shows what is called the ability to conserve; when presented with the same problem, he will recognize that the two pieces still have the same amount of clay in them, based on his awareness that liquids and solids do not change in amount or quantity merely because their external shape changes. The seven-year-old is able to reverse an event in thought and knows that the sausage can be reshaped back into the original ball without a loss or gain in the total amount of clay. The knowledge that one can reverse one state of affairs into a prior state, which is called conservation, is a mark of this new stage of development.

Another cognitive advance children make during the concrete-operational stage is the knowledge that hierarchical relationships can exist within categories. This is illustrated by the ability to arrange similar objects according to some quantified dimension, such as weight or size. This ability is called seriation. A seven-year-old can arrange eight sticks of different lengths in order from shortest to longest, indicating that the child appreciates a relation among the different sizes of the objects. Seriation is crucial to understanding the relations between numbers and hence to learning arithmetic. Children in the concrete-operational stage also appreciate the fact that terms such as taller, darker, and bigger refer to a relation between objects rather than to some absolute characteristic.

One implication of the stage of concrete operations is that the child is now able to compare himself with other children in such qualities as size, attractiveness, intelligence, courage, and so on. Hence, the formation of the child's sense of identity, or self-concept, proceeds at a faster rate because he is able to compare his characteristics with those of other children.

Formal-operations stage

The final stage of cognitive development, called the stage of formal operations, begins at about age 12 and characterizes the logical processes of adolescents and adults. A child who has reached this stage of logical thinking can reason about hypothetical events that are not necessarily in accord with his experience. He shows a willingness to think about possibilities, and he can analyze and evaluate events from a number of different possible perspectives. A second hallmark of the stage of formal operations is the systematic search for solutions. Faced with a novel problem, the adolescent is able to generate a number of possible means of solving it and then select the most logical, probable, or successful of his hypotheses. The formal thinking of adolescents and adults thus tends to be self-consciously deductive, rational, and systematic. Finally,

adolescents typically begin to examine their own thinking and evaluate it while searching for inconsistencies and fallacies in their own beliefs and values concerning themselves, society, and nature.

Symbolic ability and imitation. Symbolic ability, which appears at about one year of age, can be observed when a child imaginatively treats an object as something other than it is—pretending a wooden block is a car or using a cup as a hat. By the middle of their second year, children impart new functions to objects; they may turn a doll upside down and pretend it is a salt shaker or try to use a wooden block as if it were a chair. Many three-year-olds are capable of simple metaphor and will play with two wooden balls of different size as if they were symbolic of a parent and a child. Children's drawings also become symbolic during the second and third years and begin to contain forms that look like (or at least are intended to represent) animals, people, and various objects.

Imitation may be defined as behaviour that selectively duplicates that of another person. Like symbolism, it is a basic capacity that is inherent in human nature. Infants engage in selective imitation by seven or eight months of age, and their imitations become more frequent and complex during the next two to three years. One-year-olds already imitate the gestures, speech sounds, and instrumental actions that they see performed by people around them. They also become capable of imitating an act some time after they have actually observed it; for example, one-year-olds may imitate an action they witnessed one day earlier. Children often imitate the instrumental behaviours of parents, like cleaning or feeding, but are less likely to imitate emotional expressions or parental behaviours that have no instrumental goal. Children are also more likely to imitate their parents than their siblings or characters they see on television.

Children imitate others for a variety of reasons. They are most likely to imitate those acts over which they feel some uncertainty regarding their ability to perform. If they are too uncertain, they will cry; if they are absolutely certain they can perform an act, they are less likely to imitate it. Children also imitate actions that win parental approval or attention or that enhance their similarity to other persons they want to be like (*e.g.,* a boy imitating his father).

Memory. Memory, which is central to all cognitive processes, involves both the storage of traces of past experience and the retrieval of that stored information at a later time. It is useful to distinguish between short-term and long-term memory processes. Short-term, or working, memory may be defined as referring to traces available for a maximum of 30 seconds immediately after stimulation, but typically for a much shorter period. The ability to remember a phone number while redialing it is a good example of short-term memory. Long-term memory, or permanent memory, refers to stored information that is potentially available for relatively long periods of time, extending up to a lifetime.

Two-year-olds can usually hold in short-term memory only one or two independent units of information, while 15-year-olds can remember seven or eight units (numbers or words, for example). Both children and adults tend to perform much better when they have to recognize than when they have to recall, but this difference is most dramatic in young children. Thus, a four-year-old child can usually recognize almost all of 12 pictures he has seen but may be able to recall only 2 or 3 of them. A 10-year-old, by contrast, who recognizes the 12 pictures can also recall as many as 8 of them.

Besides improvements in capacity, older children demonstrate an increasing speed of recall and can search their memory for information more quickly. Another improvement in memory ability is selectivity. As they grow older, children become adept at choosing more important items to remember—*i.e.,* at distinguishing fundamental from merely incidental information. In addition, older children acquire more efficient strategies for the coding, rehearsal, and retrieval of information that younger children do not possess. By eight or nine years of age, for example, most children know that it is easier to relearn a text passage than to learn it for the first time. Generally, older

Imitation

Improvements in recall

children are better able to plan their own behaviour, formulate problems, monitor their ability, control distraction and anxiety, and evaluate the quality of their cognitive products. And because older children have a more accurate understanding of their own abilities, they are better able to assess and predict the cognitive abilities of other people.

The makeup of intelligence. Controversy exists over whether children can be said to differ in a unitary abstract ability called intelligence or whether each child might better be described as possessing a set of specific cognitive abilities. Some children are especially proficient with verbal problems and less proficient at problems involving spatial relations or mathematical reasoning, for example. The American psychologist J.P. Guilford suggests that cognitive abilities can be classified along three dimensions: the content of the information (symbolic, semantic, behavioral, or figural); the operation performed on the content (memory, evaluation, convergence, divergence, or cognition); and finally the product of the cognitive work (a unit, a class, a relation, a system, a transformation, or an implication). This theory predicts that there are a very large number of different cognitive profiles, not just one.

EMOTIONAL AND SOCIAL DEVELOPMENT

Personality traits. Although earlier theorists believed that personality traits evident in the first three years of life would persist into later life, research indicates that this claim is exaggerated. Long-term studies that follow children from infancy through adolescence and into adulthood indicate that lasting personality traits do not emerge until after six or seven years of age and that most of the differences seen in children in the first three years of life are not preserved. The one possible exception to this claim holds for the temperamental qualities of inhibited and uninhibited to the unfamiliar. Children who are extremely inhibited or uninhibited in the first three years of life are more likely than others to retain those qualities through late childhood.

Self-awareness and empathy. Perhaps the most important aspect of children's emotional development is a growing awareness of their own emotional states and the ability to discern and interpret the emotions of others. The last half of the second year is a time when children start becoming aware of their own emotional states, characteristics, abilities, and potential for action; this phenomenon is called self-awareness. Two-year-old children begin to describe their own actions as they are performing them, can recognize a reflection of themselves in the mirror, and may become possessive with their toys for the first time. This growing awareness of and ability to recall one's own emotional states leads to empathy, or the ability to appreciate the feelings and perceptions of others. Young children's dawning awareness of their own potential for action inspires them to try to direct (or otherwise affect) the behaviour of others. This change is often accompanied by the urge to test the standards of behaviour held by parents, and, as a result, children's second and third years are often called the "terrible twos."

With age, children acquire the ability to understand the perspective, or point of view, of other people, a development that is closely linked with the empathic sharing of others' emotions. Even six-year-olds are aware that other people have different perspectives, thoughts, and feelings from their own, and they are able to empathize with the characteristics they observe in others. By eight to nine years of age a child recognizes that people can become aware of others' point of view, and he likewise knows that others can become aware of his own perspective. By 10 years of age the child can consider a social interaction simultaneously from his own point of view and from that of another person. Owing to this increased awareness, children from age seven on are more conscious of what others think of them and show more concern over others' opinion of their behaviour. Finally, older children understand that a person's genuine emotions can be stronger or different from those he actually reveals, and they thus appreciate that a person can disguise his emotions.

One major factor underlying these changes is the child's increasing cognitive sophistication. For example, in order to feel the emotion of guilt, a child must appreciate the fact that he could have inhibited a particular action of his that violated a moral standard. The awareness that one can impose a restraint on one's own behaviour requires a certain level of cognitive maturation, and, therefore, the emotion of guilt cannot appear until that competence is attained.

A moral sense. Empathy and other forms of social awareness are important in the development of a moral sense. Morality embraces a person's beliefs about the appropriateness or goodness of what he does, thinks, or feels. During the last few months of the second year, children develop an appreciation of right and wrong; these representations are called moral standards. Children show a concern over dirty hands, torn clothes, and broken cups, suggesting that they appreciate that certain events violate adult standards. By age two most children display mild distress if they cannot meet standards of behaviour imposed by others. After age two they will playfully violate rules on acceptable behaviour in order to test the validity of that standard. One of the signs of the child's growing morality is the ability to control behaviour and the willingness to postpone immediate gratification of a desire.

Childhood is thus the time at which moral standards begin to develop in a process that often extends well into adulthood. The American psychologist Lawrence Kohlberg hypothesized that people's development of moral standards passes through stages that can be grouped into three moral levels. At the early level, that of preconventional moral reasoning, the child uses external and physical events (such as pleasure or pain) as the source for decisions about moral rightness or wrongness; his standards are based strictly on what will avoid punishment or bring pleasure. At the intermediate level, that of conventional moral reasoning, the child or adolescent views moral standards as a way of maintaining the approval of authority figures, chiefly his parents, and acts in accordance with their precepts. Moral standards at this level are held to rest on a positive evaluation of authority, rather than on a simple fear of punishment. At the third level, that of postconventional moral reasoning, the adult bases his moral standards on principles that he himself has evaluated and that he accepts as inherently valid, regardless of society's opinion. He is aware of the arbitrary, subjective nature of social standards and rules, which he regards as relative rather than absolute in authority.

Thus the bases for justifying moral standards pass from avoidance of punishment to avoidance of adult disapproval and rejection to avoidance of internal guilt and self-recrimination. The person's moral reasoning also moves toward increasingly greater social scope (*i.e.,* including more people and institutions) and greater abstraction (*i.e.,* from reasoning about physical events such as pain or pleasure to reasoning about values, rights, and implicit contracts). This transition from one stage to another is characterized by gradual shifts in the most frequent type of reasoning; thus, at any given point in life, a person may function at more than one stage at the same time. Different people pass through the stages at varying rates. Finally, different people are likely to reach different levels of moral thinking in their lives, raising the possibility that some people may never reach the later, more abstract, stages.

The evidence for these theoretical stages comes from children's answers to moral dilemmas verbally presented to them by researchers, rather than their actual behaviour in time of conflict. Scientists have argued that many children display a more profound moral understanding than is evident in their responses on such tests. Others have argued that because even rather young children are capable of showing empathy with the pain of others, the inhibition of aggressive behaviour arises from this moral affect rather than from the mere anticipation of punishment. Some scientists have found that children differ in their individual capacity for empathy, and, therefore, some children are more sensitive to moral prohibitions than others. There is evidence suggesting that temperamentally

Emergence of moral standards

Shifts in moral reasoning

inhibited children whose parents impose consistent socialization demands on them experience moral affect more intensely than do other children.

Self-concept, or identity. One of the most important aspects of a child's emotional development is the formation of his self-concept, or identity—namely, his sense of who he is and what his relation to other people is. The most conspicuous trend in children's growing self-awareness is a shift from concrete physical attributes to more abstract characteristics. This shift is apparent in those characteristics children emphasize when asked to describe themselves. Young children—four to six years of age—seem to define themselves in terms of such observable characteristics as hair colour, height, or their favourite activities. But within a few years, their descriptions of themselves shift to more abstract, internal, or psychological qualities, including their competences and skills relative to those of others. Thus, as children approach adolescence, they tend to increasingly define themselves by the unique and individual quality of their feelings, thoughts, and beliefs rather than simply by external characteristics.

Gender
identity

One of the earliest and most basic categories of self to emerge during childhood is based on gender and is called sex-role identity. Children develop a rudimentary gender identity by age three, having learned to classify themselves and others as either males or females. They also come to prefer the activities and roles traditionally assigned to their own sex; as early as two years of age, most children select toys and activities that fit the sex-role stereotypes of their culture, and during the preschool years they begin to select same-sex playmates. Another component of a child's self-concept concerns the racial, ethnic, or religious group of which he is a part. A child who is a member of a distinctive or specific group has usually created a mental category for that group by five to six years, and children from ethnic minorities tend to be more aware of ethnic differences than are nonminority children.

One of the important processes that mediates a child's self-concept is that of identification; this involves the child's incorporation of the characteristics of parents or other persons by adopting their appearance, attitudes, and behaviour. Children tend to identify with those persons to whom they are emotionally attached and whom they perceive to be similar to themselves in some way. They seem to identify most strongly with parents who are emotionally warm or who are dominant and powerful. The role models children adopt may have negative as well as positive characteristics, however, and can thus influence children in undesirable as well as beneficial ways.

Influence
of siblings

More than 80 percent of American children have one or more sisters or brothers, and the presence of these siblings can influence a child's personality development. Parents tend to be more involved and attentive toward the firstborn, stimulating him more (in the absence of other children) but then expecting and demanding more from him (as their oldest child). Because of this, firstborns tend to identify more closely with their parents, conform more closely to their values and expectations, and generally identify more closely with authority than do their younger siblings. Firstborns tend to be more strongly motivated toward school achievement, are more conscientious, more prone to guilt feelings, and less aggressive than those born later. A high proportion of eminent scientists and scholars have been firstborns, perhaps owing to the aforementioned traits, but firstborns also tend to be less receptive to ideas that challenge a popular ideological or theoretical position.

Peer socialization. During the first two years of life, infants do not spontaneously seek out other children for interaction or for pleasure. Although six-month-old infants may look at and vocalize to other infants, they do not initiate reciprocal social play with them. However, between two and five years of age, children's interactions with each other become more sustained, social, and complex. Solitary or parallel play is dominant among three-year-olds, but this strategy shifts to group play by five years.

Problems in development. An estimated 6–10 percent of all children develop serious emotional or personality problems at some point. These problems tend to fall into two groups: those characterized by symptoms of extreme anxiety, withdrawal, and fearfulness, on the one hand, and by disobedience, aggression, and destruction of property on the other. The former set is called internalizing; the latter is termed externalizing. As indicated earlier, some fearful, timid, socially withdrawn children inherit a temperamental predisposition to develop this form of behaviour; other children, however, acquire it as a result of a stressful upbringing, experiences, or social circumstances.

Aggressive
behaviour

Sex-linked differences in aggression are evident from about two or three years of age, with boys being more aggressive than girls. Although young children sometimes fight and quarrel, usually over possessions, such behaviour is generally not a serious problem in the first three or four years of life. Aggressive behaviour can become a serious problem in older children, however, and by seven years of age a small proportion of boys do display an extreme and consistent tendency to be aggressive with others. Children who are highly aggressive by age seven or eight tend to remain so later in life; these children are three times more likely to have police records as adults than are other children. By age 30 significantly more members of this group had been convicted of criminal behaviour, were aggressive with their spouses, and abused or severely punished their own children. Although biological factors can play a role in producing extreme aggression, the role of the child's social environment is critical. Parents' use of extreme levels of physical punishment, imposed inconsistently, is associated with high levels of aggression in children, as are extreme levels of parental permissiveness toward a child's own aggressive acts. Psychologists frequently help parents deal with aggressive children by teaching them to observe what they do and to enforce rules consistently with their children. Parents can thereby learn effective but nonpunitive ways of controlling their aggressive children.

Although precise information is difficult to obtain, it is estimated that each year about one million children in the United States are abused by their parents or other adults. Child abuse is more common in economically disadvantaged families than in affluent ones but occurs in all social classes, races, and ethnic groups. The abuse of children is often part of a pattern of family violence that is transmitted from parent to child for generations. Children who were abused as infants tend to show much more avoidant, resistant, and noncompliant behaviour than do other children.

Parents and the socialization of the child. Parental behaviour affects the child's personality and his likelihood of developing psychological problems. The most important qualities in this regard are whether and how parents communicate their love to a child, the disciplinary techniques they use, and their behaviour as role models. There are, of course, cultural and class differences in the socialization values held by parents. In most modern societies, well-educated parents are more concerned with their children's academic achievement and autonomy and are generally more democratic than are less well-educated parents. No single area of interaction can alone account for parents' influence on a child's behaviour and social functioning. One investigator has emphasized four factors, however: (1) the degree to which parents try to control the child's behaviour, (2) the pressures imposed on the child to perform at high levels of cognitive, social, or emotional development, (3) the clarity of parent-child communications, and, finally, (4) the parents' nurturance of and affection toward the child. Those children who appear to be the most mature and competent tend to have parents who were more affectionate, more supportive, more conscientious, and more committed to their role as parents. These parents were also more controlling and demanded more mature behaviour from their children. Although the parents respected their children's independence, they generally held firm positions and provided clear reasons for them. This parental type is termed authoritative. A second class of children consists of those who are moderately self-reliant but somewhat withdrawn. The parents of these children tended to use less rational control and relied more heavily on coercive discipline. These parents were also slightly less affectionate, and they did not encourage the discussion of parental rules. This parental type is termed authoritarian. The least mature children had parents who were lax in discipline and noncontrolling but affectionate. They made few demands on the children for mature behaviour and allowed them to regulate their own activities as much as possible. This parental type is termed permissive.

The effects of divorce on children appear to be very complicated. The major adverse impact of divorce on children is evident during the first year after the divorce and seems to be a bit more enduring for boys than for girls. Preschool children seem to be most vulnerable to the effect of divorce and adolescents the least.

In most modern industrialized countries, the proportion of working mothers with children under 18 greatly increased in the last few decades of the 20th century, to the point that one-half of all mothers with children under 5 are in the workforce. However, there is no clear evidence that this change in Western society has had a profound influence on child development, independent of other historical changes during this same period.

BIBLIOGRAPHY. Authoritative texts on all stages of human development include MARC H. BORNSTEIN and MICHAEL E. LAMB (eds.), *Developmental Psychology: An Advanced Textbook*, 3rd ed. (1992); URIE BRONFENBRENNER, *The Ecology of Human Development: Experiments by Nature and Design* (1979); RICHARD M. LERNER, *Concepts and Theories of Human Development*, 2nd ed. (1986); RICHARD M. LERNER and DAVID F. HULTSCH, *Human Development: A Life-Span Perspective* (1983); DANIEL J. LEVINSON et al., *The Seasons of a Man's Life* (1978, reissued 1985); LAWRENCE KOHLBERG, *Essays on Moral Development*, 2 vol. (1981–84); and ROBERT PLOMIN, *Development, Genetics, and Psychology* (1986).

The major theories of human development discussed in the article are presented in SIGMUND FREUD, *An Outline of Psychoanalysis* (1949, reissued 1989; originally published in German, 1940); ERIK H. ERIKSON, *Childhood and Society*, 2nd ed. rev. and enlarged (1964, reissued 1985); and JEAN PIAGET, *The Origins of Intelligence in Children* (1952, reissued 1974; also published as *The Origin of Intelligence in the Child*, 1953, reprinted 1977; originally published in French, 1936).

Aspects of development in the infant, child, and adolescent are presented in ALAN F. GUTTMACHER, *Pregnancy, Birth, and Family Planning*, rev. and brought up to date by IRWIN H. KAISER (1986); DAPHNE MAURER and CHARLES MAURER, *The World of the Newborn* (1988), a highly readable account of what psychologists have learned about the prenatal and early postnatal periods; JUDY F. ROSENBLITH, *In the Beginning: Development from Conception to Age Two*, 2nd ed. (1992), an excellent summary of basic research on the infant; JEROME KAGAN, *The Nature of the Child* (1984), a collection of essays on child development; JANE B. BROOKS, *The Process of Parenting*, 3rd ed. (1991), a practical guide to child-rearing techniques; PAUL HENRY MUSSEN, JOHN JANEWAY CONGER, JEROME KAGAN, and ALETHA CAROL HUSTON, *Child Development and Personality*, 7th ed. (1990); MARC H. BORNSTEIN and WILLIAM KESSEN, *Psychological Development from Infancy: Image to Intention* (1979); MARGARET B. SPENCER, GERALDINE KEARSE BROOKINS, and WALTER RECHARDE ALLEN (eds.), *Beginnings: The Social and Affective Development of Black Children* (1985), a collection of recent psychological studies; JOHN BOWLBY, *Attachment and Loss*, vol. 1, *Attachment* (1969, reissued 1982), a classic work, summarizing his theoretical ideas on the subject; ALEXANDER THOMAS and STELLA CHESS, *Temperament and Development* (1977), summarizing the research of two psychiatrists who reintroduced the concept of temperament; WILLIAM DAMON (ed.), *Social and Personality Development: Essays on the Growth of the Child* (1983), a comprehensive account of the social, familial, and cognitive determinants of a wide range of personal characteristics; JUDY DUNN, *Sisters and Brothers* (1985), a survey of the impact of siblings on a child, and *The Beginnings of Social Understanding* (1988), presenting information based on observations of the home during the second year; JOHN H. FLAVELL, PATRICIA H. MILLER, and SCOTT A. MILLER, *Cognitive Development*, 3rd ed. (1993), an excellent text; and JEAN BERKO GLEASON (ed.), *The Development of Language*, 3rd ed. (1993), an excellent summary.

Journals include *Human Development* (bimonthly), published in Switzerland; *Developmental Psychology* (bimonthly); *Developmental Review* (quarterly); *Child Development* (bimonthly); and *Journal of Experimental Child Psychology* (monthly).

JEROME KAGAN. Professor of Psychology, Harvard University, Cambridge, Mass. Author of *Unstable Ideas: Temperament, Cognition, and Self* and many others.

World of Medicine Contributors

George J. Annas, J.D., M.P.H.
Special Report Human Subjects: Used or Abused?
Edward R. Utley Professor of Health Law, Boston University Schools of Medicine and Public Health

Richard L. Atkinson, M.D.
Obesity
Professor of Medicine and Nutritional Sciences, University of Wisconsin Medical School, Madison

Donna C. Bergen, M.D.
Epilepsy
Senior Attending Neurologist, Rush-Presbyterian-St. Luke's Medical Center, Chicago

Abraham B. Bergman, M.D.
Pediatrics
Director of Pediatrics, Harborview Medical Center; Professor of Pediatrics, University of Washington School of Medicine, Seattle

Thomas W. Bice
Health Policy (coauthor)
Assistant Vice President, MetLife HealthCare Management Corp., Westport, Conn.

Sir Roy Y. Calne
Transplantation
Professor of Surgery, University of Cambridge, England

Sabra Chartrand
Medical Technology
Journalist and "Patents" column writer, *New York Times,* Washington, D.C., bureau

Bryan Christie
Medical Education
Health Correspondent, *The Scotsman,* Edinburgh; Correspondent, *British Medical Journal*

Oscar B. Crofford, M.D.
Diabetes
Professor of Medicine and Director, Division of Diabetes and Metabolism, Vanderbilt University School of Medicine, Nashville, Tenn.

Geoffrey Dean, M.D.
Special Report ALS: Patterns and Progress
Emeritus Director, the Medico-Social Research Board of Ireland, Dublin; Member, International Medical Advisory Board of the World Federation of Multiple Sclerosis Societies; Director of the Study on Amyotrophic Lateral Sclerosis based on the Oxford (England) Record Linkage Scheme

Margo A. Denke, M.D.
Diet and Nutrition
Associate Professor, Center for Human Nutrition, University of Texas Southwestern Medical Center at Dallas

Kay Dickersin, Ph.D.
Special Report Meta-analysis: Nuisance or New Science? (coauthor)
Assistant Professor, Department of Epidemiology and Preventive Medicine, University of Maryland School of Medicine, Baltimore

Alexander Dorozynski
Special Report Health Care in France: Saving the System
Science Writer, Recloses, France; Associate Editor, *Science et Vie;* Correspondent, *British Medical Journal*

Marc K. Effron, M.D.
Cardiovascular Disease
Staff Cardiologist and Director of Echocardiography, Scripps Memorial Hospital, La Jolla, Calif.; Associate Clinical Professor of Medicine, University of California at San Diego, La Jolla

Danielle Foullon
Pharmaceuticals (coauthor)
Biotechnology Editor, F-D-C Reports, Inc., Chevy Chase, Md.

George A. Freedman, D.D.S.
Dentistry
Dentist in private practice, Markham, Ont.; Adjunct Associate Professor, Case Western Reserve University School of Dentistry, Cleveland, Ohio; Past President, American Academy of Cosmetic Dentistry

Barbara A. Gilchrest, M.D.
Skin Cancer (coauthor)
Chairman, Dermatology Department, Boston University School of Medicine; Chief of Dermatology, University Hospital of the Boston University Medical Center, and Boston City Hospital

Jane Gitschier, Ph.D.
Genetics
Assistant Investigator, Howard Hughes Medical Institute; Associate Professor of Medicine and Pediatrics, University of California at San Francisco

Richard M. Glass, M.D.
Mental Health and Illness
Clinical Associate Professor of Psychiatry, University of Chicago Pritzker School of Medicine; Deputy Editor, *Journal of the American Medical Association*

Steven N. Goodman, M.D., Ph.D.
Special Report Meta-analysis: Nuisance or New Science? (coauthor)
Assistant Professor of Oncology and Epidemiology, Johns Hopkins University School of Medicine, Baltimore, Md.

Robert P. Heaney, M.D.
Osteoporosis
John A. Creighton University Professor, Creighton University School of Medicine, Omaha, Neb.

Michael A. Kaliner, M.D.
Asthma
Medical Director, Institute for Asthma and Allergy at the Washington Hospital Center, Washington, D.C.

Zaven S. Khachaturian, Ph.D.
Alzheimer's Disease (coauthor)
Associate Director, Neuroscience and Neuropsychology of Aging Program, National Institute on Aging, National Institutes of Health, Bethesda, Md.

Howard K. Koh, M.D.
Skin Cancer (coauthor)
Associate Professor of Dermatology, Medicine, and Public Health, and Director of Cancer Prevention and Control, Boston University Schools of Medicine and Public Health

Daniel R. Kuritzkes, M.D.
AIDS
Assistant Professor of Medicine, Microbiology, and Immunology, University of Colorado Health Sciences Center, Denver

Philip J. Landrigan, M.D., M.Sc.
Special Report Perspective on Pesticides
Ethel H. Wise Professor of Community Medicine and Chairman, Department of Community Medicine, Mount Sinai School of Medicine of the City University of New York

Bernard Levin, M.D.
Gastrointestinal Disorders
Professor of Medicine and Chairman, Department of Gastrointestinal Medical Oncology and Digestive Diseases, University of Texas M.D. Anderson Cancer Center, Texas Medical Center, Houston

Shôn W. Lewis, M.D.
Special Report Making Sense of Schizophrenia
Professor of Adult Psychiatry, University of Manchester (England) Medical School; formerly Senior Lecturer and Honorable Consultant, Department of Psychiatry, Charing Cross and Westminster Medical School, University of London

Robert Marshall, Jr., Ph.D.
Smoking (coauthor)
Chief, Applied Tobacco Research Section, National Cancer Institute, National Institutes of Health, Bethesda, Md.

Carol Nicholson
Pharmaceuticals (coauthor)
FDA Editor, *F-D-C Reports: "The Pink Sheet,"* F-D-C Reports, Inc., Chevy Chase, Md.

Arnauld E. Nicogossian, M.D.
Aerospace Medicine (coauthor)
Chief Medical Officer, Office of Space Flight, National Headquarters, National Aeronautics and Space Administration, Washington, D.C.

Russell R. Pate, Ph.D.
Physical Fitness
Professor and Chairman, Department of Exercise Science, University of South Carolina, Columbia

Alex Poteliakhoff, M.D.
Special Report Worn Out, but Why?
Retired physician, London; Coauthor, *Real Health: The Ill Effects of Stress and Their Prevention*

Thomas O. Pyle
Health Policy (coauthor)
Chief Executive Officer, MetLife HealthCare Corp., Westport, Conn.

Teresa S. Radebaugh, Sc.D.
Alzheimer's Disease (coauthor)
Director, Division of Extramural Programs, National Center for Nursing Research, National Institutes of Health, Bethesda, Md.

Howard J. Schneider, Ph.D.
Aerospace Medicine (coauthor)
Mission Scientist, Johnson Space Center, National Aeronautics and Space Administration, Houston, Texas

Terry T. Shintani, M.D., J.D., M.P.H.
Special Report Ancient Ways for Modern Ills: Hawaiians Go on a Diet
Director, Preventive Medicine, Waianae Coast Comprehensive Health Center, Waianae, Hawaii; Clinical Faculty, University of Hawaii John A. Burns School of Medicine and School of Public Health, Honolulu

Donald R. Shopland
Smoking (coauthor)
Coordinator, Smoking and Tobacco Control Program, National Cancer Institute, National Institutes of Health, Bethesda, Md.

David E. Trentham, M.D.
Rheumatology
Chief, Division of Rheumatology, Beth Israel Hospital; Associate Professor of Medicine, Harvard Medical School, Boston

George O. Waring III, M.D.
Eye Diseases and Visual Disorders
Chairman, Department of Ophthalmology and Director of Research, El-Maghraby Eye Hospital, Jiddah, Saudi Arabia; Professor of Ophthalmology and Director of Refractive Surgery, Emory University School of Medicine, Atlanta, Ga.

Gertrude M. Webb, Ed.D.
Special Report Doors Opening for Children with Disabilities
Distinguished Professor, Curry College, Milton, Mass.; President, Webb International Center for Dyslexia, Waltham, Mass.

Derek Yach, M.B.Ch.B., M.P.H.
Special Report Focus on Health in a Changing South Africa
Group Executive, Essential Health Research, Medical Research Council, Pretoria, South Africa; Public Health Adviser, Development Bank of Southern Africa

HealthWise Contributors

William J. Anderson, M.D.
Wrists at Risk
Hand and Orthopedic Surgeon in private practice, Lewisville and Flower Mound, Texas; Medical Consultant, Disability Determination Division, Texas Rehabilitation Commission, North Texas Region; Former Guest Adjunct Professor, School of Music, Southern Methodist University, Dallas, Texas

Barry A. Franklin, Ph.D.
Getting the Upper Hand on Exercise (coauthor)
Working up a Cold(-Weather) Sweat (coauthor)
Director, Cardiac Rehabilitation and Exercise Laboratories, William Beaumont Hospital, Royal Oak, Mich.; Associate Professor of Physiology, Wayne State University School of Medicine, Detroit, Mich.

Roger Goldingay
Keeping Healthy on Campus (coauthor)
Photojournalist, Malibu, Calif.; Coauthor, *Campus Health Guide*

Barbara Ladenheim, Ph.D.
Through Children's Eyes (coauthor)
Codirector, Pediatric Visual Assessment Service, The New York Hospital-Cornell University Medical Center; Guest Investigator, Rockefeller University, New York City

Marcia H. Magnus, Ph.D.
Nutrition for the Later Years
Associate Professor of Dietetics and Nutrition, Florida International University, Miami

Joelle Mast, Ph.D., M.D.
Through Children's Eyes (coauthor)
Assistant Professor of Pediatrics and Neurology, Cornell University Medical College; Assistant Attending Physician in Pediatrics and Neurology and Director, Pediatric Visual Assessment Service, The New York Hospital-Cornell University Medical Center, New York City

Mark Messina, Ph.D.
Vegetarianism Comes of Age (coauthor)
Nutrition Consultant, Mount Airy, Md.; formerly a Program Director, National Cancer Institute, National Institutes of Health, Bethesda, Md.

Virginia Messina, M.P.H., R.D.
Vegetarianism Comes of Age (coauthor)
Nutrition Consultant, Mount Airy, Md.; Coauthor, *The No Cholesterol Vegetarian Barbecue Cookbook*

Frances Munnings
Getting the Upper Hand on Exercise (coauthor)
Working up a Cold(-Weather) Sweat (coauthor)
Freelance Writer, Minneapolis, Minn.

Carol L. Otis, M.D.
Keeping Healthy on Campus (coauthor)
Director, Specialty Clinics, University of California at Los Angeles Student Health Service; Coauthor, *Campus Health Guide*

Mary Pullig Schatz, M.D.
PosturePerfect
Medical Staff President, Centennial Medical Center, Nashville, Tenn.; Author, *Back Care Basics: A Doctor's Gentle Yoga Program for Back and Neck Pain Relief*

Ruth Andrea Seeler, M.D.
Hemophilia
Associate Chief of Pediatrics, Michael Reese Hospital and Medical Center; Professor of Pediatrics, University of Illinois at Chicago College of Medicine; Cofounder and Medical Director, Camp Warren, a camp in Illinois for boys with hemophilia

Bruce D. Shephard, M.D.
Say No to Drugs (in Pregnancy)
Clinical Associate Professor of Obstetrics and Gynecology, University of South Florida College of Medicine, Tampa

Joe Sweeney
Active Vacations: Exercise Your Options
Freelance Writer; Speaker, Trainer, and Consultant, Sweeney & Associates, San Diego, Calif.

Title cartoons by Richard Laurent

Index

This is a three-year cumulative index. Index entries to World of Medicine articles in this and previous editions of the *Medical and Health Annual* are set in boldface type; *e.g.,* **AIDS**. Entries to other subjects are set in lightface type; *e.g.,* alcohol. Additional information on any of these subjects is identified with a subheading and indented under the entry heading. The numbers following headings and subheadings indicate the year (boldface) of the edition and the page number (lightface) on which the information appears. The abbreviation *il.* indicates an illustration.

All entry headings are alphabetized word by word. Hyphenated words and words separated by dashes or slashes are treated as two words. When one word differs from another only by the presence of additional characters at the end, the shorter precedes the longer. In inverted names, the words following the comma are considered only after the preceding part of the name has been alphabetized. Examples:

        Lake
        Lake, Simon
        Lake Charles
        Lakeland

Names beginning with "Mc" and "Mac" are alphabetized as "Mac"; "St." is alphabetized as "Saint."

Dark type numbers refer to the year of the edition, *e.g.,* **95**–264 for the 1995 edition, page 264.

481

Dark type numbers refer to the year of the edition, *e.g.,* **95**–264 for the 1995 edition, page 264.

Dark type numbers refer to the year of the edition, e.g., **95**–264 for the 1995 edition, page 264.

483

Dark type numbers refer to the year of the edition, *e.g.,* **95**–264 for the 1995 edition, page 264.

485

Dark type numbers refer to the year of the edition, *e.g.*, **95**–264 for the 1995 edition, page 264.

Dark type numbers refer to the year of the edition, e.g., **95**–264 for the 1995 edition, page 264.

487

Dark type numbers refer to the year of the edition, *e.g.,* **95**–264 for the 1995 edition, page 264.

Dark type numbers refer to the year of the edition, *e.g.,* **95**–264 for the 1995 edition, page 264.

489

Dark type numbers refer to the year of the edition, *e.g.,* **95**–264 for the 1995 edition, page 264.

491

Dark type numbers refer to the year of the edition, *e.g.,* 95–264 for the 1995 edition, page 264.

493

Dark type numbers refer to the year of the edition, *e.g.*, **95**–264 for the 1995 edition, page 264.

Dark type numbers refer to the year of the edition, *e.g.*, **95**–264 for the 1995 edition, page 264.

495

Dark type numbers refer to the year of the edition, e.g., 95–264 for the 1995 edition, page 264.

497

Dark type numbers refer to the year of the edition, *e.g.,* **95**–264 for the 1995 edition, page 264.

Medicare (U.S.)
health care policy and costs **95**–299; **94**–322; **93**–310
senior citizen health care **94**–227
medication: *see* drugs; Pharmaceuticals
Medicine in the Community (Cuba)
health care system (special report) **94**–359
medicine man: *see* shaman
medieval physician
animal testing **95**–102
Medina sickness: *see* guinea worm disease
Mediterranean
diet and nutrition **94**–273
medroxyprogesterone acetate (drug): *see* Depo-Provera
MedWatch (FDA program)
pharmaceuticals **95**–363
melanoma **95**–379; **94**–251
deaths **93**–260
gene therapy (special report) **94**–314; **93**–304
U.S. death rate **95**–380
vaccines (special report) **93**–267
melatonin (hormone)
body clock **95**–33
Mellaril (drug): *see* thioridazine
melodic intonation therapy
music and the brain (special report) **94**–400
Meltzoff, Andrew
television violence **95**–95
memory
repressed memory syndrome **95**–330
men
gynecologists and obstetricians **94**–16
Japan's demography (special report) **93**–337
midlife development **95**–64
musical savants (special report) **94**–403
see also Men's Health
meningitis: *see* Haemophilus influenzae meningitis
menopause
cholesterol levels (special report) **94**–277
hormone therapy **94**–226
midlife development **95**–65
Men's Health 94–353
age-associated problems **94**–223
alcohol
marketing **93**–152
warning labels (special report) **93**–168
birth-defect role **94**–304
childhood obesity effects **94**–452
cholesterol levels (special report) **94**–275
diet and nutrition **94**–269
diseases and disorders
AIDS **95**–216; **94**–236, 238
appendicitis **93**–425
body dysmorphic disorder (special report) **93**–365
cancer **94**–256
cardiovascular disease **95**–243
congestive heart failure **94**–437
coronary heart disease **93**–42
gastrointestinal disorders **95**–281
hemophilia **94**–457
hypertension **94**–334
Jerusalem syndrome **94**–131
multiple personality disorder (special report) **93**–362
multiple sclerosis **94**–363
obesity **95**–339
overwork in Japan **94**–374
sexually transmitted diseases **93**–453
skin cancer **95**–380
stroke death rate and prevention **93**–396, 399
exercise testing **95**–371; **93**–473
Maryland (U.S.) death rate **93**–315
sexual behavior and reproductive health **93**–209
smoking **95**–389
student health **95**–452
weight-reduction research **94**–459
menstruation
Depo-Provera effects **94**–394
Mental Health and Illness 95–325; **93**–354
aquatic exercise **93**–430
body dysmorphic disorder (special report) **93**–363
chronic fatigue syndrome **93**–272
exercise effects **94**–471
housing conditions **93**–202
Jerusalem syndrome **94**–126
South Africa (special report) **95**–312
taste and smell disorders **93**–403
see also Psychology
Merck & Co. (drug co.)
Costa Rica **93**–136
Mercury, Freddie
U.K. AIDS-prevention impact **93**–112, *il.*
Merson, Michael
AIDS-prevention programs **94**–239
mesenchyme
tooth formation (special report) **94**–266
mesentery
children's appendicitis diagnosis **93**–427

mesoridazine, *or* Serentil (drug)
psychoactive drugs and the elderly (special report) **94**–233
messenger RNA, *or* mRNA
cancer research **94**–250
meta-analysis (special report) **95**–383
environmental health **94**–288
metabolic equivalent, *or* MET
exercise testing **95**–447; **93**–474
metabolic stress
Alzheimer's disease **95**–226
metabolism
Alzheimer's disease **95**–224
burn injuries **93**–253
children and medicine **93**–434
energy and fatigue (special report) **95**–350
exercise effects **94**–458
obese children **94**–453
metal
taste disorders **93**–403
metastasis
cancer **94**–253
Metcalf, Donald **95**–21
Metchnikoff, Élie **94**–462
methamphetamine
obesity drugs **95**–340
method
exercise regulation **95**–418
methotrexate
rheumatoid arthritis **95**–375
metolazone (drug)
heart disease treatment **94**–442
Mevacor (drug): *see* lovastatin
Mexico
Africanized bee stings (special report) **93**–282
cholera epidemic **93**–76
ethnic cuisines and coronary heart disease **93**–46, 56, *il.*
occupational health **94**–368
MHR: *see* maximum heart rate
Michigan (state, U.S.)
occupational health **94**–369
physician-assisted suicides **94**–349
Michigan, Lake (lake, U.S.)
contaminated water **94**–287
Michigan, University of (Ann Arbor, Mich., U.S.)
AIDS treatment research **94**–237
genetics research **93**–304
overweight children study **94**–452
Michiko (empress of Japan) **95**–16
microabrasion
dentistry **95**–255
microarchitectural deterioration
osteoporosis **95**–343
microbe
infectious diseases **94**–339
microbiology
strep infections **94**–425
microchimerism (biochem.)
transplantation **95**–397
microencapsulation
child immunization **94**–43, *il.* 44
MicroGeneSys (co., U.S.)
AIDS vaccine research **95**–221
gp160 testing **94**–238
microgravity
aerospace medicine **95**–210
micronutrient
dietary role **95**–264
microsatellite DNA
cancer research **94**–254
microscopy
pathology **94**–64
microsomal enzyme
cancer **94**–252
microvillar cell
olfactory system **93**–404
Mid-Century White House Conference on Children and Youth
child care **94**–259
middle ear
infections **94**–467
Middle East (reg., As.)
ethnic cuisines **93**–57
see also individual countries and regions by name
middle temporal gyrus
autoscopy **94**–128
"Midlife: The Crisis Reconsidered" (feature article) **95**–61
midwifery **93**–371, *il.* 372
premature births **94**–152
mifepristone (drug): *see* RU-486
migraine, *or* migraine headache, *or* sick headache
drug-treatment approval **94**–376, *il.*
migration
hunger **94**–170
South Africa (special report) **95**–314
mild hypertension **94**–334
milk, *or* cow's milk
dietary fat source **94**–410; **93**–44
disease controversy **94**–15
infant diet recommendations **94**–413, 454
yogurt production **94**–462

Miller, Daniel S.
"Hunger in the Midst of War" **94**–156
Miller, James
"Raising Spirits: The Arts Transfigure the AIDS Crisis" **95**–124
Miller, Leon
musical savants (special report) **94**–403
Miller, Zell
physical fitness *il.* **93**–389
milrinone
heart disease treatment **95**–244
Milwaukee (Wis., U.S.)
contaminated water **94**–287
gastrointestinal disorders **95**–285
mind
body dysmorphic disorder (special report) **93**–363
mind-body dualism
medical terminology **95**–326
"Mind, Mood, and Medication in Later Life" (special report) **94**–229
"Minds of Billy Milligan, The" (Keyes)
multiple personalities **93**–362
mineral
bone mass **95**–344
bread **93**–447
eye disease prevention **93**–295
taste disorders **93**–403
mineral supplement
diet, nutrition, and health **94**–424
Minnelli, Liza
AIDS anthem **95**–127
Minnesota (state, U.S.)
public health care policy **94**–325
minocycline
rheumatoid arthritis **95**–375
minority
alcohol advertising **93**–155
alternative medicine **94**–131
bone marrow transplantation **93**–249
medical education **93**–343
midlife development **95**–63
United States
children's future **94**–214
health care policy and costs **94**–320
life expectancy **93**–311, 315
see also specific minorities
minoxidil, *or* Rogaine (drug) **93**–381, *il.*
"Mir" (Russ. space station)
biomedical research **95**–215
"Miracle Worker, The" (film)
temper tantrums *il.* **94**–479
mirror
body dysmorphic disorder **93**–365
miscarriage, *or* spontaneous abortion
illness during pregnancy **93**–442
video-display-terminal exposure **94**–371
misidentification, delusions of: *see* delusions of misidentification
misoprostal, *or* Cytotec (drug)
abortion use **94**–376
gastrointestinal protection **95**–377
Missouri (state, U.S.)
public health (special report) **94**–329
Mitchell, George **95**–8
Mitchell, Malcolm
cancer research **93**–267
mite
allergies **95**–238
MMR vaccine: *see* measles/mumps/rubella vaccine
Moban (drug): *see* molindone
moderate-intensity physical activity
physical fitness **95**–373
Moertel, Charles G. (obit.) **95**–23
Mogadishu (Som.)
hunger **94**–156, *ils.* 169–177
Mohr, Lawrence C.
Clinton appointment **94**–9
molar
leucite-reinforced porcelain **95**–256
mold
allergens **95**–238
molecular biology
cancer **94**–250
child immunization **94**–30
DNA (special report) **94**–305
pathology **94**–69
pediatrics **95**–354
Molimard, Robert
French antismoking law **94**–391
molindone, *or* Moban (drug)
hypertension treatment **94**–334
psychoactive drugs and the elderly (special report) **94**–233
Molloy, Bryan B.
Prozac development **95**–21
Monette, Paul
AIDS and the arts **95**–135
mongolism: *see* Down syndrome
MONICA (UN project)
coronary heart disease study **93**–46
monkey
AIDS research use **94**–238
arterial damage studies **94**–421
Depo-Provera research use **94**–393
monoamine oxidase A
aggressiveness genes **95**–295

monoamine oxidase inhibitor, *or* MAOI
depression **95**–329
panic disorder **93**–358
monoclonal antibody
cancer treatment **94**–255
transplantation **95**–396
mononucleosis
student health **95**–451
monosodium glutamate, *or* MSG
Chinese cuisine **93**–55
monounsaturated fat
blood cholesterol level **93**–47
diet and nutrition **94**–273
monozygotic twins: *see* identical twins
Montagnier, Luc
AIDS research **94**–13, *il.*
Montignac, Michel
French diet **94**–274
mood
temper tantrums **94**–478
moon citrus, *or* Murraya paniculata (plant)
Chinese remedy **93**–142
Moore, Thomas
midlife development **95**–64
Morgagni, Giovanni Battista
pathology **94**–59, *il.* 60
Morgan, Thomas Hunt
hemophilia **95**–457
Morillon, Philippe
Bosnian relief **95**–152, *il.* 154
morning-after pill (contraception)
RU-486 abortion pill **94**–397
morning paralysis: *see* polio
morphology
pathology **94**–53
Morris, John M.
obituary **94**–23
mortality
AIDS **95**–53; **94**–236
blood cholesterol role **94**–278
cancer **94**–250
breast **94**–398
prostate **94**–354
exercise effects **94**–475
obesity **94**–451
overwork (special report) **94**–373
yogurt benefits **94**–462
mortality rate: *see* death rate
mosquito
disease transmission **95**–49; **94**–340
eradication **94**–282
infections in pregnant women **93**–443
mosquito netting
disease prevention **95**–43
motherhood: *see* maternity
motion sickness
travel during pregnancy **93**–442
motivation, human: *see* "Human Motivation"
motor neuron disease, *or* motor neurone disease: *see* amyotrophic lateral sclerosis
motor vehicle
childhood injuries **93**–335
injury prevention **93**–332
senior citizen accidents **94**–224
South Africa (special report) **95**–311
teenage and young adult injuries **95**–455; **93**–336
travel
accidents **95**–37
pregnancy **93**–441
see also airplane; automobile
mouse (rodent)
aging and immunity research **93**–392
cancer vaccine research **93**–265, *il.* 266
gene therapy (special report) **94**–314
genetically engineered animals **94**–19, *il.* 20
mouth
cancer death toll **93**–259
strep infections **94**–425
mouth-to-mouth
cardiopulmonary resuscitation **95**–194
Moynihan, Daniel Patrick **95**–8
Mozambique
hunger **94**–161
MREs: *see* Meals, Ready-to-Eat
MRI: *see* magnetic resonance imaging
mRNA: *see* messenger RNA
MS: *see* multiple sclerosis
MSG: *see* monosodium glutamate
mucosal immune system
child immunization **94**–44
mucus
olfactory system **93**–405
Mudd, Samuel A.
Lincoln assassination **94**–18, *il.*
Mullis, Kary B.
polymerase chain reaction **95**–292, *il.* 293
multiculturalism
midlife **95**–62
multipayer system **93**–314
multiple drug resistance, *or* MDR
cancer treatment **94**–257
multiple personality disorder (special report) **93**–359
"Multiple Personality: Illness or Act?" (special report) **93**–359

Dark type numbers refer to the year of the edition, *e.g.*, **95**–264 for the 1995 edition, page 264.

499

studies
AIDS treatment **93**–382
alternative medicine **94**–241
obese children **94**–452
New Mexico (state, U.S.)
public health (special report) **94**–330
New Orleans (La., U.S.)
yellow fever outbreak **94**–343
New York (state, U.S.)
AIDS and health care workers **93**–234
drinking water **94**–288
public health care reform **94**–325
New York, Declaration of: see Declaration of
New York
New York City (N.Y., U.S.)
"AIDS and the Arts" **95**–126
child care **94**–259
health care *il.* **93**–311
historical living conditions **93**–194, *il.* 195
pesticides and health (special report)
95–253
New York Hospital Association
public health care reform **94**–326
newborn infant: see neonate
"Newsmakers" **95**–7; **94**–6
"Newsweek" (Am. mag.)
AIDS epidemic **95**–134
NF1: see von Recklinghausen
neurofibromatosis
NFL (U.S.): see National Football League
NGF: see nerve growth factor
NHANES (U.S.): see National Health and
Nutrition Examination Survey
NHLBI (U.S.): see National Heart, Lung, and
Blood Institute
NHS (U.K.): see National Health Service
Ni-Hon-San Study
diet and coronary heart disease **93**–47
niacin: see nicotinic acid
Nice Touch (device)
stethoscope warming *il.* **94**–17
nicotine
FDA regulations **95**–13, 390
nicotine patch
new formulation **93**–381, *il.* 382
nicotinic acid, *or* niacin
cholesterol reduction **94**–281
NIDDM: see non-insulin-dependent diabetes
mellitus
Nigeria
guinea worm disease **94**–284
mobile vaccination team *il.* **94**–37
Nightingale, Florence
energy and fatigue (special report)
95–348, *il.* 349
NIH (U.S.): see National Institutes of Health
NIMH (U.S.): see National Institute of Mental
Health
nine-banded armadillo
animal research **95**–113, *il.*
Ninth International Conference on AIDS
(Berlin) **95**–219
NIOSH (U.S.): see National Institute for
Occupational Safety and Health
Nipent (drug): see pentostatin
Nippon: see Japan
nitric oxide
cardiovascular disease **95**–241
male impotence role **94**–355
nitroprusside
heart disease treatment **94**–444
nitrous oxide
occupational health **94**–370
Nixon, Nicholas
AIDS photographs **95**–138
NMR: see magnetic resonance imaging
NMSC: see nonmelanoma skin cancer
NNDSS (U.S.): see National Notifiable
Diseases Surveillance System
"No Magic Bullet: A Social History of
Venereal Disease in the United
States Since 1880" (Brandt)
chemical prophylaxis **93**–118
"No Pity: People with Disabilities Forging a
New Civil Rights Movement" (work
by Shapiro) **95**–291
No Smoking Day (U.K.)
public health efforts **93**–104, *il.* 103
no-smoking policy
occupational health **94**–371
Nobel Prize
genetics **95**–292
NOCSAE (U.S.): see National Operating
Committee on Standards for Athletic
Equipment
Nolvadex (drug): see tamoxifen
non-Hodgkin's lymphoma
pesticides and health (special report)
95–254
non-insulin-dependent diabetes mellitus,
or type II diabetes, *or* maturity onset
diabetes, *or* NIDDM, *or* adult-onset
diabetes **95**–259
exercise benefits **95**–371; **94**–474
genetic research **94**–302
vegetarian diets **95**–404
nonfat dry milk
yogurt production **94**–463

nonmelanoma skin cancer, *or* NMSC
95–379
nonnucleoside analog (biochem.)
anti-HIV drug research **95**–219
nonprescription drug: see over-the-counter
drug
Nonprescription Drug Manufacturers
Association, *or* NDWA (U.S.)
adverse drug reactions and warning
labels **94**–381
noodle
world cuisines **93**–48
Noone, Ahilya
"HIV/AIDS" **95**–52
"Normal Heart, The" (play by Kramer)
AIDS and the arts **95**–138
Norplant (drug)
Depo-Provera comparison **94**–394
Norpramin (drug): see desipramine
North American Free Trade Agreement, *or*
NAFTA
occupational health **94**–368
North American Symptomatic Carotid
Endarterectomy Trial
stroke-prevention study **93**–398
North Carolina (U.S.)
smoking restrictions **95**–395
Northwestern University Medical School
(Chicago, Ill., U.S.)
AIDS survival studies **94**–238
nortriptyline, *or* Pamelor (drug)
psychoactive drugs and the elderly
(special report) **94**–231
Norway
alcohol advertising **93**–167
nose
basal cell carcinoma *il.* **95**–381
ear infection role **94**–467
strep infections **94**–426
nosocomial infection, *or* hospital-acquired
infection
patient deaths **94**–341
Notel (research study)
television violence **95**–96
Novello, Antonia
advertising industry **93**–163
AIDS and adolescent health **93**–208
NRA: see National Rifle Association
NRDC: see Natural Resources Defense
Council
NSAID: see nonsteroidal anti-inflammatory
drug
NSC: see National Safety Council
NTD: see neural tube defect
nuclear magnetic resonance: see magnetic
resonance imaging
nuclear medicine
medical imaging **93**–350
nuclear weapon
radioactive-waste disposal **94**–290
nucleoside analog (biochem.)
anti-HIV drug research **95**–219
nucleotide
DNA structure (special report) **94**–306
Nuland, Sherwin B. **95**–20
Nuremberg Code
human experiments (special report)
95–230
Nureyev, Rudolf
AIDS death **95**–134, *il.*; **94**–11
Nuromax (drug): see doxacurium
nursery school
child care **94**–259
Nurses for National Health Care
U.S. public health reform **94**–327
Nurses' Health Study
diet and nutrition **95**–265
nursing
AIDS legal issues **94**–315
premature births **94**–152
South Africa (special report) **95**–315
nursing home
Alzheimer's patients **93**–298
Japan's aging population **93**–340
psychoactive drugs and the elderly
(special report) **94**–233
urinary incontinence in the aged **94**–225
nut (food)
vegetarian diets **95**–405
NutraSweet: see aspartame
nutrient
eye disease prevention **93**–295
nutrition: see Diet and Nutrition
"Nutrition Action Healthletter" (med. pub.,
U.S.)
nutrition quiz **94**–8
Nutrition Labeling and Education Act (1990,
U.S.)
food-labeling regulations **94**–269
Nutrition Screening Initiative
senior citizen health **95**–442
nutritionist
sports medicine **93**–179

nylon hose
claw toe role **94**–448
"NYPD Blue" (television program) *il.* **95**–99
nystagmus
multiple sclerosis occurrence **94**–364
Nyswaner, Ron
"Philadelphia" **95**–144

O

OAM (U.S.): see Alternative Medicine,
Office of
OAR (U.S.): see AIDS Research, Office of
Obesity 95–337
children **94**–451, *il.* 452; **93**–386
diet and nutrition **94**–271
exercise programs **94**–457, 474
Hawaiian diet (special report) **95**–271
health hazards
endometrial cancer **93**–259
hypertension role **94**–333
insulin resistance **95**–260
U.S. public health (special report) **94**–331
vegetarian benefits **95**–403
Obesity Research Center (N.Y.C., N.Y.,
U.S.)
diet-resistant patients **94**–271
observation
pathology **94**–54
obsession
body dysmorphic disorder **93**–363
obsessive-compulsive disorder, *or* OCD
body dysmorphic disorder comparison
(special report) **93**–368
Obstetrics and Gynecology 93–369
HIV transmission during birth **95**–216
men's roles **94**–16
postpartum mood disorders **95**–327
premature birth **94**–139
RU-486 delivery use **94**–397
travel during pregnancy **93**–439
U.S. abortion funding **93**–317
see also pregnancy; sexual and
reproductive health
obstruction
appendicitis **93**–424
coronary artery disease **93**–320
smell disorders **93**–403
stroke **93**–396, *il.* 400
occipitotemporal gyrus
autoscopy **94**–87
occlusion
coronary disease **93**–324
stroke treatment **93**–399
occult blood
gastrointestinal disorders **95**–282
Occupational Health 94–368
amyotrophic lateral sclerosis (special
report) **95**–367
U.S. public health (special report) **94**–330
see also Environmental Health
OCD: see obsessive-compulsive disorder
ocean liner
travel during pregnancy **93**–442
odds ratio
meta-analysis (special report) **95**–386
Odone family
adrenoleukodystrophy **94**–14, *il.* 15
genetic research **94**–302
odorant
smell experience **93**–404
OECD (Fr.): see Economic Cooperation and
Development, Organization of
oil
Persian Gulf war **93**–37
South Africa (special report) **95**–314
Okinawa (is., Japan)
diet and health **93**–45
Oklahoma (state, U.S.)
premature births **94**–139
old age: see Aging; senior citizens
Oldham, Kevin
AIDS death **94**–12
O'Leary, Hazel
U.S. radiation experiments (special
report) **95**–229
oleic acid
diet and nutrition **94**–273
Olestra
fake fats **95**–341
olfaction: see smell
olfactory mucosa
cat allergens **93**–480
olfactory receptor cell
taste and smell disorders **93**–401
olfactory system
smell disorders **93**–403
olive oil
diet and nutrition **94**–273
Italian cuisine **93**–47
omega-3 fatty acid
diet and coronary heart disease **93**–45
premature births **94**–149
omentum
appendicitis in infants **93**–427
"On Airs, Waters, and Places" (Hippocrates)

travel medicine **95**–26
"On the Mode of Communication of
Cholera" (Snow) **94**–344; **93**–83
"Once Stung, Twice Shy?" (special report)
93–281
oncogene
cancer research **94**–251
ondansetron hydrochloride, *or* Zofran (drug)
FDA approval **93**–380
1A rating
pharmaceuticals **93**–380
1B rating
pharmaceuticals **93**–380
1C rating
pharmaceuticals **93**–381
"One Year of AZT and One Day of AZT" (art
exhibit)
AIDS and the arts **95**–136, *il.* 137
Onik, Gary
cryosurgery techniques **94**–355
oocyst
toxoplasmosis transmission **93**–462
open carpal tunnel release (med.
procedure) **95**–412
open-heart massage
cardiopulmonary resuscitation **95**–194
operational tolerance
transplantation **95**–397
ophthalmology **95**–276, *il.* 277; **93**–293, 419
opioid (biochem.)
diet and nutrition **94**–273
opium
drugs **93**–137
opportunistic infection
AIDS association **95**–216; **93**–232
HIV-related eye disorder **93**–296
tuberculosis (special report) **93**–244
optic nerve
multiple sclerosis effects **94**–363
optic neuritis
multiple sclerosis occurrence **94**–363
optotype
pediatrics **95**–434, *il.*
oral cancer
causes and treatments **94**–254
oral hygiene: see hygiene
oral immunization, *or* oral vaccine **94**–24
oral polio vaccine *il.* **94**–46
oral prostaglandin
abortion use **94**–396
oral rehydration salts, *or* ORS
cholera treatment **93**–90
oral rehydration therapy, *or* ORT
cholera treatment **95**–57; **93**–88
oral tolerance
rheumatoid arthritis **95**–374
oral vaccine: see oral immunization
ordeal bean: see Calabar bean
Oregon (state, U.S.)
public health care reform **94**–324
yews **93**–130
"Ordeal of Gilbert Pinfold, The" (Waugh)
schizophrenia (special report) **95**–332
Oregon Health Sciences University
(Portland, Ore., U.S.)
dietary experiment **93**–47
organ
pathology **94**–53
organ donation
bone marrow transplantation **93**–246
ethics **95**–399
heart transplantation **93**–322
liver transplantation **93**–9
organelle
pathology **94**–65
organic mental disorder
medical terminology **95**–326
Ornish, Dean **95**–20
orphan drug **93**–380
ORS: see oral rehydration salts
ORT: see oral rehydration therapy
orthopedic shoe **94**–449
orthopedic surgeon
sports medicine **93**–176
orthopedics
corrective footwear **94**–449
robotic surgery **94**–17
orthose, *or* orthotic device
foot pain treatment **94**–449
orthostatic hypotension
psychoactive drugs and the elderly
(special report) **94**–233
orthostatic intolerance
spaceflight biomedical research **93**–226
orthotist
corrective footwear fabrication **94**–450
O'Shaughnessy, William Brook
cholera research **93**–87
osseointegration
dental implants (special report) **94**–265
osteoarthritis **95**–376
Osteoporosis 95–342
bones and dietary calcium **95**–405
drinking water **94**–288
exercise effects **94**–473
genetic origins **95**–294
menopause association **94**–226
yogurt consumption effects **94**–463

Dark type numbers refer to the year of the edition, *e.g.*, **95**–264 for the 1995 edition, page 264.

501

Dark type numbers refer to the year of the edition, *e.g.,* **95**–264 for the 1995 edition, page 264.

Dark type numbers refer to the year of the edition, *e.g.,* **95**–264 for the 1995 edition, page 264.

503

Dark type numbers refer to the year of the edition, *e.g.*, **95**–264 for the 1995 edition, page 264.

Dark type numbers refer to the year of the edition, e.g., **95**–264 for the 1995 edition, page 264.

505

Dark type numbers refer to the year of the edition, *e.g.*, **95**–264 for the 1995 edition, page 264.

Dark type numbers refer to the year of the edition, *e.g.*, **95**–264 for the 1995 edition, page 264.

507

Dark type numbers refer to the year of the edition, e.g., **95**–264 for the 1995 edition, page 264.

Dark type numbers refer to the year of the edition, e.g., 95–264 for the 1995 edition, page 264.

509

Dark type numbers refer to the year of the edition, *e.g.,* **95**–264 for the 1995 edition, page 264.

Dark type numbers refer to the year of the edition, e.g., **95**–264 for the 1995 edition, page 264.

511

Dark type numbers refer to the year of the edition, *e.g.,* **95**–264 for the 1995 edition, page 264.